THE SOCIAL PSYCHOLOGY
OF ORGANIZATIONS

DANIEL KATZ
Department of Psychology
and Survey Research Center
The University of Michigan

ROBERT L. KAHN
Survey Research Center
and Department of Psychology
The University of Michigan

SECOND EDITION

JOHN WILEY & SONS
New York   Santa Barbara   Chichester   Brisbane   Toronto

Library of Congress Cataloging in Publication Data:

Katz, Daniel, 1903–

   The social psychology of organizations.

   Bibliography: p.
   1. Organization. 2. Social psychology.
I. Kahn, Robert Louis, 1918– joint author.
II. Title.
HM131.K35   1978   301.18'32   77-18764
ISBN 0-471-02355-8

Printed in the United States of America

10 9 8 7 6 5

■ PREFACE ■

Our first edition championed the cause of the open system approach to the study of organizations. Today that point of view has gained wide acceptance in organizational research and theorizing. Research is no longer contained within the boundaries of a single organization but crosses those borders to deal with environmental forces, relationships with other systems, and the effects of organizations on individual members as human beings and members of the larger society. That social psychological principles can be applied to all forms of collective organized effort is now acknowledged in many disciplines. Industrial psychology has moved toward becoming organizational psychology and not only studies behavior of people in many organizational settings but on occasion recognizes organizational or system variables in shaping that behavior.

In this revision we have attempted to take account of developments within the field since our first edition, both new concepts and fresh findings. The present volume includes chapters on the organization and its environment, conflict and its management, organizational effects on members (work and health), organizational models, and a greatly expanded treatment of organizational change. Other chapters have been revised to include recent research. The growth has been so great that we have had to be selective in citing relevant literature, and we have tried to maintain our perspective of a comprehensive system approach.

As in our first volume we are indebted to the Institute for Social Research for institutional support and to some of the same ISR staff members for advice and stimulation; namely, John R. P. French, Jr., Edward E. Lawler, Stanley Seashore, Basil Georgopoulos and Arnold Tannenbaum. To this list should be added the names of Linda Argote, Cortlandt Cammann, Stephen Nelson, Mark Peterson, Robert Quinn, Graham Staines, Lorraine Uhlaner, and Eser Uzun, all of whom we consulted to our advantage on many problems.

During the year 1976–1977, our work was greatly facilitated by the Netherlands Institute for Advanced Study (N.I.A.S.). Robert Kahn spent the year in Wassenaar as a N.I.A.S. Fellow, and Daniel Katz was there for two weeks as a visiting scholar. It is a pleasure to acknowledge the unusual opportunity that N.I.A.S. provides, the dedication of its staff, and the foresight and generosity of the Dutch government in funding such a facility. Our thanks go particularly to its Director, Professor H. A. J. F. Misset, and the Associate Director, Mrs. J. E. Glastra van Loon.

The production of a book takes form as an organized effort through the expertise and devotion of the people actually in charge of typing, referencing, checking, and other related chores. Helene Hitchcock proved a gifted administrator and Grace Stribley an exceptional secretary. Mrs. Stribley with occasional excellent help from Susan Wood Paz typed numerous versions of many chapters and organized the materials at various stages of preparation. Without her help the volume would still be in manuscript form.

We also wish to thank the following publishers for permission to use excerpts, tables, and figures in this book: American Psychological Association, American Sociological Association, Basic Books, Brookings Institution, Dorsey, Doubleday, Free Press, Harcourt Brace Jovanovich, Harper and Row, Harvard University Press, Industrial and Labor Relations Review, Industrial Relations Research Association, Richard D. Irwin, Jossey-Bass, McGraw-Hill, Mental Health Research Institute, University of Michigan, Mentor, Pergamon, Personnel Psychology, Plenum Press, Rand McNally & Co., The Rationalization Council, SAF, LO, Russell Sage Foundation, Swedish Employers Confederation, Tavistock Publications, John Wiley and Sons, and Yale University Press.

Matters of language and style are of great importance for authors and readers, but they are seldom discussed in prefaces. On the whole, we concur with this practice; sins and virtues of expression are revealed in the text and no prefatory comment can atone for the first or add to the second. It may be appropriate, nevertheless, to say something here about our forms of reference to men and women, minorities, and other groups.

Almost every disadvantaged group, as it gains strength, attempts to set the language by which it is willing to be designated. We know that those preferences change and that all members of the affected groups are not of one mind. We have attempted to follow the dominant preferences as we understand them, and especially to avoid the use of male terminology when both men and women are included in the meaning. To be more specific, we use the plural pronoun (they) wherever appropriate; where the singular is necessary, we use the phrase he or she. We cite historical facts and quotations as they originally appeared; and we use male or female terms when doing so adds information. If a population under study is described as *salesmen*, therefore, we are referring to a sales force made up only of men. We occasionally use a term that is sex-specific in form and not meaning, but only if there is no synonym in good currency; *man-machine* system is an example of such a term. We hope that such decisions serve the convictions of our readers.

Daniel Katz   Robert L. Kahn

This book had its origin in the program of research on human relations in organizations launched by Rensis Likert in 1947 as one of the major programs of the Survey Research Center of The University of Michigan. From its inception, this series of researches has been concerned with problems of morale and motivation, productivity and effectiveness, power and control, and leadership and change processes in large-scale organizations. The research findings from the program and related work in the Institute for Social Research were well summarized several years ago by Rensis Likert, whose original work on organizational problems and whose contagious enthusiasm for research have been extremely helpful to us. This book is in part an effort to provide a more general theoretical treatment of some of the same issues which he considered in *New Patterns of Management* (1961), and we have drawn on some of the same materials and experience.

In our attempts to extend the description and explanation of organizational processes we have shifted from an earlier emphasis on traditional concepts of individual psychology and interpersonal relations to system constructs. The interdependent behavior of many people in their supportive and complementary actions takes on a form or structure which needs to be conceptualized at a more appropriate collective level. Classical organization theory we found unsatisfactory because of its implicit assumptions about the closed character of social structures. The development of open-system theory, on the other hand, furnished a much more dynamic and adequate framework. Hence, our effort, in the pages to follow, is directed at the utilization of an open-system point of view for the study of large-scale organizations.

Many individuals have provided ideas and approaches to the complex problems of organizational life, and we have benefited from many. We are particularly indebted to Floyd H. Allport, whose original theoretical approach to problems of social structure inspired this book even though it reflects but faint and distorted versions of his thunder. Herbert Thelen and John R. P. French, Jr. have by means of many discussions and through their own work improved the quality of ours. Others who have wrestled with problems of organizational theory to our considerable advantage are Chris Argyris, Sidney Cobb, Stanley Seashore, and Floyd C. Mann. They, along with Angus Campbell,

Gerald Gurin, and Arnold Tannenbaum, commented on parts of this manuscript, as did Ellen Baar and Shirley Ball. John DeLamater provided valuable assistance in the preparation of the manuscript.

We are grateful for the support provided by the National Institutes of Health, by the Carnegie Corporation, and by the research fund of the Horace H. Rackham School of Graduate Studies. We want also to thank our colleagues in the Survey Research Center, particularly Angus Campbell, for making possible occasional periods during which the usual demands of ongoing research and administration could be eliminated in favor of writing. During the year 1960 to 1961 our work was greatly facilitated by the Ford Center for Advanced Study in the Behavioral Sciences. Daniel Katz spent the year there as a Fellow (a fellowship supported by National Institutes of Health) and Robert Kahn the summer as a visiting scholar. We are glad to acknowledge the good effects of that unique environment and to express our thanks to its director, Ralph Tyler, for having created and sustained it.

Various people have typed and proofread numerous drafts of the fourteen chapters of this book. Most of the work has been done, however, and done with excellence and unfailing good spirit, by Mrs. Rita Lamendella. She deserves a share of whatever pleasure and satisfaction attend the completion of the book. Mrs. Nancy Abbey and Marcia Kahn were her able assistants.

We also wish to thank the following publishers for permission to use excerpts, tables, and figures in this book: American Psychological Association, Basic Books, Dorsey, Doubleday, Free Press, Harcourt, Brace and World, Industrial and Labor Relations Review, Industrial Relations Research Association, McGraw-Hill, Mental Health Research Institute, University of Michigan, Mentor, Pergamon, Tavistock Publications, and John Wiley and Sons.

Daniel Katz
Robert L. Kahn
September 1965

CONTENTS

To Floyd Henry Allport

1

POINT
OF DEPARTURE

OUTLINE

Open System Theory

Forerunners of Open System Theory
Marxian Theory
Talcott Parsons and the Structural Functionalists
Allportian Event-Structure Theory
General Systems Theory

Growth of the Field of Organizational Studies
Sociological Case Studies
Scientific Management and Traditional Industrial Psychology
Mayo and the Rediscovery of Informal Group Processes
Comparative Analysis of Organizations
Surveys of Morale and Motivation

The Problem of Levels

Summary

The psychological approach to the study of problems in the social world has been impeded by an inability to deal with the facts of social structure and social organization. Societies in their very nature represent organized groupings of people whose activities are institutionally channeled. The exercise of power and control in a society is largely a function of its institutional structure. Yet the dominant tradition in psychology has included the implicit assumption that individuals exist in a social vacuum. Students of personality have recognized the importance of familial patterns of behavior for the development of character, but they have neglected the fact that people behave not only as grown-up children but as adult members of social systems. Social psychologists, too, have been guilty of negligence of the facts of social life. Their partial attempts to include social variables reflect a curious alternation between the most global of all influences, that of culture, and the most minute of group influences.

The great central area of human behavior in organizations and institutions has been ignored. Yet in the modern world people spend the greater part of their waking hours in organizations and institutional settings. The usual textbook in social psychology consists of three parts—a consideration of individual cognitive processes (that are of possible social significance) such as attitude change, cognitive dissonance, and causal attribution; an account of personality development and socialization; and a treatment of interpersonal and intragroup processes.

This type of book, in our opinion, leaves off where the most important problems of social psychology begin. A second volume is necessary to move beyond the introduction to the field and to deal with the psychological aspects of social structures. The present work is an attempt to supply such a second book in social psychology.

Psychologists halt their study with the individual in the small-group setting in great measure because they lack conceptual tools for venturing into more complex areas. Although the need for dealing with structure and organized forms has been acknowledged in all scientific disciplines, there have been basic weaknesses in most of the theoretical approaches popular in social psychology. Behaviorism, psychoanalytic theory, and field theory have been too individual in orientation and hence of very limited usefulness in dealing with social-structural problems. Nor have the older societal theories of the other social sciences provided the answers.

OPEN SYSTEM THEORY

Through the application of open system theory, we are beginning to move toward a social psychology concerned with social structure.

This approach emphasizes two aspects of social behavior patterns: (1) their *system character*, so that movement in one part leads in predictable fashion to movement in other parts, and (2) their *openness to environmental inputs*, so that they are continually in a state of flux.

Open system theory emphasizes the close relationship between a structure and its supporting environment. It begins with the concept of entropy, the assumption that without continued inputs any system soon runs down. One critical basis for identifying and understanding social systems is therefore their relationship with the energic sources for their maintenance. For almost all social structures, the most important maintenance source is human effort and motivation. If we wish to understand the maintenance of social systems, we are at the social-psychological level. The carriers of the system cannot be ignored; they furnish the sustaining inputs.

The other major emphasis in open system theory is on throughput: the processing of production inputs to yield some outcome that is then used by an outside group or system. Thus the hospital meets the health needs of the community, and the industrial enterprise turns out goods or furnishes services. In any given system, these functions can be identified by observing the cycle of input, throughput, and output. That cycle is sometimes described in terms that abstract it from the human beings involved—so many tons of raw materials and so many finished products. The moment, however, that we deal with the throughput cycle in ways that include the organization of people in the system, we are again at the social-psychological level. Thus open system theory furnishes a useful framework for examining social structures from a social-psychological point of view, and social psychology informs the open system approach to human organizations.

The continuing transactional relationships with the environment point up the contingent character of social systems. From an open system point of view the constancy of environmental inputs cannot be assumed but must continually be the subject of investigation. Thus the nature of the environment—its stability, turbulence, and degree of organization, for example—becomes a critical area of study. The behavior of an organization is contingent upon the social field of forces in which it occurs and must be understood in terms of the organization's interaction with that environmental field.

Another aspect of open system theory is its inclusion of different levels of systems and their interrelationships. A pattern of collective behavior with a limited specific function may tie into other patterns to achieve a more general outcome, as in the case of work groups whose cooperative relationship insures a final product. These interconnected groups may form the technical or production subsystem of an organization. In addition, however, these behavior patterns are crisscrossed by cycles of behavior from the managerial subsystem. There is a hierarchical ordering of the many parts of the organizational structure such that actions at higher levels are dominant over actions at lower levels. Most transactions with the environment are monitored through the managerial system, so the external relationships of an organization's officers comprise a critical set of variables for predicting the effectiveness and survival of the organization itself. Individuals in strategic positions are therefore not excluded from scrutiny, but they are studied as people in specified roles subject to the social milieu of those roles.

Because of the hierarchical relationship of system levels and the functional relationships of system parts, the optimal strategy in social discovery is to look upward in the system. In natural science we look down for explanation, expecting that physiology will account for psychological processes, and biochemistry for physiological processes. In social science, however, our first search should be at the more complex system level. For example, a certain small automobile company has had a record of industrial harmony and few strikes. We could go down to the individual level to find out if the leaders on both sides tend to be nonaggressive people; we might even try to examine their socialization history in terms of early weaning and toilet training. But if we go to the next higher systemic level, we discover that the company is marginal in the industry, that it cannot afford a costly strike, and that both labor and management have agreed to follow the compromises reached between the larger producers and the United Auto Workers.

FORERUNNERS OF OPEN SYSTEM THEORY

The roots of open system theory go deep, and the lines of historical development are not clear. Four past conceptualizations, however, have paved the way for present interest in the system view of organizations:—(1) Marxian theory, (2) Parsons and the structural-functionalists, (3) Allportian event-structure theory, and (4) the general systems approach.

Marxian Theory

Perhaps the most systematic as well as challenging attempt to deal with social structure and its social-psychological aspects is Marxian theory. Because of its confusion with propagandistic doctrine, the theory itself has sometimes received summary treatment from social scientists. In some senses it was an effort at a field theory of society in which social relationships rather than individual characteristics were the determining forces and in which structural dynamics were expressed as the dialectic. It was more a theory of the internal dynamics of social structures than of the mutual influencing of system and environment, as in open system theory. Marx saw the social relations of production as the key institutional system of a society leading to its class stratification, its conflicts, both internal and external, and their resolution. The primary motivating factor was not so much individual self-interest as the role the individual played in the production process and the group interest of people playing similar roles. Behavior in common roles came first; then ideology developed as a weapon to handle common role interests. In other words, social stratification preceded class consciousness. Other subsystems of a society, such as the school, the church, and the state, were built around the social relations of production.

The strength of the Marxian theory was its breadth and depth. It took account of societal organization, specified its apparent critical institutions, and yet related its structural analysis to the carriers, or human beings, of the system and their interactions. It proposed that the major determinant of ideas and values was not economic status as such but key economic roles, the way in which men and women related to their fellows in the productive process through selling their labor or some other commodity or buying the labor of others. The workers who no longer owned their tools in a large factory system and who were exploited in the sale of their labor power were alienated from the dominant values of the society. Marxian theory asserted that social interaction among workers in urban factory centers would facilitate the development of ideology. It further claimed that overt behavioral conflict was necessary to crystallize group ideology. Hence demonstrations, strikes, and confrontation would facilitate such ideological development. Thus Marxian theory made assumptions about social interaction, social reinforcement, the playing of behavioral roles, alienation, and the conditions producing group solidarity.

The weakness of Marxian theory for social science purposes is twofold. First, it was tied too specifically to certain conditions Marx had observed at one period in history and in certain localities. Marx did not generalize his notion about the significance of role settings in determining behavior, but narrowed it down to the role relationship he considered primary—the social relations of production in privately-owned uncontrolled industry, and the resulting class conflict. Second, Marxian thinking concentrated too much on internal dynamics; social change was seen as the working out of built-in contradictions. The changing environment and its potential for affecting institutions received insufficient attention. The capacity of a system to use its environment to handle its internal conflicts was recognized, but only as a delaying, temporary expedient. Open system theory, on the other hand, would attempt long-range predictions about social structures only in terms that included environmental factors. In an uncertain and constantly changing environment, such predictions take the form of contingent statements.

Talcott Parsons
and the Structural Functionalists

Like the Marxians, the structural functionalists, headed by Talcott Parsons (1960), have examined social structures from the point of view of the functions they serve. The Parsonians also resemble Marxians in that they seek the function of a system not so much in the limited operations of its subsystems as in its impact on the whole society. But unlike the Marxians, they do not make social dysfunction a central concern. Instead they see our society as integrated by a common set of values and they are interested in how the parts of the system contribute to these values and are affected by them. Marx focused on social change. His theory was formulated to account for radical transformations, especially the predicted transformation from capitalism to socialism. Parsons' interest is more in social stability and the adjustments made within the societal supersystem to keep it functional and to preserve that stability. For that reason Parsonian theory has been criticized as establishment-oriented and unable to deal with change.

In examining the operation of social structures, however, Parsons has contributed conceptual tools for delineating subsystems and their specific functions. The interrelationship of these subsystems and the nature of the "break" as we move from one subsystem of an organization to another have thus become areas of study. It is only a step from this analysis to the notion of boundary systems and boundary roles. Although Parsons' writings do not provide the operational procedures for dealing with environmental transactions, they do move us away from the older sociological theories of a closed system character.

Allportian Event-Structure Theory

F. H. Allport (1954, 1962, 1967) is one of the few psychological theorists to deal with problems of social structure at their own level. He believes that patterned human activity cannot be adequately described in biological metaphors. Social groupings have no separate anatomical structures that parallel their functions as the parts of the body parallel the functions of the organism. Nor does the physical arrangement of buildings describe the structure of the social organization. Yet there is something out there that can be identified objectively. It is the form of human interaction, the shape of the patterned behavior. Allport conceptualizes social structure as a cycle of events which return in circular fashion to reinstate the cycle. This pattern occurs in the real world and not just in the head of the social scientist. Events are the observable nodal points in such cycles, and can be conceptualized as structures.

Instead of linear behavior of A stimulating B and B responding, Allport believes that a continuing series of events must complete a cycle before we have social structure. Moreover, cycles can crisscross or can be tangential to one another, and they can vary in size. These complex patterns need to be identified if one is to understand social behavior.

Allport's earlier thinking along these lines contributed the concepts of partial inclusion, potency of involvement, and structural relevance. Partial inclusion, which to date has been the most useful, refers to the fact that organizational membership and role behavior generally include only a piece of personality. Organizations are thus composed not of people but of common behavioral segments. Potency of involvement refers to the strength of an individual's attachment to a collective structure, which is measured in terms of the effort that person would put forth to maintain the structure if it were threatened. Relevance is the extent to which attitudes and actions affect the structure in question.

The implications of the Allportian approach for the study of social organizations are threefold. First, it calls attention to the fact that social systems as forms of behavior involving people have no anatomical structure. The function itself is the structure. Thus social systems are more contrived than biological systems and have no dependable life cycle. Their parts can be indefinitely replaced as long as human beings exist. It follows that open system theory, if it is to be fruitful for social research, must avoid the fallacy of biological analogies.

Second, the development of open system theory requires the identification of patterns of social behavior by following cycles of events as individuals complete their circles of repetitive interactions. In this search we should look for the activity that can reinforce or modify the original pattern. Observations of this sort establish future possibilities, not past accomplishments.

Third, Allport's work implies that the usual causal approach of seeking the impact of single variables in a complex field should be replaced by examining the ongoing structure of interacting events. Factor A may have a dramatic effect on factor B in the laboratory, but in the real world, if factor B is part of a field of forces, A may have little or no influence. The introduction of a planned change in an organization may have unanticipated consequences or none at all, depending on the nature of the ongoing system processes.

Allport's point of view is well summarized in his own words:

Causation, in the structural view, is not historical, nor linear, but continuous, time independent and reciprocally cyclical. One looks for it neither in society nor in the individual, as traditionally seen as separate levels or agencies, but in the compounded patterns of structuring which are the essential reality underlying both. (1962, p. 19)

General Systems Theory

Several decades ago von Bertalanffy (1950, 1956) proposed the idea of a general system theory that would embrace all levels of science from the study of a single cell to the study of a society. It would seek generalizations that would hold at all levels so that the methodological unity of science would be accompanied by a substantive unity of principles and laws. General system theorists might not deny conceptualizations specific to a given level but would emphasize the fundamental similarities across levels and the possibility of a unified science. They therefore reject the traditional barriers between the various academic disciplines. Miller (1955, 1965a, 1965b) and his colleagues further developed the general systems approach to show that a single set of concepts could be applied across different sciences. Methods of handling information overload, boundary crossing, subsystem coding, feedback, the transactions of input, throughput, and output are proposed as characteristics of all "living systems."

As formulated by von Bertalanffy, the general systems approach postulates the openness of every system; general system theory should be open system theory. It is easier in practice, however, to take account of stable relationships than dynamic interactions of input, throughput, and output, and many approaches labeled systemic are in fact closed and static. Systems engineering, for example, constructed models of man-machine arrangements that made simplistic and unchanging assumptions about human beings. Much of the systems engineering approach has embodied the fallacies of Taylor's scientific management and is not properly open system theory.

Another difficulty with the general systems approach is its preoccupation with biochemical and biological levels of phenomena and explanation. This is true of the original formulation, as well as of the work of the Miller group. Boulding (1956) has described a hierarchy of systems representing eight levels of complexity:

1. frameworks of static structure
2. the clockworks of physics and astronomy
3. the control mechanism or cybernetic system
4. the cell or self-maintaining structure
5. the genetic or plant level
6. the animal level with purposive behavior and self-awareness
7. the human level
8. social organization or individuals in roles

He believes, moreover, that the phenomena to be explained become more complex at each successive level and that adequate theoretical models have been developed only for the first four. Even if this evaluation is pessimistic, it does indicate why the natural sciences have dominated the thinking of students of systems. The danger, however, is that analogical thinking will replace concepts derived from the direct study of the higher levels of phenomena.

**GROWTH OF THE FIELD
OF ORGANIZATIONAL STUDIES**

Organizational research has had major inputs from five sources: (1) the case studies of sociologists, (2) traditional industrial psychology inspired by scientific management theory, (3) the Mayo exploration into small group processess and related work in group dynamics, (4) comparative studies of social organization, and (5) surveys of morale and motivation.

Sociological Case Studies

Organizational behavior as a field of study owes much to the early case studies of sociologists who took an almost anthropological approach in their emphasis on depth of understanding of a single social unit. In a series of studies, many of which appeared in the decade of the fifties, industrial sociology came into its own and provided rich materials for the formulation of organizational hypotheses. Among the better known of these early case studies are Selznick's account (1949) of the Tennessee Valley Authority, Gouldner's investigation (1954) of a coal mine, Stanton and Schwartz's study (1954) of a hospital psychiatric ward, Blau's comparison (1955) of two government agencies, Lipset's collaborative work with Trow and Coleman (1956) in describing a labor union, and Sykes' graphic account (1958) of a prison. Although no longer popular, the tradition of the organizational case study has persisted in the insightful work of a number of investigators such as Stotland and Kobler's depiction (1965) of the life and death of a mental hospital. And Brown (1960) has followed up the work of Jaques (1951) with a continuation of the change story in a British metal works.

Although strong in qualitative observation and penetrating in their insights into social processes, these case reports were weak in quantification and so provided little opportunity for establishing relationships between variables. Case studies need not exclude measurement, but the early trend was for comprehensive qualitative coverage and little quantification.

Scientific Management
and Traditional Industrial Psychology

Industrial psychology began with a narrow focus; it accepted organizational variables as givens and tried to learn how people could best be selected and adapted for the required organizational roles. The orientation was pragmatic, and the organization was viewed as a machine. The dominating interest, explicit or implicit, was how the organization could be made more efficient. The scientific management school of Frederick Taylor (1923) conducted time and motion studies, investigations of temperature and illumination, rest intervals, and other conditions of work—always in relation to the criterion of productivity. This concern with ways of increasing productivity went hand in hand with personnel procedures for developing an appropriate fit between a particular role and its incumbent, preferably without modifying the role. In short, industrial psychology before World War II contributed some knowledge about the behavior of individuals in work organizations but little about the behavior of organizations. It was more a branch of applied individual psychology and, in fact, had many of the same founders as other branches of applied psychology. It did not include system variables, told us almost nothing about the nature of organizations, and was silent about problems of organizational change.

Mayo and the Rediscovery
of Informal Group Processes

Whereas early industrial psychologists took the formal organizational chart as an account of organizational structure, sociologists and social psychologists were interested in the interpersonal processes and emerging group norms of organizations as ongoing systems. The experiments of Elton Mayo and his followers (1933), originally designed to investigate problems of scientific management (optimum conditions of illumination), ended up by dramatizing the importance of the small informal group. Even under poor working conditions female employees in a group enjoying special status and special privileges improved their productivity, whereas male employees with their own established norms about productivity were relatively unaffected by such treatment (Roethlisberger and Dickson, 1939). The increased productivity, known as the Hawthorne effect, has been ascribed merely to giving more attention to workers—an interpretation that misses the central part played by participation and group norms (Kahn, 1975).

The Mayo tradition was paralleled by the group dynamics movement, which had a different theoretical heritage—the work of Kurt Lewin (1947). Lewin and his associates developed research and theory on group process much more systematically than the Mayo school. Both approaches went beyond the industrial psychology of the time in seeing people in organizations not merely as individuals responding to the formal requirements of their roles, but as group members developing their own norms and their own cohesion. Although this was a great advance, it still did not deal with individuals as organization members.

The small group was as far as many disciples of group dynamics were willing to go. In England, however, the Tavistock research group, also influenced by Lewin, pursued a rather different line of investigation and opened the door to a consideration of system variables. They conceived of the organization as a sociotechnical system dependent on the character of the social environment (Trist et al., 1963).

Comparative Analysis of Organizations

Sociologists have supplemented their case studies of organizations with comparative analyses in which they seek to find relationships among characteristics of organizations themselves, or between organizational characteristics and aspects of the environment. By studying two or more organizations at a time, the investigator attempts to make generalizations at the organizational level—for example, between size and differentiation, or between an uncertain environment and flexible organizational structure, or between rate of growth and the proportion of employees in administration and in production. The organization, not the individual, is the unit of analysis.

Such studies clearly focus on the system and furnish a valuable counterpoint to the older industrial psychology. Their weaknesses have been less conceptual than methododological, in that their measures of organizational variables have often come only from secondary sources, such as organizational records, or from expert opinion. Too often the investigator lacks the resources to assess adequately the factors under investigation. Nor do researchers agree either about what should be studied or how, even if resources were ample. Nevertheless, the approach of the comparative study must engage the organizational researcher of the future, because comparative analysis is especially appropriate for furnishing information about the primary adaptation of the organization to its social and technological setting (Udy, 1965). Already in 1965 Udy, in his review of the work in this area, was able to report on over 100 studies, an encouraging sign. It should be added that the survey method can also contribute to the comparative analysis of organizations, provided that more than one organization is involved in the research design and the surveys are directed at organizational variables. The work of Tannenbaum (1974) illustrates the use of survey methods for comparative organizational research.

Surveys of Morale and Motivation

The advocates of scientific management assumed that people in organizations accepted the formally prescribed roles much as they themselves did. But people evaluate their environment according to their own perceptions and interests. Their evaluations, their satisfactions, and the resulting motive patterns contribute to their behavior in organizations, and in the aggregate affect the morale of the system. During World War II, when industrial productivity in the United States became a national concern, two government units, one headed by Rensis Likert and the other by Elmo Wilson, conducted studies of morale and motivation in relation to absenteeism and productivity. These studies used multi-organizational designs and quantitative procedures; for example, Hyman and Katz (1947) in a study of absenteeism used a carefully drawn sample of 18 plants and a sub-sample of some 100 workers in each plant.

The use of surveys for examining industrial problems was extended by Likert and his colleagues, a number of whom moved to the University of Michigan in 1946 to found the Survey Research Center. Surveys began to include theoretical issues as well as practical problems. It soon became apparent from a series of studies in large organizations that leadership patterns at the first level influenced employee satisfaction and productivity, and that the relationship between first-line supervisors and employees was in turn heavily influenced by relationships at other echelons in the hierarchy. In other words, these investigations suggested the importance of variables characterizing the system rather than characterizing single personalities or pairs. This recognition led to one of the first large-scale field experiments in organizational psychology, in which the major independent variable manipulated was the degree of hierarchical control in the system (Morse and Reimer, 1956).

A rewarding example of the survey approach to studying organizational properties can be seen in the work of Arnold Tannenbaum (1968) on control in organizations. He selected a critical set of variables concerning power and its distribution in organized structures. These variables, though systemic in their conceptualization, were measured at the individual level and system attributes were determined by the agreement across levels in the organization. The propositions with which Tannenbaum was concerned have been pursued and tested in a variety of settings, culminating in a cross-national (1974) set of studies in which the same relationships were examined in cultures that differed markedly in degree of democratic values and practices, legal context, and worker expectations.

THE PROBLEM OF LEVELS

Organizational psychology, like the social sciences in general, has suffered from a confusion about levels of description and explanation. The older industrial psychology, as we have said, emphasized the individual level and neglected the collective level. Sociologists would say that it dealt with micro rather than macro variables. But what do we mean by the collective or macro level as compared to the micro or individual level? Are we not dealing with the behavior of individuals in both cases? For the most part we are, but differently. We start with different theoretical orientations, are therefore directed to different aspects of human behavior, and make different uses of individual responses.

In referring to levels, then, we must distinguish between levels of conceptualization and levels of phenomena. The level of phenomena refers to that which can be encountered, observed, measured, and manipulated. The conceptual level has to do with ideas and theories about phenomena. Now in the natural sciences levels differ both with respect to phenomena and with respect to concepts. There is an emergence of phenomena as we ascend the ladder from physics to psychology—the psychological experiences of color vision are not identical with the underlying physiological processes. In the social sciences, however, the distinction between levels is less clear. The product of an industrial plant is the output of a group of people and in that sense it is an emergent phenomenon rather than a mere aggregation of individual acts. But what is directly observable in creating that output are the interrelated acts of individuals. Much of what is regarded as at the sociological level is human behavior of this kind. It is at a higher level conceptually, but not phenomenologically.

Our thesis, then, is that the study of organizations should take the social system level as its conceptual starting point, but that many of the actual measures will be constructed from observations and reports of individual behavior and attitude. Concepts at the system level tell us what particular individual data to gather and how to use them. In studying the introduction of a new piece rate into an industrial enterprise, an individually-oriented psychologist might concentrate on the worker's needs for economic gains. The system-oriented social psychologist would look for the group norms that legitimate production rates. Both researchers would have to observe the behavior of individuals and both would have to put their questions to individuals, but their foci of inquiry and their inferences from data would be different.

Open system theory permits the use of both levels, the conceptual level for macro or system variables, the phenomenal level for the actual facts to be gathered. In looking at the actions of Castro and his followers overthrowing the Batista regime in Cuba in 1958, for example, psychologists would talk about the deprivations and frustrations motivating people to take action against the visible sources of their difficulties. Sociologists might talk about an unstable social system in which a semifeudal society held together by military force collapsed when an agrarian revolution destroyed the military force. Two observations are immediately possible from this example. The sociological analysis is much broader in scope and attempts to bring into focus a much wider range of related facts. It can do this by the use of such concepts as semifeudal system, which refers to a societal patterning of economic, social, and power relationships. Moreover, the sociological frame of reference, broader in scope, calls attention not so much to a different level of phenomenal facts as to more and different facts of human behavior at the same phenomenal level. The narrower scope of psychological theory again would give us not so much facts of a different level, but more detail about facts that might be passed over very quickly in any sociological description. The trend in sociological research has been in the direction of using the same field methods of study as those of the psychologist, sampling and interviewing and the use of quantitative methods in the observation of behavior. The main difference is that the more global, more all embracing theories of the sociologist are directed at an understanding of the total pattern of events.

Constructs at the macro level, however operationalized, may be too blunt or gross to account for the psychological dynamics at work in social systems. For example, we know in general that a nation in the process of shifting from secondary, or production industry, to tertiary, or service types of industry, will experience changes in the character of its political parties and in the voting behavior of its citizens. Precise predictions of the changes themselves will require knowledge of such factors as the fixation of people upon the identity and values of their old groups, the conditions that facilitate realistic perception of the changes taking place, and the attachment to group values that have no direct relation to occupational clustering. The macro approach is invaluable, however, in underlining the significant problem and directing our attention to areas in which variables need more careful formulation.

The weakness of the micro approach in the past has been twofold. It has dealt with too few of the significant variables in the total situation. It has often seized upon inappropriate variables and has pushed too hard in the direction of showing the universality of some fundamental principle such as reinforcement in the learning theory approach to social problems. This reductionistic emphasis in its very character tends to lose the problem with which it should be concerned. We are limited in our understanding of an organizational outcome such as a strike vote by a union when we try to reduce it to the principles of laboratory learning. We can use learning principles profitably, however, if we can identify a learning problem in the social system in which it arises.

We contend that these weaknesses in the micro approach are readily overcome if we combine this psychological attack with the concepts available from the macro approach. This procedure involves the translation of the sociological concepts into a host of micro concepts which are concerned with the same area of social behavior. The translation is made easier by the fact that the two levels by and large do not have different types of facts to worry about. The physiological and the psychological can be correlated but not translated; the sensation of blueness always remains distinctive as a factual datum from the neuro-chemical process upon which it may be dependent. A role system can, however, be translated into the interdependent and shared values and expectations of legitimate behavior of a group of people.

SUMMARY

Past approaches to the study of social problems and social behavior have been limited by a lack of adequate conceptual tools. This limitation has been manifest both in psychology and sociology, although in different ways.

Psychologists have been characteristically unable or unwilling to deal with the facts of social organization and social structure. Societies and organizations consist of patterned behaviors, and the behavior of each individual is determined to a considerable extent by the requirements of the larger pattern. This context is not often incorporated into psychological theories. Some such theories—the psychoanalytic, for example—deal with the influence of the family on the individual. Others take some account of the small group as the individual environment, and still others are concerned with the influence of culture, that most global of environmental concepts. Even social psychology, however, has neglected the organizational and institutional level, and textbooks of social psychology typically conclude with some treatment of small face-to-face groups. This book is an attempt to extend such discussions by beginning where they leave off—with the behavior of people in organizations. It is in that sense a second book in social psychology.

To remedy the shortcomings of psychological theorizing, we propose to follow the approach of open system theory, which emphasizes the system character of social relationships and the transactions of systems with their environment. This theoretical approach is not yet fully developed but important contributions to its growth can be found in the dialectic of Marx, the general systems theory of von Bertalanffy and J. G. Miller, the event-system conceptualization of F. H. Allport and the sociological theory of Talcott Parsons. Open system theory seems to us to permit breadth without oversimplification. It emphasizes, through the basic assumption of entropy, the necessary dependence of any organization upon its environment. The open system concepts of energic input and maintenance point to the motives and behavior of the individuals who are the carriers of energic input for human organizations; the concept of output and its necessary absorption by the larger environment also links the micro and macro levels of discourse. For all these reasons, open system theory represents the point of departure for the chapters that follow.

Open system theory can provide a comprehensive framework for bringing together the advances in organizational research which in themselves are limited and incomplete. Five major sources of input can be readily identified in the history of the field; sociological case studies of individual organizations, traditional industrial psychology of scientific management, the Mayo work and the rediscovery of informal group processes, comparative analysis of organizations, and surveys of morale and motivation.

The problem of scientific levels, specifically of the macro versus the micro approach, is solved once we recognize the common error of confusing theoretical concepts with data. The macro level for the social psychologist is one of theory, of system constructs. The micro level is one of data, of the measurement of human behavior. The varieties and patterns of behavior are many and the events of human behavior can be aggregated and combined in many ways. Concepts from the macro level tell the social psychological observers where to look and how to utilize and combine their observations. But the observations themselves are usually at the micro level; the basic data of social psychology are the acts of human beings.

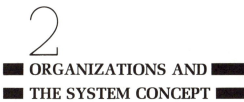

2
ORGANIZATIONS AND THE SYSTEM CONCEPT

The aims of social science with respect to human organizations are like those of any other science with respect to the events and phenomena of its domain. Social scientists wish to understand human organizations, to describe what is essential in their form, aspects, and functions. They wish to explain cycles of growth and decline, to predict organizational effects and effectiveness. Perhaps they wish as well to test and apply such knowledge by introducing purposeful changes into organizations—by making them, for example, more benign, more responsive to human needs.

Such efforts are not solely the prerogative of social science, however; common-sense approaches to understanding and altering organizations are ancient and perpetual. They tend, on the whole, to rely heavily on two assumptions: that the location and nature of an organization are given by its name; and that an organization is possessed of built-in goals—because such goals were implanted by its founders, decreed by its present leaders, or because they emerged mysteriously as the purposes of the organizational system itself. These assumptions scarcely provide an adequate basis for the study of organizations and at times can be misleading and even fallacious. We propose, however, to make use of the information to which they point.

THE DEFINITION AND IDENTIFICATION OF ORGANIZATIONS

The first problem in understanding an organization or a social system is its location and identification. How do we know that we are dealing with an organization? What are its boundaries? What behavior belongs to the organization and what behavior lies outside it? Who are the individuals whose actions are to be studied and what segments of their behavior are to be included?

The common-sense answer to such questions begins with the organizational name. The fact that popular names exist to label social organizations, however, is both a help and a hindrance. These labels represent socially accepted stereotypes about organizations and do not specify their role structure, their psychological nature, or their boundaries. On the other hand, these names help in locating the area of behavior in which we are interested. Moreover, the fact that people both within and without an organization accept stereotypes about its nature and functioning is one determinant of its character.

The second key characteristic of the common-sense approach to understanding an organization is to regard it simply as the epitome of the purposes of its designer, its leaders, or its key members.[1] The tele-

---

[1]See Chapter 15 for a further discussion of the problem of organizational goals.

ology of this approach is again both a help and a hindrance. Since human purpose is deliberately built into organizations and is specifically recorded in the social compact, the by-laws, or other formal protocol of the undertaking, it would be inefficient not to utilize these sources of information. In the early development of a group, many processes are generated that have little to do with its rational purpose, but over time there is a cumulative recognition of the devices for ordering group life and a deliberate use of these devices.

Apart from formal protocol, the primary mission of an organization as perceived by its leaders furnishes a highly informative set of clues for the researcher seeking to study organizational functioning. Nevertheless, the stated purposes of an organization as given by its by-laws or in the reports of its leaders can be misleading. Such statements of objectives may idealize, rationalize, distort, omit, or even conceal some essential aspects of the functioning of the organization. Nor is there always agreement about the mission of the organization among its leaders and members. The university president may describe the purpose of the institution as turning out national leaders; the academic dean sees it as imparting the cultural heritage of the past, the academic vice-president as enabling students to move toward self-actualization and development, the graduate dean as creating new knowledge, the dean of students as training young people in technical and professional skills which will enable them to earn their living, and the editor of the student newspaper as inculcating the conservative values that will preserve the status quo of an outmoded capitalistic society.

The fallacy here is equating the purposes or goals of organizations with the purposes and goals of individual members. The organization as a system has an output, a product or an outcome, but this is not necessarily identical with the individual purposes of group members. Though the founders of the organization and its key members do think in teleological terms about organizational objectives, we should not accept such practical thinking, useful as it may be, in place of a theoretical set of constructs for purposes of scientific analysis. Social science, too frequently in the past, has been misled by such shortcuts and has equated popular phenomenology with scientific explanation.

In fact, the classic body of theory and thinking about organizations has assumed a teleology of this sort as the easiest way of identifying organizational structures and their functions. From this point of view an organization is a social device for efficiently accomplishing through group means some stated purpose; it is the equivalent of the blueprint for the design of a machine that is to be created for some practical objective. The essential difficulty with this purposive approach is that an organization characteristically includes more and less than is indicated by the design of its founder or the purpose of its leader. Some of the factors assumed in the design may be lacking or so distorted in operational practice as to be meaningless, while unforeseen embellishments dominate the organizational structure. Moreover, it is not always possible to ferret out the designers of the organization or to discover the intricacies of the design which they carried in their heads. The attempt by Merton (1957) to deal with the latent function of the organization in contrast with its manifest function is one way of dealing with this problem. The study of unanticipated consequences as well as anticipated consequences of organizational functioning is a similar way of handling the matter. Again, however, we are back to the purposes of the creators or leaders, dealing with unanticipated consequences on the assumption that we can discover the consequences anticipated by them and can lump all other outcomes together as a kind of error variance.

It would be much better theoretically, however, to start with concepts that do not call for identifying the purposes of the designers and then correcting for them when they do not seem to be fulfilled. The theoretical concepts should begin with the input, output, and functioning of the organization as a system and not with the rational purposes of its leaders. We may want to employ such purposive notions to lead us to sources of data or as subjects of special study, but not as our basic theoretical constructs for understanding organizations.

Our theoretical model for the understanding of organizations is that of an energic input-output system in which the energic return from the output reactivates the system. Social organizations are flagrantly open systems in that the input of energies and the conversion of output into further energic input consist of transactions between the organization and its environment.

All social systems, including organizations, consist of the patterned activities of a number of individuals. Moreover, these patterned activities are complementary or interdependent with respect to some common output or outcome; they are repeated, relatively enduring, and bounded in space and time. If the activity pattern occurs only once or at unpredictable intervals, we could not speak of an organization. The stability or recurrence of activities can be examined in relation to the *energic input* into the system, the *transformation of energies within the system*, and the *resulting product or energic output*. In a factory the raw materials and the human labor are the energic input, the patterned activities of production the transformation of energy, and the finished product the output. To maintain this patterned activity requires a continued renewal of the inflow of energy. This is guaranteed in social systems by the energic return from the product or outcome. Thus the outcome of the cycle of activities furnishes new energy for the initiation of a renewed cycle. The company that produces automobiles sells them and by doing so obtains the means of securing new raw materials, compensating its labor force, and continuing the activity pattern.

In many organizations outcomes are converted into money and new energy is furnished through this mechanism. Money is a convenient way of handling energy units both on the output and input sides, and buying and selling represent one set of social rules for regulating exchange. Indeed, these rules are so effective and so widespread that there is some danger of mistaking the business of buying and selling for the defining cycles of organization. It is a commonplace executive observation that businesses exist to make money, and the observation is usually allowed to go unchallenged. It is, however, a very limited statement about the purposes of business.

Some human organizations do not depend on the cycle of selling and buying to maintain themselves. Universities and public agencies depend rather on bequests and legislative appropriations, and in so-called voluntary organizations the output reenergizes the activity of organization members in a more direct fashion. Member activities and accomplishments are rewarding in themselves and tend therefore to be continued without the mediation of the outside environment. A society of bird watchers can wander into the hills and engage in the rewarding activities of identifying birds for their mutual edification and enjoyment. Organizations thus differ on this important dimension of the source of energy renewal, with the great majority utilizing both intrinsic and extrinsic sources in varying degree. Most large-scale organizations are not as self-contained as small voluntary groups and are very dependent upon the social effects of their output for energy renewal.

Our two basic criteria for identifying social systems and determining their functions are (1) tracing the pattern of energy exchange or activity of people as it results in some output and (2) ascertaining how the output is translated into energy that reactivates the pattern. We shall refer to organizational functions or objectives not as the conscious purposes of group leaders or group members but as the outcomes that are the energic source for maintenance of the same type of output.

The problem of identifying the boundaries of an organization is solved by following the energic and informational transactions as they relate to the cycle of activities of input, throughput, and output. Behavior not tied to these functions lies outside the system. Many factors are related to the intake of materials into a structure but only those activities concerned with the actual importation of energy or information are part of that structure. Similarly, many processes are associated with the reception of outputs by the environment, but only those activities having to do with export of products are behavioral patterns of the organization. Obviously there is less difficulty in identifying the patterns of behavior responsible for the throughput of the system than for the boundary subsystems that deal with the environment. These subsystems do not always have clearly identifiable borders. Nor can the problem be handled by regarding any behavior of an organizational member as organizational behavior. A person in a boundary role may interact with members of another system as if he or she belonged to that system. Even the production worker's behavior, although physically taking place within the factory, at times may be social interaction with friends unrelated to the work role. In searching for criteria to define the boundaries of a system one looks for some qualitative break in the nature of the behavior pattern under scrutiny or some sudden quantitative change. These changes can be noted as the same people step out of their organizational roles and behave in radically different fashion or as we move to different people operating in different role systems.

This model of an energic input-output system is taken from the open system theory as promulgated by von Bertalanffy (1956). Theorists have pointed out the applicability of the system concepts of the natural sciences to the problems of social science. It is important, therefore, to examine in more detail the constructs of system theory and the characteristics of open systems.

System theory is basically concerned with problems of relationships, of structure, and of interdependence rather than with the constant attributes of objects. In general approach it resembles field theory except that its dynamics deal with temporal as well as spatial patterns. Older formulations of system constructs dealt with the closed systems of the physical sciences, in which relatively self-contained structures could be treated successfully as if they were independent of external forces. But living systems, whether biological organisms or social organizations, are acutely dependent on their external environment and so must be conceived of as open systems.

Before the advent of open system thinking, social scientists tended to take one of two approaches in dealing with social structures; they tended either (1) to regard them as closed systems to which the laws of physics applied or (2) to endow them with some vitalistic concept like entelechy. In the former case they ignored the environmental forces affecting the organization and in the latter case they fell back upon some magical purposiveness to account for organizational functioning. Biological theorists, however, have rescued us from this trap by pointing out that the concept of the open system means that we neither have to follow the laws of traditional physics, nor in deserting them do we have to abandon science. The laws of Newtonian physics are correct generalizations but they are limited to closed systems. They do not apply in the same fashion to open systems which maintain themselves through constant commerce with their environment, that is, a continuous inflow and outflow of energy through permeable boundaries.

The essential difference between closed and open systems can be seen in terms of the concept of entropy and the second law of thermodynamics. According to the second law of thermodynamics, a system moves toward equilibrium; it tends to run down, that is, its differentiated structures tend to move toward dissolution as the elements composing them become arranged in random disorder. For example, suppose that a bar of iron has been heated by the application of a blowtorch on one side. The arrangement of all the fast (heated) molecules on one side and all the slow molecules on the other is an unstable state, and over time the distribution of molecules becomes in effect random, with the resultant cooling of one side and heating of the other, so that all surfaces of the iron approach the same temperature. A similar process of heat exchange will also be going on between the iron bar and its environment, so that the bar will gradually approach the temperature of the room in which it is located, and in so doing will elevate somewhat the previous temperature of the room. More technically, entropy increases toward a maximum and equilibrium occurs as the physical system attains the state of the most probable distribution of its elements. In social systems, however, structures tend to become more elaborated rather than less differentiated. The rich may grow richer and the poor may grow poorer. The open system does not run down, because it can import energy from the world around it. Thus the operation of entropy is counteracted by the importation of energy and the living system is characterized by negative rather than positive entropy.

COMMON CHARACTERISTICS OF OPEN SYSTEMS

Though the various open systems have common characteristics by virtue of being open, they differ in other characteristics. If this were not the case, we would be able to obtain all our basic knowledge about social organizations through studying biological organisms or even through the study of a single cell.

The following ten characteristics seem to define all open systems.

1. *Importation of energy.* Open systems import some form of energy from the external environment. The cell receives oxygen from the bloodstream; the body similarly takes in oxygen from the air and food from the external world. The personality depends on the external world for stimulation. Studies of sensory deprivation show that a person placed in a darkened soundproof room, with minimal visual and auditory stimulation, develops hallucinations and other signs of mental stress (Solomon et al., 1961). Deprivation of social stimulation also can lead to mental disorganization (Spitz, 1945). In other words, the functioning personality is heavily dependent upon the continuous inflow of stimulation from the external environment. Similarly, social organizations must draw renewed supplies of energy from other institutions, or people, or the material environment. No social structure is self-sufficient or self-contained.

2. *The throughput.* Open systems transform the energy available

to them. The body converts starch and sugar into heat and action. The personality converts chemical and electrical stimuli into sensory qualities, and information into thought patterns. The organization creates a new product, or processes materials, or trains people, or provides a service. These activities entail some reorganization of input. Some work gets done in the system.

3. *The output.* Open systems export some product into the environment, whether it be the invention of an inquiring mind or a bridge constructed by an engineering firm. Even the biological organism exports physiological products such as carbon dioxide from the lungs, which helps to maintain plants in the immediate environment. Continuing to turn out a system product depends on the receptivity of the environment. The stuff that is pumped into the environment may not be absorbed—either the primary product which surfeits the market or the secondary product which pollutes the surrounding air and water.

4. *Systems as cycles of events.* The pattern of activities of the energy exchange has a cyclic character. The product exported into the environment furnishes the sources of energy for the repetition of the cycle of activities. The energy reinforcing the cycle of activities can derive from some exchange of the product in the external world or from the activity itself. In the former instance, the industrial concern utilizes raw materials and human labor to turn out a product which is marketed, and the monetary return is used to obtain more raw materials and labor to perpetuate the cycle of activities. In the latter instance, the voluntary organization can provide expressive satisfactions to its members so that the energy renewal comes directly from the organizational activity itself.

System structure, or the relatedness of parts, can be observed directly when the system itself is physically bounded and its subparts are also bounded within the larger structure. The human body and its various organs constitute such a system. But how do we deal with social structures, where physical boundaries in this sense do not exist? The genius of F. H. Allport (1962) contributed the answer, namely that the structure is to be found in an interrelated set of events that return upon themselves to complete and renew a cycle of activities. It is events rather than things which are structured, so that social structure is a dynamic rather than a static concept. Activities are structured so that they comprise a unity in their completion or closure. A simple linear stimulus-response exchange between two people would not constitute social structure. To create structure, the responses of A would have to elicit B's reactions in such a manner that the responses of the latter would stimulate A to further responses. Of course the chain of events may involve many people, but their behavior can be characterized as showing structure only when there is some closure to the chain by a return to its point of origin, with the probability that the chain of events will then be repeated. The repetition of the cycle does not have to involve the same set of phenotypical happenings. It may expand to include more subevents of exactly the same kind or it may involve similar activities directed toward the same outcomes. In the individual organism the eye may move in such a way as to have the point of light fall upon the center of the retina. As the point of light moves, the movements of the eye may also change but to complete the same cycle of activity, that is, to focus upon the point of light.

A single cycle of events of a self-closing character gives us a simple form of structure. But such single cycles can also combine to give a larger structure of events or an event system. An event system may consist of a circle of smaller cycles or hoops, each one of which makes contact with several others. Cycles from other types of subsystems may also be tangential to one another. The basic method for the identification of social structures is to follow the energic chain of events from the input of energy through its transformation to the point of closure of the cycle.

5. *Negative entropy.* To survive, open systems must reverse the entropic process; they must acquire negative entropy. The entropic process is a universal law of nature in which all forms of organization move toward disorganization or death. Complex physical systems move toward simple random distribution of their elements and biological organisms also run down and perish. In the long run all open systems are subject to the law of entropy; they lose inputs or the ability to transform them, and die. While they live, however, the entropic process is arrested or reversed. The cycle of input, transformation, and output is essential to system life, and it is a cycle of negative entropy.

Open systems vary in their ability to survive even brief interruptions in this cycle. Some storage capacity, however, is characteristic. By importing more energy from its environment than it expends, the open system can store energy and acquire negative entropy. Within the limits of its storage capacity, an open system tends to maximize its ratio of imported to expended energy, to survive and, even during periods of crisis, to live on borrowed time. Prisoners in concentration camps on a starvation diet will carefully conserve the expenditure of energy, in order to make the limited food go as far as possible (Cohen, 1954). Social organizations will seek to improve their survival position and to acquire in their reserves a comfortable margin of operation.

The entropic process asserts itself in all biological systems as well as in closed physical systems. The energy replenishment of the biological organism cannot maintain indefinitely the complex organizational structure of living tissue. Social systems, however, are not anchored in the same physical constancies as biological organisms and so are capable of almost indefinite arresting of the entropic process. Nevertheless the number of organizations that go out of existence every year is large.

6. *Information input, negative feedback, and the coding process.* The inputs into living systems do not consist only of energic materials that become transformed or altered in the work that gets done. Inputs are also informative in character and furnish signals to the structure about the environment and about its own functioning in relation to the environment. Just as we recognize the distinction between cues and drives in individual psychology, so must we distinguish between informational and energic inputs for all living systems.

The simplest type of informational input found in all systems is negative feedback. Information feedback of a negative kind enables the system to correct its deviations from course. The working parts of the machine feed back information about the effects of their operation to some central mechanism or subsystem which acts on such information to keep the system on target. The thermostat that controls the temperature of the room is a simple example of a regulatory device which operates on the basis of negative feedback. The automated power plant would furnish more complex examples. Miller (1955) emphasizes the critical nature of negative feedback in his proposition: *"When a system's negative feedback discontinues, its steady state vanishes, and at the same time its boundary disappears and the system terminates"* (p. 529). If there is no corrective device to get the system back on its course, it will expend too much energy or it will ingest too much energic input and no longer continue as a system.

The reception of inputs into a system is selective. Not all energic inputs can be absorbed into every system. The digestive system of living creatures assimilates only those inputs to which it is adapted. Similarly, systems can react only to those information signals to which they are attuned. The general term for the selective mechanisms of a system by which incoming materials are rejected or accepted and translated for the structure is coding. Through the coding process the "blooming, buzzing confusion" of the world is simplified into a few meaningful and basic categories for a given system. The nature of the functions performed by the system determines its coding mechanisms, which in turn perpetuate this type of functioning.

7. *The steady state and dynamic homeostasis.* The importation of energy to arrest entropy operates to maintain some constancy in energy exchange, so that open systems that survive are characterized by a steady state. A steady state is not a motionless or true equilibrium. There is a continuous inflow of energy from the external environment and a continuous export of the products of the system, but the character of the system, the ratio of the energy exchanges and the relations between parts, remains the same. The catabolic and anabolic processes of tissue breakdown and restoration within the body preserve a steady state so that the organism from time to time is not the identical or-

ganism it was but a highly similar organism. The steady state is seen in clear form in the homeostatic processes for the regulation of body temperature; external conditions of humidity and temperature may vary, but the temperature of the body remains the same. The endocrine glands are a regulatory mechanism for preserving an evenness of physiological functioning. The general principle here is that of Le Châtelier (see Bradley and Calvin, 1956), who maintains that any internal or external factor that threatens to disrupt the system is countered by forces which restore the system as closely as possible to its previous state. Krech and Crutchfield (1948) similarly hold, with respect to psychological organization, that cognitive structures will react to influences in such a way as to absorb them with minimal change to existing cognitive integration. The initial adjustment to such disturbances is typically approximate rather than precise. If it is insufficient, further adjustment in the same direction will follow. If it is excessive, it will be followed by a counteradjustment. The iterative process will then continue to the point of equilibrium or until the process is broken by some further disruptive event. A temporal chart of activity will thus show a series of ups and downs instead of a smooth curve. Moreover, the system itself is in motion. Its equilibrium, as Lewin (1947) put it, is quasi-stationary, more like the constant depth of a flowing river than a still pond. *The basic principle is the preservation of the character of the system.*

The homeostatic principle must be qualified in one further respect in its application to complex living systems: in counteracting entropy these systems move toward growth and expansion. This apparent contradiction can be resolved, however, if we recognize the complexity of the subsystems and their interaction in anticipating changes necessary for the maintenance of an overall steady state. Stagner (1951) has pointed out that the initial disturbance of a given tissue constancy within the biological organism will result in mobilization of energy to restore the balance, but that recurrent upsets will lead to actions to anticipate the disturbance:

> We eat before we experience intense hunger pangs.... energy mobilization for forestalling tactics must be explained in terms of a *cortical tension* which reflects the visceral-proprioceptive pattern of the original biological disequilibration.... *Dynamic homeostasis* involves the maintenance of tissue constancies by establishing a constant physical environment—by reducing the variability and disturbing effects of external stimulation. Thus the organism does not simply restore the prior equilibrium. A new, more complex and more comprehensive equilibrium is established. (p. 5)

Growth is one form of this tendency toward equilibria of increasing complexity and comprehensiveness. In preserving its character, the system tends to import more energy than is required for its output, as we noted in discussing negative entropy. To insure survival, systems operate to acquire some margin of safety beyond the immediate level of existence. The body will store fat, the social organization will build up reserves, the society will increase its technological and cultural base. Miller (1955) has formulated the proposition that the rate of growth of a system—within certain ranges—is exponential if it exists in a medium that makes available unrestricted amounts of energy for input.

In adapting to their environment, systems will attempt to cope with external forces by ingesting them or acquiring control over them. The physical boundedness of the single organism means that such attempts to control the environment affect the behavioral system rather than the biological system of the individual. Social systems will move, however, toward incorporating within their boundaries the external resources essential to survival. Again the result is an expansion of the original system.

Thus, the steady state, which at the simple level is one of homeostasis over time, at more complex levels becomes one of preserving the character of the system through growth and expansion. The basic system does not change directly as a consequence of expansion. The most common growth pattern is a multiplication of the same type of cycles or subsystems—a change in quantity rather than in quality. Animal and plant species grow by multiplication. A social system adds more units of the same essential type as it already has. Haire (1959) has studied the ratio between the sizes of different subsystems in growing business organizations. He found that though the number of people increased in both the production subsystem and the subsystem concerned with the external world, the ratio of the two groups remained constant. Qualitative change does occur, however, in two ways. In the first place, quantitative growth calls for supportive subsystems of a specialized character not necessary when the system was smaller. In the second place, there is a point where quantitative changes produce a qualitative difference in the functioning of a system. A small college that triples its size is no longer the same institution in terms of the relation between its administration and faculty, relations among the various academic departments, or the nature of its instruction.

In short, living systems exhibit a growth or expansion dynamic in which they maximize their basic character. They react to change or they anticipate change through growth which assimilates the new energic inputs to the nature of their structure. In terms of Lewin's quasi-stationary equilibrium, the ups and downs of the adjustive process do not always result in a return to the old level. Under certain circumstances a solidification or freezing occurs during one of the adjustive cycles. A new base line is thus established and successive movements fluctuate around this level, which may be either above or below the previous plateau of operation.

8. *Differentiation.* Open systems move in the direction of differentiation and elaboration. Diffuse global patterns are replaced by more specialized functions. The sense organs and the nervous system evolved as highly differentiated structures from the primitive nervous tissues. The growth of the personality proceeds from primitive, crude organizations of mental functions to hierarchically structured and well-differentiated systems of beliefs and feelings. Social organizations move toward the multiplication and elaboration of roles with greater specialization of function. In the United States today medical specialists now outnumber the general practitioners.

One type of differentiated growth in systems is what von Bertalanffy (1956) terms progressive mechanization. It finds expression in the way in which a system achieves a steady state. The early method is a process that involves an interaction of various dynamic forces, whereas the later development entails the use of a regulatory feedback mechanism. He writes:

> It can be shown that the *primary* regulations in organic systems, that is, those which are most fundamental and primitive in embryonic development as well as in evolution, are of such nature of dynamic interaction. . . . Superimposed are those regulations which we may call *secondary,* and which are controlled by fixed arrangements, especially of the feedback type. This state of affairs is a consequence of a general principle of organization which may be called progressive mechanization. At first, systems—biological, neurological, psychological or social—are governed by dynamic interaction of their components; later on, fixed arrangements and conditions of constraint are established which render the system and its parts more efficient, but also gradually diminish and eventually abolish its equipotentiality. (p. 6)

9. *Integration and Coordination.* As differentiation proceeds, it is countered by processes that bring the system together for unified functioning. Von Bertalanffy (1956) spoke of progressive mechanization in the regulatory processes of organic systems, the replacement of dynamic interaction by fixed control arrangements. In social systems, in contrast to biological systems, there are two different paths for

achieving unification, which Georgopoulos (1975) calls coordination and integration.[2] Coordination is analogous to von Bertalanffy's fixed control arrangements. It is the addition of various devices for assuring the functional articulation of tasks and roles—controlling the speed of the assembly line, for example. Integration is the achievement of unification through shared norms and values.

In organisms, hormonal and nervous subsystems provide the integrating mechanisms. In social systems, without built-in physical mechanisms of regulation, integration is often achieved at the small group level through mutually shared psychological fields (see chapter 12). For large social organizations, coordination, rather than integration, is the rule for providing orderly and systematic articulation—through such devices as priority setting, the establishment and regulation of routines, timing and synchronization of functions, scheduling and sequencing of events.

10. *Equifinality.* Open systems are further characterized by the principle of equifinality, a principle suggested by von Bertalanffy in 1940. According to this principle, a system can reach the same final state from differing initial conditions and by a variety of paths. The well-known biological experiments on the sea urchin show that a normal creature of that species can develop from a complete ovum, from each half of a divided ovum, or from the fusion product of two whole ova. As open systems move toward regulatory mechanisms to control their operations, the amount of equifinality may be reduced.

SOME CONSEQUENCES OF VIEWING ORGANIZATIONS AS OPEN SYSTEMS

Like most innovations in scientific theory, the open system approach was developed in order to deal with inadequacies in previous models. The inadequacies of closed system thinking about organizations became increasingly apparent during the midcentury decades of rapid societal change. The limitations of empirical research based on closed system assumptions also pointed up the need for a more comprehensive theoretical approach. The consequences, or rather the potentialities, of dealing with organizations as open systems can best be seen in contrast to the limitations and misconceptions of closed system thinking. The most important of these misconceptions, almost by definition, is the failure to recognize fully the dependence of organi-

---

[2]This distinction is similar to the one formulated by Nancy Morse on *binding-in* and *binding-between* functions—the binding-in referring to the involvement of people in the system, the binding-between referring to the ties between system parts. (Unpublished manuscript.)

zations on inputs from their environment. That inflow of materials and energy is neither constant nor assured, and when it is treated as a constant much of organizational behavior becomes unexplainable. The fact that organizations have developed protective devices to maintain stability and that they are notoriously difficult to change or reform should not be allowed to obscure their dynamic relationships with the social and natural environment. Changes in that environment lead to demands for change in the organization, and even the effort to resist those demands results in internal change.

It follows that the study of organizations should include the study of organization-environment relations. We must examine the ways in which an organization is tied to other structures, not only those that furnish economic inputs and support but also structures that can provide political influence and societal legitimation. The open-system emphasis on such relationships implies an interest in properties of the environment itself. Its turbulence or placidity, for example, limits the kinds of relationships that an organization can form with systems in the environment and indicates also the kinds of relationships that an organization will require to assure its own survival.

The emphasis on openness is qualified, however. There is a duality to the concept of open system; the concept implies openness but it also implies system properties, stable patterns of relationships and behavior within boundaries. Complete openness to the environment means loss of those properties; the completely open organization would no longer be differentiated from its environment and would cease to exist as a distinct system. The organization lives only by being open to inputs, but selectively; its continuing existence requires both the property of openness and of selectivity.

The open system approach requires study of these selective processes, analysis of those elements in the environment that are actively sought, those disregarded, and those kept out or defended against. The basis of these choices, the means employed for their implementation, and the consequences for organizational effectiveness and survival becomes topics for research. In well-established organizations the internal arrangements for making and implementing such choices are highly developed, a fact that often allows such organizations to withstand environmental turbulence better than the reform or revolutionary movements that seek to displace them. Sustained supportive inputs are less predictable for groups attempting social change.

A second serious deficiency in closed system thinking, both theoretical and pragmatic, is overconcentration on principles of internal functioning. This could be viewed as merely another aspect of disregard for the environment, but it has consequences of its own. Internal moves are planned without regard for their effects on the environment and the consequent environmental response. The effects of such moves on the maintenance inputs of motivation and morale tend not to be adequately considered. Stability may be sought through tighter integration and coordination when flexibility may be the more important requirement. Coordination and control become ends in themselves, desirable states within a closed system rather than means of attaining an adjustment between the system and its environment. Attempts to introduce coordination in kind and degree not functionally required tend to produce new internal problems.

Two further errors derive from the characteristic closed system disregard of the environment and preoccupation with internal functions— the neglect of equifinality and the treatment of disruptive external events as error variance. The equifinality principle simply asserts that there are more ways than one of producing a given outcome. In a completely closed system, the same initial conditions must lead to the same final result; nothing has changed and therefore nothing changes. In open systems, however, the principle of equifinality applies; it holds true at the biological level, and it is more conspicuously true at the social level. Yet in practice most armies insist that there is one best way for all recruits to assemble their guns; most coaching staffs teach one best way for all baseball players to hurl the ball in from the outfield. And in industry the doctrine of scientific management as propounded by Taylor and his disciples begins with the assumption of the one best way: discover it, standardize it, teach it, and insist on it. It is true that under fixed and known conditions there is one best way, but in human organizations the conditions of life are neither fixed nor fully known. Such organizations are better served by the general principle, characteristic of all open systems, that there need not be a single method for achieving an objective.

The closed system view implies that irregularities in the functioning of a system due to environmental influences are error variances and should be treated accordingly. According to this conception, they should be controlled out of studies of organizations. From the organization's own operations they should be excluded as irrelevant and should be guarded against. The decisions of officers to omit a consideration of external factors or to guard against such influences in a defensive fashion, as if they would go away if ignored, is an instance of this type of thinking. So is the now outmoded "public be damned" attitude of business executives toward the clientele upon whose support they depend. Open system theory, on the other hand, would maintain that environmental influences are not sources of error variance but are integral to the functioning of a social system, and that we cannot understand a system without a constant study of the forces that impinge upon it.

Finally, thinking of organizations as closed systems results in failure to understand and develop the feedback or intelligence function, the means by which the organization acquires information about changes in the environment. It is remarkable how weak many industrial companies are in their market research departments when they are so dependent on the market. The prediction can be hazarded that organizations in our society will increasingly move toward the improvement of the facilities for research in assessing environmental forces. We are in the process of correcting our misconception of the organization as a closed system, but the process is slow.

Open system theory, we believe, has potentialities for overcoming these defects in organizational thinking and practice. Its potentialities, however, cannot be realized merely by acknowledging the fact of organizational openness; they must be developed. Open is not a magic word, and pronouncing it is not enough to reveal what has been hidden in the organizational cave. We have begun the process of specification by discussing properties shared by all open systems. We turn next to the special properties of human organizations, as one category of such systems.

SUMMARY

The open system approach to organizations is contrasted with common-sense approaches, which tend to accept popular names and stereotypes as basic organizational properties and to identify the purpose of an organization in terms of the goals of its founders and leaders.

The open system approach, on the other hand, begins by identifying and mapping the repeated cycles of input, transformation, output, and renewed input which comprise the organizational pattern. This approach to organizations represents the adaptation of work in biology and in the physical sciences by von Bertalanffy and others.

Organizations as a special class of open systems have properties of their own, but they share other properties in common with all open systems. These include the importation of energy from the environment, the throughput or transformation of the imported energy into some product form that is characteristic of the system, the exporting of that product into the environment, and the reenergizing of the system from sources in the environment.

Open systems also share the characteristics of negative entropy, feedback, homeostasis, differentiation, coordination and equifinality. The law of negative entropy states that systems survive and maintain their characteristic internal order only as long as they import from the environment more energy than they expend in the process of transformation and exportation. The feedback principle has to do with information input, which is a special kind of energic importation, a kind of signal to the system about environmental conditions and about the functioning of the system in relation to its environment. The feedback of such information enables the system to correct for its own malfunctioning or for changes in the environment, and thus to maintain a steady state or homeostasis. This is a dynamic rather than a static balance, however. Open systems are not at rest but tend toward differentiation and elaboration, both because of sub-system dynamics and because of the relationship between growth and survival. Finally, open systems are characterized by the principle of equifinality, which asserts that systems can reach the same final state from different initial conditions and by different paths of development.

Traditional organizational theories have tended to view the human organization as a closed system. This tendency has led to a disregard of differing organizational environments and the nature of organizational dependency on environment. It has led also to an overconcentration on principles of internal organizational functioning, with consequent failure to develop and understand the processes of feedback which are essential to survival.

3
DEFINING CHARACTERISTICS
OF SOCIAL ORGANIZATIONS

OUTLINE

The Nature of Social Systems
    The Contrived Nature of Social Systems
        Symbiotic Patterns versus Social Organizations
    Production and Maintenance Inputs
    Types of Forces Reducing Human Variability

Major Social System Components: Roles, Norms, and Values
    Three Bases of System Integration
    Role Systems and the Role Concept
        The Concept of Partial Inclusion
    System Dynamics
        Acquisition and Extraction
        Organizational Climate

Generic Types of Subsystems
    Production or Technical Subsystems
    Supportive Subsystems
    Maintenance Subsystems
    Adaptive Subsystems
    Managerial Subsystems
    Subsidiary Concepts
        Leading Subsystems
        Organizational Space

The Organization in Relation to Its Environment
    Systems, Subsystems, and Supersystems
    System Openness, System Boundaries, and System Coding
    Intrinsic and Extrinsic Functions

Summary

System theory in its general form, as Kenneth Boulding (1956) has observed, furnishes the framework or skeleton for all science. It remains for the various disciplines to supply the flesh and blood, to provide a viable model for the understanding of phenomena at their own level of analysis. We are indebted to general system theory for some useful concepts and for the basic approach that emphasizes the principles of mutual influence in a fluid field of forces. But in the search for an all-encompassing dialectic, general theories often neglect essential characteristics of each particular field of forces. Our discussion of the common characteristics of all open systems should not blind us to the differences that do exist between biological and social systems. The stuff of which a system is constituted—the cells of a biological organism or the human beings in the social system—needs careful study. Otherwise we could know all there is to know about the political state from the science of cytology.

THE NATURE OF SOCIAL SYSTEMS

Biological structures have a physical boundedness that social structures lack. The biological structures are anchored in physical and physiological constancies, whereas the social structures are not. The skin of the body, the walls of the cell, even the less visible boundaries of the magnetic field represent a kind of structural location and definition for which there is no close social analogue.

Social structures are of course not found in a physical vacuum. They are tied into a concrete world of human beings, material resources, physical plants, and other artifacts, but these elements are not in any natural interaction with each other. In fact the social system has considerable independence of any particular physical part and can shed or replace it. The communication network of a social organization bears only a distant and figurative resemblance to the physical structures, such as the circulatory and nervous systems, by which the subparts of a biological organism are integrated. Too often such loose metaphors have prevented sociologists or even biologists, turned social theorists in their declining years, from grasping the essential differences between organism and society. The constancies of mutual influence among the subparts of a social system are fewer and less perfect than among the parts of a biological system.

A social system is a structuring of events or happenings rather than of physical parts and it therefore has no structure apart from its functioning (Allport, 1962). Physical or biological systems such as automobiles or organisms have structures that can be identified even when they are not functioning. In other words, these systems have both an anatomy and a physiology. There is no anatomy to a social system in this sense. When the biological organism ceases to function, the physical body is still present and its anatomy can be examined in a postmortem analysis. When a social system ceases to function, there is no longer an identifiable structure. It is difficult for us to view social systems as structures of events because of our needs for more concrete and simple ways of conceptualizing the world. Hence we tend to identify the buildings, the technological equipment, and the people they contain as the structure of an organization.

There has been no more pervasive, persistent, and futile fallacy handicapping the social sciences than the use of the physical model for the understanding of social structures. The biological metaphor, with its crude comparison of the physical parts of the body to the parts of the social system, has been replaced by more subtle but equally misleading analogies between biological and social functioning. This figurative type of thinking ignores the essential difference between the socially contrived nature of social systems and the physical structure of the machine or the human organism. So long as writers are committed to a theoretical framework based on the physical model, they will miss the essential social-psychological facts of the highly variable, loosely articulated character of social systems. They will ignore in the future as they have in the past the significance of system openness with respect to maintenance and production inputs and will neglect the overriding importance of maintenance inputs for social systems. They will see social organizations in terms of machine theory, or they will go to the opposite extreme of interpreting social outcomes as individual decisions and behavior in organizational roles as the mere expression of individual personality.

The Contrived Nature of Social Systems

Social structures are essentially contrived. People invent the complex patterns of behavior that we call social structure, and people create social structure by enacting those patterns of behavior. Many properties of social systems derive from these essential facts. As human inventions, social systems are imperfect. They can come apart at the seams overnight, but they can also outlast by centuries the biological organisms that originally created them. The cement that holds them together is essentially psychological rather than biological. Social systems are anchored in the attitudes, perceptions, beliefs, motivations, habits, and expectations of human beings. Such systems represent patterns of relationships in which the constancy of the individual units involved in the relationships can be very low. An organization can have a very high rate of turnover of personnel and still persist. The relationships of items rather than the items themselves provide the constancy. Biological systems are also patterns of relationships but their constituent parts are sufficiently stable so that the system itself can be readily identified and physically encountered. Our use of the term system, however, for describing a pattern of relationships is a conceptual definition rather than a term for a simply perceived or encountered aggregation of parts. Biological systems have the advantage, from the research point of view, of fixed physical boundaries and relatively small size, so that they are easily perceived as physical realities. Social systems are more difficult to locate, bound, and comprehend.

In short, social systems are characterized by much greater variability than biological systems. Three aspects of this variability will concern us especially throughout this book. (1) Social systems can be readily devised for a tremendous range of varying objectives, and any given system can acquire new and different functions during its life history. (2) The variable elements of the social system are not held in place by any set of biological givens, and many control mechanisms are introduced to hold the organization together. Much of the energy of organizations must be fed into devices of control to reduce the variability of human behavior and to produce stable patterns of activity. (3) The predictable growth curves of biological systems do not necessarily apply to social structures. Organizations are both more vulnerable to destruction and more long-lived than biological organisms. There is an internal determination of the life cycle of an organism based upon its genetic constitution. Built-in resources and forces for growth in the organism foster its survival and development in a normal environment. The social organization in its initial stages may or may not possess internal resources, and so may or may not survive its first few weeks or months of existence. The mortality rate of new enterprises and new organizations is significant, even in times of marked prosperity (Statistical Abstract of the United States, Bureau of the Census, 1963 and Survey of Current Business, U.S. Department of Commerce, September 1964). On the other hand, the social system has the great advantage of readily replacing elements or parts so that it can continue to operate within an unlimited future. All biological organisms have built-in entropy forces; their parts wear out and, despite a few dramatic surgical exceptions, basically cannot be replaced.

Symbiotic Patterns Versus
Social Organizations

The contrived nature of social systems warrants closer examination, for the nature of the contrivances further specifies the system properties of particular social structures. Though all social systems are dominantly of a contrived character, they vary in the degree to which the interdependent patterning of behavior is culturally fabricated or biologically based. The reciprocal behavior of mother and child in the feeding process reflects some social learning, but it is maintained basically by the physiological satisfactions that both child and mother obtain in the process. The interdependence of sexual partners is another instance of the biological basis of a social institution. Social psychologists have traditionally made the family the basis of their theorizing because the social tie—the bond that maintains people in constant relationship—is most compelling in the symbiotic patterns of sexual behavior and mother-child interactions. In most social systems, however, the social tie is not reinforced by direct biological gratification deriving from the acts of responding to others. To what extent it has its basis in early family experience, to what extent it grows out of the incorporation of *significant others* into our self-conceptions, and to what extent it is instrumental to needs wholly removed from the interaction process will depend on the particular social pattern in question. For the present, we will be content with pointing out the differences between the biologically sustained symbiotic pattern and the interrelated role activity in a sociotechnical system maintained by sanctions and external rewards. In the symbiotic pattern, one derives physiological gratification not only from one's own responses, but from the reciprocal responses of one's partner. In role relationships, there is also satisfaction from the mutual rewarding of expectations, but these gratifications are but a faint reflection of the intense rewards of the symbiotic relationships.

The difference between symbiotic and social ties can be seen clearly in the biological history of the individual. Between the embryo and the body of the mother there is a fixed physiological interdependence. At birth the physical separation of mother and offspring has profound consequences for the relationship, which becomes increasingly psychological. At first biological ties persist in the symbiotic relationship of the nursing infant and the feeding mother. Soon, however, the ties between mother and child are wholly psychological in character and the social relationship is a far cry from the early biological relationship. The range and complexity of possible patterns of relationship between parent and offspring are great compared to the fixed regularities of the physiological tie between embryo and the body host of the mother. Some psychoanalysts have marred the understanding of adult relationships by failing to see their socially distinctive character. These theorists attempt to explain the behavior of adults as an extension of the symbiotic pattern of infancy, and sometimes they even push back into intrauterine life for their interpretations. It is possible, of course, with adequate imagination to relate everything in this world to everything else, but the remote connections between the behavior of individuals in biological systems of early life and their behavior as members of social systems account for a negligible amount of the total variance. In other words, the major explanation of the malfunctioning of people in social systems is to be found at the level of social systems and not at the level of their infantile symbiotic patterns of nursing.

Production and Maintenance Inputs

It follows from the contrived nature of social systems that special attention must be given to the means by which the contrived pattern is maintained—that is, to their maintenance inputs. All open systems, of course, require *maintenance* as well as *production* inputs. *Maintenance inputs* are the energic imports that sustain the system; *production inputs* are the energic imports that are processed to yield a productive outcome. In social systems, however, the maintenance problem is more complex than in biological systems because the maintenance requirements are much less clearly specified in social systems. Certain minimum nutritive and caloric input is necessary to keep the biological organism functioning. Science can specify these inputs with precision, and most organisms show a good deal of primitive wisdom about staying alive even without such specifications. By contrast, the motivations that will attract people to a social system and keep them functioning in it are varied, the relationship between organizational inducements and the required role behavior is indirect and mediated by many factors, and too little is known either at the practical or at the scientific level about maximizing productive output in relation to maintenance input. Moreover, physical and physiological systems with a given physical structure can lie dormant and still maintain their basic character when revived; the social system, once it ceases to function, disappears. This difference means that the social system is more open than physical systems; its needs for production and maintenance materials are in some respects unique.

Biological systems also require nourishment and maintenance. Food, water, air, and certain conditions of pressure and temperature are essential to life. But the preservation of the physical structure is not a problem from the point of view of the parts leaving the whole. Cells do not wander away from the organs in which they are imbedded; organs do not leave the body any more than the spark plug of an engine goes absent without leave. Human beings do drift away from social systems, do go on strike, and do stay at home. Hence the social sciences must go further than natural sciences in order to take into account two types of system openness: openness with respect to production inputs and openness with respect to maintenance inputs. The trend in the social sciences, however, has been to focus as does the physical scientist on one type of openness—namely, the openness to production inputs. The natural scientist can concentrate solely on the learning function of rats in a maze and treat the walls of the maze as a constant. In the social system the walls of the maze are not constant because they are made up of human behavior. Classic organization theory with its machine concepts has been concerned almost exclusively with the single type of openness and has attempted to develop principles of organizational functioning as if the production input and the methods of processing it were the only variables. Holding the human parts in the system and mobilizing their energies in prescribed patterns do not represent constant factors in the equation and cannot be ignored. The distinction we are emphasizing between production and maintenance inputs is similar to R. Cattell's (1951) differentiation between effective synergy and maintenance synergy in his discussion of the dynamics of groups. Synergy he defines as the sum total of the energy that a group can command. That part of the energy used to keep the group in being is maintenance synergy and that part used to carry out the objectives of the group is effective synergy.

Studies of influence processes in unstructured groups report a similar dichotomy in leadership functions. Bales (1958) found that leadership activity is of two types: *socioemotional* leadership supportive of group maintenance, and *task* leadership oriented toward getting the work done. Most individuals who contribute to group leadership are high in either socioemotional support or task direction but not in both.

Types of Forces Reducing Human Variability

The possibility that individual members of a social system may leave it is the most dramatic example of the special maintenance problems of social systems, and human history offers a long list of arrangements, benign and malignant, for preventing such departures—feudalism, slavery, conscription, imprisonment, indenture, apprenticeship, contractual agreements, passport controls, and an almost infinite list of rewards and punishments. The continued existence of a social system, however, requires not only the physical presence of human beings but their enactment of particular behavior patterns. Such patterns, in their uniformity and synchronization, contrast sharply with the variety of spontaneous individual behavior. Indeed, one can define the core problem of any social system as reducing the variability and instability of human actions to uniform and dependable patterns. Thelen[1] has proposed a model that distinguishes three types of control pressures or forces that have this variance-reducing effect: environmental or task requirements in relation to needs, demands arising from shared expectations and values, and the enforcement of rules.

1. *Environmental pressures.* The problem in the objective world

---

[1]Personal communication to author, 1960.

requires a coordinated effort of people for its solution. The residents of a village without a fire department may work as a group to extinguish a fire in the home of any member. Division of labor arises naturally to meet the demands of the situation. A volunteer fire department may result in which activities are coordinated in relation to the task to be accomplished. Even in more complex organizations, the task requirements, or the pressures from the external environment, induce coordination of group effort.

2. *Shared values and expectations.* People have some goals in common and mutual expectations about how they should behave to achieve these common objectives. Some members of the community become convinced of the importance of fluoridating their water supply. They discuss the problem, hold meetings, and form action committees. The cooperative activity engendered grows out of the shared values more than out of the imperative demands of an objective task. Voluntary groups are formed on this basis, and social organizations also depend on this pressure though less exclusively than voluntary groups.

3. *Rule enforcement.* Variability is also reduced by rules, the violation of which calls for some form of penalty or negative sanction. Formal prescriptions develop in social systems in which the functions carried out are remotely and indirectly related to the needs of the members. People observe the regulations of the governmental agency or the company for which they work because they want to hold their jobs.

Extrinsic rewards might be considered a fourth force commensurate with these or, as Skinner's theory of operant conditioning would assert, prior to all of them. For our purposes, however, it seems appropriate to treat extrinsic rewards as functionally analogous to penalties—that is, as adjunct to rule enforcement.

In all social systems, variability of individual behavior is brought under control by one or more of these three mechanisms. Community movements and voluntary groups are based much more on the first two processes than on the third. Large-scale organizations employ all three. Sociologists have rightly called attention to the fact that organizations utilize cooperation based on shared values much more than one would expect from studying their formal tables of work organization and work schedules. The concept of informal organization is sometimes used to emphasize this aspect of group functioning. Nevertheless, rules and their enforcement are also a very significant aspect of organizations. The essential difference between social organizations and less structured social systems is the greater reliance on formal prescriptions of acceptable versus unacceptable behavior in the organization. In a voluntary movement the common values arise from sources prior and external to the association; like-minded people find one another. By contrast, the formal organization indoctrinates its members with its own system norms. To understand social organizations, we need to describe the formal patterns of behavior achieved through rule enforcement—that is, *roles*—and the ideological basis of roles in *norms* and *values*.

MAJOR SOCIAL SYSTEM COMPONENTS: ROLES, NORMS, AND VALUES

The social-psychological bases of social systems comprise the *role* behaviors of members, the *norms* prescribing and sanctioning these behaviors and the *values* in which the norms are embedded. Roles describe specific forms of behavior associated with given positions; they develop originally from task requirements. In their pure or organizational form, roles are standardized patterns of behavior required of all persons playing a part in a given functional relationship, regardless of personal wishes or interpersonal obligations irrelevant to the functional relationship. Norms are the general expectations of a demand character for all role incumbents of a system or subsystem. Values are the more generalized ideological justifications for roles and norms, and express the aspirations that allegedly inform the required activities. That operators of a drill press should get blank stock from the person to their left, should drill holes in 240 pieces of such stock each hour, and should put the completed pieces on a moving belt at their right are examples of role requirements. The statement that all members of the organization shall follow to the letter the work instructions of their superiors or be penalized for insubordination is a norm; it is systemwide in its application, and it reinforces the role requirements. If the notion of obeying orders is embellished and elaborated as an expression of natural law and a means to national security, the appeal would be to values beyond the norms themselves, and an ideology would be in process of development.

Roles, norms, and values differ also in degree of abstractness. In most systems, the major requirements of roles are stated in relatively specific terms; ambiguity in role definition occurs and can be troublesome, but clarity is the dominant characteristic. Norms, in attempting to state requirements of membership more widely applicable than those of roles, often use language so abstract as to lead to varying interpretations. Values carry the process of abstraction still further, and the problems of interpretation and translation are correspondingly greater. The banners of liberty and justice may be borne with equal conviction by opposing armies.

Roles, norms, and values thus differ with respect to the type of justification mobilized to sanction behavior. At the level of role behavior it is simply a matter of expectancy about task performance; at the level of norms it is a matter of following the legitimate requirements of the system; at the level of values it is a matter of realizing higher moral demands.

Three Bases of System Integration

Roles, norms, and values furnish three interrelated bases for the integration of social systems. (1) People are tied together because of the functional interdependence of the roles they play; for example, the newspaper reporter, the linotype or photo-offset operators, the press operators, and the drivers of delivery trucks must perform in accordance with a particular sequence and time schedule. Because the requirements of different roles are interrelated, people who perform them are bound together and, as a result, the organization achieves a degree of integration. (2) The normative requirements for these roles add an additional cohesive element; for example, the worker not only plays a part in the interdependent chain of activities but accepts the norms about doing a satisfactory job. (3) Finally, the values centering about the objectives of the system furnish another source for integration; for example, the political activist may be dedicated to the liberal or conservative values of the party.[2]

The integrative contributions of roles, norms, and values combine in the ongoing life of organizations. Nevertheless, the relative importance of the three components is different in different systems. The assembly line may give greater weight to task requirements or role performance, the research agency to the norms of rigorous scientific procedure, and the political party to saving the country from ruin. In primitive society, as Durkheim (1947) has observed, social integration was based on a common value system. With little division of labor and few subsystems, there was a mechanical solidarity based on a collective conscience or a common morality manifested by all societal members and appropriate to all situations. With a highly differentiated social structure containing many subsystems there is less of a simple universal moral code, and societal integration is based more on normative practices and role interdependence.

Role Systems and the Role Concept

Although organizational integration is a fusion of role, norm, and value components, it is useful to consider them separately for analytic purposes. Chapters 7 and 12 attempt this analysis in detail; this section describes the major properties of each of the three concepts.

---

[2]Organizational leaders may epitomize system values, and identification with such leaders can be a powerful integrative force. The charisma of leaders also enhances and strengthens the integrative effects of roles and norms.

In all those situations in which complementary activities are not a direct function of symbiotic biological needs or obvious situational requirements, people have devised the expedient of sanctioning certain forms of behavior that are required of individuals by virtue of their position in social relationships. Thus, the person who calls the meeting to order and recognizes speakers does so in the role of chairman. One individual may play this role in a heavy-handed and partisan manner; another may be scrupulously fair and conscientious. But the role of chairman is the central fact for understanding the behavior of the individual presiding over the group. It makes incumbent on that person certain types of decisions and also sets definite limits to his or her behavior in the group meeting. Standardized or institutionalized behavior of this sort is termed *role behavior*. The person in a social system who plays a role is under the demands of that role to act in many of the ways he or she does.

Bureaucratic organizations represent the clearest development of a pattern of interlocking roles in the sense that roles are employed without the encumbrances of socially inherited status or personality contamination. Moreover, the roles in such organizations represent prescribed or standardized forms of activity. The network of standardized role behaviors constitutes the formal structure of an organization. A *formalized role system* is one in which the rules defining the expected interdependent behavior of incumbents of system positions are explicitly formulated and sanctions are employed to enforce the rules. Formalization or standardization of role performance is a matter of degree, but in organizations individuals have less freedom to transform their roles to coincide with the expression of their personalities than in other social settings. For example, a man or woman may play the role of citizen in a democratic state in a great variety of ways, from voting occasionally in a national election to running for an elected office. In fact, in nonorganizational settings, they are generally unaware of the social roles they play. Within the organization, however, the specific demands of the role compel awareness.

A role abstracts the behavioral requirement from the satisfactions accruing to the individual for enacting the behavior. Whether or not the individual enjoys carrying out the expected task becomes irrelevant. There are many other ways of making behavior stable and reliable, ranging from the primitive's fear of the tribal chief to the modern organization man's (and woman's) generalized sensitivity and obedience to "what is expected." Such mechanisms can be built into the processes by which the individual is socialized into the culture.

Roles are found in their purest form when they are completely divorced from the personalities of role incumbents and from any motivational tie that could encumber the role relationship. The slave and master who have reciprocal affection for one another interfere with the functioning of the system of slavery as such. *The general development of role systems has been in the direction of getting rid of surplus elements in role relations.* In some older societies role requirements became mixed with their sanctioning sources, as in the case of sanctity of economic practices; or with the personalities of role incumbents, as in the case of the semi-divine character of monarchs; or with the monopoly of physical force by the owning group, as in the case of slavery. The full utilization of roles came only with the development of bureaucratic structure where the role could be set up, abolished, or changed as part of the rules of the game—where it could be observed as a role and nothing more. The economic version of history, which makes the creation of the free market the pivotal point in the development of modern western society, is only a partial statement of the facts of the matter. The free market was the economic expression of the discovery that roles could be developed as roles in all types of human endeavor.

The Concept of Partial Inclusion

At the individual level the role concept implies that people need be involved in system functioning only on a segmental or partial basis. Unlike the inclusion of a given organ of the body in the biological system, not all of the individual is included in organization membership. The organization neither requires nor wants the whole person. Even where the person cannot withdraw physically from a social system, as in the case of military service, the individual's psychological life space covers much more than military duties. People belong to many organizations and the full engagement of their personalities is generally not found within a single organizational setting. Moreover, they frequently shift their membership in organizations. F. H. Allport (1933) developed the concept of *partial inclusion* to refer to the segmental involvement of people in social groupings.

The concept of partial inclusion helps us to understand many of the problems of social organization. The organizational role stipulates behaviors that imply only a "psychological slice" of the person, yet people are not recruited to organizations on this basis; willy-nilly the organization brings within its boundaries the entire person. The organizational demand on the individual to put aside some parts of the self for the sake of performing a role is literally a depersonalizing demand; in this sense the individual who joins with others to create an informal "organization within an organization" is fighting for his or her identity as a person.

The concept of partial inclusion is relevant also to the special boundary problems of social organizations. Since individuals are involved in a social system with only part of themselves, they might readily behave less as members of any given organization and more in terms of some compromise of their many segmental commitments unless special circumstances make salient the demands of the particular system. There must be clarity of demands and constraints so that they will give unto Caesar what is Caesar's. In other words, the boundary conditions which insure that behavior patterns within a system are appropriate to that system are largely psychological in character. Individuals must not be confused about which system they are psychologically in at any given moment. They must realize when they have crossed over into an area where behavioral alternatives are limited or nonexistent. The more time individuals spend in the boundary condition either because of frequent crossings, because this is their permanent place in organizational space, or because of competing cross pressures from two or more organizations, the more necessary it becomes for the organization to utilize mechanisms insuring their allegiance.

In trivial instances the failure of an individual to recognize when he or she has crossed an organizational boundary is mere gaucherie and provides a common kind of humor. For corporations with far-flung operations the boundary problem is by no means a subject of humor, and people are rotated from one location to another or brought back to the parent location at regular intervals as a way of preventing them from "going native"—that is, becoming influenced by people on the wrong side of the organizational boundary. When an analogous situation occurs across a national boundary, we call it treason and it becomes a matter of life and death.

Organizations, as we have said, consist of patterned behavior; if members misperceive the organizational boundary and misbehave in terms of it, they threaten the very life of the organization.

System Dynamics

The tendency of organizational functions to determine system norms (See chapter 12) can be seen as part of a more complex dynamic for maintenance and survival. Lacking the built-in stabilities of biological systems, social organizations resort to a multiplication of mechanisms to maintain themselves. We have already observed that they develop specific role expectations and penalties for failure to meet them, rewards to bind their members into the system, norms and values to justify and stimulate required activities, and authority devices to control and direct organizational behavior. In other words, there is an overdetermination of the behavior necessary to preserve the organization. People are not only rewarded for taking their roles, they receive constant reminders from the incumbents of adjacent interdependent roles, and they share an ideological environment in which their role behavior is legally appropriate and morally right. In an effectively functioning system the field of forces determining the behavior of the members is not dependent on one motivational source nor on a single individual. There is a cumulative pattern of many reinforcements exerting pressure in a single direction. The occasional deviant, or the occasional failure of a single reinforcement, is not especially important. In inexact popular parlance we say that the system is greater than the individual.

This overdetermination arises as an organizational defense in depth against failure and loss of system character. It often has the side effect, however, of not merely maintaining but intensifying that character. We shall use the term *system dynamic* to refer to such functionally derived characteristics of social organizations. Both the major system and the component subsystems are characterized by their own dynamic or complex of motivational forces that move a given structure toward becoming more like what it basically is. For example, a hospital for mental patients organized as a custodial institution tends over time to become more of a custodial institution unless it is subject to new inputs from its supporting environment, and even then the system dynamic may resist movement from the custodial homeostasis (Zald, 1962).

Acquisition and Extraction

The operation of system dynamics can be seen in the acquisitive and extractive mechanisms employed by systems and subsystems. Much of the organizational literature on this subject is apolitical and antiseptic (with the exception of the work of such political theorists as Harold Lasswell). It is strangely silent, except in the case of the simple economic model, about how a social system acquires the input necessary to maintain itself and carry on its functions. Social organizations, however, employ many mechanisms for acquiring energic input besides the sale of their product in a free market. It is characteristic of any organization to try to place itself in an advantageous position with regard to environmental resources and competing groups. Even a charitable organization will struggle to get as favorable an allocation from the United Fund as possible or will go outside the Fund to conduct its own moneyraising campaign if this appears as the more effective way of securing an adequate budget.

In the beginning there is no guaranteed reservoir of energy for the social organization. If it is to survive, it must secure some continuing supply of materials and people. Acquisitive and extractive procedures are thus the primitive mechanisms by which negative entropy is attained. The general law of entropy states that any system will tend to run down, lose its differentiated structure, and become one with its environment. These death forces are countered in the most direct and simple manner in social systems by taking over and exploiting natural resources and by taking away the possessions and even the labor power of other groups—whether by persuasion, guile, or force.

The mechanisms for acquisition of energic input are directed both at securing advantages in obtaining raw materials and a ready market and at utilizing human energy as effectively and with as little cost to the organization as possible. Such acquisition mechanisms include the obtaining of legal priorities or monopolies on sources of supply or on markets; the influencing of the public through persuasion, information, and propaganda; transactions or deals with leaders of other groups; developing distinctive capabilities that will place the organization in a monopolistic position; maneuvers and price wars to liquidate rivals, and the development of reward systems within the organization to maintain a favorable ratio between organizational costs and organizational gains. Within the national state, organizations compete through such mechanisms. Outside national boundaries, there is also the resort to threat, intimidation, and organized force. Nor is the acquisitive self-interest in organizations limited to profit-making institutions. Universities and colleges scramble to receive support from the federal government as well as from more traditional sources. And universities, like business organizations, raid one another for top talent.

Well-established organizations also develop protective mechanisms to guarantee their advantageous position regarding energic input. They may acquire ownership of the sources of supply or they may invest a great deal in the maintenance of the status quo, which is favorable to them. Similarly, subsystems within an organization seek to perpetuate their favorable position vis-a-vis other subsystems. In the field of liberal education it took fifty years before the sciences could obtain equality with the humanities because of the protective devices of required courses and the fixed budget allocation to various departments. It is tempting to regard these protective devices as defense mechanisms similar to the defense mechanisms of individuals. Although it is of interest to establish genotypical similarities between categories, the more specific the prediction, the greater the danger in jumping from the individual to the collective level. The organizational persistence in holding to its established pattern in spite of some social change can affect social reality in a manner in which the individual cannot. A strong, well-entrenched organization is in fact part of social reality, and the self-fulfilling prophecy holds at the collective level much more than at the individual level.

The substructures of acquisition and defense against the acquisitions of others are most conspicuous at the national level, where defense looms large in almost every budget. A good deal of organizational structure is built around the acquisitive and protective self-interest of systems at lesser levels, however. In most organizations there are special units concerned with procurement of materials, recruitment of personnel, public relations, and relations with outside elite groups. Top management and leadership, with special staff help, will devote considerable time to the full exploitation of environmental resources and organizational capabilities.

Organizational Climate

Norms and values about defense and acquisition, exchange and reciprocity are common to all organizations because they derive from functions common to all. The general proposition that norms and values develop around dominant ongoing activities, however, implies that to some extent each type of organization and even each specific organization will develop distinctive norms and values. A particular organization will share certain norms with others of its type and some norms with organizations in general, but it will also have its own taboos, folkways, and mores.

Hospitals and universities, factories and government agencies, armies and political parties, although they share certain bureaucratic activities and norms, develop different and distinctive normative climates. It is an insult to tell an academic dean that a university is being run like an army, but the army general would be at least as offended at the alleged equivalence.

The normative climate of a particular organization reflects such differences, but more. Organizational climate reflects also the history of internal and external struggles, the types of people the organization attracts, its work processes and physical layout, the modes of communication, and the exercise of authority within the system. Just as a society has a cultural heritage, so social organizations possess distinctive patterns of collective feeling and beliefs passed along to new group members. In an industrial concern with a long history of amicable union-management relations there may be no stigma attached to the union steward who becomes a supervisor, no feeling that talking to a company officer is an attempt to curry favor, and no countenancing of sabotage or stealing of company materials. Educational institutions also show marked differences in climate and culture. Even a casual visitor can detect differences between the atmosphere of Antioch, Swarthmore, City University of New York, the University of Oklahoma, and Princeton University.

In spite of the obvious differences between the cultures of organizations performing essentially the same types of functions, it is not easy to specify the dimensions of such differences. Though the subculture of the organization provides the frame of reference within which its members interpret activities and events, the members will not be able to verbalize in any precise fashion this frame of reference. They will be clear about the judgments they make, but not about the basic standards or frames they employ in reaching a judgment. The many subtle and unconscious factors that determine a frame of reference are not susceptible to direct questioning. The technique of observation has thus been more revealing about organizational climate than the typical survey. What is needed ideally for the study of organizational climate is sustained observation to supply the insightful leads and systematic interviewing of appropriate population samples within the organization to insure adequate coverage. Such work might also facilitate the development of adequate conceptual and operational definitions of organization climate, so that this potentially valuable research concept might become more than a vague borrowing from meteorology.

GENERIC TYPES OF SUBSYSTEMS

When we encounter the culture of a particular organization, we find some norms and values common to all social life, some common to all bureaucratic systems, and some specific to the particular functions of the organization. This tendency for functions to create distinctive subcultures continues within the organization, but in ways that also reflect the cross-organizational commonalities of subsystems.

Social organizations like other systems have a throughput or a transformation of the energic input. Those activities concerned with the throughput have been called *production or technical subsystems* (Parsons, 1960). To insure existence beyond a single cycle of productive activity, there must be new materials to be worked on. *Production-supportive structures* develop in a surviving system to provide a continuing source of production inputs. They are of two kinds. One is the extension of the production system into the environment by activities that procure raw materials and dispose of the product. The second type is at the more complex level of maintaining and furthering a favorable environment through relations with other structures in the society—the institutional function, in Parsons' terms.

In addition to the need for production inputs, special attention must be given to maintenance inputs, that is, to insuring the availability of the human energy that results in role performance. If the system is to survive, *maintenance substructures* must be elaborated to hold the walls of the social maze in place. Even these would not suffice to insure organizational survival, however. The organization exists in a changing and demanding environment, and it must adapt constantly to the changing environmental demands. *Adaptive structures* develop in organizations to generate appropriate responses to external conditions. Finally, these patterns of behavior need to be coordinated, adjusted, controlled, and directed if the complex substructures are to hold together as a unified system or organization. Hence, *managerial subsystems* are an integral part of permanent elaborated social patterning of behavior.

Thus we can describe the facts of organizational functioning with respect to five basic subsystems: (1) production subsystems concerned with the work that gets done; (2) supportive subsystems of procurement, disposal, and institutional relations; (3) maintenance subsystems for tying people into their functional roles; (4) adaptive subsystems, concerned with organizational change; (5) managerial systems for the direction, adjudication, and control of the many subsystems and activities of the structure.

Production or Technical Subsystems

The production system is concerned with the throughput, the energic or informational transformation whose cycles of activity comprise the major functions of the system. Organizations are commonly classified according to their main productive process, for example, educational, if concerned with training, political, if concerned with affecting power relations, economic, if concerned with the creation of wealth. In the following chapter we examine the operation of production systems in more detail, especially their relationships to the other subsystems of the organization.

Supportive Subsystems

Supportive subsystems carry on the environmental transactions of procuring the input or disposing of the output or aiding in these processes. Some transactions are a direct extension of the production activities of the organization, importing the material to be worked on or exporting the finished product. Others are indirectly related to the production cycle but supportive of it, maintaining a favorable environment for the operation of the system.

Relating the system to its larger social environment, for example, by establishing external legitimation and support, is sometimes referred to as the *institutional* function. In general, the top echelon of an organization, such as the Board of Trustees, would be responsible for this function and would often have some degree of membership in outside structures. Thus, supportive subsystems concerned with environmental transactions include the specific procurement or disposal activities as well as the more general activities of securing favorable relations with larger structures.

Maintenance Subsystems

Maintenance activities are not directed at the material being worked on but at the equipment for getting the work done. In most organizations, much of the work consists of patterned human behavior and the "equipment" consists of human beings. The arrangement of roles for interrelated performance does not guarantee that people will accept or remain in these roles performing their functions. Hence, subsystems for recruitment, indoctrination or socialization, rewarding, and sanctioning are found in enduring social structures. These subsystems function to maintain the fabric of interdependent behavior necessary for task accomplishment. They tie people into the system as functioning parts. They are cycles of activity that are tangential to, or crisscross, the production cycles. Individuals may play both production and maintenance roles, as when members of a college faculty move from their teaching roles to meet as an exeutive committee to decide on promotions and salary increases for faculty members. In effect, they move from one subsystem function to another. Many systems do not permit such moves, or the combination of different subsystem functions in the same role. Instead they emphasize the separateness of subsystem specialties. Thus maintenance roles, for example, must be filled by specialists in the maintenance function, even if they are quite naive about the major differentiating function of the organization. The person serving as an administrator in a maintenance structure becomes a specialist in terms of that function, but a generalist in that the same function is required in many organizations. Indeed, a director of personnel or training in a given company probably could move more easily and with less strain to a functionally comparable position in another company than to a different subsystem in his or her own organization.

Whereas the supportive systems of procurement and disposal are concerned with insuring production inputs, that is, materials and resources for the work of the organization, the maintenance system is concerned with inputs for preserving the system either through appropriate selection of personnel or adequate rewarding of the personnel selected. We have already noted the neglect of the maintenance function in traditional thinking, which accepts social structures as objective and fixed in nature as biological relationships. The same neglect characterizes the world of practical action in which attention is centered on the production system and its inputs. Problems of personnel both on the recruitment and morale sides have received belated and inadequate recognition and the position of the director of these operations is generally low in the management hierarchy, whether the organization is industrial or governmental.

Rewards and sanctions, utilized to maintain role performance, are major maintenance devices and the rules for their allocation and use are among the most important organizational properties. In social organizations rewards and sanctions are employed with respect to specific performances and infractions according to a set of rules. In feudal systems sanctions and rewards tended to be invoked in a more capricious manner. In the small agrarian community punitive actions toward a transgressor were based on the outraged morality of community members and were not finely attuned to a set of particulars established about the transgressing act.

Social organizations, at least in our culture and era, move toward emphasis on rewards rather than punishments. To hold members in an organization and to maintain a satisfactory type of role performance means that people's experiences in the system must be rewarding, particularly if they have freedom to move in and out of organizations. Often one set of rewards develops to attract and hold members in a system and another to achieve some optimum level of performance.

In keeping with the relative neglect of maintenance functions is the blindness in most organizational theorizing to a significant characteristic of the reward system, namely its *allocation parameters*, or who gets what and why. The allocation of rewards in most organizations in western nations (and to a greater extent than realized in communist countries as well) is highly differential between members of various subsystems. The problem is one of keeping people in the organizational system and keeping them motivated to perform when there are conspicuous differences in the amount of return to various subgroups in the organization. Rewards are not only monetary; they also include prestige and status, gratifications from interesting work, identification with group products, and satisfactions from decision making. The distribution of all these types of rewards is basic for understanding how an organization operates. There is a substantial correlation among the various kinds of reward; the members who are paid the most generally have the highest status, the most interesting jobs, and the opportunity to make decisions. Hence, the differentials in rewards to people at different levels and in different subsystems are even greater than the differences in monetary return would suggest.

Adaptive Subsystems

Nothing in the production, supportive, and maintenance subsystems would suffice to insure organizational survival in a changing environment. Except for the functions of procurement and disposal, these subsystems face inward; they are concerned with the functioning of the organization as it is rather than with what it might become. The risks of concentrating attention and energies inward are directly proportional to the magnitude and rate of change in the world outside the organization. External changes in taste, in cultural norms and values, in competitive organizations, in economic and political power—all these and many others reach the organization as demands for internal change. To refuse to accede to such demands is to risk the possibility that the transactions of procurement and disposal will be reduced or refused, or that the processes of maintenance will become increasingly difficult. In most formal organizations there arise, therefore, structures that are specifically concerned with sensing relevant changes in the outside world and translating the meaning of those changes for the organization. There may be structures that devote their energies wholly to the anticipation of such changes. All these comprise the adaptive subsystem of the organization and bear such names as product research, market research, long-range planning, research and development, and the like.

Managerial Subsystems

These systems comprise the organized activities for controlling, coordinating, and directing the many subsystems of the structure. They represent another slice of the organizational pattern and are made up of cycles of activities cutting across the structure horizontally to deal with coordination of subsystems and the adjustment of the total system to its environment. The functions of top management require actions affecting large sectors of organizational space, the development of policies rather than their implementation, the formulation of rules rather than the specific invoking of penalties for recalcitrant members. The exercise of the management function is observable, however, at all levels of the system. Two major types of managerial substructures that deserve further description are *regulatory mechanisms* and the *authority structure*.

Our basic model of a social system is a structure that imports energy from the external world, transforms it, and exports a product to the environment that is the source for a reenergizing of the cycle. Substructures may develop that gather and utilize intelligence about these energic transactions. Such devices function to give feedback to the system about its output in relation to its input. Management in modern organizations operates in good part through such *regulatory mechanisms*. When a system operates without a specialized feedback or regulatory mechanism, we shall refer to it as a primitive group rather than a social organization. Voluntary groups, for example, may form from time to time and may carry on some cooperative activity. The accomplishments of such a group depend on the number of members and their enthusiasm at the moment and will vary greatly from time to time. The group is not guided by any systematic information about its impact on the world or any intelligence about the contributions of its members. It may not even have a roster of its members and its new chairman may search in vain for the records of what was done by his or her predecessor, how it was done, and what the outcome was. A voluntary group becomes an organization when it acquires systematic methods for regulating its activities on the basis of information about its functioning. Operationally a voluntary group is identified as an organization when it has a permanent secretariat or some equivalent device for maintaining stability in the offices of secretary and treasurer with respect to membership rolls, finances, and records.

In some profit-making organizations, regulatory mechanisms are highly developed and information about sales and markets is used constantly to control production schedules and the purchase of raw materials. Regulatory mechanisms vary in complexity and sophistication, however, and very primitive mechanisms of regulation may direct the activity of large, complex systems. A medical school may base its admissions on the number of available microscopes or the size of its laboratories, rather than on the need for physicians.

The dominant tendency is toward complexity in regulatory mechanisms. Industrial concerns utilize increasingly detailed estimates of economic trends in planning the capture of new markets. A highly significant development in modern industry is the use of computers to guide or regulate directly the activities of the enterprise at a number of levels. Indeed, the development of computer technology has set the pace for the increasing sophistication of regulatory mechanisms in large corporations. The storage capacity and speed of the computer makes it possible for vast amounts of information about the internal functioning of the organization and its environment to influence decisions at the highest levels.

The regulatory cycle is closed when information output from the computer is coupled directly to an operating cycle of the organization; we then have an automated or self-regulating device. Computers are used extensively for such purposes at lower organizational levels, especially in continuous process technologies such as oil refining. To what extent the seemingly autonomous decisions of top management are similarly regulated is an important researchable question. The mystique of the computer sometimes leads people to forget that it is limited by the quality of the information introduced into its memory and by the logic of the programs written to arrange that information. The intraorganizational clients of computer output should take as their own the hard-headed motto of computer specialists: "Garbage in, garbage out."

Problems of inferior quality and inappropriate utilization, however, emphasize rather than contradict the central point. The systematic use of information to guide organizational functioning is the *sine qua non* of an organization. The implications of such regulatory mechanisms are far-reaching. They include the elaboration of the role structure to provide for such a continuing function, and they imply the addition of other structures to coordinate the incoming information with the ongoing activities. The social system of feudalism rested more on status relationships than on highly developed role concepts and relied for stability on a combination of physical force and the mysticism of the masses. Modern role systems, however, need an intelligence function to maintain themselves.

Organizations need not be authoritarian in character, but they must possess an established and definitive form of decision making about organizational matters. We will use the term *authority structure* to describe the way in which the managerial system is organized concerning the sources of decision making and its implementation. Decisions are accepted if made in the proper manner, whether by democratic vote or by an edict from duly constituted authority. The essence of authority structure is the acceptance of directives as legitimate, that is, either the acquiescence or approval by people of rules of the game. The rules may be arrived at through a democratic process or they may be promulgated from above, but they are accepted as binding on the members of the system. They are properties of the system and not of the dominance-submission patterns of individual personalities. We recognize this when we say that a person has exceeded his or her authority. The person has gone beyond the legitimately defined limits of the position.

The clear theoretical distinction between authority and authoritarianism is obscured in practice by the tendency of authoritarian personalities to select themselves or to be selected for positions of power in social systems. Their personality traits may lead them to abuse this legal power, especially in areas where it is difficult to check on their actions. Agents of law enforcement—local police, internal revenue officers, immigration authorities, and customs officials—are entrusted with carrying out the rules of the game, but often have a reputation for officiousness or overstepping their authority.

A further confusion of authority and authoritarianism stems from the very human tendency to personalize relationships. People impute personal despotism to the orderly functioning of the social system, and call the exercise of legal authority authoritarian. Since authoritarianism is bad by definition and opposed to liberty and democracy, it serves as a battle cry against any rules that an individual does not relish.

A structure of authority implies that organizational decisions shall be abided by until a change is effected through legitimized channels for change. Those channels differ greatly, of course, in different organizations, from majority rule in a simple democratic group to the choice of the top figure in an unmodified hierarchy. All organizations, democratic or hierarchical, face the continuing task of carrying out organizational decisions, a process that involves a proliferation of lesser choices.

We may say that every organization therefore has an *executive structure* within the managerial subsystem for carrying out policy and implementing administrative decisions. In a democratic organization there is in addition a separate *legislative structure*, with the power vested in the membership to select top executives officers, set policy, choose between alternative leadership policies, or veto policy proposals. In authoritarian organizations, the executive and legislative functions tend to be combined within the managerial subsystem; the top executives do the legislating for the organization. It is also possible for an authoritarian structure to have separate legislative and executive systems, in which an appointed or self-perpetuating board of directors sets policy and a manager and subordinates execute it. *The essential difference between a democratic and an authoritarian system is not whether executive officers order or consult with those below them but whether the power to legislate on policy is vested in the membership or in the top echelons.*

There is an interpenetration of the authority and reward systems of an organization. The authority structure allocates decision making, and decision making is rewarding in two senses: (1) its exercise is in itself gratifying to the needs of people for participation and autonomy, and (2) it is instrumental in its power potential for achieving other objectives. Hence, an authority structure democratically based in a legislative system involving the membership has a built-in reward mechanism not found in an authoritarian system. There are some advantages to an authoritarian system but its problems of maintenance are often great and very different from those of the democratic system. Organization theorists apart from political scientists have given scant attention to this critical difference between organization forms. In the industrial world the appeal of the unions to workers is often a mystery to industrialists who have failed to grasp the significance of democratic structure and its reward character, even in imperfect manifestation.

Ordinarily the developmental processes by which groups acquire a regulatory mechanism and an authority structure are not independent but interactive. With a regulatory mechanism goes the need for decision making about the uses to which the information will be put. So long as a primitive group can operate in terms of the enthusiasm of its particular adherents at a given time and drop to another level of activity with less motivated followers at another time, it requires only task direction that can be generated within the group itself. But when it moves over to the utilization of information about maintaining some effective ratio of energy input to energy output and some stability in the level of its operations, it needs a more permanent and definitive form of decision making. Thus, the authority structure grows in response to the development of a regulatory maintenance mechanism. And conversely, as authority comes to be vested in positions in the group, its exercise is dependent on information feedback about its functioning. The officers charged with staffing an organization need information about the amount and causes of turnover, and about the kind of people who are lost relative to those who are retained. Some regulatory feedback mechanism is needed to maintain the quantity and quality of personnel that the operations require. The top officers are concerned with the total efficiency of the operations and they will institute cost accounting systems to aid them in the exercise of their authority.

There can be a power structure in primitive groups in terms of the superior personality force of a leader, whether because of physical prowess, mental alertness, or persuasiveness. This is not, however, the same as authority structure in which the order is followed because it comes from the legitimized position in the structure rather than from a certain personality. The soldier salutes the uniform of the superior officer, not the person. The informal group of teenagers on the corner may start as a primitive group with leadership a matter of the interplay of the strongest personalities in the group. After a time a leader may emerge and the group may develop norms about how the leader's authority should be exercised. It becomes an organization when leaders and followers decide on membership and procedures for admitting novices to membership. This process is one of regulating group functioning through information about its component parts.

The authority structure in feudal and semi-feudal systems was clear and legitimized but was less a matter of role and more a combination of role and status and personality. The noble was obeyed because of inherited status as a noble, which is irretrievably mixed up with the person because of the confusion of biological and social inheritance. It is the modern bureaucratic organization, as Max Weber pointed out, that has developed an authority structure of the rational-legal type, whereby the rules and prerogatives of authority are quite separated from the person and personality of the wielder of authority. Some structure of authority, some criteria for allocating it, and some rules for its exercise are, however, among the common characteristics of all human organizations.

Subsidiary Concepts: Leading Subsystems and Organizational Space

LEADING SUBSYSTEMS

Our identification of the five major subsystems of organizations (and some of their further subdivisions) has been made in functional terms, beginning with the organizational throughput. All these subsystems perform functions vital for the organization in that the failure of any would in time incapacitate the organization itself. The significance of the different subsystems nevertheless varies at different times in the life cycle of the organization and in different environmental circumstances.

The subsystems within an organization, regardless of how essential they are to the organization as a whole, are not equipotential in their influence on the total system. Thelen (1960) uses the concept of leading system to designate "a component system whose output exerts the greatest influence on the inputs of other component systems, and through this, controls the interactions of the suprasystem." He further observes that subsystems may vary in this characteristic during periods of rapid organizational growth, though a coordinating system having inputs and outputs to most or all of the other systems in the organization may be permanently leading. During growth, the leading system may be the latest system to develop "in the sense that it tends to be the 'executive seat,' for it obtains feedback and stimulation from all the other systems; it is the system best able to mediate between internal and external demands, and thus to guide the locomotion of the organism as a whole."

The circumstances that make a certain subsystem leading are various. One of the most obvious is the possession of a technology or skill that assumes major importance because of larger developments in the organizational environment. In the 1940s population sampling represented such a technique for social research and the subsystem incorporating this function became the leading subsystem in many research organizations. More recently, the development of computer technology has nominated a new kind of subsystem for leadership, with implications yet to be worked out.

Organizational Space

The view of organizations as consisting of five functional subsystems is fundamental, we believe. It is not, however, the only way of viewing the suborganizational components of an organizational system—components larger than roles and role activities but smaller than the organization as a whole. Organizational space, like physical space, can be divided in many ways.

The complex set of interrelated activities comprising the social organization can be coordinated to a social map that we shall call organizational space. By organizational space we refer to the locus of the various organizational activities and the behavior distances between members in carrying out their many organization-related tasks. Sectors of organizational space can be identified objectively by observing the behavior of members. Organizational space is not identical with physical space, though physical space is one of its components. The head supervisor of the foundry might be physically closer to the foundry workers than to the plant manager, yet the foundry supervisor's frequency and closeness of contact with the plant manager might be greater than with the foundry workers. Inferences about behavioral distances can also be made from the psychological or perceived separations reported by organizational members.

Organizational space is the social transformation of the physical or objective space that provides the topography of the organization. It is the use of physical space for social objectives. This is obvious in the business enterprise that not only has separate offices for its differing staff levels but separate dining rooms for these levels, so that there is one dining room for executives, another for supervisory personnel, and a cafeteria for rank-and-file employees. Geographical spread and separation, moreover, must occur in organizational operations since they cannot be conducted in a vacuum. And such spread of activities over physical space tends to make for behavioral and psychological separation as well.

There are four types of separation of organizational members with respect to organizational space. The first derives from *geographical separation*, which makes constant communication difficult if not impossible. The workers in the foundry and the sales force in the field are so separated by geographical arrangements that each group can know little about the sector of organizational space occupied by the other. In addition to geographical separation, we have a *functional* separation in this case. Even if the salesagents and foundry workers could have a common dining room, they would still eat with their own associates. Common interests, problems, and language of the occupation would pose barriers to communication just as great as physical separation.

A third type of separation has to do with the *status or prestige* of position and function. White-collar workers may communicate more freely with other white-collar workers than with blue-collar workers because they do not want to lower their status in the eyes of other white-collar workers. Or secretaries may sit by themselves in the lunch room rather than mingle with their bosses because it would be presumptuous to assume that they have equal status with the executives. Finally, there is a separation on the basis of *power*, which is related to status and prestige but not identical with it. The authority hierarchy of the organization sets a pattern for the flow of communication. The formal functioning of a hierarchy permits a worker to raise questions with his or her immediate supervisor but not with the supervisor's boss. The same pattern will carry over into informal patterns of communication, so that the hourly employee will not seek out the general manager for a luncheon date.

The reason for introducing the concept of organizational space is twofold. We do not encounter an organization in its entirety from any single observational point, and we need a concept that permits us to see the organization in a number of different ways. Interpretations both by theorists and practitioners have been based too often on experiences within one sector of organizational space. The discovery of informal structure by the Mayo group, for example, called attention to some sectors of the organization as experienced at the floor of the factory (Roethlisberger and Dickson, 1939). However, Mayo's followers have been occupied too exclusively with such limited segments of organizational space. Even more common is the error of the management consultant who perceives the sector of the organization most available to the level of management he or she is serving. There have been few attempts to study organizations by systematic observations that encompass the whole of organizational space.

Since top leadership in any large organization is remote in organizational space from many of its operating sectors, it is a fiction to expect that the intelligence and wisdom of the top officials enables them to assess intuitively the impact of a change in one sector on other sectors. Opening channels of communication from below (more often advocated than accomplished) is one way of giving policy makers access to larger sectors of organizational space, so that they do not become captives to the information provided by the official bureaucrats around them.

The second reason for introducing the concept of organizational space is that many of the internal problems of organization, such as intrasystem conflict and strain, can be understood by an appreciation of where people stand in terms of that space. Just as the outsider overgeneralizes his or her observations of an organization from one limited perspective, so the organizational member sees the organization in terms of the functioning of his or her sector. Studies show that most supervisors are rather poor judges of the perceptions, attitudes, and motivations of rank-and-file workers, and that the phenomenon of differential perception becomes more pronounced as the intervening organizational space becomes greater (Kahn, 1958; Likert, 1961).

The tendency of any group of people occupying a given segment of an organization is to exaggerate the importance of their function and to fail to grasp the basic functions of the larger whole. Some of this may be defensive, and some of it is related to circumscribed visible horizons (Tannenbaum and Donald, 1957). Loyalties develop to one's own organizational sector rather than to the overall organization. Conflict between departments can become bitter and persistent because the members of each do not accept common organizational objectives but only the specific tasks that comprise their daily lives.

**THE ORGANIZATION IN RELATION
TO ITS ENVIRONMENT**

Organizational functioning must be studied in relation to the continuing transactions with the supporting environment. The concepts of subsystems and supersystems, system openness, boundaries, and coding are all concerned with aspects of this relationship. Indeed, the function of the organization as a whole can be defined in terms intrinsic to the organization or in terms of its contribution to some aspect of the environment.

Systems, Subsystems, and Supersystems

Social systems as open systems are dependent on other social systems; their characterization as subsystems, systems, or supersystems is relative to their degree of autonomy in carrying out their functions and to the particular interests of the investigator. From a societal point of view the organization is a subsystem of one or more larger systems, and its linkage or integration with these systems affects its mode of operation and its level of activity.

If our focus of interest is a manufacturing concern, the company in question can be considered as the system; its organizational activities of production, marketing, recruiting, and holding employees are then subsystems, and the industry and larger community constitute the supersystem. In spite of the high degree of autonomy implied by doctrines of national sovereignty, the dependence and openness of a social system does not stop at national boundaries. The student of national policy toward foreign affairs, as Singer (1961) points out, should consider international relationships as the relevant system and nations as subsystems. The open-system approach dictates a strategy of research that is in basic opposition to reductionism or the immediate pushing to some more elementary level for an understanding of social-psychological phenomena. The first step should always be to go to the next higher level of system organization, to study the dependence of the system in question upon the supersystem of which it is a part, for the supersystem sets the limits of variance of behavior of the dependent system. More analytic study can then explore the contributions of subsystems to this limited range of variance. For example, if we want to study patterns of cooperation and conflict within an industrial company, our first step would be to study the position of the company in the community and in the industry as a whole, not to look at the informal standards in work groups. The company's marginality or leadership position in the field, the position of its local union with respect to the larger organization of unions, and other such relationships will be reflected in the internal life of the organization.

Apart from the practical interests of the investigator, the characterization of systems can be specified relative to degrees and types of autonomy. There must be some degree of freedom for decision making on such key issues as fiscal policy, admission of members, type of product, or distribution of rewards to justify integrity as an organization. A practical criterion is legal responsibility, although it is not infallible. Corrections will have to be made for those subsystems that are still under the complete control of the larger organization in spite of their nominal independence. For example, a manufacturing concern making parts for an automobile company may be completely under the domination of that company even though it is legally separate and independent. On the other hand, subunits of a larger organization that are legally bound to it may be granted considerable organizational autonomy. The establishment of "profit-centers" (subunits responsible and autonomous with respect to many organizational functions) exemplifies this assertion. The locus at which profits may be accrued and the locus at which decisions to use such profits may be made are additional criteria of obvious practical significance for assessing organizational independence from the supersystem.

A fully satisfactory set of theoretical criteria for such assessment is not available, but it might well include such factors as the following: power to stipulate sources of input rather than accepting sources prescribed by the supersystem; power to choose target populations for export of the organizational product; development of internal mechanisms for organizational regulation, including positive and negative feedback. It may be that many of these criteria will be reflected in a single aspect of organizational life: the ease or difficulty of moving across a boundary. The more difficult such a move and the more extensive the changes which it implies, the greater the degree of organizational autonomy.

System Openness, System Boundaries, and System Coding

These three concepts are interrelated and have to do with the relative autonomy of system functioning and with system differentiation from the surrounding environment. *System openness* is the most general of these concepts and refers to the degree to which the system is receptive to all types of inputs. Systems vary in the range of inputs they can absorb and in their openness to particular types of inputs.

Either of the major American political parties would be an example of a system open to a fairly wide range of influences. Many types of individuals can move into the organization, bringing with them different ideas and interests. The party accepts contributions and help from many sources. As a result, American political parties tend not to present distinctive action or ideological programs or distinctive candidates. They are not highly differentiated from one another or from the surrounding environment of community activities concerned with the exertion of influence. Eisenhower was sought as a presidential candidate by both parties. It has been proposed, and from an improbable source (Luce, 1964), that the history of American political parties can be understood as a cyclical process in which the tendency of the parties to become increasingly open and undifferentiated from each other is occasionally and dramatically interrupted by some historical issue that either polarizes them or creates a realignment of forces and a new pair of parties.

System coding is the major procedure for insuring specifications for the intake of information and energy, and it thus describes the actual functioning of barriers separating the system from its environment. One of the significant characteristics of any system is the selective intake of energy and information and the transformation of that input according to the nature of the system. Social systems develop their own mechanisms for blocking out certain types of alien influence and for transforming what is received according to a series of code categories. Though the coding concept can apply to the selective absorption and transformation of all types of input into a system, it is characteristically employed for the processing of information.

The procedure for excluding information may be deliberately and rationally developed. The judicial system, for example, has codified rules that define the nature of the evidence admissible. Hearsay evidence is excluded; so too are confessions obtained under duress; and in some states the results of lie detection tests are ruled out. Most organizations have not developed their rules for the exclusion of information in as systematic a manner, but they do possess *formal criteria* for rejecting some types of input. These criteria may specify that only information relevant to the questions posed by organizational leaders will be accepted, or that only members of a certain status or functional position will be heard on certain questions. The more general practice is to have specialized structures for the reception of information so that any message will have to traverse and survive the "proper channels" in order to get a hearing.

System boundaries refer to the types of barrier conditions between the system and its environment that make for degrees of system openness. Boundaries are the demarcation lines or regions for the definition of appropriate system activity, for admission of members into the system, and for other imports into the system. The boundary constitutes a barrier for many types of interaction between people on the inside and people on the outside, but it includes facilitating devices for the types of transactions necessary for organizational functioning. The barrier condition is exemplified by national states, with their border guards and customs offices that restrict the flow of people and goods across their boundaries. Within a national state, organizations are similarly characterized by boundaries, both physical and psychological, to maintain the integrity of the system.

Psychological separation is maintained by visible symbols, such as uniforms, dress, and insignia (e.g., fraternity pins), and even more subtly by speech patterns and other distinctive forms of behavior. Without such special provisions, organizational members at the boundaries would be dysfunctionally susceptible to outside influence. The incursion of environmental influence would be uncontrolled and would vitiate the intrasystem influences. Where physical space can be employed to create separation, there is protection against such external forces. But since the organization must have interchange with its supporting environment, some of its members must occupy boundary positions to help in the export of the services, ideas, and other products of the system and in the import of materials and people into the system. Since these members face out on the world and deal with the public, they are subject to the conflicting pressures of their own organization and the social environment. Because of their greater acquaintance with opportunities outside the organization as well as the conflicting demands of their roles, one would expect greater personnel turnover in these boundary positions than in the central production structure. Many other evidences of the stressfulness of boundary positions have already been produced (Kahn et al., 1964; Adams, 1976).

The boundary condition applies also to the process by which outsiders enter and become members of the organization. They may be physically within the organization for some time before they cross the psychological boundary and become part of the organization. Before foreigners are admitted to citizenship in the United States, they must have resided within its physical boundaries for five years, have passed required tests, and taken an oath of allegiance. Many organizations have formal induction and socialization procedures for instilling the behavior, attitudes, and values that differentiate the system from the outside environment (Dornbusch, 1955).

We have been speaking mainly about the boundary condition with respect to maintenance inputs. Environmental transactions on the production side are also controlled by organizational boundaries. In system theory it is common to define the boundary as the area where a lower interchange of energy or information occurs than in the system proper. In social systems it is also a matter of qualitative breaks between the activity within the system and the activity on the outside.

Intrinsic and Extrinsic Functions

We have defined structure in social systems in terms of relationships between events. Function refers to the outcomes of structured activity, and outcomes must be located with respect to some ongoing system. The distinction between intrinsic and extrinsic functions is the beginning of such specification. *Intrinsic function* refers to the immediate and direct outcome of a system or subsystem in terms of its major product. It should be distinguished from *extrinsic functions,* which are the system outcomes as they affect other systems or subsystems to which the structure in question is related.

A given system may have a number of extrinsic functions if it has different impacts on various adjacent systems. For example, the automobile factory has the intrinsic function of making automobiles. In relation to the stockholders it has the *extrinsic* function of making profits, in relation to the government the function of furnishing tax revenues, in relation to the union the function of providing gainful employment. This is not so much a matter of differential perception as of differential effect of its output as experienced by observing the throughput of a system as it evolves into a product. Extrinsic functions call for assessment of consequences with respect to a larger systemic context.

Although there may be many specific consequences of an organization's outputs for the surrounding environment, the major extrinsic function is the part the organization plays as a subsystem of the larger society. We shall refer to this functioning in relation to the larger structure as the *genotypic function* of the organization. Thus, the research organization has an adaptive function in furnishing information so that the larger system can survive in a changing environment. The political party has a representative and compromise function in aiding the governmental structure to make decisions about the allocation of resources; the manufacturing concern has a productive function in creating goods. The relationships of organizations to their environments are treated more fully in Chapters 5 and 6.

■ SUMMARY

All open systems share certain properties, but these are insufficient for adequate characterization of specific systems. It is useful therefore to create categories of open systems and to attempt some delineation of their distinctive properties.

Social systems, for example, lack the fixed physical structure of biological and other physical systems. Social systems have structure, but it is a structure of events rather than physical parts, a structure therefore inseparable from the functioning of the system.

This unique aspect of social structure as compared with physical structure implies great importance to *maintenance inputs* (which sustain the system), in addition to *production inputs* (which are transformed and exported as the system functions). This aspect of social structure reminds us also that social organizations are contrived systems, held together by psychological bonds. The contrived quality of social systems and their quality of event-structure mean that they can be designed for a wide range of objectives, that they do not follow the growth curves typical of the life cycle of physical systems, and that they require control mechanisms of various kinds to keep their component parts together and functioning in the required interdependent fashion.

Three types of forces are involved in reducing human variability to the patterns required for organizational functioning: environmental pressures generated by the direct, observable requirements of a given situation, shared values and expectations, and rule enforcement.

The formal patterns of behavior achieved through rule enforcement are *role* behavior, sanctioned by *norms*, which are justified in their turn by *values*. Roles, norms, and values thus furnish three interrelated bases for the integration of organizations.

The integration process is complicated by the different dynamics of the major organizational subsystems. These include the production or technical subsystem, primarily concerned with the organizational throughput; the production-supportive subsystems of procurement, disposal, and institutional relations; the maintenance subsystem for attracting and holding people in their functional roles; the adaptive subsystem, concerned with organizational change; and the managerial subsystem, which directs and adjudicates among all the others. The presence of these subsystems and the formal role pattern in terms of which they function are among the major defining characteristics of social organizations as a special class of open systems.

GROWTH OF ORGANIZATIONAL █████████
STRUCTURES AND SUBSYSTEMS █████████

A description of the growth of organizational structures may take several forms, depending on the terms of reference. It may be the biography of a particular organization, or perhaps a synthetic biography that describes no single organization but attempts a kind of ontogenetic generalization. On the other hand, it may be phylogenetic and describe a historical process that accounts for the dominant forms of organizations at a particular stage in human history without suggesting that each new organization must follow the same path of development. Finally, the growth of organizational structures can be described in terms that emphasize their logical derivation and elaboration without implying that each step in that development can be identified and dated as a historical event.

GROWTH STAGES

The description that follows is something of a hybrid. Using the basic concepts of the previous chapter, we apply an open system approach to explaining the development of organizational structures. The input and output transactions of the open system in commerce with its environment are supplemented by interactions within the boundaries of the system between role incumbents and between suborganizations. The patterns of these events constitute the functioning of the organization, take place in specific environmental settings, and involve specific people. These settings and the events going on within them are the determinants of subsequent events and organizational structure (Figure 4-1).

Our main purpose is the explication of present organizational forms in these terms, but we have not knowingly violated the accounts of historians and anthropologists. And we find in the growth of specific contemporary organizations some recapitulation of these developments. The following stages can be recognized: (1) primitive collective response to common problems, (2) insurance of stability of structure, and (3) elaborated supportive structures.[1]

---

[1]These stages are intended as a general phylogenetic logic of development, not as an exact historical account of existing organizations. In its struggle to survive, it is not necessary for every organization to go through the same set of experiences as other systems have because it can take advantage of what others have learned. Trotsky (1936) referred to this general principle as the law of leaping development in his description of Russian economic progress in moving fairly directly from feudalism into large-scale capitalism.

"The privilege of historical backwardness ... compels the adoption of whatever is ready in advance of any specified date, skipping a whole series of intermediate stages .... Unevenness, the most general law of the historic process, reveals itself most sharply and completely in the destiny of backward countries. Under the whip of external necessity their backward culture is compelled to make leaps (p. 5)."

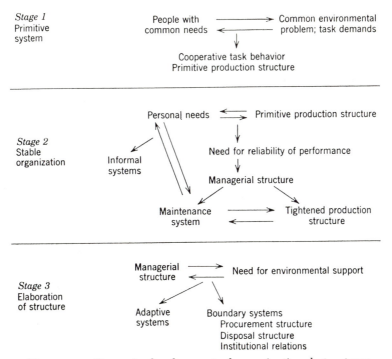

Figure 4-1 *Stages in development of organizational structures.*

Stage 1. Primitive Collective Response to Common Problems

The two major sets of determinants in the initial stages of an organization are the *environmental pressures,* or the common environmental problem, and the *needs and abilities of the population.* The environmental pressures generate task demands, which are soon met by appropriate *production* or *technical structures.* The requirements of the objective task thus exert pressures for the patterning of activities that will complete the task. A primitive system emerges in which the basis for the productive activities is the cooperative response of people based on their common needs and expectations.

Stage 2. Insurance of Stability of Structure

The primitive production structure that emerges from the task requirements does not necessarily constitute a social organization. It depends on the fit between the needs of people, their shared values, and their immediate cooperative effort in solving a common problem; as a result, it lacks consistent role performance and effective coordination of roles.

In addition to those common needs around which they cooperate, the people involved in the production system have their individual needs, aptitudes, and aspirations. Every step of the productive process of the organization, though carried out by individual human beings, is not necessarily going to coincide with their immediate needs. Moreover, the role requirements for stability and uniformity are not consistent with the facts of human variability. The closure of the first cycle of activities in task accomplishment does exert a pressure toward its repetition but there are the counter pressures of the many other interests and activities of the people involved.

The bases of the primitive production structure are the shared values and expectations of people dealing with a common problem. These are not enough to guarantee stability of socially patterned behavior. The urgency of the common problem and individual perceptions of urgency may vary over time. There will be idiosyncratic interpretations of the expectations about cooperative behavior. A host of individual decisions will arise about the kind of participation in the joint undertaking: precisely what each person is to do, how and when it should be done, and the like. Around the first crude cooperative efforts will be built devices for formulating and enforcing rules—in other words an *authority structure.* As the source of binding pronouncements and the locus of decision-making process, the authority structure is the basis of the managerial system. People no longer merely do what the task demands of them; they follow the rules that are seen as binding on members of the system. We have emphasized the development of rules, but it often happens that variability in behavior is first brought under control by a strong personality. Many early groupings are held together by such individual leadership. Organizational progress comes, however, from a development of a system of impersonal rules.

Though the authority structure is the first manifestation of the managerial subsystem, another major arm soon develops. This is the maintenance subsystem, whose specialized function involves keeping track of the rules, socializing new members into the system and its regulations, and administering rewards and sanctions.

The interaction between the primitive production structure and the variable character of human beings results in the development of a maintenance function. Considerable energy is expended to preserve the technical or production structures for task accomplishment. Special arrangements are required to insure that people will stay within the system and will carry out their roles in a reliable fashion. The maintenance structure develops, administers rewards, and mediates between the demands of the members and the requirements imposed by the technical structures. The maintenance structure thus faces both toward the people in the system and toward task requirements.

The systematic use of rewards is ancillary to the establishment and operation of a set of rules prescribing certain forms of behavior. The maintenance structure relies heavily on *rule enforcement*. Thus to the original *shared values* and *task requirements* is added the third and essential component for stable social organization. With rules and rule enforcement the loose, primitive production structure becomes elaborated and tightened.

Informal Structures

Although the maintenance arm of the managerial subsystem, if successful, does reduce the variability in performance, it does so at some cost to the personalities of the people in the system. Maintenance mechanisms generally do not seek to cope fully with the personal needs of people but only to effect some workable compromise between the task requirements and the psychological wants and gratifications of those on the job. The inevitable conflict between collective task demands and individual needs is sometimes erroneously attributed to the fact that human beings are inherently lazy and have to be bludgeoned into productive performance. The real reason is that the technical systems for getting work done are set up to insure predictability, efficiency, and coordination of the efforts of a great many individuals. The uniformity, the routinization, and the fragmentation of behavior run counter not only to the factor of individual differences but to the needs of people for self-determination, spontaneity, accomplishment, and the expression of individual skills and talents.

The usual compromises brought about by the maintenance structures are of two kinds. The first and most common is the imposition of external rewards, especially money, to make the intrinsically unsatisfying job more desirable. The second is to introduce some minor reform in the character of the work itself. The first method keeps people performing but does not meet their basic needs; the second is too slight to affect many people deeply. The consequence of this organizational frustration is the development of an informal structure among the people in the system. They interact, make decisions of their own, cooperate among themselves, and so find some gratification for their needs for self-determination and self-expression. To their work-oriented supervisor, they may be job holders, fillers of organizational roles; to their fellows they are personalities. Every group thus develops its own pattern of communication, interaction, and informal norms to meet the social and emotional needs of its members. Informal structure of this type is not necessarily in opposition to the basic objectives of the organization, but it frequently is in contradiction to the prescribed institutional paths for reaching those goals. One continuing problem for organization practice is how to direct the enthusiasm and motivation of informal groupings toward the accomplishment of the collective task.

Stage 3. Elaborated Supportive Structures

The fact that the organization is an open system means that it is constantly interacting with its environment to dispose of its product, to obtain materials, to recruit personnel, and to obtain the general support of outside structures to facilitate these functions. There is a constant need for environmental support. Hence subsystems develop at the boundaries of the organization to institutionalize environmental relationships and guarantee such support. An organization will often have separate departments for merchandising, advertising, and selling; for recruiting and selecting personnel; for procuring raw materials; and for public relations and contact with the larger society.

Although different organizations will assign different names and, to some extent, different functions to these departments, three types of boundary subsystems can be identified: procurement, disposal, and institutional relations.

The procurement operation is divided into the function of obtaining the input of materials to be converted and the input of personnel to get the job done. These two functions are characteristically found in separate bureaus or divisions of the organization. Theoretically part of the boundary subsystems, in practice the procurement of materials usually is tied into the production structure and the recruiting of personnel into the maintenance system. The basic condition for this allocation is a fairly abundant supply of materials and people in the external environment. When materials and personnel are difficult to obtain, the structures responsible for their procurement must face more completely toward the outside world and divorce themselves in part from the production and maintenance functions. Thus the securing of personnel for given periods of time in industrial organizations through contracts with unions is not handled through the personnel officer but through a vice president in charge of industrial relations.

The disposal function of marketing the product is found in its most exaggerated form in profit-making organizations with elaborate merchandising and sales systems. The primary emphasis is on inducing the public to purchase the product of the organization, but feedback on the success of this effort will lead to changes in the product itself. Many nonbusiness organizations expend little energy in direct product disposal. They are not in the position of having their source of input support tied directly to the disposal of their output. For example, educational institutions have as their product the imparting of knowledge and the increase of knowledge, and they do little to market their graduates.

All organizations have as their essential boundary subsystem what Parsons (1960) calls the *institutional system* or relations with the larger community or society. The operation of any organization depends not only on the specific reception of its product but on the support and legitimation of its activities by the larger social structure. Corporations deal with the federal government with respect to policy and practice on mergers and monopolies and tax laws, among other things. Corporations also relate to the general public regarding support for private enterprise and restrictions on private power. Corporate officers and board members are much concerned with the image of the company in the public mind. In similar fashion, the public school interacts with the community it serves through its Board of Education. An educator named as president of a large university soon finds little time available for educational administration within the university. The president of a university is primarily its external representative, dealing with alumni groups, foundations, potential donors, governmental officers, civic and other public groups. The term *public relations* tends to be restricted to institutional advertising, and is not an adequate concept to cover this important function of relating the organization to the total social system of which it is a part.

Changing Environmental Pressures and Adaptive Subsystems

Organizations do not exist in a static world. The surrounding environment is in a constant state of flux, and a rigid technical system, even if protected by excellent support structures, does not survive. The pressures for change are communicated most sharply to the organization when there is no market for its output. This is often too late for organizational survival and so many organizations develop *adaptive structures* whose function it is to gather advance information about trends in the environment, carry out research on internal productive processes, and plan for future developments. The maintenance activities are directed at survival in the limited sense of preserving the organization as it is. They are internally oriented and mediate conflicts between internal demands and existing production structures. The adaptive mechanisms face out on the world and are concerned with solving the conflicts that arise between present organizational practices and future environmental demands. Their internal message is almost always— change. Research and development departments of organizations are easily recognized as adaptive structures, but not all adaptation occurs within such formally designated units.

Our account of organizational growth is consistent with Blau and Scott's (1962) summary statement of organizational development, specifically:

> Large and complex formal organizations do not spring into existence full-blown but develop out of simpler ones. . . . Some in-

ferences can be drawn concerning the early development of organizational complexity from Udy's study (1958) of production organizations on nonliterate societies.[2] His cross-cultural comparisons suggest that a hierarchy of authority, in which persons in the lower levels are dependent for their rewards on those in the higher levels, tends to develop early in simple production organizations. There is also some indication that such rudimentary bureaucratic hierarchies are rooted in the ascribed status system of the community, inasmuch as these hierarchies were more frequently found in organizations where membership was based on kinship or political status rather than on a voluntary contract. Specialization typically evolves only in organizations already characterized by hierarchical differentiation, and it, in turn, tends to precede the development of more complex institutional arrangements, such as gearing rewards to contributions, and introducing contractual agreements to replace community status as the basis for defining the terms of membership participation (pp. 224–225).

THE VERTICAL (HIERARCHICAL) DIMENSION OF ORGANIZATIONS

We have described the articulated subsystems of organizations with regard to the flow of work and the specialized mechanisms for carrying it out. Work flow can be thought of as a horizontal dimension of organizational structure that locates people according to their membership and function in the production, maintenance, boundary, or adaptive subsystems. The location of individuals in this flow determines in part their view of the organization, the demands it makes of them, and the opportunities it offers.

Work flow, however, is only one dimension of organization. We can think also in terms of a vertical dimension, which differentiates people according to the power, privilege, prestige, and rewards of their organizational positions (Figure 4-2). To some extent these differences are associated with membership in the managerial subsystem, but most organizations have other categorical distinctions of a vertical kind. In many industrial companies, for example, people are classified as hourly employees or salaried employees, and the latter receive material benefits not available to the former group. In the army there is a sharp

---

[2] See in particular, Stanley H. Udy, Jr., "'Bureaucratic' Elements in Organizations," *American Sociological Review*, 23, 1958, pp. 415–418, and "Technology, Society, and Production Organization" paper read at the meetings of the American Sociological Association, New York, 1960.

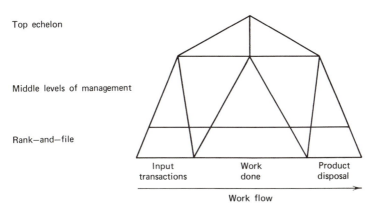

Figure 4-2 *Dimensions of organizational structure.*

distinction between enlisted soldiers and commissioned officers; in universities between academic staff and nonacademic employees.

Finer gradations are clearly visible in all these organizations, but they merely emphasize the division of positions and people according to this basic vertical gradient of privilege. Although there is a correlation between managerial authority or power and the various perquisites of prestige, privilege, and reward, it is not a perfect correlation and we cannot equate the vertical dimension with the managerial system. Professional staff members, for example, may be well paid and may enjoy all the privileges of the organization and may still be low in the power hierarchy.

The reason for calling attention to this dimension of organizational structure is that it has implications for organizational functioning. Even though the members of a vertical organizational class, like the hourly workers in industry, do not ordinarily represent an articulated subsystem of the organization, they do have attitudes, values, and interests in common with their fellows and at some variance with the salaried members of management. Since there is usually little formal representation of their interests within a firm, they often become members of an outside organization, namely the union, to represent their interests. The point we are making is, however, a general one. The vertical structure of an organization is not merely a gradient of reward; it frequently divides members of the organization into two or more classes. The *dynamic* or common motivation of a group of members is determined both by their work function and by their hierarchical position in the structure. An employee is both carpenter and rated hourly worker, for example. Attempts at organizational change designed to improve organizational functioning frequently examine only the horizontal dimension of the organization, the flow of work. They do not inquire into the arrangements whereby the hierarchical distribution of rewards creates classes of varying patterns of motivation.

The more general postulate that underlies our concern for the horizontal (functional) and the vertical (hierarchical) dimensions of organization is that one's position in organizational space is a powerful determinant of perceptions, attitudes, motivation, and behavior. The question that arises immediately on accepting this postulate is how many dimensions are needed to define a position in an organization. Or to put it more formally, what n-dimensional space is adequate for the representation of an organization.

Our answer to this question is that the two dimensions of function and hierarchy are most important. The first locates the position in the work flow of the organization and the second represents a fusion of status, power, and material rewards. One could imagine organizations in which this fusion would not exist, and organizational space would become correspondingly more complex. It might also be objected that two dimensions suggest a kind of organizational flatland. That is an objection which evokes some sympathy, but we believe that the problem lies with the reality of organizations rather than with the representation. It follows then that any significant organizational reform must take into account the two dimensions of function and of hierarchy.

GROWTH AND DECLINE OF ORGANIZATIONS

Four Kinds of Growth

We have had several occasions to remark the flexibility of organizations compared to biological organisms. Flexibility is particularly apparent in the processes of organizational growth, which can be of at least four kinds: increase in unit size, increase in number of parallel units, increase in differentiation, and merger. Let us consider them in that sequence.

1. An organization may grow simply by increasing the size of existing units without other structural change. For example, a supermarket may add a clerk or two if customer demand increases; a construction crew may add a few laborers if the work is falling behind schedule; or workers may be added to an assembly line to relieve positions that are under-timed. Growth in these terms has obvious physical limitations,

and organizations with significant growth demands or opportunities are likely to move to other modes.

2. An organization may grow by increasing the number of units doing identical work—growth by intraorganizational replication. Continued expansion of customer demand is likely to lead the supermarket chain to open additional stores, not merely add clerks to existing stores. Continued pressure for production will lead to putting on another crew of construction workers, another shift on the assembly line, or even a second line. This is the simplest way to meet increases in demand that can no longer be accommodated within the old structure. It involves *no restructuring save for the multiplication of units.* It is a common form of growth where an organization reaches out geographically to obtain more clients as in opening new branch offices, supermarkets, and so on. Even on the production side there is some advantage in multiplying units over the country so as to be less dependent on a given labor supply and closer to local markets. Much of the growth of the automobile companies follows this pattern. Such expansion is more evident for social than biological systems. Genetic factors rigidly restrict biological growth so that mutations are necessary to produce a body with two hearts or three kidneys. At the biological level the addition of parallel units is only possible by the creation of whole new biological entities, as in population increase. In social structures it is not necessary to create a whole new system in order to achieve expansion.

3. Another common form of organizational growth occurs through differentiation and specialization. Increases in system size can be attained not only through adding identical units to those already existing, but through adding units and then reallocating functions among all units. Some minimal size is required before differentiation is economically feasible, but following the Weberian model of technical specialization has resulted in gigantic economic gains. Ours has become an organizational society and it still has to be demonstrated that our level of productivity can be achieved without a high degree of differentiation of function. Technology and functional differentiation interact. Without functional differentiation only a crude technology is possible. Specialization of function leads to technological development and technological growth leads to further differentiation. Once set upon this course, we have an escalating spiral of organizational growth.

This process, is, however, checked by two forces. One is the external environment where natural resources are limited, competing values are expressed, and competing social systems exist. The second is internal to the organization, where differentiation has to be countered by integration to provide for coordination of activities and for system maintenance. Specialized activities are fractionated and must be brought together at certain points. A new specialization develops and new positions are created in the administrative and supportive subsystems for coordinating the system. Thus the problems of size are met by increasing still further the size of the system as the organizational dialectic runs its course.

4. Another form of growth is not the internal increase of similar or differentiated units but the merger with other organizations. Two organizations may combine, as in the case of Western Reserve University and Case Institute. Or a large organization may take over a small one, as in the growth of many business enterprises. The move toward monopolistic growth in the economic field has led to attempts at restriction through federal legislation. As a national pastime, however, trust busting has been more often popular than effective.

Each of these four forms of organizational growth (intraunit growth, unit replication, internal differentiation, and external amalgamation) has advantages and disadvantages. The latter two are in themselves forms of organizational restructuring, whereas the first two are not. Moreover, the latter two call for even more restructuring of the system to bring together the diverse parts. It is true that setting up parallel units, as with adding supermarkets to the chain, does call for some additional centralized machinery. But the administration of parallel units is less complicated than the coordination of specialized divisions. The profit-loss sheet can be more readily utilized as a criterion in monitoring parallel than diverse units. Moreover, demands for supplies and supportive services are more difficult to assess equitably where units are not parallel.

The greater productive efficiency of specialization is countered to some extent by the maintenance advantages of less specialized parallel units. A unit with multiple functions offers more opportunities for cohesion, provided that the unit is relatively small. Because its members have to carry out a number of activities, the work is less routine and the workers can relate to one another in performing it. A smaller unit with a number of tasks can thus be more attractive to its members. This dynamic of self-renewal is lost to the larger unit performing a single function.

Organizational growth seldom proceeds at the same rate across all subsystems. The first push is toward expansion of the production function. To have capital to plough back into the system, to get over the economic hump, and to build some reserve means giving high priority to expanding productive capacity. As production increases, however, so do the maintenance mechanisms for recruiting people, training them for role performance, and holding them with system rewards. Personnel departments follow production departments, although in most organizations personnel chiefs are not on a par with production heads. Very early supportive structures grow to insure the procurement of raw materials and to market what is being produced. These extensions of the organization into the environment are checked from without by contact and conflict with organized and unorganized groups.

The managerial function is at first fused with the production function but over time becomes differentiated from it. The organizational emphasis is no longer merely on production problems of turning out more cars or moving more coal, but becomes a more complex affair of policy formulation and implementation which assesses the recommendations of the various specialists and adjudicates competing claims.

Organizational Decline and Death

Growth, expansion, and development of organizations has received more attention in research studies and theoretical treatments than breakdown, decline, and death. This is in part due to the optimistic value orientation of behavioral scientists but also in part to the fact that organizations have a low mortality rate. In the only systematic study of the survival rate of federal governmental bureaus in the United States, Kaufman (1976) reports impressive powers of endurance. Of 175 such organizations that existed in the year 1923, about 85 percent were still going 50 years later and the majority of these had preserved their original administrative status. Moreover the 27 deaths of governmental units in this population were heavily outweighed by the birth of 246 new units, which were still alive in 1973. These figures include all executive departments but defense and postal service. At the departmental level, mortality was zero. During the 50-year period, no department went out of existence, but the status of the postal service shifted. (See Table 4-1.)

But does this confirmation of the popular stereotype about the immortality of gevernmental bureaus have any implications for other types of bureaucratic organizations? Statistics show that business enterprises, once they are past the threat of infant mortality, also have an excellent survival rate, although not as great as governmental bureaus. The average annual rate of business failures for the years from 1924 to 1973 has been only 57 per 10,000 firms. The comparable figure for deaths of governmental bureaus is 28 (Kaufman, 1976, p. 53). In our organizational society it seems easier to start than to terminate an organization, for many more are born each year than perish.

The conditions making for organizational survival or death constitute a relatively unexplored research area. The Kaufman report suggests that either extreme, flexibility or rigidity, is related to organizational morbidity; survival apparently calls for some stability of structure but also some flexibility to meet changing environmental conditions.

TABLE 4-1 Organizational Births, Deaths, and Survivors of U.S. Federal Governmental Bureaus by Age Group, 1923–1973

Age Group	1923 Population	Deaths 1924–73			Number Surviving in 1973	Number Surviving from 1923	Births, 1924–73	1973 Population
		By Age in 1923	As Percent of 1923 Population	By Age at Death				
0–9	35	8	23	3	27	—	120	120
10–19	38	5	13	5	33	—	33	33
20–29	17	2	12	1	15	—	56	56
30–39	15	2	13	2	13	—	30	30
40–49	10	2	20	3	8	—	7	7
50–59	16	2	13	3	14	27	—	27
60–69	13	2	15	2	11	33	—	33
70–79	8	0	0	2	8	15	—	15
80–89	2	1	50	0	1	13	—	13
90–99	6	2	33	4	4	8	—	8
100–109	2	0	0	1	2	14	—	14
110–119	2	0	0	0	2	11	—	11
120–129	0	0	—	0	0	8	—	8
130–139	11	1	9	0	10	1	—	1
140–149	—	—	—	0	—	4	—	4
150–159	—	—	—	1	—	2	—	2
160–169	—	—	—	0	—	2	—	2
170–179	—	—	—	0	—	0	—	0
180–184	—	—	—	0	—	10	—	10
Total	175	27	—	27	148	148	246	394
Median age	27	22	—	44	27	77	10	27

From Kaufman, 1976, p. 35.

THE DYNAMICS OF
ORGANIZATIONAL SUBSYSTEMS

Formal structures, once created, generate pressures for their own survival and enhancement. Organizations cannot be understood wholly in terms of the interaction of past, present, and future environmental requirements and personal needs of members. The very structures created to meet these demands exert a force in their own right. Once developed, a production system will profoundly influence the rest of the organization. Once developed, maintenance structures will be a powerful force for conservatism in the perpetuation of existing practices. One reason why the findings and concepts of small group experimentation within the laboratory are not adequate for an understanding of organizational functioning is that they deal with momentary pressures and not with the potency of formalized structures having historical depth and breadth. The dynamic of a structure derives, as we noted in Chapter 3, from the common interests of its members sharing a common fate, from the common norms for carrying out their functions, and from the common values which rationalize and provide a rationale for their activities. The dynamics contributed by different organizational subsystems will appear as we examine these structures in greater detail (Table 4-2).

Production or Technical Structures

The production subsystems of organizations develop a *dynamic of technical proficiency*. The force field is generated by task requirements and the ideology is directed toward task accomplishment. The concentration on completing the task has the consequence of developing standards of skill and method. This does not mean, however, that the production structure will automatically move to the highest level of technical efficiency. It may well become arrested at a stage of development that falls far short of optimal functioning. Nor are the proficiency standards of the production department all-inclusive criteria for organizational costs as a whole. Technically proficient workers may be so negative in their attitude toward the company that they contribute to high employee turnover or do not step out of their technical roles to cooperate on matters important to the organization. They may blink their eyes to stealing of company materials or other forms of cost and waste. In other words, although technical proficiency arises as a natural value from the production system, that fact does not guarantee overall organizational efficiency. Nevertheless, in the name of efficiency the organization of people to get the job done generally moves in the direction of specialization and fractionation of the component elements of the work process. More emphasis has been placed on breaking down a

TABLE 4-2 Formal Subsystems of Organizations: Their Functions, Dynamics, and Mechanisms

Subsystem Structure	Function	Dynamic	Mechanisms
I. Production: primary processes	Task accomplishment: energy transformation within organization	Proficiency	Division of labor: setting up of job specification and standards.
II. Maintenance of working structure	Mediating between task demands and human needs to keep structure in operation	Maintenance of steady state	Formalization of activities into standard legitimized procedures: setting up of system rewards; socialization of new members.
III. Boundary systems			
A. Production-supportive: procurement of materials and man-power and product disposal	Transactional exchanges at system boundaries	Specifically focused manipulation of organizational environment	Acquiring control of sources of supply; creation of image.
B. Institutional system	Obtaining social support and legitimation	Societal manipulation and integration	Contributing to community, influencing other social structure.
IV. Adaptive	Intelligence, research and development; planning	Pressure for change	Making recommendations for change to management.
V. Managerial	Resolving conflicts between hierarchical levels	Control	Use of sanctions of authority.
	Coordinating and directing functional substructures	Compromise vs. integration	Alternative concessions; setting up machinery for adjudication.
	Coordinating external requirements and organizational resources and needs	Long-term survival; optimization, better use of resources, development of increased capabilities	Increasing volume of business; adding functions; controlling environment through absorbing it or changing it; restructuring organization.

task into minute specialties than on division of labor into functional units of meaningful size.

The scientific management school of Taylor (1923) addressed itself to the problems of rational analysis of the productive process and the appropriate forms of coordination. Standards for every aspect of behavior were set on the basis of time and motion studies. Performance control was provided by records completed at the end of every day and transmitted up the line for the scrutiny of the higher offices. The supervisor had daily records on worker performance, the division chief had records on the sections under the supervisor, and so on to the organizational summit. The older industrial psychology was largely concerned with the efficiency of carrying out given tasks and devoted considerable attention to the physiology of fatigue, time and motion studies, and the influence of temperature and lighting on the work process. The modern extension of this approach can be seen in the concept of man-machine systems.

A comparable approach is the administrative theory of Gulick (1937). He examined the principles of organization of the work process and concluded that the basic factors for departmentalization were purpose, process, person, and place. Jobs could be allocated to a department on the basis of their general purpose, their similarity in terms of process, the people who would carry out the assignments, or the place and clientele to be served. Gulick's conclusions were that the factor most appropriate for a given system was contingent upon circumstances and upon the results desired. A small organization might have to forego purpose specialization in favor of process specialization. For example, if there is not enough work for a private secretary assigned to each officer, it is more efficient to have a central secretarial pool. In a large organization, however, a full-time secretary can be assigned to each officer. Moreover, no matter which factor is selected for primary organization, the other factors must be taken into account for secondary types of organizational structure. Gulick's early theoretical formulation has not been followed up by more refined analysis nor by systematic research to find the conditions under which one organizing factor rather than another could be judged superior.

Maintenance Structures

The maintenance structures are motivated toward *maintaining stability and predictability* in the organization. The dynamic here is one of preserving a steady state of equilibrium. This may take the form of a tendency toward organizational rigidity, the preservation of the status quo in absolute terms. Or it may take the form of preserving the pattern of existing relationships by adjustments of processes and parts according to some constant ratio of energic transaction. For example, the volume of business may be increased with no appreciable shifts in the patterning of activities. The maintenance dynamic in turn results in pressures toward formalization or institutionalization as the simplest method of achieving stability.

Many specific mechanisms are developed in the interests of preserving a steady state in the system. Selection procedures are employed to screen out applicants who do not seem likely to adapt to the system. Socialization or indoctrination practices are used to help fit new members into the organizational mold. System rewards are provided for membership and seniority in the system. Regulatory mechanisms are developed to give some automatic corrections to departures from the norm of organizational functioning. Rules are elaborated and provisions made for policing. Decisions are made on the basis of precedent. Uniformity becomes the ideal, and standard operating procedures are worked out for human relations as well as for production requirements.

The most general statement that can be made about all the mechanisms for maintaining stability is that they seek to *formalize or institutionalize* all aspects of organizational behavior. If a standard operating procedure has been legitimized for all relevant human behavior in the system, then the problem of predictability and stability has been logically solved. All organizations move toward formalization and role prescription to insure appropriate selection from the vast realm of possible behaviors within the structure. Unfortunately this logical solution for decreasing variability and change is too much of a tour de force to be a complete psychological solution. It runs the risk of substituting organizational ritualism for genuine functionalism.

At most moments in organizational history the easiest way to insure survival, at least for the short run, is to maintain things as they are and permit no changes. This is the characteristic tendency of the maintenance substructure.

Pressures to change often come from external demands which imply altering the character of the organizational task. These pressures are felt first by the sectors of the organization closest to the environment, the marketing and sales groups and the leaders who deal with the outside world. Next in sensitivity to external pressures is the production department concerned directly with the primary tasks to be done. The maintenance structures are the most insulated from such forces. The maintenance people face inward upon the organization. If the company cannot sell huge cars with nonfunctional body styling in large numbers, the production people may grumble but they will turn to changing their product. The secondary structures of maintenance are threatened in two respects. Some large segment of their activities may no longer be required, or demands may be made on them for which they lack the resources to cope. In other words, the maintenance structures are as concerned with their own preservation as with the survival of the organization as a whole. In fact, the typical complaint from the production departments is that the administrative services do not facilitate the production operations but throw up roadblocks to efficient functioning. Exaggerations in the criticism of administrative services are apparent, but there may also be some spark of fire that produces the smoke.

Complications arise when the maintenance subsystem, which has the primary function of sustaining existing organizational patterns, acquires a secondary function of organizational change. This can occur when members of a maintenance substructure—say the personnel department—find that some managerial policy or practice is causing unintended instability, high turnover on particular jobs, or high grievance rates in particular departments. It can also occur when professionals in the maintenance substructure bring into the organization points of view acquired through their extraorganizational professional associations. In such circumstances the maintenance substructure, perhaps in the name of long-term stability, attempts an additional function of adaptation. Its members may see themselves as agents of organizational change, and find increased satisfaction in their expanded role. It is nevertheless a complicated and hazardous one.

Boundary Structures
of Procurement and Disposal

The functions of procurement and disposal, although directly supportive of production structures, have to do with transactional exchanges with the environment. They are directed at environmental manipulations of a specific kind and their function is largely unidirectional. The marketing and advertising divisions of an enterprise are concerned with influencing the buying public. Their attention is directed outward toward clients as malleable objects to be influenced. The primary job of the people in these structures is to break through whatever resistance the consumer may show. Public resistance and consumer need may affect the organization so that it will change its product or service, but decisions of this type are made in the managerial structure. Within fairly wide limits there is no easy method of determining in advance the exact outcome of a vigorous and ingenious production and sales campaign. Hence the initial push in the marketing and sales structure is toward influencing the client, not toward influencing the company to change its type of product. If these efforts are not attended by success, then management will evaluate the situation and will use as relevant data the reports from the marketing division about their difficulties with the public. To this extent the boundary structures have a secondary function that brings information into the organization and has implications for organizational change.

Adaptive Structures

Since maintenance subsystems face inward on the organization and even inward on themselves, and the procurement and disposal subsystems are concerned primarily with sustaining the production cycles as they exist, the survival requirements of the system in a changing world lead to the creation of units and departments concerned with problems of adjustment. For example, there may be a small planning group working closely with the heads of the organization, or small research units to gauge the needs of the outside market, or a large department of research and development engaged in experimentation on new processes, new products, and product improvement. These functions of planning, research, and development, which permit the organization to exploit a changing environment rather than to be exploited by it, are essentially the role responsibilities of the top leadership. In large organizations and especially in technical systems the governing group needs the help of specialists devoting their full time to research, development, and planning. A large enterprise like the General Electric Company will apportion a sizeable chunk of its resources to various forms of research for increasing basic knowledge in the physical sciences, applying such knowledge to the manufacture of new and improved products, and investigating the needs of the changing world which the company serves. Sometimes these adaptive functions will be vested in the traditional departments concerned with maintenance functions; sometimes they will be adjuncts to existing task units either in production or sales; sometimes they will be located in new departments serving directly as one arm of top management.

The type of output and the type of dependence on the external environment affect the form of adaptive activities. In contrast to General Electric, automobile companies deal with a single complex product which calls for little basic scientific research. They are, therefore, more concerned with the utilization of knowledge than with the development of new knowledge. Research and development are geared into existing production and sales units, and tend to lag behind the changing world instead of anticipating its changes.

Most universities have relatively indirect transactions with their external environment and are poorly staffed for gathering information about changing demands and for determining how to utilize their resources to meet these demands. To criticize educational institutions alone for failure to anticipate foreseeable developments is to ignore the fact that they have lacked resources and incentives for this type of research and planning. Universities have enjoyed considerable autonomy in their academic functioning and have not had to develop many specialized adaptive mechanisms. There are many ways in which education gains by being free from the "market test" with which industry is continuously confronted. An indirect and unintended effect of this freedom, however, is the poor adaptive response of educational institutions to those occasional massive demands that cannot be denied.

The adaptive function, like the maintenance function, is directed toward the survival of the organization. Although the maintenance function faces inward and the adaptive function faces outward, they are similar with respect to another basic tendency. Both move in the direction of preserving constancy and predictability in the conditions of organizational life. The maintenance function moves toward a constant set of internal structures. The adaptive function tends to achieve environmental constancy by bringing the external world under control. One method is to extend the boundaries of the organization so that it incorporates more of the external world. If rival companies can be swallowed up, the major company will have better control over what had been a competitive market. If raw materials present problems of fluctuation and unpredictability, the company will attempt to set up subsidiaries which own the sources and process the raw materials. Where it is not possible to incorporate pieces of the external world into the organization, the trend is to control external forces so that they lose their independence as external forces.

The adaptive function, however, can move in both directions. It can strive to attain control over external forces and maintain predictability for its operations in this fashion, or it can seek internal modification of its own organizational structures to meet the needs of a changing world. Both tendencies will be at work in the same organization and the apparent illogic of organizational action is sometimes due to the compromises effected between these opposing trends. The hypothesis seems tenable that the dominant tendency in the powerful organization will be to seek control over the environment rather than to modify internal structures to accord with external changes. Foreign competition is answered with a demand for import duties and restrictions. Legislation for control of automotive emissions evokes immediate requests for modification—of the legislative requirements and effective dates. Large organizations proceed on the principle that it is easier to make the world adjust than it is to adjust to the world, and the latter alternative will be adopted only if the first offers small hope of success.

The limiting variable is the relative openness of the system to external influence. The American Medical Association, with its restriction of apprentices and its prestiged and privileged position in the body politic, is less open to outside influence than a political party constantly seeking the majority endorsement of a capricious public. Hence the American Medical Association will attempt to change society first and its own internal program second. The present complex system of delivery and payment for medical care in the United States, an elaborate combination of public and private "third-party" insurers and guarantors, can be seen as an attempt to extend medical service without requiring major changes within the profession itself.

The choice between internal and external change does not only depend on degree of openness; it also depends on the extent of the needed modification. Sometimes the modification requires changing both people and organizational structure (the multidetermined patterns of interaction), and sometimes just people, or certain of their specific practices and ideas. If the problem can be met by changing people's specific behavior, that form of change is likely to be adopted in preference to a solution that involves changing both specific behavior and generalized institutional practices. Thus if an organization is confronted with the alternative of changing some preferences in its clientele or changing its own structure and personnel, it will take the former path. If, however, it must change outside structures and personal habits, as against a limited internal change in practice, it is more likely to seek the latter solution. In general, structural change means radical change in what is considered legitimate and proper; it implies new role prescriptions, new roles, and the task of getting people to accept their new roles and even to like them. This has been one of the reasons for the difficulty of achieving racial integration of schools. Not only must many people come to accept a new pattern of legitimacy for blacks, but some of them must also favor the changes themselves. Otherwise a tough minority of people who dislike the changes and who will not accept their legitimacy can exert more influence than a larger group moved only by a willingness to abide by a new law which they personally dislike.

Both the maintenance and the adaptive function have the effect of expanding the original organization. As the adaptive function is recognized, it leads to such new and specialized structures as departments of research and development. As it seeks control of the external world, it calls for bringing more of the outside into the organization, for developing activities to control the external forces, or at least for obtaining continuing information from outside. Hence it creates a powerful dynamic for organizational growth.

Both the maintenance and adaptive subsystems share also a certain vulnerability. Their contribution to organizational survival is for the most part long-run rather than short-run, indirect rather than direct, and they therefore are obvious targets when drastic economies must be introduced. The characteristic ups and downs of personnel, training, and research units provide continuing evidence of the short-term marginality of these subsystems.

Managerial Structure

As we have already indicated, the managerial system cuts across all the operating structures of production, maintenance, environmental support, and adaptation. It is the controlling or decision-making aspect of the organization and its parts. We have traced its origin to the need for stability and predictability in the cooperative efforts at solving a common problem. The first managerial function of maintaining the system occupied the attention of management in the beginning and then became elaborated into the maintenance structure. The insurance of continuing inputs and a market for outputs were the next concerns of management, and again supplementary subsystems developed to implement top decision making. Institutional relations remain, however, as a continuing concern of the management structure. The adaptive mechanisms were once the exclusive province of the people at the top of the hierarchy. Again organizational elaboration created specific groups to help in this function. The complexity of organizational structure implies that the functions of management are also complex. Three basic functions can be distinguished: (1) the coordination of substructures, (2) the resolution of conflicts between hierarchical levels, and (3) the coordination of external requirements with organizational resources and needs.

The four types of dynamics created by the substructures of the organization (proficiency, stability, environmental manipulation, and internal change) are often in conflict and must be resolved or kept in bounds by the managerial structure. Management not only has the function of coordinating current environmental pressures with internal organizational forces, but also adjudicates between the demands of the substructures of the system. Overall control is maintained by decisions that either resolve the differences between the subparts or keep them sufficiently localized and quiescent so that the organization preserves some semblance of unity. The adjudication function more often than not moves in the direction of a *dynamic of compromise*. It is much easier for management to meet conflicts on a day-to-day basis, making concessions first to one part of the organization and then to another part, than to attempt the thorough reorganization that abstract logic might dictate. The alternation of concessions in response to the mobilization of forces means that organizations often move by jerks and jumps. They will be inactive about change too long and then move too rapidly on a single dimension of change. Movements in one direction will be counteracted by movements in another direction. Such uneven progress is often found in large complex organizations and is the result of compromises between the various substructures in the total system. To avoid some of the consequences of abrupt shifts in policy and to give continuity to decision making, adjudication procedures will develop in organized groups. This is particularly true in political and labor organizations, is somewhat true of educational institutions, and is perhaps of less consequence still in industrial organizations.

The dynamic of compromise handles conflicts between hierarchical levels as it does between substructures. It is easier to meet the demands of one subclass with a concession than to try to solve the problem by organizational restructuring. In organizations in which representative democracy is not operative, the demands of those at the lowest levels tend to be muted in the long hierarchical passage to the top of the structure. What does reach top management are the indirect effects of the hierarchical conflict or the demands transmitted from outside organizations of employees.

In addition to its internal adjustment function the managerial structure has the major task of coordinating external requirements with organizational resources and needs; that is, it must set and implement policy with respect to the problems under study by the adaptive structure. In some organizations there is no separate adaptive subsystem, and management either gathers its own intelligence or acts with little systematic information about external problems. Any overall consideration of the relationship between the organization and its surrounding environment generally leads to decisions that attempt to optimize this relationship. The optimization may be in the direction of insuring the stability of the system, of utilizing resources more effectively in its ongoing operations, or taking advantage of potential capabilities of the system to do additional things.

The dynamic for change generated in the adaptive structures is usually implemented through the managerial structure. This is so because change will affect the whole organization and top management cannot delegate the responsibility for modifications in basic policy without transforming the organization itself. When the adaptive substructure develops in an organization, the decision-making power with respect to adaptation remains with management; it is the intelligence function—the gathering and assimilation of data, and perhaps the making of recommendations—which is delegated to the new substructure. The implementation of proficiency for productive processes and of stability for the maintenance process does not necessarily call for obvious changes in organizational structure, however, and so will often be carried out by the substructure itself.

At any given time management may be more influenced by one

substructure than another. Top management positions, for example, may be held by people who have moved up from the production rather than the adaptive structure. In general, where the management structure has been more influenced by the production and maintenance subsystems than by research development and planning departments, it has met its problems by accepting the formalization dynamic of its maintenance unit and the technological way of thinking of the production people.

The Institutional System

Parsons (1960) has made a case for distinguishing between the managerial structure concerned with internal administration and allocation of resources within the organization, and the decision-making centers occupied with broad problems of external relations. He reserves the term *managerial system* only for the former and adds the label *institutional system* for the latter. In addition he would subsume under a third level, *the technical system*, most of the functions we have described under the headings of production, maintenance, procurement and disposal, and adaptation.

In Parson's words:

> But not only does such an organization [a formal organization] have to operate in a social environment which imposes the conditions governing the processes of disposal and procurement, it is also part of a wider social system which is the source of the "meaning," legitimation, or higher level support which makes the implementation of the organization's goals possible. Essentially, this means that just as a technical organization (at a sufficiently high level of the division of labor) is controlled and "serviced" by a managerial organization, so, in turn, is the managerial organization controlled by the "institutional" structure and agencies of the community. (pp. 63–64)

Thus a business enterprise enters into the institutional system through its board of directors rather than its manager, the school system through the board of education rather than the school superintendent, and a university through its board of trustees and president rather than its deans and other internal administrators.

In small organizations, where the division of labor is not great, the same officers may operate at the technical, managerial, and institutional levels. The president of a small college may move from one to another of these functions, dealing successively with alumni, with internal managerial problems, and with technical problems of curriculum. These different activities, however, involve different kinds of information, different skills, and different problems. The president of a large university is unlikely to have either time or expertise for all of them. External relations usually claim most of the president's time, and vice-presidents take over the functions of internal management, academic and nonacademic.

Parson's analysis of the three system levels (the technical, the managerial, and the institutional) led him to challenge an often-invoked principle: unity of the chain of command. Machine theory postulates a single chain of command, with orders coming down the line from the top authority figure. Parsons, however, points out that there are significant breaks in the chain between each pair of the three system levels. For many problems the managerial executive is not competent to make decisions that professional experts can make. The executive can hold them responsible for the consequences of their decisions, or can veto their recommendations. To propose alternative or even meaningful changes, however, may require information or training the executive does not have.

Parsons (1960) sums up his approach in these words:

> I may generalize about the nature of the two main breaks in line authority which I have outlined by saying that at each of the two points of articulation between subsystems there is a *two-way* interchange of inputs and outputs. What has to be "contributed" from each side is qualitatively different. Either side is in a position, by withholding its important contribution, to interfere seriously with the functioning of the other and of the larger organization. Hence the *institutionalization* of these relations must typically take a form where the relative independence of each is protected. Since, however, there is an actual hierarchy, since in some sense, the "higher" authority must be able to have some kind of "last word," the problem of protection focuses on the status of the lower-order element. Accordingly, we find that such institutions as tenure serve, in part at least, to protect professional personnel from pressures exerted by management—pressures that are often passed on down from board levels. (p. 69)

Although we have not followed Parsons' nomenclature or his formal differentiation of the managerial subsystem, we share his emphasis on the importance of institutional or external relations and his view that responsibility for them is concentrated at the apex of the organizational hierarchy. A similar emphasis can be found in the work of Selznick (1957) and Rice (1963). Both theory and research have tended to neglect the complicated external transactions of organizational life.

BOUNDARY SUBSYSTEMS AND THE
BARGAINING PROCESS

Procurement, disposal, and institutional subsystems all call for activities at the boundaries of the organization, or, to be more precise, such activities comprise boundary subsystems. The behavior of people in such boundary roles is subject to two main influences, pressures from members of their own organization and the behavior of their counterparts in other organizations—competitors, suppliers, and the like. The people in boundary roles represent their own organizations but also try to maintain a continuing interaction with their opposite numbers in other interdependent organizations. There are relatively few studies of organization boundary systems in industrial research, but Adams (1976) has developed a structural conceptualization of the factors involved and, with his students, has launched a number of important experiments. His model of boundary systems is presented in Figure 4-3, in which he shows the boundary role person of Organization A interacting with the constituents of that organization and the boundary role person of Organization B similarly interacting with a set of constituents. In addition, the two boundary role representatives interact with one another to form a boundary transaction system.

The model provides a basis for identifying the classes of variables that determine boundary role behavior. These include attributes of the components of the model and attributes of the relationships among components. Specifically they are characteristics of the two organizations, the two sets of constituents, the two boundary role representatives, the boundary transaction system, the general environment, as well as the relationships among these components.

Adams has applied his paradigm to a central area of boundary behavior—bargaining and negotiating between organizations. Exam-

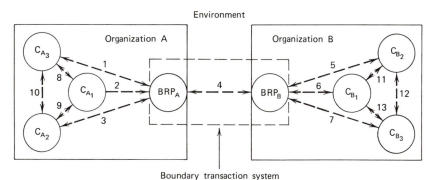

Figure 4-3 *Structural model of organization boundary systems. (From Adams, 1976, p. 1180.)*

ples of the variables suggested by his structural analysis would be the trust of the constituents in the boundary role person, the perception of the opposing role boundary person as cooperative or exploitative, the visibility of the boundary role person to his or her constituents, and the norms developed in the boundary transaction system.

Frey and Adams (1972) set up a simulated labor-management negotiation in which trust and cooperation were manipulated. They found that an exploitative counterpart was reacted to with more demanding messages than a cooperative counterpart. Trust, however, was a mediating variable and a boundary role person distrusted by his or her constituents made smaller concessions even to a cooperative counterpart than a trusted person to an exploitative counterpart. In a more complex study Frey (1971) found that conciliatory verbal behavior, if not backed by actual concessions, produced few concessions under conditions of distrust. When a boundary role person was directed by constituents to be exploitative and encountered an opponent, who though verbally conciliatory bargained exploitatively, he or she (the first boundary role person) reacted by taking a very tough line with the counterpart.

Holmes (1971) has investigated the effects of pressure from the constituent group on the bargaining behavior of the role representative under varying conditions of message content, counterpart behavior, and consensus. The main effects were that (1) competitive pressure from constituents was more potent than cooperative pressure in producing corresponding behavior in the role representative; (2) perception of the cooperative or competitive stance of one's opponent significantly modified the response to constituent pressure, and (3) in-group consensus had more influence than dissensus. Where the constituent group was not in full agreement about a cooperative stance, the role representative responded competitively if his or her counterpart was perceived as competitive. This occurred even though the majority of the group were sending cooperative messages to their representative. When there was consensus in the constituent group about cooperation the role representative behaved in a more conciliatory manner if his or her opponent was perceived as cooperative.

THE MAXIMIZATION PRINCIPLE

The managerial structure, like all the subsystems of the organization, has a self-maintenance dynamic. The structures that we have called maintenance (training and indoctrination, the administration of rewards and promotions, rule enforcement, and morale building activities) seek to develop and preserve stable patterns for the whole organization. But every subsystem also attempts to maintain itself. The managerial structure, as the decision-making group for the whole system, is thus concerned with the preservation of the entire organization, as well as the preservation of the management structure itself. Since the maintenance dynamic is all-pervasive throughout the organization, why is it not sufficiently potent to result in highly rigid and unchanging structures? Without question there is considerable resulting stability, but there is also growth, expansion, and change in almost all social systems. In fact, one of the basic properties of social systems of the bureaucratic type is that they move toward maximization, toward growth and expansion. Parkinson (1957), in noting this tendency, contends that increases in personnel and positions are not accompanied by increases in productivity.

The maximization principle can and frequently does override the maintenance dynamic for five basic reasons: (1) the proficiency dynamic leads to an increase in organizational capabilities; (2) expansion is the simplest method of dealing with problems of internal strain; (3) expansion is also the most direct solution in coping with problems of a changing social environment; (4) bureaucratic role systems in their nature permit of ready elaboration; and (5) organizational ideology encourages growth aspirations.

The Proficiency Dynamic and Maximization

The task requirements generate a proficiency dynamic for getting the job done. Although maximum efficiency may not be achieved, competitive pressures from outside the organization and experience with the task within the organization tend to produce technological improvements in the work process. These improvements result in increased capabilities of the plant for greater output with resulting increases in the sales and supportive functions. An example of such technological expansion in the steel industry was reported in the *Wall Street Journal* (January 31, 1961) as follows:

> "We don't particularly want to expand capacity, but we can't help ourselves, every step we take to raise efficiency seems to increase our capacity," one steel executive says. Equipping steel-making furnaces to use oxygen cuts costs but also lifts capacity. Pure oxygen is used in furnaces to speed the process.
>
> Bethlehem Steel Corporation is raising the capacity of its big Sparrows Point plant ten per cent to a million tons a year, mainly by equipping open hearths to use oxygen. (p. 1)

Even when the steel industry was operating at some 50 percent of its total capacity because of lack of markets, it was still expanding capacity for more steel production. That such growth might have consequences harmful to the industry and lead to further reduction in operations did not prevent the development of increased capabilities. And the statement of the steel executive that they were operating in a situation beyond their control is highly significant. The maximization dynamic is not the expression of a few ambitious personalities at the top of the organization but the outcome of the total field of forces of the sociotechnical system.

Expansion as a Simple Solution to System Strain

The contrived character of a social system means that its subsystems are rarely coordinated so as to produce completely harmonious functioning of the whole. System strain inevitably occurs because of the inability of any mode of organization to meet all the demands placed on the system. As Gulick (1937) pointed out, in the use of either purpose, process, person, or place as the basis of departmentalization, one criterion is selected at the expense of other criteria. And as has been demonstrated in the above paragraphs, the various substructures have their own characteristic dynamics which are often in conflict with one another.

The typical method of dealing with internal system strain is compromise. The compromise solution tends to make concessions to subsystems rather than requiring them to give up essential functions or resources. If one department brings pressure against a second department because the second unit seems overstaffed and overprivileged with respect to status and frequency of promotions, the tendency of management is not to cut back the one department but to upgrade the other. The compromise solution also makes for expansion when conflict between two departments is handled by setting up liaison offices between the two units. Because each subsystem will mobilize all its forces for self-preservation, it is easier for management to meet internal problems by adding rather than by subtracting. Forces for stability in the system thus generate forces for expansion.

Another method for dealing with the system strain evidenced by conflict between substructures is to create a larger structure that will absorb the contending units and so reduce their identity and semiautonomy. This was the solution attempted in the unification of the armed services of the United States. Although some duplication of functions was eliminated by defense unification, the total structure expanded to include an overall defense department above the three subsystems of the army, navy, and air force. Without entering into the controversy over the merits of unifying the armed services, we do want to point to the strength of the forces mustered by each subsystem to preserve its basic functions. Reorganization in the interests of streamlining operations can result in further expansion.

It is more probable that organizations will deal with internal problems by encapsulating them in expanded structures than by eliminating parts. The basic political maneuver is to create a new committee rather than to abolish the old one, or to increase the size of the committee and thus immobilize some of the old sources of strain.

To control the dissatisfactions of informal groups within the system, formal status may be accorded to some mechanism for their expression. Management may respond to the complaints of employees with a formal grievance committee or an elaborate suggestion system. Again internal strains of a system result in an enlargement of the structure.

Expansion and Environmental Demands

The third basic reason for the strength of the maximization principle stems from the demands and uncertainties of the external environment. Organizations are not self-contained, as we have seen, and survival requires both that they develop reserves to endure occasional disruptions in supply and demand and that they act to minimize such disruptions. One way of building reserves is to increase the volume of business and thus obtain a greater absolute profit. There are limits to this process, of course; markets saturate, competitors compete, and increases in volume bring diminishing increments in returns.

A more direct way of dealing with environment disruptions is to control the environment, which also implies growth through the absorption of suppliers and competitors, the addition of organizational units to educate or deceive the public, and the like. There is, however, an alternative strategy for dealing with environmental uncertainty; an organization may spread the risks by relying more extensively on outside suppliers. Large organizations are likely to use both strategies, sometimes simultaneously. General Motors absorbed many of its early competitors, along with its suppliers of automobile bodies, batteries, and electrical components. Nevertheless, it uses an extensive network of smaller manufacturers as suppliers of parts. On balance, the uncertainties of the environment must be counted among incentives to organizational growth.

The dynamic of expansion in response to environmental demands and opportunities is expressed by the specialization of top management. In a small enterprise the head may have a generalized role of handling all problems and of dealing with a small staff on a personal basis, and may be content with keeping the business small. In large organizations the top leaders are more concerned with specialized roles of assessing and increasing the organization's capabilities in relation to the changing environmental forces. Their roles and careers are tied into the success of the organization and success is rarely associated with organizational suicide. In fact, in those organizations whose demise is assured by their accomplishment of their mission, there are special problems with respect to the motivation of leaders and followers as they approach their goal. Because of their special position with respect to knowledge of the functioning of the organization, the leaders are more likely to understand the advantages of increased capability of some substructures of their organization by relatively slight improvements and expenditures of energy.

In addition to expansion in the volume of business and in the structures for controlling the external environment, the organization may take on new functions and new structures to meet new demands made upon it. It generally will do this, however, without abandoning its existing structures. Any existing structure represents an investment and has a maintenance dynamic of its own. It can be modified but not easily obliterated from the larger system. In all national emergencies the United States government has responded to changing needs not by abolition of old line departments but by the creation of new agencies.

Since organizations do not drop activities and structures as readily as they acquire them, organizations that survive tend to expand. Almost any organized group that has survived over the years is the accretion of all sorts of activities and practices. The Protestant churches have added social service functions and perhaps these comprise their major activities. But the minister still gives sermons on Sunday, and Sunday school classes are held for children as if the theological function of the church were of undiminished significance. The oldest organization of them all, the Roman Catholic Church, is a remarkable collection of institutional techniques and organizational devices reflecting its long history of operation.

Bureaucratic Structure and Expansion

Another reason for the expansion of organizations is the very nature of bureaucratic structure. Bureaucracy is a rational social device for dealing with problems by legitimizing a role system. The immediate response to any evidence of system strain or externally induced pressure is the creation of new roles and new rules. If management finds workers poorly informed about the company, the personnel department may be authorized to issue a house organ to remedy this gap in organizational communication. In governmental areas we pass a law, or issue an administrative edict, and in other organizations equivalent action is taken to legitimize new roles. So prevalent is this tendency that additional functions or roles are carefully scrutinized by the budget bureau, or its equivalent, to determine whether or not there will be additional expenses. Although the proposers of expansion generally answer in the negative, the additional activities will be used in another year as the basis for requesting additional budget. In universities academic departments will ask for new courses, hopefully stating that existing personnel can handle the task, only to find that the emergency arrangements for handling the extra work are no substitute for permanent additional budget.

It is customary to satirize our readiness to pass a law to solve any problem, but the facts of the matter are that every year our state and federal governments literally pass thousands of laws, many of them leading to some form of bureaucratic expansion either within or without the government structure. As a bureaucratic society we are likely to see more rather than less growth of organizational structure in the future.

Organizational Ideology and Maximization

Finally, a factor making for maximization in organizations is the ideology generated to provide justification for the organization's existence and functions. This ideology not only suffers from inaccuracies as a scientific description of the organization but as ideology it is more pretentious than any specific organizational objective. The labor union may have the objective of advancing the interests of the workers in collective bargaining with the company, but the general ideology of unionism may support the functions of insurance, of recreational facilities, or even of political activities on a national scale. In America there is a positive cultural value placed on bigness and growth.

In addition to the general conditions that foster the maximizing principle in organizations, some social systems have a built-in device for maximization. If the transactions with the external environment can be so managed as to give the organization a greater return for its output than the energy required for its production, then the system will move toward maximizing this favorable type of exchange. The profit-making organization is the pure example of this sort of built-in maximization. In this case there is a measurable form of feedback and the trend is toward increasing the activities of the organization to insure greater profits. This is true whether the profits go to the managers, the absentee owners, or the members of a cooperative. The greatest profits in such organizations occur during a period of rapid growth, and stock market investors are constantly looking for such growth stocks. After the period of rapid growth and high profit, the organization is driven to further expansion and greater activity. This is due to the need to preserve absolute profits by a greater volume of business. Even where the profit motive is not operative, organizations with visible measures of feedback on their operations are spurred toward maximizing their functioning. University departments in the various disciplines seek to attract more or better students into their courses this year than last, turn out more Ph.D.'s, improve the quality of their graduate training so they can place their graduates in better positions, or increase the research productivity of their staff.

The maximizing principle operates differently, however, where the output system is not in competition with other systems and where restricting the number of members increases the privileges and powers they enjoy. Under this condition, there will be resistance to growth in size, as in the days when trade unions of skilled workers restricted the number of apprentices, or in the days of rapid population growth when the medical profession followed equivalent practices. But even in these instances the maximization principle is operative in directions other than membership growth. The monopolistic power position of the group is increased by the development of functions in the political spheres of life.

Not all the new functions and the expanded activities of organization are effective devices for controlling their external environment. The maximization principle in itself cannot predict the efficacy of these attempts. But it does predict that organizations will attempt to control their environment not by subtraction but by addition of substructures and functions. They will also attempt to utilize available sources of energy efficiently in order to attain a better strategic position vis-à-vis outside forces as well as to provide a margin for any added functions.

In short, the maximizing principle means that the organization seeks to acquire more of the resources that furnish energy for its activities, to employ these energies more efficiently in its productive output, and to improve the ratio of return to the organization for the energy invested in its output. Maximization pushes in the direction of growth and expansion, of control over energy sources outside the organization both with respect to intake and output; it results in mergers and the assumption of more and more functions; it is the principle behind the attempt to create favorable social conditions for the organization in the external environment; it can be seen in the staff activities of research, planning, and development by which the organization controls the future as well as the present.

In recent years the principle of maximization has begun to be challenged, not as a present fact but as a social value and as a basis for human organizations of the future. Limits to population growth, limits to natural resources, and limits to the disposal of waste have begun to get the wide discussion they deserve. What changes in the design of organizations themselves and the larger social environment would be necessary to alter the maximization dynamic are not yet clear. We will consider some of the speculative answers to such questions in Chapter 21. The present power of the maximization principle, however, is beyond argument.

THE CONFLICT DYNAMIC

In keeping with the structural-functional approach, we have emphasized the factors that create and maintain stable organizational systems. We have not viewed organizational systems as static but as moving toward a closer approximation of their ideal form. Nevertheless, the effect of our analysis may be to reify organizational forms into absolutes of social behavior. Our interest in what ties people together in a system should not lead to the assumption that social ties, once explained, can thereafter be accepted as *fixed entities* in a study of organizations. The patterned relationships as the compromise outcome of antagonistic forces continue to reflect the essential conflicts that they have compromised. We have indicated that authority structure arises to maintain predictability but that informal structure arises to maintain the conflict between rules and regulations and human needs. We have also pointed out the fundamental cleavage in organizations based on differentials in the hierarchical gradients of power, prestige, and reward. Although people in the lower ranks accept their lot to the extent of minimal conformity to organizational demands, they are often individually in rebellion against the organization, and sometimes they collectively attempt to modify it. Finally, there are competitive conflicts between the many functioning subsystems of the organization.

Dahrendorf (1958) has contended that the structural-functional approach in sociology, with its orientation toward problems of integration, neglects conflict processes. The facts of social disruption in general strikes or in race riots are too readily dismissed as unintentional and dysfunctional. Dahrendorf maintains that models of social structure must include recognition of built-in conflict associated with the dichotomy of positive and negative dominance roles—a dichotomy produced by the necessary authority structure.

The general point is that organizations are less integrated than biological systems; their patterns of cooperative interrelationships also represent constrained adjustments of conflict and struggle. The adjustment is not only the compromise of past antagonisms but also of immediate differences of feeling, belief, and interest. The contrived character of organizations means that by nature they contain built-in sources of conflict. Many facts of organizational life can be readily understood if the model of organizations is one which views social patterns not as fixed and rigid interrelations but as the outcome of a continuing tug of war. The implication of this model is that organizations are always in process of change and that the constancy attributed to the system is exaggerated by the fact that the verbal label for describing an organization remains the same even when the processes of organization do not. For example, the Democratic Party in the United States is the same organization from year to year, or from state to state, more in name than in the processes going on within the structure. Another implication of this approach is that the nature of the built-in conflicts in a given organization should be studied for an adequate understanding of its present functioning and future stability.

Conflict can have both dysfunctional and functional consequences, as Coser (1956) has pointed out. It can lead to heightened morale within a subsystem and it can lead to solutions that move more in an integrative than a compromise direction. Organizations generally develop mechanisms to handle internal struggles and devices to dull the sharp edges of conflict. As we have already noted, in large complex organizations one of the main functions of top management is the adjudication of competing claims and conflicting demands. Conflict within and between organizations is the main topic of Chapter 18. We have introduced the subject here to emphasize the fact that the conflict dynamic is an important force in organizational growth and development, and that it persists in organizational maturity.

DIFFERENTIATION AND INTEGRATION

The development of organizational structures can be conceptualized as differentiation and integration. These processes can be found in all living systems but their social manifestations require study in their own right. As we have indicated, functions once carried out by the organization as a whole become specialized tasks of subsystems. Some minimal increase in numbers and resources is necessary to provide a safe margin for such separation of functions and their institutionalization. Once past this critical point, the greater effectiveness and return to the organization resulting from a differentiated structure lead to further growth and differentiation. In ongoing systems differentiation can be measured in terms of division of labor, occupational titles, job descriptions, subunits of the organization carrying out different tasks, and number of hierarchical levels.

The history of modern society is a history of a continuing differentiation and specialization of functions. Both basic and applied sciences have become increasingly fractionated, with narrowing areas of interest for the many fractions, whether molecular biology, biochemistry, auditory physiology, or cognitive expectancy theory. In medicine we have fewer general practitioners and more specialists who are experts in limited areas such as heart surgery, vascular functioning, or arthritic problems. Even in organized sports professional teams recruit for the specialist rather than the all-around athelete, for example, in football for the field goal kicker, the punter, or the passer (the days of the triple threat man are gone). There are, of course, diminishing returns to overspecialization, but what is impressive is not the occasional check imposed by diminished effectiveness but the continuing trend toward differentiation.

The other general principle in organizational development is the complementary tendency toward coordination. As organizations become divided into subsystems, devices become necessary to integrate subsystem actions and interactions. Coordination and control thus become significant functions of the management structure. Increasingly, in large organizations a major function of management becomes one of bringing together the activities of the many divisions and from this derives the role of the executive in adjudicating and compromising internal conflicts and divergences. (See pages 91–92.) Coordination, like differentiation, has its costs. The most obvious is the increase in administrative personnel in the organization. Less noticeable is the difficulty in achieving coordination without sacrificing the human resources in the system. Russia, with its five- and ten-year plans, has attempted to program in a coordinated way the productivity of the various industries and even individual plants. These ambitious attempts at coordination have, however, been far from successful.

Just as specialization can be pushed too far in terms of the effectiveness of the outcome, so too can coordination be extended beyond the point of maximum system return. Hence, when we talk about the coordination in an organization, we should differentiate between the amount of coordination demanded by the objective nature of the situation and amount of coordination decreed by management philosophy or historical accident. This was the essential point made by Alfred Sloan (1964) when he was head of General Motors. He saw real advantages in decentralizing on a divisional basis (Chevrolet, Pontiac, Buick, etc.), with no coordination with respect to sales, advertising, or production schedules. The controls he saw as essential were budgetary. In general, the less the formal machinery for coordination, the greater the opportunity for autonomy of subsystems and the greater the possibilities of corrective adjustments as a subsystem interacts with its relevant environment.

A general principle in organizational design should be to question the need for every coordination device contemplated. It is almost always possible to make a case for coordination but often the costs are greater than the gains. It is frequently advantageous to have decisions made at lower levels in the system so they do not apply to the organization as a whole. There are many occasions when a single policy determination for many diverse units is not necessary. We can create problems for the organization by seeking coordination for all its activities. Moreover, some attempts at coordination may be ineffective and others dysfunctional in that they postpone decisions to the point of no return.

In short, organizational growth is a complex process. It always promises gains of some kinds—that is why it is undertaken—and it frequently delivers. Nevertheless, all organizational growth involves costs, at least in terms of coordinating additional persons or units. The issue in any growth decision is therefore always a question of net gain, a balance of potential costs and benefits. That calculation is further complicated by the fact that many criteria are likely to be involved, and the question of loss and gain will be answered differently depending on the weighting of those criteria. The criteria of efficiency, profit, resource utilization, and worker satisfaction may suggest different optima for organizational size in a particular case. The decision to grow, and the mode of growth to choose, will depend inevitably on a choice or weighting of these criteria.

To complicate the decision further, the cost curves are not smooth. The costs of coordination, for example, show a stepwise function with increases in size. Adding a worker to a unit will probably be handled by increasing the load on a particular supervisor, with no conventional cost to the organization. Adding a unit requires an additional supervisor, and the added cost of coordination becomes immediately visible. Small wonder that decisions about growth are often handled as if they were nearer the artistic end than the scientific end of the managerial continuum.

SOME ISSUES IN ORGANIZATIONAL GROWTH

Is Surplus (Margin) or Size the Basic Variable in Organizational Growth?

Organizational growth is dependent on some margin or surplus realized by the system as a result of its organized effort. A surplus does not have to be used for organizational expansion but it does allow for the *first organizational choice*—whether to grow or to use the margin for other purposes. The robber barons in the early days of American capitalism often did not plough back much of their profits into organizational development. But the choice was there. Without some slack or margin there is no choice. This is one of the problems of India and some of the other underdeveloped nations today. There is little or no surplus in the system and hence the great difficulty of getting over the critical hump in economic development.

Since size can be so readily measured, it is often utilized as the critical variable in research on organizations. Peter Blau (1970) has built his formal theory of organizations around size, and hypothesizes that increasing size generates structural differentiation along various dimensions at decelerating rates. But size is an effect of differentiation as well as a factor enabling differentiation—necessary but not sufficient. Surplus productivity is the essential element. The division of labor of course requires a certain minimum number of people. The real problem, however, is how to incorporate them into an organized system. India does not suffer from a lack of bodies—quite the contrary. What India lacks is the capital to place its people into the differentiated roles of a productive economic system.

Organizations grow in size as they become differentiated and some critical mass is necessary for each developing specialized function. An enterprise typically does not recruit more workers and then find ways of breaking down old tasks into fractions to take advantage of its surplus labor. If it has the resources and if greater returns are in prospect, it multiplies old functions by further division of labor and adds new ones. Then it recruits staff to meet its new table of organization. School systems seem an exception in that increases in student enrollment are often followed by the addition of specialized teachers and supportive personnel. However, it is not the increase in pupils as such but the increase in budgetary allocation from the state that permits additional hiring.

The underlying dynamic in growth is the productivity or effectiveness of the system and the consequent accumulation of surplus. There are economies of scale such that large organizations can be more effective than small organizations with respect to certain criteria. But again the payoff comes from the way people are organized in a sociotechnical system in which advantage is taken of technology and of role arrangements. Size is not without importance in that a system that integrates successfully the efforts of many people will be more effective in the accumulation of surplus than a system that integrates the efforts of fewer people. It is that surplus margin, however, that allows for the organizational decision to grow.

What Problems Result from Size?

Size, though neither the primary determinant of organizational characteristics nor the immediate antecedent of growth, has significant consequences, once given magnitudes of organization are attained. Problems that arise from the sheer number of people involved in a collective enterprise are manifold but we shall concern ourselves with four major types: (1) the loss of the primary group in motivating people to achieve organizational goals; (2) inadequacies and errors in communication among organizational members and subgroups;

(3) weaknesses in integration, that is, in utilizing the skills, knowledge, and experience of organizational members; and (4) problems of social traffic and congestion. In addition, organizational attempts to handle these difficulties through formalization create additional problems.

Members of small face-to-face groups interacting about a common task can develop a strong unity of purpose and feeling, based on a shared psychological field. People will submerge themselves in their group identity and devote all their energies to the group goal. The necessary conditions are, however, face-to-face association over time among people with a common fate. The power of the peer group has long been remarked and derives from the shared expectations, perceptions, and attitudes of others with whom one can identify. In a large organization, however, many people do not know one another; others have only a nodding acquaintance, and very few are closely associated in continuing interaction. Primary groups develop but they do not embrace all organizational members nor is their cohesiveness necessarily tied to achieving organizational goals.

Communication problems increase, moreover, in that there are more relays and wider loops in the information circuits. Even though communication is restricted to organizational tasks, more links are required with more people. Especially in the upper levels of the hierarchy, people are subject to information overload and its accompanying errors. Organizations frequently fail to utilize relevant information in the system for coping with their problems. With small numbers, the possibility of interaction among people introduces a corrective device for communication errors. Face-to-face discussion can iron out differences in interpretation but numbers are a limiting factor in such interchange.

With large numbers it is difficult to utilize fully the wide range of skills, experience, and specialized knowledge represented in organizational members. This failure is further aggravated by the greater routinization characteristic of larger systems. Except for the performance of their specialized roles, people become spectators of the organization rather than members in a more active sense. Barker's (1965) intensive study of big versus small schools provides a vivid example of this phenomenon of size.

Finally, the mere piling up of active bodies creates noise, confusion, and collision. Rules and restrictions are necessary with the increase in numbers to hold down the level of air pollution, of noise, of encounters unrelated to a task. To add members means more than additional punch cards. It means new human beings with their complexes of common and individual traits. The organizational answer is partial inclusion through role prescription but people do bring with them other than role-prescribed behavior. The larger the system, the more it can be encumbered by the inevitable presence of the formally excluded portions of the personalities of human beings.

The federal government is frequently taken to task for its inability to handle the communication and coordination problems of size, with its multitudes of units engaged in similar or redundant functions. The many coordinating devices such as overlapping committees, clearance procedures with related agencies, interlocking directorates, and new superstructures may just not be adequate to bring together the many subunits. Moreover, the integrative problems in carrying out a unified policy are intensified when a new policy must be formulated or when immediate decisions are required. The foreign policy apparatus of the U.S. government has been cited as an example of poor coordination due to dispersal and gigantism, or in Stanley Hoffman's words (1968) "fragmentation and elephantiasis." J. F. Campbell, in 1971, described the situation as follows:

> For Washington has not one but many foreign offices, autonomous organizations chartered in the late 1940's to wage the cold war on separate fronts. Diplomacy, military force, economic subvention, propaganda, and clandestine operations and research are pursued by the separate entities of the State and Defense Departments, AID, USIA, and CIA. Four dozen other units of the executive branch, including the Treasury, Commerce and Agriculture Departments, have foreign staffs and programs. White House committees and staffs, including a National Security Council, try to coordinate the competing offices beneath (p. 13).

How Should Surplus Be Used for Effective Development?

If the first organizational choice is whether or not to use a surplus for growth, the second choice is the selection of means for an effective pattern of development. Priority can be given (1) to a further division of labor in the production process, (2) to the development of production supportive functions such as marketing, sales, procurement of raw materials, (3) to maintaining the role system through creation of a personnel department, (4) to adding mechanisms of coordination and control in managerial structure, (5) to new roles for relating to the social environment, or (6) to the creation of an adaptive structure such as a research and development unit.

The logic of the situation with respect to environmental forces and the stage of organizational development narrow the choices that can be made. The most likely alternative in the beginning is a further division of labor in the production process itself. What has worked with a high degree of visibility before will be repeated. This process of continuing specialization of production tasks is checked, however, as existing technological knowledge is used up. The organization must either seek new technology from the outside or develop its own research activities. In either case a new subsystem emerges.

The production-related processes of marketing and of procurement of raw materials and labor also have a high priority in the early history of the organization—a priority, moreover, that continues over time. The substructures which grow around these activities are governed in part by environmental circumstances. An assured market carries different implications for the growth of a sales and advertising department and a market research division than does a highly competitive market.

Disproportionate Change and the Need for
Additional Coordination

The greater the division of labor and the more the subunits carrying out specialized activities, the greater the need for additional mechanisms of coordination. In his theory of organization Blau (1970) has made this his second major hypothesis, namely: "Structural differentiation in organizations enlarges the administrative component." The rationale behind the proposition is twofold in character.

In the first place, the many subunits cannot be adequately synchronized by a programming operation in most organizations. There has to be some more flexible set of mechanisms for relating their activities and allowing a margin of correction within a subunit itself. Otherwise, the failure of a single part could result in the collapse of the whole system. The cost of differentiation is increased coordination. No organization process is without its cost. The cost of increased coordination is further coordination. Coordinating committees are set up to coordinate the coordinators.

In the second place, the growth process does not proceed evenly for all parts of a living system, whether biological or organizational. As early as 1917 the Scottish biologist D'Arcy Thompson formulated the principle of nonproportional change and Kenneth Boulding (1953) has applied it to social systems. Environmental demands do not affect an organization uniformly; they affect different parts of the organization to different degrees. Although substructures do not respond automatically to such pressures, there is some degree of substructure responsiveness in many organizations in the interests of profitability and survival. In addition to differential growth based on environmental demands, different activities may follow different curves of growth because of their essential nature. But the point is that disproportionate changes in subsystems can create strain for the larger system and can call for compensatory coordination. Smaller units may need protection to preserve their essential autonomous functions against the encroachment of the large dominant units. Hence uneven growth can result in greater increases in the administrative component than even growth. In fact, Boulding maintains that there is a point beyond which the organization cannot compensate for the nonproportional changes in subsystem size, and so must limit its expansion.

We have to be careful, however, in accepting Boulding's assumption of critical internal stress produced by disproportionate change. It is aesthetically satisfying to assume a norm of harmonious proportions and it is true that in the biological organism uneven growth rates produce dysfunction and even death. But aesthetics and biology only furnish analogies, and the hypothesized strain resulting from disproportionate growth in social systems needs further explanation in theory and confirmation in empirical research to justify Boulding's formulation. There is no *a priori* reason for believing that the personnel department of a business enterprise has to grow as rapidly as the production department when the labor market is not tight. Nor does the production department have to grow as rapidly as the research division if present technology has reached a point of diminishing returns. Disproportionate growth can have compensatory outcomes for the system as a whole. Moreover, it is more important for subsystems in some organizations to be in balance with their appropriate sector of the environment than with one another.

What, then, are the sources of strain created by disproportionate growth that require administrative coordination? The critical factor determining internal stress is the nature of the interdependence of the subsystems of the larger structure. The most extreme case of interdependence is the convergence of all subsystem activities upon a single objective at a single point in time, as in the work of the space agency getting a man on the moon. The other extreme could be a university. The output of its colleges, departments, and research centers is numerous and diversified. The various units are interdependent at the general level of contributing to the training of students, but in a loose fashion. Not all departments can present their course offerings only on Monday, Wednesday, and Friday at 10 to 12 in the morning. The interdependence between research units and teaching departments is at the level of general values, not specific operations. The real source of system strain is not on the throughput side but in the competition for resources. A growing department will struggle for more of the budget and a static department will try to hold its own. Different rates of growth, which would jeopardize the space agency's mission, are normal for a university. They do not produce undue strain in the academic institution. The administrative mechanisms of the university developed for uniformity and coordination may, in fact, be a cause of whatever stress is created by sudden growth of a given unit. For example, a research center may have to conform to personnel and budget policies of the larger system which are inappropriate and inefficient for its productive functioning. An organization can increase in size without strain if all of its activities require only modest integration, and if that fact is reflected in its management. Diverse activities can be made governable not only by increasing the governing staff but by redefining the meaning of governance.

Between the convergence model and the diversity model we can have varying degrees of interdependence with respect to a number of dimensions such as work flow, timing, interaction with sectors of the environment, and budgetary processes. The belief and even the practice of adding coordination devices and personnel need to be justified then, not on the basis of a general principle, but an analysis of the specifics of the organizational setup and its environment.

Is Organizational Growth Accompanied by Increased Administrative Intensity?

An issue that has generated considerable discussion and even some research is the alleged disproportionate increase in bureaucratic and administrative staff as organizations grow. Parkinson's law has it that the less the amount of work in an organization, the greater the number of bureaucrats. His dramatic example was drawn from statistics about the British navy, which showed a 31 percent decline of officers and men between the years of 1914 and 1928, accompanied by a 78 percent increase of Admiralty officials for the same period. As Blau (1962, p. 226) points out, however, this example is misleading in that it took no account of technological changes in warfare or the shift from wartime to peacetime. Nonetheless, the Parkinson doctrine has become a strongly established popular belief, reinforced by the media and reiterated by presidential pronouncements if not actions. The old proposition of Baker and Davis (1954) that the staff of an organization grows geometrically while the line grows as a linear function was punctured by the empirical work of Haire (1959). Haire found that the rate of proportionate increase of staff compared to line varied according to the stage of growth under investigation, with an equal rate of increase for staff and line in late but not early growth stages. The research evidence that we shall presently consider is generally not supportive of the hypothesis that administrative intensity (proportion of personnel in administration) increases with organizational size.

Part of the debate is that two opposed tendencies are at work as organizations grow. One is the economy of scale at the administrative level, with supervisors increasing their span of control. To handle a substantially greater volume of work requires additional production workers but not necessarily more executives or supervisors. Blau (1970) furnished empirical support for this proposition from his study of 53 relatively autonomous state agencies in the United States, responsible for administering unemployment insurance and providing public employment. These agencies included 1,201 local branches and 354 headquarters divisions. Blau found that span of control expanded with increasing organizational size, for all levels of managers and supervisors and for agencies, headquarters divisions, and local offices.

The opposing principle is that, as organizations grow, they require more coordination, as recognized in Blau's second generalization concerning organizational development (1970). The greater the number of subunits, the more complex the system, and the more diversified and specialized the tasks, the greater will be the need for communication and controlled interaction within the system. As is often the case with general tendencies of a contradictory character, we need to know the other factors in the situation that can help to specify the conditions or the range of phenomena for which each principle will be dominant. Blau believes that feedback from administrative costs and overhead counteract the trend toward adding administrative personnel for purposes of coordination. An important factor, then, in administrative intensity is the marginal productivity of added administrative personnel at given periods of organizational growth. New coordinating positions may be set up until diminishing returns set in.

A second factor affecting the relative size of the administrative component is the essential throughput of the organization—its product or service. These can vary in complexity, in difficulty of production without costly error, in molding materials or people, and in the acceptability of error. Quality control in the production of drugs and the rendering of health services requires more supervisory checks than turning out pieces of furniture. There is a wide variation in span of control for different industrial enterprises. L. R. Pondy (1969) reports that administrative personnel per 100 production workers ranges from 8.7 for the logging industry to 131.1 for the drug industry. More than span of control is involved in these figures, but they illustrate the more basic point that the various supportive and supplementary activities of an enterprise are dependent on the nature of the throughput. As Freeman observes, "A brewery and a chemical firm may use very similar production systems, but one would expect the chemicals firm to have a wider variety of products, a more diverse set of raw materials, and a more elaborate research and development operation. Administrative intensity may be higher, then, because administrative functions are linked to these product-related variables." (1973 p. 761)

A related consideration is the accessibility of the production process to technological advances in automation and computerization. Organizations processing materials can be more readily mechanized than human service organizations. Supervisory control and administrative coordination can be taken over by programming and monitored by computers more fully in the production of automobiles than in providing medical care. It is of interest that the use of teaching machines, of programmed learning and of mechanical aids has been so poorly received in our educational systems.

A fourth factor in administrative intensity is the heterogeneity or homogeneity of the many subunits of the system. An increase in subunits may involve functional differentiation, wide spatial separation, or neither. An organization with many similar subdivisions can increase in size with a decrease in administrative intensity but heterogeneous system face a more difficult problem.

A fifth and critical issue in the relation of growth to administrative intensity is the degree of interdependence among the parts of the organization with respect to turning out a single product. We have already discussed the varying nature of the interdependence of the subsystems of an organization.

In the sixth place, the type of environment in which the organization operates can affect administrative intensity. A stable predictable environment imposes fewer requirements on the management of an organization than an uncertain, changing environment. The society or suprasystem can also affect the scope and intensity of administrative efforts of an organization by direct order as in the mandating by statute of positions and subunits in some agencies (e.g., departments of finance). On the other hand, the federal government may expand administrative tasks for private organizations indirectly by multiplying rules and regulations with which the private concern must comply or attempt to circumvent.

Finally, the fourfold characterization of organizations (Blau and Scott, 1962) according to the type of principal beneficiary is relevant in dealing with administrative intensity. An organization benefitting its owners and managers will consider administrative increases or decreases in relation to marginal profitability. An organization of a mutual benefit type such as a labor union or political party may encounter difficulties in increasing its administrative component because it must turn to its members for resources. A commonweal organization like a government department lacks the constraints of the marketplace and of an active constituency. Such organizations are loathe to reduce administrative staff even with a decline in volume of work. A service organization like a social welfare agency will require little coordination if it is structured to provide a great deal of autonomy for its case workers.

It is not surprising, then, that the research evidence on the relationship between organization size and administrative intensity is not clear and compelling. What is surprising is that, with no attempt to examine systematically the many factors discussed above, there is some degree of consistency in the findings of investigations in a wide variety of settings. In general, these findings just do not support Parkinson's law. Exceptions are to be found in which size is accompanied by a disproportionate increase in the number of bureaucrats, but most of these exceptions can be questioned regarding the measurement of the administrative component.

We have suggested that the lack of more definitive findings may be due to an attempt to establish a general principle without specifications about type of organization, stage of development, or nature of environment. Another problem has been the lack of agreement about the definition of administrative intensity. Blau's formulation was clear in restricting administration to managerial and supervisory personnel and thus dealing specifically with the issue of overbureaucratization in organizational growth. Other writers have lumped together all personnel except workers in direct production as the administrative component. Thus the salesman, the copywriter in advertising, the research scientist, the secretary, the maintenance worker, and the janitor all fall into the administrative category. There is some interest in knowing what happens to the ratio of direct production workers to all other employees as organizations grow, but this is not the issue of administrative intensity.

Almost all studies show a decline in proportion of workers in direct production as organizations increase in size. This is consistent with our account of organizational development, which emphasized the addition of various supportive subsystems as coming later in time than the production system. Bendix (1956), for example, has reported that for the manufacturing industries in United States, Germany, France, Great Britain, and Sweden, since the beginning of the century the ratio of salaried employees to hourly workers has consistently increased. In other words, even in secondary industry there were changes taking place comparable to the shift in occupational structure in the larger society from blue collar to white collar jobs.

What would be more interesting than further documentation of the trend toward relatively fewer production workers as organizations grow, would be specific accounts of the proportionate increase in employees carrying out different organizational functions such as research, institutional relations, marketing, and personnel activities. Here research opportunities abound in that we have so few systematic investigations. A promising start has been made by Kasarda (1974) in his examination of 178 school systems in Colorado, in which he distinguished the following four functions: (1) managerial (superintendents, assistant superintendents, principals, assistant principals, directors, assistant directors, administrative assistants, business managers, coordinators, supervisors); (2) professional and technical (guidance counsellors, librarians, psychologists, social workers, speech therapists, school nurses); (3) communicative (secretaries and clerical personnel), and (4) teaching (all classroom teachers in the system). The findings were (a) that professional and technical activities increased disproportionately with the size of the school system; (b) that an even greater increase occurred in communicative functions, and (c) that the size of the managerial component decreased relative to system size. Kasarda concludes that as systems grow in size and complexity, communication becomes a paramount issue.

Child (1973b) has also shown that aggregate measures of indirect employment cover a heterogeneous number of supportive activities, some of which increase with organization size more than others. For example, he found that over 50 percent of the variance in the numbers of people in sales and service was accounted for by the size of organization, but only 20 percent of the variance in market research and personnel.

It should be noted that the Kasarda study reports a proportionate decrease in the administrative component with increasing size when administration is defined by managerial and supervisory roles. This contradiction of the stereotype about officials multiplying with bureaucratic growth is confirmed by the majority of investigations that separate administration from other supportive activities. Although Bendix (1956) found an expansion of nonproductive personnel in large organziations, he also found that in Germany where the data could be separated for administrators and technicians, it was the technicians who increased their numbers with organization size. In fact, the proportion of administrators dropped as organizations expanded. In 1933, for example, the proportion of administrators was 10 percent in enterprises employing 51 to 200 workers and only 7 percent for those employing over 1,000 workers. This accords with Melman's early analysis (1951) of data from manufacturing concerns which shows a negative correlation between size and percentage of administrators. The Blau study (1970) of employment security agencies also revealed a decrease in proportion of administrative personnel with increases in size of local offices. There was a decelerating curve with a rapid drop occurring before an office size of 50 was reached and a slower rate of decrease after the size of 100. The correlation between size of office and proportion of supervisors was −.46. Blau accounts for the deceleration as due to the greater need for coordination in larger units.

Cross-sectional studies, among their other limitations, do not show the effects of size independent of rate of growth. A large organization studied at one point in time may be smaller than it was in previous years and a small organization larger than it had been. Hence the work of Hendershot and James (1972) in their survey of school districts in the United States is of special significance in that it included measures of the same units taken at two points in time, 1949–1950 and 1955–1956. Moreover, they differentiated administrative staff from other non-production workers. Their results supported cross-sectional studies in showing a decrease in administrative intensity with increased size. Size and growth rate, however, contributed independently to this effect. Administrative intensity decreased with rapid growth but not with slow growth. Hendershot and James (1972) also point out that the component of the organization most affected by environmental pressures will grow the most rapidly. More teachers had to be added in the 1950s to meet the postwar baby boom whereas administrators could be added more gradually. If, on the other hand, there were a large increase in school funds without an enrollment increase, the expectation would be that there would be an expansion in administrative staff.

Three conclusions from research studies on organizational growth can be drawn:

1. As organizations grow in size the proportion of workers in direct production decreases, but not as a monotonic function.
2. As organizations grow in size the proportion of members in managerial and supervisory positions (administrative intensity) decreases but at a decelerating rate. The Parkinson law and the popular stereotype about overbureaucratization are incorrect.
3. Although administrative intensity tends to decrease with organizational growth, the correlations account for only a small part of the variance. Better-than-chance predictions can be made about administrative intensity if we know the size of an organization, but not very much better than chance.

Predictions can be greatly improved, however, if we know (1) the rate of growth, (2) the shifting environmental pressures on the organization and its component parts, (3) the marginal productivity of the various organizational components, (4) the nature of the throughput, (5) organizational complexity, and (6) the type of organization. Some of this information is difficult to obtain, such as figures on marginal productivity for various functional units in the system. Nor, at the present time, do we know how to assess the effects of some of these variables, such as the forces toward oligarchy in a commonweal organization compared to a service or business concern. In other words, the studies generated by the issue of administrative intensity have suggested new areas for organizational research. The interrelationships of the above variables, as well as their effects on the size of the administration component, would provide a continuing research program for a challenging series of investigations. In such a program complexity or differentiation needs just as much attention as does size as a major independent variable. In an investigation of British labor unions, British business organizations, and engineering firms, John Child (1973a) discovered that degree of complexity itself had a more direct relationship with formalization than did size, but size was the major predictor of decentralization.

◼ SUMMARY ◼

Three stages of organizational development are considered. At Stage 1 certain characteristics of a human population and some common environmental problem interact to generate task demands and a primitive production structure to fulfill them. At Stage 2 devices for formulating and enforcing rules appear. An authority structure emerges and becomes the basis for managerial and maintenance subsystems. Stage 3 sees the further elaboration of supportive structures at the organizational boundaries—structures for procurement, disposal, and institutional relations.

Each of these organizational subsystems develops its own dynamic tendencies—technical proficiency in the case of the production subsystem, stability and predictability in the case of the maintenance subsystem, external control and internal change in the case of the boundary and adaptive subsystems, and compromise, control, and survival in the case of the managerial subsystem.

These dynamic tendencies of subsystems are not always manifest in the same terms nor with the same strength. Moreover, there are tendencies that characteristically dominate in organizations. One of the most important of these is the maximization principle, which reflects organizational efforts at insured survival and environmental control. The tendency toward maximization, which solves at least temporarily many problems of internal strain and external threat, is often overriding in human organizations.

Four forms of growth can be distinguished: increases in personnel without structural changes; increases in the number of units doing identical work; differentiation and specialization; and merger with other organizations. Differentiation gives rise to the complementary need for integration. This need is usually met by new administrative positions and other coordinative devices, which are sometimes successful but sometimes add to the managerial structure without performing an integrative function.

Among the issues in understanding the process of growth in organizations are:

the underlying dynamic that is expressed by growth;

the unintended problems resulting from growth;

the bases for allocating growth opportunities within organizations;

the question of administrative intensity (the allegation that overall organizational growth is accompanied by disproportionate growth in bureaucratic functions and staff).

5

■ ENVIRONMENT ■

OUTLINE

Four Ways of Conceptualizing Environmental Forces
Five Environmental Sectors
Four General Dimensions of Environment
    Stability-Turbulence
    Diversity-Homogeneity
    Clustered-Random
    Scarcity-Munificence

Turbulence in Relation to Sector of the Environment

Organizational Responses to Reduce Uncertainty
    Direct Control and Incorporation
    Indirect Attempts at Control
    Structural Changes and the Temporary System
    Research Studies of Organizational Response to Environmental Change

The Technological and Informational Sector: the Issue of Technological
    Determinism
Measuring Organizational Dependence
Summary

Open system theory assumes continuing interaction of an organization with its environment; such interaction is what it means for a system to be open. The study of organizations therefore should include the relationships between characteristics of the environment and characteristics of the organization. In fact, however, theory and research too often deal with only one term of the relationship, namely, the organization. Research on administrative intensity, for example, has concentrated on the relationship between overall organizational size and relative size of various organizational components, with little attention to the dynamic process of interaction with environmental factors. The research seeking relationships among other organizational variables such as complexity, coordination, and centralization is similarly limited.

Even when aspects of the environment have been included in organizational research, the treatment implies one-way causality rather than dynamic interrelationship. The effects of competition or uncertainty, for example, have sometimes been taken into account as factors in organizational decision making, but without considering also the external effects of such decisions. Only in the world of politics, as people begin to grapple with such issues as the exhaustion of resources or the pollution of air and water, do we see a concentration on the environmental effects of organizational demands and outputs.

The concept of environment is itself a kind of arbitrary, organization-centered formulation, which involves a convenient and misleading implication. Everything in the universe, except for the organization under study, is treated under the single category of environment. More specifications and better conceptualizations are badly needed.

FOUR WAYS OF CONCEPTUALIZING ENVIRONMENTAL FORCES

Attempts to characterize the environment of organizations more precisely encounter theoretical and methodological difficulties. Part of the problem is that we should be seeking patterns of interrelationships rather than lists of external characteristics to be correlated with lists of internal characteristics. Such lists can be interminable, and the correlations they engender can appear and disappear in apparently capricious fashion. Four types of emphasis can be found in the work of writers who have struggled with conceptualizing environmental variables.

1. In dealing with the issues of environmental forces, Emery and Trist (1965, 1973) have concentrated on such overall properties as turbulence and stability. They seek generalizations that apply to all organizations and contribute to organizational theory. They stress the

importance of studying environmental characteristics in their own right. Their analysis yields four types of environment, classified according to the "causal texture" affecting organizations: (a) a placid randomized environment, implying no difference between tactics and strategy on the part of an organization dealing with it; (b) a placid but clustered environment, which calls for strategy in addition to tactics, in order to benefit from the patterns of clustering; (c) a dynamic clustered environment, in which competition between similar kinds of organized groups makes demands beyond ordinary tactical and strategic considerations, as each act of an organization must take into account the acts and responses of others, and (d) a turbulent field, which in its complexity and multiple interconnections generates its own dynamic properties. The resulting uncertainty, according to Emery and Trist, can be countered only by acceptance of overarching values by competing groups.

2. Empiricists seeking readily measurable environmental characteristics have examined such specifics as size of budgets provided by suprasystem, number of competing organizations, increases in potential client populations, proximity of location to raw materials or markets, and state of the economy. The merit of this approach is that it can dig into the particulars of the relationship between an organizational system and its milieu with respect to economic interchanges.

3. Other writers have given their attention to a single level of environmental phenomena, albeit an important one—the relationships of the focal organization to other organizations. In their concern with the organizational web or network they assume that organizations talk only to their own kind. W. M. Evan (1966), following the lead of Blau and Scott (1962), has developed the concept of organizational-set to refer to the relationship of an organization to other organized systems much as the concept of role-set describes the interrelationship of roles within a single system. Adams (1976) has suggested a refinement in this approach by distinguishing between a first-order environmental organization as one that has a direct influence on the focal organization and a second-order organization in which the influence is mediated through one of the first type.

4. Finally, there are those who see the major issues of environmental context as the relationship between the organization and the society or suprasystem in which it is found. The suprasystem in turn might be described in terms of its politics (e.g., a totalitarian state or a political democracy), social institutions (e.g., private enterprise versus socialism), or culture (e.g., value patterns stressing empirical orientation versus theoretical or artistic orientation).

The approach we are suggesting would utilize some of the concepts developed in these four approaches to the organizational environment but would emphasize the kinds of relationships existing between an organization and its world. We want to identify those aspects or sectors of the environment that are most important as determinants of organizational structure and function, and to characterize those environmental sectors in terms of a limited set of descriptor variables. The conceptualization and measurement of organizational dependence on the environment would then proceed within each such sector. Such a framework has never been fully developed, and the work on measurement is even less advanced. The following material is intended to contribute to such theoretical and methodological development.

FIVE ENVIRONMENTAL SECTORS

A framework for conducting research and for understanding relationships with the environment should provide some of the generality of the Emery-Trist conceptualization and yet not ignore the specific problems emphasized by the more particularistic approaches. This dual objective can be accomplished if we keep in mind the types of functional relationships that organizations establish with different sectors of the environment as well as the dimensions applicable to more than one environmental sector. All organizations function (1) within the *value patterns* of the cultural environment in which they are embedded, (2) within the *political structure* or *pattern* of legal norms and statutes that define their formal legitimacy and limit their activities, (3) within the *economic environment* of competitive markets and competitive sources of input such as labor force and materials, (4) within the *informational and technological environment*, which can also be competitive in nature, and (5) within the *natural or physical environment* of geography, natural resources, and climate. In other words, organizations exist and adapt to five environments—the cultural, the political, the economic, the technological, and the ecological. All five sectors can vary on some of the dimensions described by Emery and Trist, such as turbulence or randomness, and each may vary independently of the others. A very placid political environment does not necessarily mean a placid economic environment. The similarity or dissimilarity of our five environmental sectors on the Emery-Trist dimensions is an interesting question for empirical research. Moreover, different kinds of organizations may be differentially affected by uncertainty or turbulence in these several environmental sectors.

FOUR GENERAL DIMENSIONS OF ENVIRONMENT

We believe that four dimensions can be applied to most environmental sectors. They are stability-turbulence, uniformity-diversity,

Environmental Sectors or Types of Functional Relationships	Stability-Turbulence	Uniformity-Diversity	Clustered (Organized)-Random	Scarcity-Munificence
1. Societal values: cultural legitimation				
2. Political: legal norms and statues				
3. Economic: markets and inputs of labor and materials				
4. Informational and technological				
5. Physical: geography; natural resources				

Figure 5-1 *A framework for examining organizational relations with the environment specifying both environmental sectors and general dimensions.*

clustered-randomized, and scarcity-munificence. Our use of these dimensions owes much to the classic paper of Emery and Trist. Figure 5-1 presents the four dimensions in relation to the five environmental sectors or aspects described earlier. The environment of an organization would be described by a score in each of the 20 cells shown in the figure.

Stability-Turbulence

The stability-turbulence dimension refers to the changing nature of the environment. At one extreme would be a constant field of forces, in the intermediate ranges some constancy in rates of change so that the immediate future is predictable, and at the turbulent extreme changes difficult or impossible to predict. The turbulent field is made up of many interdependent factors that can affect one another to produce bewildering complexity. The economy of Western nations in the 1970s was turbulent, with inflation and recession—ordinarily forces that counter each another—both increasing at unpredictable rates.

An example at the other extreme—great stability—is provided by social institutions during the feudal period. They operated on the basis of a predictable environment within the larger society. Societal values worked to preserve the social order by an emphasis upon precedent, tradition, and acceptance of authority. The church as the dominant institution permitted little in the way of dissidence or deviation from official doctrine. The economic arrangements of a peasantry bound to the great estates were integral to the static feudal system.

Diversity-Homogeneity

The environment can also vary with respect to its diversity-homogeneity. An organization faces different problems if its surround is all of one piece, so to speak, than if it is confronted by a variety of structures and processes. Coping with diversity requires more adjustment than dealing with a uniform environment. An automobile company that attempts to predict and produce for all markets (small-car, intermediate, and large) has a more difficult task than a company that concentrates on only one of those market sectors. The company attempting to produce for all three markets may have a particularly difficult time if it has competitors that are more specialized—although they of course will be more affected by any instability in the one market on which they concentrate.

A more important aspect of homogeneity or diversity involves the congruence of an organization with the surrounding environment, particularly the political and value sectors. Utopian communities have had a notoriously hard time surviving in most societies precisely because they incorporate values and politics that diverge from those of the larger society. The kibbutz communities of Israel have prospered in part because the public sector includes some 42 percent of the Israeli economy. Moreover, the *Histadrut* (federation of trade unions) owns or operates many enterprises and the *moshavim* (cooperative farm communities) have some following. The small minority of kibbutz members, some three percent of the population, thus have sympathy and support from larger segments of the society with which they share some values and elements of life-style (Katz and Golomb, 1974). Furthermore, the kibbutz communities are consistent with the larger society in their orientation toward productivity, reclamation of the land, and national defense.

Clustering-Randomness

The significance of diversity between an organization and its environment depends in part on another environmental characteristic, the degree to which the environment itself is organized. Environments differ in the degree of structuring or clustering, as contrasted to anarchy or randomness. At one end of this dimension we can imagine a totalitarian political system that presents any organization with a powerful and highly structured set of demands and constraints. The price of survival is compliance; organizations that deviate from the requirements and values of the suprasystem are altered or destroyed. At the other extreme, we can imagine a poorly organized, almost anarchic, society in which the lack of order makes further diversity easily tolerated. An organization might be in conflict with one aspect of such a society, but that diversity would not be construed as a general and intolerable deviancy. Such a society would be likely to have a variety of other problems, especially with regard to its overall productivity and civil order, but these are not our present concern.

There are practical implications of the fact that the environment of organizations tends to be other organizations. It is true that organizations often turn out a product or render a service for an unorganized public but in reaching that public they frequently go through organized outlets—wholesalers, advertising agencies, retailers, mass media, and so on. One reason why market research is limited is that it deals with an aggregation of individuals whereas what often counts is the organized outlet. A product or a political candidate can be presented on national television to a mass audience but the agencies and channels for reaching this audience are highly organized and can exert as much influence on the nature of the message as feedback from the public itself. In other words, organizations more often deal with a clustered environment of other organizations than is generally realized.

Scarcity-Munificence

Finally, the dimension of scarcity-munificence is important. This becomes especially clear when we examine the physical environment on which the organization depends for materials and labor. The niggardliness or the abundance of the natural environment is the ultimate determinant of necessary input for any organization. It was once assumed, and not without cause, that rich river valleys were the likely sites for the rise of early civilizations.[1] The direct influence of the natural environment was soon modified by technological advances that could turn distant and apparently barren lands into rich preserves. But natural resources, when exploited by modern technology, are not limitless and ecologists today are again voicing concerns about environmental overutilization as well as pollution. Now the questions of resource

[1]Charles A. Beard and Mary R. Beard, *Rise of American Civilization*, New York: Macmillan, rev. college edition, 1934. "For three thousand years or more the clash of ancient races and empire builders had as its goal, possession of the rich valleys of the Nile and the Euphrates, where food for congested populations could be won with ease and ruling classes could be readily founded on servile labor." (p. 5)

utilization are posed in more sophisticated fashion, including recycling forms of energy rather than conservation as such. For some purposes an organization is judged not only by its effective use of materials but by its total expenditure of energy (including transportation to and from the market) in relation to its contribution to the renewal of material resources.

The concept of abundance applies to other aspects of the environment than natural resources. Information and technological know-how are also environmental resources, and they are of great consequence to an organized system. Sophistication in knowledge and technology is more important than sheer amount but some critical volume is usually needed before an advance can be made from one stage to another. With respect to the economic environment, size is often an important factor. Industrial enterprises have achieved high levels of efficiency by capturing a mass market. Not only is the absolute size of the client population for a service or product important: so also is the size relative to the number of organizations in competition with one another. Indeed, these considerations of size, amount, and abundance may require more than a single dimension. We should leave this question open until research studies demonstrate the independence or unity of these concepts.

The dimension of scarcity-munificence of the environment was discussed by March and Simon (1958) as it affected intraorganization conflict. They proposed that under conditions of scarcity, subgroup competition for resources took the form of a zero-sum game. It remained for Staw and Szwajkowski (1975) to study this environmental factor as it affected company interrelationships, market practices, and legally questionable activities. In an ingenious use of secondary data they took as a measure of munificence the financial performance of industries as indicated by *Fortune's* list of the 500 largest companies in the country. As a measure of unfair market practices the investigators examined companies cited in *Trade Cases,* a publication reporting decisions and consent and litigated decrees for cases involving possible violations of antitrust laws and the Federal Trade Commission Act. A sample was drawn for the years 1968–1972 of companies in such areas of litigation as price discrimination, "tie-in" arrangements, exclusive dealing, franchise violation, price fixing, allocation of markets, monopoly, and conspiracy. The hypothesis tested was that organizations in scarce environments, in their search for additional sales and resources, would be much more likely to commit illegal action than firms in munificent environments. The results show that this was the case: "the industrial environments of the companies cited for illegal acts were less munificent than those of other companies in the *Fortune* 500."

TURBULENCE IN RELATIONSHIP TO
SECTORS OF ENVIRONMENT

We have shown the four major environmental dimensions separately for each of the specific types of environment in Figure 5-1 because such descriptive dimensions can have different scores for the various specific sectors. The economic sector may show a different level of turbulence than the political or cultural, and the technological sector may show more diversity than the cultural. There may also be a trend toward consistency, so that a turbulent environment in one sector will tend to be matched by turbulence in another sector, but the extent of such convergence remains to be determined. Moreover, the more interesting problems may occur where there is a discrepancy between environmental characteristics for different sectors—for example, where political uniformity is found together with economic diversity.

We believe that there is a dynamic relationship among the five sectors of the environment, especially with regard to turbulence. Attempts are made to restore stability as we move up the ladder at each higher level of sector complexity. As the physical environment no longer guarantees an assured supply of raw materials and energy and is poisoned by our industrial complex, we turn to new technology and scientific development to provide a new physical balance. Technology and science in their over-concentration on physical versus human problems in turn are checked at the level of political norms and societal values. The economic sector with its big corporations, interlocking financial and business directorates, and price rigging also furnishes some measure of predictability and control against a technology run wild in the hands of large numbers of entrepreneurs. Economic breakdowns, supposedly the sign of capitalistic collapse, have been controlled at the political level, through the policing of bankruptcy, indirect redistribution of wealth, controls of banking, and other such measures. Finally, the overarching values of a society have contributed some cohesion to the political, economic, and technological sectors. The most potent control, although perhaps not the most pervasive, has been political. Government may not be fully responsive to societal and individual needs, but in the Western democracies it is the most responsive mechanism that we have to environmental turbulence. When the political system itself becomes truly turbulent, then we have a state of anarchy to be followed either by social collapse or revolution.

National political systems have the function of reducing turbulence within nations. Each encounters difficulties outside its own national boundaries. In an older period of colonialism direct ownership and military power assured to certain Western countries control of resources and people throughout an empire or sphere of influence. With political independence and the creation of new national states, the international environment has become less predictable at the very time the world has shrunk and interdependence among national systems has increased. The oil embargo in the early 1970s is an example of the uncertain international environment. It illustrates the dynamic relationships among the five environmental sectors and confirms the Emery-Trist assertion that turbulence is the wave of the immediate future.

In other words the larger environment itself needs to be organized for a predictable universe. Emery and Trist (1975) recognize this problem and propose the necessity of an overarching set of values that national and international organizations will embody in their programs and policies. This proposal reminds us that internationalists and pacifists have long sought a world order based on values that cut across national and economic boundaries. They have favored any mechanisms or procedures that would bring people of differing national loyalties into communication and contact with one another. International organizations like the United Nations, however, lacking supranational powers, often can do no more than array blocs of nations against one another, thus increasing the intensity of conflict among nations. The creation of a new level of organization means a reduction of autonomy at the level it supercedes. Nations wanting an international order without relinquishing any sovereignty are seeking a goal that is something of a contradiction in terms.

ORGANIZATIONAL RESPONSES TO REDUCE UNCERTAINTY

The persistence of organized activities implies reduction of uncertainty. Any organized activity, in order to persist, must have some degree of predictability of interdependent internal activities and interdependent activities with its environment. Unless a business organization can depend on people with appropriate skills and training to operate and maintain the machines, materials fed into the system will not be appropriately transformed. Unless customers can be counted on to buy a product or service, there is no point in producing. Organizations need some degree of certainty with respect to internal and external factors to operate at all. This fact has been widely recognized by modern organizational theorists, as typified by March and Simon (1958) in recognizing the powerful organizational pressures to reduce uncertainty. Thompson (1967), too, has called attention to the organizational measures taken to reduce environmental uncertainty. A direct demonstration of this tendency appears in the work of Macaulay (1963), who found a relationship between environmental uncertainty and a firm's attempts to engage in long-term contracts with other firms.

The first impact of the environment is direct feedback of a positive or negative kind regarding support for an organization's major function. Is an industrial enterprise selling its products or services, is a university getting financial support from the government or the public, is a political party gaining votes and attracting financial support? But the organization not only has today's feedback to deal with, it must also gauge tomorrow's response. It must be able to predict, at least in some crude fashion, whether the environmental forces will grow more or less favorable. Hence, it seeks to reduce uncertainty either by controlling what will happen to its inputs and outputs, or by predicting and adjusting to changes it cannot control.

Direct Control and Incorporation

The main organizational responses to uncertainty involve control, direct or indirect. Direct control can take two forms: internal regulation and external incorporation. Internal controls are aimed at producing a disciplined, unified system that can move quickly to meet environmental threats or changes.

Another form of direct control is aimed at the environment. If the environment can be controlled, it need not be predicted. Thus, an organization moves to incorporate critical parts of its milieu into itself. It extends its boundaries, for example, by purchasing the source of its raw materials, building a company town, or taking over competing firms. It attempts to influence clients and consumers, if not to control them directly, through expenditure on information and advertising.

Indirect Attempts at Control

Organizational attempts at direct control are often limited by the reactive character of an environment. It, too, has some organized character and the ability to fight back. The organization may therefore attempt to make itself less dependent on specific environmental conditions by building up some margin of reserve in its good years and diversifying its products or services in poor years. It may also seek to build support in the unorganized public and in organized groups through extensive public relations campaigns against some future crisis. In general, indirect attempts at control have replaced more direct forms as in the case of the developed nations and their industrial giants abandoning gunboat tactics for economic and technological measures.

Finally, organizations can reduce environmental certainty by gearing into larger systems, in order to take advantage of control mechanisms more powerful than their own. Every organization falls back on the larger systems of societal values and legal norms to secure both general legitimacy for its activities and specific laws or edicts to buttress its position. Manufacturers try to keep foreign imports at a minimum by backing tariff laws. Corporations in the past have contributed to both major political parties in the United States, in the hope that they will be dealt with kindly by whichever party is in power.

Within a nation state, almost all organizations will take account of their environment by interaction with the political sector to assure legitimacy for themselves, to protect themselves against unfavorable legislation, or to gain economic advantage. Often these activities will be handled through secondary organizations such as professional associations, trade organizations, or organized lobbies.

Organizations thus use two strategies for overcoming the uncertainties of a changing world. The first we have described as direct control and environmental incorporation. An organization can expand beyond its original specialized function and seek to become a conglomerate, an educational institution, a political territoriality, or a welfare state. The second organizational strategy for controlling uncertainty is to maintain the boundaries around its main organizational function, and handle the many other tasks of political, informational, and supportive economic adjustment through interactions with outside organizations that specialize in these activities. As these interactions become stabilized, the organization in a sense becomes part of a larger social system.

Structural Changes and the Temporary System

Even before turbulence characterized many environmental sectors, organizations frequently faced new problems, for example, those created by war or economic depression. The older answer to organizational problems was to respond with more organization—a new committee, a new commission or a new body. The administration of Franklin Roosevelt was notorious for setting up new alphabetical agencies to cope with problems not handled by old-line government departments. In the more turbulent environment of the 1970s more radical suggestions have been made, antithetical in direction and even more oversimplified. Their core idea is that, as the environment approaches anarchy, organizations can reply in kind and create a kind of anarchy within themselves. One form of this doctrine, popular among some members of the new left, calls for a dissolution of organized forms and proposes to fall back on individuals and their spontaneous goodness and wisdom.

A more sophisticated form of the antiorganizational argument would keep organizations in name but transform them into highly malleable unbureaucratic systems. Thus, turbulence in the environment is paralleled (and somehow made more bearable) by turbulence in the organization. Bennis and Slater make an interesting case for such "nonbureaucratic" organizations in their volume *Temporary Society* (1968). They propose that organizations in a turbulent environment continually create task forces composed of members who as a group possess the mix of skills needed to cope with the problems of the moment. Such groups can be drawn from any part of the organization or any rank or any geographical location, so long as they possess the necessary knowledge, expertise, or skill. There should be no fixed hierarchy in the overall organization. Once the problem for which a task force has been created is solved, the group is dissolved. It, or other groups, can be assembled in other ways, with other organizational members, to solve new problems. The authors' key term for the social structure of organizations of the future is *temporary*. "There will be adaptive, rapidly changing temporary systems. These will be task forces organized around problems to be solved by groups of relative strangers with diverse professional skills. The group will be arranged on an organic rather than mechanical model: it will evolve in response to a problem rather than to programmed role expectations . . . Adaptive, problem solving, temporary systems of diverse specialists, linked together by coordinating and task-evaluating specialists in an organic flux —this is the organizational form that will replace bureaucracy as we know it." (1968, pp. 73–74). Although the authors claim the trend toward temporary systems is already visible in the aerospace and construction industries, they offer no evidence about its growth or extent nor do they suggest techniques for its measurement. It could be maintained with equal plausibility that for every step taken in this new direction organizations have taken two steps in more conservative directions to deal with problems of environmental change. Empirical studies of multiorganizational design are much needed to settle such arguments and improve on such predictions.

Research Studies of Organizational Response to Environmental Change

A pioneering research approach to the relationship between organizations and their environment can be found in the study of Burns and Stalker (1961). The management practices of 20 manufacturing concerns in Scotland and England were compared with respect to the stability of their environments as determined by rates of change in the relevant markets and in technological innovations in the larger industry. The investigators utilized intensive interviews with managers and supervisors, observational techniques, and documentary data. In stable environments they found that management practices followed the traditional machine model. In environments changing in markets and technology, the common practice was for increased lateral communication, more decision making down the line, less clearly defined roles in

TABLE 5-1   **Relative Uncertainty of Environmental Sectors**[a]

Environmental Sector	Clarity of Information	Uncertainty of Causal Relationships	Time Span of Definitive Feedback	Total Uncertainty Score
Scientific	3.7	5.3	4.9	13.9
Market	2.4	3.8	2.8	9.0
Techno-economic	2.2	3.5	2.7	8.4

[a] Higher scores indicate greater uncertainty.
From Lawrence and Lorsch, 1967, p. 29.

the hierarchy—what Burns and Stalker term an organic model. Their conclusion was not that the mechanistic model was inferior to the organic model under all conditions but that each model was appropriate to a different environment; in a stable environment the mechanistic system had its merits.

The findings of the Burns-Stalker investigation were confirmed by the more systematic quantitative study of Lawrence and Lorsch (1967). The first phase of the Lawrence-Lorsch research was conducted in six firms in the plastics industry, which was chosen as having an uncertain and changeable environment. The second research phase involved the comparison of a highly effective company and a less effective competitor in each of two industries—standardized containers and processed foods. The container industry, in contrast to plastics, was at the stable end of the continuum and the food industry was intermediate regarding the changing character of its environment. Data were obtained about internal organizational functioning from questionnaires and interviews with between 30 percent and 50 percent of the upper-level and middle-level managers in each organization; data on the environments of the three industries were obtained from interviews and questionnaires with only the top executives in each organization.

In the plastics industry innovations in products and in processing were critical for success. Three environmental areas were especially relevant for the industry—the scientific sector, the market, and the technoeconomic sector. The investigators computed uncertainty scores for these sectors (see Table 5-1) on the basis of clarity of information, uncertainty of causal relationships, and time span of definitive feedback. Formality of organizational structure was found to be definitely and negatively related to uncertainty; departments with lower uncertainty scores, like production groups, tended to have more formal structure than the less certain departments, like research. But there was no one-to-one correspondence between environmental demands and departmental characteristics. By and large, the correlation held for effective departments but not for ineffective departments. Effectiveness was measured by three criteria: change in profits over the past five years, change in sales value over the past five years, and sales of new products introduced as a percentage of total current sales.

Organizations that responded to changing external demands with departmental differentiation in formal structure were high on performance. Organizations with more stable environments could emphasize formal integration and still be high in performance. Informal integration through personal contact rather than prescribed roles characterized the plastics firms but not the food processing enterprises. There was also significantly more spread of influence or decision making down the line in the plastics industry than the food industry. In light of these findings, Lawrence and Lorsch proposed a contingency theory of organizational structure, namely, that the effective organization is the one that parallels in its own departments the characteristics of the most relevant sector of their respective environments. (See Table 5-2.)

The findings of the Burns-Stalker and the Lawrence-Lorsch studies lend some support to the theory of Bennis and Slater. A shift from rigid bureaucracy toward more informal and flexible mechanisms does foster effectiveness in a more turbulent environment. But the companies in uncertain environments, while moving in the predicted direction, did not make drastic changes in major structure. The modifications were within subsystems and did not affect the overall bureaucratic pattern. Moreover, they were not addressed to the Bennis hypothesis that environmental turbulence is the wave of the future and the future is now.

The contingency-structural model of Lawrence and Lorsch with its hypothesis of organizational effectiveness resulting from an appropriate fit between environmental and organizational characteristics has not had widespread research support. In fact, the operational measures of these investigators have been challenged for unreliability and subjectivity. Tosi, Aldag, and Storey (1973) found the Lawrence-Lorsch uncertainty scale inadequate on the basis of internal reliability assessment and factor analysis. Pennings (1975) reports that strong support for the Lawrence-Lorsch thesis comes only from studies utilizing sub-

TABLE 5-2 Comparison of Units Required and Actual Attributes

| | NUMBER OF POSITIVE COMPARISONS | |
Industry	High-Performing Firms	Low-Performing Firms
Foods	10[a]	2[a]
Containers	8	4

[a] Difference significant at .05 (Fisher's exact test).
From Lawrence and Lorsch, 1967, p. 105.

jective measures rather than objective data. In his own investigation, using both objective and subjective data, Pennings did not find corroborative evidence for the contingency model. He studied 40 widely dispersed branch offices of a large brokerage organization and found no strong pattern of relationships between environmental variables and the mechanistic or organic structure of the organization. The hypothesis that goodness of fit between environment and organizational structure would determine organizational effectiveness, a central part of the theory, received no support—in fact, the best predictors of effectiveness were the internal structural characteristics of the organization. The concept of appropriateness of organizational structure to the character of the environment is still of interest but it needs considerable elaboration and specification. The adoption of a simple isomorphism, a matching of internal to external characteristics, may not be an appropriate way for an organization to deal with its environment. An uncertain environment does not call for an uncertain organizational structure. In fact the reverse can be the case. A military organization in a strange country confronting unconventional guerilla fighters does need unusual mobility and adaptability but it may require greater unity of command.

TECHNOLOGICAL AND INFORMATIONAL SECTOR: THE ISSUE OF TECHNOLOGICAL DETERMINISM

The issue of technological influence on organizations is both important and confused. It is important because the technological sector has been the leading subsystem of many societies for many years, and it has become confused because technology exists both in the environment and in the organization. These are not the same, however; there are two technologies, the internal technology actually used by the organization and the external technology potentially available to it in the larger environment.

When writers include the machinery and equipment within the organization as part of its technological environment, they confuse internal and external technologies. The term environment should be reserved for impinging or potentially impinging factors outside the organization.

A debated question in environmental influence concerns the importance of technology as a cause of organizational change. There are those who argue for a technological determinism by showing relationships between the kinds of machinery and equipment within the organization and its social structure. But this is beginning the story in the middle because the organization with a given technology has already made a decision to accept it. The term environment should not refer to elements already taken into an organization, but to factors outside it. At the individual level, for example, we do not speak of the nervous system, or the sensory receptors that mediate stimuli, as part of the environment.

Pugh and his colleagues (1973) lump internal and external factors together as "contextual variables." Lawrence and Lorsch (1967) want a term to cover the task requirements, or the nonhuman aspect of production, and so talk of the technoeconomic environment. Here they shift their frame of reference from the organization as a social system to the individual level and do not differentiate between environmentally generated and internally generated forces. Starbuck (1976) identifies at least 20 different uses of the term environment, many of them in fact referring to intraorganizational properties. We prefer to use *technological environment* to refer to the knowledge about technical processes and machine design existing outside the organization itself, more precisely as a specific type of informational milieu. An organization may import some of this knowledge unchanged or may adapt it. In either case, some elements of external technology then become part of the organization itself. How an organization reacts to technological changes outside of its boundaries is itself an important area for investigation. Often an enterprise will react positively to the introduction of new technology in its field of activity, especially if it is in a very competitive industry in which its rivals are adopting or developing technological changes. Until an organization imports it, however, the technology is part of the environment. The state of technology in the larger industry or in the society is an environmental influence on a specific organization as its internal technology is an influence on its social structure, but we must differentiate between the technology that is part of the organization and the technology of the larger milieu.

One reason for the confusion in the literature is, as Porter, Lawler, and Hackman (1973) suggest, the renewed interest in theories of technological determinism. According to this conception, technology is the major causal factor affecting other organizational attributes, intraorganization activities, and interorganizational behavior. Marxian theory made *technical conditions of production* an important determinant of individual well-being, but not as critical as the *social relations of production* (social and political institutions). The technocrats assume, however, that if they know the state of technical advance in any given industry, whether the society is capitalistic or communist, they can predict the organizational consequences.

Both proponents and opponents of technological determinism can invoke historical examples to buttress their position. The method of yoking oxen, perhaps as early as 4000 B.C., revolutionized agriculture and made possible subsequent economic development; the transistor radio and the automobile have altered the developing nations in our own time. On the other hand, China for many centuries resisted technological advances.

Research can contribute partial answers to the issue of technological determinism if we circumscribe the problem to a limited number of organizations and variables. Joan Woodward (1965) moved the field forward by attacking the global question as a research problem of a more restricted type. She examined the internal technology of 100 manufacturing firms in southeast England in relation to other structural characteristics and to their relative effectiveness. She employed in the main a threefold classification of technologies, listed in order of increasing complexity: (1) small batch and unit production (e.g., producing units or small batches on customers' orders), (2) mass production or large batches (e.g., assembly lines for automobiles), and (3) process production (e.g., continuous flow production of chemicals or gases). Her findings were:

1. Number of levels of authority increased with technical complexity.
2. Ratio of managers to total personnel increased with technical complexity.
3. Labor costs (as a proportion of total costs) decreased with technical complexity.
4. Span of control of first line supervisor increased from unit to mass production, and then decreased from mass to process production.
5. The successful firms tended to bunch toward the middle of a given organizational characteristic for each of the three technology categories: Thus the successful unit-production firms clustered around the median on measures of formalization for unit producers; the successful mass producers clustered around the median for mass producers. In other words, there was evidence for the appropriateness or goodness-of-fit theory already discussed in the work of Burns and Stalker and Lawrence and Lorsch.
6. The mass production firms, moreover, followed the mechanistic model of Burns and Stalker, showing more rigid bureaucratic practice than the unit and process firms, which were closer to the organic model with fewer rules, more delegation of authority and more flexible interpersonal relations. Again the more successful or effective concerns were those following the more *appropriate* policies and procedures for their level of technology.

Unfortunately the findings of the large scale study of Hickson, Pugh, and Pheysey (1969) of 46 firms are not consistent with those of Woodward. In their judicious review of the literature Porter, Lawler, and Hackman suggest that the discrepancy can be explained by the size of the concerns under study. Few large companies fell in the Woodward sample. The Pugh-Hickson group themselves believe that small organizations are more affected by technology than large organizations. In larger systems technological effects will not necessarily be found in the structural variables more remote from the job itself (e.g., hierarchical and administrative structure.) Porter, Lawler, and Hackman conclude their review by stating, "it [technology] does have some relationship to certain features of structure. But it is particularly difficult to estimate how many of the structural features have been caused by technology, how much technology has been the effect of structure, and, especially, how much other factors have affected or caused both the nature of the technology and the design of organizations. With respect to this latter point, it cannot be emphasized too strongly that individuals in organizations are not helplessly dependent upon the particular existing technology. While it may be difficult to change certain features of technology in a given organization, it is not impossible. Actions can be taken by individuals to change the technology and make it responsive to human choice."

In a detailed study of the Polaris Missile Program, H. M. Sapolsky (1972) reports the interaction of technology, structural factors, and policy issues in the success of the project's development. He points out that there was a convergence between the technological imperative from the objective side and a unanimity about policy alternatives from the decision-making side that resulted in an effective program. He rejects the idea that "when technology beckons, men are helpless" (R. Lapp, 1970) and agrees with Schmookler (1966) that the adoption of technology is less influenced by available supply than by societal demand.

MEASURING ORGANIZATIONAL DEPENDENCE

Implicit in the discussion of environmental influence on organizational structure and behavior is the concept of organizational dependence. With independence from competitive systems and an abundant physical environment organizations could ignore many environmental demands or influence attempts. It is understandable that the studies show some disagreement on technological determinism, in that organizations vary in their margin of independence. Dependence may take many forms: dependence on a parent company, on governmental support, on a single type of consumer market, on the calibre and nature of competition, on the money market for recapitalization, on suppliers of materials, labor, and so on. Hence it has proved difficult to measure.

In the Aston study conducted by Pugh, Hickson, and their associates (1969a), utilizing data from 52 English organizations, an attempt was made to assess dependence and its relationship to other organizational variables. A distinction was made between dependent relations with parent organizations or owning groups, and with other organizations. For the former relationship four scales were used to show (1) the relative size of the focal organization compared to its parent; (2) its status as subsidiary, head branch, or independent company; (3) its representation in policy-making bodies of parent system; and (4) number of specializations contracted for outside the system. Where the dependence was not upon a parent organization, five subscales were used to measure (1) integration with suppliers in terms of ownership and control; (2) production geared to customer order, to stock supply, or to schedule; (3) contractual ties to customers; (4) percentage of output taken by largest consumer; and (5) percentage of largest customer's needs taken care of by organization. These five subscales were combined to give a summary measure of *vertical integration*. In addition, two other dimensions were scaled: public accountability of parent organization and the origin of the focal enterprise as an individual or organizational undertaking.

Factor analysis of these seven scales yielded a large first factor of *dependence*, with loadings of about .7 on six of the seven scales accounting for 55 percent of the variance. The four subscales with the heavist factor loading on dependence were (1) number of specializations contracted out, (2) representation in larger organizational group's policy-making bodies, (3) relative size of the focal organization in the group, and (4) status of the focal organization. The data thus suggest positive relationships among various types of dependence but they are far from establishing a unitary factor of dependence. It is encouraging to find one factor accounting for more than half of the total variance, but it does not justify neglecting the rest of the factor structure. Moreover, not all the measures predicted in the same fashion to other organizational variables as would be the case if they were measuring the identical factor of dependence.

The most telling criticism, however, of the Aston measurement of dependence comes from S. E. Mindlin and H. Aldrich (1975), who point out that the final scale used by Pugh and his colleagues was a measure of dependence on the parent organization rather than other organizations. Conceptually, there is ambiguity in both the concept of environment and the kind of relations under scrutiny, for example, resource procurement or market control. Mindlin and Aldrich propose to improve research procedures by dealing more specifically with boundary spanning functions. They also suggest a distinction between levels of interorganizational dependence: interdependence between *pairs* of organizations, between focal organizations and their organizational sets, and among all organizations in a network of organizations.

■ SUMMARY ■

Open system theory gives priority to the interrelationships of organizations and their environments. Four types of emphasis can be found in attempts to conceptualize environmental characteristics. Some writers stress overall properties of the milieu, such as turbulence and clustering as in the causal texture theory. Other more empirically oriented writers seek any measurable specific characteristic. Still others see the environmental surround as consisting of other organizations or the organizational set. Finally there are those who concentrate on the suprasystem—the cultural values of society or the · character of the political state. A different approach is to seek the functional relationships that organizations establish with different sectors of the environment—such sectors as the natural or physical environment, the informational or technological, the economic, the political, and the cultural milieu. Whether a given characteristic such as turbulence affects all environmental sectors uniformly is a problem for research. It can be hypothesized that, as we move up the levels of sector complexity, there are attempts to control events by activities at the next higher level. For example, problems at the natural environmental level are met by technological adjustments, and technological instability is checked at the economic and political levels.

The lack of assurance of sustained inputs and continuing markets for outputs leads to various forms of organizational response to reduce uncertainty. The first attempt is to control the environment directly and to incorporate it within the system. Then come efforts at indirect control through influencing other systems by means of political manipulation or economic bargaining. Or the organization may move to change its own structure to accord with environmental change. The concept of the temporary society can be considered in this context for it calls for adaptive, problem-solving task forces, fluid and changing in nature, to replace rigid structures.

Research studies of organizational response to change lend some support to the hypothesis that a shift from rigid bureaucracy toward more informal and flexible mechanisms tends to increase effectiveness in a turbulent environment. Conclusive support for the related proposition of the importance of an appropriate fit between environmental and organizational characteristics—the contingency-structural model—is lacking. An isomorphism or matching of internal to external characteristics does not take account of the complexities of interaction of a system and its environment.

Technological determinism assumes that "when technology beckons, men are helpless." But the importation of technology from the environment into the organization is a matter of human decision and unless the larger system has made a broad commitment to technology the issue may be open. The critical question is whether the great national powers have already made such an uncritical commitment to technology that there is no turning back.

A TYPOLOGY
OF ORGANIZATIONS

An eminent British scholar of an earlier century, on seeing a steam engine for the first time, is said to have exclaimed, "It is a giant with a single idea!" Some such exaggerated statement might also be made about human organizations. In comparison to communities or societies, organizations are created with limited functions, and their claim to survival is their greater efficiency in carrying out a single significant task.

In an uncertain environment, however, they cannot confine themselves to a single function without being extremely vulnerable to outside forces. They respond, as already suggested, in two basic ways. First, they develop differentiated subsystems with functions other than their primary mission; for example, an industrial firm will establish its own research unit for adapting external technology to internal needs. Second, they try to establish relatively enduring relationships with other organizations, so that their internal needs are met without compromising organizational autonomy. Nevertheless, the independence is only partial, and organizations tend to become subsystems of larger organizational sets as specialized organizations become the environmental field for one another.

It is useful to describe such organizational networks by the types of specialized organizations involved, as determined by their major or genotypic function. By genotypic function we refer to the work that gets done, to the nature of the throughput as it leads to an output which in turn recycles energy for the continuing work of the organization. Thus we differentiate economic from political or from research institutions. There are practical advantages to such a typology, in that once we know we are in an industrial plant or in a political party we can anticipate forms of activity. Within the typological categories, the variance in intraorganizational behavior will be reduced.

GENOTYPIC FUNCTIONS

We propose to consider genotypic functions from the point of view of the activity in which the organization is engaged as a subsystem of the large society. Thus we are concerned with the throughput in relation to its contribution to the surrounding social structure. Just as we considered the substructures of production, maintenance, adaptation, and management as they related to the total organization, so we shall describe organizations as they assume a production, maintenance, adaptive, or managerial role in the society.

Organizations then fall into four broad classes, though minor subtypes can be distinguished within each broad category.

1. *Productive* or economic organizations are concerned with the creation of wealth, the manufacture of goods, and the provision of services for the general public or for specific segments of it. These organizations can be subdivided into the primary activities of farming and mining, the secondary activities of manufacture and processing, and the tertiary activities of service and communication. For the society as a whole they provide an instrumental integration. They provide the output—food, clothing, shelter, and the rest—for some of the most basic human needs. They also provide the extrinsic rewards or inducements for people to keep the collective order working.

2. *Maintenance* organizations are devoted to the socialization of people for their roles in other organizations and in the larger society. Schools and churches are the major maintenance structures of the social order. Again a subdivision is possible between (a) the direct function of maintenance, as in education, indoctrination, and training, and (b) the restorative function, as in health and welfare activities and institutions of reform and rehabilitation. All these activities help to keep a society from disintegrating and are responsible for the normative integration of society. The groundwork for the maintenance structures has been laid in the early socialization process of the family.

3. *Adaptive* structures create knowledge, develop and test theories, and, to some extent, apply information to existing problems. Universities (in their research activities) and research organizations carry on this adaptive function for society as a whole. Less direct and less organized adaptive activities can be found in artistic endeavor through which there is an enriching of experience and the creation of new conceptualizations of experience.

4. Finally, there is the *managerial* or *political* function, the organizational activities concerned with the adjudication, coordination, and control of resources, people, and subsystems. At the apex of political structures is the state, which provides a specific form of legitimation in its legal statutes and which has a theoretical monopoly on the use of organized physical force for mobilizing the society against external enemies and internal rebels. The state is thus the main authority structure of society. In addition to the various formal governmental subsystems, there are such adjunct political structures as pressure groups, labor unions, and organizations of other interest groupings, such as farmers, educators, manufacturers, and doctors. Penal institutions, as instruments of law enforcement, are political

organizations. They represent the repressive side of the law in their punitive and custodial aspects. As rehabilitation agencies, however, they have a socialization or normative function.

Society is sustained (1) through the rewards of its economic system, which provides powerful instrumental motivation toward socially required behaviors; (2) by the maintenance structures of education and religion, which inculcate general norms and specific behavioral codes; and (3) by the political structures that pass and enforce laws. These three important types of integration are a more complex expression of the three bases of social systems (task requirements in relation to needs, shared values and norms, and rule enforcement), and to their respective motivational patterns (economic gain, value consensus, and political compliance).

In brief, for a society to endure there must be economically productive activities that meet basic needs and provide basic services. There must be a central set of values and norms, with socializing agencies to inculcate these belief systems and to provide general and specific training for social roles. To insure some workable integration or compromise among organized groups and interest publics, there must be an authoritative decision-making structure for the allocation of resources. Finally, in an advanced society specialized agencies develop for the creation of knowledge and for fostering artistic endeavor.

These major tasks are distributed among organizations, which generally specialize in a single function but make supplementary contributions in other areas. Industrial organizations, for example, although concentrating on the economic function, contribute scientific knowledge; in the physical sciences organizations have their own laboratories concerned with increasing knowledge. Many business organizations develop political ways of dealing with their environment to insure a favorable allocation of resources. The manufacturing industries press for high tariffs to rule out competition from foreign producers. The oil industry seeks favored tax treatment in depletion allowances. The airlines try to acquire governmental subsidies through mail contracts or outright grants.

Every organization depends in part on the contributions of other types of organizations to maintain itself. An industrial company depends on educational institutions to mold people for its operation, on the political structure to preserve its position in the scheme of things, or on health and welfare organizations to aid in the well-being of its personnel. Many organizations supplement the functions of outside agencies by special subsystems within their own boundaries. A company may extend the work of the public schools by developing its own procedures of socialization, extend the ethical system by developing its own values, and extend the political system with internal mechanisms for self-protection and allocation of resources.

Some organizations take on two or more functions, not in the sense of supplementing a major task, but in the sense of attempting more than one significant job. Universities are concerned both with the training or socializing function and with the creation of new knowledge. Custodial institutions often attempt to rehabilitate their inmates as well as to remove deviants from the social or political scene. Organizations attempting more than one main function seem to have special problems in integrating their tasks. Universities tend to split their research and teaching functions, and then to suffer endless discussion of relative priorities and entitlements. Custodial institutions have had little success in rehabilitating inmates and still giving maximum emphasis to their custodial responsibilities (Goffman, 1961; Zald, 1962). It is difficult to be at one and the same time the punitive arm of the political system and the rehabilitation agency of the educational system.

Even organizations that concentrate on a single genotypic function are complex systems and develop the familiar ancillary subsystems— production, maintenance, boundary transaction, adaptation, and management. The same generalized frame of reference can thus be used at the level of the organization and at the societal level. Activities centering around the throughput, societal or organizational, are *productive;* around the human input, *maintaining;* around coordination and control, *managerial;* and around discovering solutions to problems, *adaptive.*

People in a given type of organization will have some factors in common because of its genotypical function. For example, members of an industrial enterprise, whether engineers in the plant, personnel people in the office, or managers around the board table, will all embrace in some degree the proficiency dynamic of getting on with the job, of turning out goods that can be sold in large quantities. There will also be factors in common between members of a substructure in one organization and their counterparts in another organization. A manager from industry might experience some difficulty in moving into a management position in a university but less difficulty than a production engineer making the same move.

Most people accept these facts as truths. This acceptance is reflected in the frequency of individual moves from one organization or organizational type to another, but within the same functional substructure. We did not think it odd that the board of the Chrysler Corporation, during a financial crisis some years ago, chose as chairman and president protem a man whose industrial background was in coal mining; it was the function and experience in general management that made the move rational. Whether the degree of commonality within an organization is greater than the commonality between corresponding substructures of several organizations is difficult to predict unless we specify more about the organizations we are dealing with. In general the larger and the more complex the organizations, the greater will be the commonality of their management substructures.

SECOND ORDER CHARACTERISTICS

In addition to their genotypic or first order functions, organizations can be described in terms of their structure, their transactions with the environment, their internal transactions, and many other second order characteristics. We shall confine ourselves to two such characteristics: (1) the nature of the throughput and (2) the processes for insuring the maintenance input of human personnel.

The Nature of the Throughput:
Transformation of Objects
versus Molding of People

A dimension of organizations that differentiates many economic from noneconomic structures is the nature of the work being done. The basic energy transformations in organizations involve the processing of objects, the rendering of a service, or the molding of people.[1] The problems facing the manufacturer of material objects are not the same as those confronting the director of an insurance office or the principal of a school. Human beings as objects of a change process require different organizational procedures than materials transformed in a manufacturing plant, although hospitals have been slow to realize the implications of this distinction. Human beings are reactive, participating subjects as well as objects in any molding process. In most organizations, the decision to enter and remain is voluntary, and assumes some initial level of cooperation (Goffman, 1961). Moreover, the cooperation of subjects in all educational and most therapeutic procedures is essential to a successful outcome. Parsons (1960) describes the educational organization as follows:

> The school class is a social system with an important degree of integration between teacher and pupils. Teaching cannot be effective if the pupil is simply a "customer" to whom the "commodity" of education is "turned over" without any further relation to its purveyor than is required for the settlement of the

---

[1]We do not intend to imply that economic organizations can always be distinguished from noneconomic solely by this criterion. Many tertiary economic structures are concerned with molding people.

terms of transfer—as in the case of the typical commercial transaction . . . There must be a long-standing relation between a pupil and a succession of teachers. . . . This difference between the processes of physical production and various types of "service" has much to do with the fact that the *products* of physical technology in our society tend to be disposed of through the process of commercial marketing, while services—with many variations, of course—are much more frequently purveyed within different kinds of nonprofit contexts. (pp. 72–73)

Hasenfeld and English (1974), in their analysis of human service organizations, have introduced a useful distinction between *people-processing* organizations and *people-changing* organizations. An employment placement office would be an example of the first type and a mental hospital an example of the second. In people processing there is no attempt to change basic personal attributes, but such alterations are the main purpose of people-changing organizations. This is an important distinction because of the implications for organizational procedures in dealing with clients. Where change is the objective there must be a considerable area of discretionary power for organizational personnel. The reactive nature of subjects or patients requires reciprocal spontaneity on the part of the staff. Open prisons, where such spontaneity is a basic aspect of the staff approach toward inmates, report significantly lower rates of escape and recidivism (Scudder, 1954).

On the other hand, people-processing organizations, which provide only benefits and services based on the status or objective entitlement of people, need to restrict the discretionary power of staff members so that all recipients of service are treated equitably, according to their objective entitlement. The Social Security Office, for example, treats each claimant in similar fashion according to age, contributions to the system, and number of dependents. There is little room for the personal judgment or spontaneous response of the Social Security officer. This dependable, uniform, and equitable treatment of clients by Social Security offices is one reason why Social Security receives much higher marks from the public than public assistance agencies (Katz, Kahn, Gutek, and Barton, 1975). When we shift from people-processing to people-changing organizations, a larger more flexible role is desirable for staff members.

The external transactions of people-processing and people-changing organizations are not those of the marketplace in any immediate or direct sense. The expense of most educational institutions and hospitals is borne in part by the larger community, through public subsidy, endowment campaigns, and exemption from taxation. Such organizations are therefore less open to the immediate influence of the marketplace and more concerned with long-range outcomes. This insulation from immediate external pressures, at least those of the marketplace, justifies and intensifies the insistence of the public that people-molding organizations such as hospitals and schools be guided by norms of somewhat gentler, more individually oriented nature than might be imposed on an economic, object-molding organization. We make the same argument for occupations and professions concerned with training and therapy even when the test of the marketplace is also applied. For example, we expect medical doctors to manifest norms of truthfulness and benevolence in excess of television pitchmen, even though both market their services.

Hasenfield and English (1974) also point out that a key characteristic of human service organizations is their ideological character: their goals are defined in terms of values. Such goals are more easily announced in principle, however, than made specific and operational. The necessity of stating them in specific and task-relevant terms often leads to conflict within the system. Client needs may not coincide with staff goals, and abstract organizational goals may suffer a value transformation as operational criteria are developed. The resulting discontinuities are too often reduced by selecting clients whose problems and aspirations conform to staff goals, convenience, and superficial criteria of organizational success. More deviant and more needy candidates for service are rejected.

The contrast between object-molding and people-molding organizations is not absolute, because organizations concerned primarily with the manufacture of physical products must nevertheless deal appropriately with the human tools for getting the physical job done. In hiring, training, and motivating employees such organizations encounter many of the same problems and are subject to much of the same logic as organizations whose product is wholly human. Employees are subjects as well as social objects; they cannot be bought and sold like commodities. They are never passive, never mere role occupants, and never characterized by the same lack of reactivity as the machines that can replace them for many tasks.

The central error of the machine theory of organization is the assumption that people are tools for accomplishing a given purpose and that their work can be planned without consideration for human variability and reactivity. Machine theory is highly appropriate for the processing of material objects through the use of tools. Its weakness in applying the same logic to human instruments in factory production is often compensated for by its efficiencies in dealing with the processing of materials. Where the materials being processed are human beings, this compensatory factor is lacking.

The Expressive versus the Instrumental Cycle

We noted in Chapter 4 that social systems have the dual task of self-maintenance and productive activity. The factory, for all its semiautomated machinery, ceases to run if the workers and technicians walk off the job. What, then, holds people to the performance of their roles? Their activities in the system must carry either some intrinsic rewards, some instrumental or extrinsic rewards, or some combination of the two. When the intrinsic rewards are part and parcel of the major productive activities of the system, we are dealing with an expressive cycle; when people perform in their roles because they will be paid or because they like their fellow workers or for other extraneous considerations, we are dealing with an *instrumental cycle.*[2] More formally, in the expressive cycle the energic input, throughput, and output constitute a cycle of events that return directly to the initial point so that the output itself provides the energy for renewing the cycle.

The simplest social system would consist of so-called expressive organizations in which the members meet for the purpose of self-enjoyment, as in the case of the bridge club, the bird-watching society, or the sports club. In these cases, we are dealing primarily with a simple cycle of energic input and return which renews input. The club activity is rewarding in itself. It provides satisfactions directly, and these satisfactions are the basis of the continuation of the activity. In most organizations, however, the cycles of energy exchange are more complex. The product must be sold in an external market, and the money obtained is used to pay wages and purchase materials for the continuation of the production process. The organization and membership in it are instrumental to the attainment of other objectives. Many cycles may intervene between working and consuming those things for which work was undertaken. In the expressive cycle we are dealing with a much simpler system, more self-contained in its activities and requiring few transactions with the external environment.

The expressive-instrumental distinction can be thought of as a single dimension, with one extreme represented by an activity that provides only immediate and direct satisfaction, and the other extreme represented by some job that offers no satisfaction beyond the paycheck. Intermediate on such a scale would be activities that are neutral or dissatisfying in the immediate sense but experienced as part of a more complex cycle which is expressive. For example, although dropping bombs is immediately satisfying only to a war lover, as John Hersey (1959) has reminded us, military service can provide such expressive satisfactions as demonstrating love of country, defending one-

---

[2]See the discussion of *Gemeinschaft* and *Gesellschaft* in Chapter 9.

self against tyranny, and the like. Some managements, realistically recognizing the expressive limitations of the assembly line, have sought to inculcate identification with the organization as a whole in an effort to invest the most monotonous jobs with expressive value. The failure of most such efforts is not a failure of principle but a result of the feeble, overly economical devices used to accomplish the task.

Few organizations are pure types. Most productive organizations are characterized by complex and indirect energy transactions that involve wage payment and contractual exchange for effort, but even in such organizations there are subcycles energized by satisfactions from the work process itself. Some members of industrial organizations do find expressive as well as instrumental satisfactions in their work. Similarly, the expressive organization may have to enter into commerce with the environment to insure adequate facilities and uninterrupted time for members to pursue their expressive activities; in the process it acquires a treasury and a paid staff and suffers consequent losses in its simplistic expressive character.

Some of these complications can be accommodated if we think of the expressive and instrumental nature of a role or an organization as represented by two independent dimensions, each ranging from a maximum negative to a maximum positive value, with a midpoint at zero. The resulting two-dimensional space allows for the possibility of activities that have both expressive and instrumental value, either without the other, or neither (although it might be argued that even the most coerced activities occur only when some positive value attaches to doing as compared to refusing them).

The expressive or instrumental nature of activities is directly related to the three bases of organization—task requirements, value consensus, and rule enforcement. Where the task generates its own motivation or where people are carrying out activities in accordance with their own shared values, the opportunities for expressive satisfaction are maximized. Where performance is in response to rules that must be followed to insure rewards (wages) and to escape penalties, the satisfactions tend to be instrumental. Almost every organization tends to employ all three bases to insure effective performance, but the relative emphasis on them varies greatly from organization to organization, with industrial enterprises at one extreme and voluntary organizations at the other.

Voluntary organizations are often built on an expressive cycle in which many of the members enjoy playing their roles or derive direct gratification from the success of the organizational mission. But such organizations may have many members who join for reasons that maximize their own satisfactions without incorporating organizational goals. Not all the members of a political party are there because they find it rewarding to organize and agitate for their beliefs. Many are there because of the social satisfactions associated with party work (Valen and Katz, 1964).

The expressive versus the instrumental cycle has to do with the character of the commitment of people to the system. Where the organizational activity is intrinsically rewarding, it is directly expressive of the needs and values of the individuals involved. Members cannot be easily lured away from such organizations, since competing systems must furnish the same type of activity or offer extrinsic rewards in overwhelming amount. Where members are bound in by extrinsic reward, the possibility of defection increases.

RELATIONSHIP BETWEEN GENOTYPIC FUNCTION AND SECOND ORDER CHARACTERISTICS

Productive Systems

We have defined the economic or productive function as the creation of wealth in direct fashion, either through extracting materials from the environment, transforming them for consumption, or rendering some services related to these activities.

Because the economic function as expressed in primary and secondary production activity is directed at the molding of objects and not people, its structural elaboration tends to be better attuned to things, not people. Its immediate adaptive procedures are concerned with research on product development and testing, not on the human beings and relationships within the organization. Even its research on its marketing public is extremely limited. According to current estimates, more than 20 billion dollars are spent on advertising each year in the United States. The same sources estimate the annual budget for market research at only a small fraction of that amount. Clearly the emphasis is on shaping consumer preference rather than on discovering that preference and modifying the organization in accordance with it.

Dealing with material things and tangible services, the economic organization has the criterion of the marketplace to guide it. This constant pragmatic check reinforces the proficiency dynamic of the system, so that economic organizations have set the pace for other bureaucratic structures, with their elaborate division of labor, systematic controls on operations, and ready institutionalization of new technical procedures.

The greatest problem of the productive structure is the appropriate handling of maintenance inputs. Since mechanization is the dominant principle of the economic organization, the human tools tend to be adapted to this principle. Rank-and-file members are held in the system by an instrumental cycle rather than an expressive cycle. Economic organizations do have opportunities for binding in their top personnel, both administrative and professional, through intrinsic as well as extrinsic rewards. And the more simplified, routinized, unsatisfying roles are increasingly being automated. One solution for the future then is to take advantage of the decreasing size of the staff required in some organizations, and to make the remaining members first-class citizens in the operation. Such a solution is more feasible in an automated power plant with 20 technicians than in a nonautomated plant with 400 workers.

The industrial organization does not stimulate the all-or-nothing loyalty of rank-and-file members that is common in many political groupings. Workers form friendships on the job and may develop emotional ties to their neighborhood or community. In general, however, the economic orientation of the organization permeates its members. If another enterprise pays more and economic considerations of seniority and security do not interfere, people will move to the higher paying posts.

Conflicts of interest between economic organizations competing for the same markets are also expressed in economic terms rather than direct attack. Product design, selling price, and sales appeal are the weapons, rather than direct attempts to incapacitate or interfere with the opposing organization. In short, competition rather than conflict is the basic economic method for getting favorable returns from the environment. Conflict implies direct interference with the other party; competition implies that each party attempts to surpass the others running roughly parallel paths toward the same goal. Business organizations do engage in conflict activities through their use of pressure groups, but these actions illustrate the political rather than the economic side of organizational life.

Profit-making organizations are also characterized by the principle of immediate accountability for operational costs and efficiency. The worth of an executive is assessed not by loyalty to the organization but by the ability to run a tight shop. Immediacy of return as the yardstick of success makes for difficulties in long-range planning and the consideration of distant goals. A manager may maximize short-term returns by neglecting recruitment, training, and innovation. Even such a revolutionary development for profit-making as automation has been adopted more slowly than efficiency alone would have dictated.

The leading part of the economic organization will shift from time to time, as different parts represent differential potentials for profit. As Piel (1961) has pointed out, at one time the economically significant industrial property was the machine, then it became the design, and now it is fast becoming "the capacity to innovate design in process and product." Under these circumstances research and development becomes the leading organizational subsystem, and economic organizations would be expected to respond more quickly and appropriately to changes in their situation.

The principle of maximization also characterizes economic structures, whether they are publicly or privately owned. The proficiency dynamic means fuller exploitation of an ever-expanding technology. Economic organizations operate more profitably if they can control their sources of raw materials, if they can produce in substantial quantity, and if they can plan without market interference from undercutting competitors. Hence they move in the direction of mergers, cartels, and monopolies. It is a paradox of private enterprise that its dynamic reduces the number of competitors and ultimately may lead to public regulation as the few large organizations in any field become quasi-public institutions.

Some social theorists, especially the Marxians, have considered the economic structures of a society as its leading subsystem. The organization of economic activities is seen as more of an independent than a dependent variable in relation to political, educational, religious, and other organizations. Changes in the economic structure are alleged to affect political realignment, the nature of education, and the character of religion much more than changes in the latter activities will affect the economic structure.

A more modest formulation of the principle of the priority of material change is the generalization that change is more readily accepted in the technological than in the social sphere. There are at least two reasons why this may be so, one involving the visibility of technology and the second its instrumentality. An improved technique for tilling the soil or a more efficient machine for harvesting the crops can be readily demonstrated in ways that are perceived by the senses. An atomic bomb is visibly more powerful than an ordinary explosive, a hydrogen bomb superior in a terrible way to an atomic bomb. Social change is more complex, less observable in its immediate effects, and hence much less compelling.[3]

Moreover, social change is impeded in ways that technical change is not. We invest more emotion and more personal values in specific political and religious ideas than in specific technical devices. We value our automobiles as instrumental means for increasing our control of our immediate environment, but we will quickly abandon the old

[3]Erasmus (1961) cites evidence from a number of anthropological field studies which indicates the importance of the "demonstration effect": demonstrating the superiority of a new technique in a manner which is readily perceivable markedly increases its chances of acceptance (p. 19).

model for a new one or for a helicopter if that would serve our purposes better. Our attachment to political and religious beliefs is less instrumental, however, and more expressive of our own values. To the extent that they are thus expressive, we resist changing them even when rationality urges change.

Since it is difficult to effect changes directly in the nonmaterial culture, political, educational, and religious systems are modified indirectly through changes in the material culture. This is the thesis of Ogburn (1922), who presented historical evidence of the differential rate of change in the two types of culture. A more current instance of this thesis can be seen in the development of armaments. The technical changes in moving from conventional weapons to hydrogen bombs have profoundly affected our political and international systems. To what extent those systems can control nuclear technology remains to be seen.

Although it is plausible to look for the source of change in the developments of material culture, these developments do not encompass all of societal dynamics. The control of change is often political and the rate and the direction of change may be affected by educational, religious, and other social agencies. Our own approach to the larger problem of social change and stability would emphasize the interactional or field relationships of economic and noneconomic structures. Their interaction is more important for understanding and improving the social world than is the historical question of which came first.

Maintenance Systems: The School

The school is the organizational counterpart of the family in training children for their adult roles. It helps build in the patterns of values and norms that facilitate the assumption of roles in adult life. In addition it contributes to the knowledge and skills necessary for adult roles. Increasingly our mass bureaucratic society depends on people with a generalized role readiness—an ability to meet the demands of many organizational settings with the proper cooperation. These requirements may shift from situation to situation, and individuals must be able to pick up their cues and play their part. Riesman (1950) contrasted this other-directedness unfavorably with the inner-directedness of an earlier period. Such generalized role readiness, however, is essential to the operation of large bureaucracies in a mass society with its norms of reciprocity and coordinated activity. Children pick up these patterns in the school situation both through value indoctrination and through assuming the many roles the modern school assigns. Much has been made of the economic and social deprivations of blacks in northern cities as the causal background of rioting and violence, and rightly so. A contributing factor is the lack of socialization of young people in an adequate school system. Many of the rioters are teenagers, and many of them have not been brought into the social system through a first-rate educational program.

The school as an important maintenance subsystem of society is, in its very nature, a mechanism for preserving the status quo so that in a nation with class and group inequities it functions to maintain those inequities. This is often obscured by those who exaggerate its opportunity function. Underprivileged youngsters can improve their status relative to their parents but not necessarily relative to improved standards of living for the country as a whole. In many European countries a system of different educational tracks has abetted class stratification in that it is difficult for those not graduating from the academic gymnasium to enter a university. Where social mobility does occur it may not so much remove class inequalities as siphon off some of the leadership of the underprivileged groups without affecting the nature of the system. Such instances of upward mobility, though exceptional, can lend credibility to an egalitarian ideology.

Getzels' Congruence Model

The congruence of factors affecting the learning of children in the school system is the focus of J. W. Getzels' (1969) work with the social psychology of education. Getzel differentiates four factors: A, the culture or values of the larger society, B, the role expectations for the pupil in school, C, the personality or individual disposition of the student, and D, the values of the family and subculture. For the majority middle-class child, all four are congruent. The subculture and larger culture (A and D) are consistent; D and C are congruent in that personal dispositions follow the values of the subculture; A and B are congruent in that the role expectations of the school are in agreement with societal values, and B and C are congruent in that the role expectations of the school are compatible with the personal dispositions of the students. Hence the learning behavior of the child tends to be both effective and efficient. In the case of the socially deprived, minority lower-class child the pattern of congruence can be broken in a number of ways. A and D can be incompatible; similarly D and C may be in conflict, and so too A and B, and finally B and C. Hence the child's school behavior tends to be dysfunctional from the point of view of the culture and the school. Moreover the interrelatedness of system factors and individual dispositions makes improvement difficult unless attempted change is system oriented and takes account of all four factors.

The research findings of Gurin and Epps (1975) show the importance of distinguishing between the values of the larger society and the values of the subculture, as in the Getzels model, for the motivation and achievement of black college students. This program of research included cross-sectional studies taken at four points in time as well as panel interviews with students at the beginning of their freshman year and at the end of their senior year. In all, some 6,000 students in 10 predominantly black colleges were included. The collective racial commitment for some black students, designated by Gurin and Epps as *activists*, dominated their aspirations for academic success and future careers. This group had lower job aspirations as seniors than they had as freshmen. Another group, the *committed achievers*, were able to maintain and even increase their emphasis on achievement while developing a stronger collective consciousness. In fact the *committed achievers* were higher than a third group, the *individualistic achievers*, in their preference for difficult and nontraditional jobs.

These findings raise questions about the conventional measuring instrument for internal-external control of reinforcements—the Rotter scale. The assumption in this scale is that internality-externality is a single dimension and that people vary in the extent to which they attribute control either to their own efforts or the capriciousness of fate. But the Gurins and their colleagues (Gurin, Gurin, Lao, and Beattie, 1969) have pointed out that a realistic appreciation of such external forces as racial discrimination is not the opposite of feelings of internality. People can believe in themselves and still be aware of the social constraints affecting their lives. Factor analysis of the responses of black students to an internal-external scale did show that internality and externality were two factors rather than one. The Gurins have developed the concept of *system blame* for a social ideology which takes account of group forces outside the individual restricting his opportunities. People who accept this ideology can still be heavily committed both to individual achievement and to group goals.

Janowitz's Aggregation Model

Applying social science concepts and findings and drawing on his own involvement in educational and research programs during the sixties, M. Janowitz (1969) has proposed an aggregation model to replace the more traditional specialization model (see pages 160–161) as a strategy for change in urban education. Table 6-1 outlines the basic dimensions of these two models as they deal with the specifics of operating a school system. Janowitz goes on to say:

> The notion of the aggregation model is relevant to the entire social structure. In suburban areas, the "crisis" in public education presents an equivalent disarticulation between the academic goals and socialization goals. The growth of hostility toward educational authority and patterns of personal disorganization derive from an overemphasis in high school on narrower and

narrower criteria of test achievement, from a prolongation and uninterrupted period of higher education, as well as from a separation of the life experience of the school from the community. In particular, the aggregation model should serve to produce a more integrated and varied educational experience and should help blend school with nonschool experience, through community service and work service in a fashion most compatible to the needs of the inner city. (p. 121)

Since educational institutions are concerned with the molding of people rather than the transformation of objects, the motivation of students and teachers presents special problems not encountered in economic organizations—at least with respect to throughput. The same generalization holds, of course, for the restorative organization, whether it be a hospital or social welfare agency. The role of the teacher or of the therapist could be heavily prescribed if one were concerned only with the technical aspects of learning. But learning and reeducation are not only determined by techniques of spacing material and of mechanical reinforcement but also by deeper motivational processes. Therefore, a wider area of discretionary power is necessary for the staff member in the maintenance type of organization. This makes possible an optimum interaction between pupil and teacher, and between patient and therapist. Teaching machines with their programmed learning and television lessons piped into the classroom are important adjuncts to the educational process, and can provide more options for the student. Their impersonality, however, has its cost. In the past many students from underprivileged economic groups have gone on to successful college and professional careers because of the special guidance and inspiration of the gifted secondary school teacher. Proposals for educational change should be designed to increase the likelihood of such relationships.

The success of the economic model of organization has led many educational and hospital systems to follow the organizational forms of elaborated role structure, mechanization and institutionalization of procedures, control devices, and centralization of power. Nevertheless, these forms have not been simulated faithfully and the gap between the paper blueprint and the empirical system is great. In many universities, for example, the amount of decentralization is much greater than in industrial firms. Departments are powers in their own right and make many of the decisions in fact that are reserved for the Board of Regents in legal form. Individual instructors have considerable autonomy in what they teach, how they teach, and what scholarly activity they engage in. The norm of academic freedom and the organizational device of tenure, although not absolute guarantees of autonomy, are relatively

TABLE 6-1   Basic Dimensions of Specialization and Aggregation Model[a]

Dimension	Specialization Model	Aggregation Model
Strategy of Change	Incremental innovation by specific programs. Piecemeal change based on demonstration programs.	Holistic reorganization reflecting concern with organizational climate and minimum standards. Based on top level managerial direction.
Organizational Goals	Priority of academic over socialization; socialization stressed but segregated.	Interdependence of academic and socialization goals.
Division of Labor	Emphasis on increased division of labor and increased used of specialists.	Emphasis on increased authority and professional competence of classroom teacher.
Investment Pattern	Capital intensive techniques; high investment on the new media	Labor intensive techniques; stress on subprofessionals and volunteers.
Organizational Format	School district central office levels with central office exercising administrative control.	Schools under sectors' administrative control, with central office planning control.
Authority Structure	Fractionalized.	Centralized policy-making and decentralization based on professional autonomy.
Curriculum Construction	External and centralized construction; independent hierarchy of curriculum specialists in school system.	Balance between external construction of materials and faculty involvement in curriculum construction; curriculum specialists as resource personnel.
Grading System	Fixed class levels, periodic grading on systemwide criteria.	Continuous development system, flexible system of grading which include both systemwide criteria and specific indicators of achievement.
School Districts	Specific and single boundaries with trend toward specialized schools.	Multiple and flexible boundaries and emphasis on adaptation of comprehensive high school.
Principal's Role	Administrative specialist.	Principal teacher.

[a] Janowitz, 1969, pp. 44–45.

continued

ABLE 6-1   Basic Dimensions of Specialization and Aggregation Model[a] (*continued*)

Dimension	Specialization Model	Aggregation Model
eacher's Role	(a) Teacher specialist; specialized skills and subject matter oriented;	(a) Teacher manager balance between subject matter skills and interpersonal and managerial competence;
	(b) Academic and vocational training.	(b) Coordinator of social space of youngster and of community resources.
lassroom Management	Reduction of class size.	Flexible educational groupings depend on program.
eaching Style	Solo practitioner.	Group practice; peer group support and use of subprofessionals and volunteers.
ubprofessionals and Volunteers	Limited involvement and narrow definition of tasks.	Strong emphasis; seen as general resource with teaching responsibilities.
sychology of Learning	Cognitive psychology.	Impact of institutional setting and normative order.
ontrol of Deviant Behavior	Emphasis on specialized personnel and specialized structure.	Maximize classroom management and teacher skills.
valuation	Pupil oriented.	Teacher and system oriented.
lew Media	Centralized control, used for regular instruction, for maximum audience manned by media personnel.	Decentralized control use for specific audiences as a supplement to regularized instruction.
ommunity Contacts	Specific, directed through principal and specialized community agent.	Diffuse and involvement of all educational staff members.
eacher Education	Specialized education in education and classroom practice teaching.	Liberal arts education plus clinic exposure to diversified experiences in community and educational practice.
service Training	Under the control of school of education and linked to degrees.	Under public school system control and linked to professional development and curriculum development.

Janowitz, 1969, pp. 44–45.

effective in giving staff members a wide range of discretion in their activities.

Changing Functions of Higher Education

The broad functions of higher education according to the analysis of Robert J. Havighurst (1967) are production, opportunity, and consumption. Before 1970 colleges and universities in the United States were mainly concerned with the production and opportunity functions. They trained people to be productive workers, skillful technicians, and needed professionals. They were also sources of upward social mobility—a good education was a means of rising in the social system. But in recent years and even more in the years ahead, education is also becoming a consumption good. With more leisure time available, people want education to be able to enjoy that leisure, to be more appreciative and expressive in the arts, and to utilize their college experience not for productive roles but for their lives as citizens and as self-actualizing individuals. The Havighurst theory helps explain the disagreements between faculty members and students during the 1960s. Most faculty members saw higher education in relation to its production function, the training of apprentices in skills that would enable them to play the usual roles in established society. Many students, however, were more interested in education as a consumption good, and self-expression and self-actualization were primary considerations. Hence they opposed old practices, which not only emphasized the greater expertise and professional knowledge of faculty members but also granted them greater political power in running the university and defining the goals of higher education.

Maintenance Systems: The Hospital

Hospitals have long been involved in the training of nurses and doctors. Because of their historical linkage with the military and the church, however, and because of their special problems of ready mobilization for emergencies and of protecting against the disastrous effects of error, hospitals resemble industrial organizations more than educational institutions. There has been elaborate and rigid role prescription for attendants and nurses, an emphasis on rules and regulations for predictable performance, and a tendency to treat patients as objects rather than as people. Nevertheless, hospitals do differ from industrial systems in several important respects, three of which are deserving of special mention.

In the first place, there is no single line of authority in many hospitals. The board of trustees, the doctors, and the administrator comprise three centers of authority, so that there is a delicate balance of power rather than a single hierarchical line of command (Georgopoulos and

Mann, 1962). In the second place, there is a professionalization of the two principal types of workers, namely, the doctors and the nurses. Professional workers in industry tend to be staff people but in the hospital they represent the major line activities. As professionals they are less subject to lay authority and are part of their own professional system as well as members of the hospital. In Parsons' terms, the break between the managerial and technical systems would occur at a very high level in the organizational structure of the hospital. The professionalization of staff means that the expressive rather than the instrumental cycle characterizes many staff members. They obtain much of their reward directly from the exercise of their professional skills, as well as indirectly through salaries and fees. Moreover, the objectives of the organization of preserving life and combatting illness are easily assimilated to the corresponding values of the individual organizational member. Professionalization also means that, in spite of the potency of involvement in the hospital, the individual is heavily involved in a profession as the larger system. In any competition between the values of the two systems, the medical profession takes priority over the hospital administration.

In the third place, hospitals, especially mental hospitals, differ from many industrial organizations in the attitudinal orientation of staff members. An overriding value for these people should be one of hope, the belief that they or their institution can help the patient. The patient also needs to have hope. If staff members do not believe in the helpfulness of what they are doing, their lack of faith is communicated directly or indirectly to the patient. Stotland and Kobler (1965) furnish dramatic documentation of this point in their case study of the life and death of a mental hospital. The hospital lasted ten years, and its demise followed the breakdown of morale among staff, a rebellion by adolescent patients, and an epidemic of suicides among patients. Central to the decline of the institution was the erosion of faith in its ability to cure patients, which in turn was caused by factionalism among professionals, feuding between professionals and administrators, and conflicts between the Board of Trustees, administrators, and professionals. The high hope with which the institution began deteriorated as the staff itself no longer believed in its mission and the patients reflected the staff's beliefs.

The contemporary hospital thus has more than its share of organizational dilemmas. It is a highly complex institution based on the mutual cooperation of a large and heterogeneous assortment of interdependent professional, semiprofessional, and nonprofessional members, subject to lines of authority that are sometimes parallel and sometimes conflicting. The military model of control and hierarchical authority has lost some of its force in our society and hospitals have had to adapt to this as well as to other social changes. Yet they are still under the constraints of the most critical of all services—the preservation of life and the improvement of health. It is no wonder, then, that studies of hospitals have multiplied and number in the hundreds in less than a ten-year span. In his review of the research literature on hospitals Georgopoulous (1975) notes that for the decade of the sixties some 68 percent of the hospital studies utilized a survey design—but only 11 percent of all studies were propositional or hypothesis testing. He also found an imbalance in the areas researched. Problems of effectiveness, resource allocation, and organizational integration accounted for some 72 percent of the studies, while adaptation to the environment, coordination, and system strain accounted for only 13 percent. The relative neglect of system strain is of particular interest, because the early landmark study of the general hospital (Georgopoulos and Mann, 1962) found intergroup tensions common and extensive. Such tensions characterized the entire interaction structure of the organization: relationships within the medical staff itself, between doctors and nurses, between doctors and administrators, and between nurses and administrators.

Nevertheless, measures of system strain were found to have only weak correlations with an index of goal attainment or patient care in general hospitals (Georgopoulos and Matejko, 1967). Of a possible 50 correlations (between ten measures of strain and five of patient care), only 8 percent showed statistical significance. On the other hand, the measure of coordination (programming and interrelating activities) was strongly linked with patient care, with 76 percent of the correlations statistically significant. This study was based on a national probability sample of 41 general hospitals and some 2,400 respondents, representing the medical, nursing and administrative staffs.

The complexity of hospital functioning is demonstrated in an extensive study of Smith and King (1975) of state mental hospitals. In a sample of 18 such hospitals involving interviews, questionnaires, and ward observations these investigators established the importance of goals that went beyond the treatment of patients. In those hospitals where the goals included research and training as well as treatment, a greater level of effectiveness was achieved than in single goal establishments, especially with respect to patient care, staff morale, and organizational flexibility. The more effective hospitals, moreover, had decentralized patterns of influence down to the nursing level. But this did not mean an abdication of leadership at the top echelons, for support from high-ranking administrators was a critical element in hospital performance. The researchers themselves conclude:

> In the last analysis, it is the patients themselves and life as it actually occurs on the ward that determines whether hospital

organization and processes of coordination and decision-making will eventually contribute to patient movement and rehabilitation. Hospital organization provides structure and direction that can partly compensate for the chronically ill patient population that these hospitals serve under conditions of very limited resources. If such processes of coordination and decision-making can encourage and make treatment efforts a reality, the patients in the wards may experience a viable rehabilitation process. In addition to such conditions, the nursing staff must effectively interact with the patients.... While our results are modest in scope they do essentially confirm the notion that through the proper utilization of both organizational and administrative processes a truly therapeutic community can be realized. (1975, p. 170)

During the past decade fairly radical reforms have been taking place in the administration of some hospitals. The creation of the therapy team and the movement toward an open hospital are indications of the rethinking of organizational structure in this field. Nevertheless, hospitals, like other maintenance organizations, have been slow to respond to changes in the larger society.

Economic organizations, because of their technological orientation and their feedback from the marketplace, are generally better equipped to deal with change than are organizations that emphasize the maintenance function. The economic enterprise has its research and development department and its program and planning staffs geared to meet immediate changes in input and the reception of output. It is difficult to find an educational institution or a hospital with similar adaptive structures.

Maintenance systems also have special problems with respect to the hierarchical separation of power, privilege, and reward, in that there is likely to be a line of cleavage between the staff and the population of subjects to be taught or treated. This line, moreover, is between the authority to make organizational decisions and the requirement to submit to them; to have a fair degree of autonomy in working out one's role and to be assigned specific directives about one's conduct; to administer sanctions and to receive punishments; to enjoy privileges and to be deprived of them. The older philosophy for molding and influencing people followed the *carrot and stick* principles. The staff, occupying the power positions, meted out rewards for correct behavior and punishments for incorrect behavior by the subordinate subject population. This was the pattern in the school, the old mental hospital, and even the church with its imposition of penances. People can be molded in this fashion under conditions in which the institution has complete control over the behavior of its inmates and is supported by the values of the overall society. An additional facilitating condition in schools is the youthfulness of the subject population, in that identification with the aggressor occurs more readily among the weak and helpless.

Today, when children and even mental patients are regarded as having rights of their own, the simple punishment-reward pattern has been altered. The expectation is that people, whether young or old, should cooperate in learning, reeducation, or therapy not on the basis of extrinsic rewards and penalties, but on the basis of intrinsic motivations of their own. Punishment and reward should be cues for the direction or redirection of behavior rather than incentive patterns. School teachers who operate conspicuously on the old principle soon find themselves in conflict with the family, the parent-teacher organizations, and the community.

The general strategy of involving the subject population in the organization implies some obscuring of the line of cleavage of power and privilege. Students will not be eager to accept and enforce rules in which they had no voice. Nor will they be highly motivated to follow prescribed courses of study that stifle their own intellectual interests. On the other hand, subject populations, whether students, patients, or church audiences, are there to be guided by those with superior skills and knowledge. Their resentment of nondirective teaching (and therapy) is considerable and, in our view, justifiable. The appropriate areas of freedom for the second grade student or for the graduate student do not lend themselves to easy definition. In fact, the emphasis on precise definition of these areas should be replaced by an emphasis on participation toward common objectives by both staff and subject populations.

Maintenance systems like the school and the church not only impart special skills and knowledge but also teach the values and norms of the society. In a sense, then, their major function is one of preserving the stability of the social structure, of tying people into the normative system. But this is true in general more than in specific terms; the stability they encourage is for the type of society they operate in rather than for particularistic rules. Thus in a democratic society like the United States the norms inculcated produce less respect for specific laws than respect for law itself as the outcome of a democratic process. Similarly, a church will emphasize the Christian way of life more than its specific theology. Such generalized norms are more often an idealized set of values than a description of existing practices in the society or a realistic prescription of what they are expected to be. Hence there is the paradox that the maintenance institutions by their emphasis on general norms furnish some dynamic for social change. By making salient the moral and rational character of a democratic way of life and of Christian ethics, the school and church provide a positive force for changing practices inconsistent with these values.

In Russian society as well, the ideology of educational systems is rationalized in more idealistic terms than many of the existing practices. Probably this condition had some effect in facilitating changes away from the repression of the Stalinist era. But are these examples too selective to make the point? What of a societal set of norms which justifies slavery, the divine right of kings, or other antisocial goals? Even here the general rule would indicate movement in the direction of a broader, more ethical basis involving the interests of more people than the specific privileged group in power. The divine right of kings went beyond the tyranny of one man; by linking the ruler with religion it also placed on him the responsibility of a demigod for the welfare of his people.

Political Systems

In any society the political system has the three functions of allocating resources and handling internal conflict through policy formulation or legislative decisions; implementing such decisions through an executive arm; and mobilizing the society for relations with other nations—whether cooperative, competitive, or conflictual. In a nondemocratic society all three functions are exercised by a single ruler or a small ruling class, whereas in a democratic society the legislative function is directly or indirectly in the hands of the people.

There would be small need for a political system if there were unanimity among people about goals and the means for reaching them. Any one person could voice the wishes of the group and receive immediate assent. The state and its subsystems exist because people are neither homogeneous nor neatly complementary with respect to their roles, their interests, their perceptions, and their values. Homogeneity of interests and goals are not enough to make for automatic solution of problems. There must also be unanimity about the specifics of problem solution.

Political scientists use the concept of *scarce resources* to call attention to the basis for political organization. Thus Easton (1961) writes:

> The reason why a political system emerges in a society at all—that is, why men engage in political activity—is that demands are being made by persons or groups in the society that cannot all be fully satisfied. In all societies one fact dominates political life: scarcity prevails with regard to most of the valued things.... Only where wants require some special organized effort on the part of society to settle them authoritatively may we say that they have become inputs of the political system. (p. 85)

Political machinery provides the means for reaching some consensus among the differing groups, and the political arena is the place where the mutual influencing process goes on before decisions are reached. Marx held that the political state was necessary only in societies with social classes, that is, conflicting interest groups. In a classless society, the state would wither away because there would be a ready consensus of shared convictions on all issues of importance. The facts are, however, that individual and group differences of opinion do not rest merely on class differences. In those countries that call themselves socialist, the political state has shown no signs of withering away but has, if anything, taken a new lease on life.

To achieve a consensus, all the means of influencing people are employed in the political arena, from the use of organized force, through debate and bargaining, to persuasion and integrative problem solutions. Within a society, organized force is restricted to the police and the military. Those out of power, unhappy as they may be with the actions of the power structure, generally refrain from violence. When such violence does take place, we speak of rebellion, riot, coup d'etat or revolution. Ordinarily, there is a consensus that legitimized decisions (those reached through following the rules of the game) are binding upon all members. This legitimizing of the rules for decision making, so that conflicts can be handled without internal strife and anarchy, is at the core of the political system. The only effective way to prevent wars between nations is through international systems that legitimize procedures for handling conflict so that all nations bind themselves to accept the verdict or outcome. To extend political systems in this fashion across national boundaries is extremely difficult because it means a genuine revision in thinking with respect to national sovereignty.

In the modern democracy the principal mechanisms for achieving decisions are accommodation and compromise. In the top decision-making body of elected representatives, differences in interest and ideas are subject to debate, persuasion, and bargaining. The final policy arrived at may not have the enthusiastic approval of the major contending forces, but each group will have achieved some measure of what it wanted or some assurance of a payment in kind on another issue. Moreover, the whole process is facilitated by the compromises already achieved within political parties. Especially in a two-party system as in the United States, each party operates to achieve compromise among the interests of its own subgroups so that not all interest conflicts are reflected to their full extent in the top national decision-making body.

The same logic of compromise extends to the selection of candidates representing a political party at the various levels within the structure. The nominee is often a compromise candidate in the sense that no individual ideally represents all of a given electorate but some one person must be selected. The higher the office, the more must the official take into account the compromise nature of the mandate from the electorate. Officials must see themselves as representing the broad electorate that put them in power rather than the narrow sector whose views coincide with their own. This is particularly true at the national level. Otherwise the official will be utilizing a system based on compromise and accommodation to push the views of a small minority. In democratic politics the electorate itself has a check upon this abuse at the very next election. A dictator, however, can take advantage of the system, as Hitler did after he was called to office by President Hindenberg. Once at the head of the state, he violated the implicit mandate of representativeness and corrupted the system so that it became solely the voice of his own Nazi party.

The value systems of political structures reflect the important functional requirements of internal compromise, representativeness, and in-group patriotism. On the one hand, the national government has the ideology of representing all the people, doing something for everybody. Modern political parties seek to be national parties in terms of nationwide appeal to many sectors of the population. Within the system compromise is the order of the day, and politics is recognized as "the art of the possible." On the other hand, the ideology of the political system has a radically different set of values regarding those outside the system. The ideas and interests of outsiders are not to be accommodated within the system. Instead, all system members tend to unite in their loyalty to their own group and to reject the intruder and the foreigner—whether from another party, another state, or another country. The realistic give-and-take conception of internal functioning is in marked contrast to the absolutistic, militant conception of external relations. This dual set of beliefs about the political system can make for confusion and outrage when one political group turns the nationalist values regarding people outside the nation against subunits within the nation.

Easton's Analysis of Levels of Support For The Political System

Support for the national political system is not of one piece, as Easton (1965) has emphasized in calling attention to three levels of system cohesion. In the first place he postulates a sense of political community at the interpersonal level in that people must be able to trust one another and cooperate with one another to achieve some common objective. In the second place there is some degree of regime support or allegiance to the particular authorities in power. In the third place there is support of a more generalized type, expressed in terms of commitment to basic constitutional or governmental forms.

Easton further maintains that diffuse support for political institutions can hold the system together when various groups have been alienated because they feel they have been short-changed on specific privileges and benefits. One of the few studies of the levels of support for the national political system has suggested the usefulness of the Easton approach as well as complexities that go beyond his model. In a national survey people were interviewed about their evaluation of various aspects of the national system as well as about their own experiences with political bureaucracy (Katz, Gutek, Kahn, and Barton, 1975). More dimensions of support were found than the three-level model Easton proposed, in that factor analysis revealed some seven factors of attitudinal approval or disapproval of the national system. In addition to the sense of political community there was evidence that people discriminated among beliefs reflecting general confidence in public bureaucracy, the helpfulness of government workers, evaluation of their own experience with government offices, negative stereotypes about public office, confidence in national political leadership, and symbolic nationalism.

The Easton hypothesis that diffuse support for the national structure works to keep people attached to the established order in spite of the erosion of specific support for particular groups was not confirmed. Instead favorable responses to the helpfulness of particular government services counteracted a negative reaction at the more general or diffuse level. Many people who believe public bureaucracy in general is poorly run still feel their own problems have been well taken care of. What seems to be a more general principle than that suggested by Easton is that various groups are tied into the system in different ways or at different levels. For example, lower income groups were more nationalistic than higher income groups, whereas the more affluent expressed more confidence in political leadership in Washington.

To the extent that organizations are political in character, they show in more intense forms many of the attributes of all organizations. The in-group–out-group dichotomy, for example, becomes sharper in political structures. In other sectors a person may belong to a variety of groups; but when the organization is basically political, the individual can belong to only one such group, and the members of other political organizations are enemies. One cannot belong to both the Republican and Democratic parties. The in-group–out-group dichotomy thus accentuates organizational membership and endows organizational loyalty with an all-or-nothing quality. If people accept membership, they cannot reserve to themselves any decisions or discretion once policy has been decided. A member cannot choose to "sit this one out." Each faces the questions: "Are you with us?" and "Which side are you on?" The resulting affective identification with the political organization means that relations with members of opposition groups are often accompanied by heated argument and emotional outbursts.

Actions of an antisocial nature are sanctioned toward members of the outgroup; aggression is countenanced and even encouraged. Unless checked by the larger social structure, such actions will assume the form of physical violence. The labor union members may have highly moral and cooperative attitudes toward other human beings, but scabs or strikebreakers do not fall into this category, and almost any harsh treatment of them is justified. The burglary of the Democratic Party office at Watergate, which began the demise of the Nixon administration, is a further example of this dichotomous political morality.

Moreover, the tendency in a political struggle group is to regard all outsiders as members of the opposition. The outgroup is expanded to include not only the formal opposition but all outsiders as well. The neutral category is often dismissed with the view that if you are not for us, you are against us.

The political organization, which exists primarily to influence and control outside groups, is sometimes assumed to be the pure type of all complex organizational forms. Some students of history maintain that the origin of complex authority structures is to be found in the struggle of one group to maintain its interests against those of another. They assert that much of modern political structure was developed and elaborated as the military forces of one or another tribe mobilized for purposes of conquest and confiscation. Oppenheimer (1914) and other social theorists hold that the political state itself arose in this fashion and that even today the organizational forms of national states show the character of their struggle origins. In any case, the presence of an authority structure to coordinate all activities of the system, the all-or-nothing involvement of members, and the treatment of outsiders as adversaries rather than competitors are seen most clearly in political groupings.

The major political system, the national state, though built on the segmental involvement of its citizens, has priority in its demands on them. Most citizens of a modern nation have only peripheral contact with their government during the greater part of their lives. They pay taxes, obey the laws, vote, and on occasion show ritualistic respect for national symbols. The nation state as a functioning system is remote from the pattern of their daily activities.

Nevertheless, there is great potency of involvement in the nation state because it is the one system the individual cannot withdraw from without becoming an outcast, an exile, or a prison inmate. Its legal requests take priority over membership in any other system—religious, economic, or familial. Not only is this priority established through the early socialization process, it is maintained by the nature of the organization of the state as the one system that embraces all other organizations in the society. The state is both the authority structure and the supersystem of the society. All other organizations must work within its rules. In times of emergency it can even take over its subsystems in direct fashion, incorporating the militia into the armed forces, nationalizing key industries, and the like. The nation state represents the means for maintaining the basic way of life for its citizens. Although individuals belong to many organizations, they all have common membership in the nation state. If it were to be destroyed or overthrown, its people would face a different way of life. We are speaking here, of course, of the established nation state. In newly emerging nations there is often no universal maintenance structure such as the school to inculcate nationalistic ideology and allegiance to national symbols, no political institutions to cut across or integrate tribal organization; in short, potency and priority of involvement have not as yet been achieved.

Political Parties

Political parties are often subsystems of the state, and party membership has some of the same segmental character. There is, however, less commitment to the subsystem than the state, and the boundaries are more permeable. Admission into the party is of course easier than admission to citizenship, and departure from it is not uncommon.

Nevertheless, the majority of the people in the United States, which has a very loose party system, remain in the same party throughout their lives. The segmental involvement in the political party belies the strength of allegiance to it. Although not politically active, many people find it difficult to desert their traditional political allegiance in spite of an occasional splitting of ballots. Political activists are bound into the organization at the local and national level in interdependent ways so that even when the party organization is in the hands of their opponents, they tend to stay with it.

Older studies (Campbell et al., 1960) found that two-thirds of American voters who could remember their first vote for president still identified with that party. More recent research shows that although the number of independents (those not identifying with either major party) has increased, few people shift their allegiance from one party to the other. Moreover, party identification remains an important predictor of voting behavior (Converse, 1975; Converse, 1976). The American findings on party identification have been replicated in a number of European countries (Borre and Katz, 1973), and Converse has demonstrated for five nations a positive relationship between average intensity of party identification and age of uninterrupted democracy in the political system (1969).

Perhaps because the political system represents the key decision-making structure of the society, it is generally provided with built-in defenses to preserve its characteristic form—as a constitutional monarchy, an oligarchy, or a democracy. In an authoritarian political society, the state controls not only the military force, but also the political parties or party, the school system, and even the economic structures. Even in a democracy, which legitimizes change, there is a series of checks and balances to prevent rapid change. In the United States the compromise dynamic within political parties and within the national government is aided by the institutional provisions of (1) distribution of powers between federal and local government and (2) separation among the legislative, executive, and judicial branches of government. Part of the pattern of restraints is the legal process whereby law making, administration, and adjudication are public events open to public inspection. In addition, administrative officials must justify their actions by reference to the appropriate enabling legal statutes. To make legislative control of executive agencies even more stringent, some units of government must allocate every expenditure to a specific and appropriate line in the officially authorized budget. Public accountability is thus carried to such a logical extreme that it can become self-defeating in a misplaced emphasis on detail.

Penal Institutions

The negative aspect of the political system is the penal institution for punishing and confining lawbreakers. Goffman (1961) has used the concept of total institution to refer not only to prisons but to mental hospitals, to military organizations, and to monasteries. He writes:

> Their encompassing or total character is symbolized by the barrier to social intercourse with the outside that is often built right into the physical plant.... In total institutions there is a basic split between a large managed group, conveniently called inmates, and a small supervisory staff.... Social mobility between the two strata is grossly restricted; social distance is typically great and often formally prescribed. (pp. 4–7)

Goffman's emphasis is thus on the control exercised by the staff over inmates, and his total institutions are organizations in which there is massive control over all aspects of the inmates' lives by the supervising staff. We shall consider penal institutions, including concentration camps and prisoner-of-war camps, as being the most representative of this control dimension of total institutions. Although the training of the nun or the monk in the monastery does involve complete control over the novices, they enter of their own accord, can leave of their own accord, and after their indoctrination, can move up in the structure. The mental hospital, it is true, was once more of a custodial and penal institution than a rehabilitation center, and some of this older character still persists. Nonetheless, the modern hospital has moved toward openness, with more contact with the outside world and fewer barriers between staff and inmates.

The penal institution often shows some deviation from the official objective of total control over inmates. A system develops in which an informal leadership pattern among the prisoners is tacitly encouraged by prison officials, so long as it is not directed against them. Transactions occur between leaders and wardens which are of course not officially recognized. Sykes (1958) has used the concept of *inmate cohesion* to refer to the pattern of cooperative getting along which helps to maintain the equilibrium of the prison society. The violent, aggressive, unstable elements are held in check by the informal leaders. The pattern of getting along does not, of course, mean informing on fellow prisoners or accepting the custodial point of view. One factor in prison riots is the undermining of this inmate cohesion by efforts of the custodial force to enforce rules strictly and to crack down on all violations.

Penal systems are organizational devices for handling deviants from the legal order, and their objectives have been traditionally threefold: (1) to protect society by removing the dangerous offender, (2) to deter potential deviants, and (3) to reform the offender through punishment or more enlightened means of treatment. Partly because the objectives of protection and deterrence have not been adequately realized through punishment and imprisonment, and partly because of a changed cultural ideology, the penal institution is seen increasingly as a rehabilitation agency.

The penal institution is thus supposed to perform two essentially incompatible functions. As part of the political system, it should protect society by isolating deviants who have a nuisance value or who constitute a threat. As a maintenance subsystem, it should retrain such deviants. The two functions of incarceration and rehabilitation have incompatible elements. An efficient custodial organization would place emphasis on high walls, electrically charged barriers, and machine guns. Given scarcity of resources, it would place lower priorities on the health and welfare of its inmates, so that minimal diets and health standards would be the order of the day. In the most extreme case, the inmates are regarded as expendable, save that the population has to be maintained at some critical point to insure continued appropriations and maintain the institution. The prisoner-of-war camp is the pure case of this sort of custodial institution. The camp fails precisely to the degree that prisoners escape, and succeeds to the degree that escape is prevented at low cost. Other considerations are less relevant or completely immaterial.

Rehabilitation, on the other hand, is the most difficult of educational tasks. It has to do not only with inculcating knowledge and skills but also with change in character habits. To bring about such change requires a different relationship between staff and inmates than is called for by the custodial function (Zald, 1960). Staff members no longer serve as guards but must interact with prisoners in a personal fashion in which their authority is not the dominant factor determining the relationship. Within our prisons, little is attempted in the way of rehabilitation save for occupational training. And partly as a result, recidivism is the modal pattern; older prisoners compromise a population with records of many previous incarcerations.

It is encouraging to find some positive results in shifting from a custodial to a treatment setting in dealing with young offenders. The traditional custodial pattern produces, or at least reinforces, values of solidary opposition to the official system and staff, as a review of some 35 studies of correctional institutions indicates (Sykes and Messinger, 1960). But David Street (1970) compared inmates of two custodial institutions with two treatment institutions and found significant differences between the two types consistent with their policies and practices. In the treatment institutions with less emphasis on negative sanctions and more positive behavior of staff toward inmates, the juvenile offenders scored higher in their attitudes toward the institutions and themselves, and lower in "prisonized" attitudes about the best way to get along and to receive a parole or discharge.

The conflict between incarceration and rehabilitation can perhaps be reconciled if a longer temporal frame of reference is accepted by prison authorities, legislators, and the public. The costs of rehabilitation are much heavier in the short run, in requiring more and better trained personnel for prisons; over time, however, they could be assessed against the heavy costs of recidivism. The same long-run time perspective needs to be used with respect to the few inmates who escape the institution concerned with rehabilitation. The tendency is to give undue weight to the exceptional case. In time, rehabilitation may prove more effective in protecting society, and so meet the objective which has so long been used to justify incarceration.

Adaptive Systems
Adaptive systems are of two types: the research and development adjuncts of the government and of business enterprises; and the independent research agencies and universities. In general, the first type concentrates more on operational research, the second more on basic research. This is a matter of relative emphasis and not a qualitative distinction. Universities have many contracts with government and business for operational research, and some business organizations conduct basic research in the physical sciences.

Operational research can be systematically organized. Organizations carrying on this applied type of research, however, function better with less separation in the hierarchical dimension of power and privilege than economic or productive systems. Freedom is the factor that has most regularly been discovered to predict research productivity (Meltzer, 1956; Pelz and Andrews, 1966). The break in the line of command between the technical and managerial levels should come high in the structure. The researchers should be making the decisions about research, and management should allow them to translate the operational problems to be solved into researchable terms on the basis of their technical skill and experience.

It is, of course, necessary to maintain some linkage between research activities and other organizational subsystems of the society, but this can be done at least as well by introducing some research people into larger decision-making functions as by permitting managers without research background to enter authoritatively into research activities.

Basic research requires even more freedom than operational research. It is difficult to institutionalize basic research since it deals with yet undiscovered areas of knowledge. An organizational framework, with its role prescriptions and control devices, is based on existing knowledge. One can program the production of an automobile, since all parts of the productive process and their contribution are well known, but scientific discoveries in the very nature of the case cannot be programmed. This fundamental fact about the nature of the throughput in scientific organizations is often recognized but not as often acted upon because we fall back on the familiar in making organizational decisions.

In research groups we are dealing with an easy maintenance problem for the larger profession of scientists, but with a difficult problem for specific organizations. Research scientists get significant rewards from their scientific activity, so that an expressive as well as an instrumental cycle is at work. Moreover, the involvement of research scientists in their profession is heavy. But their gratifications come less from being members of a particular university or governmental agency and more from their activities as scientists. Hence research scientists are fairly mobile people and can be hired from one organization to another by promises of a better laboratory, better equipment, more graduate assistants, and the like.

Colleges and universities were large-scale teaching organizations before they became large-scale research enterprises. Again we have the problem of the single organization, the institution of higher learning, attempting both a socializing or teaching function and an adaptive or research function. The organizational forms of higher education were built on teaching rather than on research. College professors received their title and tenure because of teaching. In the major institutions they were also supposed to give some marginal time outside of classes to scholarly research. The basic academic budget for a department within a university traditionally has carried little if any funds for research. Hence, to conduct research, the professor had to obtain funds outside the regular budget of the university. The flow of federal funds to support research has become so great that universities are changing their rules to give more status to the research operation. Some schools are even planning to extend academic tenure to their top research personnel.

The inclusion of research in the university structure has made it a more open system and has increased its relations with the larger society. The ivory tower of scholastic learning is remote from the large-scale modern university with its bustling campus, its many research institutes, its conferences for industrial, institutional, and governmental personnel, its ties to professional organizations, and its support from foundations, business, and government. Its many staff members are engaged in a diversity of activities other than teaching, such as serving on the President's Council of Economic Advisers, launching action research on population problems in India, carrying on operational research for industry, conducting research on government programs for energy conservation and pollution control, cooperating with clinical agencies on problems of training, and placing graduate students in professional jobs in universities, business, and government. To carry on such activities requires freedom of movement, since staff members must spend time away from the campus and take frequent leaves of absence. Thus they serve as members of subsystems other than those of their own university.

The description of teaching and research as separate functions is an oversimplification. Some of the best training and teaching occurs in the research laboratory. And the college that neglects research soon becomes a dead place even for teaching. Its teachers merely regurgitate the ideas of those whose research is now outmoded. The creative spark of discovery and of scholarship is lost. On the practical side the problems that arise in integrating teaching and research are twofold. Teaching can be geared to mass learning. Research cannot if it is to become a good training vehicle. For purposes of mass education, there is an economy in inculcating fundamentals before students become apprentices in research. Whether this is a false economy is a debatable issue. The other practical obstacle to combining research and teaching is the typical organizational form of the college or university, which at present is not geared to integration of these two functions. In concentrates on general education and on professional training, and research experience is not regarded as basic to either one. Moreover, to integrate research experience with these other activities would require a great increase in the freedom allowed both to the teacher and the student.

Apart from the constraints of the educational institution, research in university settings is often handicapped by the organizational requirements of the larger system. In a state university where public accountability of public funds has resulted in an item line budget, the research project must divert time and energy to meeting requirements not appropriate to its activity. An outstanding example of misplaced governmental control is the federal law requiring a budget office review and approval of any questionnaire, interview, or research instrument, whether the research is basic or applied, and whether it is conducted by a governmental agency or a university receiving a governmental contract.

It seems to us that two great problems of articulation between adaptive organizations and other subsystems of society are to some extent inherent in the adaptive function. The adaptive subsystem is by definition a source of change inputs to the larger society, but society must be selective in its acceptance of those proposals for change and in the rate at which accepted proposals are implemented. The adaptive organization that generates some new bit of knowledge or technology cannot be the ultimate judge of its side effects, ramifications, and social acceptability. To implement fully and rapidly each new research finding would create a state of bankruptcy and anarchy. Research workers become accustomed early to the failure of hoped-for discoveries; to some extent they must become accustomed to the failure of discoveries to be utilized. Human survival requires increasingly that we shall not do all the things of which we are capable.

The complementary problem of articulation between adaptive organizations and the rest of society involves the kinds of knowledge sought. Research has its own dynamics; the process of discovery and theory-construction to some extent sets its own problems. Adaptive organizations tend, therefore, to answer questions that other subsystems may not have asked, and to be often unable or unwilling to answer questions that are urgent in other subsystems. Even when research organizations attempt to be responsive, the answer to some social or medical problem may lie at the end of a long sequence of studies that are themselves significant only within the terms of the disciplines that guide them. The problem of setting research goals and the problem of utilizing research results are thus aspects of the larger issue of articulation of the adaptive subsystem with other societal subsystems. The first problem is felt most keenly in the world of practice: why don't researchers solve *our* problems? The second question is more often put by the research workers: why have our knowledge and discoveries not been used?

The larger society influences the goals of research in many ways—by the enunciation of national goals and other system-permeating aims, by the inclusion of adaptive suborganizations in productive structures, and by the control of resources. Scientists want freedom and funds (Meltzer and Salter, 1962); the larger society more often grants either than both.

The influence of research on the larger society has in recent years become the subject of intensive study (Havelock, 1972; Rogers and Shoemaker, 1971). The process of research utilization is extremely variable in different nations and in different substantive domains. In the already industrialized nations, the general pattern has been for relatively rapid and uncritical adoption of technical innovations, and relatively slow response to social and behavioral findings. The optimal articulation of the adaptive function is a crucial issue for a technological society.

Art and Leisure Time Pursuits

There is an area of life, outside these major organizational structures, where individuals follow their own bent and express themselves through hobbies, sports, art, the enjoyment of the art of others, or the vicarious experiences of watching others perform, on the stage or in the sports arena. This is the world of leisure time activities.

Even here, however, we have organized structures to meet these individual needs for recreation, for vicarious living, or for enriching experiences. Organized sports operate as a large-scale business, as do cinema and television. Other areas are not as well organized.

But the world of art by definition does not follow the same rigid codes as other areas. Since this is the world of make believe, of *as if*, there is much more freedom for movement and for the expression of ideas. Moreover, in this less conventional, coded aspect of life not all of the restrictions apply in the same measure as in political and economic affairs. Members of minority groups barred from any but the lowest positions in other structures traditionally were able to rise in this field.

And the ideas generated in the world of art can either buttress and rationalize the status quo, as they have been required to do in the more controlled and totalitarian societies, or they can be critical of the existing society, innovative, and a source of change and adaptation. More significant organizational changes are anticipated by creative artists who help to furnish the rationale for their later acceptance.

The Dominance of the Supra-Political System

We need to take account of an important dynamic in organizational societies: the penetration of subsystems by the suprasystem. With more and more specialization and growth, interdependence among subsystems and the need for coordination at higher levels in the system has also increased. Moreover, technical advances in communication and transportation increase the extent and frequency of individual contacts and make uniform rules imperative to avoid physical and psychological collisions. Then too, the problems that affect individuals have grown beyond the scope of their own control or of local controls. Environmental pollution and energy shortage cannot be handled at the local level. Public controls at a national level are necessary not only to guard against environmental dangers, to protect people from hazards of contaminated foods, deadly drugs, and disease, but also to regulate the monopolistic tendencies of industry and to protect people against the invasion of their individual rights.

The political suprasystem, which develops in complex industrial societies, can be viewed in two lights. It can be seen as a monstrous complex of computers and bureaucrats controlling more and more of the lives of the people and burdening them with heavier and heavier taxation. Or it can be viewed as a set of controls over the exploitative practices of aggressors so that people have guarantees of equality of opportunity, of due process of law, and of their rights as citizens. Both images have some factual basis, with the mix varying for different countries and political regimes.

The picture of the federal government of the United States as a bureaucratic monster is not a figment of populistic imagination. In the 50 years from 1923 to 1973 the mortality rate of government organizations studied by Kaufman (1976) of the Brookings Institution was only 15 percent, while the birth rate was many times that percentage (see pages 81–82). Moreover, the growth rate was not affected by whether a Republican or Democratic administration was in power. In 1976 the Democratic and Republican presidential candidates vied with one another in denouncing the Washington establishment; localism or control at the community level became the stereotyped form of the new populism. The problem, however, is that people are mobile and localities are interdependent. Even social services encounter difficulties when handled at the local level. Part of the financial plight of New York City is that it attempted a local solution of the broader issue of helping the indigent and deprived. New York City's public colleges offered free admission; its standards of economic assistance to the poor were high, and so were its taxes. Corporations and their more prosperous employees left for the suburbs or more distant parts, but the inmigration of the poor continued. In the resulting financial crisis, only the intercession of the state and federal government averted bankruptcy.

The social recognition of the second picture—the federal government as protector—appears in many ways. One is the demand of the individual for citizen's or public rights even though employed by a private organization. Business enterprises must not only preserve certain minimal health conditions in their plants, they must also pay minimum wages to employees, limit the hours of work for the individual, and must not discriminate in the recruitment or promotion of people on the basis of race, religion, or sex. Other organizations, such as hospitals and universities, must follow the same standards. What were once private organizations are now quasi-public in character. They are answerable in courts of law and to federal regulatory commissions. Moreover, they are involved in attempts to influence legislation in direct and indirect ways. The liaison of nongovernmental organizations with government may be interpreted as the private sector taking over the public sector, but the critical fact is the increasing penetration of the suprasystem into the various subsystems of society.

We are not assuming that a society represents a perfect integration or even a balance of organizations performing different functions. Not all the groupings within a society represent subsystems making a functional contribution to its maintenance and survival. Nor are we assuming a single societal goal, such as the democratic ideal of the greatest good for the greatest number or the oligarchical enhancement of the military industrial complex. We are assuming a plurality of subsystems, some supportive of one another, some antagonistic, and some with very little relationship to one another. We are assuming some minimal consensus on societal values and legitimate authority, so that elementary rules of the game are observed, from driving on the right side of the road to utilizing the courts to redress wrongs. In addition we believe that this acceptance of legitimacy to some extent replaces the common collective conscience which Durkheim (1947) felt was undermined by the division of labor. Equity with its empirical referents replaces a morality from above, and the political state becomes the recognized arbiter of conflicts.

Finally, we believe there is some functional interdependence among many (although not all) of the organizations in society, and a dependence of those organizations on the political suprasystem. To be independent of the society in which it exists, an organization would need dominant control of its market or clientele and of the supply of labor and raw materials; in addition, it would require political hegemony. Obviously these conditions are not met in a technological society, and it is meaningful to speak only of the relative independence and dependence of a given organization in certain areas of operation. The major way single organizations secure some degree of control over their own fate is to form alliances, compromise conflicts, and acquire satellite organizations.

THE ARGUMENT OF COUNTERPRODUCTIVITY

We have discussed organizational typology from a functional point of view—the kind of work done within a subsystem and its legitimation by the norms and needs of the larger system. But is it possible that this is an ideal model and that in the real world the very opposite state of affairs exists? Illich (1976) has advanced the counterproductive argument with some documentation, namely, that organizations not only fail to carry out their expected functions but that they make worse the problems they are supposed to solve. Thus he contends that schools foster generalized incompetence, organized medicine threatens public health, and reformatories and prisons breed crime. "Specific or paradoxical counterproductivity," Illich writes, "is a negative social indicator for a diseconomy which remains locked within the system that produces it.... Specific counterproductivity is an unwanted side effect of increasing institutional outputs that remains internal to the system which itself originated the specific value" (p. 8). Such negative effects are the result of overproduction which paralyzes autonomous action.

The Illich thesis of counterproductivity, in spite of the interesting evidence he presents, is far from proved but it does suggest that many of the beliefs we accept about organizational functions are really researchable questions rather than established truths. We are surprised to encounter functional illiteracy in high school graduates, shocked at the recidivism rate of the penal institution and startled by the degree of health required to survive hospital treatment. But this may be less because these are great exceptions to the rule and more because we lack objective feedback about organizational outcomes.

■ SUMMARY ■

Some of the inherent difficulties of organizational typologies are discussed, including the often-overemphasized uniqueness of individual organizations, and the inability of pure types to account fully for the variability encountered among organizations. Further difficulties include the absence of logical limits to the process of creating categories, and the fact that some organizational properties are readily conceptualized as continuous variables, others as dichotomies, and still others in neither set of terms.

A typology of organizations is proposed, based on genotypic (first-order) factors and second-order factors. The genotypic function is the function an organization performs as a subsystem of the larger society. Four such functions are defined, with four types of organizations identified on this basis:

Productive or economic organizations—These organizations are concerned with providing goods and services, and include mining, farming, manufacturing, transportation, and communication.

Maintenance organizations—These organizations are concerned with the socialization and training of people for roles in other organizations and in the society at large. Schools and churches are the main examples of maintenance organizations.

Adaptive organizations—These are organizations intended to create new knowledge, innovative solutions to problems, and the like. The research laboratory is the prototype of such organizations, and universities (as research organizations rather than teaching organizations) would also belong in this category.

Managerial-political organizations—These organizations have to do with the coordination and control of people and resources, and with adjudicating among competing groups. The national state and the agencies of government at lesser levels are examples of this category, although pressure groups, labor unions, and other special-interest organizations would also be classified as managerial-political.

Organizations, although of one type in genotypic function from a societal point of view, are also microcosms of the larger structure in possessing ancillary subsystems of the larger society. Thus an economic organization centers about turning out products or rendering services but still has its own mechanisms for maintenance, management, and adaptation.

Second-order characteristics can reflect aspects of structure, the nature of environmental transactions, internal transactions, and limitless other organizational properties. A discussion of several second-order characteristics is offered in the following terms:

Nature of organizational throughput—a distinction between objects and people as the end products of organizational functioning. A further distinction can be made between people-processing and people-changing institutions, as between an unemployment insurance office and a mental hospital. Each has its own logic and the traditional model of bureaucracy applies least well for people-changing organizations.

Nature of maintenance processes—a distinction between expressive (intrinsic) rewards and instrumental (extraneous) rewards as ways of attracting and holding members in organizations.

Maintenance systems such as the school are discussed with reference to the congruence model of Getzels and the aggregation model of Janowitz. Political systems are described with attention to Easton's analysis of levels of support and the dominance of the suprapolitical system. Finally, the argument of counterproductivity is considered—namely, the claim that organizations operate to defeat their genotypic function.

7

■ THE TAKING OF ■
■ ORGANIZATIONAL ROLES ■

OUTLINE

The Organization as a System of Roles
    Definition of Role Behavior
    The Process of Role-Sending
    The Received Role
    The Role Episode
    The Context of Role-Taking
    Multiple Roles and Multiple Activities

Research on Role-Taking
    Role Expectations
    The Relationship Between Role Expectations and Response
        Role expectations and role-sending
        Sending and receiving
        Expectations and performance
        Role conflict
        Role ambiguity
    The Feedback Effect of Role Behavior on Expectations
    Organizational Factors as Determinants of Role Expectations
    Personality Factors as Determinants of Role Expectations
    Properties of the Focal Person as Mediators
    Personality as Affected by Role Behavior
    The Significance of Interpersonal Relations in Role-Taking
    Role Socialization and Role-Making

Summary

What scientists seek reflects their frame of reference, and each discipline teaches its own. To the outsider the divisions and subdivisions of other fields are likely to appear minor and the differences among them trivial. To the dweller within each specialized area, however, the boundaries are important and the differences may be irreconcilable. Certainly psychologists and sociologists have strung a good deal of intellectual barbed wire along the boundary between their disciplines, with each group implying that there is something slightly suspect if not superfluous about the level of explanation the other has chosen for its own. On top of this ideological fence sit the social psychologists, striving to look as comfortable as the metaphor will allow. All too often they ease their pain by avoiding the synthesis of sociological and psychological levels of discourse that should be the hallmark of their hyphenated trade.

To the extent that choice of concepts can contribute to so complex a synthesis, the concept of role is singularly promising. It is the summation of the requirements with which the system confronts the individual member; it is the example most frequently given when one asks for a concept uniquely social-psychological and, for a concept in the vocabulary of a young science, it has a long history. Park wrote, as early as 1926, that "everyone is always and everywhere, more or less consciously, playing a role... It is in these roles that we know each other; it is in these roles that we know ourselves" (p. 37). Mead (1934) used role to explain the origins of social behavior and Moreno (1934), as a concept in psychotherapy. Linton (1936) gave it a central place in anthropology; Newcomb made it the key concept in his theoretical approach to social psychology (Newcomb, 1951; Newcomb, Turner, and Converse, 1965). Parsons (1951) and Merton (1957) consider it essential to understanding social action and social structure. It has been argued (Nieman and Hughes, 1951) that the literature of role is more distinguished for conceptual promise than research fulfillment. Subsequent reviews, however, in both sociology and psychology show a large and still-growing body of empirical work.[1]

We have given the role concept a central place in our theory of organizations. We have defined human organizations as role systems (Chapter 3), and the effectiveness of such systems will be discussed (Chapters 8 and 12) in terms of the allocation of tasks to roles and in terms of the motivation to fulfill the requirements of those roles. It remains for this chapter to link the organizational and individual levels by making explicit the social-psychological processes by which organizational roles are defined and role behavior is evoked in the ongo-

---

[1]See for example, Rocheblave-Spenle, 1962; Turner, 1956; Biddle and Thomas, 1966; Van Maanen, 1976; Graen, 1976; Sarbin and Allen, 1968.

ing organization. More specifically, we will review briefly the implications of viewing the organization as a system of roles. We will consider role-sending as a continuing cyclical process by means of which each person is socialized into a particular organizational role, informed about the acceptability of his or her behavior in relation to the requirements of that role, and corrected as necessary. We will examine some of the properties of the organization that determine the nature of specific roles. Finally, we will consider the extent to which the process of role-taking is modified by enduring properties of personality and interpersonal relations.

THE ORGANIZATION AS A SYSTEM OF ROLES[2]

In defining human organizations as open systems of roles, we emphasized two cardinal facts: the *contrived nature* of human organizations, and the unique properties of a *structure consisting of acts or events* rather than unchanging physical components (Chapter 3). There are, of course, many ramifications of these facts. It follows, for example, that human organizations attain constancy and stability in terms of the patterned recurrence of such acts rather than in terms of the persons who perform them.

Indeed, one of the chief strengths of formal organization is its constancy under conditions of persistent turnover of personnel. It follows also that, since the units of organization are not linked physically, they must be linked psychologically. Because the organization consists of the patterned and motivated acts of human beings, it will continue to exist only so long as the attitudes, beliefs, perceptions, habits, and expectations of human beings evoke the required motivation and behavior. In short, each behavioral element in the pattern is to a large extent caused and secured by the others. These facts in turn imply that human organizations are characterized by a paradoxical combination of durability and fragility. They remain intact only so long as the psychological cement holds, and yet their intactness and longevity is independent of the life-span of any and all organizational members. There is a variability and flexibility to these social contrivances that free them from the biological cycle of birth, growth, and death.

The emphasis on interdependent acts as the substance of organization is reminiscent of symbiotic relationships, as we observed earlier (Chapter 3). Formal organizations, however, involve no symbiosis in

---

[2]The exposition of role and related concepts draws heavily on Chapter 2 of *Organizational Stress*, Kahn et al., Wiley, 1964, and on Role Stress: A Framework for Analysis, Kahn and Quinn, in *Mental Health and Work Organizations*, A. McLean (ed.), Rand-McNally, 1970.

the strict sense of that term; it is not instinct and immediate biological gratification that motivates role behavior in organizations. Rather, it is a process of learning the expectations of others, accepting them, and fulfilling them—primarily for the extrinsic rewards of membership, although many other motives enter into the taking of organizational roles. There is intrinsic satisfaction in the skillful and successful meshing of our own efforts with those of others, in meeting their expectations as they meet ours, especially if the process affords the expression of valued abilities or the acquisition of new ones.

When we observe an organization in motion, its systemic nature is immediately visible, especially if we think in terms of the organizational throughput. That characteristic transformation of material or energy, and the associated functions required to sustain it, informs the pattern of human acts that we observe. And we have only to look beyond the buildings and grounds, and the individuals present, to see that what literally is organized are acts—the behaviors of people acting on materials, acting on machines, but above all interacting with each other.

Such behaviors are neither disembodied nor anonymous; they are enacted by individuals. Moreover, in any organization we can locate each individual in the total set of ongoing relationships and behaviors comprised by the organization. The key concept for doing this is *office,* by which is meant a particular point in organizational space; space in turn is defined in terms of a structure of interrelated offices and the pattern of activities associated with them. Office is essentially a relational concept, defining each position in terms of its relationship to others and to the system as a whole. Associated with each office is a set of *activities* or expected behaviors. These activities constitute the *role to be performed*, at least approximately, by any person who occupies that office.

Each office in an organization is directly related to certain others, less directly to still others, and only remotely related to some offices in the organization. The closeness of such relationships is defined by the work flow and technology of the organization, and by the lines of authority (managerial subsystem).

Consider the office of press foreman in a factory manufacturing external trim parts for automobiles. The offices most directly related to that of the press foreman might include the general foreman of the trim department and the superintendent of sheet-metal operations. From these offices emanate the work assignments to the office of press foreman, and to these offices the foreman turns for approval of work done. Also directly related to the office of press foreman might be that of the stock foreman, whose section provides sheet-metal blanks for the presses, the inspector who must pass or reject the completed stampings, the shipping foreman whose section receives and packages the stampings, and, let us say, 14 press operators whose work the press foreman directs. Imagine the organization spread out like a vast fish net, in which each knot represents an office and each string a functional relationship between offices. If we pick up the net by seizing any office, the offices to which it is directly attached are immediately seen. Thus the office of press foreman is directly attached to 19 others—general foreman, superintendent, stock foreman, inspector, shipping foreman, and 14 press operators. These nineteen offices make up the *role-set* (Merton, 1957) for the office of press foreman.

Similarly, each member of an organization is directly associated with a relatively small number of others, usually the occupants of offices adjacent in the work-flow structure or in the hierarchy of authority. They constitute the member's role-set and typically include the immediate supervisor (and perhaps the supervisor's immediate supervisor), the subordinates, and certain members of the same or other departments with whom the member must work closely. These offices are defined into the member's role set by virtue of the work-flow, technology, and authority structure of the organization.

Definition of Role Behavior

Generically, role behavior refers to the recurring actions of an individual, appropriately interrelated with the repetitive activities of others so as to yield a predictable outcome. The set of interdependent behaviors comprise a social system or subsystem, a stable collective pattern in which people play their parts.

When we abstract some of the essential persisting features from the specific acts comprising role behavior we speak of roles. For example, we can speak of the role of the quarterback on a football team in general terms of play selection without specifying the particular signals he barks to his teammates or the specific plays with which they respond. This general description applies to roles both within and outside formal organizations. The various members of the family interact in consistent ways in their roles as father, mother, son, daughter, husband, and wife. In formal organizations many of the functionally specific behaviors comprising the system are specified in written and coded presentations. Moreover, in formal organizations the roles people play are more a function of the social setting than of their own personality characteristics. The basic criterion, then, for studying role behavior is to identify the relevant social system or subsystem and locate the recurring events that fit together in converting some input into an output. This can be done by ascertaining the role expectations of a given set of related offices, since such expectations are main elements in maintaining the role system and inducing the required role behavior.

The Process of Role-Sending

All members of a person's role-set depend on that person's performance in some fashion; they are rewarded by it, judged in terms of it, or require it to perform their own tasks. Because they have a stake in that person's performance, they develop beliefs and attitudes about what he or she should and should not do as part of the role. Such prescriptions and proscriptions held by members of a role-set are designated *role expectations*; in the aggregate they define the role, the behaviors expected of the person who holds it. The role expectations held for a certain person by a member of his or her role-set will reflect that member's conception of the office and its requirements, modified in some degree by the member's impressions of the abilities and personality of the officeholder.

The content of role expectations consists mainly of preferences with respect to specific acts, things the person should do or avoid doing. But role expectations may also refer to personal characteristics or style, ideas about what the person should be, should think, or should believe. Role expectations are by no means restricted to the job description as it might be given by the head of the organization or prepared by some specialist in personnel work, although these individuals are likely to be influential members of the role-sets of many persons in the organization. Moreover, people well up in the organizational hierarchy also exercise an indirect effect on the roles of others through decisions about the choice of products, technology, and formal division of labor.

The mention of influence raises additional issues of definition and theory. Role expectations for a given office (and its occupant) exist in the minds of members of its role-set and represent standards in terms of which they evaluate the occupant's performance. The expectations do not remain in the minds of members of the role-set, however. They tend to be communicated or "sent" to the focal person.[3] Moreover, the numerous acts that make up the process of role-sending are not merely informational. They are attempts at influence, directed at the focal person and intended to bring about conformity to the expectations of the senders. Some of these influence attempts (for example, those from superiors) may be directed toward the accomplishment of formally specified responsibilities and objectives of office. Others (perhaps from peers or subordinates) may be directed toward making life easier or more pleasant for the senders themselves, in ways unrelated or even contrary to official requirements.

---

[3]The term *focal person* is used to refer to any individual whose role or office is under consideration. In referring to role expectations as sent to the focal person we are following the formulation of Rommetveit (1954). He refers to members of a role-set as role senders, and to their communicated expectations as the *sent role*.

The messages of role-sending are of many kinds—instructions about preferred behaviors and behaviors to be avoided, information about rewards and penalties contingent on role performance, and evaluations of current performance in relation to role expectations. The statements of role-sending may be specifically behavioral—"As the completed parts come from your machine, you must put them immediately on the overhead rack"—or they may refer to some less tangible matter—"You won't get along here if you think you're too good for the rest of us." In the former case, the focal person knows exactly what he or she must do to meet expectations. In the latter case, the expectation-satisfying behavior must be inferred, as the role sender inferred the objectionable attitude.

As a communicative and influential process, acts of role-sending can be characterized in terms of any of the dimensions appropriate to the measurement of communication and influence. Some of the more important ones proposed by Gross, Mason, and McEachern (1958) include sign (prescriptive or proscriptive), magnitude (strength of the influence attempt), specificity (extent to which the expected behaviors are made concrete and detailed), intensity (extent to which the focal person is allowed freedom of chioce in complying or refusing compliance), and range of conditions under which compliance is intended. As our treatment of power, communication, and leadership implies, our interest in the role-sending process centers upon magnitude or strength of the influence attempt. We are interested also in the psychological basis of influence on which different acts of role-sending depend. Every attempt at influence implies consequences for compliance or noncompliance. In organizations, as we have seen, these commonly take the form of rewards or sanctions—gratifications or deprivations that a role sender might arrange for the focal person, depending on that person's having conformed to the sender's expectations.

The concept of legitimacy, and its acceptance by organizational members, makes the actual use of negative sanctions infrequent in many organizations. (See Chapter 10 for discussion of this concept.) Members obey because the source of the command is legitimate and its form and subject matter are appropriate to the source. All three—source, form, and substance—are thus congruent with the member's own concept of organizational membership and role requirements. The availability and visibility of extrinsic rewards and sanctions are important, nevertheless. The sanctions may be seldom used, perhaps seldom promised or threatened, but they are important. Even in the least punitive of organizations, the enactment of a role within the limits of tolerance of the role-set is a condition for holding the associated office. The person who fails utterly to meet the expectations of the role is thus confronted with the most logical of sanctions, removal from office. One can think of exceptions, in which the nonperforming office-holder continues to hold the office by reason of some personal claim, ownership or nepotism or seniority too great to be denied. But the rule is more important than the exceptions; bureaucratic organizations are systems of achieved rather than ascribed roles, and one validates possession of an office by enactment of the associated role.

Thus, each individual in an organization acts in relation to and in response to the expectations of the members of a role-set, not because those expectations constitute some mentalistic field of forces but because they are expressed in explicit behavioral ways. The expression need not be continuous; human memory can be long, and adults in our society have graduated from a lengthy period of training and socialization in organizational role-taking. They have learned a quality and technique of role readiness that lets them anticipate many of the role expectations of others with few cues. As a result, they learn new roles quickly, absorbing a great deal of role-sending during the early days of their occupancy and retaining much of it without repetition. When the behavior of the focal person is thus appropriate and compliant in the eyes of the role senders, they and their expectations may be quite inconspicuous. But let a person stop performing within the range of such acceptability, and there will immediately become visible the membership of the role set, the expectations which they hold, and the means of enforcement at their disposal.

The Received Role

To understand the response of any member of an organization to the complex pattern of role-sending addressed specifically to him or her, we must regard the organization from the vantage point of that person's office. When we do so, we see that the members of the role-set for that office, and the influential pressures which they direct to its occupant as a focal person, are part of that person's objective environment. To consider the compliance of the focal person with the sent role or the deviations from it, however, takes us immediately beyond the objective organization and environment. Each individual responds to the organization in terms of his or her perceptions of it, a subjective or psychological "organization" that may differ in various ways from the actual organization.

Thus for each person in an organization there is not only a sent role, consisting of the influential and communicative acts of the appropriate role-set; there is also a *received role*, consisting of that person's perceptions and cognitions of what was sent. How closely the received role corresponds to the sent role is an empirical question for each focal person and set of role-senders, and will depend on properties of the senders, the focal person, the substantive content of the sent expectations, the clarity of the communication, and the like.

It is the sent role by means of which the organization communicates to each of its members the do's and don'ts associated with his or her office. It is the received role, however, that is the immediate influence on each member's behavior and the immediate source of his or her motivation for role performance. Each sent expectation can be regarded as arousing in the focal person a motivational force of some magnitude and direction. This is not to say that these motivational forces are identical in magnitude and direction with the sent influence attempts that evoked them. Messages may be misunderstood or defensively distorted.

Furthermore, when sent-role expectations are seen by the focal person as illegitimate or coercive, they may arouse strong resistance forces that lead to outcomes different from or even opposite to the expected behavior. It is such processes, repeated for many persons over long periods of time, that produce the persistent component of unintended effects in organizational behavior. Pressures to increase production sometimes result in slowdowns. Moreover, every person is subject to a variety of psychological forces in addition to those stimulated by pressures from the role-set in the work situation. Role-sendings from that set are only a partial determinant of the person's behavior on the job.

Additional sources of influence in role-taking are the objective, impersonal properties of the situation itself. The taking of roles may be aided by the nature of the task and the previous experience of the individual with respect to similar tasks. The soldier in combat seeks cover when under fire not so much because of the expectations of members of his role-set as because of the demands of the situation. The worker on the assembly line tightens the bolt on the passing car both because he has been told that it is his job and because the structuring of his work situation is a constant reminder of what he is supposed to do. People can be conditioned to play their roles by cues other than those of the communicated expectations from other system members. Nevertheless, in most organizations, role behavior is largely dependent on role-sending.

In addition to the motivational forces aroused by sent expectations and other cues, there are important internal sources of motivation for role performance. For example, there is the intrinsic satisfaction derived from the content of the role. The concert pianist has many motives that encourage performance; one of them is probably the intrinsic psychological return from exercising a hard-won and valued skill.[4] But there is, in addition to intrinsic satisfaction in expressing

---

[4]The patterns of motivation for role behavior, together with the organizational conditions that evoke them and the organizational outcomes they produce, are discussed in Chapter 13.

valued abilities, another kind of "own force" important in the motivation of role behavior. In a sense each person is a "self-sender," that is, a role-sender to him or herself. Each individual has a conception of the office he or she occupies, and a set of attitudes and beliefs about what should and should not be done by an occupant of that office. Each individual has some awareness of the behaviors that will meet the responsibilities of that office, contribute to the accomplishment of organizational objectives, and further his or her own interests. A person may even have had a major part in determining the formal responsibilities of his or her office, especially if it is a line or staff position well up in the hierarchy.

Moreover, some of the persisting motives of the individual are likely to include the sector of organizational behavior. Through a long process of socialization and formal training within the organization and in the larger culture of which both person and organization are parts, the individual will have acquired a set of values and expectations about his or her own behavior and abilities, about the nature of human organizations and the conditions for membership in them. In short, as Miller (1962), Dai (1955), and others have observed, the person has an occupational self-identity and is motivated to behave in ways that affirm and enhance its valued attributes. The individual comes to the job in a state of what we have previously referred to as role-readiness, a state that includes the acceptance of legitimate authority and compliance with its requests, a compliance that for many people extends to acts that they do not understand and that may violate many of their own values. Milgram's finding (1965) that two-thirds of the adult subjects in an experiment obeyed an instruction to administer what they believed to be electrical shocks of several hundred volts to groaning and protesting victims only highlights the phenomenon of compliance in role behavior.

That phenomenon is frequently underestimated, perhaps because of biases inherent both in everyday organizational life and in organizational research. The meeting of expectations is by definition expected and requires no corrective action. It is therefore likely to go unremarked by formal leaders and unobserved by research workers. Managers and research workers, for their own respective reasons, share an interest in deviant organizational behavior. Admittedly, deviance, both as failure and as inspired success, can teach us a great deal. But the dominant defining property of human organizations is the recurrence of expected behavior patterns, and that recurrence reflects individual compliance with the expectations of organizational roles.

The Role Episode

Our description of role-sending and role-receiving has been based on four concepts: *role expectations*, which are evaluative standards applied to the behavior of any person who occupies a given organizational office or position; *sent-role,* which consists of communications stemming from role expectations and sent by members of the role-set as attempts to influence the focal person; *received role*, which is the focal person's perception of the role-sendings so addressed, including the reflexive role expectations that the focal person "sends" to himself or herself; and *role behavior,* which is the response of the focal person to the complex of information and influence thus received.

These four concepts can be thought of as constituting a sequence or role episode. The first two, role expectations and sent role, involve motivations, cognitions, and behavior of the members of the role-set; the latter two, received role and role behavior, have to do with the cognitions, motivations, and behavior of the focal person.

To list the concepts in this order emphasizes one direction of causality—the influence of role expectations on role behavior. There is also a feedback loop; the degree to which a person's behavior conforms to the expectations of the role-set at one point in time will affect the state of those expectations at the next moment. If the response of the focal person is a hostile counterattack, the role-senders are apt to think and behave in ways quite different than if the focal person were submissively compliant. If the focal person complies partially under pressure, they may increase the pressure; if he or she is obviously overcome with tension and anxiety, they may "lay off." In sum, the role episode is abstracted from a process that is cyclic and ongoing: the response of the focal person feeds back to each sender in ways that alter or reinforce that sender's expectations and subsequent role-sending. The current role-sendings of each member of the set depend on that member's evaluations of the response to his or her last sendings, and thus a new episode begins.

The Context of Role-Taking

Role sending and role behavior are thus seen as events in an ongoing and interdependent cyclical process. That process does not occur in isolation; it is itself shaped by several additional or contextual factors—individual, interpersonal, and organizational. The role episode and its context are shown in Figure 7-1. Arrow 1 represents the process of role-sending, and Arrow 2 the process of feedback by which role-senders estimate the degree of compliance with their previous communications and prepare to initiate another cycle. The role episode is thus at the core of the figure, Boxes A to D and the connecting arrows 1 and 2.

The circles in Figure 7-1 represent the context in which such episodes occur: relatively enduring states of the organization, the person, and the interpersonal relations between focal person and role-senders. Such enduring properties are for the most part abstractions and

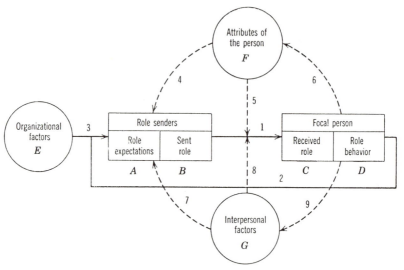

Figure 7-1. *A theoretical model of factors involved in the taking of organizational roles.*

generalizations based upon recurrent events and behaviors. For example, characterizing a relationship as supportive means simply that the parties to the relationship have behaved in a supportive manner toward one another on a sufficient number of occasions so that we feel justified in inferring supportiveness as a quality of the relationship. Such repetitions and patterns of events provide the basis and context within which each new occurrence can best be understood.

To a considerable extent the role expectations held by the members of a role-set—the prescriptions and proscriptions associated with a particular office—are determined by the broader organizational context. The technology of the organization, the structure of its subsystems, its formal policies, and its rewards and penalties dictate in large degree the content of a given office. What the occupant of that office is supposed to do, with and for whom, is given by these and other properties of the organization itself. Although human beings are doing the "supposing" and rewarding, the structural properties of organization are sufficiently stable so that they can be treated as independent of the particular persons in the role-set. For such properties as size, number of echelons, and rate of growth, the justifiable abstraction of organizational properties from individual behavior is even more obvious. The organizational circle (E) in Figure 7-1 represents the set of such variables. Some of them characterize the organization as a whole; others describe some part of it. Arrow 3 asserts a casual relationship between certain organizational variables and the role expectations held about and sent to a particular position.

Enduring attributes of the person (circle F) refer to all those variables that describe the propensity of an individual to behave in certain ways—his or her motives and values, defense preferences, sensitivities, and fears. Such factors affect the role episode in several ways. First, some traits of the person tend to evoke or facilitate certain evaluations and behaviors from role-senders (arrow 4). Second, the same sent-role can be experienced differently by different people; that is, personality factors act as conditioning variables in the relationship between the role as sent and the role as received and responded to (arrow 5). Finally, we propose that role behavior has effects on personality (arrow 6). This is simply the hypothesis that we become what we do, and in a sense we un-become what we do not do. The person who is required to play a subservient role, for example, cannot do so over an extended time without consequent changes in personality. Most abilities atrophy if unexercised.

As Figure 7-1 indicates, interpersonal relations (circle G) fulfill functions parallel to those already described for attributes of the person. The expectations held for and sent to a focal person at a particular time depend to some degree on the quality of the interpersonal relationship already existing between that person and the members of his or her role-set (arrow 7). The focal person will also interpret differently the sent expectations of the role set, depending on his or her continuing interpersonal relations with the senders (arrow 8). Praise and blame have one set of meanings when they come from a trusted source, another when they stem from untrusted sources. Finally, the behavior of the focal person feeds back to and has effects on his or her interpersonal relations with members of the role set (arrow 9). If the focal person suddenly and persistently refuses to comply with their role-sendings, we would predict not only an immediate change in their evaluation of the role behavior itself (arrow 2), but an enduring change in their liking for the focal person (arrow 9).

Multiple Roles and Multiple Activities

The process of organizational role-taking is simplest when a role consists of only one activity, is located in a single subsystem of the organization, and relates to a role-set all of whose members are in the same organizational subsystem. It can become more complex, however, in several ways: by the addition of activities, subsystem involvements, and role-senders, and in rare circumstances the addition of other organizational roles to be enacted by the same focal person. The first of these requires little explanation. Every activity added to a role constitutes a kind of complexification, although there is ample evidence (Katzell, Yankelovich, and others, 1975; Quinn and Shepard, 1974) that most people who enact work roles with few activities prefer some additional complexity.

Roles also become more complex when they require the focal person to be simultaneously involved in two or more subsystems, since each is likely to have its own priorities and to some degree its own subculture. The crossing of subsystem boundaries may be physically required of the focal persons themselves or it may consist in the coordination of persons whose roles are located in different organizational subsystems. The professor who spends half-time in a teaching department and half-time in a research unit of the same university quickly discovers the added complexity of additional subsystem involvements. But the academic vice-president who must somehow respond to the heads of both units will have made that discovery long since.

The role complexification and the expansion of role-sets that come with involvement in two or more subsystems exemplify processes that occur as well across system boundaries. The role-set of a sales clerk is likely to include customers, especially "regular" customers. The role-set of a purchasing agent is likely to include suppliers as well as the heads of the intraorganizational departments that pay for and use the supplies. Moreover, the members of a person's work role-set—his or her role-senders for the work role—may include people who are not themselves members of the work organization or any of its subsystems. When people are asked to name members of their role-sets—those persons whose expectations about how the job shall be done represent a continuing source of influence—the responses sometimes include friends and union officers, husbands and wives.

The inclusion of multiple activities and multiple subsystem involvements is increasingly evident as we move up the hierarchy in most large organizations. The first-line supervisor, for example, is of course responsible for the quantity and quality of production in the immediate task force of which he or she is the formal leader, but is likely also to train new workers, perhaps to plan work for the unit as a whole, to negotiate with the supervisors of adjacent units, and the like. In addition, the supervisor takes direction from the next higher level of management and perhaps represents the interests of his or her own work group to that level. The supervisor is thus a member of two subsystems—the managerial structure and the unit supervised. The conflicts inherent in this dual membership have given rise to a literature of their own, beginning with Roethlisberger's (1945) vivid characterization of the foreman as "master and victim of double-talk."

The diverse demands of such subsystem involvements can be thought of as two subroles, which together constitute the role of foreman. Members of middle management are likely to be similarly involved in the crossing of subsystem boundaries—in relations with the various productive, procurement, and marketing units, for example. And as Mann and Dent (1954) and Likert (1961) have pointed out, people at every supervisory level in the hierarchy (except for the very top) are members of groups at two hierarchical levels—one at which they supervise and one at which they are supervised. The boundary between the rank-and-file and the managerial structure, however, has a unique significance and poses unique problems for first-level supervisors, who must somehow reconcile the demands of their two subroles.

It is possible for one person to hold more than one office, and thus enact two or more work roles in the same or related organizations. The Dean of the Graduate School may also be the University Vice-President for Research. The Premier of the Soviet Union may also be the Secretary of the Communist Party. The professor who divides his or her time between a teaching department and a research institute may have two titles, two offices, and perhaps two different salary rates.

Whether such enactments are designated as the person's holding two quite separate roles and offices, or as the fusion of two previously separate roles into a single new office and subroles, is a matter of organizational choice. It is interesting, however, that we generally regard the holding of multiple offices in an organization as indicating something amiss or at least in transition: a seizure of power, as when a dictator picks up for himself the portfolios of several cabinet ministers; a lack of qualified people; or an inadequacy in the formal organizational plan. There is less tendency, however, to be critical of the same basic process of multiplying the roles played by a single person when all of them are tied as subroles to a single office. The essential dilemma is that there is no escape from the coordinative needs resulting from specialized subsystems and fractionated jobs.

We have suggested that the simplest organizational arrangement occurs when one activity defines role and office. In fact, a general trend in organizations is to move toward such simplification and to fractionate many jobs into their component activities. The more such role specialization develops at one level, however, the greater the need for coordination at a higher level. Thus, the very organization that follows the simplified arrangement of one activity, one role, and one subsystem for its assembly-line workers must adopt a more complex plan for higher offices, multiplying their activities and subsystem involvements. The many specialized subsystems must be interrelated and hence offices created in which these various substructures intersect. In short, the less the coordinative demand within roles, the greater the demand for some means of coordination between roles. That means usually the creation of a new coordinative office.

RESEARCH ON ROLE-TAKING

The research evidence for this model of role-taking in organizations is irregular in quality and relevance. It is, however, substantial in quantity and gaining in other respects. These tendencies are especially characteristic of the last decade, and give some support to the advocates of role as a concept particularly useful for the study of human behavior in organizations.

An elementary assumption in such research is that the occupants of different roles show characteristic and distinctive attitudes, values, and behaviors. That assumption has been part of human experience and folk wisdom for time beyond recollection, and it has been well-documented in the organizational context over a period of thirty years. Officers are more favorable toward army life than enlisted men (Stouffer et al., 1949). Foreman are more favorable toward the employing company than are workers, and stewards are more favorable toward the union (Jacobson, in Guetzkow, 1951).

Moreover, role-related patterns are not only characteristic of attitudes and values, but of perceptions. Mann found differences of 60 percentage points between supervisors' perception that they "always or almost always get their subordinates' ideas in the solution of job problems" and the perceptions of the subordinates that they were so consulted (Likert, 1961). Tannenbaum (1968) reports sizable differences in perceptions of control in organizations, with rank-and-file members typically wanting more and seeing themselves as having less than those at more advantaged locations in the hierarchy want for them or perceive them to have (Tannenbaum, 1968). Such differences are so well-established and so consistent across organizations and across industrial societies that there is little purpose to citing additional examples.

Nor is there great purpose to enlarging the stock of such data. These role-descriptive findings, important in their time, lend themselves to either of two interpretations, or more likely to both: one can argue that the role shapes the attitudes and perceptions of the individual or that the individual is selected for goodness of fit to the role requirements. Organizations make a sustained effort, in fact, to do both these things, and both have become important fields of applied psychology—training and selection (Guion, 1976; Hinrichs, 1976). Our concern, however, is with the dynamic processes of role-sending, enactment, and evaluation that begin after the formalities of selection and training have taken place.

Role expectations
The idea of role as a set of expected activities associated with the occupancy of a given position assumes substantial agreement among the relevant people as to what those activities are. Research on role conflict has investigated deficiencies in that agreement, but the dominant fact is the expectational agreement rather than the deficiencies.

Such agreement has been demonstrated for many roles, social and organizational, for many organizations, and for a number of cultures. Moreover, it has been demonstrated by means of different research techniques. Sarbin and Jones (1956) present such data for the role of daughter, using a 200-word checklist to identify the role expectations. Thomas, Polansky, and Kounin (1955) describe similar results for the role of social worker, with expectational agreement measured by means of sentence-completion procedures. Sherwood (1958), using an essay task to generate data, reported significant agreement on the role expectations for Bantu clerks.

Even research that has concentrated on problems of role conflict shows agreement as the modal pattern among members of the role-set. Agreement is characteristically less than complete, however, and other forms of expectational inadequacy are also common. Such variance in expectation patterns constitutes the first element in the model of role-taking presented earlier in this chapter. We now examine the empirical evidence for that model, following in sequence the categories of relationships identified by number in Figure 7-1.

The Relationship Between Role Expectations and Response (Arrow 1).

As Figure 7-1 suggests, a sequence of three relationships is involved in the linkage of role expectations to role performance. There is the relationship between the expectations held by members of the role set and the expectations as actually sent to the focal person, the relationship between those sent by the set and those received by the focal person, and the relationship between the expectations so received and the subsequent response (both as role performance and side effects). The empirical research on roles was not designed to provide explicit tests of this sequence, however, and the evidence for its several links is uneven. We will review it in the order suggested above, and then consider the research on various inadequacies in organizational role-sending and role-taking.

Role Expectations and Role-Sending

It is often assumed that all role expectations are communicated from role-senders to the focal person, a proposition more distinguished for its convenience than its plausibility. The concepts of organizational research reflect many such assumptions and many subsequently discovered intrusive realities—formal versus informal organization (Roethlisberger and Dickson, 1939); official versus operative and operational goals (March and Simon, 1958); espoused managerial theories versus theories-in-action (Argyris, 1975). Little is yet known of how role expectations as actually sent compare to expectations in the minds of the role-set.

We do know that a great deal of communication goes on in the course of getting work done in organizations—communication by means of gestures and the manipulation of objects as well as by the written and spoken word—and we know that much of the flow of communication falls within the definition of role-sending. Horsfall and Arensberg (1949) reported 20.9 acts of communication per worker per hour among 28 shoe workers, Miller (1958) 19.3 acts among 23 glass workers, Stieber (1956) 16 acts among German steel workers. Such rates are affected by technology, pacing, spatial arrangements, and the like, but the main facts are clear: communication among work-related peers is sustained and frequent. Communication between supervisors and workers is also frequent; Turner (1955), Walker (1956), and Meissner (1976) show the same modal response in widely disparate industries— "between twice a day and under once an hour." Meissner (1976) presents these data in detail.

Sending and Receiving

In an organizational society, people acquire a kind of general expertise in the taking of organizational roles, a process that has been more studied in the laboratory than in organizations. Sarbin and Williams (1953) conducted a laboratory experiment that demonstrated something of the expertise that people acquire in receiving and understanding communications from role-senders. The subjects of the experiment listened to 38 sentences, each conveying some role expectation; their task was to determine the age, sex, and role of the sender, the intended receiver, and the action or role behavior that was being requested. Performance of the experimental subjects was so accurate that the resulting distributions showed the typical J-curve of conforming behavior. Cline and Richards (1960) reached similar conclusions from quite different experiments, as did Orne (Orne, 1959; Orne and Scheibe, 1964).

General expertise in such matters does not imply unfailing congruence between sent and received roles in organizations. Messages may be misunderstood or defensively distorted. High expectations may be comfortably scaled down by the focal person. Moreover the agreement between sent and received roles may be spuriously high in the laboratory situation because the motivations to defend or distort are relatively weak. Kraut (1965), in a study of salesagents and managers in 151 offices, obtained estimates in dollars of the amount of sales that the manager expected of each salesagent, the amount that each agent thought the manager expected, and the amount that the salesagent considered appropriate. Kraut took the difference between the manager's actual expectations and the saleagent's own standard of appropriateness as a measure of objective role conflict. The subjective role conflict was measured in terms of the difference between the agent's own standard and the manager's expectations as perceived by that sales-agent. There was a strong tendency for agents to underestimate the expectations of managers, and thus the amount of the conflict. On the average, subjective conflict was about half as large as objective conflict.

Such discrepancies are more common among low performers than high, either because better performance makes defense unnecessary or because a more accurate receiving of expectations induces higher performance. For our present purposes, the significant fact is the gap itself; the role as received cannot be assumed identical with that sent.

Expectations and Performance

Orne's work provides evidence for the power of role expectations, as well as expertise in role enactment. Subjects instructed to simulate hypnosis do so well enough to deceive expert observers, a fact that suggests completeness and potency of role-sending as well as skill in role-taking. Other research on experimenter-subject relationships has demonstrated the power of the experimenter's role-sending in opposition to the other cues available to the subject. Subjects have experienced sensory deprivation when there was none, discriminated nonexistent differences, and the like.

Milgram's (1965) well-known experiments on obedience to authority, in which many subjects administered what they believed to be painful or dangerous electric shock to other subjects, often in contradiction to their own expressed values, are perhaps the most dramatic examples of the power of this sort of role-sending (see Chapter 10). Gage (1953) was perhaps closer to the realities of organizational role-sending in comparing the accuracy with which behavior could be predicted from knowledge of role expectations with prediction from knowledge of individual idiosyncrasies. Role expectations provided the better predictive base.

General evidence for the power of role-sending lies all around us in the patterned behavior of organizational life itself. All forms of role-sending are not equally effective, however, nor are they equal with respect to undesirable side effects. Research on role-sending in organizations has thus far concentrated more on side effects than main effects (that is, role enactment per se), and more on particular inadequacies in the expectational pattern and sending process (conflict, ambiguity, overload) than on constructive elements. Least research has been done on the important question of what kinds of role-sending evoke most effective performance and fewest undesirable side effects, although it could be argued that this question is included in some more comprehensive lines of research, organizational and nonorganizational. Likert (1961, 1967), for example, proposes the principle of supportive relationships as underlying effective supervision, but implies that it is equally applicable to peer relationships. Skinner (1948, 1971) proposes the principle of reinforcement and its embodiment in operant conditioning as sovereign in human behavior, including organizational design and management.

We need research, however, at the level of specific role sending and enactment. An example is the experimental work of Luchins and Luchins (1966), in which subjects were required to learn a social role by means of several different kinds of role sending. Learning was much more efficient when an overall description of the role and its requirements was provided than when expectations were communicated step by step without such a survey. Consistent with this was their finding that an opportunity to observe and imitate successful role enactment was conducive to rapid and effective learning. Replication and extension in organizational settings would be welcome.

Role Conflict

We define role conflict as the simultaneous occurrence of two or more role expectations such that compliance with one would make compliance with the other more difficult. Such conflicts may be differentiated regarding the degree of mutual interference; in the extreme case compliance with one excludes absolutely compliance with the other. They may also be differentiated in terms of the importance of the interference, the number of role-senders whose expectations are affected, and the like. Role conflict is typically envisaged as a disagreement between two or more role-senders, but two or more expectations of the same role-sender may be in conflict, and conflict can occur between expectations of the role-set and those of the focal person for himself or herself. Conflict may also be generated between two or more roles held by the same person—for example, the role of worker and mother—although the study of such inter-role conflicts takes us outside the immediate boundaries of the organization.

Empirical research on role conflict has tended to choose roles for which some polarization of differences among role-senders seemed likely, and has then demonstrated that such differences existed and were stressful for the persons involved, especially the focal person. Among the studies that fit this description are some that concentrated on the role of industrial foreman, industrial superintendent, staff officer, elective official, military chaplain, scientist, salesperson, military officer, minor government official, teacher, and manager. In every occupational category, such conflicts were associated with negative psychological responses on the part of the focal persons.

Little research has been done on the effects of role conflict on members of the role set, but one would predict strain and hostility there as well, moderated by the visibility of the focal person's behavior and the focal person's coping strategy, among other factors. Bible and his colleagues (Bible and Brown, 1963; Bible and McComas, 1963), in a study of teachers, investigated the side effects of role conflict on the role set and found that consensus among members of the set regarding the focal role was associated with satisfaction among them as well as with the satisfaction of the focal person (teacher).

Studies of role conflict that utilize objective or independent criterion measures are also less common than they should be, although there are implications that role conflict leads to decrements in performance. Getzels and Guba (1954) found role conflict to be associated with reduced teaching effectiveness in nine air force training schools, and Bible and McComas (1963) reported similar findings for teacher effectiveness in other settings. Role conflict has also been studied in relation to various measures of physiological strain. (This research is summarized briefly in Chapter 17; for more extensive reviews see Kahn and Quinn, 1970; McLean, 1970, 1974.)

Data on the incidence and prevalence of role conflict are difficult to interpret. Most studies include only small and unrepresentative populations and depend wholly on self-reported measures. Moreover, different methods of measurement have given substantially different results. All agree, however, that the experience of role conflict in the work situation is widespread. In a nationwide study of male wage and salary workers, Kahn and his colleagues (1964) found nearly half to be working under conditions of noticeable conflict. Forty-eight percent reported that from time to time they were caught between two sets of people who wanted different things from them, and 15 percent reported this to be a frequent and serious problem. Thirty-nine percent reported being bothered by their inability to satisfy the conflicting demands of their various role-senders. The hierarchical and depersonalized nature of large-scale organization is also reflected in these data: 88 percent of all role conflicts reportedly involved pressures from above, and in 57 percent of these cases the spontaneous description of the source of the pressure was given in such impersonal terms as "the company" or "management."

Quinn and his colleagues (1974), using a card-sorting technique with two national samples of adults, report results of slightly lesser magnitude: in 1969 31 percent of all employed people reported themselves as subject to (not free from) "the conflicting demands that other people make" in the work situation; in 1973 the corresponding figure was 43 percent. Studies of more limited populations (Kahn, 1974; French and Caplan, 1973) have reported substantially higher proportions among administrators, scientists, and engineers in certain agencies of the government.

Role Ambiguity

In its prototypical form, role ambiguity simply means uncertainty about what the occupant of a particular office is supposed to do. But there may be uncertainty as well about many other aspects of a role, including the membership of the role-set, the ends to be served by role enactment, and the evaluation of present role behavior.

Research on the consequences of role ambiguity has discovered some side effects similar to those for role conflict—low job satisfaction and high tension—and some that seem more specific to the ambiguity experience—low self-confidence and a sense of futility (Kahn et al., 1964). There is also substantial evidence that role ambiguity reduces the effectiveness of performance: Cohen (1959) reports that the accomplishment of experimental tasks is reduced when instructions are unclear, and Smith (1957) found similar effects when "nonsending role-senders" (silent unidentified stooges) were introduced into an experimental situation. Weitz (1957) found ambiguity of role expectations was related to turnover in a variety of jobs. Torrance (1954) found that ambiguity of role allocation and definition in air force crews under stress was a significant factor in survival.

Such research began with the assumption that ambiguity frustrates the human need for clarity or structure in the environment, accordingly regarded it as a stressor, and sought evidence of resulting strain and performance decrement. The findings are consistent with this approach, but they do not imply that maximum specificity is maximally desirable in organizational life. The preference of most people for general rather than close supervision, autonomy in pacing their work, and choice in the method of doing it argue against the simplistic assumption that ambiguity is an unmitigated evil. Jackson (1960) and Hollander (1964) have demonstrated that some degree of ambiguity—"acceptable ranges of role expectations"—facilitates the management of role conflict. We need research on different aspects and ranges of role ambiguity as they affect role enactment and the well-being of focal persons.

Little can be said about the prevalence of role ambiguity. National samples over a ten-year period report percentages of employed persons experiencing substantial role ambiguity as ranging from 11 to 35. Studies of more limited populations have produced higher proportions: French and Caplan (1973) obtained reports of role ambiguity from 60 percent of the men employed by a government agency, although an agency with a conspicuously difficult and complex mission. And Graen (1976) found that 80 percent of the administrative recruits to a service arm of a public university did not know "what the supervisor wanted," even after nine months in role. We conclude only that role ambiguity is a significant organizational problem by any count and measure yet taken, that its incidence varies widely, and that for some populations and organizations it is the modal condition.

The Feedback Effect of Role Behavior on the
Expectations of Role-Senders (Arrow 2).

The model of role-taking that we have proposed is cyclical, and consists of two core processes or components. One is role-sending; the other is the feedback of information about role enactment from the focal person to members of the role-set. Such feedback in turn influences the next cycle of role-sending, and so the process continues. Research to study this hypothesized process adequately would be longitudinal in design in order to show how the performance of the focal person in successive cycles of role-sending and response leads to modifications of the expectations and role-sendings of the members of the set. Such research has yet to be done, but some data on the feedback component in role-taking are available.

A series of experiments by Adams and his colleagues (Adams, 1976; Wall, 1972; Wall and Adams, 1974) identifies at least two kinds of information used by role-senders in evaluating role enactment of the focal person: success (making or losing money, for example) and conformity to instructions and directives from the role-set. The effects of these two kinds of information were essentially additive, although there were some unique effects. Either deviation of the focal person from prescribed methods or failure in outcome (loss of money) resulted in subsequent more intensive monitoring by members of the set. Members of the role-set also made inferences about the focal person's loyalty on the basis of both kinds of information, although a conforming "loser" was rated higher on loyalty than a nonconforming "winner." Losers, however, tended not to be chosen by the role-set for further (hypothetical) missions.

The implication is that unsuccessful enactment of a role compels some action, corrective or compensatory, by the role-set. The usual assumption is that failure to enact the sent role is unintentional and that dismissal or corrective action by the role set is unwanted by the focal person. This need not be the case; the focal person may want to leave the role or, more often, to induce changes in it.

Goffman (1961) has proposed the concept of role distance or "distancing" as a process by which a focal person makes manifest his or her unwillingness to enact a certain role or role component, and thus confronts the role-set with the necessity of taking some alternative action. One such action is reallocation of the functions within the role set. Perry, Silber, and Bloch (1956) describe such reallocation within families when a child takes over functions usually belonging to one or another parent. It would be useful to know whether reallocation occurs mainly when the faulty performer must nevertheless be kept within the set, as in the family, or whether reallocation within role-sets is common in the organizational situation as well.

The finding that deficient role performance leads to increased monitoring by the role set is plausible, as an alternative to removal of the focal person. It is consistent with the earlier finding (Stouffer and Toby, 1951) that close observation by members of the role-set does in fact lead to increased conformity by the focal person. It is not consistent, however, with the finding by Kahn and his colleagues (1964) that rigidity on the part of the focal person was associated with reduced intentions on the part of the role-set to bring about change.

It is likely that members of role-sets make sophisticated judgments about different kinds of performance deficiencies and their amenability to different role-sendings. Roy (1952, 1955), for example, described the refusal of role-sets to teach required skills until the focal persons had shown themselves to be "trustworthy." Finally, the feedback arrow reminds us that the focal person is not merely the passive recipient of role-sending, but to greater or lesser degree modifies the role and the expectations of the role-set by the manner of role enactment. Graen (1976) refers to the cycles of role-sending and feedback as role-making, and argues that the feedback loop (arrow 2) has received inadequate attention. He emphasizes the proactive behavior of the focal person in defining or negotiating the expectations to which he or she will subsequently be held. The negotiation occurs mainly during the early weeks of role occupancy, and is described as consisting of three phases—initial confrontation, working through, and integrating. Longitudinal studies of office workers (Graen, Orris, and Johnson, 1973) and managers (Danserau, Graen, and Haga, 1975) confirm this early negotiating process between focal person and role set.

Organizational Factors as Determinants of Role Expectations (Arrow 3).

This category of findings reminds us that role expectations and the process of role-sending do not arise as spontaneous and idiosyncratic expressions on the part of role-senders nor as simple responses to some previous behavior of the focal person to whom the expectations were sent. Such factors serve only to mediate the major determinants of role-sending, which are to be found in the systemic properties of the organization as a whole, the subsystem in which the role-senders are located, and the particular position occupied by each.

The study of organizational effects, however, requires multiorganizational designs. These are difficult, relatively expensive, and still rare. The most ambitious and tenacious effort along these lines has been that of Pugh and his colleagues (Pugh et al., 1963; Payne and

Pugh, 1976), who in an extensive series of field studies in Britain and the United States are attempting to specify the effects of what they call organizational context (purpose, size, ownership, etc.) and organizational structure (structuring of role activities, etc.) on the immediate environment (task and social) of the individual. The effects of size on role structure and enactment are better documented than other links in this scheme, although even size effects are not uniform in all studies. Payne and Pugh (1976) report six multiplant studies conducted in three countries, all of which found substantial correlations (.34 to .80) between organizational size and role differentiation (the extent to which the organizational task was divided into specialized roles). Role differentiation was in turn correlated with the specificity of role definitions and expectations. Finally, size is associated with various measures of individual role behavior and well-being. Kahn et al. (1964) report an almost linear relationship between organizational size and the amount of reported role conflict and tension in the organization. Porter and Lawler (1965), summarizing the available research on organizational structure and job behavior, report that as size increases, so do tardiness, reported sickness, and turnover.

Other investigators report results generally consistent with these, but modified to some extent by other factors. Thus, Hall and Tittle (1966) find modest positive correlations between size and six dimensions of bureaucratization chosen to operationalize Weberian theory. Blau and Schoenherr (1971), in a study of 53 government agencies, find that structural differentiation increases with organizational size, but at a decelerating rate; the relationship is curvilinear. This finding of curvilinearity is consistent with earlier evidence that the number of administrative and coordinative roles increases with organizational size, but the proportion of such roles decreases (Terrien and Mills, 1955; Anderson and Warkov, 1961; Haas, Hall, and Johnson, 1963).

The greater differentiation and structuring that comes with size does not imply greater consensus. On the contrary, size is associated with reduced consensus about role expectations in school systems, service agencies, hospitals, and industries.

Few studies are sufficiently intensive to explain these relationships, although Barker's findings (Barker, 1963; Barker and Gump, 1964) that students in small schools have greater opportunity for role elaboration and choice, and enact roles of greater variety, are suggestive. We need research that deals simultaneously with organizational size, organizational shape, and subunit size, at least. And we need organizational models that make explicit the properties of organizations as such, in distinction to groups and other organizational components. Such organizational properties will include normative as well as structural characteristics.

Kahn and his colleagues (1964) identified five dimensions of normative expectations that appeared to be characteristic of organizations as systems rather than of individual persons or roles. These included the extent to which one is expected to obey rules and follow orders, the extent to which supervisors are expected to show personal interest in and nurture their subordinates, the closeness or generality with which supervision is to be accomplished, the extent to which all relationships are conducted according to general (universalistic) standards, and the extent to which organization members are expected to strive strenuously for achievement and advancement. Little empirical work has been done to replicate or refute these findings, however.

We have more evidence linking role expectations to position within the organizational structure than to the properties of the structure as a whole. Location in vertical (hierarchical) terms and location in terms of nearness to an organizational boundary have been studied as factors affecting role expectations, role behavior, and psychological tension. The Kahn study (1964) found positions deep within the organizational structure to be relatively conflict-free; positions located near the skin or boundary of the organization were likely to be conflict-ridden. Jobs involving labor negotiations, purchasing, selling, or otherwise representing the organization to the public were subjected to greater stress. Living near an intraorganization boundary—for example, serving as liaison between two or more departments—revealed many of the same effects but to a lesser degree. Adams (1976) and others (Organ, 1970; Miles, 1976) have replicated these findings experimentally and extended them in a number of ways, including the specification of subsystem and system properties that reduce or intensify the stressfulness of boundary positions. These suborganizational properties include the visibility of the boundary role to members of the role-set, and such related characteristics as physical separation, whether created by physical distance or legal rules (as in closed-session bargaining). In general, boundary persons who were less closely observed deviated more from organizational norms and experienced less tension in the role.

Among the organizational norms that affect the experience and behavior of the boundary person is the organizational norm of "short-term maximizing" versus "longer-term optimizing." Holmes (1971) found in laboratory experiments that the norm of longer term optimization, which gave the boundary person greater flexibility, also produced more agreements between the boundary person and his or her extraorganizational antagonists, and produced greater net returns to the organization over time. Replication of this research in the field situation would be particularly useful.

Relationships between hierarchical position and role-taking experience are less consistent. Increases in hierarchical position are associated with increasingly positive perceptions of role and organization (Schneider, 1972; Payne and Mansfield, 1973; Gorman and Malloy, 1972), but the rewards of advancement in the hierarchy are many and the interpretation of such findings is correspondingly difficult. Responsibility in the usual sense of the term certainly increases in linear fashion with hierarchical ascent, but symptoms of strain do not. Nor is the often heard assertion that the lowest levels of supervision are subjected to the greatest conflict always borne out. Kahn et al. (1964) report a curvilinear relationship in which the maximum of conflict occurs at the upper middle levels of management. Supervisory responsibility, both direct and indirect, is associated with conflict among role senders with respect to the appropriate style and requirements of the role.

The significant principle reflected by all these specific data is that characteristics of the organization as a whole, of its subsystems, and of the location of particular positions act to determine the expectations that role-senders will hold and communicate to the occupant of a particular job. The holding and sending of such expectations is personal and direct; their content is nevertheless shaped by systemic factors.

Personality Factors as Determinants of Role Expectations (Arrow 4)

The influence of personality on role-sending is one of those undeniable facts of organizational life that nevertheless awaits measurement and documentation. Anyone who has worked under a number of different bosses has become a student of such personality differences; anyone who has supervised a number of subordinates has discovered how differently they respond to uniform tasks and supervisory behavior. Results of research undertaken thus far can be summarized in terms of four patterns of findings, perhaps best presented as hypotheses: that roles tend to attract people who are suited to them, that role expectations are modified by the characteristics of focal persons in various ways, that much role conflict can be understood as conflict between the expectations of the role set and the properties of the focal person, and that properties of the focal person may be a source of stress for the individual independent of the expectations of the role-set.

The tendency of persons to choose roles and organizations that fit their needs and abilities is confounded with three other mechanisms that make for such goodness of fit—selection by others (as contrasted to self-selection), adaptation and socialization in role, and role modification by the focal persons themselves. The gross tendency toward goodness of fit seems clear, however, especially in academic settings. Hutchins and Nonneman (1966) found a strong association between student personality and academic climate in 28 medical schools. Schools with "encapsulated" training climates tended to have students low in needs for achievement, autonomy, and aggression, but high in needs for order, abasement, and nurturance. Medical schools with training programs more reliant on intrinsic motivation had students with opposite need patterns. Similar findings were reported by Stern (1970) and by Astin (1964) for colleges, and by George and Bishop (1971) for public schools.

The tendency of role-sets to moderate or raise their expectations according to the attributes of the focal person is more obvious in practice than demonstrated in research. Hage and Aiken, in a study of 16 welfare agencies, reported that agencies with higher proportions of professionally trained people showed less requirement for strict rule observation, and more participation of employees in decision-making. But the dynamics of these relationships were not documented at the level of role-expectations and role-sending. Kahn and his coauthors (1964) reported a more complex pattern in the industrial context. They found that people who were flexible rather than rigid were subjected to greater pressures to change by their role-senders. The behavior of role-senders toward extremely rigid focal persons seemed to reflect a judgment of futility and acceptance and the abandonment of continuing attempts to influence behavior in the direction of ideal performance. Role expectations and role-sending were also related to the achievement orientation of the focal person. The greater the achievement-orientation, especially when such orientation took on a cast of neurotic striving, the more likely were role-senders to apply increased pressures to change the style of the focal person. We have emphasized in theory the importance of the focal person's own attributes in setting reflexive role expectations—expectations like any others in substance, but unique in that they are "sent" from the focal person to himself or herself. There is evidence that people often have the sense of responding to the role expectations of others against their own "better judgment." Forty-five percent of the employed adults in a national sample (Kahn et al., 1964) acknowledged such behavior. At the same time, the values, judgment, and explicit reflexive expectations of focal persons are a major source of role conflict.

Finally, the attributes of the focal person may lead to the setting of reflexive role expectations that are not sources of conflict within the role-set, but are causes of strain or conflict for the individual. Mueller (1965), for example, found that the overload of university professors was self-induced, at least in the opinion of the professors themselves and of their spouses.

Properties of the Focal Person as Mediators
Between Role Expectations and Response
(Arrow 5)

The empirical evidence for the mediating influence of enduring properties of the focal person (including demographic, experiential, and personality characteristics) has been accumulating for decades, and the general proposition is beyond question. One could regard the whole literature of personnel selection as a continuing attempt to identify those personal attributes that enhance the enactment of specific roles. Studies cast more explicitly in terms of role theory have emphasized three kinds of attributes as heightening or reducing the quality of role enactment and the vulnerability of the focal person to its various side effects: values, personality characteristics, and a postulated general aptitude for role-taking.

The first of these emphases came early in research on organizational roles. Stouffer and Toby (1951), in an experiment based on Stouffer's earlier work (1949), found that the chosen behaviors indicated by their experimental subjects in hypothetical situations of role conflict tended to express the predisposition of subjects to the norms of universalism or particularism. Jacobson and his colleagues in the same year (1951) found that the conflict experience of foremen was higher among those who had previously served as stewards, presumably because they had internalized the values of the earlier role. Gross and his colleagues (1958) utilized attributes best described as value-orientations with some success in predicting the conflict-resolving behavior of school superintendents in four hypothetical situations, involving hiring and promotion, time allocation, salary recommendations for teachers, and budget recommendations. The personality predictor was based on a categorization of the superintendents as moralists, moral-expedients, or expedients—according to their predisposition to emphasize legitimacy or sanctions in response to a series of test items. Smelser (1961) conducted laboratory experiments to show the moderating effects of personality in relation to specific role demands. He constructed roles requiring dominant and submissive behavior patterns in a two-person cooperative task, and tested subjects independently for dominance and submissiveness. Role enactment was then measured for all possible pairings. As predicted, the assignment of congruence (dominant person in dominant role; submissive person in submissive role) maximized role enactment; the reverse assignment minimized it, and the mixed situations fell between these extremes. This pattern was clearest in the initial trials, and became less sharp thereafter, presumably because processes of learning and "role-making" diluted the personality effect.

Much of the work on personality as a moderating factor in role-taking has been concerned with factors that handicap performance under stressful conditions. Inappropriate cognitive patterns (Lazarus, 1966) have been studied in these terms, as has rigidity, anxiety, intelligence (lack of it), and need for achievement (beyond what the role allows). This work is summarized in Kahn and Quinn (1970) and

McGrath (1976). Finally, there is an early research effort, intermittently revived, to demonstrate a generalized aptitude for role-taking, irrespective of specific role requirements, goodness of fit between person and role, or stressfulness of role damands. Sarbin and various colleagues (Sarbin and Allen, 1968) engaged in a series of laboratory experiments showing that the ability of individuals to respond appropriately to role expectations was a function of various personality attributes. The ability to perceive accurately demands of a role was related to a measure of neuroticism based on self-description. Role-taking ability was also related, apparently via the capacity to empathize, to such dimensions as equalitarianism-authoritarianism, and flexibility-rigidity. Extreme inability to take roles was manifested by schizophrenics and psychopaths, a finding consistent with Gough's (1948) earlier theory of psychopathy. He proposed that the characteristic problem of the psychopath is inability to empathize, that is to respond in the focal role *as if* the person understood and felt the forces to which the role-senders were subjected. Such an interpretation of psychopathy was given some support by Baker's (1954) small comparative study of psychopathic and nonpsychopathic prisoners. Questioning these subjects in terms that others used in appraising and describing them, Baker found that the psychopaths had significantly greater difficulty recognizing in themselves the ascribed traits. The evidence seems clear for some threshhold ability of interpersonal perception as necessary for role enactment, but thereafter the shape of the function and the relevance of other variables are in doubt.

Personality as Affected by Role Behavior (Arrow 6)

Psychologists tend to treat the characteristics of adult personality as relatively fixed, having been formed during earlier years of life and by earlier experiences. We believe that personality is essentially the product of social interaction, and that the process of personality formation therefore continues throughout life. The empirical evidence for this dynamic process is admittedly thin; few studies show unambiguous effects of role experience and behavior on personality.

The association of role and personality, on the other hand, has been long established. Waller (1932) noted the attributes of pedantry and officiousness among school teachers (in the days when teachers could dare to be either), and Merton's (1940) observation of impersonality and compulsiveness among long-time bureaucrats gave title to a now well-known personality syndrome. More unambiguous findings for the effect of the role came later. Gough and Peterson (1953) found that deficiencies in role performance led to an increasing inability to see oneself in objective terms and to identify with the views of others.

In an extended experiment involving the manipulation of the level of decision-making in a large clerical operation, Tannenbaum (1957) showed that both the autonomous and the hierarchical conditions produced significant changes in personality. The personality changes were in the direction of increasing congruence between role and person.

Lieberman's (1956) study remains in many respects the clearest demonstration of change in the person caused by changes in role. He was able to measure the perceptions and attitudes of employees in two appliance plants three times during a period of three years: once when all were rank-and-file workers, a year later when 23 had become foremen and 35 had been elected stewards, and two years later still when about half of the new foremen and stewards had reverted to nonsupervisory jobs and half had continued in their new roles.

In their rank-and-file days, there were not significant differences between future foremen and future stewards, although both groups were more ambitious, more critical, and less unquestioningly loyal to the company than were the workers destined to become neither foremen nor stewards. On becoming foremen, Lieberman's subjects tended to report more favorably about the company as a place to work, to be more favorable in their perceptions of top management, and to endorse the principle of incentive pay. Those who became union stewards became, according to their responses, more favorable toward unions in general, toward the top officers of their own union, and toward the principle of seniority rather than ability as a basis for wage payments. Those foremen and stewards who subsequently returned to the worker role tended also to revert to the perceptions and attitudes of workers; those who remained as foremen and stewards showed more sharply as time passed the kinds of differences described above. Mean differences between future foremen and future stewards on the numerous scales used were less than one percentage point at the time when all subjects were workers; 48 percent between the foremen and stewards after one year in role, and 62 percent after three years in role.

Even these data, however, leave unsupported many of the linkages stipulated in the model. Lieberman's data argue strongly for a causal relationship between the offices individuals occupy in an organization (foreman, steward) and expressed attitudes on job-relevant matters. Whether the characteristic changes in attitude are brought about because of the causal sequence of different role expectations, the sending of these expectations as attempts at influence, the receiving of such communications, and subsequent response to them remains untested by Lieberman's research. Moreover, the interpretation of the criterion variables is not easy. Almost certainly there were changes in attitude, but were there changes of deeper kinds in values and personality? If so, were they manifest in other roles, as well as at work? And did they show greater stability than the more obviously job-related attitudes?

Merton (1957) concluded his exposition of bureaucratic structure and personality with a plea for "studies of religious, educational, military, economic, and political bureaucracies dealing with the interdependence of social organization and personality formation . . . ." The conclusion remains appropriate today.

The Significance of Interpersonal Relations in Role-Taking (Arrows 7, 8, and 9)

In theory, enduring properties of the interpersonal relationship between a focal person and members of the role-set enter into the process of role-sending and response in ways analogous to enduring properties of the person. That is to say, we expect that the interpersonal relations between focal person and role-senders will help to determine their role expectations, will intervene between sent-role and received role, and will in turn be affected by the role behavior of the focal person.

There are few data to support or to challenge such predictions. Cohen (1959), in an experimental study testing the effects of ambiguity on role enactment, found that task and instructional ambiguity not only had the expected decremental effect on performance but also tended to impair interpersonal relationships among those involved. A field study of the labor force (Kahn et al., 1964) produced similar findings, especially when the ambiguous expectations of the role-set were expressed in evaluative rather than prescriptive terms. Wall (1972) found that boundary role persons (salespersons) in a laboratory experiment were considered less loyal when they lost money in the experimental task than when they gained, and less trustworthy when they deviated from the sent-role (irrespective of their success) than when they complied. Wall's findings refer unequivocally to the effect of role behavior on interpersonal relations (arrow 9). The other research cited does not allow us to differentiate between the effects of role behavior and those of role expectations on interpersonal relations in the role-set.

The evidence is somewhat richer for the moderating effect of interpersonal relations in the role sequence (arrow 8), both in positive and negative terms. Cobb (1976) has reviewed completely and persuasively the effects of interpersonal support on role response under conditions of externally imposed stress. The buffering effect of interpersonal support is highly significant, especially in reducing symptoms of strain and physical debility. Gross and his co-authors (1958) had found earlier that members of school boards (as focal persons) met the expectations of the school superintendent (as role-sender) more fully when they felt liking, admiration, and respect for the person. Kahn et al. (1964) found a general tendency for close interpersonal relationships to intensify the effects of role conflict on the focal person. And Organ (1970) found that distrust by members of the role-set had the effect of heightening the conformance of the focal person to their role expectations. In short, every investigation that has sought such interaction effects appears to have found them, but the effects are widely assorted.

The implication is that interpersonal relations enter into the role sequence in many ways, and that hypotheses of a general form—interaction, buffering, or intensification—will have to be replaced by more specific predictions. Adams (1976) provides an example of such a hypothetical sequence in his interpretation of findings to date regarding the behavior of boundary role persons. He proposes that an initial decrement in trust leads to increased closeness of monitoring and evaluation by role-senders (arrow 7), that closer monitoring under conditions of reduced trust induces more stereotypic conformity to role expectations (arrow 8), that such rigid enactment of the role evokes opposition from people outside the organization and therefore produces less successful outcomes, and that reduction in successful enactment leads to reduced trust (arrow 9). In a series of experiments, Adams and his colleagues have demonstrated each of these links (Strickland, 1958; Organ, 1970; Frey and Adams, 1972; Gruder, 1968; Wall, 1972). It remains to combine them in a single research design, replicate the laboratory findings under field conditions, and extend them beyond the special case of boundary roles.

Role Socialization and Role-Making

Most research on the taking of organizational roles either studies the ongoing role relationships in organizations or creates brief encounters in the laboratory. In the former case the accommodation of person to role and the shaping of role to person has already occurred, and in the latter case there is usually neither time nor motive for such efforts to take place. The open system view of organizations would treat the entry of a person into an ongoing organization as a new intersection of two existing systems, with the area of intersection characterized by cycles of behavior that in some respects continue the previous history of each system and in some respects are unique products of their coming together. Thus, the person who enters an organization and takes a job to replace someone who has retired, resigned, or been dismissed encounters a role-set and an array of role expectations ready made. But the new job-holder also has a history and an ongoing life, a set of expectations about jobs in general and even perhaps the particular job, a pattern of motives and beliefs about work roles, and an array of other roles and obligations.

Assuming that this particular person-in-role intersection is to continue, some accommodation must be reached. The process of accommodation between person and organization, which continues for the duration of the organizational membership but is concentrated in its early phases, can be partitioned into two aspects: the socialization of the person and the modification of the role. There is less research on either aspect than is needed, in spite of an earlier sociological interest in occupational socialization (Hughes, 1958), but each has been the subject of a recent review (Van Maanen, 1976; Graen, 1976).

The methods by which organizations socialize individuals include selection, training, apprenticeship, debasement experiments, anticipatory socialization, and what is sometimes referred to as "trial-and-error" (Caplow, 1964; Porter, Lawler, and Hackman, 1975). In terms of our model of role-taking, the last of these is the most relevant. It is simply a specific instance of what Brim (1966) defines as the general process of adult socialization: "the manner in which an individual learns the behavior appropriate to his position in a group, through interaction with others who hold normative beliefs about what his role should be and who reward or punish him for correct or incorrect actions." Empirical research on socialization into work roles makes two main points—the importance of early socialization experiences in the role, and the stressfulness of the process. Berlew and Hall (1966), for example, found that the performance of managers in several industries depended significantly on experiences during the first year, especially with respect to the challenge of the job. Their general finding is consistent with others, in positions from executive offices to jail cells (Schein, 1965; Denhart, 1968; Vroom and Deci, 1971). Moreover, the early period on a job is often regarded as conditional on both sides, and is marked by a large number of employees quitting and being dismissed (Saleh, Lee, and Prien, 1965; Graen, 1976).

The mutuality of the early accommodation process is described by Graen, Orris, and Johnson (1973) in a longitudinal study of eight departments of a large public university. Over a six-month period they obtained repeated measures from new focal persons in clerical and secretarial positions and from their supervisors. Measures included the supervisors' preferred enactment of the role, and their perceptions of actual enactment, the focal persons' own preferred enactment, and their perceptions of supervisors' preferences. The main findings are convergence over the six-month period, with the process of convergence gradual and asymmetrical. The amount of convergence varies for individual pairs, however, and is much greater for focal persons whose initial stance was role-acceptance. Research on the stresses of socialization have emphasized disillusionment (Graen, Orris, and Johnson, 1973; Vroom and Deci, 1971) and symptoms of strain (McGrath, 1970). The major antidote or preventative for both would appear to be advance opportunities for observance of role enactment, trial, and the like.

The concept of role-making as the other side of the socialization coin is both old and new. It is new as a label, and as a proposed post-bureaucratic response to organizational transience and rapid change; it is familiar as role elaboration, altercasting, and the creation of microsocial systems (Goffman, 1961). Any role can be thought of as including not only a set of prescribed (and proscribed) behaviors, but also an area of option in which the occupant can exercise choice with respect to activities, methods, and style. A focal person's exercise of such options is to some extent personal and unique, and constitutes that person's elaboration of the role. The area available for elaboration varies with the role, particularly its position in the organizational hierarchy; hierarchical ascent confers a relatively greater area for role elaboration, a fact universally recognized by the excitement that attends succession of heads of state or heads of major organizations.

Goffman (1961) has emphasized the fact that every taking of a role requires complementary adjustments by members of the role set. He proposes that the attainment of mutual adjustment by each focal person and role set constitutes a microsocial system with certain idiosyncratic properties, and yet merged with the macrosystem that represents the more general requirements of the role. The success of the focal person in bringing about such complementary adjustments to the process of his or her own socialization appears to depend on two elements of behavior—giving evidence of successful enactment and showing actively a desired area of latitude (Ziller, 1965; Dansereau, Graen, and Haga, 1975).

We would predict that initial indications of successful enactment are essential to establish trust within the role set, and reassurance that their own interdependent role performance will not be handicapped. But proactive behavior by the focal person would nevertheless be necessary to establish the range or latitude within which role elaboration will be tolerated: it is inevitably a negotiated boundary. In sum, the empirical evidence of recent years, some of it developed in response to the model of role-taking we have proposed and some developed in wholly other frameworks, is generally compatible with the model and has done much to fill its empty conceptual categories with the data of organizational reality.

■ SUMMARY

The concept of role is proposed as the major means for linking the individual and organizational levels of research and theory; it is at once the building block of social systems and the summation of the requirements with which such systems confront their members as individuals. Each person in an organization is linked to some set of other members by virtue of the functional requirements of the system that are heavily implemented through the expectations those members have of the person; he or she is the focal person for that set. An organization can be viewed as consisting of a number of such sets, one for each person in the organization.

The process by which the expectations of members of a role-set are linked to the behavior of the focal person for that set is described in terms of role episodes. The role episode in turn consists of a sequence of events involving members of a role-set and the focal person. The sequence begins with the role expectations held by members of the set for the focal person; these are activities that they require of the person to perform their own roles or to maintain their own satisfactions. The next step in the role episode is the sending of these expectations from the members of the set to the focal person, the communication of role requirements in terms intended to influence his or her behavior.

With the communication of role expectations from role-set to focal person, the first half of the role episode is completed. The second half has to do with the perceptions and behavior of the focal person. He or she receives, with greater or lesser distortion, the role expectations sent. It is the received role that is the immediate source of influence and motivation of behavior (insofar as it is influenced by members of the role-set). Finally, the focal person acts; he or she behaves in role, showing some combination of compliance and non-compliance with the expectations of the role-set. Members observe and evaluate the person's behavior in relation to their expectations and needs, and thus the cycle moves into another episode.

Several complications are considered in connection with the treatment of organizational role in these terms. One role may involve many activities; multiple roles may be incorporated in a single office, that is, intended for performance by a single individual. Moreover, one person may hold a number of offices. Each of these elaborations adds its own complications to the simple situation in which a single recurrent activity comprises a role, which in turn comprises an office occupied by a person without additional organizational commitments.

Three oversimplifications of the role episode are considered: the fact that organizational life is continuous rather than made up of discrete episodes, the fact that members of a role set are often in disagreement among themselves with respect to what the focal person should do, and the fact that the role episode occurs within and is shaped by a matrix of organizational influences.

Research evidence for the relationships specified by the framework of the role episode has been accumulating and puts some flesh upon the bones of the skeletal model of role-taking. For example, studies agree that role conflict in work situations is widespread and a nationwide survey found nearly half of the male population to be working under conditions of noticeable conflict. Such conflict is often associated with anxiety, tension, and reduced effectiveness.

Finally, role-making or the elaboration of the role by the individual, as the other side of the socialization coin, is greatly restricted by hierarchical level. It also is dependent on initial indicators of successful enactment to establish trust within the role-set.

8

THE CONCEPT OF ORGANIZATIONAL EFFECTIVENESS

To be effective means literally to have effects, but more than that is usually meant. When we say that something is effective, we usually mean that it has effects that we desire or that we recognize as intentional in the design of the thing in question. If we call aspirin effective, we probably mean that it relieves our headaches. If we call a television set effective, we probably mean that it provides a clear picture and a reasonable reproduction of sounds. Such examples and definitions serve in those simple cases in which the system under study has few outcomes, and the relevant actors and observers are agreed on what is intended in design and wanted in use. When the system in question is more complex, with many outcomes wanted and unwanted by different constituencies, a unitary concept of effectiveness is inadequate. Such is the case for human organizations.

PROBLEMS OF DEFINITION

The research evidence for this complicated state of affairs began to accumulate some years ago, and continues to do so. A study using expert rankings to determine the effectiveness of 20 successful and 20 unsuccessful insurance agencies developed signs of internal contradiction in the course of analysis. These resulted from the fact that the concept of organizational effectiveness was understood as multidimensional by the expert raters who were in some disagreement with respect to the weighting of the various dimensions. Moreover, they were unaware of their disagreements. A factor analysis of 70 measures of performance obtained from these agencies (independent of the ratings) demonstrated that the effectiveness concept utilized in the research contained no fewer than seven independent factors, and that the expert judgments of effectiveness corresponded very badly to any of them.

A study of 32 operating units of a nationwide service organization was designed to evaluate leadership practices in relation to unit effectiveness, the latter based on managerial rankings. The data for five criteria of effectiveness (overall ratings, productivity as measured by time study, chargeable accidents, unexcused absences, and observed errors) were analyzed separately, after an attempt to predict according to the overall rankings showed an overlarge unexplained variance. The correlations among the five criteria of effectiveness were generally low, with fewer than half of them reaching significant levels. Even more disturbing was the fact that the magnitude of the intercorrelations varied greatly within the 32 organizational units. For example, the relationship between productivity and effectiveness varied from $-.56$ to $+.83$, and the relationships among the other criteria were no less erratic (Seashore et al., 1960).

A later effort by Yuchtman and Seashore (1967) involved repeated factor analyses of 76 performance variables over a period of 11 years. The data were obtained from 75 independently owned and managed life insurance agencies located in different communities throughout the United States. This analysis generated ten factors of considerable stability: business volume, production cost, productivity of new members, youthfulness of members, business mix (i.e., unit size of transactions), labor force growth, management emphasis, maintenance cost (i.e., cost of maintaining clients), member productivity, and market penetration (in comparison with estimated population potential). This is a long list for seekers after a single criterion, and the authors point out additional and less obvious problems: the ambiguous meaning, probably specific to particular circumstances of market and organization, of youthfulness, for example. They note also disagreements between and within organizations with respect to the preferred position on some of the factors, and ponder the implications:

> how can some choice as to preferred type of business be said to be a goal of these organizations when the people themselves do not agree on whether one end of the scale is "better" or "worse" than the other?

Friedlander and Pickle (1968), in a study of small businesses, developed a different set of effectiveness criteria in the course of an attempt to identify outcomes of importance to owners, employees, creditors, suppliers, customers, "governmental regulators," and the host community. Like Seashore and Yuchtman, they found many low and some negative correlations across these criterion measures.

The examples could be continued, but they need not. Campbell (1974) has reviewed studies that focus on a single criterion of organizational effectiveness, and has identified 19 different variables that have been so used. Steers (1975) surveyed 17 studies that used multiple criteria of effectiveness and described his findings as follows:

> One of the most apparent conclusions emerging from a comparison of these multivariate models is the lack of consensus as to what constitutes a useful and valid set of effectiveness measures. While each model sets forth its three or four defining characteristics for success, there is surprisingly little overlap across the various approaches. (pp. 547–549)

The problem of developing satisfactory criteria of organizational performance is clear enough; its solution is much less obvious, although attempts at conceptual clarification have been even more numerous than major empirical studies. Thus, Argyris (1962) defines organizational effectiveness as that condition in which "the organization, over time, increases outputs with constant or decreasing inputs or has constant outputs with decreasing inputs" (p. 123). Seashore and Yuchtman (1967, p. 393) concluded the research described earlier by defining organizational effectiveness as the "ability (of an organization) to exploit its environment in the acquisition of scarce and valued resources to sustain its functioning." Other definitions have emphasized goodness of fit between the organization and selected aspects of the environment (Perrow, 1972; Mohr, 1973; Pennings, 1975).

Recent efforts seem to have abandoned the conceptual struggle at this level, and instead offer frameworks within which one may make any of an assortment of choices in the name of effectiveness. Scott (1976), for example, offers such choices in terms of three broad conceptualizations of human organizations that he designates as the rational, the natural, and the open-system models. The open-system approach to organizations that we have proposed in earlier chapters is less tolerant perhaps, but we believe that it offers a basis for solving some of these old problems and defining others as no longer problematical. With this approach in mind, let us consider the meaning of organizational effectiveness, beginning with one of its few widely agreed upon components, efficiency.

THE EFFICIENCY OF ORGANIZATIONS

As open systems, organizations survive only as long as they are able to maintain *negentropy*, that is, import in all forms greater amounts of energy than they return to the environment as product. The reasons for this are obvious. The energic input into an organization is in part invested directly and objectified as organizational output. But some of the input is absorbed or consumed by the organization. In order to do the work of transformation, the organization itself must be created, energized, and maintained, and these requirements are reflected in an inevitable energic loss between input and output. Electric motors and transformers are relatively efficient machines, but they extract an energic price (recognizable as heat) in the process of changing electrical energy to mechanical, or alternating current to direct. The vacuum tube must be heated before it can do its work; even the transistors and the microcircuits that replace them pass on less energy than they receive.

For all open systems, it is appropriate to question the amount of this cost. How much of the energic input from the outside into the system emerges as product, and how much is absorbed by the system? In other words, what is the net energic cost of the transformation?

The ideal answer to this question would be provided by a system which exported as intended output 100 percent of the energy that it received. For such a system the efficiency ratio of output/input would be 1.00 or 100 percent.

There is a convenient simplicity to examples like that of the electric motor or transformer. They are systems for which the input is a single energic form—electricity—and the intended output is a single but different energic form—the kinetic energy of a rotating shaft in the case of the motor, and an altered electric current in the case of the transformer. In such cases the efficiency concept (ratio) is relatively obvious in meaning and easy in computation. In all human organizations, however, there are many additional complications, and in private industry there is the special complication of profit and its relation to efficiency.

One of the major and characteristic complications of human organizations lies in the multiple forms in which energy is imported. Almost all organizations take in energy in at least two forms: *people*, as energy sources; and *materials*, which already contain the energic investment of procurement, extraction, or partial manufacture. Many organizations also import energy in other forms such as steam, electricity, or the movement of water.

Direct and Indirect Components

Rough distinctions are often made among energic sources and among the uses to which each may be put. For example, it is customary to refer to the energic input of people as *direct* or *indirect*, according to its closeness to the basic transformation in which the organization is engaged. In general, direct labor refers to all energy that acts directly on the materials being put through the organization. (Forming metal, grinding corn, and selling groceries are direct labor.) Energy that acts directly on other members of the organization (supervision or staff services), or on materials not part of the organizational throughput (accounting, running time studies, or planning future requirements), we are accustomed to call indirect labor. Most positions in the production and production-supportive subsystems thus tend to be in the category of direct labor, and most positions in the adaptive and maintenance subsystems tend to be indirect. Positions in the managerial subsystem are indirect by definition. It has been a long-standing convention of industry, although one occasionally challenged by labor unions and reduced in significance by the continuous processes of the newer technologies, to pay for direct labor by the hour and indirect labor by periods of time ranging from a week to a year.

A distinction in some ways similar to that between direct and indirect labor is made with respect to materials. Reflecting primarily their directness of use in the organizational throughput (that is, the rapidity with which they are consumed in the productive process), they are classified as *supplies* or *equipment*. The ideal supply is completely consumed in the process of organizational transformation; it emerges transformed and without waste as product or output. The ideal equipment, on the other hand, is eternal and indestructible; it facilitates the organizational throughput but is not transformed. In practice, of course, the distinction blurs; the electric utility uses up its generators and steam turbines no less than the coal or oil that feeds them—but more slowly.

Units of Measurement

A further complication in studying the efficiency of human organizations stems from the inadequacy of our methods of accounting and reckoning. The measurement of organizational input and output is not often done in energic terms, nor in any other common denominator that might be translated readily into some energic measure. We speak in tons, board feet, hours, or gallons, according to the material or commodity in question. The nearest we come to a common measure of these diverse units is the dollar (cost), which is not necessarily commensurate with energic input and output. It is interesting, perhaps even ironic, that economists have long recognized the disadvantage of using money as a unit of measure in circumstances that really require measures of energic investment and psychic return. Most economists have nevertheless become so convinced of the elusiveness of such concepts that they have given up trying to make operational their psychic concept of utility and have preferred to be guided by its distant and distorted fiscal echo.

Such measurement inadequacies in turn reduce the efficiency of organizations. To the extent that organizational decisions are guided by data, they reflect the limitations of those data, including errors of commission and omission. Most current attempts to improve the measurement of organizational functioning have taken the form of bringing previously unaccounted events into the framework of dollar accounting. Human asset accounting, for example (Hermanson, 1964; Likert, 1967; Brummert, Flamholtz, and Pyle, 1968) attaches dollar estimates to the value of training, experience, commitment, and other characteristics of the human organization. These estimates are made specific to positions, and treated as assets. Like other assets, they can be increased or depleted, and it becomes part of the accounting function to measure such changes.

No sovereign unit of measurement is at hand, however. The assessment of organizational functioning will continue to involve many different modes of measurement, and dollar costs may well be the most nearly comprehensive of them. The conversion of organizational measures to energic terms would be a tremendous task, and not one justified for practical purposes. Even if the cycles of organizational life were reduced to an energic common denominator, some conceptual problems of organizational effectiveness and efficiency would persist. Miller (1960) has argued that human organizations must be regarded both as information-processing and energy-processing systems, and in subsequent chapters on communication and policy making we will be concerned more with informational than with energic processes. And Galbraith (1967) has reminded psychologists of organization that human energy is not like other scarce resources, because of the basic human need for expressive activity. To the extent that organizational roles offer opportunity for such activity, their energic demands will be welcomed within broad limits, and a reduction in those demands might be experienced as psychic loss rather than gain.

Nevertheless, we can advance our understanding of organizational efficiency by thinking of it as analogous to that of a motor and asking the question suggested by that analogy:

How much output do we get for a given input?

How much input must we invest to assure a given output?

How can we judge the relative efficiency of two or more similar organizations?

An Example of Comparative Efficiency

Imagine two modest establishments engaged in the manufacture of wooden baseball bats, one producing the bats entirely by hand, and the other making use of a lathe, power saw, and power sander. One immediate measure of the relative efficiency of these two establishments could be had by comparing the energic input required by each to produce a finished bat. It is likely, however, that these quantities would not be readily available, and we might therefore make use of an approximation: the number of worker-hours of input required to produce a bat, assuming for the moment that the energic input of the hand-worker during an hour was equal to that of the tool-worker. (We assume, in other words, that the lathe-hand is working as "hard" as the worker using a spoke shave.) If we found that the lathe-hand made one bat during each hour of an eight-hour day, while the hand-worker made only one bat during an entire day, we would conclude that the lathe system was eight times as efficient as the hand system for the manufacture of baseball bats.

The example would have to be elaborated in many respects before it would begin to do justice to the complexities of our subject. The two manufacturing operations do not permit such simple comparisons. They both make direct use of human labor and of wood. But the lathe system uses lathes, and the hand system does not. True, the lathe system does not use up the lathe very fast; it may last, let us say, for the manufacture of 100,000 bats. Nevertheless, it is part of the input, and 1/100,000 part of the energic cost of creating a lathe must be included in the energic cost of each bat. The advantage will still lie with the lathe system over the hand system. But an important principle is involved: our first comparison disregarded entirely the cost of the physical plant; our second comparison at least raised the problem of computing and including such costs. Obviously a complete energic accounting, like a complete cost accounting, would include all inputs—labor, electricity, plant, equipment, and the rest.

The system theorist is not rigid about such matters, however; the inclusion or exclusion of any input is a problem of frame of reference. It is permissible (and it is sometimes very useful) to compare the efficiency of two systems with each in a prime ongoing state, without regard to the cost of achieving and maintaining that state. If you do not want to accept the physical equipment of a system as given, or if (which amounts to the same thing) you want to measure efficiency over a period of time longer than the life of the equipment, then the energic cost of replacement must be included in your calculations. Efficiency becomes a matter not only of labor input and materials (direct costs) but also of plant and equipment (indirect costs). For most purposes, any statement regarding efficiency must include both direct and indirect costs, especially in light of the increasing rate at which industrial equipment becomes obsolete.

The problem of defining spatial boundaries for some purpose of organizational analysis is much like the temporal problem. How much space (what activities) are we to include in the system under analysis? The nature of this problem can be readily illustrated by means of the previous example, if we bring into the manufacture of baseball bats the additional issue of wood supply and procurement. Suppose that the Lathe Bat Company is located in New York City and imports its wood from an average distance of 500 miles. The Hand Bat Company is located next to a mature ash grove and brings its wood an average distance of 500 yards. If our comparison of efficiencies is defined solely in terms of the manufacturing process, the facts of location are irrelevant. If we are interested in a larger organizational space of procurement-plus-production, then nearness to source of materials is important. In this example, the relative efficiency of the Lathe Bat Company as compared to its competitor is less because of its location. Analogous arguments with respect to location could be made for any other needed resource, and for any other environmental transaction, including marketing.

The spatial and temporal boundaries to system analysis are characteristically interdependent. Suppose we specify that our analysis of bat manufacture is to apply in perpetuity, or at least for a time period of great and indefinite length. To guarantee a permanent supply of the appropriate wood, the bat company may find it necessary (as some large lumber companies do) to extend its boundaries to include operations which will guarantee renewal of major supplies at a rate which balances their consumption in manufacture. Thus the bat company must grow ash trees as fast as it cuts them down and uses them, and a subsystem of reforestation becomes part of the total energic cost of bat manufacture and part of the system for manufacture.

Which frame of reference, or definition of system boundaries in space and time, is appropriate depends on what we want to do. If we want to make an overall comparison between two companies or predict their profitability, the legal boundaries of the establishment may be appropriate for our purpose. But suppose that our efficiency study is intended to determine whether or not the Hand Bat Company should install lathes. For this purpose the comparison of manufacturing operations per se is most appropriate. Similarly, a decision about plant location would involve efficiency comparisons with respect to procurement and marketing, with manufacturing procedures as such largely irrelevant. Empirical studies of industrial mobility have documented the considerations that enter into the location and relocation of companies (Katona and Morgan, 1950; Mueller and Morgan, 1962). The costs of inputs, especially raw materials and labor, are important factors, as are tax levels. The costs of bringing raw materials to the organization and transporting the organizational product to market are carefully computed. On the other hand, the dollar value of employee travel between home and work probably will not have been estimated, either in terms of direct transportation costs or the opportunity costs of time spent commuting. Such costs are not ordinarily borne by the enterprise and therefore are not included in its accounts.

The accounting of industrial mobility is selective in other respects as well. Closing a plant in one location and opening it in another involves costs to the people who lose their jobs and to the community that provides support during the period of their unemployment. The physical and psychological costs are unlikely to be measured at all, although they are substantial (Cobb, 1974, 1976). The dollar costs will appear in the family accounts and in those of community agencies for job-finding and economic assistance. They will not appear in the books of the company, even if its management was concerned about the impact of its decision to move. The system view of organizations does not solve such problems by including all costs in its computations. Attention to system boundaries, however, serves to remind us of the limits of our analyses at any given time, and makes it more probable that we will set those limits in terms appropriate to the problem. In principle there is no limit to such inclusion, no limit to the extension of time-space boundaries in the study of human systems, since all seemingly independent and separate human systems are linked together into the total system of human life. The human enterprise as a whole represents a system of great negative entropy. It persists only by means of massive importation of energy—first of all from the sun, on a continuing basis, and second from other natural processes—some of time long past, like the formation of coal and oil, and some continuing, like the power of rivers and waterfalls.

POTENTIAL AND ACTUAL EFFICIENCY

The efficiency ratio tells us how well the organization uses the energy at its disposal, how much energic investment in all forms (labor, supplies, power, and the like) is required for each unit of output. This concept of efficiency, in turn, can be resolved into two distinct components: the potential efficiency of the system design, and the extent to which that potential is realized in practice.

Suppose that two plants identical in technology are set up with different organizational structures, one plan calling for a supervisor for each ten workers and the other calling for a supervisor (putting forth equivalent effort) for each twenty workers. If both plants operate as designed, let us say to produce 1000 television sets in an eight-hour shift, clearly the more efficient system is the organization with fewer supervisory positions. It is achieving the same output with less energic input. Furthermore, its superior efficiency is intrinsic in the organization *design*. Each system is operating as designed, but one design is more efficient than the other.

The example might not work out this way, of course. If the thinness of supervision in the "20:1" plant were reflected in higher scrap loss and lower production, so that this plant produced only 800 working television sets per day, the efficiency comparison between the two plants would be different. One plant would have the more economical (efficient) organizational plan, but would be unable to fulfill in practice the production that the plan called for; the other organization would have a more costly (less efficient) plan, but its operation would meet fully the specifications of the plan. Which of the two plants was more efficient overall would be an empirical question.

This kind of distinction between components of efficiency is common enough. Every automobile enthusiast will assure us that an engine with overhead camshafts, fuel injection, and extensive use of weight-saving alloys is inherently more efficient than a flat-head, side-valve, cast-iron engine of the same displacement. If both engines are in prime condition and properly tuned, the facts of this comparison can be readily demonstrated in terms of speed, economy, and other criteria of performance and efficiency. One engine is simply a better, more elegant design than the other; it is a superior system for transforming gasoline into transportation. But what if the superior automobile has been badly driven, inadequately maintained, or otherwise abused, so that its actual performance falls far short of its potential efficiency? It may realize so little of its potential that it will in practice be less efficient than its plebeian competitor. There are, in short, two quite separate aspects of the efficiency of any functioning system: the potential or abstract efficiency in the system design, and the extent to which that efficiency is realized in the concrete instance. The two aspects are not wholly independent, of course. Some organizational designs are more fragile than others, some more accident-prone, some inherently easier for human beings to bring to life. Optimal design, of engines or organizations, must be design for use, which means taking into account the situation and characteristics of users as well as the thing used.

Social scientists have been slow to deal with organizational designs in general, let alone the ease or difficulty of their realization. The approach to organizations as man-machine systems (Chapanis, 1970, 1976) is a partial exception because it is concerned with both aspects of design—ideal efficiency and the practicability of attaining that ideal with human beings under realistic conditions of work. The study of man-machine systems, despite its title, has been the study of specific tasks; it designs jobs rather than organizations. The concept of the organization as a sociotechnical system (Emery and Trist, 1960) emphasizes the importance of designing organizations to meet social-psychological as well as technological criteria, so that human beings will be willing and able to enact the organizational roles. Current experiments in this and similar frameworks (Chapters 17, 19, and 20) suggest the possibility of an optimistic convergence—the readiness of some managements to acknowledge organizational inadequacies, the interest of some unions in the quality of the work experience, and the involvement of some social scientists in the design of organizations for use.

PROFIT AND EFFICIENCY

Let us turn to the special but extensive case of the profit-making organization. We said that the efficiency of an organizational system is given by the ratio of its energic output (or product) to its energic input (or cost). We stipulated also that total cost per unit of production includes procurement, marketing, maintenance, depreciation of plant, and the like. Will this efficiency ratio also define precisely the profitability of the plant? No.

An increase in efficiency will tend to make a plant more profitable, since its greater efficiency means a lesser cost per unit of product and implies no immediate reduction in selling price. Prices tend to be set by what consumers will pay and correspond roughly to the production costs of the least efficient producers. In almost every category of business, the most profitable companies report rates of return at least double those of their less successful competitors (*Fortune*, May and June, 1976). The usual ordering of American automobile manufacturers—General Motors, Ford, Chrysler, and American Motors—illustrates the pattern. Many factors enter into such profit advantage, the efficiencies of size and volume prominent among them. A gain in the efficiency of a particular company is likely to mean an increase in profit.

But other considerations must be introduced even into an elementary discussion of profit, considerations that have little to do with system efficiency. Suppose that a manufacturer of television sets has two plants in different parts of the country, and that the plants are technologically identical. The dollar investment in plant and equipment is identical, and the costs of procuring supplies and marketing the finished product are the same. In Plant A, however, the employees work 25 percent harder than in Plant B, and they produce 25 percent more sets. As a result, Plant A is certainly more profitable than Plant B, and there is a presumption that it is better managed. Is it also 25 percent more efficient as a system?

In the energic terms of reference we have employed, it is not. Plant A uses the same number of energy units for each product unit as does Plant B. Plant A is simply getting a greater energic input from each worker. Suppose that employees in Plant A worked ten hours each day instead of eight (an alternative way of obtaining a 25 percent increase in energic input from each worker). Would this increase in hours of work make Plant A more efficient than Plant B as a producing system? Of course not—at least not in the terms in which we have defined efficiency. Efficiency has to do with the ratio of energic output to input; increasing the output by running the system longer or by increasing the rate of energic input does not per se alter the efficiency ratio.

Only in certain limited respects would such changes in operation tend to affect efficiency. The plant in which workers are suddenly motivated to work 25 percent harder and produce 25 percent more has not had a 25 percent change in the energic ratio of output/input, since both numerator and denominator have increased. There will have been some genuine gain in efficiency, insofar as the greater output is obtained from the same plant and equipment without a corresponding increase in its rate of depreciation. There will be greater differences between these two plants in profitability, however. The company which has induced its employees to increase output by 25 percent has probably realized a profit increase of much greater magnitude, unless the production increase has involved a corresponding increase in the wage bill. The important point is that profitability and efficiency are not synonomous, as energic and dollar accounting are not synonomous, although they are certainly related.

In dollar accounting, free resources increase efficiency because they are not included as costs in the computation of inputs. Any method of reckoning, of course, counts some things and ignores others. An increase in output that results from some uncounted increase in input improves the input/output ratio and is interpreted as a gain in efficiency within those terms of reference. The open-system approach to organizations accommodates such differences in terms of boundary definition and boundary transactions. Suppose that we view Plants A and B not only as energy-transforming systems but as energy-procuring systems. We then ask how much of the organizational output must be expended in order to secure new inputs. Plant A, which obtains the energy of labor at a lower rate per unit, is more efficient in that exchange; it is not more efficient in utilizing the energy so obtained, except for the more intensive use of plant and equipment.

EFFICIENCY AND SURVIVAL

The discussion of efficiency has so far made little reference to the dimension of time. The definition of efficiency as an energic ratio can be applied at any instant of time; the cost of the organizational transformation of inputs into product can be computed for any span of time. Short-term analyses are, as is often the case, easier and more obvious. The previous examples of organizations differing in efficiency have stipulated some of the major short-term advantages of the more efficient organization in comparison to its competitors. The more efficient organization can lower prices and thus gain a larger share of the market. Or it can, at a given market price, make more gross profit than its competitors. It can, as a result, increase the return to the members of any or all of its subsystems. The more efficient organization, in short, is in the process of acquiring an energic surplus, because the terms of its input and output transactions are set by its less efficient competitors.

This operating advantage has long-term implications of importance, beginning with the storage of energy. Efficiency gives a margin over the organizational hand-to-mouth condition in which the return from product is barely sufficient to purchase the inputs needed to repeat the productive cycle. This margin can be immediately distributed as wage payments, bonuses, or dividends. In American industry executive bonuses and dividend payments vary sharply with changes in relative efficiency and gross profits; wage payments are more likely to be set by industrywide standards of collective bargaining, although they too respond to increases or decreases in the margin between organizational income and outgo.

Organizations seldom distribute all of the surplus of income over cost of production, however; they use it to provide *organizational slack* (Cyert and March, 1963). This means the storage of energy in any of a variety of forms. Funds may be set aside for specific purposes— expansion of facilities, replacement of equipment, or fiscal emergencies. Materials may be stockpiled as protection against unexpected interruptions in supply. Staff members may be retained beyond present needs, in order to take advantage of future opportunities.

The most important long-range outcomes of efficiency-generated surpluses are therefore organizational *growth* and increments in the *survival power* of the organization. The storage of energy permits the organization to survive its own mistakes and the exigencies of its environment. For the organization without such storage, every untoward event, internal or external, is in some degree incapacitating, and mishaps of size can be deadly.

The contribution of efficiency to growth is not a one-way or a one-time organizational event; it is a cycle that continues over a wide span of time and a wide range of organizational circumstances, sizes, and structures. Efficiency begets growth, and growth brings new gains in efficiency. There are limits, of course; for any criterion there is some optimum organizational size, and Schumacher (1973) has put the case eloquently for those criteria in terms of which "small is beautiful." But the cost-optimal size for sophisticated technologies and extensive markets is apparently very large, and the relationship of production costs to size can for many purposes be regarded as a linear function.

In the auto industry, for example, the costs of retooling for a substantial change in style or mechanical specification run to hundreds of millions of dollars. General Motors spent $1.1 billion to reduce the size and weight of its 1977 cars. The more units produced during the year by a given company, the lower the cost of retooling that must be borne by each unit. This is an elementary kind of arithmetic, but inexorable. There is, of course, that theoretical point at which size becomes a handicap—a point that seems to come quite early for some attitudinal measures, but very late for production costs and still later for profits. For most organizations, the long-range effects of efficiency are growth and survival, and the effect of growth is likely to be increased efficiency.

EFFICIENCY IN NONPROFIT ORGANIZATIONS

The foregoing analysis was developed in the course of exploring the relationship of two common measures of organizational effectiveness, efficiency and profitability. To what extent is the analysis applicable to human organizations which do not sell products and accumulate profits or losses? We can answer this question by posing another: What does profit signify? It means merely that people "want" the organizational product enough to forego other things and choose it, that is, buy it at a price that covers the costs of production, including profit. This is one way by which the larger social environment permits an organization to import energy—that is, hire people, build plants, and buy materials. If there is an overwhelming preference for other organizational products, or if people lack the economic means to signify their wants by buying, then in effect the organization is denied the means to import energy and it must reduce its operations or go out of existence.

Business organizations differ, of course, in the advantageousness of their environmental transactions. As they become more efficient, they require less energic return in order to maintain their operations. There are also the many forms of special advantage bestowed by location, by exclusive production of certain goods, or by reserves built up from past efficiencies. The basic equation remains, however; in the long run the organization must receive its necessary quantum of energy from outside or it must cease to be, and a business receives this input by selling its product.

For other kinds of organizations, the life-giving or death-dealing energic decisions are made in quite different fashion. A community college does not typically operate at a profit. In a sense, perhaps, the students "buy" its product, and some economists and sociologists have attempted to demonstrate that these decisions to buy are made in terms of the probable increment in lifetime earnings. But the students in the community college (and in most other institutions of higher education, for that matter) do not pay a tuition high enough to permit the organization to hold its faculty and maintain its plant. The real sale of the college product is to the public, and the decision that the organization shall continue is given by the city council or other legislative body which appropriates the funds for operating the college. The legislature has, in effect, "chosen" the product of the community college in preference to other products which might have been had for the same appropriation. In so doing, the legislature makes it possible for the college to import the energy it requires.

The environmental decision to support the college differs in many respects from the decision to support the business establishment. The decision about the college is made formally and explicitly by a legislative body which has the legitimate power to appropriate funds or refuse them, power which in turn has been given to the legislature by the body politic and which can be withdrawn (at least from specific legislators) at the next election. In the case of a business, no purchaser of goods makes the decision to sustain the establishment or commit it to organizational ruin, and yet the sum of individual consumer decisions adds up to that determination.

For some other nonbusiness organizations, the picture is still more complicated. The military, for example, is sustained in part as is the college; it is awarded tax funds by legislative act. Under extraordinary circumstances it may be permitted to import human energy in a more direct fashion by conscription. This, too, in our society requires legislative sanction, but the legislation takes the form of a direct awarding of human energies to the military organization, rather than an awarding of money which enables the organization to attract people. With this important exception, inputs are acquired by the military as by other organizations, through negotiation and purchase.

Organizations to which people offer inputs for instrumental or extrinsic reasons must meet the terms of the exchange by providing extrinsic payments and rewards. In voluntary organizations, on the other hand, the behavior of members is expressive rather than instrumental and the decision to give or withhold organizational inputs is individual and direct. A student weighs the decision to join the Chess Club, wondering whether the psychological return will be sufficiently great and its probability sufficiently high to make it "worth while" to join and invest energy in the activities of the club. If a sufficient number of students decide in favor of the club, it will have an organizational existence. If it fails to return enough psychic satisfaction to its members to motivate their continuing investment of energy, it will go out of existence. The "efficiency" of the club and its prospects for survival are given by the amount of such return to members in relation to the demands made on their time and energy.

The concept of efficiency does not have meaning only for business organizations, and the survival benefits of efficiency are not limited to profit-making organizations. These notions are inherent in the characteristics of human organizations as open systems. They remind us that the ultimate decision to give or withhold the needed organizational inputs lies in the environment, and that the larger social environment in this way holds the power of life and death over every organization.

Under these circumstances, efficiency cannot guarantee survival but almost certainly improves the probability of organizational survival over the long run.

EFFICIENCY AND EFFECTIVENESS

The immediate consequences of a gain in efficiency are, other things being equal, the creation of surplus in some form and therefore the choice of how it shall be used. Some solutions to this problem of allocation are obvious, because they reflect the competing interests of visible constituencies. A company that has become more efficient than its competitors can allocate the resulting gains to its clients by reducing the price or increasing the quality of its product. It can allocate the gains to its owners or stockholders in the form of profits and dividends. It can allocate the gains to its members in any of a variety of ways, from an equal wage increase to all employees, to a bonus given to top management only.

But there are other constituencies and other forms of allocation are possible, although admittedly less probable. The company might make some major public donation or create some facility for the community as a whole, a museum or library, for example. The energic demands of work might be reduced, either by shortening the number of hours required or reducing the pace of the work itself. One can even imagine a decision to increase the variety and challenge offered by jobs in ways that reduce efficiency, thus exchanging those previous gains for potential increases in other organizational outcomes. Gains in efficiency can also be used within the organization, to generate still further gains, by expanding capacity or improving technology. Or they may simply be held as fiscal reserves, to increase the ability of the organization to deal with future uncertainties.

Which of these choices or which combination of them will be taken in a particular situation is a nice problem in the prediction of organizational behavior. Our present problem, however, is to determine which of these choices would constitute an increase in organizational effectiveness. Is one organization more effective than another if it pays higher wages, gives larger managerial bonuses, lowers prices, sends out larger dividend checks, improves technology, makes work more interesting, or adds to the public facilities of the community? The common-sense answer and in this case a helpful one, is that it is a matter of definition; it depends on the goals in terms of which effectiveness is to be assessed.

To define effectiveness in terms of goal attainment, however, is to exchange one difficult definitional problem for another. A goal is a desired or preferred end-state and, if we are to avoid a naive personification of the organization, that means desired or preferred by somebody. Two questions therefore arise: Can organizational effectiveness be defined in terms that go beyond the goals and preferences of some constituent group? If not, on what basis can we choose among the competing preferences of constituencies? We will consider five different ways in which organizational theorists have attempted to answer these questions and thus develop a satisfactory definition of organizational effectiveness: (1) the preferential ordering of constituencies, (2) the linear programming solution, (3) survival as the sovereign criterion, (4) throughput as the organizational goal, and (5) the organizational contribution to the suprasystem.

Preferential Ordering of Constituencies

This approach to the definition of organizational goals and therefore organizational effectiveness begins with the assumption that different constituencies inside and outside the organization will have different goals for it. The approach proceeds by setting criteria for ordering these goals. There is, of course, a position of complete relativism, which acknowledges the differential goals of various organizational constituencies but denies any basis for choosing one over another as a criterion of effectiveness. The relativist position in this case, as in so many others, is logically unassailable but theoretically and pragmatically unsatisfying. It does not explain the complex compromised outcomes of organizational life; it gives no help to those who must choose and wish to choose wisely, nor to those who seek some comprehensive organizational theory; it merely imposes the criterion of competing self-interests and awaits the outcome.

Various ideologies have been invented to support the claims of one or another constituency on the grounds of its numbers and consequent maximization of utility, its need, its alleged moral qualities, or its emergent historical role. Such criteria are essentially normative; a constituency is chosen and organizational effectiveness is defined in terms of its special claims. Pennings and Goodman (1976), however, drawing on the work of Cyert and March (1963) and Thompson (1967) have proposed the concept of the *dominant coalition* as a more sophisticated basis for ordering the incompatible goals of multiple constituencies.

Imagine an organization as a set of individual members who form subsets of interest groups or constituencies. Such groups reflect real conditions of organizational life, especially the distinctive patterns of inducement and contributions (rewards and role requirements) associated with different positions. Each such constituency develops goals for the organization—that is, domains of activity and future states toward which it would prefer the organization to move. These goals reflect the experience, perceptions, and interests of the constituency that develops them and are unlikely to be identical to those of other constituencies. The goals express the values of the constituency, and provide a preference ordering of organizational outcomes that applies both to quantitative differences on particular dimensions and to qualitative differences between dimensions. Thus a constituency would be likely not only to have a position on the desirability of more or less productivity, but also on the relative desirability of more profit versus higher wages.

The political problem of any constituency has been well epitomized by Thompson (1967, pp. 127–128) in the contrast of two phrases: goals *for* the organization and goals *of* the organization— political preferences versus political actualities. The constituency works at its problem with the various means of influence available to it, from collective bargaining to executive negotiation, and typically discovers that its wants exceed its power. Constituencies thus exist under conditions that invite coalition formation.

It is the process of coalition formation that permits an organization to act in spite of differential and incompatible interests and constituencies. Pennings and Goodman (1976) are particularly concerned with the structure and process of such decision making, the transformation of competing goals *for* the organization into the goals *of* the organization. New contracts and agreements are adopted, affiliations and mergers are accepted or refused, acquisitions are made or rejected, fulfilling the wishes of some constituencies and frustrating those of others in varying degrees. Such decisions are formally taken by management and are accepted by the various organizational constituencies; from those facts we infer the goals of the organization. The effectiveness of the organization is then measured by its success in reaching those goals.

How and by whom are the goal-setting decisions really made? In answer Pennings and Goodman propose the concept of the *dominant coalition*. They suggest that for any organization at any given time there is a combination of constituencies, identifiable by their relationship to the basic process of input-transformation-output, which is the ultimate source for ordering goal states, choosing the means for attaining them, and thus defining a scale of organizational effectiveness. The dominant coalition may accept, reject, or modify the proposals of any constituency, but it includes and somehow represents all constituencies. It does not, of course, include all the influential groups outside the organization (blacks, environmentalists, or feminists, for example) but it must be aware of them and cannot avoid responsibility for organizational actions toward such groups.

The concept of the dominant coalition is appealing as a description of organizational functioning. To the extent that factional differences must be resolved, the creation of a dominant coalition can be considered as a necessary condition for organizational effectiveness. The empirical work that might establish its importance, however, remains to be done. That work will require further specification of how members of the dominant coalition can be identified at any moment and how the membership of the coalition changes in response to changes in the environment or in the organization itself. Indeed, it remains to be seen whether the dominant coalition exists as a social entity in organizations, or whether it is merely a construct for describing the bargaining process among constituencies.

The Linear Programming Solution

The notion of effectiveness as a process of optimization among competing criteria suggests the model of linear programming, in which an optimal solution is sought by setting certain constraining conditions and then seeking to maximize (or minimize) some outcome within those constraints. For example, a business organization must pay taxes to several branches of government, must meet minimum wage standards, must maintain certain limits of temperature and air flow within its work place, must dispose of waste products in certain ways, and of course must find a market for its product. What remains after these and other constraining conditions have been met is profit, and profit is the outcome that business organizations are said to maximize. It is the single outcome most often cited by managers as the criterion of effectiveness, the "bottom line." Can we accept that formulation, and use profitability as the criterion of effectiveness, at least in making comparisons among business organizations?

Herbert Simon (1964) argues persuasively against doing so, on the grounds that setting any one of the constraining conditions of organizational life as "the criterion" is arbitrary, a matter of linguistic and analytic convenience. He proposes that these constraints are essentially symmetrical, and uses the example of a manufacturer of cattle feed to demonstrate the equivalence of describing the goal as the production of the best quality possible at a given price or the best price possible at a given quality. His epigrammatic conclusion is that "if you allow me to determine the constraints, I don't care who sets the optimization criterion." Many a business executive has made the same point as a complaint against the constraining conditions imposed before profit maximization, and James Reston's hypothetical newspaper reader, Miss Nomer, showed a grasp of the point from an opposite political position when she described herself as "in favor of private enterprise but in favor of regulating the hell out of it" (*International Herald-Tribune*, September 30, 1976).

Simon believes that every constraint is a "functional requisite for survival," something the organization must by definition do and continue doing in order to survive. Thus,

> in the decision-making situations of real life, a course of action, to be acceptable, must satisfy a whole set of requirements, or constraints. Sometimes one of these requirements is singled out and referred to as the goal of the action. But the choice of one of the constraints, from many, is to a large extent arbitrary. For many purposes it is more meaningful to refer to the whole set of requirements as the (complex) goal of the action. This conclusion applies both to individual and organizational decision-making. (p. 7)

It can be argued that, if the organizational goal is thus plural and complex, there is no definitive basis for weighting or assigning values to the varied dimensions of constraint. Organizational effectiveness consists in meeting or exceeding constraints and becomes a profile rather than a number. There is a counterargument, however, that can be made in terms of the linear programming model. All constraints are not of one kind. Some set standards that must merely be met; performance beyond the standard is inappropriate or unrewarded. Other constraints set minima but imply that more is better. Moreover, organizations are loosely coupled systems and many of the constraints they face are easily met. There is therefore a great deal of internal discretion about the dimensions of performance that are to be maximized. One could incorporate such distinctions into the definition of organizational effectiveness. Thus, paying taxes would be a constraint on a business organization but the maximization of profit would be a goal. Effectiveness would be measured in terms of the latter.

Defining effectiveness in terms of profit maximization, of course, is at best applicable to only one kind of organization and economic system. For other kinds of organizations, the linear programming model requires the identification of some other constraint in terms of which organizational maximization is characteristically attempted. Simon (1964) gives at least limited support to making that identification in terms of hierarchical structure:

> In view of the hierarchical structure that is typical of most formal organizations, it is a reasonable use of language to employ organizational goal to refer particularly to the constraint sets and criteria of search that define roles at the upper levels. Thus it is reasonable to speak of conservation of forest resources as a principal goal of the U.S. Forest Service, or reducing fire losses as a

principal goal of a city fire department. . . . (Similarly) it would be both legitimate and realistic to describe most business firms as directed toward profit making—subject to a number of side constraints. (pp. 21–22)

This procedure meets the requirement of linear programming for a "variable to be maximized," but it is less than satisfactory in other respects. For example, it puts us in the position of measuring the effectiveness of a privately owned airline in terms of profit maximization and of a publicly owned airline in terms of service. This surely oversimplifies the dynamics of both organizations. The linear programming model is powerful when its assumptions are met, but it turns back to us the question with which we began: How does one identify the organizational variables to be maximized?

Survival as the Sovereign Criterion

The limited applicability of the profit criterion, even if it were otherwise acceptable as the measure of effectiveness, urges the search for some concept of wider relevance. Given the multiple outcomes of organizations and the numerous preferences of organizational constituencies, the solution of the sovereign criterion seems particularly attractive. If such a criterion can be discovered or invented, other organizational outcomes will be included or excluded from the index of organizational effectiveness according to their empirical association with the sovereign variable. Such a variable should be subject to precise definition, should be susceptible to empirical measurement, and should be persuasive beyond argument—to the students of human organizations if not to the members of the various constituencies.

Organizational survival has been proposed as such a variable, the sovereign goal of all organizations and the appropriate criterion of organizational effectiveness. Certainly organizational survival has the virtue of finality, and it is intuitively satisfying to define the quick as more effective than the dead. Moreover, organizations behave "as if" survival were a major goal. The business response to the exhaustion of markets is to change products, not to disband. Nonprofit and voluntary organizations (Sills, 1957) seem to exhibit similar efforts at continuity of form, even at the costs of altered function.

The disadvantage of survival as the test of effectiveness, like its appeal, has to do with finality. The demise of an organization is by definition a unique event in its history. Moreover, the life span of organizations is often very long and, if the assessment of effectiveness had to wait in each case until the duration of that span was known, the empirical difficulties would be extreme. We need leading indicators of effectiveness, indicators that are based on the continuing states and outcomes of the organization but predict its survival, much as indicators of morbidity predict mortality. One significant argument for taking the maximization of return as the measure of organizational effectiveness is its hypothesized prediction of organizational survival. There are problems with so organization-centered and exploitative a definition, including the likelihood that a supremely return-maximizing organization might exhaust its sources of supply and thus perish rather than survive.

This problem can be handled in temporal terms; short-term maximization might mean catastrophe in the longer run, therefore effectiveness can be defined as long-term maximization. Yuchtman and Seashore (1967) dealt with the same problem by defining effectiveness as the organization's "ability to exploit its environments in the acquisition of scarce and valued resources to sustain its functioning." (p. 393) In emphasizing the *ability* to maximize rather than the fact of maximization, however, they encounter a problem in measurement; it is difficult to measure the ability of the organization except through its actions. Nevertheless, the notion of effectiveness as some organizationally controlled state of optimization in relation to the environment remains attractive.

Throughput as the Organizational Goal

As a special category of open systems, all organizations share certain properties and confront certain constraints (Chapters 3 and 4). When we wish to make distinctions and comparisons among organizations, however, to understand what the organization "does," we look to the throughput. The throughput of an organization is its response to the objective task posed by the needs of the environment.

One could argue therefore that the throughput embodies the primary goal that the external environment has set for the organization, and that organizational effectiveness ought to be defined in terms of success in attaining that goal. By this criterion the effectiveness of a public utility engaged in the conversion of coal or petroleum to electric power would be measured by the quantity and cost of this throughput (leaving aside for the moment the problem of the relative weighting of these measures). A privately owned electric power company—say Consolidated Edison of New York—and a publicly owned producer of electric power—say the Tenessee Valley Authority—would thus be assessed using the same criterion of effectiveness. The differences in their situations would be described in terms of the constraints they face regarding the accumulation and disposition of surplus. The public agency must presumably break even; the private company must do enough better than that to attract investors.

Approaching the definition of organizational effectiveness in this way is useful and consistent with the systemic view of the organization as itself part of a larger system. Admittedly, to define effectiveness in terms of throughput takes little note of the conflicting definitions of different constituencies, may fail to describe the motivations of management, and may not acknowledge fully the importance of differing constraints (the importance of the profit dynamic in the previous example). Nevertheless, the ultimate justification of an organization's existence and its claim on scarce resources is its throughput, its transformation of energy and material into forms and locations valued for reasons and by individuals outside the organization. The more the throughput, the better its quality, and the less consuming the transformation process, the more we call the organization effective. If one insists on a single effectiveness criterion, the maximization of throughput under specified constraints is a defensible choice.

Organizational Contribution
to the Suprasystem

Parson's proposed analysis of social structure (1956, 1960) would locate each organization by its contribution to the functioning of the next higher order of social structure. The effectiveness of a given organization would then be judged as the magnitude of that contribution. Yuchtman and Seashore (1967; 1973, pp. 495–496) quote the summary passages:

> Since it has been assumed that an organization is defined by the primacy of a type of goal, the focus of its value-system must be the legitimation of this goal in terms of the functional significance of its attainment for the superordinate system, and secondly, the legitimation of the primacy of this goal over other possible interests and values of the organization and its members. . . . For the business firm, money return is a primary measure and symbol of success and is thus part of the goal structure of the organization. But it cannot be the primary organizational goal because profit-making is not by itself a function on behalf of the society as a system.

The basic question in assessing the effectiveness of an organization thus becomes "how well the organization is doing for the suprasystem." It is an appropriate criterion. Organizations are contrived systems, and that fact implies some purpose external to the organizations themselves. There are two problems in defining organizational effectiveness in this way, one of them involving the multiplicity of organizational outputs and the other the nature of the relationship between the organization and the suprasystem. The outputs of complex organizations are usually numerous and their ramifying effects on the larger system are correspondingly many and difficult to trace. As a result the conceptual neatness of Parson's phrase—the functional significance of the organization's attainment for the superordinate system—becomes somewhat ragged in application to specific ongoing organizations. Does the functional significance of a large private airline consist in the facilitation of business transactions, the creation of jobs, the maintenance of dispersed kinship structures, or the improvement of international relations? Functional significance is only slightly less diffuse a term than organizational effectiveness.

The second difficulty with the Parsonian formulation was discussed by Gouldner (1959) shortly after its publication, and involves the issue of autonomy and interdependence. To define organizational effectiveness solely in terms of the contribution of the organization to the functioning of the suprasystem, Gouldner argues, emphasizes the interdependence of parts and the organization as a part. In so doing, this definition neglects the autonomy of the organization, its partial independence, and its exercise of choice.

The concept of effectiveness as functional contribution to the next superordinate level of organization fits best as a characterization of closely coupled systems in which each part has a single function and no independence. The function of the spark plug in an internal combustion engine is to ignite the mixture of gas and air at the peak of the compression stroke. It is effective if it does so invariably, and becomes less effective as variance increases. Nothing is lost when we define that performance as the effectiveness of the plug. But the organization has many outcomes, some of which can be described as functional contributions to the larger society, some of which can best be described at the level of the organization itself, and some of which are of significance primarily to the individuals of whose behaviors the organization is comprised. The range of organizational choice includes the possibility of trade-off across such outcome levels. Seashore and Yuchtman (1967) overcorrect for this emphasis on the organization as part of the suprasystem, we believe. As they put it, the crucial question shifts from the Parsonian query, "How well is the organization doing for the superordinate system?" to "How well is the organization doing for itself?" This definition of effectiveness as maximization at the organizational level deserves some further consideration.

MAXIMIZING RETURN TO THE ORGANIZATION

We have seen that efficiency in organizations increases the possibility for energy storage, and is conducive to long-run growth and survival. Efficiency, however, is a criterion of the internal life of the organization, especially the economic and technical aspects. By itself, it takes inadequate notice of the openness of human organizations. This is especially true when the efficiency concept is applied for a short time-span and a single location.

When we concern ourselves with longer time periods and comparisons among different locations, it is clear that organizational success depends not only on internal efficiency but also on the advantageousness of boundary transactions. Such transactions involve persuasion and the use of influence. The terms of purchase and sale must be negotiated. We can generalize this point by stating that environmental transactions are in some degree *political;* they involve the making and engineering of choice on grounds other than economics and efficiency in an open market.

The pursuit of organizational advantage by political means is prevalent, and a most natural outcome of the dynamics of organization. The very achievement of internal organizational efficiency promotes growth and, if continued, dominance with some degree of monopolistic control over the terms of procurement and marketing. But even where that degree of internal efficiency has not been attained, a company has much to gain in overall effectiveness by using political tactics. Some of these tactics have been outlawed for almost a century (although the simultaneous existence of antitrust and "fair-trade" legislation suggests confusion and ambivalence in these matters). Conspiracy in restraint of trade, monopolistic dominance in an industrial field, price fixing among major producers, and the like are illegal. They are nevertheless live legal issues, and few years pass without trials and suits of substantial scope. Political advantages in sale and purchase are pressed, and the number of corporations (and corporate executives) that choose to live dangerously near the legal margin gives testimony to the rewards of doing so.

Many forms of political influence in the service of organizational goals are judged legitimate by the larger society. We are indignant at side-payments and prosecute some forms of bribery. It is considered appropriate, however, for an organization to attempt to bring about advantageous environmental relationships by persuasion of influential people or by formal lobbying. The resulting advantages may take the form of subsidies, as in the case of airlines and the merchant marine, or special tax arrangements, as for oil and gas producers. They may take the form of tariffs and duties or legislation to weaken union influence on the conditions under which business is conducted. It is no less an example of political means in the service of organizational goals, of course, when labor unions create their own legislative programs and political campaigns.

Political and economic transactions merge in some instances. A company with sufficient resources to afford the maneuver may reduce prices below the cost of production for a time, in order to eliminate or make more tractable a competitor who lacks the cushion of stored resources to survive such a program. This is essentially a political tactic, although the immediate means involve economic manipulation.

It is not necessary for our present purposes to attempt a catalogue of political extensions of organizational control over the environment. It is important to recognize such extensions as inevitable outcomes of the organizational dynamic for maximizing returns from the environment and thus prospects for growth, security, and survival. The textbook path to organizational survival is internal efficiency: build the better mousetrap or build the old trap less expensively. There is, however, a whole class of alternative or supplementary solutions—the political devices that maximize organizational return at some cost to other organizations or individuals. These alternatives we have called political, in contrast to the economic or technical alternatives.

Economic-technical solutions are reflected as increases in organizational efficiency. They make the organization a more efficient system for the transformation of energy and thereby contribute to its growth and survival. They do not necessarily make the organization more efficient in the acquisition of inputs and the disposal of outputs. Political solutions complement economic ones by dealing with problems of input and disposal in other ways, usually involving direct manipulation of the environment. Both economic and political means contribute to profitability and to the maximization of return to the organization.

The examples of political activities we have offered have dealt entirely with external transactions—with arrangements to maintain price levels, to get subsidies or other preferments, to eliminate or restrict competition, or to get some commitment to obtain inputs on advantageous terms. The use of political means to obtain organizational advantage need not be directed outside the organization, however. We would also define as political rather than technical most devices for getting more energic investment from the worker for each wage dollar. Extreme cases make the point obvious: slavery is a political institution, a set of political means for guaranteeing labor input to organizations concerned with agriculture and construction. The institution of indenture provides another example.

We would argue also that, if one firm pays lower wages than another, or induces its workers to work longer hours, or to work harder, all these would constitute political increments to organizational return. And the opposition to such attempts takes political forms—in terms of the demand for collective bargaining, for a minimum wage, for a contractual agreement about hours of work and speed of work.

There is admittedly a certain arbitrariness in deciding where to draw the line between increments in organizational return that will be considered gains in efficiency and those that will be considered the result of political advantage. It is tempting to draw it at the organizational boundary. This would have the effect, however, of defining as efficiency all internal arrangements that increased the organizational return—whether by improvements in the energic ratio of input required to create a given amount of product, or by devices for inducing increased energic input from organizational members. We prefer to distinguish between these two kinds of increments, keeping the term efficiency to describe the former and including the latter with other, externally oriented political approaches.

There is in this distinction no implication that to increase organizational return by means of efficiency gains is virtuous and to do so by political means is reprehensible. The value issues involved require separate argument and justification. The neutrality of the political classification can perhaps be illustrated by those programs which are designed to induce greater energic input from organizational members and also to increase the psychological return to those members. If such a program were successful, it would have increased the return to the organization by political means rather than by improving the efficiency ratio.

Maximizing the return to the organization has certain common effects, regardless of whether it results from increments in efficiency, from advantageous transactions with various outside agencies and groups, or from similarly advantageous bargains with members of the organization itself. Increased return contributes to the immediate profitability of the enterprise and to its growth and survival power for the longer term. Short-term advantages in such matters tend to be reinforced and made "permanent" by precedent and legal recognition. Moreover, economic and political factors interact; causes in one category may have consequences in the other. Organizational returns that accrue because of efficiency, for example, may permit successful political initiatives that could not otherwise be carried out. And political advantages, say in procurement or sales, have economic consequences; they are undertaken for that reason.

The preceding exposition of efficiency and political transactions in the short term and the longer run is summarized in Figure 8-1.

FRAMES OF REFERENCE AND
ORGANIZATIONAL EFFECTIVENESS

We have been discussing the maximization of return to the organization, as determined by a combination of its efficiency as a system and

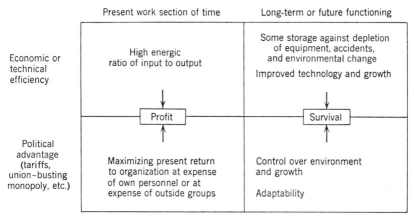

Figure 8-1 *Maximization of organizational return.*

its success in obtaining on advantageous terms the inputs it requires. We have distinguished between such maximization in the short-term and the long-term sense, and we have identified the marks of long-term maximization as storage, growth, control over the environment, and survival. The discussion has taken place primarily within the organizational frame of reference, and maximization at that level constitutes one definition of organizational effectiveness. It is probably the definition that comes nearest to the "organizational" point of view, at least as expressed by owners and managers. From this frame of reference, the only limitation on the maximization principle is that the organization shall not incapacitate its environment as a source of inputs and a receiver of outputs, since doing so would reduce its own effectiveness or even its power to survive.

Maximization to that seemingly self-destructive point is by no means uncommon. The hardwood forests of northern Michigan were destroyed to smelt ore and produce lumber, and the organizations engaged in those activities did not survive the destruction of those local inputs. Similar examples could be provided with respect to soil depletion for the sake of some large-scale cash crop. And the destruction of fishing grounds by ships that are semi-automated factories for the gathering and processing of herring, tuna, and other ocean fish has become a serious international problem.

We have attempted to deal with this anomaly in the definition of organizational effectiveness by extending the time frame; the organization that maximizes in perpetuity must avoid depleting its environment. Yuchtman and Seashore (1967) handled the problem with similar results by defining effectiveness as power unexercised; the maximally effective organization has "the ability . . . to exploit its environment in the acquisition of scarce and valued resources," but exercises that ability to the optimum rather than the maximum. Optimum "is the point beyond which the organization endangers itself, because of a depletion of its resource-producing environment or the devaluation of the resource, or because of the stimulation of countervailing forces within that environment." These definitions are attempts to retain the organizational level as the systemic frame of reference and to satisfy—or optimize—the requirements of other systemic levels as well. Such a happy convergence of optima requires a breadth and depth of perspective seldom attained within organizations—renunciation of short-term organizational maximization in favor of long-term and supra-organizational considerations. Hardin (1968) has dramatized this point in his discussion of the "tragedy of the commons," the publicly owned ground in New England towns of another day, which any farmer could use for pasture (See Chapter 17.) The best strategy for any individual acting as an individual at any particular moment in competition with other individuals was to seek a greater share of this common resource. Unfortunately, when all individuals so acted, the common resource was depleted and all suffered from its depletion.

Milsum (1972) has examined the principle of maximization as it applies to the ecological performance of biological species, and concludes that survival seems "to be related more to *stability* of living systems than . . . to maximization of biomass." He says that "if particular subsystems of a larger system operate so as to optimize their own individual 'good' (performance indices), the net result will almost never be overall system optimization." The implication, for Milsum, is that the operation of systems at each level must be subject to constraints that represent the requirements for well-being at the next higher level in the systemic hierarchy.

This is persuasive, but it leaves unanswered the question of how those requirements for the good of the larger system are to be assessed and by what organizational means they are to be imposed, if necessary, on other human organizations. There are times when societal needs, especially in the short term, seem very clear and the larger society can therefore impose limitations or inefficiencies on organizations with very broad agreement for doing so. In effect, the society asks the organization to become less effective or efficient in its own terms in order to become more effective in meeting the needs of the suprasystem. The sharpest examples can be found in the wartime operation of industry. The short-term demand of the larger society for maximizing gross product takes precedence over all the usual criteria of organizational efficiency. Production costs become almost irrelevant; criteria of employee selection are rewritten. The cost-plus contract is not merely a pressing of organizational advantage for purposes of profit; it symbolizes the abandonment of one set of criteria and frame of reference for another.

A less belligerent but perhaps more controversial example is provided by the massive effort of organizations, public and private, that culminated in the landings on the moon. Bauer and his colleagues (1967), in analyzing the impact of these activities on American society, raise many questions of the ultimate ratio of costs to benefits. Nevertheless, the NASA effort exemplifies the modification of some criteria of organizational effectiveness in the service of goals enunciated at a higher (or at least different) organizational level in the society.

We can imagine a similar imposition of supersystem criteria with respect to any goal of great social importance. The identification of such goals is essentially a problem in values rather than organizational theory as such. We might decide, for example, that the importance of discovering causes and cures for cancer in the least possible time is far more important than making such discoveries at the least possible cost, or in ways that conform to the usual signs of organizational efficiency. The indications of such a decision would be the availability of massive inputs for cancer-related research, willingness to support conflicting approaches simultaneously instead of in some sequence of learning, tolerance of duplication, and many other violations of the etiquette of efficiency. It is interesting that the word *war* (war on disease, war on poverty) is in general use to indicate the abandonment of the organizational frame of reference and the launching of a major effort in which the societal frame of reference defines effectiveness.

These examples, it could be argued, impose certain losses in efficiency but do not entail deviations from the principle of organizational maximization. To the contrary, the meeting of public needs seems often to have been rewarded with organizational growth and private fortune. It remains to be seen whether societal needs that challenge the maximization principle of organizations more directly—energy conservation and pollution control, for example—can be successfully incorporated into the organizations themselves.

The conflict between the organizational and societal frames of reference is primarily spatial; it has to do with the number of organizations, roles, and individuals to be considered in setting and applying the criteria of effectiveness. It has also a temporal aspect; short-term maximization and long-term dissolution is a conceivable organizational strategy; at the societal level it is pathological.

In short, if we accept the value premise of the greatest good for the greatest number for the longest time, the principle of organizational constraints would seem to follow. The problem, of course, is how such constraints shall be exercised. Certainly we cannot assume that the successive levels of control in the social hierarchy necessarily embody

successively broader societal interests. Greater wisdom and benefi-
cence are not necessarily exercised at the level of the nation-state than
the community, nor at the United Nations than the nation-state.

The principle of the greatest good for the greatest number and the
longest time may be acceptable as principle, but it requires omniscience
in application. In the absence of such an ideal state, the use of multiple frames of reference for the assessment of organizational effectiveness seems to us inevitable. At the organizational level, the
maximization dynamic will be dominant, and the needs of other and
larger social aggregations (community, nation, human race, ecosystem)
must enter the organization as constraints on maximization.

Such constraints will in turn represent the goals of other organizations, public, private, and voluntary. The relationship among human
organizations is thus less the well-ordered hierarchy that Milsum describes in other contexts, and more a network in which each organization has for its environment a set of other and constraining organizations. Organizational effectiveness consists of maximization within
these constraints.

SUMMARY

Organizational effectiveness has been subject to numerous
and conflicting definitions. An attempt is made to resolve such
conflicts by distinguishing among several components of organizational effectiveness.

Organizational efficiency is the first such component, and is defined as the ratio of energic output to energic input. Efficiency thus
tells us how much of the input of an organization emerges as product and how much is absorbed by the system. Further distinctions
are made between human energy and materials as organizational inputs, between direct and indirect uses of human energy in organizations, and between the use of materials as supplies and as equipment. The computation of organizational efficiency is shown to be
dependent on the spatial and temporal definitions of organization.

A further distinction is introduced between the potential efficiency of an organization and its actual efficiency. This distinction
contrasts the elegance of a given organizational design with the
degree to which a given design is realized in organizational practice.

Efficiency is also distinguished from profit, although the two are
asserted to be strongly related. The contribution of efficiency to survival is discussed in terms of the storage of energy which efficiency
permits and the consequent margin for error which it provides.

The choice an organization makes in the allocation of its resources is subject to varying theoretical assumptions. One such postulation is of some sovereign criterion of effectiveness such as survival. Another is in terms of meeting its essential function or throughput. A third theory would emphasize contributions to the suprasystem. A fourth invokes linear programming, which first meets important constraints such as taxes and other obligations before maximizing benefits. Finally, there is the empirical solution of the decisions of the dominant coalition in the system.

The chapter concludes with an explication of organizational effectiveness as the maximization of return to the organization by all means. Such maximization by economic and technical means has to do with efficiency; maximization by noneconomic or political means increases effectiveness without adding to efficiency. Increases in effectiveness by both means are typically observable as storage of energy, organizational growth, organizational endurance and survival, and as organizational control of the surrounding environment. All definitions of effectiveness involve some assumptions with respect to frame of reference. Two such frames are considered, that of the organization as a system in its own right, and that of the larger society or system of which the organization is a subsystem.

■ ORGANIZATIONAL
■ MODELS

OUTLINE

Community versus Organization
Classical Bureaucratic Models
    Machine Theory
    Basic Assumptions in Weberian Theory
        Neglect of Maintenance Subsystem in Weberian Model
    Unanticipated Dysfunctional Consequences
        The Merton Model
        The Gouldner Model

Talcott Parsons and the Structural-Functionalists
    Barnard's Equilibrium Model

Theories of Conflict: Marx and Dahrendorf
    Blau's Classification Based on Prime Beneficiary
    The Reimer Modification

The Chinese Experience and the Maoist Ideal
Socio-Technical Systems
The Human Relations Approach and the Likert Model
The Aggregation Model of Janowitz and
the Temporary Society of Bennis and Slater
The Etzioni Model of Compliance and Power
Organizational Models and Their Limitations
A Threefold Categorization of Motivational Patterns
for Organizational Functioning
    Compliance with Rules
    Responsiveness to Economic Returns and External Rewards
    Value Consensus and Intrinsic Rewards

Relationship of Motivational Framework to Other Concepts of
Organizational Functioning
Unintended Consequences of Emphasis on a Given Motivational Pattern
Summary

COMMUNITY VERSUS ORGANIZATION

Our organizational society with its fractionation and its multiplicity of specific associations is often contrasted with an older folk society where the dominant social unit was the community and the dominant form of authority was traditionalism. The community consists of the social interaction of people in primary group settings, where persons react to one another in good part as personalities and not just as role incumbents. Organized groupings similar to the community are marked by their *expressive* rather than their *instrumental* functions. Ferdinand Tönnies (1887) developed his famous ideal types of *Gemeinschaft* and *Gesellschaft* to differentiate between the group that is held together by *common ties of feeling* and the organization that integrates roles around *instrumental objectives*.[1] A mutual aid and admiration society, such as a college fraternity, exemplifies a *Gemeinschaft* and an industrial firm that manufactures automobiles illustrates a *Gesellschaft*. The distinction is captured nicely by Rudolf Heberle (1968) in his statement:

> Certain entities, for example, social clubs or religious sects, result from mutual sympathy habits, or common beliefs, and are willed for their intrinsic value; other entities, for example, most business associations, are intended by their constituents to be means to specific ends. (p. 100)

Historically, we can also understand our organizational age by contrasting it with what was the dominant social institutional pattern of many folk societies—namely feudalism. A feudal system is distinguished from a developed capitalistic society in a number of ways. The most important of these involves the nature of authority, as Weber's classic analysis made clear. Where the source of authority is traditional and is sanctioned by the customs of the past, there is little leeway for progressive modifications based on empirical outcomes. A way of doing things is right not because it works but because it was ordained as the proper way in tribal teaching. Tradition bound individuals and their descendants to obligations to the end of time. A landowner yielded the use of land to a vassal on condition that the produce from it was entailed forever. Not only was there a blanket, long-running com-

---

[1]To use Tönnies' own language: "The sharpest contrast, then, arises if affirmation of a social entity for its own sake is distinguished from an affirmation of such an entity because of an end, or purpose which is extraneous to it." From page 65 of "The Concept of Gemeinschaft" as found in the English translation in *Ferdinand Toennies on Sociology: Pure, Applied and Empirical; Selected Writings;* edited by Werner J. Cahnman and Rudolf Heberle, Chicago: University of Chicago Press, 1971. The original paper *Gemeinschaft* and *Gesellschaft* was in manuscript form in 1880–1881.

mitment but the vassal was obligated to remain on the land, and the lord was obligated to afford him protection. Instead of a simple cash transaction specific to some function, we have a cumbersome arrangement that confuses personality and role. The older pattern involved fewer sets of relationships for individuals but those arrangements were more complex.

Traditional authority was outmoded as it competed with the rational authority of bureaucracy in the seventeenth and eighteenth centuries, and its demise was marked by the English, American, and French revolutions. The bureaucratic model distinguished between people and the many roles they might play, and it made roles an impersonal set of requirements for all who happened to play them. Entrance into these roles and promotion into the role system was a matter of technical training and proficiency. Moreover, the criteria for selection and promotion were universalistic—they applied to all candidates. *Acquired*, and not *ascribed*, characteristics were all-important. Awarding a medical degree was justified not upon ascribed status, such as being born in a noble family, but upon competence in medical studies. Roles were differentiated and coordinated according to their contribution to the outcome of some collective effort. In other words, functional contribution toward task accomplishment became the overriding consideration.

CLASSICAL BUREAUCRATIC MODELS

The rise of bureaucratic structures in the early capitalistic era inspired the classical model of Weber (1947) and its derivatives in the public administration theory of Gulick (1937) and the scientific management approach of Taylor (1923). Weber's concern was with the fundamental processes of formalization and legitimation by which role systems are elaborated and sanctioned. The public administration school and the advocates of scientific management, although both derived from Weber's basic assumptions, were more interested in the practical problems of organizing for effective functioning.

It will be recalled that there are primary tasks confronting organizations: (1) environmental transactions to insure the supply of material inputs and the acceptance of outputs; (2) production, creating the throughput or work that gets done, and (3) maintenance, or attracting, holding, and motivating people to perform. Most classical theories addressed themselves to one of these three sets of issues, production problems.

Machine Theory

Machine theory (Worthy 1950) is a graphic name for several production-emphasizing accounts of bureaucratic functioning, especially those of Weber, Gulick, and Taylor. The organization, although it consists of people, is viewed by all three as a machine, and they imply that just as we build a mechanical device with given specifications for accomplishing a task, so we construct an organization according to a blueprint to achieve a given purpose. Human needs and abilities enter mainly as physiological limits or constraints. More recent writers have labeled machine theory the mechanical as opposed to the organic conception of organizations (Burns and Stalker, 1961).

Basic Assumptions in the Machine or Weberian Model

The major assumptions, explicit or implicit, in the classical Western model of bureaucracy are:

1. *Process specialization of tasks.* Efficiency can be attained by subdividing any operation into its elements. These partial tasks can be taught, expertness in their execution can be readily attained, and responsibility for their performance can easily be fixed.

2. *Standardization of role performance.* As tasks become fractionated, their performance becomes standardized. There is one best way to perform a task, and it should be taught and enforced. Such institutionalization of functions also protects against costly blunders. At higher levels in the organization the same logic is followed by prescribing not only the purpose of the role but the means for achieving this purpose.

3. *Unity of command and centralization of decision making.* The organization is conceived of as a machine, but it is not necessarily self-directing. To maintain the coordination of the whole, decisions must be centralized in one command, and to attain perfect coordination there should be *person-to-person responsibility* down the line. There should be no bypassing of a hierarchical level as messages are relayed up and down the line. To further insure unity of command there must be *a limited span of control*, so that no person at any hierarchical level has more immediate subordinates than he or she can control.

4. *Uniformity of practices.* Not all behavior in the organization can be prescribed by task standardization. Much behavior must be controlled by the specification of uniform institutionalized practices. Thus the same personnel procedures should be followed with respect to all individuals in a given status.

5. *No duplication of function.* One part of the organization should not duplicate functions being performed by another. Operations for the whole organization should be centralized. The army,

navy, and air forces should not have separate purchasing departments. Different departments in an enterprise should not have their own travel and transportation units but should have their needs met by one centralized section.

6. *Rewards for merit.* Selection and promotion of personnel should be on the basis of technical proficiency for the task and achievement in its performance. This means recruiting and upgrading people for performance and formal qualifications, not on the basis of personal friendship nor *ascribed status.* Membership in a social class or race is irrelevant; in theory meritocracy replaces either personal or institutional favoritism.

7. *Depersonalization of office.* The office is independent of the particular incumbent, who is responded to not because of personal attributes but because he or she occupies an official position with limited and prescribed perogatives.

The net effect of these assumptions is to produce a system that is universalistic rather than particularistic. It is government by rules and regulations, and not by individuals. All people are entitled to equal treatment under the law and equity becomes a central concept in Weberian bureaucracy. This describes the ideal model; in practice departures from the model are common.

These concepts are seen at their clearest in military organizations. Machine theory has also been especially applicable to large-scale organizations engaged in the mass production of goods and commodities. The assembly line is an example of the efficiency that is sometimes attainable through the use of this approach to organization. The concepts of machine theory have, however, infiltrated thinking about almost all types of organizations.

An application of the machine model to administration in general can be seen in Gulick's analysis (1937) of administrative functions, in which he presented a contentless list of activities cutting across all organizations—activities assumed relevant regardless of the knowledge or technical expertise of the tasks performed by a specific enterprise. Gulick named these general executive functions: planning, organizing, staffing, directing, coordinating, reporting and budgeting.

The scientific management approach probably pushed more strenuously than the other classical models toward specification of how tasks should be organized. It envisaged people, in the words of March and Simon (1958), as "adjuncts to machines." Time and motion studies were its principal tools. Rest periods during the working day were studied in terms of the optimum recovery from psychological fatigue. Wages and incentive pay as the sources of motivation were conceived of in terms of a model of economic man. Moreover, the scientific management approach dealt almost exclusively with the production structure of the organization and had little to say about the maintenance, institutional, and managerial structures, except that the same rational economic man was assumed to inhabit all of them.

"Scientific management," in Taylor's sense of the term, continues to dominate the field of industrial engineering and factory design, although its principles are increasingly contested. Moreover, the newer field of man-machine systems (usually called ergonomics outside the United States) incorporates many of the same assumptions. Chapanis (1976) describes its concept of the worker "as a biological and psychological constant with many innately determined abilities and limitations." The task then becomes one of "changing the machines and the tools with which man worked, or the environment in which he worked, to make the job better suited to the man." But "suited" in this context means merely within the range of individual capacities, physiological and psycho-physiological.

Machine theory was sometimes wrong and sometimes right in its basic tenets, but it was almost always inadequate in dealing with the complexities of organizational structure and functioning. It lacked the power of open system theory to deal with significant organizational variables. Specifically, (1) it took little account of the constant commerce of the system with its environment. Constantly changing environmental influences necessitate constant changes in the organization. (2) It neglected many types of input-output exchange with the environment. It restricted input to raw materials and labor power. That input also consists of the values and needs that people bring with them into the organization was ignored. That input, in addition, consists of the social support of surrounding structures and of the public was also ignored. On the output side there was a similar exclusion of all outcomes besides the physical product exported. (3) The concepts of machine theory paid little attention to the subsystems of organization with their differential dynamics and their own interchange within the organization. In the process of interchange each subsystem codes and filters its input according to its own characteristics. The mutual influencing of the different subsystems and the problems of their interrelationships are dealt with sparsely, if at all, in the older theories. (4) The semiformal and informal structures created within the formal organization, often as a reaction to its inadequacies, were also conspicuously neglected. Merton (1957) and other sociologists have described the unintended and dysfunctional consequences of organizing according to machine principles. (5) Machine theory conceived of organizational constancy as a rigid, static arrangement of parts. Open systems, and all organizations are open systems, are indeed characterized by the maintenance of a steady state, but this maintenance is a dynamic process of preserving patterns of relationships by constant adjustments.

March and Simon (1958) sum up many of the weaknesses of machine theory when they state:

> It is because activities are conditional, and not fixed in advance, that problems of organization, over and above the assignment problem, arise. For convenience, we may make the following specifications, without interpreting them too strictly:
> (a) the times of occurrence of activities may be conditional on events external to the organization or events internal to the organization;
> (b) the appropriateness of a particular activity may be conditional on what other activities are being performed in various parts of the organization;
> (c) an activity elaborated in response to one particular function or goal may have consequences for other functions or goals. (p. 27)

Neglect of Maintenance Subsystem in the Weberian Model

The Weberian model was developed to take account of the production subsystem of organization instead of the maintenance subsystem. The maintenance side includes the rewards and returns for staying in the system, the socialization of people in the system, and the recruitment of people for elite positions. But traditional bureaucratic standards of functional specificity, of universalism, of rewards for achievement rather than ascription are developed more for the technical production subsystem than for the managerial or maintenance subsystems. In the managerial and maintenance subsystem the meritocracy of the production subsystem is diluted by particularism and ascription. In the production subsystem workers may be paid according to the amount they produce or the number of hours they work. Engineers are recruited, promoted, and paid on the basis of technical proficiency. In the managerial subsystem ascription often operates in that managers may be recruited from a small group of graduates from highly selective institutions. Non-ability factors (Quinn et al., 1969) enter significantly into promotions.

The rewards, moreover, that the maintenance system uses to recruit and hold people are not necessarily based on proficiency in task accomplishment. In fact, here we encounter one of the basic contradictions in the Weberian model. The procedures to achieve technological efficiency are not conducive to maximizing motivation to produce. For example, the set speed of the assembly line prevents individual workers from affecting the quantity of their performance. Moreover, jobs are set up and standardized so that individuals are easily replaceable. Differences in performance within the same role are negligible because the system has been set up to eliminate such differences. It is a model designed to make motivational differences irrelevant.

Different roles may carry different responsibilities, and there is some basis here for different levels of reward. Nonetheless, the great majority of people within an organization may be so interdependent in the production process that it is difficult to work out justifiable wage differences. In other words, as the production subsystem develops along the lines of the Weberian model, it closes over the possibilities for tying performance to motivation to perform. A similar contradiction can be seen in the pyramidal structure of the organization, which is necessitated by the need for unified coordination and control. A pyramidal structure in general permits very few chances for promotion.

Another basic contradiction in the model is that the stated requirements for a position in the production subsystem are only the training and skills for doing a technical task. In this model the functional specificity of a job defines the technical proficiency involved, but does not take into account psychological qualities that will make the person a dedicated and loyal member of the organization. The Chinese apparently sacrifice some technical proficiency for the motivational advantages of internalized group goals (see pages 273–276). Thus even at the level of first line supervision political purity of the applicant is a criterion. The Chinese model then takes criteria from the maintenance system as well as criteria from the production system for the recruitment of people to leadership positions.

Older models of organization combined the production and maintenance (motivational) functions in a somewhat different fashion. Leadership groups were recruited from elite categories or were especially trained and socialized for leadership roles. They came into given organizations already incorporating the social values and collective goals that would make them dedicated organizational members. The British recruited their leadership in this fashion as did many of the colonial powers. The Ottoman Empire gave special attention to recruiting promising youngsters from its subject populations for special training. These elite groups, either because of organizational ascription or because of their special training, were then accorded a status within the organization that could not be achieved by the rank and file. The great bulk of the organizational members were kept in line by the power of the elite groups, which had control of information, of rewards, and of sanctions. The Chinese pattern essentially broadens the base of this type of system by making upward mobility possible through achievement. The achievement, however, includes absorbing political values as well as technical skills.

Unanticipated Dysfunctional Consequences

A number of sociologists, following the lead of Robert Merton, have pointed out the inadequacies of machine theory. They emphasize the dysfunctional consequences of unanticipated, yet logical, outcomes of bureaucratic structure. These theorists have made valuable contributions to our understanding of organizations but they have limited themselves to single, though different, aspects of organizational dysfunctioning. March and Simon have presented an incisive analysis of these models and the following account summarizes their analysis.

The Merton Model

The Merton model (1957) starts from the problem, already described, of reducing the variability of human behavior to predictable patterns necessary for organizational functioning. From this demand for control comes the emphasis on reliable behavior, for which the resort is to rule enforcement. Standard procedures are outlined and supervision instituted with penalties for deviant behavior. The anticipated consequence is achieved when people follow role prescriptions and use categorization as a basis for making decisions. Problems are approached in terms of some ready organizational precedent rather than a thorough search for alternatives. The emphasis on role and position decreases personalized relations (Figure 9-1).

The unintended consequences of such reliance on rules and their enforcement include a rigidity of behavior which in turn increases the amount of difficulty with clients. The official follows the easily invoked rule even though it may not be the most appropriate response to the problem presented by the client. Rigidity reduces organizational effectiveness, and risks the support of clientele. It is no accident that the sales division of an organization tries to counteract this tendency by adopting the motto that the customer is always right. On the other hand, as long as rule enforcement continues to be the main emphasis in the organization, rigidity of behavior is fostered by the easy defensibility of individual action which adheres to the rules. The difficulty this rigidity creates with clients only reinforces the original pattern of lack of discriminating behavior on the part of the organization members. Since they are challenged in the performance of their duties, their defense is to fall back on some highly visible rule to prove that they have only been doing their duty as prescribed by statute. They are primarily concerned not with solving the problem of the client, but with the defensibility of their own behavior. Hence the client problem becomes aggravated.

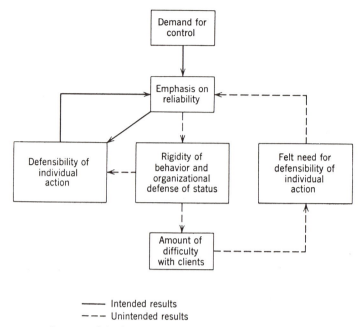

Figure 9-1. *The simplified Merton model. (From* Organizations, *James G. March and Herbert A. Simon, New York, Wiley: 1958, p. 41.)*

The Merton model rightly calls attention to an important unanticipated dysfunctional consequence of the heavy reliance on rule enforcement to insure reliable patterns of behavior. But it is a simplified model dealing with one unanticipated consequence of one major type of control employed in organizations. The increased problem with clients growing out of rigidity of organizational behavior is a specific illustration of the failure to recognize the true character of organizations as open systems in constant interaction with a dynamic environment.

The Merton example applies primarily to the members on the boundaries of the organization who deal with the outside public. The same rigidity, however, can develop among the people on the inside of the organization in their observance of rules. The unintended consequences can be similar to those Merton emphasizes with respect to clients. There can be increased problems of one subsystem of the organization relating to another subsystem with resulting failures in cooperation, communication, and coordination. Another dysfunctional consequence within the organization itself is the lack of innovative and spontaneous behavior necessary for effective organizational functioning. It is impossible to prescribe role requirements precisely and completely or lay down rules with sufficient specificity to cover all contingencies arising in a single week of work of a complex organization. An enterprise must rely both on stable role patterns and the spontaneous actions of people directed toward the accomplishment of organizational goals. An almost exclusive emphasis upon rule enforcement, with its resulting rigidity, can destroy this innovative aspect of organizational functioning.

In Chapter 3 we pointed to three sources of patterned cooperation which account for the existence of organizations: (1) interdependence with respect to task accomplishment, (2) shared norms and values, and (3) rule enforcement. Machine theory neglects the *shared values* and disregards the group parameters of task interdependence. Reliance on *rule enforcement* limits the attainment of organizational objectives either because it fails to call into play some of the needed types of behavior (it may in fact inhibit them) or because it leads to other types of dysfunctional consequence.

The Gouldner Model

A similar attempt to spell out one type of dysfunctional effect of machine theory is found in the work of Gouldner (1954). The Gouldner model, like the Merton model, starts with the demand for control being met by the use of general, impersonal rules. Gouldner stresses the impersonal nature of the rules, which decreases the visibility of power relations within the group. (In a democratic society it is assumed that members of an organization will be more highly motivated when their supervisors are not arbitrary authority figures.)

The unanticipated consequence of the general, impersonal rules, however, is the creation of minimum acceptable standards of organizational behavior. The minimum standards of performance tend to become the common pattern of most organization members and thus become the maximum standards as well. The person who deviates in the direction of higher performance is the rate buster, the eager beaver, the company man or woman. Minimum performance, however, leads to a discrepancy between organizational goals (held by leaders) and organizational accomplishment. Pressure is put on supervisors to check more closely on subordinates. This increases the visibility of power relations within the group, leads to an increase of interpersonal tension, and disturbs the equilibrium of the system (Figure 9-2).

The Gouldner model correctly calls attention to some of the self-defeating effects of reliance on rule enforcement. It does not, however, inquire into the psychological inputs into the organization which account for the dysfunctional outcomes. Nor does it deal with consequences other than the acceptance of minimal standards and the increased tension in the group growing out of close supervision.

The specific models described above have pointed out the de-

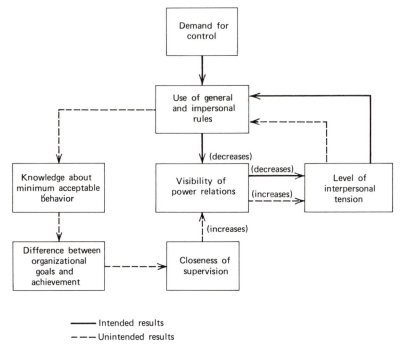

Figure 9-2. *The simplified Gouldner Model. (From Organizations, James G. March and Herbert A. Simon, New York: Wiley, 1958, p. 45.)*

ficiencies of machine theory in operation but have been too limited in scope to provide an adequate basis for the prediction of organizational behavior. Another approach to organizational theory is to abandon the closed-system approach of the machine model and to examine more directly the interrelationships between the subsystems of a structure and between the total system and its environment.

TALCOTT PARSONS AND THE STRUCTURAL-FUNCTIONALISTS

A wider framework for the study of social systems is provided by Talcott Parsons (1951, 1960) and the so-called structural-functionalists. These theorists were heavily influenced by Weber (Parsons is his leading disciple) but instead of concentrating on organizational design for efficient production as in the machine model they have taken a societal perspective. They have sought social functions both direct and indirect for social structures and have shown a tendency to regard a given social form as serving a broad social purpose rather than the self interests of a narrow group. For example, the function of an industrial concern is seen not as making profits for its owners but as providing jobs for workers and contributing to the economy of the community. In other words sufficient consensus of interests among the subgroupings in a society to maintain social stability and equilibrium is assumed (as in Barnard's theory, see below). A weakness in this approach is the failure to acknowledge social conflict and coercion by dominant groups, and a corresponding underemphasis of problems of change. There is a bland neglect of the unequal distribution of economic rewards and political power. There is also the danger of circularity in structural-functionalism, in that every structure is seen as societally necessary because of the various functions it performs. Even if a subsystem appears to be predatory or exploitative, it is possible to identify some secondary effect as its justifiable purpose. Whether in fact the structure came about or remains in being because of such a secondary function has to be proved rather than assumed.

Although Parsons has been criticized for his scant recognition of conflicting interests and values, he has contributed heavily to an understanding of organizations by his careful analysis of the significant internal functions they must perform. Here he shifts his frame of reference from secondary societal effects to the primary tasks of the organization itself in attempting to survive. We have followed his lead in identifying and describing the productive, maintenance, adaptive and institutional (boundary) subsystems of organizations.

Barnard's Equilibrium Model

The recruitment of personnel and their retention in the system—what we have referred to as maintenance inputs—is slighted in machine theory. The focus on organizational design in the classical approach gives little attention to the rewards offered by the organization and the motivations of its members. Barnard (1938), whose work preceded that of Merton, Gouldner, and Parsons, explicitly recognized the problem and offered an equilibrium hypothesis to describe it. He maintains that people will join organizations and contribute their energies to organization functioning in exchange for the monetary and other rewards that they receive. If the alternative to a low-paying job is no job, people will accept the low-paying job. From a Marxian point of view there is an imbalance between the return to the workers and the effort they expend, but to Barnard the system is in balance so long as individuals prefer to stay in the organization rather than leave it. Over time many organizations have shown the stability assumed in the equilibrium hypothesis. But there are also periods of change, and there is some reason for distinguishing between a balance that is essentially a tug-of-war and a balance that is an integrated resolution of conflict.

Kurt Lewin (1948), in his discussion of quasi-stationary equilibria, dealt with this issue by recognizing that states of balance differed not only in their static or dynamic character but also in their tension level. He pointed out that opposing forces of relatively equal strength could exist at different levels of intensity. All equilibria require equal and opposing forces, but in one equilibrium the forces may be great and in another, small. The less intense the conflicting forces, the less is the tension in the situation. When change attempts were directed at altering the equilibrium level by strengthening one set of forces, there tended to be corresponding mobilization of the opposing set and hence increased tension. When, however, these attempts were directed at reducing the strength of the restraining forces as well as increasing the positive forces, there could be stabilization at a new level of equilibrium with lessened tensions created by opposing forces.

THEORIES OF CONFLICT: MARK AND DAHRENDORF

The classical theorists of organization and the structural-functionalists tended to treat conflict as a peripheral issue or to disregard it entirely. Some theorists concerned with economic and political constraints, on the other hand, have viewed organizations as conflictual systems. Their interest has been less in problems of production and more with the vulnerability of the system to divisiveness and dissolution because of the unequal returns to rank and file and leadership. Marx made economic opposition fundamental in his conception of the warring interests of those who sell their labor power as against those who purchase the labor of others. Political conflict flowed from the economic clash. Thus, Marx felt that eliminating the economic opposition of interests through the abolition of private property would result in the erosion of political conflict. But after more than half a century Soviet Russia has not succeeded in eliminating the political dynamic with its rule enforcement and sanctions.

Another theorist, Dahrendorf (1959), has avoided this Marxian assumption of economic determinism in his own conflict theory of organizations. Dahrendorf views political differences in organized systems between those with power and those without power as the critical dynamic in understanding how social systems function. He does not rule out economic differences, but for him the strategic factor is the exertion of authority, with differential psychological outcomes for those in positions of domination or superiority and those in positions of submission and compliance. For him the superior-subordinate relationship is essentially conflictual in nature.

Dahrendorf asserts the inadequacy of a general equilibrium principle. He takes Parsons and the structural-functionalists to task because he believes they make only one kind of assumption, namely the consensual or Utopian. This appears in four guises:

1. Every society is a relatively persistent stable structure of elements.
2. Every society is a well-integrated structure of elements.
3. Every element has a function; that is, it contributes to maintenance of the system.
4. Every functioning structure is based on a consensus of values.

Dahrendorf prefers a conflict model, which makes opposite assumptions:

1. Change is ubiquitous.
2. Social conflict is ubiquitous.
3. Every element contributes to disintegration and change.
4. Every society is based on coercion.

Dahrendorf concedes that both the consensual and conflict models are partial views and that both are necessary for a full understanding of all types of social problems. He prefers the conflict model partly because of its neglect in conventional social science. In attempting to understand organizational life, the Dahrendorf approach would begin with conflicts of interest but would also give priority to the tensions created by hierarchical arrangements of any sort.

Blau's Classification
Based on Prime Beneficiary

A more specific conflict model than that of Dahrendorf has been developed by Blau and Scott (1962) in their direct examination of the primary beneficiary in organizations. These writers are noted exceptions among system theorists in calling attention to differences among organizations with respect to their main beneficiary. The query who benefits the most, who gets what from whom, is generally bypassed because its primitive character seems to question established enterprises and institutions. But it is a fundamental question and Blau suggests a fourfold typology based on whether the system is run primarily for the benefit of the owners or managers, *business concerns;* for the benefit of all its members, *mutual benefit associations;* for the clients being served, *service organizations;* or for the benefit of the public at large, *commonweal organizations.* Although more than one of these groups may gain from a given organization, the benefits to one party are the reasons for its existence. A business firm is run in the interests of its owners and managers, even though rank-and-file workers are compensated for their work. If profits are threatened, workers will be laid off.

Mutual benefit associations include fraternal organizations, political parties, labor unions, professional organizations, clubs, and veterans' organizations. Service organizations primarily benefit the client, and in this category fall social work agencies, hospitals, and schools. Commonweal organizations, in which the public-at-large is the main beneficiary, would include many governmental branches affording protection, such as fire and police departments.

The importance of this classification is that it points up the different problems faced by different types of organizations. The mutual-benefit association faces the critical problem of maintaining internal democratic processes to prevent apathy among its members and the growth of oligarchy. The business firm has as its salient concern maintaining its competitive position through increased efficiency. In service organizations the dilemma is maintaining a high level of professional competence without running the service for the benefit of the professional and administrative staff. For commonweal organizations the key issue is that of power and control, the development of democratic procedures which give to the outside public some ability to check and guide the agency.

Blau and Scott state:

> Note also that the criticism that an organization is "over-bureaucratized" means quite different things in the four types of organizations. In the case of mutual-benefit associations, such as unions, overbureaucratization implies centralization of power in the hands of officials. Here it does not refer to inefficiency; indeed, bureaucratized unions are quite ruthlessly efficient. But in the case of business concerns overbureaucratization implies an elaboration of rules and procedures that impairs operating efficiency, and here the term is not used in reference to the power of management officials to decide on policies, since such managerial direction is expected and legitimate. Finally, service and commonweal organizations are considered overbureaucratized if in consequence of preoccupation with procedures rigidities develop which impede professional service to clients or effective service of the public interest. (p. 45)

The Reimer Modification

Reimer (1971) has also pointed out that organizations differ critically in their definitions of the client relationship, on a dimension ranging from autonomous to manipulative. Some organizations provide a service of which people can avail themselves, as with a library. Other organizations, including most businesses, seek out clients and urge them to accept a service or product over which the clients have no control. The key difference is the amount of autonomy of the public in accepting a service, defining or modifying within limits, and using it. In the library the reader-consumers are active in selecting books and absorbing information or entertaining themselves. With most organizations, however, consumers play a more passive role; once they have made a commitment, they must accept the product or service without question. The contrast can be seen when one uses a library and when one joins some book-of-the-month club. In the latter case the options of the consumer close over; the options are fewer and it is even difficult to get off the mailing list once one's name is entered. The service organization in Reimer's sense of the term not only gives the consumer an active role in the use of the service or product; it does not pressure the consumer to buy because it is relatively free to all comers. Hence we need to examine organizations from the point of view of how much they deceive, control, and dictate to their publics. This influence starts with high-pressure advertising and exploitation of needs and fears to bring potential consumers within the purview of the system, and continues with products and client relationships which manipulate their lives.

In the true service organization as Reimer defines it, clients in effect become members but on a special voluntary basis. Their activities comprise an organizational function but the clients themselves are not organized.

THE CHINESE EXPERIENCE AND THE MAOIST IDEAL

Social experience as well as theory suggests the need for change in the classical bureaucratic model, and modifications, real and alleged, are being propagated in many parts of the world. For example, the kibbutz communities of Israel violate many of the assumptions of Western bureaucracy in their rotation of personnel in official positions, their group decision making, their equality of rewards, and their departures from universalistic criteria in personnel selection. Nevertheless they compete very effectively with the private sector of Israel's agriculture and economy, which is more bureaucratized.

The Maoist conception of organization has points of similarity with conventional Western models but also critical points of difference. An American political scientist and student of Chinese politics and cultures lists these specifics of commonality and difference (Whyte, 1973, p. 157; see Table 9-1).

TABLE 9-1. Conceptions of bureaucracy.

CONTRASTS

Western Conceptions	Maoist Conceptions
1. Use criteria of technical competence in personnel allocation	1. Use both political purity and technical competence
2. Promote organizational autonomy	2. Politics takes command, and openness to outside political demands
3. Legal-rational authority	3. Mass line participative-charismatic authority
4. Informal social groups unavoidably occur	4. Informal groups can and should be fully coopted
5. Differentiated rewards to office and performance encouraged	5. Differentiated rewards to office and performance deemphasized
6. Varied compliance strategies needed, depending on the organization	6. Normative and social compliance should play the main role everywhere
7. Formalistic impersonality	7. Comradeship
8. Unemotionality	8. Political zeal encouraged
9. Partial inclusion and limited contractual obligations of officeholders	9. Near total inclusion and theoretically unlimited obligations
10. Job security encouraged	10. Job security not valued, and career orientations not encouraged
11. Calculability through rules and established procedures	11. Flexibility and rapid change valued, rules and procedures looked on with suspicion
12. Unity of command and strict hierarchy of communications	12. Collective leadership and flexible consultation

SIMILARITIES

1. Organizations have specific goals	1. Same
2. Organizations utilize a hierarchy of specialized offices	2. Same
3. Authority and rewards greater at the top of an organization	3. Same, although efforts to deemphasize
4. Universalistic hiring and promotion criteria	4. Same, although criteria differ
5. Files, rules, and written communications regulate organizational life	5. Same, although not always viewed positively
6. Offices separated from officeholders	6. Same

From Whyte, 1973, p. 157.

Even when characteristics are listed as similar, such as *universalistic rules* for hiring and promotion, the specific criteria differ. In China political beliefs are given greater weight than in Western bureaucracy, perhaps greater weight than technical competence. Admission to Chinese universities is based in part on commitment to Communist ideology, whereas scholastic aptitude would be considered more relevant for the American university.

To what extent the Chinese have achieved their model in practice is not known. A monolithic Communist party is still central in political decision making and monolithic control tends to reduce internalization of values. Edicts from above lack the spontaneity and enthusiasm of autonomously generated ideas. The Chinese leaders have countered this tendency by mobilizing face-to-face small groups to give vitality to the position of the Communist party. They have thus attempted to combine two seemingly opposed principles: *small group process* calling for spontaneity and expressive involvement and *hierarchical control* requiring conformity and regimentation.

Whether these two emphases can be integrated is far from clear. Some success in improving the morale and performance of the Chinese army has been reported by Alexander George (1967) and Doak Barnett and Ezra Vogel (1967). Military activities were politicized and ideological indoctrination insured by small cohesive discussion groups with regular political rituals, group criticism, and mutual consultation between officers and men. On the other hand, the investigation of Barry Richmond (1969), who gathered data on 38 industrial enterprises in China, is far from conclusive on the relative effectiveness of Maoist model. In comparing the figures from China with those of India, the Soviet Union, Japan, and America, Richmond found greater efficiency in China than India but less than in the other countries. China may be more bureaucratic in the Weberian sense than India. Generalizing more from his broad knowledge of the Chinese situation than from his survey data, Richmond suggests that small amounts of organizational "Maoism" are productive of increased worker motivation but large amounts are counterproductive.

Other Sinologists are more negative, and insist that egalitarian ideals have not altered greatly the pattern of bureaucratic rights and privilege. Leys (1977) asserts that "the Maoist bureaucracy today has thirty hierarchical classes, each with specific privileges and prerogatives." He reports that even the May Seventh schools, which were inventions of the Cultural Revolution intended to provide political correction to bureaucrats by requiring them to experience peasant life directly, have become institutionalized: "Their inmates plant cabbages and feed pigs, granted, but they do it with *other bureaucrats*, on the school grounds."

The conflict between small group process and hierarchical control is met in part by resort to the Chinese use of role modeling—a traditional mechanism in Chinese socialization. Peers are held up as examples of proper behavior in achieving social goals. Munro writes

> One of the most striking phenomena about exemplars in China is the pervasiveness of model selection throughout all organizations right up the chain of command and the quantity of the exemplars chosen. In 1959, in the country as a whole, some 3,000,000 "advanced producers" and over 300,000 advanced units were selected. (Munro, 1975, p. 344)

Thus involvement in one's group is obtained through the use of peers as models but hierarchical control is maintained in that the examples are selected from above.

Concluding his thoughtful discussion of the contrasts between Weberian bureaucracy and the Chinese model, Whyte (1973) writes

> Weekly sessions for the study of Mao's thought for factory workers may not simply interfere with production by tiring people out. Insofar as this activity strengthens a sense of organizational cohesion and identification, it may contribute to production. At the same time, it is not clear that the Maoist ideal is a panacea for all organizational problems, or that it can even be very easily applied. In real Chinese organizations its application may result in some cases in both political involvement and internal efficiency, in others in political involvement without greater efficiency, or perhaps in failure in both areas. It would take much better information than we have available now to specify the conditions required for successful application of the Maoist ideal. The suggestion that this ideal is appropriate for all circumstances may be just as dubious as the suggestion that organizations modeled after Weber's ideal type will be the most efficient in all circumstances. Thus claims that China has found a route to modernization without bureaucratization, or that the Maoist ideal solves the problem of how to modernize without sacrificing revolutionary social goals, must continue to be treated skeptically. But this skepticism should not blind us to the opportunity to broaden our understanding of organizational dynamics by a closer scrutiny of Chinese organizational innovations. (p. 162–163)

SOCIOTECHNICAL SYSTEMS

Whereas the classical Western models of bureaucracy emphasized the technological aspects of organizations not the social-psychological, the Maoist ideal (if not the Chinese practice) makes social values primary and technology secondary. A different approach to the dilemma of making either the production function or the maintenance function dominant was developed by social scientists at the Tavistock Institute. Their conceptualization of the organization as a sociotechnical system defines integration of social and technological factors as the core problem, not the determination of their priority. The concept originated in the first mining study of the Tavistock Institute (Trist and Bamforth, 1951) and was utilized in further Tavistock studies, including Rice's experiments in the Indian textile industry (1958). Rice puts the matter in these terms

> Any production system requires both a technological organization—equipment and process layout—and a work organization relating to each other those who carry out the necessary tasks. The technological demand places limits upon the type of work organization possible, but a work organization has social and psychological properties of its own that are independent of technology. While industrial production systems are, of necessity, designed in accordance with technological demand, there has been a tendency to project the technological into the associated work organization. The assumption is then made that there is only one work organization that will satisfy the conditions of task performance. (p. 4)

The conclusion, then, is that organizations can avoid much of the conflict between productive efficiency and alienated workers by examining the various possible work arrangements for given tools and machinery. With the same technical equipment there may be some ways of organizing the work that will achieve more in terms of production and morale than other ways. Since a sociotechnical system includes people as well as tools it is appropriate to ask how well it utilizes tools and how well it utilizes the abilities of people and meets their needs.

The success of the Tavistock group in redesigning systems to take account of both their technical and social dimensions has been paralleled by the work of investigators in other countries (Walker and Guest, 1951; Westerlund, 1952; and Touraine, 1955; Thorsrud et al., 1976). Although the Tavistock researchers have concentrated on the primary work group, their conceptual approach can be applied at all levels of organizational functioning. There are severe limitations in organizational change if we confine ourselves to the lowest level in the production subsystem and omit the managerial and institutional subsystems.

Sociotechnical analysis, then, moved beyond man-machine theory to allow for social-psychological processes at the primary group level. Whereas man-machine theory was content to take account of physiological and individual factors, sociotechnical theory included group parameters as integral. The sociotechnical approach is discussed in greater detail in Chapter 19.

THE HUMAN RELATIONS APPROACH AND THE LIKERT MODEL

In retrospect, the Human Relations approach can be seen as a sort of compensatory movement. Individual motives, goals and aspirations, which had no significant place in the Weberian conceptualization of organization, were put at the center of things. Organizational success was explained in terms of individual motivation and interpersonal relationships, especially the relationship between supervisor and subordinate.

McGregor's *Human Side of Enterprise* (1960) is perhaps the prototype of this approach to organizations and to organizational change. It tells us that improving interpersonal relations and persuading the supervisory hierarchy to model itself after the hypothetical "Manager Y" constitute the path to effective organizational functioning. Manager Y, in McGregor's theory, in contrast to old-fashioned Manager X, is a supportive, understanding human being who trusts people and has confidence in them. The hypothetical Manager Y begins with a different set of assumptions, a different "theory" about human nature and motivation. He or she therefore treats people differently and they, being treated differently, behave differently. The implication is that if we convert the authoritarian Manager X's into empathic Manager Y's, they will treat their subordinates more considerately and even institute the organizational reforms necessary to make life more satisfying within the enterprise. But followers of the human relations approach generally do not address themselves to the need for structural changes in the organization to facilitate better interpersonal relations. These writers neither start nor end with an organizational theory. They remain personality theorists or small group theorists at heart. An outstanding exception is to be found in Rensis Likert (1961, 1967), whose earlier work on interpersonal aspects of organizational life was followed by the brilliant integration of structural concepts and principles of human relations which he calls the linking-pin theory.

According to the linking-pin model, organizations should consist of "families" that are tied together through their common members, who act as linking pins. Each such organizational family consists of a supervisor (at any level in the hierarchy) and the people who report directly to that supervisor. The organizational family takes group responsibility for its work and makes group decisions concerning its task. Each formal leader of such a group is the linking pin in that he or she belongs to two organizational families and helps tie them

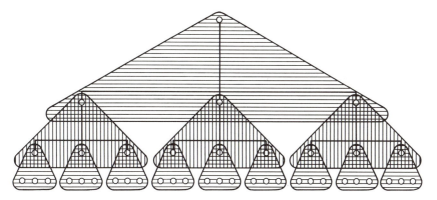

Figure 9-3.   The overlapping group form of organization. Work groups vary in size as circumstances require, although shown here as consisting of three persons. (From New Patterns of Management, *Rensis Likert, New York: McGraw-Hill, 1961, p. 105.)*

together. Each formal leader is thus the head of a group of subordinates and also a member of a group of peers who meet with their own superior. (See Figures 9-3, 9-4, and 9-5.)

For example, the president of an organization would meet with the vice presidents as the top organizational family, and as a group they would work through many problems ordinarily handled by the president alone, or by the president meeting separately with one or another

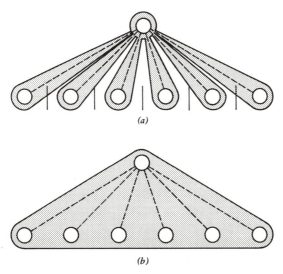

Figure 9-4.   (a) Person-to-person and (b) group patterns of organization. (From New Patterns of Management, *Rensis Likert, New York: McGraw-Hill, 1961, p. 107.)*

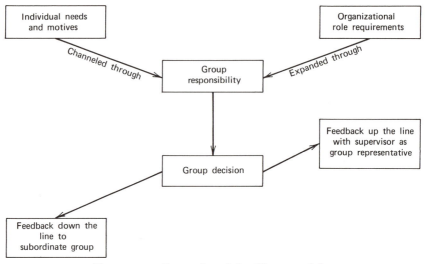

Figure 9-5. *Dynamics of the Likert model.*

of the vice presidents. In turn each vice president meets with his or her department heads and again the problems at this level are met through group process, with the vice president forming the link to top management and interpreting company policy. Department heads meet with their division heads and so on down the line. When a department head meets with his or her peers and their superior, the vice president, the department head functions not only as a member of that group but as a representative of his or her own group of division heads. These meetings take on a task-oriented character, facilitated by the continuing use of research and measurement on the activities of the group itself.

Decisions are made at the level of the structure that is the relevant locus for the organizational space involved. If a decision affects only the people within a subunit, then it should be made in that subunit. Thus top management is relieved of many small decisions that can be made as well or better down the line. Every member of the organization except those at the very top and bottom levels thus serves as a linking pin and functions as a member of two organizational families. The bond between organizational levels is always personally mediated. Every group in the organizational structure has a voice in decision making. It decides how its task should be implemented. Although its task is set primarily by the level above it, it also has some participation at this higher level through its representative.

The Likert theory is based on four essential concepts: (1) the efficacy of group process and group responsibility in maximizing motivation of organization members, (2) the channeling of this motivation toward group goals by the use of overlapping organizational families, (3) the key role of each member of two families as a linking-pin function, and (4) the development of short feedback cycles through the use of research on the functioning of both the social and the technical systems. This theory thus takes account of the hierarchical authority structure of organizations, but it ties every individual into the organization through attachment to a primary work group, and presumably integrates the needs of all subgroups through the overlapping structure of decision making.

At least five possible advantages are explicitly stated or implied in the Likert volumes (1961, 1967):

1. The organizational dilemma of the clash between the informal or primary group structures, and the formal or secondary structures, is solved. The primary group now functions to move toward organizational goals, not to set limits on organizational performance.

2. Internal organizational conflicts between competing officers and competing units are minimized. The head of a unit cannot rely on private lines to the boss but must work together with his or her coordinates in a group that includes the superior officer. In turn, the boss cannot play off one subordinate against another by maintaining separate vertical lines of communication. Horizontal communication is maintained at the appropriate group level. Hence the jockeying for position is obviated, and the time spent in getting privileged pieces of information from upper levels is saved.

3. The effective flow of information is increased and the barriers to communication are removed. There may not be a greater total exchange of information, but the information exchanged will be more functional for the organization. The old problem of blocks to upward communication is taken care of by the fact that it is not only the privilege of the unit head to talk about the problems of his or her own group, but it is normal and required. Downward communication is facilitated by the fact that the members who leave their "upper" group to interpret policy to their subordinates really understand and appreciate the decisions because they have been involved in them.

4. The most valuable resources of the organization, the skills and motivations of its members, are more effectively utilized. There is a characteristic failure in most organizations to tap the resources of members.

5. Decisions are more effectively implemented. They would have acceptance by the group because the group is often involved in making them. As Maier (1952) has demonstrated, there is a built-in acceptance of group decisions, which are in a sense the group member's own decisions.

There are, however, difficulties with the Likert theory—not because of the nature of the approach but because the approach is not pushed far enough in dealing with the walls of the maze—the structure of the system. Specifically, the following problems still remain:

1. The voice of the rank-and-file member of the organization is greatly attenuated in its representation up the line. By the time the ordinary member's voice is reinterpreted through several levels of the organizational structure, it may be so faint as to be ghostlike.
2. A related weakness is that the Likert model is primarily directed at the technical and task problems of the organization. The interest group conflicts in organizations over the distribution of rewards, privileges, and perquisites between hierarchical levels are difficult to meet in this system of organizational families. Overlapping hierarchical groups cannot substitute for the labor union, which cuts across all organizational families at the rank-and-file level and is still the workers' best chance of gaining representation of their interests. Legitimate differences in interests between groups may in fact be obscured by an application of the Likert model.
3. The problem of the determination of the area of decision making for each organizational family is not automatically solved by the criterion of relevance to a given sector of organizational space. Decisions about specific tasks are perhaps not difficult to handle by this criterion, but decisions about the distribution of rewards, about the impact of the decision of one organizational family on another, present knotty questions.
4. Finally, a group process that is kept to a limited set of decisions, especially when the limits are imposed on the group, can prove unsatisfactory. Workers may prefer their own unions, where officers are elected and must stand for reelection on the basis of their performance, to work groups where they do not elect their leaders and have only a remote voice in larger issues. Group process generates its own dynamic and people involved in it want to go beyond their limited directives.

THE AGGREGATION MODEL OF JANOWITZ AND THE TEMPORARY SOCIETY OF BENNIS AND SLATER

The Tavistock and Likert models developed as efforts to correct the overemphasis on production and technology in the theories of Weber and his followers. An equally serious deficiency in classical theories of organization is the disregard of the environment of organizations. This constitutes an acute problem in theory and practice when a turbulent and uncertain environment makes organizational flexibility a requirement for survival. Two leading attempts to deal directly with this problem are the aggregation model proposed by Janowitz and the temporary system suggested by Bennis and Slater.

Janowitz (1969), concerned with problems of reform in urban education, has suggested an *aggregation model* to replace the *specialization* model of machine theory. The more traditional specialization approach fractionates tasks and limits each role to one specialty with little overlap of role functions. It thus does not provide any role with the complexity and challenge of an interesting holistic task or perspectives. The aggregation model provides flexible role boundaries and allows people to aggregate different aspects of the functional requirement that fulfills the organizational purpose. For example, in a school system teachers should not be just subject matter specialists and pupils spongelike learners, but both should participate in the teaching-learning process. Administrative tasks should not be relegated to administrative specialists but should involve all members of the system. The many tasks of counseling, disciplining, formal training, and extracurricular activities should be shared team responsibilities and not segmented role prescriptions.

Bennis and Slater (1968) independently have carried the Janowitz thinking to its logical conclusion for all organizations facing an uncertain and unpredictable environment. They propose a continuing sequence of temporary arrangements to meet the changing exigencies of the external situation. The emphasis is on task forces cutting across the horizontal and vertical system dimensions. Role flexibility is to replace ritualism, informal communication to replace prescribed channels, and task orientation to replace rules and regulations—all temporary. The problem with the transient approach of Bennis and Slater is that the changes proposed are likely to be transient, and the many forces contributing to the established structure are likely to persist. Thus a task force may well be dissolved after the emergency and instead of a new arrangement being set up to anticipate a future crisis, the old structure will take over.

THE ETZIONI MODEL
OF COMPLIANCE AND POWER

Dahrendorf's strictures against the unrealistically harmonious state of affairs in equilibrium models of organization find a sympathetic response in the writings of Etzioni (1971, 1975). Etzioni sees three bases of compliance to produce the coordinated patterns of social behavior known as organizations: (1) coercive force, the application or threat of physical sanctions, (2) control over material resources and rewards through allocation of salaries and wages, fringe benefits, services, and the like, and (3) normative control through the manipulation of symbolic rewards such as esteem and prestige. Moreover, he views all three as forms of power. Etzioni's theory is that while most organizations use all three kinds of power, each organization tends to rely heavily on one, and the type of power relied on depends on the nature of the organization. This pattern occurs because one form of power tends to neutralize another. In prisons, for example, coercion produces alienation and hence makes it extremely difficult to apply normative power, which is one of the reasons why rehabilitation is difficult to achieve in a penal institution. The use of economic or remunerative power similarly undermines the appeal to normative values. Etzioni further suggests that there are three types of involvement of people in organizations, corresponding to the kind of power utilized; alienative for coercion, calculative for economic reward, and moral for normative powers.

His major hypothesis is that effective organizations will be those in which there is a congruence between type of commitment sought and type of power utilized. For example, a business organization will be more effective if it relies on a good wage and salary scale than if it attempts to use normative or moral persuasion; a church will be more effective if it uses moral teaching than coercion or remuneration. The compliance theory has been further elaborated to describe relationships between forms of commitment and other organizational variables, including recruitment, socialization, communication, goal-setting, and the attainment of consensus. Many research studies supply bits of evidence consistent with the theory but there has been no systematic test of its major hypothesis that congruent organizations with respect to form of power and type of involvement will be more effective than noncongruent organizations.[2]

There is some validity to the notion that not all motives can be

---

[2]Gamson (1968) has utilized a similar theoretical framework for problems of social change in proposing that constraints as a means of social control produce resentment toward authorities; inducements or material benefits produce a calculative orientation; and persuasion alone is consistent with maintaining a positive trust orientation provided that an initial level of trust is already there (p. 28).

appropriately combined. Nevertheless Etzioni's theory of the incompatibility of the motive patterns of coercion, material rewards, and normative values is too general a statement to hold for organizational behavior. A combination of sanctions and material rewards may make for a more effective penal institution than coercive force by itself. Similarly, material and psychic rewards can produce better results than either one alone. We shall discuss this problem further in the concluding section of the chapter.

ORGANIZATIONAL MODELS AND THEIR LIMITATIONS

The many organizational models illustrate the differing aspects of systems in which social theorists have been interested, and the difficulty of bringing a very complex set of phenomena into a single framework. Weber, Taylor, Gulick and other machine theorists have been concerned with organizational design in the interests of efficiency and have given little attention to the effects upon the people in the system or to changing environmental inputs. Merton and Gouldner have demonstrated some of the unintended consequences this neglect has for individual performance, and Marx and Dahrendorf have shown the consequences of vertical conflict within systems. The neglect of changing environmental forces is met by Bennis and Slater in their temporary society and Janowitz in his aggregation model. Some human relations proponents and group dynamicists have turned to issues of motivation but have taken no account of structural factors. Some theorists have attempted to deal with both structural and motivational problems. Among them the Tavistock researchers have been in the forefront, with the sociotechnical system approach. They contend that there are a number of possible organizational designs to accomplish a given purpose with given equipment; the choice of an organizational design should take account of the social structure it will produce. Likert has proposed organizational modifications to accord with principles of motivation and group process. Etzioni has proposed a congruence theory, namely that organizations, to be effective, should employ the form of power congruent with their function and thus maximize the appropriate motive pattern.

A THREEFOLD CATEGORIZATION OF MOTIVATIONAL PATTERNS FOR ORGANIZATIONAL FUNCTIONING

Since motivational patterns have not received adequate consideration in organizational theory, we propose a threefold categorization

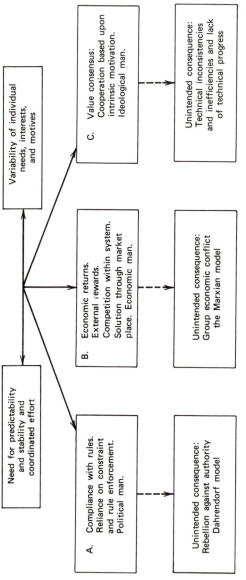

Figure 9-6. *Framework for organizational models.*

(see Figure 9-6) which will furnish the basis for detailed treatment in the next four chapters. Organizational design cannot be dictated solely by the seeming requirements of efficiency and effectiveness; the blueprint on paper may not work in practice or may be made to work only at great cost. Nor can the design of an organization be set once and for all. Human beings are too variable from time to time and person to person to be readily fitted into stable, precise patterns. Moreover, the environment is also variable, so that the pattern that made an organization effective yesterday may not make it effective today. For these reasons we need to distinguish among the major forms of motivation, their nature and their consequences, intended and unintended, for organizational functioning. Three motive patterns are particularly important in models of organization: (1) compliance with rules; (2) responsiveness to economic returns and external rewards, and (3) value consensus and intrinsic rewards.[3]

Compliance with Rules

The coordinated behavior of organization members may stem from enforced compliance with the rules and regulations of the system. There is recourse to authority and sanctions. Members can be fired, fined, or disciplined for failure to observe organizational rules. They can also quit the organization but they often have little option with respect to other economic opportunities. Moreover, the organization has the legal system of the society behind it. The culture of the society also sets value on doing one's duty and complying with all forms of authority whether in school, industry, or nation state. Rule enforcement is the political means for insuring the coordination of activity, and industry has not been blind to the example of the military in the heavy use of rule enforcement to insure the carrying out of interdependent tasks. This pattern assumes a political model of human life in which leaders are power brokers. Although rule compliance makes the acceptance of legitimate edicts and regulations a value, its ultimate sanction is the exercise of force. Laws that are not enforced become dead letters on the statute books.

---

[3]These models are ideal types in that specific organizations in practice will represent some mix of the three patterns. The relative emphasis on a given pattern may vary considerably across cultures or from historical period to period and will have important implications for the understanding of differences in organizational functioning. One of the clearest accounts of the uses of typologies with respect to ideal models and empirical referents can be found in Miner's article on "Community-Society Continua" (1968) which is also cited here because of its scholarly presentation of concepts related to the above distinctions between consensual, pragmatic, and political models (p. 1).

Responsiveness to Economic Returns and External Rewards

Organizations in the Western world have relied heavily on the external rewards of economic gain to attract and hold members. Free land and the opportunity to compete as an independent artisan or professional are not realistic alternatives for many people and the corporation wins out in the marketplace in obtaining their services. The group interests of most people in organizations are given by their roles in the productive process—for example, blue-collar hourly workers, white-collar office personnel, professionals, and managers and owners. Organizational models based on external rewards are not only economically competitive in attracting members in the first instance but remain competitive in that, for the most part, the internal groupings are rivals for the rewards from their cooperative efforts at producing goods or rendering services. The owners and managers try to pass along to the consumers the cost of increased wages to the workers but this is not an automatic process and does not necessarily remove the opposition of economic interests between the internal divisions of the enterprise.

Value Consensus and Intrinsic Rewards

People with common values find it intrinsically rewarding to work for the fulfillment of their beliefs, a fact of life demonstrated perpetually by the so-called dedicated members of some voluntary organizations. This motivational underpinning assumes that the human being is something of an ideological creature, and so runs counter to traditional Western bureaucracy in practice and theory. Nevertheless, this motive pattern is regarded as critical for leadership groups in an organization, who supposedly embody the values of the system even though the rank and file may show less internalization and less agreement concerning organizational objectives.

Systems achieve internalization of values in four main ways:

1. The use of intrinsically rewarding tasks, that is, the development of meaningful and satisfying roles.
2. The tying together of system objectives through small face-to-face groups (thus generating social reinforcement from friends and colleagues and the expressive satisfactions in relating to members of one's own group).
3. Democratic participation in goal setting and goal implementation. People see as their *own*—as part of their own doing—policies and practices in which they have helped make the important decisions.
4. The sharing of rewards from common effort.

Values can be implanted by indoctrination and socialization practices but unless they are also rooted in one or more of the above practices they will lack depth of internalization. The Nazi ideology was maintained by a monopoly of information and by severe sanctions, but with military defeat it showed no inner strength and collapsed overnight.

Two motivational patterns of social consequence are not specifically included in the above framework: emotional attachment to symbols, as in patriotism and chauvinism, and identification with leaders, as in hero worship and charisma. In any realistic attempt to deal with variance in organizational functioning these two patterns need to be taken into account. They are not explicitly included in our paradigm because they are mediating processes of social influence, rather than direct ties between organizational requirements and individual motivation. Moreover, they are dependent in good part on the motivational sources of intrinsic or extrinsically rewarding activities. The concept of emotional symbolism has been used to account for the vitality of nationalistic movements and the stability of religious institutions but has not been systematically related to organization structure. The concept of charisma was employed by Weber to deal with leadership of a nonorganizational character. In other words, these two motivational patterns have had an existence independent of organizational theory with the possible exception of Etzioni's writing.

RELATIONSHIP OF MOTIVATIONAL FRAMEWORK TO OTHER CONCEPTS OF ORGANIZATIONAL FUNCTIONING

The three patterns of motivation—coercive compliance, external rewards, and value consensus—are found in varying degrees in different organizations. For example, penal institutions are high in coercive compliance, business concerns high in economic rewards, and political systems employ all three. Most of the theoretical models we have discussed do not concern themselves with motivational matters, although this lack often involves the theorist (or the practitioner who follows) in difficulties. The classical accounts of Weber and his school assumed that compliance and external rewards could be stuck into an otherwise depersonalized organizational design and would somehow make the organization functional. Merton and Gouldner in their closer examination of machine theory show that this assumption is incorrect and that dysfunctional consequences are the result.

In a sense Barnard bypasses the motivational problem. His equilibrium hypothesis assumes that people will not be attracted to or remain in productive roles in an organization unless the rewards balance the costs. Marx and Dahrendorf were interested in motivational factors but as centrifugal forces that tear social systems apart. From Dahrendorf's point of view an increase in the use of coercion or even material rewards would bring about more resentment of the established hierarchy. From Marx's point of view differential rewards and hierarchical control were inimical to value consensus. The Chinese theorists have tried to go beyond Marx and to combine value consensus with material reward and compliance. Every person belongs to a primary group where he or she participates in discussion and in some decision making. Official policy comes through the hierarchy but in theory the individual citizen has been involved in the process of policy formulation. Whether or not the Chinese are successful over time in fusing value consensus with compliance they have explicitly directed themselves to motivational issues. They reward the overt social expression of values and thus lay down the conditions for the internalization of beliefs.

Janowitz in his aggregation model, and Bennis and Slater in their model of the organization as a temporary system, suggest organizational changes that will give greater opportunity for value consensus to take place. They call for drastic reforms in machine theory such that people will have more chance to show their ability, to be involved in decisions, and to communicate more freely with one another. All these participative measures will make organizational tasks more attractive and, in a changing environment, perhaps more effectively carried out.

The approach of sociotechnical systems is also aimed at bringing value consensus into the picture. What is suggested here is examining possible technologies and work arrangements from the point of view of both the task and the social consequences of the productive system. The use of the group rather than the individual as the responsible unit can provide a sociotechnical system that allows for value internalization. Again the logic is similar to that of Janowitz and of Bennis and Slater.

Finally, the Likert model deals explicitly with motivational matters, and in terms that include the entire organization rather than the work group. Systematic feedback up the line is an essential feature of this normative model; every member actually participates in some decisions and is represented at the next level in the system by a person he or she may be able to influence. Likert makes explicit how word moves up and down in the structure—something we can only guess at in most other models. The ideological or value appeal of the Likert proposal is weak and constrained, or at least not made explicit. Nonetheless, the ideological involvement of people in a system would be greater if Likert were to supplant the machine theorists.

UNINTENDED CONSEQUENCES OF EMPHASIS
ON A GIVEN MOTIVATIONAL PATTERN

The unintended consequences of these several patterns of control have been the subject of considerable theorizing by social scientists. Marx saw the outcome of a Weberian society based on different group interests and different roles in the production process as revolutionary. His conceptualization has had more predictive success, however, for the developing countries than for advanced industrial societies, and for turmoil rather than resolution. Nonetheless the implicit disaffection in a system of economic and political constraints can never be ignored in any realistic account of societal processes. In the United States it has led, however, to the organization of workers not to change the system but to gain a greater share in the returns. Business unionism rather than revolutionary unionism has dominated the American scene since the late nineteenth century.

The unintended consequences of rule enforcement, as Dahrendorf observed, have been to create resentment and rebellion against authority. The resort to threats and the use of sanctions breed resistance, as the frustration-aggression hypothesis suggests. The aggression may be repressed but only if there is an overriding fear of penalties. The logic of punishment calls for increasing the severity of penalties to maintain a required level of fear—a process that is costly and tragic but unfortunately tenable for indefinite periods of time.

The indirect effects of reliance on value consensus may be inefficiencies in operation and lack of adaptability to objective feedback. The bureaucratic model assumes that through programming with rule enforcement and external rewards every role in the organization can be tuned to a satisfactory level of performance. (The use of value consensus frequently implies some democratic processes to insure internalization. People share those beliefs in which they have had a part in formulating and implementing.) External rewards or sanctions are employed to achieve role definitions that are not intrinsically satisfying to people. Value internalization calls for more meaningful tasks and value consensus generally implies some democratic process to insure voluntary acceptance. People see as reflecting the ideology of their own kind those beliefs that they have had a part in formulating and implementing. Hence instead of the bureaucratic selection and training of people on the basis of technical proficiency, ideological criteria of the commitment of people to certain values enters into selection and promotion procedures. At one time the United States Department of State would pass over a more technically qualified scholar for a Fulbright professorship, in favor of a less qualified candidate whose ideas were more congruent with conventional American values. The Chinese criteria for promotion go beyond technical aptitude, and include intensity of conviction about the values of the Chinese system as a critical element of political fitness. When people are selected and promoted on a basis other than technical competence, they may prove less efficient and reliable in performance than when the priority is given to proficiency for the task in question. Moreover, the ideologically pure may show individual differences in the means they employ for reaching the common goal. Hence there may be some sacrifice in overall efficiency among the ideologically committed even though they show a high level of motivation toward the end objectives.

To the extent that people are ideologically motivated they may be less willing to accept feedback from the objective world or from their superiors in the organization. The system based on value commitment may be more rigid and less adjustable than the conventional bureaucratic model with its rule enforcement and pragmatic feedback. This point is often neglected because social movements urging change present themselves as opposed to an existing rigidity. But among the revolutionaries themselves there is an almost religious orthodoxy. It is hard for the outsider to understand why religious or radical sects will fight more bitterly among themselves over minor doctrinal differences than they will fight their obvious enemies, but the pattern is too common to be denied. Ideological commitment leads to organizational rigidity, more often than not.

When organizations can fuse all three forms of commitment, so that people get material benefits from following rules the justification for which reflects their own basic values, the resulting lift in motivation is marked. The individual often balances the costs against the gains in undertaking an activity but when the same line of conduct satisfies many motives, the effect can be multiplicative rather than additive. Certain periods in history show such confluence of motive patterns for certain groups, and they seem to be periods of fabulous cultural development, fantastic technological progress, or unparalleled growth. Historians like Hayes (1926) tell us that development of nation states in the last century was facilitated by the enthusiasm of the middle classes for whom the new nation state meant a better way of life, more power, and more self-expression through their national identity. The same integration of motive patterns can be found in the anticolonialism movement in developing countries today, where fires of nationalism are fed by material interests, group identity, and psychological gratifications. This is one reason why the new national aspirations of the developing countries have proved irresistible. It is a question as to how much Chinese revolutionary values are based on social idealism and how much upon a narrow nationalism.

■ SUMMARY ■

Our organizational society with its many instrumental groupings can be contrasted with an older folk society where the dominant social unit was the community and the dominant form of authority was traditionalism. In our organizational age technological developments affect the nature of theories and a machine theory type of thinking has been pervasive in the classical bureaucratic model of Max Weber and its derivatives—the scientific management approach of Frederick Taylor and the public administration account of Luther Gulick. All three have common elements, including an emphasis on process specialization of tasks, standardization of role performance, centralization of decision making, uniformity of practice, and avoidance of duplication of function. These emphases are descriptive in the case of Weber; they have the quality of advocacy in the theories of Taylor and Gulick.

Unanticipated dysfunctional consequences in the actual operations of machinelike systems have been pointed out by Merton and Gouldner and have challenged the structural-functionalists to demonstrate latent societal functions for various forms of organized activity. These theorists, led by Parsons, have assumed a value consensus in society and have pointed out how subsystems can contribute to societal goals. On the other hand, conflict models, such as those of Marx and Dahrendorf, make assumptions contrary to those of the structural-functionalists and view the social scene as the struggle or potential struggle of opposing groups. To the extent that society is held together, it is held together by coercion. Where equilibrium is achieved it is the tug of war of opposed forces and not a harmonious resolution.

The theory of Mao also makes a number of assumptions not consistent with the Weberian model in advocating total rather than partial inclusion of personalities and ideological commitment. Whether Maoist ideas have been realized significantly in Chinese experience is another question.

The sociotechnical system of Trist and Emery seeks the optimum combination of technical and social subsystems in carrying out the organizational mission. A technical system may appear efficient in its blueprint form but the social system that accompanies it may make it much less effective than its promise. Hence both social and technical aspects of organized arrangements need to be considered in overall system design.

Likert has moved from an individual human relations approach to his System 4 model, which has as an essential feature the combining of group process and structural variables. He would replace one-to-one hierarchy of machine theory with a hierarchy of small groups and an overlapping of these groups through representatives functioning at more than one level.

The aggregation model of Janowitz and the temporary society of Bennis and Slater are also attempts at an organic rather than a mechanical conception of organization. Janowitz would reverse the fractionation and role specialization in the school system, would urge flexible role boundaries, and would allow people to aggregate different aspects of a functional requirement. To handle environmental uncertainty, Bennis and Slater propose shifting, flexible task forces with a deemphasis on rules and formal channels of communication.

Finally, the Etzioni model distinguishes between three ways of producing compliance: coercive force, economic control over material resources and rewards, and normative control through the manipulation of symbols. His theory is that while most organizations employ all three forms of power, the effective organization is the one which relies heavily on the form of control appropriate to its nature.

Organizational research and theorizing has not been sufficiently analytic in distinguishing among three motivational patterns, namely compliance with rules, responsiveness to external rewards, and internalized motivation. Machine theory assumes that rule enforcement, or coercive compliance, is the fundamental pattern. Dahrendorf holds that rule enforcement creates its own antithesis. Marx also holds that differential reward and hierarchical control are inimical to internalized motivation. Likert, Janowitz, and Bennis and Slater all focus on value internalization. Systems theory must at some point deal explicitly with motivational patterns and the problem of their utilization for various organizational tasks.

10

POWER AND AUTHORITY:
RULE ENFORCEMENT

The exposition of power and authority in human organizations has been forecast to some extent by three themes of earlier chapters: the defining characteristics of such organizations (Chapter 3), the development of organizations from primitive to complex structural forms (Chapter 4), and the nature of organizational roles (Chapter 7). We defined the organization as an open social system, distinguished from other open systems in that it is a structure of events or human acts rather than of physical components. An array of such acts intended for performance by an individual we defined as a role, and the organization is therefore a system of roles.

It follows that a continuing requirement for all human organizations is the motivation of role behavior, that is, the attraction and retention of individual members and the motivation of those members to perform the organizationally required acts. As Merton (1957) has stated, the reliability of role behavior is the requirement intrinsic to human organizations. To state that requirement in other terms, every organization faces the task of somehow reducing the variability, instability, and unpredictability of individual human acts.

THE REDUCTION OF HUMAN VARIABILITY
AND THE J CURVE OF CONFORMING BEHAVIOR

The general success of organizations in achieving this reduction is obvious to the most superficial observer. Within an organization, members behave in ways which they would not do outside the organization. They may wear uniforms or costumes that they would not otherwise wear. They are likely to adopt certain styles and formalities in interpersonal relations which are not elsewhere in evidence. Above all, their behavior in organizations shows a selectivity, a restrictiveness, and a persistence that is not to be observed in the same persons when outside the organization. The most elementary examples of behavior can illustrate this point: Consider the regularity in the time of arrivals and departures of employees of a company. Some minutes before the appointed hour in the morning workers begin to stream through the plant gates and move to their places, in most plants pausing at the time clock en route. Just before the required hour, the traffic through the gates hits its peak (the timing reflects the superb assurance of long practice), and then there is an abrupt reduction in flow. A small proportion of workers come a few minutes late, and then the traffic stops altogether until the complementary surge outward in the afternoon.

The same employees, were we to survey their preferences for hours of waking and sleeping or their behavior on weekends and vacations, would show the distribution of human differences typical on almost any characteristic—height, weight, intelligence or what you will. The distribution of such attributes over a large population almost always generates that bell-shaped curve that reminds us of the variability of human preferences and characteristics, the bulking up of most cases in the middle ranges and the symmetrical tapering off to both extremes.

The behavior of employees in the organization, however, shows a different configuration. The extreme cases reduce in number, the bell shape sharpens to a peak, and the distribution becomes asymmetrical; it is more permissible to be early than late. The normal curve is transformed into the J curve, the curve of conformity that is characteristic of organizationally determined acts (Allport, 1933, 1934). As the organization becomes larger, more complex, more specialized in its parts, the behavior patterns required of members are not merely uniform. The generalized requirement of conforming to the requirements of one's role and the expectations of the people who constitute one's role set continues, however.

Indeed such conformity is a more insistent and vital requirement in sophisticated organizations than in primitive ones, precisely because of the greater interdependence in the complex organizations. If one field hand in a group of 100 fails to meet the requirements of the role, total productivity is reduced from 100 percent to 99. If one assembly-line worker in a group of 100 stops performing, not a single completed unit is produced. The total amount of work done may drop by only one percentage point, but the completed product has dropped to zero. Small wonder that the essential corporate requirement on the individual is for dependable role performance, that the employee who so performs is called responsible, and that deviation from meeting role expectations is defined as irresponsibility.

In certain circumstances a visible and dramatic environmental situation may be enough to stimulate such coordinated effort among people. At other times the values and expectations shared by various individuals may be sufficient to bring them into some state of cooperation. These, however, we have asserted to be more characteristic of ad hoc, voluntary groups than of formal organizations. Members of formal organizations of course respond to visible environmental pressures and are often motivated by shared values; the dominant organizational solution to the problem of achieving reliable performance, however, is to promulgate and enforce rules of conduct. The organizational solution to the problem of achieving lawfulness is to pass laws. Indeed, that is the meaning behind the definition of an organization as a system of roles. Each role consists of a set of prescriptions or behaviors to be performed and typically includes in addition a set of proscriptions or behaviors to be avoided. In the process of creating such prescriptions and proscriptions we have seen the beginnings of the managerial subsystem of an organization.

Some of the organizational prescriptions are very broad and apply to every position in the system. Some apply to subparts of the system, and some apply only to a single role or position. For example, getting to work by 8 o'clock each morning may be a law that applies to all day-shift jobs below the level of superintendent. Keeping the floors clean is an injunction that may apply only to the job of janitor. "Don't steal company property" may be a law that is systemwide in its application. In short, these laws include all of the norms and role requirements of the organization.

FORMS OF AUTHORITY

Weber (1947) put the forms of normative compliance in historical perspective by pointing out that modern bureaucratic structures have developed a functional specificity of roles sanctioned by an authority structure of a *rational-legal type,* and that this is in contrast to the feudal system, where authority was vested in *traditional status,* and to systems dependent on *charismatic authority* or obedience to leaders because of assumed supernatural or divine qualities. In traditional and charismatic authority we thus have specific cases of blind obedience, whereas legitimate authority assumes some value consensus among system members.

In traditional authority, people are not observing enacted rules, but the directives of a person occupying a position of authority because he or she has rightfully inherited the post. In Weber's language, "A system of imperative coordination will be called 'traditional' if legitimacy is claimed for it and believed in on the basis of the sanctity of the order and the attendant powers of control as they have been handed down from the past, have always existed." Where pure types of traditional authority exist, there are no clearly defined spheres of competence for a trained administrative staff whose actions and decisions are determined by impersonal rules. Changes in the requirements of the system to meet changing conditions cannot come from new legislation. To the extent that changes develop at all, they come from the traditional person in authority who justifies them as old values to be implemented in new ways. Thus, the only orientation of traditional authority to rules is to the precedents of the group's history.

Charismatic authority is not bound by rules of any kind. The magical qualities of the leader are so unlimited that in pure form charisma would not result in any stable set of role relationships. Over time, charisma moves toward traditionalism as the manner of succession becomes established, for example, designation of a successor by the leader, or hereditary succession. Or it moves toward legalization as the disciples develop rules for the admission of novices to the group and organizational protocols describing the hierarchy of positions and their rewards.

The legal type of authority asserts that obedience is to be rendered only to the law, that is, to the impersonal order of a person in a position of authority and only within a defined area of legitimate power. Weber outlined the following characteristics of rational-legal authority:

1. A continuous organization of official functions bound by rules.
2. A specified sphere of competence based on a division of labor with authority and sanctions to ensure proper role performance.
3. A hierarchical arrangement of offices in terms of supervision and control.
4. The governing of the conduct of an office by technical rules or by norms and the requiring of specialized training for the incumbents of these offices.
5. Complete separation of the property belonging to the organization and the property belonging to the official. In fact, an official should not be an owner of company property.
6. The lack of rights to the office by the incumbent. The office-holder must not appropriate the official position for personal or private interests.
7. Administrative acts, decisions, and rules are formulated and recorded in writing. . . . The combination of written documents and a continuous organization of official functions constitute the "office" which is the central focus of all types of modern corporate action.

Weber's analysis thus emphasizes the diffuseness of roles in systems that emphasize traditional and charismatic authority as against their functional specificity in rational-legal structures. The modern bureaucracy of the industrial corporation represents a good illustration of the working out of rational-legal authority. It is true that organizations, including even the industrial enterprise, will show all types of authority patterns. Some industrial leaders may be obeyed because of charismatic qualities, and traditional status may be found in large corporations. But modern social organizations rest primarily on rational and legal grounds. Bureaucratic structure in the Weberian sense utilizes role systems in their purest form and they represent the most pliable, the most effective instruments for environmental transactions and exploitation in the evolution of social systems. For maximum utilization of the energy sources in the environment, including human sources, and their transformation into social products, the formal social organization may be the greatest social invention in history.

THE CONCEPT OF LEGITIMACY

Weber believed that the system of rational-legal authority not only insured the acceptance of rules but had the potentiality of providing an ideological basis for their acceptance, a potentiality that was realized in some cases and not in others. The key concept for this elaboration of rational-legal authority is *legitimacy*. This concept has been employed by sociologists to refer to the fact that a great deal of behavior can be readily predicted once we know the rules of the game. It is not always necessary to take extensive representative samplings of the behavior of many people to know how most of them will conduct themselves in certain situations. All we need are a few informants who can tell us the legitimate norms for given types of behavioral settings. In most European countries the simple norm of giving the right of way to the driver on the right accounts for a great deal of driver behavior. The same principle holds for all social structures. If travelers from Mars are informed about the rules of the game in any social situation, they can predict and understand a great deal of what goes on. In a baseball game they can predict that the batter after hitting the ball will run to first base, not to third, and not around the grandstand.

Psychologists have tended to ignore the concept of legitimacy and its meaning for the individual. Yet it is basically a social-psychological concept in that it refers both to social situations in which widespread compliance occurs and to the psychological processes within individuals that account for their compliance. Acceptance of the legal rules of a system is a necessary condition for participation in that system by the individual. Acceptance of them is in part a recognition of the objective social realities and in part an outcome of the socialization process in which a generalized acceptance of legal rules is developed. The objective social realities are that organized group effort cannot take place if people behave as anarchists. Rousseau's doctrine of the social contract, according to which people voluntarily exchange some of their individual rights for the benefits of social cooperation, is not necessarily an accurate description of the origin of social systems. It does, however, contain the profound truth that the involvement of people in social systems entails generalized obligations to follow systemic demands.

Legitimacy exists at three levels: (1) formal law, (2) legal norms, and (3) societal or moral justification, as embodied in social norms.

1. At the formal level we encounter statutes enacted by legislative bodies and the edicts and directives issued by executives. These two aspects of formal rules can be identified not only in the political system but in the organization as well.

2. Legal norms or generalized codes transcend specific statutes. These canons of legal practice affect the way specific laws are interpreted and applied. They reflect judicial precedents, principles of jurisprudence, and accepted beliefs about proper procedures. Their interpretation is the particular concern of judges, lawyers, and others in the legal profession.

3. Relevant social norms are the more widely held beliefs of people outside the legal profession about the rightness or wrongness of alleged infractions of the law. Laws can embody moral values but there is not a complete overlap between social norms and specific laws. The law student learns very early that there are often conflicts between justice and conformity to legal requirements, and the conflicts are not necessarily resolved in favor of principles of justice. Part of the rationale for the jury system of a trial by peers is to bridge the possible gap between law and the mores.

Legitimacy means, then, more than compliance with the letter of the law. In fact judges do not deal with the cases before them by simplistic and absolutistic application of legal rules. Judges, like other mortals, are affected by the legal and social norms incorporated into their belief and value systems. Even the United States Supreme Court has reversed itself as different normative patterns have affected the nation. A historic example is the Court's rejection in 1954 of its own earlier decision that separate school facilities for blacks and whites could be equal.

Since legitimacy has a threefold basis in law, legal norms, and social values, it has great power to produce compliance. People are often more concerned about the legitimacy of a proposal than with its actual meaning. Respect for symbols of authority is supposedly characteristic of the German people but the Milgram experiments, presently to be described, suggest that it is a more universal phenomenon.

Involvement in any social structure thus means that its symbols of authority and its rules, promulgated in the prescribed manner, are accepted as binding. It is typically an all-or-nothing affair. The person cannot become involved in a system and remain the arbiter of what to accept or reject in its requirements. Members can attempt to influence or alter the system decisions but, once made, these decisions are binding upon them regardless of their own views. Even in such loosely structured organizations as American political parties, factions that were violently antagonistic at the nominating convention subsequently close ranks and accept some measure of party discipline. In more tightly organized groups there is no question about compliance with legitimately derived decisions. When they enter an organization, individuals often assume that they can control their degree of involvement and retain the right of discrimination with respect to organizational requirements. Before they are aware of it, however, they are acting like other organizational members and complying with the rules and authorized decisions.

Research evidence from the Tannenbaum (1974) study of industrial plants in five countries is relevant to the nature of compliance in organizational settings. Workers and supervisors were asked directly, "When you do what your immediate superior requests you to do on the job, why do you do it?" Six reasons were provided and the respondents could indicate from 1 (not at all) to 5 (to a very great extent) the importance of each answer. In all countries the reason given the highest rating was either, "It is necessary if the organization is to function properly," or "It is my duty." (See Table 10-1.)

Some very loose voluntary organizations show less of this all-or-nothing pattern. Such organizations often make only minimal demands on most members, who are really marginal to the group. This large marginal group is asked only to give verbal and financial support, and to maintain a favorable climate of opinion in which the small core of activists can function. For the activist, however, the demands are heavy, and failure to meet them brings relegation to the inactive marginals.

To assert that involvement in a structure means acceptance of its legitimate authority raises interesting problems of individual responsibility. If individuals must comply with the legitimate norms of their group, how can they be held responsible for their actions while carrying out prescribed duties? Executioners are not guilty of murder. As members of social systems, we do not assume full responsibility for our actions in carrying out our prescribed roles, nor is such responsibility usually imposed on us. In practice, however, we do hold people responsible for their actions as members of organizations under any of several circumstances: (1) when on their own volition they have entered a structure whose norms run counter to the political state, for example, joining the Communist Party in the United States; (2) when they have failed to exert all the influence they could muster to affect decisions in the structure, for example, the guilt of the German people in accepting the Nazi regime; (3) when they possess considerable power and latitude in formulating and implementing policy, usually as occupants of some position of formal leadership.

COMPLIANCE AND OBEDIENCE

Why should people become members of organizations and subject themselves to such laws? Why should they obey them? What shall be

TABLE 10-1 Bases of Superior's Power: Industrial Plants in Five Countries (mean scores)

Basis of Power	SMALL PLANTS					LARGE PLANTS			
	Italy	Austria	United States	Yugo-slavia	Kibbutz	Italy	Austria	United States	Yugo-slavia
(a) I respect his competence and judgment	3.2	3.6	4.2	3.7	3.5	3.4	3.8	4.1	3.9
(b) He can give special help and benefits	2.2	3.0	3.5	3.1	1.3	2.2	3.1	3.4	2.8
(c) He can penalize or otherwise disadvantage me	2.1	2.4	2.4	2.7	1.1	2.0	2.1	2.7	2.8
(d) He's a nice guy	2.5	3.5	3.4	3.3	2.0	2.5	3.2	3.1	3.2
(e) It is my duty	4.1	4.2	4.2	4.1	4.2	4.3	4.2	4.5	4.4
(f) It is necessary if the organization is to function properly	3.8	4.1	4.5	4.2	4.6	4.1	4.5	4.5	4.6

From Tannenbaum et al., 1974, p. 76.

done if they fail to obey them? The most general answer to such questions lies in the concept of authority and in the creation within the managerial subsystem of a structure of authority. By *authority* we mean simply legitimate power, power that is vested in a particular person or position, and that has the ultimate sanctions of force and punishment.

The managerial subsystem and the structure of authority are inseparable. They arise from the same organizational needs, and they develop interactively and simultaneously. Every organization must have means of insuring role performance, replacing lost members, coordinating the several subsystems of the organization, responding to external changes, and making decisions about how all these things shall be accomplished. For every organization these means include some form of managerial subsystem, some structure of authority, and some roles which have a degree of specialization with respect to these functions.

The motivational basis of compliance to authoritative coercion is fear or anxiety about the consequences of disobedience. But in spite of Etzioni's (see Chapter 9) emphasis on single patterns of motivation, the more common events in real-life situations involve intertwined sets of motives. Thus fear of the consequences of disobedience is supplemented by positive satisfactions associated with the righteousness of being a law-abiding citizen. In other words, to cover over the raw exercise of power a set of rationalizations evolve that soon supply a normative or ideological basis for compliance. The child may obey the parent or the subordinate a superior because of cultural indoctrination that given forms of authority are to be obeyed. The control over sanctions possessed by a person in a position of authority is buttressed by an ideological component or a rationale for rendering obedience.

Moreover, through the socialization process people develop a generalized acceptance of the rules of the game and the signs of authority that go with them. Each comes to have an image of himself or herself as an honest person able to play the game without cheating. Feelings of shame and guilt are associated with deviance from prescribed social standards. Deference to authority symbolizing such standards becomes deeply ingrained, as the classic work of Milgram on obedience has shown.

Milgram's Experiments on Obedience

Milgram (1965) has demonstrated that people socialized in our culture carry their institutional roles as conforming citizens to transient settings that simulate the authority settings of more permanent organizations. His experiments illustrate the docility with which people respond to instruction, even when the source of the request has not really established his or her authority and when the requests themselves are in apparent conflict with the individual's own wishes and values. Deeply concerned with what he called the Eichmann phenomenon, Milgram devised a series of experiments to answer this question: If a person is told to hurt another, under what conditions will he or she go along with the instruction, and under what conditions will he or she refuse to obey? In Milgram's experiments the question became: If an experimenter tells an experimental subject to hurt another person, under what conditions will the subject go along with this instruction, and under what conditions will he or she refuse to obey? The subjects in the initial experiments were adult men of varied ages and occupations, all in the area of New Haven, Connecticut. As the subjects arrived they were told by the experimenter that scientists knew very little about the effects of punishment on memory, and that the subjects were going to participate in experiments to learn more about this matter. They were also told that they would work in pairs, one as teacher and the other as learner. They drew lots to determine who would be the teacher and who the learner in each pair, but the experimenter had arranged things so that the teacher was always the true or naive subject and the learner always an instructed confederate of the experimenter.

The experiment proceeds. The learner (confederate) is taken into an adjacent room and strapped into an electric chair. The teacher, next door, is told that it is his task to teach the learner the proper responses to a list of words, and that he is to administer punishment to the learner whenever he makes a mistake. The punishment is administered by electric shock, controlled by the teacher. The teacher sits next to a simulated shock generator, with indicated voltages ranging from 14 to 450 and labels ranging from "slight shock" to "danger: severe shock." The learner, who is the experimenter's confederate, gives many wrong answers, according to plan. The teacher is instructed to administer one shock for each error, and to increase the voltage one step for each error. Needless to say, no electric shock is actually applied. The responses of the victim (that is, learner) are standardized. Starting with 75 volts, the learner begins to grunt and moan. At 150 volts he demands to be let out of the experiment. At 180 volts he cries out that he can no longer stand the pain. At 300 volts he refuses to provide any more answers to the memory test, insisting that he is no longer a participant in the experiment and must be freed. The experiment ends whenever the teacher-subject refuses to give the next higher level of shock.

More than 1000 people participated in these obedience experiments. Before the results were available, 40 psychiatrists were asked to predict the number of persons who would administer each of the increasing levels of shock. The psychiatrists predicted that most subjects would not continue the shocks after the victim made his first request to be freed (at 150 volts). They also predicted that only one subject in 1000

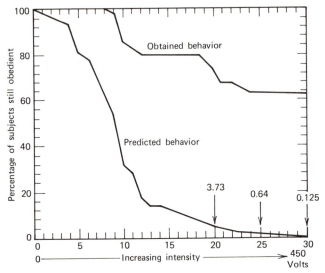

Figure 10-1 *Actual and predicted obedience in administering (fictitious) shocks. Predictions by forty psychiatrists; from Milgram, 1965, p. 260.*

would obediently administer the highest shock on the board. In fact 62 percent of the subjects (620 out of 1000) obeyed the voice of authority, met the requirements of their organizational role, and administered (as they thought) shocks of 450 volts to a moaning, protesting and then ominously silent subject (see Figure 10-1). The underestimation of compliance by the psychiatrists may reflect an occupational bias. As individually oriented therapists they probably attribute more freedom of choice to others than most people actually perceive in social situations.

In a variation of the experiment in which such sounds from the victim were not audible, virtually all subject-teachers, once commanded, went on to the end of the board, in spite of the labels "extreme shock" and "danger: severe shock." The proportion of subjects who behaved so obediently dropped to 62 percent when the moans and protests of the learner could be heard, dropped a little more when the teacher could also see his victim, and dropped to 30 percent when the teacher was compelled to touch the victim in order to administer the shock. Significant numbers continued to administer shock even when the victims claimed heart trouble.

Only one point need be added about these experiments. The teacher-subjects were not acting without feeling. On the contrary; they expressed tension, conflict of conscience, sympathy for the learner, dissatisfaction with the experiment and the research organization. But they continued to administer shocks.

There are two ways in which normative requirements can buttress the coercive power of authority: (1) There may be common beliefs concerning the desirability of obedience to laws, thus providing in some degree our third pattern of motivation, value consensus (Figure 9-6). (2) There may be blind acceptance of a slogan or symbol of obedience in which obedience to authority as such is a virtue. People following this approach do not develop their own value consensus about law, authority, and order but shift their attention to being law-abiding citizens or good organization members.

Conditions Conducive to Legal Compliance

We can identify five conditions conducive to producing legal compliance in organizations: (1) a societal background of normative socialization processes, (2) recognized and appropriate symbols of authority, (3) clarity of legal norms and requirements, (4) specific penalties and sufficient police power, and (5) expulsion or threat of expulsion of nonconformers from the system. (See Table 10-2.)

1. Organizations borrow from the socialization effects that a society and its institutions have on the growing child. Children are taught to obey their parents because they are parents. The school and church reinforce obedience as a virtue and compliance with rules as a duty. Patriotic exercises involve implicit ritual acceptance of respect for national symbols. The law is reified as a general commandant, deviation from which can lead not only to penalties but to guilt feelings as well. As individuals enter organizational settings, they carry over a generalized attitude of deference to commands, and this is specifically reinforced by the organizational rules being equated to the law and the boss made to appear as a parental figure. In a society in which the various institutions of socialization have followed the same pattern of inducing conformity in young people, the organization can readily make coercive compliance its basic source of power. In a society where socialization practices vary from family to school to church and where conformity is not the goal, it is not easy to resort to authority as a single factor for producing compliance.

2. The acceptance of directives on the basis of legitimacy requires the use of symbols and procedures that identify an appropriate source of authority in the system under consideration. The worker may grumble at the supervisor's order but recognize the right of the supervisor to give an order. Particular directives are accepted as legitimate when they conform to the authority structure of the system. In a representative democracy the policy decision of an administrator may be rejected because it lacks the legislative stamp required in that system. A company may have a union contract stating that changes in the speed of the assembly line must be agreed to by both organizations. The workers

TABLE 10-2   Conditions and Methods of Using Legal Compliance

Objective Condition	Mediating Psychological Variables
1. Normative socialization practices of societal institutions	Internalization of norms of conformity
2. Use of appropriate symbols of authority	Recognition and acceptance of symbols
3. Clarity of legal norms and requirements	Lack of subjective ambiguity permitting wishful interpretations
4. Use of specific penalties and possession of physical force	Individual expectation of being caught
5. Expulsion of nonconformers	Desire to stay within system; dependence on system for way of life

accordingly will accept a speedup in the line if it is sanctioned by union-management agreement, but not if it is the work of a general supervisor attempting to impress higher management.

The acceptance of legal rules is also restricted to their appropriate realm of activity. Union policy as formulated in its authority structure is binding upon its members only when it specifies relations with the company. The edicts of union officials on matters of desegregation or support of political parties are not seen as legal compulsions by union members. In similar fashion, employees do not regard the jurisdiction of the company as extending to their lives outside the plant. Areas of private behavior and personal taste are generally regarded in our democratic society as outside the realm of coercive laws.

3. A related condition for the acceptance of legal decisions is clarity—of authority symbols, of procedure, and of the content of the decision itself. Lack of clarity can be due to vagueness of the stimulus-situation or to conflict between stimulus cues. In some organizations, symbols of authority are sharply defined but the relationship between competing symbols lacks clarity. The armed services make visible in conspicuous fashion their authoritative symbols, but conflicts between branches of the service occur because of difficulties in unification of command. Confusion can also occur when different types of authority structure are introduced in the same social system. One difficulty of using group decision in certain parts of an otherwise authoritarian structure is that group members may not perceive the democratic procedure as legitimized by the larger structure. They will question the compelling effect of any decisions they reach, and often they may be right. Another kind of conflict arises when the exercise of power is not consistent with its substantive purpose. The classic case is that of *ordering* people to be democratic.

Procedures as well as symbols may be ambiguous. Where there are many interrelated channels for the formulation of legal rules, people may be confused as to what interpretation of the law to follow. The doctrine of interposition, used in the South to justify resistance to the Supreme Court decision of 1954 on desegregation, had the sole function of giving apparent legal support to the segregationists. Laws are promulgated at local, state, and national levels and are interpreted by state and federal courts in various ways. The procedural complexity created confusion for many Southern citizens. If they complied with the Supreme Court decision, they would in fact violate local laws. And the doctrine of interposition, which set the sovereignty of the state above that of the nation in certain areas of life, gave legal support to setting the legal structure on its head. In more recent years the simultaneous requirement to employ certain proportions of blacks and women, and also to hire without regard to race or sex, has created difficulties for those who wish to comply with the law and opportunities for those who do not.

Specific laws can also be ambiguous in their substance. They can be so complex, so technical, or so obscure that people will not know what the law is. The multiplication of technical rulings and the patchwork of legislation with respect to tax structure motivates people to pay as little as possible without risking legal prosecution, but leaves them confused as to how little that is. Such ambiguity generates a counter dynamic to the tendency to comply with legal requirements, namely, the use of legal loopholes to defy the spirit of the law. Any complex maze of rules in an organization will be utilized by the guardhouse lawyers in the system to their own advantage.

In brief, legal compliance rests on the belief that there are specific imperatives which all good citizens obey. If there is doubt about what the imperative is, or if there are many varying interpretations, then the law is not seen as having a character of its own but as a means for obtaining individual advantage. To this extent, the legitimate basis of compliance is undermined.

4. To maintain the internalized acceptance of legitimate authority requires reinforcement in the form of penalties for violation of the rules. If there is no policing of laws governing speeding, speed limits will lose their force over time for many people. Penalties can take the form of social disapproval as well as legal action. But the very concept of law as binding on everyone in the system requires penalties for violation either from above or below. Where there is no enforcement by authorities and no sanctions against infractions from the group itself, the rule in question becomes a dead letter.

An important consideration in the use of penalties is the tying of the sanction to a given proscribed action as in a penal code. Otherwise, the negative affect generated by punishment can spread to objects and behaviors different from the intended target. The parent or teacher or boss who depends routinely on threats and penalties may become the object of resentment or avoidance, rather than the tabooed action. It is easier to build up a specific connection between a reward and a desired behavior than between a penalty and a proscribed behavior. If individuals are traumatized they may become ego defensive and fail to learn what it is they should not do. Positive reinforcement, as experiments demonstrate, is a more reliable and easier technique to administer than negative reinforcement (Maier, 1949). It is also less subject to side effects.

One way of dealing with ego defensiveness under penalties is to make punishment as objective as possible, so that it is perceived as a consequence of the situation and not of the personality of the individual in power. Specifically, this calls for equity both in the treatment of malefactors and in their detection. From this point of view one cannot completely abandon the old doctrine of the punishment fitting the crime; concentrating upon the idiosyncratic motives and intentions of the offender may represent equity of another kind, but it is a kind difficult to perceive and to justify.

5. Finally, a basic condition for legal compliance is the individual's involvement in a social system. The systems in which a person participates are part of his or her way of life. To reject the authority and rules of the system is to reject the system. The naturalized citizen takes an oath of allegiance to the new country, and many groups require similar formal commitments. Even without such formalities, there is the understanding that serious failure to accept legitimized norms will result in expulsion from the system. At some point, denial of the authority of the system becomes psychological if not legal treason. The relevant consideration is the point at which involvement in the system is threatened by acts of nonconformity. The Catholic Church, for example, makes clear that excommunication will follow overt defiance of authority as well as certain types of heresy, whereas other violations of its code can be atoned for. Political states define some category of acts as treasonable.

Many behaviors are defined differently under different circumstances. External threat to a system extends the concept of disloyalty to forms of legal infraction which are normally tolerated. A sentry who falls asleep during a peacetime maneuver will be disciplined; during war that sentry would be subjected to a court-martial. Even where external threat is not objectively documented, a climate of opinion can develop to produce the same effects—hence the well-known technique of creating a sense of systemic danger in order to destroy one's opponents by accusing them of disloyalty. In general, infractions of legal norms central to the major objectives of organizations or to the authority structure itself are most likely to lead to expulsion. In the Catholic Church one does not flaunt the authority of the Pope. In a plant devoted to defense production one does not violate security regulations. In a research organization the faking of results would be a cardinal sin.

Another way of stating the relationship between involvement in an organization and the acceptance of its legal norms is to say that such acceptance is a sign both to the individual and to his or her fellow members. Acquiescence to the authority structure is a symbol of belonging. By the same token, any act of conspicuous violation of system norms is tantamount to giving up one's way of life in the structure.

The individual is often unaware of the full significance of involvement in a social system and the strength of the compliance demand. Only when one's own actions or the actions of others create the possibility of expulsion does the real meaning of withdrawal and membership come home. The individual may then do a great deal to insure membership in the system. When even minor dissidence incurs great penalties, dissidents are few. This is why the phenomenon of McCarthyism reached such irrational limits in the United States in the early years after World War II. People did not dare take the risk of opposition when it was likely to be defined as disloyalty and therefore threaten their way of life. To oppose unsuccessfully meant loss of membership in many occupational, professional, political, and social structures. It is not surprising that most revolts in social structures are easily quelled by invoking the symbols of authority, or that rebels make rejection by certain social systems tolerable by building their own alternative structures. For it is the presence of alternative systems that makes nonconformity within a given system possible. The political party will not cater to the needs of a faction that has nowhere else to go on election day. A business concern may choose an area where workers have no alternative to employment. The unique power of the nation-state over its citizens stems in part from the depth of their involvement in its many subsystems, but also from the difficulty of moving to another country.

The Compliance Model
as a Punishment Model

Negative sanctions, expulsion from the system, and the invoking of authority all suggest that coercive compliance has the limitations and strengths of motivating behavior through threats, intimidation, fear, and the induction of guilt. There is a long and successful history of such regimentation. The police state, internal espionage, and military force are more the rule than the exception even in modern times. Nevertheless, there is growing recognition of the weaknesses of regimes and organizations that rest mainly on superior fire power. Hence positive rewards have been combined with penalties to escape the shortcomings of negative motivation. *The carrot and the stick* has replaced the old reliance on the *stick* and the majority of theorists regard positive rewards as a more reliable basis of motivation than penalties and sanctions. The modern tendency, moreover, as shown in the value-consensus model (Figure 9-6), is to move away from external measures whether positive or negative, and to attempt to gear the desired behavior to the individual's own internalized motives.

The limitations of punishment have already been noted. The negative feelings it arouses can rub off more on the authority decreeing the penalty than on the punished actions. Even where active resentment is not expressed against authority, there is a tendency to avoid the situation and to withhold active support from the system. People obeying the law because of fear of the police cannot be depended upon to help track down law breakers. They want as little to do with the matter as possible. Legal compliance means conformity and acquiescence but not enthusiastic cooperation. Moreover, an atmosphere of intimidation is inimical to organizational tasks calling for change in beliefs, attitudes, or personality. Mental hospitals, prisons, clinics, and educational institutions presumably have such tasks. Rehabilitation and education require some willingness to be changed and some internal restructuring on the part of the subject. Constraint and avoidance are not the psychological conditions for new and constructive activity. Etzioni (1961) has correctly emphasized the alienative character of coercive measures, and Skinner (if not all those who call themselves Skinnerian) excludes negative reinforcement both from his experiments and his ideal community.

THE UNIVERSALITY OF THE HIERARCHICAL PRINCIPLE

Compliance with authority is basic to what Tannenbaum (1974) has described as hierarchical control in organizations, and such control, in one form or another, Tannenbaum regards as a universal feature of organization. This is consistent with our earlier discussion of the defining characteristics of organizations, in which we postulated an authority structure as essential to decision making and its implementation in collectivities. Tannenbaum and his followers have approached the issue empirically and have found that a wide variety of organizations (from military organizations to voluntary associations, from business organizations to labor unions, from municipal agencies to colleges and universities) show similar gradients of control, with those at the top of the system exercising more power than rank-and-file members.

Still more impressive are the findings from a five-nation study in which comparisons were made among factories in Italy, Yugoslavia, the United States, Austria, and Israeli kibbutzim. Although the ideology of Yugoslavia calls for self-management by workers, substantially the same pattern of hierarchical control was found there as in the other countries. Even the factories in the socialist kibbutzim of Israel show the familiar hierarchical pattern, though to a lesser extent. Exceptions to the general principle are rare indeed.

Tannenbaum's method for measuring the degree of hierarchy is the control graph, the horizontal axis of which represents position in the organization from director to rank-and-file member and the vertical axis the amount of control exercised by each of the hierarchical echelons. The steeper the slope of the control curve, the more hierarchical is the organization. Because of practical difficulties with observational measures of the exercise of power by various echelons within the organization, Tannenbaum has used reported perceptions of organizational members. The following question is typical of this line of research:

In general, how much say or influence do you feel each of the following groups actually has in what goes on in your plant?

	Little or No Influence	Some Influence	Quite a Bit of Influence	A Great Deal or Influence	A Very Great Deal of Influence
Your plant manager	___	___	___	___	___
The other supervisors in your plant	___	___	___	___	___
The men in your plant	___	___	___	___	___

This question and related inquiries are posed for all levels of the organization and the averaged responses can be taken as a measure of control.

Perceptual measures of the type employed are subject to various sorts of error, and Tannenbaum has used three checks to establish their validity. In the first place, consensus among people at different echelons and among people who report to a common supervisor gives reassurance regarding some forms of individual and group bias. In the second place, organizations less hierarchical in nature (for example, voluntary associations) show gradients of control less steep than those of business enterprises. In the third place, within the same type of industrial plant there are differences in the slope of the control curves across five nations which accord with the ideology in and practices of those countries. The comparative study of organizations thus suggests

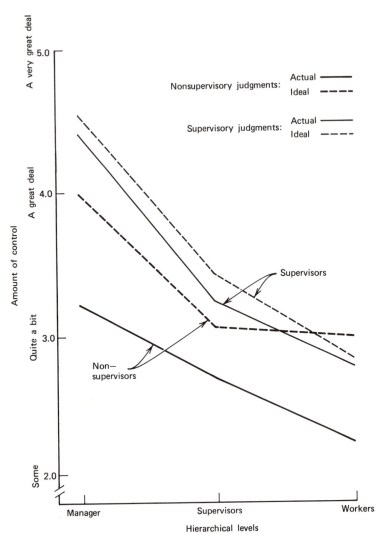

Figure 10-2 *Average control curves for 32 stations of a delivery company: actual and ideal control—nonsupervisors and supervisors.*
(From Tannenbaum, 1968, p. 78.)

the essential accuracy of the perceptual approach to the measurement of power and influence. Let us examine in more detail some of the research on control in organizations.

One great advantage of the Tannenbaum control graph is that it describes the exercise of power at the organizational rather than the individual level. It does not attempt measures of the democratic or authoritarian characteristics of specific persons but deals with the distribution of control within the organization. It illustrates how individually reported data can be used to construct measures of organizations as social systems.

Figure 10-2 presents the average control curves for 32 stations of a delivery company. Data are shown separately for rank-and-file employees and for the supervisory echelons, and separately for the actual control as perceived by people and the form of control they would ideally prefer. All four curves show a similar negative slope, with less influence attributed to lower than higher levels. Supervisors see all levels exercising more control than do the workers, and the workers want more influence than they see themselves as presently enjoying. But even this ideal pattern would give their superiors in the system more power than the workers see as desirable for themselves. According to people's perceptions as measured by the control graph, the amount of control is not a fixed sum or constant; increasing the amount of influence of one echelon does not necessarily mean decreasing the influence of another echelon. Thus organizations can be seen as varying in the *total amount of control* they utilize, as well as in its relative distribution. In this graph the men differ markedly from the supervisors in reporting *less* total control.

Figure 10-3 shows related findings from a study of 112 local leagues or branches of the League of Women Voters. Both the rank-and-file membership and members of the Board of Directors agree that the Board exercises more influence than the local president and the membership is lowest in actual control. In this voluntary organization the hierarchical principle is in evidence, but it does not elevate the local presidents above their boards of directors. Ideally, moreover, both officers and members feel that the membership itself should exercise the greatest influence.

Table 10-3 sums up comparisons of studies of voluntary associations, business-industrial concerns, and labor unions with respect to actual and desired (ideal) amounts of control. The hierarchical principle is clearly in evidence in that in all business organizations and in the great majority of voluntary associations the shape of the control curve was negative—which means less control exercised by people at the lower echelons. Not only do people in industrial enterprises report a negative slope, they also see this as a preferred state of affairs. This is less true of the rank-and-file than of their supervisors or officers, but it still holds for a majority of the rank-and-file. In the League of Women Voters, on the other hand, the majority of local chapters report a positively sloped control curve as ideal.

The five-nation study of control in organizations is sufficiently rich in research data to merit closer examination. The sample design called for matching ten plants in each of five countries by selecting a

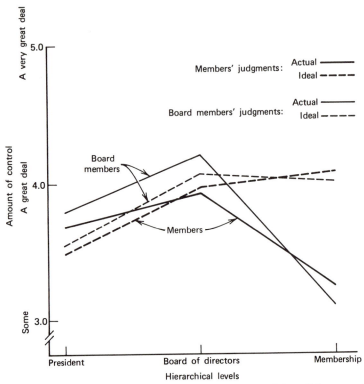

Figure 10-3 *Control curves, actual and ideal, averaged for all leagues, based on the judgments of members and board members.*
(From Tannenbaum, 1968, p. 65.)

large and a small plant in each of five industries—plastics, nonferrous foundry, food canning, metal works, and furniture. The plan could not be completely followed in the Israeli kibbutzim because all their plants are relatively small. The countries chosen represent a wide range of ideology and practice. Italy is the most traditional, and at the time of the study reflected a rigid authoritarian, family-centered pattern with a paternalistic orientation of the business elite. "Italian managers are reluctant to delegate authority and they tend to think of their authority in terms of personal power rather than in terms of a necessary function within the enterprise. The enterprise is seen as some sort of personal kingdom" (Ferrarotti, 1959, pp. 239–240. Quoted by Tannenbaum et al., 1974, p. 43). Haire, Ghiselli, and Porter (1966) have found that the Italian manager, compared to the American manager, is less supportive of a democratic ideology with respect to superior-subordinate relations.

Labor unions in Italy are more radical than unions in the United States, but their thrust is more in the direction of future revolutionary change than with running the factory today and tomorrow. American

TABLE 10-3 Organizational and Member-Officer Comparisons of Actual and Ideal Patterns of Control

	TYPE OF ORGANIZATION		
	Voluntary Association	Business-Industrial	Unions[b]
	% ($N = 112$)	% (73)	% (5)
I. Organizational type comparisons[a]			
(a) % of organization units having actual negative slope	88	100	20
(b) % of organization units having ideal negative slope	10	99	
(c) % of organization units in which ideal slope is more positive than actual slope	100	83	
(d) % of organization units in which ideal total control is greater than actual total control	89	94	
II. Member-officer comparisons[c]	($N = 112$)	(70)	(4)
(a) % of organization units in which actual slope members is more positive than actual slope officers	68*	47	0
(b) % of organization units in which ideal slope members is more positive than ideal slope officers	55	72*	
(c) % of organization units in which actual total control officers is greater than actual total control members	62*	72*	50
(d) % of organization units in which ideal total control officers is greater than ideal total control members	44	61	
(e) % of organization units in which members more often than officers indicate a more positive ideal than actual slope	41	77*	
(f) % of organization units in which members more often than officers indicate a higher level of ideal than actual total control	58	70*	

[a] Analysis based on responses of members.
[b] Measures of ideal control not obtained in the union studies.
[c] The null hypothesis in the member-officer comparisons is that $p = 50\%$.
*Significant at .01 level, 2-tailed test.
From Tannenbaum, 1968, p. 80.

TABLE 10-4 Management Principles in Industrial Plants in the Five-Nation Study

Illustrating Principles of	Kibbutz	Yugoslavia	U.S.	Austria	Italy
Ownership	Enterprise owned by the kibbutz of which the employees are members.	Enterprise owned by Society which delegates responsibility to the workers' collective consisting of all members of enterprise.	Enterprise owned by single individuals, by partners, or by shareholders.	Same as U.S. plus some state ownership.	Same as U.S. with more emphasis on family ownership.
Recruitment of managerial personnel	Elected, usually from among plant members.	Appointed and/or approved by the Workers' Council or an executive arm of the Council.	Appointed by superiors; emphasis on technical competence.	Same as U.S.	Same as U.S. with some concern for loyalty to family of owners.
Formal philosophy of management	Highly equalitarian based on socialist conception.	Highly equalitarian based on principle of self management and the definition of management as "technical coordination."	Bureaucratic and traditional tempered by human relations concerns and equalitarian cultural values.	Mostly bureaucratic and traditional with some human relations concerns.	Traditional, patrimonial, bureaucratic.

Organizational structure	Departmentalization; specialization; unity of command; scalar principle modified by participative principles and informal interpersonal relations.	Departmentalization; specialization; unity of command; scalar principle modified by principle of "self management" including Workers' Councils.	Departmentalization; specialization; unity of command; scalar principle; bureaucratic modified by informal "human relations."	Departmentalization; specialization; unity of command; scalar principle; bureaucratic.	Same as Austria with more personalized, patrimonial control
Formal decision making	Ultimate decision making power resides with the total membership.	Same as kibbutz.	Ultimate decision making power resides with owners, tempered by restraints such as unions, and legal requirements.	Same as U.S.	Same as U.S.
Reward system	Complete equality, with small financial allowance to all members. Some benefits distributed according to need.	Monetary rewards distributed according to rank and function. Medical and other benefits available to all.	Highly differentiated system of monetary rewards distributed according to rank and function. Other benefits also graded according to rank.	Same as U.S.	Same as U.S. with greater emphasis on status differentials.

From Tannenbaum et al., 1974, pp. 48–49.

unions, on the other hand, negotiate for reforms in the operation of the present system. In addition, American employees participate on an informal basis in everyday decisions more than is true in most European countries. Among the three capitalist countries, then, Italy would be the most hierarchical and the United States the least, with Austria falling between. In Yugoslavia and in the Israeli kibbutzim the formal structure involves the rank and file in making policy decisions, primarily through representative democracy in Yugoslavia with its Workers' Councils, and through direct democracy in the kibbutzim. Tannenbaum and his colleagues present a tabular summary of the differences among the five countries (see Table 10-4).

The data from the five countries on the amount of control exercised in their manufacturing plants (Figures 10-4 and 10-5) suggest the following generalizations:

1. The hierarchical principle holds for both capitalistic and socialist countries, although less for the latter than for the former. The Yugoslav plants have the flattest curves of any of the five countries, indicating greater equalization of power.
2. The slope of the control curve is very similar for both large and small plants. Only in Austria is there some tendency toward a more hierarchical pattern in large as compared to small plants.
3. The American plants are characterized by a greater amount of influence (total control) than are the plants in other countries.

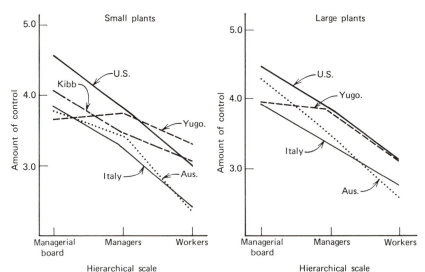

Figure 10-4   *Control distribution (all respondents). (From Tannenbaum et al., 1974, p. 59.)*

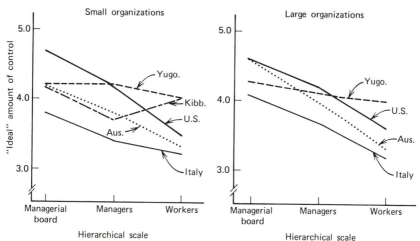

Figure 10-5   *Ideal control (all respondents). (From Tannenbaum et al., 1974, p. 63.)*

This is attributed to two factors. The top of the hierarchy is seen as having more influence than in any other country, and this is not counteracted by lesser influence at the lowest level. In fact in large plants the American factories are tied with the Yugoslav factories in showing the greatest amount of worker control.

4. There is a general tendency for the control graphs to be consistent with known structural and cultural differences among the countries, but some deviations do occur. Italy and Austria show the greatest contrasts to Yugoslavia and Israel. The United States shows considerable control at the worker level, which is in agreement with the pragmatic nature of American labor unions and with the relatively greater acceptance of informal participative procedures in American industry. One might have expected an even flatter curve among the kibbutzim in Israel than actually appears because of the ideology of these communes.

5. Discrepancies between *ideal* and actual control curves are not great in any of the five countries, but in general the ideal curve is not as steeply hierarchical as the *actual*. Again in Yugoslavia and Israel the *ideal* curve is flatter than the actual.

Is the Exercise of Power a Zero-Sum Game?

We have presented the research on control graphs as if it demonstrated compliance to coercive authority, but Tannenbaum interprets his findings to include other sources of power. It is true that in the industrial organizations studied, with the possible exception of the kibbutz, the superiors in the system have punishing sanctions at their disposal and that the duty to obey is universally recognized by subordinates. But it is also true that organizational members do not perceive influence patterns as deriving solely from binding orders from above. If they did, they would necessarily conceive of power as a fixed amount, so that the control exercised by the worker would detract from the control exercised by the boss, as in a zero-sum game. In fact, they believe that increasing the influence of the workers does not necessarily decrease the influence of their superiors in the hierarchy. This is why the total *amount* of control in organizations varies, even with the same slope of the hierarchical control curve. In Figure 10-4, for example, the United States and Italy show control curves with a similar negative slope, but the American factories show more influence at each level than the Italian factories.

The issue of power as a fixed amount or as an expandable pie has been the subject of much controversy in the social sciences, with the Dahrendorf and Marxian followers emphasizing the zero-sum nature of the game (the more you have, the less I have), and the Likert and McGregor supporters advocating the expandable amount of power.

What is central to the problem, however, is whether we are dealing with situations in which there is a community of interest or a conflict of interest. In other words, we need to know what the decisions are about, and how control is affecting the interests of the various parties. If the situation is one of commonality of interest, then we are dealing primarily with a persuasive process rather than a power struggle and the Tannenbaum thesis of an influence pie of expandable proportions is valid. Let us assume that A and B are working for the same goals, and that A will be influenced by suggestions from B and B by suggestions from A. The total influence exerted is greater than if A had merely given orders to B. And the effective outcome in productivity may well be greater and the returns to both members greater. When, however, we are dealing with a conflict of interest and A and B are engaged in a power struggle, then the more A controls a given decision the less power B has. Conflicts of interest do occur in the real world; they are not necessarily erroneous perceptions and they are not resolved by human relations assumptions that we are all brothers and sisters.

By and large the control curve of Tannenbaum can be interpreted as a gross measure of all kinds of influence exercised in organizations, whether the source is authority and coercion, economic rewards, or value realization. Coercive authority is nevertheless a central, if varying, component in compliance. The control curve reflects the authoritarian character of hierarchical systems and is flatter in situations in which value consensus is a more frequent basis of agreement.

THE EXERCISE OF AUTHORITY

We have defined authority as the power associated with a position in an organization. Let us turn to a closer examination of the pattern and nature of authority in hierarchical organizations, and the transactions by which it is exercised.

Assume that an organization is already created and ongoing. The division of labor has been accomplished and individuals assigned to specific positions in the organizational structure. For several purposes, but above all in order to see to it that the role requirements are carried out by each member, supervisory positions have been established. The supervisors are to instruct, communicate requirements for change, correct any deviations from required performance; in short, they are to influence. In turn, they are to accede to the influence of their own supervisors, and so on to the top of the hierarchy. The resulting set of role relationships constitutes the *authority structure* and provides for a highly selected and specialized set of influence transactions among the members of the organization.

First of all, the organization stipulates the *persons* who may engage in influence transactions with each other. This is done primarily by specifying the relationship of supervisor and subordinate between pairs of individuals (positions) in such a way that each person except the head of the organization has a supervisor, and each person except those at the very bottom of the hierarchy also have subordinates. The resulting structure of authority can be viewed as a set of dyadic power relationships, or it can be viewed as a set of power relationships between an individual (supervisor) and a collectivity or group (his or her subordinates). The transactions as they actually occur may be primarily between individuals or between the supervisor and the subordinate group as a whole. Likert (1961) has pointed out some of the differing consequences, for individuals and organization, resulting from these two patterns of interaction. By specifying the sets of actors among whom influence transactions are legitimized, the organization stipulates the *domain* or span of control of each supervisor, the set of persons over whom he or she has authority.

The resulting pattern of hierarchical relations is by definition *authoritative, asymmetrical,* and *transitive.* If the organization provides that A has authority over B, it follows that B does *not* have authority over A in the same affairs. Organizations need not be hierarchical in this sense, of course. The political model in the United States illustrates a kind of reciprocal power relationship between elected officials and their constituents which is neither perfectly symmetrical nor completely asymmetrical. The senator undoubtedly has certain power over his or her constituents—the indirect power of legislation and the direct power of appointment, for example. But the constituents have certain power over the senator, whom they can remove from office under special circumstances and keep from returning to office under any circumstances they choose.

Hierarchy implies *transitive* as well as asymmetrical authority. Each successive level in the hierarchy has authority not only over the echelon immediately below it, but also over *all* echelons below. There are limitations to this quality of transitivity in most organizations, as we have seen. On the whole, however, a vice-president exerts authority over his or her department heads and all persons reporting to them, and so on down the line.

Thus the formal, hierarchical organization stipulates *persons* (or agents), *domain*, *asymmetry*, and *transitivity* of authority. All these have to do with the pattern and scope of influence transactions in the organization. The organizational stipulations also include the circumstances, nature, and manner in which influence may be legitimately exerted. Perhaps the most frequent occasion for influence transactions between supervisor and subordinate is the failure of the subordinate to meet fully the requirements of the role, and the nature of the influence attempt is essentially correction. Probably the next most frequent occasion for transactions of influence between supervisor and subordinate is the introduction of change, especially the necessary local adaptation imposed by some decision arrived at higher in the authority structure. In such a transaction there is no fault implied nor any correction; the message is to do something differently because of a change in role requirements.

Influence transactions within the structure of authority are thus *role-relevant*, and the organization specifies the *range* of content that is to be so regarded. A supervisory request to a subordinate to alter mode of dress, off-the-job behavior, or choice of friends would be much resented and resisted. The basis for the resistance would be that the content of such influence attempts is out of the prescribed range, not organizationally defined as role-relevant. The supervisor has exceeded his or her authority. If the supervisor wishes to put the weight of authority behind such requests, their relevance to the subordinate's role performance must be made clear. Whether an employee chooses to spend the evening drunk or sober can be defined as a personal choice and beyond the organizational interest; the incapacitating morning hangover, however, is another matter.

The strength and form of a specific attempt will be affected by many considerations, and there is an extensive colloquial vocabulary for distinguishing among influence transactions in these respects. We speak of suggestions, requests, orders, commands, and the like. In general, however, we would expect the strength of the influence attempt to be coordinated to the organizational significance of the matter at stake, the nature of the interpersonal relationship between supervisor and subordinate, the folkways of the organization itself, and the individual personalities of the agent and recipient of influence.

The assertion that influence within an authority structure must be role-relevant points to the major *motive base* for the exertion and acceptance of influence. The presumption in an organization is that the supervisor is able to exert influence and does so because of the requirements of the role, not because of any nonorganizational caprice. The supervisor exercises authority primarily because the subordinate is doing something that is required and that the supervisor is required to see done. The motive for the influence attempt and for its acceptance have a common root—the acceptance of role in the organization and a desire to remain in that role structure. When the outraged subordinate in many an office joke says, "You can't do that to me; I quit!" he is also saying, "I am out of the system; therefore I no longer accept your authority, and I will not be influenced on that basis."

THE COSTS OF AUTHORITY

The proliferation of supervisory levels in order to reduce the risk of performance failures aggravates a problem inherent in all supervisory activity: efficiency. The language of organization is rich with reminders of the costs of supervision, and of the fact that the organizational means expended in supervision are thereby diverted from roles that contribute more directly to turning out the organizational product. We speak of direct and indirect costs of production, a relatively neutral choice of terminology. But we also speak of supervisory costs as part of the overhead expenditure of the organization, or more simply, as "the burden." The more hours of supervision per day of production, the greater is the burden. And the more supervisors who have any responsibility for overseeing a given job, the greater is likely to be the aggregate of supervisory hours invested. Organizations attempt to increase the efficiency of supervision by grouping together under a single supervisor roles which are similar in requirements or closely related in function. A supervisor may thus be assigned to supervise 20 workers, all of whom are operating identical machines, or to supervise a subassembly that involves several different kinds of jobs that are related. There is an attempt, in this way, to maximize the number of jobs that can be supervised by one person, and this attempt may persist throughout the several levels of management.

The pyramidal shape is an outcome of such proliferation of supervisory levels in order to reduce the risk of performance failure, and a concomitant effort to minimize the costs of supervision by prescribing for each supervisory office the widest feasible span of control. Much greater gain in efficiency might result from reducing the amount of supervision, perhaps stripping out whole levels of the authority structure. This, however, would require that the organization develop alternative means of insuring role performance, and the alternatives to the hierarchical application of legitimate power are relatively unexplored.

Still another of the forces that shapes the pyramid of authority is the organizational axiom that every required function must be clearly vested in some specific role. Whether this assertion deserves the status of axiom is debatable; that it enjoys that status in our culture is beyond debate. This implies that every organization must have an ultimate leader, a head of state. Suppose, for example, that a small manufacturing company has three major functional departments: manufacturing, sales, and engineering design. The efforts of the three departments must be coordinated if the organization is to produce and sell some article. The designers must create a design that can be mass-produced and sold; the manufacturing department must operate within costs that permit the sales force to dispose of the product. The need for coordination is obvious, but what are the means for coordination? The usual logic of organization says that since the three departments must coordinate, they must have a coordinator. Hence the organization acquires another level, a supreme commander.

We could object to this deduction. The three departments must coordinate; why should not the three department heads recognize this necessity and work out the necessary agreements? Such a triumvirate could be imagined, although it is easy to see how the need to break occasional deadlocks, resolve disagreements, and represent the organization to the outside world leads away from such a committee structure toward the elaboration of authority levels until the irreducible minimum has been achieved and we have a supreme level of authority with a single occupant.

A final explanation of the organizational pyramid lies in the pattern of organizational birth and growth. It is convenient for purposes of analysis to presuppose the existence of the direct productive roles in the organization, and then speculate on how this structure might be supervised. This is not the fashion in which organizations are created. Businesses typically begin with the definition of the top of the structure; the would-be founder or president is self-appointed and then tries to create the organization. The picture is somewhat different, of course, for voluntary and representative organizations, but so is the resulting structure of authority.

THE DEMOCRATIC ALTERNATIVE

It is in government and voluntary organizations that there has been developed the major alternative to the pyramidal structure for the administration of complex social organizations. That model we will risk calling democratic, in contrast to hierarchical, in spite of the value-laden nature of the terms. For the most part the subsystems of a democratic organization are the same as those of the hierarchical, other things being equal. The basic difference between the two is in the managerial subsystem, and specifically in the structure of authority.

We have said earlier (Chapter 3) that the managerial subsystem is not separate from the other subsystems of organization in terms of organizational positions (structure of offices); rather, the managerial subsystem interpenetrates the other subsystems. The shape and nature of this interpenetration in a democratic organization is very different from that in the hierarchical model. The pyramid of hierarchical organization represents a fusion of status, prestige, rewards, and power. As we ascend the pyramid, all these increase and reach their maxima at the pinnacle of the hierarchy. The president of a company typically receives the largest salary, enjoys the greatest prestige, can commit the organization to new policies, or veto such commitment. Within the limitations of law and collective bargaining, the president can hire a person into any job in the organization or fire one from any job; on the other hand, the president cannot be hired or fired by any other person in the organization. (In a public corporation, however, the president's powers may be subject to an outside board of directors.)

Particularly important to the nature of hierarchical organization is the increase in power of different kinds which characterizes each successive level in the hierarchy. Power is not only executive, having to do with the range and importance of acts of implementation; it is also legislative, having to do with the promulgation of organizational law and policy. In short, the hierarchical power includes not only the operation of the organization; it includes the definition of the organization, the power to determine that the organization shall be different tomorrow in policy and structure than it is today. It includes also, by virtue of the prerogative to hire and fire, the power to determine what combination of individuals shall play the stipulated organizational roles.

The democratic organizational model differs from the hierarchical specifically in separating those several aspects of power which are fused in the hierarchy. The distribution of power with respect to certain kinds of decisions is characteristically different in the democratic organization, being shared among the members of the body politic. Specific and crucial to the distinction between democratic and hierarchical structures is the separation of legislative from executive power. Executive power in democratic organizations usually is distributed in accord with the pyramidal structure of authority, which we have examined in detail in our discussion of hierarchy. Legislative power, however, shows a different distribution and is widely shared among the members of the organization. The fullest manifestation of this characteristic is implied in the slogan, "One member, one vote." The major criterion of democratic organizational structure, then, is the extent to which the legislative subsystem includes the entire membership of the organization. The working approach to answering this question would be to ask another: "Who makes the organizational policies?"

The distinction between policy-making (legislation) and policy implementation (execution) is not always made consistently, primarily because the view of the organization depends so much on location in the hierarchy—hence the truism "policy is what my boss decides." We propose that all organizational decisions can be arrayed with respect to three basic dimensions: level of generality, amount of organizational space affected, and extension in time.

Distinguishing between policy making and policy implementation in terms of these three dimensions implies a continuum of decisions rather than a set of discontinuous categories, with the policy-making component of decisions increasing as there is increase on these three dimensions. In general, policy decisions involve the formulation of substantive goals and objectives, and the formulation of procedures and devices for attaining goals and evaluating goal attainment. Execution involves the application of existing organizational machinery to ongoing operations, in the service of objectives already determined. (For a fuller statement of these definitions, see Chapter 15.) More specifically, if we were looking for policy decisions in the records of an organization, we would attend to decisions about the expansion or contraction of the organization itself, decisions to alter organizational structure in other ways (lines of authority, number of echelons). We would look for decisions to change the nature of the product turned out, to change the location of the organization in the larger environment, or to alter its relationship to the outside environment in other ways. Finally we would look for any decision involving a significant disbursement of organizational resources.

A second criterion of democratic structure is the veto, because it identifies the locus of ultimate organizational power. By whom, by what procedures, and under what circumstances can a given decision be overruled? The repeated presentation of an issue to successively higher levels of authority leads ultimately to the office of the president in a hierarchical organization, and to the assembled membership or their representatives in a democratic organization.

The final criterion which we propose for distinguishing hierarchical from democratic organizational forms is the basis on which selection, tenure, and dismissal are determined—especially for key executive positions. It is a characteristic of hierarchy that each level tends to have the power to name the persons who shall hold the positions at the next lower level. Where this power has been lost, its loss is keenly felt and much bewailed. The outstanding example in recent organizational history is the reduction in the hiring and firing power of the firm, and especially of the supervisor, by trade unions.

The democratic model, on the other hand, implies in its extreme form that each person shall be named to membership and position by the others. Variations on this theme are many, and not relevant for the present discussion. The crucial issue in the application of this criterion is the mode of selecting (and dismissing) the chief executive officers of the organization. The president-owner of a business is not dismissable by any power within the organization; the president of a corporation can be dismissed only by the board of directors (a quasi-external body). The president of a voluntary organization typically holds office for a stipulated term, is elected by vote of the members, and is subject to recall on the same basis.

All three of these criteria of hierarchy-democracy (the separation of legislative from executive power, the locus of the veto, and the selection of officers) are familiar in political science, although less often invoked in organizational theory. All three reflect the principle of government by the active and expressed consent of the governed.

The appropriateness of democratic and hierarchical structures to different human purposes and conditions is still unsettled. In organizational life, at least, we are inclined to the view that the advantages of hierarchy have been overstated. The military model, adopted in industry and extended with the development of machine-technology, seems to us to be overrationalized and urged by its proponents irrespective of organizational nature, purpose, and surrounding conditions. There are those who demand that every sector of life and every organization be businesslike.

We would propose as hypotheses that the hierarchical system is at its best in terms of survival and efficiency:

1. When individual tasks are minimal in creative requirements, so that compliance with legitimate authority is enough, and identification with organizational goals is not required;
2. When the environmental demands on the organization are clear and their implications obvious, so that information is redundant and can be wasted and the organization need not make use of all the potential receivers and processors of information among its members;

3. When speed in decision making is a requirement of importance, so that each additional person involved in the process adds significantly to organizational costs and risks;
4. When the organizational circumstances approximate those of closed systems, with minimal change requirements from the environment.

The advantages of democratic organizational structure reach a maximum under an opposite set of conditions, that is, when the organization is maximally open to environmental demands and when the environment is changing in ways that pose complex and difficult problems of organizational adaptation, so that great value attaches to receiving and using well all available information relevant to such changes and their implications. Democratic organization is particularly advantageous also when the correctness and appropriateness of organizational adaptations are more crucial than the speed with which the adapting decisions are made, and when the nature of individual roles involves creative efforts that require broad understanding of organizational functions and the motivation that comes from identification of one's goals with the aims of organization.

■ SUMMARY ■

A striking characteristic of behavior in organizations is the uniformity of response as documented by the J-curve studies of conformity to institutional symbols. Rule enforcement in modern bureaucratic structures is secured through a rational-legal system and the universal acceptance of the concept of legitimacy. Milgram's experiments on obedience demonstrate the power of this concept, which has a threefold basis in law, legal norms, and social values. The conditions conducive to legal compliance include: the socialization practices of the society and organization, the clarity of norms and requirements, and the use of specific penalties and sanctions.

Research has demonstrated the universality of the hierarchical principle of control in organizations. Tannenbaum and his colleagues have found that a wide variety of organized groups, from the military to voluntary associations show gradients of power based on position in the system. The same gradient was in evidence in factories in Italy, Austria, Yugoslavia, and Israeli kibbutzim, although the steepness of the control curve varied.

The exercise of authority in an organization should not be confused with authoritarianism. Organizations can have a democratic structure in which the source of legislative power is vested in the membership and the executive directives are an implementation of the wishes of the majority. Members still obey the rules. In an authoritarian system, however, both legislative and executive systems are under the control of the top echelons.

The process of insuring that each person's behavior shall be observed by another person to see that the requirements of organization are met is inevitably a source of great cost. Accordingly there are consistent efforts to minimize these costs, and the shape and process of authority reflects these efforts. The grouping of similar and related jobs under a single supervisor is a major example. This pattern, in combination with the building in of supervisory insurance by means of overlapping areas of authority (each supervisor having authority over immediate subordinates and also their subordinates, etc.), creates the characteristic pyramidal shape of the authority structure. The organizational tendency to vest each function in a single role and office makes it almost certain that the pyramid of authority will continue to the apex, at which an entire level of authority is represented in only a single office.

Rule enforcement can give us a formal hierarchical organization as an instrument of great effectiveness that can offer economies over unorganized effort. Its deficiencies must also be recognized. These include great waste of human potential for innovation and creativity and great psychological cost to the members, many of whom spend their lives in organizations without caring much either for the system (except its extrinsic rewards and accidental interpersonal relationships) or for the goal toward which the system effort is directed. The modification of hierarchical organization to meet these criticisms is one of the great needs of human life.

11

■ EXTERNAL REWARDS
■ AND INCENTIVES

OUTLINE

Types of External Rewards
Theoretical Issues
    Three Essential Conditions for a Reward Model: Valence of Goal,
    Connectedness of Behavior, Amount of Reward Relative to Effort
    Group Negotiation of Rewards
    The Concept of Expectancy
    Perception of Equity

Importance of Pay
Methods of Determining Pay:
Promotion and Advancement
    Criteria for Promotion

Praise and Recognition: Awards and Titles
Summary

The punishment model in American society has been heavily supplemented, although not replaced, by the reward model. Reinforcement theory has become the dominant form of behaviorism in psychology, and the perceived instrumentality of activities and objects is a central theme in more subjective theorizing. In schools and at work, punishments have been reduced in severity and prominence. They remain as a kind of substrate of authority; sanctions are available when other bases of influence do not suffice. But the emphasis is on rewards, especially rewards extrinsic to the desired behavior. It is in many ways a realistic emphasis.

The profit motive and competitive striving for monetary rewards is often assumed to be the dominant motivation of our society. One distinguishing mark of youthful countercultures is their questioning of the materialistic character of the older value system. In spite of this questioning, organizations are heavily instrumental in character and most members are responsive to material rewards. Owners and managers attempt to maximize profits and the rank and file attempt to maximize their individual return in exchange for labor. At the system level economic theory maintains that the marketplace produces an equilibrium between inputs and sales, and at the individual level between work and pay.

There are two extreme points of view about motivation in organizations that appear to be opposed at first glance, but are guilty of the same essential fallacy—equating the organization with the individual. The first view regards the organization as if it were an individual and attributes individual motivation to the giant over-person. The second commits this fallacy in reverse, and imputes organizational properties to persons, as if individual motivation and behavior at work merely presented in miniature the exchange of a product for a price. Both approaches involve a simplified motivational formula that takes no account either of the individual differences in behavior and drives comprising the complex organizational system, or of the behavioral outcome mediated through collective effort. Marschak (1965) has called attention to the fact that "the economists' theory of the firm has not been until very recently a theory of organization, for the theory ignored the fact that a firm is a group of individuals and dealt with the firm as if it were, in effect, a single person." (p. 447). Another challenge to the traditional view came from Cyert and March (1963), who studied the compromises and political maneuvering of subgroups within organizations and showed that the behavior of the firm is in significant degree the outcome of such pushes and pulls rather than a consistent course planned by a single individual. (See Chapter 15 for a discussion of the Cyert-March theory and research.) We require a treatment of external rewards that acknowledges their importance but acknowledges also the complexities of individual and organizational behavior.

TYPES OF EXTERNAL REWARDS

External rewards include not only monetary return, both pay and deferred benefits, but also advancement, pleasant working conditions, awards and praise from leaders, and other desired objects or aspects that are not intrinsic to the work itself. Work is often engaged in, not because it gives gratification in itself, but because it is instrumental to other objectives such as a good paycheck, the approval of prestiged people, or entitlement to health and retirement benefits.

The distinction between intrinsic and extrinsic rewards, especially in the work situation, was traditionally presented as a dichotomy. A more useful distinction, we believe, would locate the closeness of a given reward to a task in terms of three dimensions: time, space, and functional interdependence. Thus, a reward may be given immediately on completion of a task or may be long-deferred; a reward may be enjoyed at the work place or elsewhere, and a reward may be generated directly by the work activity itself or mediated by various intervening events and decisions. Pleasant working conditions are enjoyed at the time of task performance and at the place of work; one's access to them, however (short of dismissal), does not depend on quality or quantity of task performance. Monetary rewards are extremely flexible in time and functional connectedness to task performance; such rewards can be instant or long-deferred, as performance-connected as piece rates or as categorical as fellowship stipends. The exchange of money for goods and services, however, and the enjoyment of those goods and services must take place off the job. The satisfaction of artistic expression or artisanship is close to the task on all three dimensions.

THEORETICAL ISSUES

The distinction between intrinsic job satisfaction and other job-related gratifications has been neglected in recent work. It is of great theoretical and practical importance, however, and deserves a central place in any account of worker motivation. We treat the task-intrinsic motives of self-expression and internalized values in Chapter 13; this chapter is concerned with three more external types of reward: pay, promotion, and praise. In considering these external rewards, we shall also deal with such theoretical issues as the critical variables for a reward model, group negotiation of reward, the concept of expectancy and the perception of equity.

Three Essential Conditions for a Reward Model: Valence of Goal, Connectedness of Behavior, Amount of Reward Relative to Effort Expended

We shall begin with a consideration of the three essential conditions for the operation of extrinsic rewards and then see how these conditions are approximated in the organizational setting itself. (1) In the first place, since rewards are intended to induce the effort of individuals for the sake of some valued goal-object or condition, the reward must be desirable to the individual. Reward is a general concept, but all people do not find the same things rewarding, and it is the value of the reward to the individual that helps explain individual motivation. In other words, the value or desirability of the goal itself is a variable that can range from zero to some sizable magnitude and may vary for different people. Winning a gold watch or medal or certificate as a token of esteem of the company for fifty years of service has little meaning for the employee who does not care for the company's recognition. On the other hand, an increase in wages that makes possible a better standard of living can be of high value for the recipient.

(2) The second basic condition for the motivational effectiveness of an extrinsic reward is its connectedness to the required task. If the reward is to generalize to the behavior desired, it must be specifically administered for this behavior and withheld when the behavior is not forthcoming. Piece work and incentive pay run into complex problems in some organizations, but they can be more relevant to daily effort on the job than pay increases based on seniority. Performance bonuses and salary differentials have some similar potentiality for relevance. We need to take into account, as a second dimension in a reward model, the connection between the reward and the behavior actually being rewarded.

(3) A third consideration is the amount of reward in relation to the effort expended. People may see the tie between the reward and the required behavior, but may find the extra compensation a trickle compared to the flood of effort they have to expend to achieve it. Many pay incentive systems have suffered from this weakness. Jobs have been rigorously enough timed so that it requires more effort to go over standard than many workers feel is commensurate with the increase in monetary return.

Figure 11-1 presents these three dimensions of the desirability of the reward (goal), the connectedness between the required behavior and the reward, and the relationship between the amount of effort and the amount of the reward. The scale values of 1 and 2 in the figure are in a sense arbitrary; they merely indicate greater or lesser magnitudes. The zero value, however, is absolute; it signifies no reward value, no relationship between the means (task) and the goal (reward), and no probability that increased effort will bring success (Cells c, f, and i). Moreover, the model is multiplicative, which means that a strongly positive outcome requires all three factors to operate at a favorable level of response. Marked weakness of any one factor can mean the virtual failure of the reward system, and absence of any factor gives a total

	Desirability of Goal for the Individual	Connection of Means with Goal	Effort Related to Reward	Behavioral[a] Outcome
2	Very valuable (a) + 2	Very closely connected (d) + 2	Reward clearly increases with effort (g) + 2	
1	Some value (b) + 1	Fairly closely connected (e) + 1	Some relative increase (h) + 1	
0	No value (c) 0	No relation between means and end (f) 0	Reward does not increase (i) 0	

[a] Behavioral outcomes for possible patterns
$a \times d \times g = 8$
$a \times d \times h = 4$
$a \times d \times i = 0$
$a \times e \times g = 4$
$a \times e \times h = 2$
$a \times e \times i = 0$
$b \times d \times g = 4$
$b \times d \times h = 2$
$b \times d \times i = 0$
$b \times e \times g = 2$
$b \times e \times h = 1$
In addition, all other patterns containing c, or f, or $i = 0$

Figure 11-1 *Motivational Model for Rewards*

product of zero even when the other two factors are present in strength.

In the use of the multiplicative model and the consequent requirement that all the components be present to produce a motivational effect, we are following Atkinson (1958). The gold watch, to continue the previous example, may not be an effective reward even if the employee values the esteem of the company. If it is seen as a reward for growing old rather than being productive, it will not motivate productivity.

Those who use an oversimplified individual model of reward and motivation in the organizational context typically fail to take these three dimensions into account. To begin with, there is little analysis of the goals that people themselves find important. The assumption is that money is the medium into which they can translate all their objectives, and in our society the assumption is basically correct. Nonetheless, there is too much passing over other rewards, such as recognition and marks of prestige. The importance that employees sometimes attach to seemingly trivial differences—the size or position of their desks, for example, suggests a motivational pattern neglected by management.

The connection between the reward and the behavior required receives detailed treatment in Chapter 13; here we call attention to the fact that organizational rewards are often not geared to productive behavior. Nor would it be easy to bring them together. One of the complications inherent in organizational life is that productive behavior is often a collective effort, which implies that rewards for productivity would have to be collective rewards. It becomes difficult, if not impossible, to evaluate in equitable fashion for each member of the team his or her contribution to the team effort and the team outcome. A more just solution may be an equal share for all team members, as in the old place-mining system studied by the Tavistock researchers, where the members of one team were all on a common pay note (Trist et al., 1963). One reason for the difficulties with individual incentive systems is that they are often perceived as nonequitable in situations where the interdependent character of collective effort makes it difficult to assess individual contributions. Organizational theorists have often regarded the interdependence of workers as an unintended and even undesirable consequence of organizational design and technology. Yet interdependence can optimize the patterned cooperation that is the essence of an organization. In such situations the individual behavior that deserves reward is not necessarily the routine activity specified in the job description but rather those acts that are critical for the collective outcome of the group effort. The more general principle is that rewards for productivity should be allocated to the unit or level that can make a difference in productivity, whether that means individual incentives, group incentives, or an organization-wide bonus system of some sort.

Another advantage of a group reward is that it tends to change the nature of the motivation from attaining an extrinsic goal to an intrinsically satisfying activity. To participate in the accomplishment of the group means to be part of something greater than oneself and becomes more intrinsically motivating; we examine the importance of group achievement, however, in the following chapter.

Group Negotiation of Rewards

Another fact of organizational life that causes difficulties in introducing a pattern of differential rewards for individual productivity is the decision process by which reward patterns are typically established. Except for the use of piece rates, that process tends to avoid fine individual distinctions—either because they are difficult to explain and justify in practice or because the process itself involves negotiation for groups rather than individuals.

Wage levels for various types of tasks are determined in bargaining sessions between representatives of management and union representatives of workers. The settlement that is reached bears some relationship to worker productivity and worker demands, but there are many complicating factors that prevent a clear tie between individual effort and the amount of reward. For example, the strength of the union and the competitive position of the company in the industry influence the struggle, as does the skill and personality of the negotiators. In addition, the union officials are motivated by the survival and increased power of their own organization, and emphasize seniority and collective performance. Both sides find it easier to deal with classes of employees as defined by job category and seniority than to attempt an arrangement of individual rewards for individual efforts. For these reasons the use of individual extrinsic rewards has its limitations in influencing performance on the job. It is important *not* to equate the positive reinforcement of the laboratory with the use of rewards in organizational settings.

The Concept of Expectancy

At the individual level the concept of expectancy has been widely used to supplement the notion of the valence of the reward in accounting for the impulse to action. Vroom (1964) has adapted the multiplicative model of Atkinson to the work situation. Atkinson assumed that the strength of the motive multiplied by the value of the incentive and further multiplied by the expectancy or subjective probability of attaining the outcome would predict behavior. Vroom uses a similar formula in multiplying three factors: the perceived instrumentality of an action for reaching a goal, the value of that goal, and the expectation that an act will lead to a given outcome.[1] For example, a person may value becoming a doctor highly (valence of goal), may see entering medical school as an essential action toward that end (perceived instrumentality) but may have low expectancy of completing medical school (subjective probability of outcome). Lawler (1971) has proposed a slightly more elaborate model, which takes account of the subjective

[1]The Atkinson (1964) formulation has its origins in the work of Lewin (1938) and Tolman (1932), both of whom recognized the importance of expectancy and valence. Cartwright (1949) applied this approach in his principles of mass persuasion, for example, "to induce a given action by mass persuasion, this action must be seen by the person as a path to some goal he has." Peak (1955) and her students Carlson (1956) and Rosenberg (1956) emphasized the perceived instrumentality of beliefs in achieving end values as a basic principle in attitude formation and change. Georgopoulos, Mahoney, and Jones (1957) have put this hypothesis to test in an industrial setting, as has been noted on page 350. For a comparison of these formulations, see Lawler's critical discussion of theories of motivation in *Pay and Organizational Effectiveness* (1971, Ch. 4) to which he adds his own specifications (Ch. 5).

probability that effort will lead to intended performance based on the subject's self-esteem and previous personal and observed experience in similar stimulus situations. The Lawler formula also takes account of the individual's beliefs about the outcomes of accomplishment at a given level of performance, and the valence of these outcomes including negative as well as positive consequences.

The general point is that individual expectations and frames of reference play a part in the meaning of rewards. A worker may have as a frame of reference a set of expectations concerning people doing similar work and at about the same level of seniority; the worker then judges his or her own pay as low or high on this basis. We need to take account of the social context in which incentives are used, since an organization is social in its very nature and rewards are easily defined in relation to what other people are getting. Moreover, the comparisons people make can go beyond the plant to the larger industry and to other industries as well. When a union wins a wage increase in its contract negotiations, other unions make similar demands. White-collar workers have become unionized in part because they compared their lot to unionized blue-collar workers.

The frames of reference for evaluating wages and salary not only vary for employees but between employees and employers and even for employers themselves. Some administrators prefer to stress immediate performance; others give priority to promise for the future and value to the organization, or use cost replaceability in the market place as a criterion. And there are those who prefer uniform classification schemes, which can be easily defended because they avoid comparisons. Decisions made in the administrative structure often represent compromises between these various considerations.

Perception of Equity

When wages are so low that employees can barely eke out an existence, they evaluate their pay in terms of how well it meets their physical needs: whether or not it is *a living wage*. As pay increases to meet their needs, they soon use other standards, such as equity with respect to their inputs (*a fair day's pay for a fair day's work*) or with respect to what others receive (*equal pay for equal work*). Jaques (1961) years ago made the point that norms of equity take into account the relative prosperity or depression of the whole economy. His interview data also indicated that the greater the discrepancy between actual and equitable payment, the greater the individual state of disequilibrium. Jaques anticipated some recent research on equity theory in his statement, "over-equity payment [more than the accepted norm] brings about disequilibrium in the form of an insecure non-reliance upon the continuance of earnings, provokes fear of rivalry in others who are not favoured, and stimulates an anxious and selfish desire further to improve the favoured position" (pp. 142–143).

Because people do compare themselves with others, and because the resulting questions of equity are difficult to answer, many companies have followed a policy of secrecy about salaries and wages. As Lawler (1971) points out, this can lead to greater satisfaction if people underestimate what others are making but to greater dissatisfaction if they overestimate the pay of others. Research, in fact, shows that overestimation is more common than underestimation. Lawler holds that, "If pay had been well administered, the typical company would have much to gain by making pay public" (1971, p. 256).

The common expectancy and motivational models, in taking into account the individual's own psychological field, have skirted the important variable of the perception of equity. J. S. Adams (1963a, 1965) has remedied this weakness with his insightful recognition of the centrality of equity. He has postulated an imbalance in the person when the ratio of one's own perceived inputs in the work situation relative to one's returns are not equal to those of the relevant fellow workers. In other words, a person who is getting less pay for the same type and amount of work than his or her colleagues, will be upset, as Jaques (1961) suggested. Adams further held that when workers saw themselves as overpaid compared with their mates, they would suffer cognitive dissonance. In either case they could try to reduce dissonance by changing the quality or quantity of their own production. For example, workers overpaid on an hourly basis might produce more. For workers overpaid on a piece rate, producing more would increase the dissonance; hence they might turn out less work, but better quality work.

Experimental evidence from the laboratory is for the most part generally supportive of Adams' hypothesis about low productivity and high quality under conditions of inequitable pay. In the critical experimental condition, subjects were led to believe that they were unqualified to earn a standard proofreader's rate of 30 cents per page but were informed that they would be nevertheless hired and paid at that rate. The subjects made to feel poorly qualified were less productive in a two-hour period than an equitably paid control group but the quality of their work was better (Adams, 1963b, Adams and Jacobsen, 1964; and Moore, 1968).[2] There is reason for wondering how transient the

---

[2]For a review of additional research on equity theory and its application see Adams, J. S., and Freedman, S. Equity theory revisited: comments and annotated bibliography. In L. Berkowitz and E. Walster, eds. *Equity Theory: Toward a General Theory of Social Interaction, Vol. 9* of *Advances in Experimental Social Psychology.* New York: Academic Press, 1976.

findings from these laboratory experiments may be and whether they will hold on the job. In organizational settings it is not difficult for the worker to reduce cognitive dissonance produced by overpayment in other ways than through modifying the quantity or quality of work. All the worker needs do is find a reason for believing in his or her own special abilities or the lesser abilities of some colleagues, and over time such reasons can readily be found. Lawler et al. (1968) have data showing the temporary nature of dissonance produced by overpayment. After only two hours the overpaid subjects in a piece rate situation were producing at the same rate as equitably paid subjects and, of course, were earning more. The next step in research in this field is to explore directly the workers' perceptions of the equity of pay in organizational settings, the reasons for their perceptions, and the salient comparison groups they invoke when making judgments about relative fairness.

We have already suggested that a critical factor in perceived equity is the reference group with which the person compares him or herself. Thibaut and Kelley (1959) have used the concept of comparison level to refer to the standard by which an individual evaluates rewards in terms of what he or she "deserves" and in terms of realistic alternatives to present social relationships. Relevant research in industrial settings has lagged behind theory and little has been done to follow up the early work of Patchen (1961) on such questions. Patchen found a tendency for workers who are relatively low in pay to select those who earn more than themselves as comparison persons, especially if the higher earners are of similar status. The choice of a reference person was determined by the individual's relative wage position, perceived chances for promotion, and feelings of responsibility for present position. We would venture the hypothesis that people make their comparisons more frequently on the basis of their interaction and closeness with others than on Jaques' generalized other. They will evaluate their lot in relation to workers in the same plant doing similar types of work, or relatives and friends with whom they have frequent contact, rather than according to the state of the economy.

The phenomenon of the negative reference group also appears in the work of Lawler (1965), who reports that managers who see the pay differentials between themselves and their subordinates as too small are not happy about their salaries. A similar finding had been recorded by Andrews and Henry (1963) in their inquiry into pay dissatisfaction. Of the managers in the dissatisfied pay category, 87 percent thought there was not enough of a difference between their pay and that of their subordinates. Thus, the comparison process not only involves an attempt to answer the question "who am I like," but also the question "who am I not like." The answers to such questions tend to generate a scale or pattern of subjectively appropriate rewards.

It is also true that external rewards encourage an escalation of expectations. Since such rewards are highly visible and comparable (unlike the gratification of the artist in a painting), people readily become competitive in doing as well if not better than their fellows. Moreover, expectations increase because we become adapted to our old level of attainment. Years ago Hoppe (1930) demonstrated that individuals will shift their level of aspiration upward after achieving their objective and will move upward more readily after success than downward after failure. Downward mobility does not imply accepting the standards of a lower class as much as upward mobility means taking on the standards of an upper class.

IMPORTANCE OF PAY

The pecuniary accountancy of our society, to use Veblen's term, means that almost all objects, services, and qualities of life have a monetary value. In a relatively free market with a common means of exchange, the possession of money enables the possessor to satisfy a great variety of needs and wants. Hence, pay is central in the extrinsic rewards offered by the organization, for it is a common denominator for all types of desires, both materialistic and altruistic. For one person a wage increase may mean a better car, for another adequate medical treatment for a partially blind child. When employees themselves are asked to assess the importance of different incentives they are sometimes reluctant to give wages the verbal priority that their actions would imply.

Lawler (1971), in a review of 49 research studies on the relative importance of pay compared to such factors as job security, interesting job, kind of company management, appreciation of one's work, and chances for advancement, found pay to average third from the top of the list (see Table 11-1). The previous review by Herzberg and his colleagues (1957) had shown pay to be less important but Lawler's survey is more complete. The fact that pay does appear near the top of the list in many studies is all the more significant in that there is less social desirability in this response than in giving priority to interesting work.

Another method of ascertaining the importance of pay is to see how much of the variance it accounts for in other job-relevant responses. Barnowe, Mangione, and Quinn (1973) constructed a model of job satisfaction from a national sample utilizing 33 job facets and found that workers' pay was ninth in importance among such factors, and that it explained 11 percent of the criterion variance (overall job satisfaction). Campbell, Converse, and Rodgers (1976) replicated their finding in another national survey in an analysis of job attributes and personal

TABLE 11-1   Studies of the Importance of Pay

Study (by year)	Population Sampled	No. of Factors Ranked	Ranking of Pay	Terms Used for Pay	Rating Instruction
Ho (1930)	Employees quitting department store		1	Wages	Important as reason for quitting
Chant (1932)	Young men in variety of occupations	12	6		
Hersey (1936)	Factory workers	14	1	Amount of pay	Important management policy
Wyatt & Langdon (1937)	Factory workers (women)	10	4		
Watson (1939)	National sample	8	3	Pay	Important as morale factor
Blum & Russ (1942)	Males	5	3		
	Females	5	4		
Berdie (1943)	Male high school graduates	12	3		
Foreman Facts (1946)	Employees	10	5	Good wages	Important
Mayo (1946)	Male and female employees	36	1	Pay	Frequency of mention
Jurgensen (1947)	Job applicants, one company	10	6	Pay (large income during year)	Important to you
NICB (1947)	Employees, five factories	71	2	Compensation	Most important

Study	Sample	N	Very highly paid job	Rank	Choosing job
Centers (1948)	Cross section, male working population	10	Pay	6	Important to you
Jurgensen (1948)	Job applicants, one company	10	Pay	5.5	Important
Lindhal (1949)	Employees	10	Good wages	5	Important about job
Wilkins (1949, 1950)	Young men entering Army	8	Pay	2	
Evans & Laseau (1950)	GM employees		Wages	1	Frequency of mention as desirable feature
Fosdick (1950)	Retail employees	8	Pay	3	
Stagner (1950)	Employees, one large company	10	Pay rate	2	Important to you
Stagner (1950)	Workers in large firm	10	Pay rate	2	
Stromsen & Dreese (1950)	Civil servant interns		Financial rewards	3	Career problems in civil service
Worthy (1950)	Retail store employees	14	Pay	8	Important for high morale
Bose (1951)	Workers (India)	10	High pay	1	
Hardin, Reif, & Heneman (1951)	Men	10	Pay	4	Important to you
Schaffer (1953)	A typical sample of males	12	No clear pay items (one on economic security, one on economic status)		
Smith & Kerr (1953)	Employees quitting forty-eight companies	18		1	
C. Dickinson (1954)	College seniors	7	Salary	4	Importance in selecting job

continued

TABLE 11-1 Studies of the Importance of Pay (continued)

Study (by year)	Population Sampled	No. of Factors Ranked	Ranking of Pay	Terms Used for Pay	Rating Instruction
Ganguli (1954)	Factory workers (India)	8	1	Adequate earning	Rate on what wanted from job
Graham & Sluckin (1954)	Workers (England)		1	Pay	Important as job factor
Troxell (1954)	Heterogeneous sample	10	3	Good income	Important for satisfaction
Bendig & Stillman (1958)	College students	8	3.5	Good salary	Selecting job
Kahn (1958)	Workers and foremen	10	1	Steady work and steady wages	Want from job
Rosen & Weaver (1960)	Managers, one plant	24	No clear pay item		How important condition is
Porter (1961)	Middle-level managers	7	4	Pay	Important to me
Rim (1961)	Students (Israel)	12	4	Good salary	Selecting job
Bhatt (1962)		9	3	Wages	Importance of job characteristics
Dill (1962)	Masters students	12	4	Earn enough money	How preferred the characteristic is
Gruenfeld (1962)	Supervisors, eleven companies	18	9	Higher wages	Desire for rewards
Stuhr (1962)	Office workers	8	1	Recommendation for pay increase	

Study	Group				
Singh & Wherry (1963)	Factory workers (India)	10	2	Adequate earnings	Important to you
Chalupsky (1964)	Scientists	23	1	Merit salary increases	Important as an incentive
Spitzer (1964)	Supervisors	9	3	Make money in long run	Important
Heller & Porter (1966)	Managers (U.S.)	8	3	Pay	Preference
	Managers (England)	8	2	Pay	Preference
Centers & Bugental (1966)	Cross section, working population	6	1	The pay	Remaining on present job
Lahiri & Choudhuri (1966)	Workers (India)	21	1	Adequate earnings	Important to you
Lawler (1966c)	Managers	6	2	Pay	Important to you
Schwartz, Jenusaitis & Stark (1966)	Workers	10	3	High wages	Personal preference
LIAMA (1967)	College students	9	3	Good income	Important
Charnofsky (1968)	Pro baseball players		1	Personal gain	As reason for playing baseball
Poduska (undated)	Retail store executives	14	3	Pay	Importance

From Lawler, 1971, pp. 40, 41, 42.

characteristics and reported that earnings contributed 12 percent of the criterion variance.

Gupta and Quinn (1973) examined the substitutability of various rewarding job attributes in determining overall job satisfaction, and found that increases in one type of satisfaction do not necessarily affect other job facets. They state,

> ... there were no trade-offs between challenge and income in their effects on job satisfaction and lack of challenge in a job was not compensated for by high pay to obtain a specific level of job satisfaction. (p. 333)

A number of studies report that the amount of pay that individuals receive is negatively related to the importance they attach to financial rewards—that is, the poorly paid worker attaches more importance to money than the well paid worker (Lawler and Porter, 1963; Ganguli, 1954). This seems intuitively plausible and is consistent with Maslow's hierarchy of needs and motives. Hahn (1977), however, was not able to confirm this result, though she did corroborate earlier findings that blue-collar workers value financial returns more than white-collar workers (Centers and Bugental, 1966) and that union members attached more importance to pay than white-collar workers (Ganguli, 1954). When, however, Hahn looked at relative income as against absolute income, she discovered that people who were either overcompensated or undercompensated attached less importance to pay than those who were equitably treated. The measure of equity was derived from comparing actual income with that which the respondent might expect. It is easy to account for the overpaid worker attaching less importance to money since the measures are not completely independent of one another. It is not so easy to explain why the underpaid worker should evaluate pay as unimportant unless one invokes a dissonance explanation or assumes a process of self-selection by which disinterest in money leads to underpayment. It is of interest that the results for the underpaid hold for men and not for women. Among both the underpaid and overpaid, the people deprecating pay were those who reported they had little control over their compensation.

METHODS OF DETERMINING PAY

The debate over methods for determining pay probably began with the notion of payment itself, and it continues. A central issue in this debate is the use of piece rates and other such pay-for-performance formulas, in contrast to the flat wage or payment for time at work. Piece rates are used for only about 30 percent of jobs in the United States, but that is the bottom of the estimated international range—43 percent in the United Kingdom, 50 to 70 percent in Eastern Europe and the Soviet Union, 63 percent in Sweden (but 95 percent of industrial jobs in Sweden). Piece rates are reported in China, but no data are available on the extent of their use (Lawler, 1971; Lindholm, 1972; Swedish Employers' Confederation, 1975).

The argument for piece rates has been their incentive effect, the presumption of increased productivity (Hoffman, 1964; Richman, 1964; Edgren and Rhenman, 1967). The counter-arguments have been presumed side effects, such as losses in quality and negative worker attitudes (Yoder, 1947; Marriott, 1957). Data have been meager compared to the continuing richness of the rhetoric, but offer some support for both sets of presumptions. Small experiments, typically involving successive periods of some weeks at different methods of pay, present a number of methodological problems but an impressive consistency in findings over a half-century: payment for performance leads to increases in performance (Vroom, 1964; Locke, Bryan, and Kendall, 1968). Less evidence is available regarding the effects of piece rates on worker attitudes and well-being. Lawler (1971) concludes that managers favor pay for performance and that workers, while less favorable, are not opposed. Kahn (1952) found that workers in an appliance-manufacturing plant were on the whole more favorable to payment for time than for productivity, but that there was some tendency for workers to prefer the system by which they were paid and to which they were accustomed. There was general agreement that they worked harder on piece rates. Several more recent studies in Scandinavia show piece-rate payment to be associated with dissatisfaction (Ohlstrom, 1970), feelings of distress (Bohlinder and Ohlstrom, 1971), and indicators of poor mental health (Gardell, 1971). Guttormson and Smith (1971), in a study of 2700 government employees (Swedish national postal bank) found them about equally divided in their preferences, with some tendency for opposition to piece-rate payment to increase with experience and with age. There was also a decrease in feelings of well-being and comfort, a decreased propensity to help others at work, and an increase in feelings of distress.

Levi (1972) conducted an experiment handicapped by small numbers ($N = 12$) but notable for its manipulation of methods of pay in a real-life situation and for the measurement of physiological as well as psychological reactions and performance. Twelve invoicing clerks, all women between the ages of 18 and 31, worked alternate days on piece rates and on "monthly" rates. The piece rates were really a bonus or incentive paid for production above the previously established group mean, after deduction for errors. Results were unequivocal; the method of payment affected every criterion variable. Productivity doubled (from 155 to 331 invoices per hour), and there were no increases in errors. Reported psychological reactions included some feelings of being rushed, some increase in physical discomfort and fatigue (but only to "moderate" levels). Physiological reactions included increases in adrenaline, noradrenaline, creatinine, and urine flow. One subject showed doubled adrenaline output and became temporarily ill.

Generalization of the experimental results is not easy, in spite of their immediate clarity. Would the findings hold for longer periods of time? Would they hold for men as well as women, old as well as young? And would they hold for cultures less integrated and productivity oriented than the Swedish? Above all, the question of social values and social policy persists: how much stress for how much product?

Some suggestive data on this topic have been accumulated by the Swedish Employers' Confederation (Lindholm, 1972), for 73 plants that made one of three changes in the method of wage payment: from piece-work to fixed wages, from piece-work to premium systems (base wage plus premium rate for exceeding a productivity norm), or from fixed wages to premium systems. Plants in the first group (piece work to fixed wages) reported decreases in efficiency of from 15 to 25 percent, but "a universal calmer working climate has been noted." Plants in the second group reported productivity gains of 5 to 10 percent, and those in the third group reported gains of 25 to 35 percent.

This was by no means a controlled experiment, nor was it conducted by a neutral organization. The results, however, point up some of the problems, if not the answers to them.

PROMOTION AND ADVANCEMENT

Promotions generally bring with them increased responsibility, greater task complexity, and higher pay; they are therefore compounded in their impact. They represent a fusion of the rewards the organization can offer, and the opportunity for advancement can be highly motivating. Promotion, of course, has to be linked to performance in the eyes of organization members if it is to have a motivating effect. Georgopoulos, Mahoney, and Jones (1957), in their study of over 600 workers in an appliance factory, found a significant relationship between productivity and the belief that poor performance would hurt one's chances for promotion. In a steep pyramidal structure, however, promotions are extremely limited in number and very few employees can realistically think about moving up in the system. Two types of organizations are more fortunate in this respect: voluntary and rapidly growing organizations.

The voluntary organization, as we have noted (see pp. 315–317), has a flatter control curve, which means relatively more leadership positions than the business enterprise. There is also likely to be more turnover of officers in the voluntary organization and more chance for upward mobility. In American political parties, for example, new recruits who are able and hardworking soon find themselves named to more offices than they can handle, for here advancement is not compounded with pay. The rapidly growing organization also can offer many opportunities for advancement, and it often has high morale because its younger members see the possibility of quick progress in their careers. But in most organizations the lack of openings in the upper echelons creates barriers between the layers of the system. The rank and file see themselves as captives rather than as participating members of the system. This is especially true in enterprises in which the ladder of opportunity has a low ceiling, as it does when workers lack the technical qualifications to move beyond the position of straw boss and the company hires supervisors from outside applicants with different educational backgrounds.

A policy issue that confronts every management is whether to promote from the inside or to go outside the organization to fill vacancies at higher levels. The advantages of staying within the system are greater motivation and morale among members in the long run, greater stability of direction and operation, greater familiarity with the candidates, lower cost than in the comprehensive outside search. The increased morale resulting from promotion from within is accentuated if the vacancy is at a high level in a large organization, so that the promotion creates a string of vacancies down the line. Thus, White (1970) speaks of chains of opportunity, as the vacancy moves down the hierarchical line and permits a number of mobile individuals to move up. One vacancy at a high level can mean a dozen promotions.

The advantages of outside recruiting are the influx of new ideas and practices, greater range of experience and ability among candidates, the breakdown of institutional discrimination against minority groups, and the possibility of less conflict, politics, rivalry, and resentment among people on the inside. These factors take on different weightings for various organizations confronting different situations. Stability may be more important for one organization at a certain point in its history, and new directions more important for another organization. It is not always true that going outside opens up a wider range of capable candidates, and the intraorganizational variance among candidates needs to be compared with interorganizational variance. The merit of promoting from within depends on the quality of the institution compared to its competitors. A gigantic electronics firm may have more talent within its ranks than a small marginal concern, and a policy of promoting only from without would hurt the large company more than the small one. The general tendency is to try some mix of policies over time, with an emphasis on promotion from the inside. There is a self-perpetuating trend in the upper echelons of most systems and some organizations have limited self-succession in certain positions in order to insure rotation of personnel. One can hypothesize that organizations would profit from more attention to the comprehensive outside search, especially for top level positions.

The forces for the perpetuation of old ways are institutionalized in organizations and one way of dealing with environmental change is through new leadership. Moreover, there is a limit to the drastic changes that the new leader may represent, in that even an outside search is likely to be restricted to similar personnel with similar backgrounds. When a college or university seeks a new president it generally selects from the same pool of candidates being utilized by another institution also seeking a head. An interesting research project would be to examine how common such a pool of names is for given leadership posts and how these names got there.

Criteria for Promotion

The main dilemma in promotion, especially promotion from within, is what criteria to employ for evaluating candidates. Performance on the job is the best indicator of future performance, but if we look at past performance we are dealing with behavior that may not be relevant for the new position. The good production worker may not make a good supervisor. The effective college teacher may not make a good dean, and the successful research scientist may not make a good university president.

The Peter principle (1969) satirizes this point by asserting that people are promoted to their level of incompetence—they keep getting moved up from jobs they are doing well until they reach a position at which they do poorly. Thus incompetence is often encountered at high organization levels. The Peter principle overlooks two major facts. In the first place, far from rising to a position of incompetence, most people don't get promoted at all. Most production workers remain production workers, and most typists remain typists. Promotions are just not that frequent. In the second place, competence does tend to generalize, and most forms of ability show some degree of positive correlation. The mental testers have confirmed Spearman's theory of a general factor as well as specific factors in intelligence. Nonetheless the jest of the Peter principle calls attention to the necessity of taking into account the requirements of the new position in relation to the applicant's old demonstrated skills. This becomes all the more critical as affirmative action programs encounter institutional discrimination in promotion policies in which women and blacks are sometimes excluded because they apparently lack the requisite experience in more subordinate posts. The assumption is made, often without evidence, that experience at the next lower level is an important factor in successfully operating at a higher level. This may or may not be the case, and research has still to be done to determine the relevance of experience for given types of positions.

It is also true that managers entrusted with the responsibility of making decisions about promotions can lag behind the company policy on equal opportunity either because they do not believe it, because of pressures from third parties such as clients or colleagues, or because of their own prejudices. Quinn et al. (1968) conducted interviews with 130 managers in large manufacturing plants and took as a measure of discrimination the managers' own reports on their willingness to promote Jews. Although this self-report probably underestimated the amount of discrimination, it was positively related to such factors as the manager's perception that the company's actions were inconsistent with its equal opportunity policies, the manager's exposure to third party pressures, anticipation of negative responses from the potential subordinates of a Jewish candidate, and anti-Semitic attitudes and stereotypes. Discrimination in upgrading was suggested by the criteria executives said they used in determining promotion. They rated 25 traits in terms of importance for management positions. Factor analysis revealed ability dimensions as dominant but a clear pattern of nonability that can be labeled *social credentials*. This factor included the following six traits: has the right social background, belongs to the right club or lodge, lives in a good section of town, is white, is a graduate of a prestige college, and is native born.

A continuing problem for an organization is the development and use of criteria for wage increases and upgrading. Large systems like corporate business structures or big school districts move toward uniform classificatory schemes in which increments are based on seniority and other clearly visible indicators of performance. The principle of meritocracy calls for distinctions between degrees of merit, but its application creates disputes and difficulties. Ease of administration and the need to defend administrative actions results in a tendency toward improving the reliability of criteria at the sacrifice of validity. Seniority, for example, is a highly reliable measure but not necessarily a valid criterion for promotion. Hence we often find a systematic degradation of criteria for rewards.

PRAISE AND RECOGNITION: AWARDS AND TITLES

In Western culture individuals receive nonmonetary reinforcements of various sorts from praise, titles, and honorific awards. The elementary school teacher gives gold stars to pupils for learning their lessons, the football coach awards stars to be affixed to helmets for stellar performance on the field, and professional societies award gold medals to distinguished scientists. How much the effect of external rewards can be explained as operant conditioning and how much as the eliciting of the ego motive of self-esteem is an open question. Behavioral theory would account for the arousal of ego motives through the principle of reinforcement and would not seek a more subjective explanation. Many experimental findings confirm the efficacy of verbal reinforcement in modifying behavior. Verplanck (1955) has demonstrated that merely agreeing with or rephrasing a person's spoken statements will increase the frequency of expression of an opinion. He found this to be true whether the experiment was conducted in the home, a restaurant, a hospital ward, a public lounge, or over the telephone. Endler (1966) reinforced some subjects by indicating their responses were correct when they agreed with a contrived group consensus and others when they disagreed. Reinforcement for agreeing produced more conformity than reinforcement for disagreeing, and the extent of this effect was a function of the amount of reinforcement.

Earlier Greenspoon (1955) used an assenting murmur ("mmm-hmm") for some subjects whenever they used a plural noun and a dissenting murmur for other subjects for the utterance of plural nouns. The setting was a simple laboratory task in which the subject was asked to say all the words he or she could think of in 50 minutes. The assenting murmur increased the number of plural nouns spoken and the dissenting murmur decreased the number, even though subjects were unaware of their conditioning. Rowley and Keller (1962) used the word *good* as a reinforcer for one group of subjects and a smile and a nod of the head for another group. The subjects were children between 9 and 12 years and the task was to construct short sentences from words on stimulus cards including a verb and several pronouns. Sentences beginning with *We* or *I* were reinforced and resulted in more use of this class of verbal behavior than in the control group. Verbal approval, incidentally, was even more effective than the smile and head nod. The use of conditioning has been further extended by applying it to attitude formation and to nonverbal behavior. Krasner, Knowles, and Ullmann (1965), for example, have shown that the experimenter, by approving the expression of positive attitudes toward medical science, could enhance these responses and increase performance in a task requiring muscular effort.

These experiments suggest that the reinforcement of operant responses is sufficient to produce the continuation of certain behavior and the failure to reinforce can result in the dropping out of responses—in other words, behavior modification. In fact, behavior modification has become something of a cult in dealing with learning problems, eating, drinking, and smoking habits, and neurotic and psychotic disorders. Curiously, it has not been applied systematically to the improvement of organizations, although it would fit well with the machine theory of organization. But it is one thing to reinforce the correct response of a pigeon in a Skinner box and another to program supervisors so that they emit sounds of approval when the worker makes the right move. It would mean a much higher ratio of supervisors to workers than commonly found now and would entail very close supervision. This encounters the difficulty that the work process is already routinized with many employees objecting to their robotlike roles. Research has amply demonstrated that workers perform better when not supervised closely (Katz, Maccoby, and Morse, 1950).

Skinnerian reinforcement theory has something to contribute to the old debate about the relative merits of reward and punishment. It holds that the emphasis on punishment has led to ineffective learning and inadequate training. It is the violation of rules that is accompanied by penalties rather than the reinforcement of their observance by reward. Hence, people identify rules with negative sanctions rather than with positive outcomes. It would be difficult to apply the Skinnerian model to organizations in that it is so much easier to invoke a penalty for an occasional departure than to provide almost constant rewards for expected behavior. Nonetheless, the trend in Western society has been to replace punishments with rewards, and it is possible with further societal restructuring organizations may utilize Skinnerian principles more fully.

There is no doubt that praise can be an effective moderator, if not as Skinnerian reinforcement on a programmed basis, then as the elicitor of ego motives of self-esteem. The part played by the subjective evaluation of the individual personality in reacting to rewards has been shown by Galbraith and Cummings (1967) in their study of 32 workers in a plant manufacturing heavy equipment. They found that the value of outcomes multiplied by perceived instrumentality of performance in attaining the reward predicted to productivity. This was especially true when the reward was consideration and support from the supervisor. Output was highest for those workers who valued the praise from their superior and who believed such recognition was contingent upon producing well.

The use of approval to engage ego motives is widely recognized in the everyday world and this practical recognition has run far ahead of scientific acceptance and analyses of the phenomenon of social approval. One reason for the lack of application of Skinnerian principles in industry may be the alternative use of appeals to the ego as developed in the human relations philosophy of McGregor and Likert. There is little need for a mechanical system of automatic pellets for atomized responses when the whole individual can be energized toward a set of goals by engaging ego drives. Likert has recognized this in his proposed System 4 (see Chapter 19) designed to provide recognition and social support to the organization member. Approval is not conditional on the performance of a specific act as in reinforcement theory but rather is assurance and support for the individual as a fellow human being. Ego involvement, moreover, goes beyond extrinsic rewards in that the ego-rewarding activity becomes gratifying in and of itself. Hence we consider it in the following chapter on value consensus and intrinsic rewards.

SUMMARY

External rewards in organizations include pleasant working conditions, monetary return, promotions, awards, praise, and other incentives not intrinsic to the work itself. A reward model must take account of three factors: the valence of the goal toward which the reward may be instrumental, the connectedness or instrumentality of the behavior to the goal, and the amount of reward in relation to the effort expended. Organizational life makes it difficult to apply such an individual model because rewards are group negotiated through union bargaining and because the interdependence of roles often does not permit ready identification of individual effort. At the individual level the concepts of expectancy and equity are helpful in understanding how people evaluate rewards. The ratio of one's own perceived inputs relative to one's returns is compared to those of one's fellows.

Studies of the importance of pay show that it receives relatively high, but not top, ranking where employees themselves state their priorities for various job-related factors. It accounts, however, for only 11 or 12 percent of the variance in job satisfaction in national surveys. The poorly paid worker is more likely to attach importance to financial rewards than the well paid worker. Piece rates can influence productivity but only when the conditions of the reward model are met. Otherwise there can be negative effects of poor quality of work and low morale.

Promotions head the list of external rewards available to the organization because they mean higher pay, greater prestige, and more power. This is one reason why organizations may follow a policy of promotion from within. Nevertheless the advantages of outside recruiting for leaders are recognized and organizations will institutionalize devices for a national search to counteract pressures for internal promotion. The criteria for promotion have not been systematically studied. The Peter principle that people are promoted to their level of incompetence may have a grain of truth. It is easier to promote people on the basis of their past achievements than to assess the relevance of that experience for the higher job. Actual practices thus lag behind ideological commitment to equal opportunity. One study of managers in large manufacturing plants found that their ratings of traits important for management positions yielded, in addition to ability factors, a factor of social credentials.

Skinnerian reinforcement theory holds that punishment leads to ineffective learning and inadequate training. Violation of rules is accompanied by penalties but the effective procedure would be to reinforce observance of rules with reward. It would require considerable reorganization of social systems to utilize Skinnerian principles since it is easier to invoke a penalty for an occasional departure than to provide almost constant rewards for expected behavior. The use of approval can be used to engage ego motives and the eliciting of such motives belongs to the next chapter on internalized motivation.

12

▩▩ INTERNALIZED ▬▬▬▬▬▬▬▬▬▬
▩▩ MOTIVATION ▬▬▬▬▬▬▬▬▬▬

Both the punishment and reward models of motivation regard the individual from outside and, in more than one sense, from above. It is as if psychologists had imposed on the real world the familiar role allocation of the laboratory experiment. The leaders of organizations are the experimenters, in control of the aversive and pleasurable stimuli and also in control of defining the tasks. The rest of the human population is by implication assigned to the remaining role, subjects in the great experiments of reward and punishment. Many objections might be made to this characterization, not the least of them that it is indeed descriptive of the real-world situation and no invention of social science. The fact of external emphasis remains nonetheless true.

There are formidable problems in applying such models to organizational life, as we have seen, many of them having to do with the differential effects of rewards and the unintended effects of punishments. No organizational rewards have the dependable reinforcing effect of the food pellet at the end of the maze or the chocolate drop in experiments with children. External rewards are interpreted and assessed according to the subjective standards of individuals, especially those relating to equitable comparison. Punishments may be more uniformly experienced, but they are peculiarly vulnerable to unintended effects when they are imposed in situations where constraints are limited and power is possessed by those punished as well as those who impose punishment. Resentment of authority, avoidance of organizational edicts, and counterorganizational developments are familiar managerial problems.

At the other extremes from these external models are the earlier writings in the human relations tradition. Likert's *New Patterns of Management* (1961) does not include in its index the words wage, salary, money, or reward, nor any reference to punishment. McGregor's (1960) well-known contrast between Theory X and Theory Y is not merely a distinction between managerial styles but between two different sets of assumptions about human nature and human motivation. The Theory-Y manager believes in internal sources of motivation.

Management in all kinds of organizations and at all levels has always been interested in internal motivators—love of craft, commitment to doing a good job, identification with the success of the larger enterprise, and the rest. Managerial interest in such matters, however, has developed on a rather specialized basis. The operational if unspoken question has been, "How do we get people to want to do what we already want them to do?" The reciprocal questions have seldom been asked: "How can tasks be defined so that they are intrinsically rewarding to those who perform them? How can organizations be designed so that members find them worth identifying with?"

Because such questions have been so seldom asked, a great deal has been learned about building constraints and rewards and penalties into human organizations, and much less about the ways in which the enactment of organizational roles can be made self-rewarding. We will approach that issue by examining several categories of internal motivation and the contingent conditions for their expression.

SOURCES OF INTERNAL MOTIVATION

We shall not examine all the reasons why activities become self-rewarding but shall concern ourselves with those forms of behavior that are expressions of the ego or its central values. These include the broad categories of (1) *value expression and self-identification*—expressing in words and acts one's important values and thus identifying oneself and maintaining a satisfying self-concept; (2) *self-determination*—making decisions about one's own behavior and thus enabling self-expression; (3) *affiliative expression*—identifying with significant others as part of a larger whole.

Self-determination is, in a sense, a precondition for the other forms of ego motivation. The individual must feel responsibility for his or her own actions and feelings. Self-expression refers to the individual's opportunities for showing what he or she can do and is the basis of intrinsic job satisfaction. Value expression and self-identification refer to saying what one feels and thinks, and asserting what manner of person he or she is. Affiliation or identification with others goes beyond mere gregariousness to include the need of a social transcending of the physical self.

VALUE EXPRESSION AND SELF-IDENTIFICATION

The pattern of motivation associated with value expression and self-identification has great potentialities for the internalization of system goals and thus for the activation of behavior not prescribed by specific roles. In work organizations it is generally confined to the upper echelons or officers. In voluntary organizations it extends into the rank and file; in fact, most voluntary organizations depend almost entirely on a core of dedicated people. The values of the collectivity become incorporated into the individual's own value system or self-concept. As a result, satisfactions accrue to the person from the expression of attitudes and behavior reflecting his or her cherished beliefs and self-image. The reward is not so much a matter of social recognition or monetary advantage as of establishing one's self-identity, confirming one's notion of the sort of person one sees oneself to be, and expressing the values appropriate to this self-concept. A man who considers himself an enlightened conservative, an internationalist, a prudent, hard-headed business executive, or a devoted union member is motivated to actions that are overt manifestations of these values.

The expression of values not only gives clarity to the self-image but also brings that self-image closer to the aspirations of the individual. A person derives satisfaction from seeing the self-concept approach the self-ideal. Added to the need to know *who I am* is the need to realize that *I am the type of person I want to be.*

In a similar fashion Rokeach (1973) writes:

> the functions served by a person's values are to provide him with a comprehensive set of standards to guide actions, justifications, judgments, and comparisons of self and others and to serve needs for adjustment, ego-defense, and self actualization. All these diverse functions converge into a single, overriding, master function, namely, to help maintain and enhance one's total conception of oneself. (p. 216)

The socialization process during the formative years sets the basic outlines of the individual's self-concept. Parents do not train children only by the use of reward and punishment; they also utilize a mediating notion, the model of the good character they want their children to be. Children do not accept every parental injunction but they do acquire the concept of character models. In a play, a political contest, or an international conflict they want to know who are the "bad guys" and who are the "good guys." And they apply the same type of character role to themselves. In play they can quickly take over a part and become another person, but again in terms of a character model.

As adults our self-concept becomes more integrated and stable, and we can no longer move back and forth so readily between various models. Just as kind, considerate people will cover over their acts of selfishness, so too will ruthless individualists become confused and embarrassed by their acts of sympathetic compassion. One reason why it is difficult to change the character of an adult is that he or she isn't comfortable with the new "me." Group support for such changes is almost a necessity, as in Alcoholics Anonymous, so that the individual is aware of approval of his or her new self by people who share the problem and the transition.

In this fashion the individual can be activated toward the goals of the group because these goals represent his or her own personal values or self-concept. People so motivated are usually described as having a sense of mission, direction, or commitment. In most organizations there is a small core of such committed members who have internalized the values of the system.

The complete internalization of organizational goals is not as common as two types of partial internalization. The first has to do with purposes exemplified by the organization but not unique to it. Scientists may have internalized the research values of their profession but not necessarily of the specific institution to which they are attached. As long as they stay in that institution, they may be well-motivated workers. But they may find it just as easy to work for the things they believe in another institution.

A second type of partial internalization concerns the values and goals of a subsystem of the organization. It is often easier for people to take over the values of their own unit than of the larger organization. We may be attached to our own department in a university more than to the university as a whole.

Internalization of organization objectives can come about through the socialization process in childhood or through the adult socialization that takes place in the organization itself. In the first instance, a selective process initiated either by the person or the organization matches personality with system. A boy growing up in the tradition of one of the military services may have always thought of himself as a military officer. The crusader for civil liberties and the American Civil Liberties Union find one another.

The adult socialization process in the organization can build on the personal values of its members and integrate them around an attractive organizational model. People can thus identify with the organizational mission. If the task of an organization has emotional significance, the organization enjoys an advantage in the creation of an attractive image. If the task is attended by hazard (as in the tracking down of criminals by the FBI) or by high adventure (as in the early days of flying) or by service to humanity (as in the case of a cancer research unit), it is not difficult to develop a convincing model of the organization's mission.

The imaginative leader can help develop an attractive picture of the organization by some new conceptualizations of its mission. Police entrusted with the routine and dirty business of law enforcement can be energized by seeing themselves as a corps of professional officers devoted to the highest form of public service. Although reality factors limit the innovative use of symbols for the glorification of organizations, occupational groups strive to achieve a more attractive picture of themselves. Press agents become public relations specialists, and undertakers become morticians.

The image of the organization is aided appreciably by personalization or casting the model in the form of present leaders or past heroes. Political parties glorify their past warriors, and institutions constantly attempt to create charisma about their leaders. This identification with personal models may produce only partial internalization of organizational purposes. People may identify with the great figure in order to participate in a compensatory manner in his or her greatness. Nonetheless, some of the leader's virtues become their own ideals.

SELF-DETERMINATION AND SELF-EXPRESSION AS DETERMINANTS OF JOB SATISFACTION

What conditions lead to intrinsic job satisfaction? How can jobs be designed to be both satisfying and motivating for workers? Both common sense and research answer these questions in terms of variety, complexity, autonomy, and responsibility. Industrial technology has, however, given us repetitive, simplified and atomized tasks over which workers have little control. The assembly line, which is still regarded as the epitome of industrial technology, not only defines jobs in simplified and repetitive terms, but also stipulates the exact method by which the job shall be done and the pace at which it must be performed. Studies of the effects of these characteristics on satisfaction show negative relationships, especially between external control of work pace and satisfaction. In fact the bulk of the research on satisfaction with jobs demonstrates that more varied, complex, and challenging tasks are higher in worker gratification than less skilled, routine jobs. Such findings have been accumulating for almost 50 years, and the basic pattern is beyond question.

Comparisons of occupational groups show that the more skilled the vocation, the more its members enjoy their jobs. Hoppock (1935) reported that more than 90 percent of a group of 500 teachers liked their work, whereas Bell (1937) found that 98 percent of young people working in canning factories and textile mills hated their jobs. In another study by Hoppock (1935) of 309 people in a small Pennsylvania town, the greatest dissatisfaction with work occurred among the unskilled laborers. Satisfaction increased with occupational level, with the greatest satisfaction among professional groups. The relationship between job satisfaction and occupational status has also been confirmed in studies by Hull and Kolstad (1942), Thorndike (1935), Super (1939), and by Uhrbrock (1934).

A more comprehensive study, based on a national sample of the population (Gurin, Veroff, and Feld 1960), found that the greatest amount of job satisfaction occurs among the professional, technical, and managerial personnel, and the least amount among unskilled workers. (See Table 12-1) The groups intermediate in gratification are the clerical, sales, and manually skilled and semiskilled. No differences were found between these intermediate groups, either because the manually skilled job is as challenging as clerical work or because white-collar workers have higher levels of aspiration and are therefore less easily satisfied.

Intrinsic Job Satisfaction

In most of these studies, job satisfaction is used loosely to cover overall liking for the job situation as well as intrinsic job satisfaction

TABLE 12-1 Amount and Sources of Job Satisfaction as Related to Occupational Status

	Professionals, Technicians	Managers, Proprietors	Clerical Workers	Sales Workers	Skilled Workers	Semiskilled Workers	Unskilled Workers	Farmers
Job Satisfaction								
Very satisfied	42%	38%	22%	24%	22%	27%	13%	22%
Satisfied	41	42	39	44	54	48	52	58
Neutral	1	6	9	5	6	9	6	4
Ambivalent	10	6	13	9	10	9	13	9
Dissatisfied	3	6	17	16	7	6	16	7
Not ascertained	3	2	—	2	1	1	—	—
TOTAL	100%	100%	100%	100%	100%	100%	100%	100%
Number of men	(119)	(127)	(46)	(55)	(202)	(152)	(84)	(77)
Sources of Satisfaction								
Mention only ego satisfactions	80%	68%	39%	60%	54%	40%	29%	58%
Mention both ego and extrinsic satisfactions	16	20	35	29	28	31	26	17
Mention only extrinsic satisfactions	2	9	24	7	14	24	29	17
Mention no reasons for liking job	—	—	2	2	2	3	8	1
Not ascertained	2	3	—	2	2	2	8	7
TOTAL	100%	100%	100%	100%	100%	100%	100%	100%
Number of workers	(119)	(127)	(46)	(55)	(202)	(152)	(84)	(77)

From Gurin, Veroff, and Feld, 1960, pp. 159 and 163.

deriving from the content of the work process. Hence the greater gratification of the higher occupational levels can be due to the higher pay, the greater prestige of the calling, the hours, or working conditions, and the like. It is important, therefore, to hold constant factors other than the nature of the work in comparing the satisfaction derived from jobs varying in level of skill and complexity. This is, of course, not possible in dealing with broad occupational groupings where wages and conditions of work are tied to type of occupation. Within a single company, however, it is possible to make meaningful comparisons of intrinsic job satisfaction within a restricted range of differential skill levels. The company may have the same working conditions and the same program of employee benefits for all workers within this range. Moreover, the wages may take account of seniority as well as of skill level. Hence it is possible to find workers at more complex tasks earning no more than workers at less skilled jobs.

Such a situation was true for clerical workers in the home office of a large insurance company, where the tasks vary from routine filing through correspondence with policy holders to moderately complicated mathematical computations. The Survey Research Center of The University of Michigan conducted a survey of employee morale in this company in which 580 employees were intensively interviewed (Morse, 1953). Intrinsic job satisfaction was measured by an index that summarized the answers to four questions: How well do you like the sort of work you are doing? Does your job give you a chance to do the things you feel you do best? Do you get any feeling of accomplishment from the work you are doing? How do you feel about your work; does it rate as an important job with you?

In this study employees were grouped into four classes on the basis of job level: high-level technical, semisupervisory, varied clerical, and repetitious clerical. In the high-level technical group only 7 percent of their members fell into the category of low intrinsic job satisfaction, compared with 41 percent of the group doing repetitive clerical work. Moreover, this relationship was not reduced when length of service or salary was held constant. These results suggest strongly that the greater gratifications found among high-level occupational groups are not wholly a function of wages and conditions of work. People do derive important satisfaction in the expression of their skills, in interesting and challenging work, and in the sense of accomplishment from successful performance of such tasks.

In the same study, the employees who were higher on intrinsic job satisfaction tended to describe their job as having variety and as giving them some chance to make decisions. In other circumstances, this could be interpreted as a subjective phenomenon, that is, a manifestation of the ability of some people to find variety in even the most routine tasks. In this instance, however, the people who found their work varied and containing opportunities for some decision making were in fact doing more skilled and varied work.

The Morse study was ahead of its time in methodological rigor in two respects. It used an objective measure of job characteristics (complexity and responsibilities of the task) and it controlled on other aspects of the job such as pay and working conditions. Few subsequent investigations have met these research criteria, although there have been methodological advances in combining observational and survey techniques (Michigan Organizational Assessment Package, 1975) and in conducting field experiments in which job characteristics have been changed with before-and-after measures for experimental groups. We shall examine some of these studies in the following section on job enlargement and job enrichment.

The old contention that people do not like to make decisions is also answered by the findings of the Morse study. Only 24 percent of the employees were satisfied with the amount of decision making in their jobs, but satisfaction increased with decision-making, as the following figures indicate:

Proportion of employees

Making no decisions and not wanting to make any	11%
Making some decisions and not wanting to make more	13
Making no decisions and wanting to make some	30
Making some decisions and wanting to make more	46
Total	100%
N = 537	

A similar finding comes from the Survey Research Center's 1950 study of 5,700 production workers in a plant representative of heavy industry, The majority (68 percent) felt that they had little or nothing to say about how their jobs should be carried out, but wanted more (51 percent). Moreover, 65 percent thought the work would be performed better if the workers had more chance to make suggestions about such things as design, setups, and the layout of the work. When pressed further on the problem of why the workers did not make suggestions on how the work should be done, the following reasons were given:

Men don't get credit for suggestions	50%
Top management won't use suggestions men make	28%
Foremen won't use suggestions men make	23%
Other men don't think a man should make suggestions	1
Men don't know where to make suggestions	10%
Men don't know what suggestions to make	7%

Kilpatrick, Cummings, and Jennings (1964) similarly report that workers in all occupations rate self-determination high among the elements that define an ideal job. Quinn and his colleagues (Quinn and Shepard, 1974), in factor and cluster analyses of two national samples, found the intrinsic content of the job (*challenge*) to be an important determinant of job satisfaction.

The implication of these results is clear: in spite of the deadening of expectations about participation in the work process in large-scale mechanized production, the need for participation remains. Many workers experience as deprivation their lack of opportunity to apply their skill and knowledge in a full measure to their jobs. Vroom (1962), for example, obtained a correlation of .59 between job satisfaction and the perceived opportunities for self-expression for 489 blue-collar workers in a Canadian oil refinery. Self-expression was measured by a series of nine questions, such as, "How much chance to you get to use the skills you have learned for this job?" and "How much chance do you get to do the kinds of things you are best at?"

Walker and Marriott (1951) found that comparisons of factory-worker satisfaction under mechanically controlled and self-controlled conditions showed substantial differences in favor of the latter.

Other evidence is available that analyzes the nature of the work in relation to its gratification potential. Walker and Guest (1952) investigated the factor of repetitiveness versus variety in an automobile plant in terms of the number of operations the worker carried out. Of those performing more than five operations, a clear majority (69 percent) found their tasks interesting or fairly interesting. Of the workers carrying out two to five operations, only 44 percent gave similar reports on the interest of their work, and of those performing a single operation, the percentage fell to 33 percent. Many workers themselves complained about the repetitive character of the work in the groups performing few operations. Another measure of the repetitive character of work was used by Baldamus (1951) in timing the length of the work cycle. He found that the labor turnover rates for the workers with a short work cycle (less than thirty minutes) was twice as great as the workers in longer work cycles (although the sample in this study was very small).

Hackman and Lawler (1971) confirm these findings and add specifications about the types of people most affected by job enlargement. In this investigation 208 employees in a telephone company in 13 different jobs were asked about various aspects of job satisfaction. Descriptions of the variety, autonomy, task identity, feedback, and other job characteristics were made by supervisors, researchers, and the employees themselves. In addition, need strength was measured by a questionnaire asking about the various attributes and opportunities the workers would like in their jobs. Among other findings there were significant positive correlations between the job characteristics of variety, autonomy, and task identity and the level of intrinsic motivation, as well as with such specific satisfactions as feelings of worthwhile accomplishment and personal growth and development. Shepard (1970) also found functional specialization to be negatively related to job satisfaction, instrumental work orientation, and commitment to organizational goals, that is, the more atomized the job the more the alienation. His three categories of workers were from craft production, mechanized production, and automated production, and they were employed in an automobile plant and an oil refinery.

Although the bulk of the research literature finds that jobs with more variety and challenge yield higher intrinsic job satisfaction, a few studies have been cited as notable exceptions (Turner and Lawrence, 1965; Blood and Hulin, 1967; Hulin and Blood, 1968). Turner and Lawrence (1965) found that the usual relationship held for workers in small towns, but that in urban settings, workers in more challenging jobs were lower in job satisfaction than those in less demanding jobs. They interpret their results as due to the differences in cultural backgrounds of employees. Blood and Hulin (1967) and Hulin and Blood (1968) theorized that workers in cities were more alienated from middle class work norms and hence would react differently from small town dwellers, and they report some data supportive of their theory. Turner and Lawrence, however, were not dealing with intrinsic job satisfaction; their measures did not refer to the work itself but to satisfaction with the job as a whole, which can include wages and conditions of work. It is difficult to understand why their findings are seen as a reversal of the more general trend. Moreover, neither Turner and Lawrence nor Hulin and Blood had population samples which would permit generalizations about the differences between urban and small town workers. National studies of the values and aspirations of people show no such associations with social class or place of residence (Campbell, Converse, and Rodgers, 1976).

To answer the question of whether the United States has an alienated urban working class or an involved small-town-oriented proletariat requires adequate national sampling. Only if such sampling establishes the hypothesized differences can we accept this explanation of the discrepant findings of Turner and Lawrence. The facts are that every study using a national sample on job satisfaction, and the Michigan Survey Research Center has conducted a series over the past 15 years (Quinn, Staines, and McCullough, 1974), finds higher job satisfaction among higher occupational groups the country over.

Quinn and Shepard (1974), in a nationwide survey that used a measure of satisfaction with challenge (intrinsic job satisfaction), report these scores for different occupations:

	Satisfaction with Challenge[a]
Managers and administrators, except farm	3.52
Professional and technical	3.49
Sales	3.37
Craft or skilled workers	3.28
Service workers	3.01
Clerical	2.89
Laborers, except farm	2.85
Machine operatives	2.70

[a]Scores are means, based on a 5-point scale in which 5 indicates maximum satisfaction. N = 2107.

These investigators derived their measure of satisfaction with challenge from a factor analytic study of reactions to various aspects of the job. Six factors emerged: comfort (conditions of work), challenge, financial rewards, relations with co-workers, resource adequacy, and promotion. The items loading heavily on challenge or intrinsic job satisfaction were:

The work is interesting

I have an opportunity to develop my own special abilities
I can see the results of my work
I am given a chance to do the things I do best
I am given a lot of freedom to decide how to do my own work
The problems I am expected to solve are hard enough

Changing Job Design to Provide
For Job Enlargement and Job Enrichment

If variety and challenge in the job can increase intrinsic job satisfaction, we need to examine the assembly-line model to see where and how the design of work can be altered to meet the so-called higher level needs. Many organizations attempted such changes, and a kind of social movement formed around the slogan of job enlargement. Herzberg (1968) has challenged the usefulness of enlarging the job merely by adding to a worker's disagreeable task further onerous duties at the same level. He proposes job enrichment as the better concept, in that it calls not so much for more tasks but for tasks involving autonomy and responsibility on the part of the employee. The former type of change or *horizontal enlargement* calls for little modification in the power structure of the organization, whereas *job enrichment* calls for *vertical enlargement* in that some of the decision making at higher levels has to be released or shared with lower levels.

The field experiments in which job enlargement and job enrichment have been attempted have, in the main, had positive outcomes.[1] They have led to increases in intrinsic job satisfaction and (as we shall see in the next chapter) to improvements in the quantity and quality of work. Paul, Robertson, and Herzberg (1969) report four such experiments—one with laboratory technicians in an industrial research department; a second with sales representatives; a third with industrial engineers, and a fourth with factory supervisors. In the first of these experiments, some 19 technicians were increasingly involved in planning projects, assisting in other work planning and target setting. They were given financial authority to requisition materials and equipment, and responsibility for a final report. The performance of the control group of 29 technicians who were not given these advantages continued to improve for a time but was soon outpaced by the experimental group. The survey findings showed no commensurate improvement in job satisfaction, although the managers believed they saw evidence of such a change in the experimental group.

In another company an experimental group of sales representatives was given the responsibility for determining the frequency of calls upon clients, for making financial settlements up to $250 in cases of customer complaints about products, and for exercising a discretionary range of about 10 percent on the prices of most products. Although job satisfaction was already at a high level among these employees, it rose some 11 percent for the experimental group but not at all for the control group.

A similar program among design engineers gave them more independence in running their projects, more discretion in the use of project budgets, and more managerial responsibility for project staff. Before-and-after scores on a survey of job satisfaction showed increases of 21 percent and 16 percent for the two experimental groups, and no change for the control group.

---

[1]The volume *Work in America* listed 34 such industrial experiments. Others are described in two recently published volumes on the *Quality of Working Life*, by Davis and Cherns, of the UCLA Center for the Quality of Working Life (1975) and in an earlier book of readings, *Design of Jobs* (Davis and Taylor, 1972). Still others appear in a monograph series of the U.S. Department of Labor, *Improving Life in Organizations*, and in a review monograph by Katzell, Yankelovich, et al. (1975). A volume entitled *Industrial Democracy in Europe* summarizes some of the experimental developments in industries there. The Michigan Survey Research Center has become involved in the evaluation of a number of such experiments, the evaluation being directed by Seashore and Lawler in collaboration with colleagues in other universities.

The experiment on factory supervisors was really two separate studies—both in British companies and both including production supervisors on shift work and engineering supervisors on day work. The experimental changes included more involvement in planning, more on-the-spot responsibility, and more authority in financial decisions. The performance of both experimental groups of supervisors increased significantly, but only for the engineering supervisors were there increases in job satisfaction.

The experimenters concluded that their findings could be generalized to a diversity of jobs, hierarchical levels and companies. They believe that the enrichment of lower-level jobs can set up a chain reaction that leads to the enrichment of supervisors' jobs as well. They also believe that

> Individual reaction to job enrichment is as difficult to forecast in terms of attitudes as it is in terms of performance. Those already genuinely interested in their work develop real enthusiasm. Not all people welcome having their jobs enriched, certainly, but so long as the changes are opportunities rather than demands, there is no reason to fear an adverse reaction. If someone prefers things the way they are, he merely keeps them the way they are, by continuing to refer matters to his supervisor, for example. Again, there is nothing lost.... (p. 251)

The Herzberg studies were limited to supervisors and highly skilled workers; it could be argued that these are people already selected for their favorable disposition toward responsibility, and that changing their assignments in meaningful ways is easier than changing the character of the assembly line. Nonetheless the same positive outcomes have appeared with factory workers when their tasks have been expanded. In a study (Mann and Hoffman, 1960) of automation in a large public utility, the new automated plant was found to have a smaller working force than the old, but more duties for each worker and more rotation of workers through different types of jobs. One hundred percent of the workers questioned reported that their new enlarged jobs were more interesting than their old jobs. Moreover, the general level of job satisfaction was much higher in the automated plant than in another plant in the same company where the jobs followed a more repetitive and less varied pattern.

Davis (1966) has reviewed several studies of job enlargement and enrichment covering such diverse groups as operators on assembly lines in home appliance manufacture and in pharmaceutical appliance manufacture, coal miners, textile weavers, and maintenance workers. His conclusion is that job satisfaction results from such responsible autonomous job behaviors as self-regulation of work content and structure, self-evaluation of performance, self-adjustment to changes required by technological variability, and participation in setting goals for job output. Similarly, Jacobs (1975) reports that a job enrichment program at Xerox Corporation for its technical field representatives, "proved successful in increasing employee commitment and involvement" (p. 299). Before-and-after surveys "indicated an increase in positive attitudes, particularly in areas of responsibility, recognition and challenge" (p. 295) in the experimental but not the control groups.

An attempt was made to reverse assembly-line technology in an insurance company for processing data (Jansen, 1975). The company changed its division of tasks concerned with keypunching so that each operator had continuing responsibility for handling work for certain regional offices. Each operator could have direct contact with his or her client units and could take over the task, previously handled by the assignment clerk, of checking incoming documents for correctness and legibility. Moreover, operators were now permitted to correct obvious coding errors and to schedule their own activities. Again there were positive changes in intrinsic job satisfaction in the experimental but not in the control group. Jansen also reports:

> Posttrial interviews also produced considerable anecdotal evidence of improved attitudes. The frustration, boredom, and apathy found in interviews before the trial were replaced in many cases by pride in work, positive feelings about increased responsibilities, and realization that individual jobs are important to the company. Many operators report discussing their jobs with family and friends—an event that rarely occurred before the job enrichment trial.

A similar job enrichment program for key punching was put into effect at the Cummins Engine Company with similar results (Bryan, 1975). This company also had success with the enrichment of jobs in engine testing, in the fabrication machine shop, and on the automated engine-block line.

Despite this evidence of the success of job enrichment, the range of its potential has been questioned (Davis, 1976; den Hartog, 1977). The questions do not involve the internal validity of the experiments, but instead their external validity or general applicability. It is, of course, axiomatic to the systems view of organizations that changes in one sector or level cannot go far without becoming change-demands on other parts of the organization. A general program of job enrichment is inevitably a program of general organizational change. We will consider such issues in Chapters 19 and 20; the relevance of the job enrichment experiments to the present discussion is their demonstration that intrinsic job satisfaction depends on the intrinsic content of jobs.

AFFILIATIVE EXPRESSION
AND GROUP BELONGINGNESS

Affiliative expression takes account of the fact that ego expands to include significant others—family, friends, work groups, and larger associations. By being part of something beyond the physical self, the individual can achieve a sense of belongingness and can participate in accomplishments beyond individual powers. Moreover, affiliating with others can extend the ego in time as well as space, for individuals can see their contributions to the group as enduring over time even though they themselves may not survive. The core of this special extension of the ego may well be the *need for affiliation,* a concept measured by McClelland and his colleagues in projective tests (Shipley and Veroff, 1953 and Atkinson, Heyns, and Veroff, 1954). The validity of the measure was established by comparing the characteristics of stories completed under relaxed conditions with stories written under conditons designed to arouse affiliative needs—for example, after a period in which group members had rated one another. The test for need affiliation could well be adapted for research in organizational settings, so that the strength of this need and the extent to which organizational factors fulfill it could be measured in comparable terms.

The concept of *reference group* is important for understanding the dynamics of affiliative expression. It has been used, as Kelley (1952) noted, both to designate a group used by an individual as a basis for comparative judgments and a group with which the individual identifies in an affective sense—with feelings of respect, admiration, or liking. Hyman and Singer (1966) make a similar distinction, pointing out that an individual may choose a reference group in terms of its expertness, with full awareness that no bond of identification exists or is in prospect.

Our concern is with the normative or affective meaning of the concept, with those instances in which the individual feels a part of some larger social entity and recognizes a bond of identification with that entity. In political science the concept of party identification, the individual's self-perception as a staunch Republican or loyal Democrat, exemplifies our meaning. In similar fashion, studies of nationalism have used self-reports of identification with the nation-state as a measure of nationality. As these examples suggest, the reference group may be large and distant from the immediate experience of the individual. But the individual may also take as a reference group some smaller entity in which there is immediate membership and direct contact, and as Hyman and Singer (1968) pointed out, "when referent power is joined to real power, the combination is unbeatable" (p. 10).

Research in organizations had been concerned with just such situations. It has given little attention to individual identification with the organization as a whole, but a great deal to the extension of the ego to include the immediate work group. The Tavistock researchers have followed Lewin in examining the conditions and effects of group solidarity at the face-to-face level. They have shown that the individual can share in the completion of a meaningful cycle of activities by the group. The group and not the individual becomes the psychological basis for assessment of accomplishment and satisfaction.

This necessitates, however, a group organization in which individuals share in some perceptible fashion a meaningful task. It has been shown in the experimental laboratory that there is a group Zeigarnik (1927) effect. Zeigarnik originally demonstrated that an interrupted task results in frustration and leads to perseveration of the interrupted activity. People seek closure or completion of a process once begun. Moreover, if two or more people are given a common task, the logic of the Zeigarnik effect can carry over to their joint activities. One member may achieve closure through the activities of a fellow or may be stimulated to complete a task begun by a comrade. This is not conjecture. The experimental findings of Lewis and Franklin (1944) demonstrated that partners on a group task would remember the task if not allowed to complete it. If, however, one partner was allowed to finish the task, the other partner would also experience a sense of closure. And Horwitz (1954) found that groups of five college women experienced less tension for the tasks their group had decided not to finish than for unfinished tasks which the group was committed to complete. Finally, Zander and Medow (1963) have shown that the group operates as a unit according to psychological principles of individual behavior in setting levels of aspiration. With a group laboratory task, teams of boys set their level of aspiration, collectively determined, slightly above their past level of performance. They lowered it with failure and raised it with success and acted as if the group were an expended individual. It is a mistake, however, to push an individual psychology into social entities beyond the immediate group of interdependent co-workers. When Zander and Newcomb (1967) studied the changes in goals of United Fund organizations in relation to past accomplishments, they found that other variables entered the picture and that local organizations did not necessarily lower their goals after failure to achieve their quotas the previous year. Hence Zander (1971) has suggested the necessity of additional theoretical assumptions when members of a group frequently receive information from external sources.

Shared Psychological Fields

The psychodynamic basis of the group performing as an individual has been developed by Asch (1952) in his conception of shared psychological fields. According to Asch, if we have two individuals A and B, there is a special character to their interaction if:

1. A is aware of the surroundings, including B and himself
2. A perceives that B is similarly oriented
3. A acts toward B and notes that B is responding to his action
4. A notes that B's response to him sets up expectations that A will understand that B's response is directed toward him
5. The same ordering exists in B.

The coordinated interaction of dance partners or of members of any sport team who have played together illustrates Asch's contention that action is steered by phenomenal fields that are structurally similar. The basic condition, then, for shared psychological fields is twofold: (1) task interdependence of people, and (2) face-to-face interaction. Every individual in the group is dependent on the other members in playing his or her role in achieving a common goal, and this dependence is not remote and long-term but immediate and perceptible.

On the basis of experimentation with group responsibility for interdependent tasks, Rice (1958) proposes the following conditions for group involvement:

Group stability is more easily maintained when the range of skills required of group members is such that all members of the group can comprehend all the skills and, without having, or wanting to have them, could aspire to their acquisition. (pp. 37–38)

In other words the greater the differences in skill the more difficult it is for members to communicate and the harder it is to develop group cohesiveness. Similarly,

The fewer the differences there are in prestige and status within a group, the more likely is the internal structure of a group to be stable and the more likely are its members to accept internal leadership. (p. 38)

And finally,

When members of small work groups become disaffected to the extent that they can no longer fit into their own work group, those disaffected should be able to move to other small work groups engaged in similar tasks. (p. 39)

These assumptions describe the conditions under which a social-psychological system can operate to further organizational goals and to increase member satisfaction. An ideal arrangement for a sociotechnical system would be one in which the technical aspects of the work could be organized in such a manner that the immediate work group would have a meaningful unit of activity, some degree of responsibility for its task, and a satisfactory set of interpersonal relationships. And the greater the differences in skills, prestige, and status among members of the work group, the more difficult it will be to establish and maintain satisfactory interpersonal relationships.

Occupational and Organizational Identification

The factors facilitative of reference group identification with large social entities are (1) early socialization, (2) anticipatory socialization, and (3) socialization practices of organizations to which the individual belongs as an adult.

Early Socialization

At an early age, children are taught group identifications that go beyond the family. The self-image held up to them is linked to their being good group members, for example, a good Christian, a patriotic American, a loyal Republican or Democrat. This early training furnishes some of the bedrock of later organizational identification. It emphasizes general values more than the specific goals of most organizations, although many organizations attempt to embellish their narrow objectives with such common values. The reference to the company as a family, for example, has become a management cliche. In the appeal to general values, the labor union has an advantage over the company, especially among urban blue-collar workers who grew up with some consciousness of being members of the working class. For political parties, identification often begins in childhood and the majority of people vote the faith of their fathers and mothers. Some of the general character of early socialization can be seen in research findings (Valen and Katz, 1964), which show that political activism of parents is more predictive of political activism of their children than of the specific party to which the new generation becomes attached.

Anticipatory Socialization

The culture provides information and training about various adult roles so that the person aspiring toward a given role is aware of some of its requisite procedures, norms, and values. The educational system and its counseling programs and the role models featured in the mass media prepare the individual for membership in different organizations.

Socialization Practices
in the Organization Itself

The process of socialization continues after the individual enters the organization. The organization is likely to have training programs and indoctrination procedures for producing identification with it and its espoused goals. This can even take the form of identification with the aggressor in the case of total institutions. Prisons and military training units are notorious for their use of mortification procedures with new members. Less than total institutions use milder methods but also take pains to demonstrate to new members how inadequate their previous training and experience is for handling the problems of the new system. Schein (1968) puts it in these words:

> Organizations socialize their new members by creating a series of events which serve the function of undoing old values so that the person will be prepared to learn new values. This process of undoing or unfreezing is often unpleasant and therefore requires strong motivation to endure it or strong organizational forces to make the person endure it. The formation of a peer group of novices is often a solution to the problem of defense against the powerful organization and, at the same time, can strongly enhance the socialization process if peer group norms support organizational norms. (p. 6)

In a study of socialization in professional schools Ondrack (1975) examined the consistency of value patterns relevant to nursing among teachers, staff nurses, and head nurses in three otherwise comparable nursing schools. The test of socialization was the shift, during the period between entering and graduating, toward the norms of these professional groups. The amount of the shift was found to vary directly with the degree of attitude and value consistency among significant others in the school. For reports of other research on socialization into work roles, see Graen (1976) and Van Maanen (1976).

The critical condition for producing organizational identification through the activities of the organization itself is participation in decision making and the sharing of rewards. If people are involved in determining policies and share in the returns from collective effort, they regard the organization as of their own making. There is little need for convincing them through indoctrination when, in fact, the organization is theirs.

Operational Measures
of Occupational and Organizational Identification

Identification with a specific organization has been measured in various ways. Schuyhart and Smith (1972), following the work of

Morse (1953), have emphasized satisfaction with an organization as expressed in pride in it and positive attitudes toward its policies, products, public image and future prospects. They used such direct items as "I like working for this company." "I feel I am part of the company." "If I had a friend looking for employment I would recommend this company." "I believe this company's future prospects are good." "I would not want to work for any other company." "This company has good personnel policies." The index of identification based on questions of this type was found to be significantly related to a measure of job involvement among middle management employees but not to age, promotions in the company, or tenure. The conclusion reached by the investigators is that the importance of the job to the worker's self-image is associated with his or her organizational identification.

In a study of the U. S. Forest Service, Hall, Schneider, and Nygren (1970) used a related conception of organizational identification—namely, the process by which the goals of the individual and the goals of the organization become increasingly congruent. They also employed similar measurement scales, such as the feeling of pride in being part of the Forest Service, the feeling that the Forest Service is a large family in which the employees have a sense of belonging, the feeling that the Forest Service is recognized as a leader in applying principles of good land management. Occupational identification was measured by scales concerned with the opportunity for meaningful public service, the opportunity for working toward professional goals, and the opportunity for applying good land management principles. The conclusions of the investigation were that organizational identification (1) was clearly related to commitment to public service and affiliative needs, (2) was affected by length of service rather than position, and (3) was related to the satisfaction of higher order needs.

Hall and Schneider (1972) followed their study of foresters with research on two very different occupational groups: research professionals from research and development laboratories and priests in the Roman Catholic Church. Research professionals tend to follow a multiorganizational career pattern whereas priests, like foresters, follow a single-organizational career pattern. Length of tenure is a stronger correlate of organizational identification in the single-organization career group. The forester's self-image is more related to his or her organizational identification and the researcher's is more related to his or her work involvement. The authors summarize their findings: "The single-organization career thus combines security and localism with growth and cosmopolitanism, whereas in the multiorganization career the professional must choose between these alternatives" (p. 340).

Related to the notion of organizational identification is the more global concept of commitment which, in Porter's definition, includes the willingness of the individual to exert effort for the organization, a desire to stay within the system, and an acceptance of its major goals and values (Porter et al., 1974). In measuring commitment, Buchanan (1974) saw identification as one of its components, along with involvement in the work role and loyalty. His scale items on loyalty were very similar, however, to the items on identification. For example, the scale on identification included the statements: "I feel a sense of pride in working for this organization." "I really feel as if this organization's problems are my problems."

The loyalty scale contained such items as: "I have warm feelings toward this organization as a place to live and work." "I would be quite willing to spend the rest of my career with this organization."

In fact these two subscales correlated .74, whereas role involvement correlated .58 with loyalty and .65 with identification. Both empirically and theoretically, then, there is some reason for separating job involvement from organizational identification. It is of interest, however, that Buchanan found in his survey of some 279 business and government managers that years of organizational service, frequency of social interactions with peers and superiors, job achievement and promotion were associated with commitment.

In another study of organizational and occupational identification Ritzer and Trice (1969) tested Becker's side-bet theory (1960) by asking personnel managers whether they would change their companies or their occupations if given certain incentives. Becker's theory was that individuals commit themselves to an organization or calling and make side-bets to themselves about staying or leaving, the amount of the necessary enticement to leave depending on such factors as marriage and children and amount of education. In other words, structural rather than psychological factors affect commitment behavior. Ritzer and Trice (1969), however, found no support for the Becker hypotheses and suggest the importance of regarding commitment as a psychological process. Aranya and Jacobson (1975) have replicated the results of Ritzer and Trice in a study of system analysts in Israel. In this latter research, moreover, there is a high positive correlation between organizational and occupational commitment.

ALIENATION

In the sixties and seventies alienation and anomie have come to the fore as central concepts for research and discussion. It is a belated recognition of Durkheim's thesis that modern society lacks the common collective conscience provided by the internalized values of a traditional culture. From broader Marxian theory no concept has captured social psychological thinking as much as alienation, which is the negative aspect of the internalization of conventional goals in that it suggests an active rejection of them.

Alienation has been used in a number of senses but we are using it to refer to intrinsic meaninglessness of social roles to the individuals who enact them. If all that ties individuals to organizations are extrinsic factors of reward and punishment, then people may well be alienated both from their work and from society. The Marxian conception of alienation took account both of the absence of intrinsic job satisfaction and of the rejection or failure to internalize the dominant values of the society (or its ruling class). Marx saw the worker in modern society as divorced from the tools of production which were owned by others, as deprived of intrinsically meaningful work because of the robotlike requirements of the production process, and as debarred from critical decision making in the accepted institutional arrangements. Hence Marx felt that workers would rally sooner or later in organizations of their own to modify drastically the existing economic system. Three assumptions in this analysis can be challenged. First, alienation from the larger social system may not develop among all workers who do monotonous jobs at the bottom of organizational hierarchies. Especially if they are not strongly motivated toward self-determination and self-expression, increasing extrinsic rewards may keep them attached to existing social forms. If they see a better lot for themselves in the future or a better way of life for their children, this may be enough to prevent disaffection. Marx ruled out this possibility by his further assumption that the lot of the working class would grow progressively worse over the years—a prediction out of line with the facts.

Second, the prevention of alienation may not require the satisfaction of all three types of internal motivation. One type may be enough to keep people involved in their organizations. The worker who does not internalize the values of the company may have fairly interesting work. The worker who also lacks that may identify with the immediate work group, with his or her occupational group, or even with the organization as a whole.

Third, workers belong to other system-supportive groupings besides the employing organization. They may be deeply involved in one of these and hence not alienated from the larger system. Dubin, Champoux, and Porter (1975) have suggested that individuals who are not work-oriented may not be alienated. In their study of 409 employees in 37 branches of a bank and 605 employees from one division of a telephone company, these investigators found that the majority of blue-collar males and clerical females had no marked preference for work or non-work settings. Instead, they were flexible in their central life interests and not attached to a particular locus for expressing their interests. They may thus represent the adaptable individuals of a future society rather than a disaffected group.

Alienation, however, had far earlier conceptual beginnings in theology and philosophy than in Marx's writings. It has accumulated throughout its long history many meanings, all somehow involving the idea of an undesirable estrangement of the individual—from God, from nature, from society, from work, or from self. Such conceptual versatility, as Seeman (1972) has suggested, is more embarrassing than helpful; the term is invoked to explain a long list of troubles and their opposites—conformity and deviance, nonpolitical passivity and political riots, status-seeking and social retreat, suburban malaise and urban activism. By thus threatening to explain everything, as Seeman observes, the concept is in danger of explaining nothing.

Alienation from work is a more limited and more useful notion, with a history of its own. Schiller, in the eighteenth century, complaining of the division of labor into fractional subtasks, spoke of alienation in terms that anticipate Marx in the nineteenth and Fromm, Marcuse, and others in the twentieth century:

> Gratification is separated from labor, means from ends, effort from reward. Eternally fettered only to a single fragment of the whole, man fashions himself as a fragment." (Neumann, 1957, p. 271).

Seeman, in an excellent summary of research on alienation (1972), has proposed that to be alienated means to be characterized by one or more of the following feelings about oneself and the world:

1. A sense of *powerlessness*—the feeling that events and outcomes of importance to oneself are controlled and determined by external forces and not one's own efforts.
2. A sense of *meaninglessness*—the feeling that the course of events is incomprehensible and that the future cannot be predicted.
3. A sense of *normlessness*—the feeling that socially unapproved means are necessary to attain socially approved goals, and that one is therefore not bound by standards of values and morality.
4. *Social isolation*—feelings of loneliness, rejection, exclusion from valued groups or relationships.
5. *Value isolation* or estrangement—the rejection of commonly held values.
6. *Self-estrangement*—the feeling that one is engaged in activities that are not rewarding in themselves and is therefore acting in ways that are somehow not true to self and one's own needs.

A good deal is known about factors associated with such feelings of alienation.[2] For example, people feel less alienated (powerless)

[2]This summary is adapted from the chapter by Seeman already cited, *Alienation and Engagement.* (In Campbell and Converse, *op. cit.*)

when they are members of organizations that have some potential for influence in matters of importance—labor unions, professional societies, political organizations, and other voluntary associations (Neal and Seeman, 1964; Seeman, 1966; Almond and Verba, 1963). People are more likely to feel alienated (normless) if they are of low socioeconomic status—low income, low education (Meier and Bell, 1959; Bullough, 1967). As we have already indicated, there is evidence that alienation from work (self-estrangement) is more common among people doing monotonous, machine-paced, closely supervised jobs (Weiss and Reisman, 1961; Blauner, 1964; Kornhauser, 1965; Crozier, 1965; Wilensky, 1964).

Research does show a trend toward increased alienation on some dimensions in recent years in American society. Trend studies using comparable questions have been restricted, however, to a few areas of life, and there has been little systematic inquiry into alienation within the framework of what it is that people are alienated from. Thus questions dealing with trust in one's fellows, trust in government, frustrations in personal life, pessimism, feelings of control over one's fate, pragmatic satisfactions with way of life, job satisfaction, and felt political efficacy have been used as indicators of alienation. The major outcome of this work justifies three conclusions:

1. Overall there is no accumulation of dissatisfaction along lines of economic cleavage in the United States. Various groups are tied into the system in different ways. People in the lower strata are stronger than managerial groups in their nationalism and more positive in their evaluation of administrative agencies, but lower in their confidence in national and political leadership (Katz, Gutek, Kahn, and Barton, 1975).

2. From 1958 all groups in the national population showed a marked decline in trust in national political leaders (Miller, 1974). Questions concerning the competence, the integrity, the judgment, and the values of the people running the government in Washington reveal a consistent erosion of public confidence. This diminishing support for the national political establishment was noted by many political candidates in the 1976 primaries as they dissociated themselves from big government and struck a populist note. We witnessed a remarkable scene in which the official head of the government establishment, President Ford, openly attacked it for its size and intrusiveness.

3. The fall in confidence in the national leadership seems specific to that level. It does not mean generalized disaffection or profound alienation from the system. In a nationwide study, Katz, Gutek, Kahn, and Barton (1975) found that the same people who rejected government bureaucracy at the global level were often favorably disposed toward the bureaucrat they encountered in seeking service from a government agency.

Detailed data on trends in alienation and attachment to work are not available, although studies of job satisfaction have been done for many decades and some deeper inquires into the meaning of work have been repeated two or three times. The following conclusions are best regarded as tentative interpretations of this scattered material:

1. The majority of workers in the United States say they are satisfied with their jobs. Almost all studies show this pattern and, in spite of some decreases since 1960, it has been generally stable. The satisfaction response is global, however, and not specific to the intrinsic content of the job. Moreover, it is a response that is based on a complex frame of reference and a realistic appraisal of alternatives. As one worker put it, after pronouncing himself satisfied with his job,

> Don't get me wrong. I didn't say it is a *good* job. It's an O.K. job—about as good a job as a guy like me might expect. The foreman leaves me alone and it pays well. But I would never call it a good job. It doesn't amount to much, but it's not bad. (Strauss, cited in O'Toole et al., 1973). pp. 14–15

2. Questions that attempt to go deeper than such expressions of satisfaction also show substantial positive attachment of workers to their jobs. For example, about 66 percent of all workers in the United States said in 1973 that they would go on working even if they had no economic need to do so (Quinn and Shepard, 1974). Three qualifications to this positive conclusion are required, however:

a. The long-term trend indicates a reduction in such attitudes; almost 80 percent of all workers gave similar responses 20 years earlier (Morse and Weiss, 1955).

b. The positive attachment of persons to jobs is strongly related to occupation, which is the best indicator of job content available in these data sets. For example, almost half of all workers say that they would choose similar work if they "could start all over again," but the range is from 93 percent of university professors to 16 percent of unskilled auto workers (Kahn, 1974).

c. Perhaps most important for the question of alienation, the reasons that workers give for choosing to work in the hypothetical absence of economic need suggest the poverty of alternatives rather than the meaningfulness of work. The dominant response—50 percent in 1973—is the avoidance of boredom. People speak of being bored or restless without work, not knowing what to do with their time, or even of "going crazy," in the colloquial rather than the psychiatric sense of the phrase. Similarly, when people are asked what they would miss most about not working, the modal response involves social relations with co-workers; only 8 percent of all workers say they would miss doing something liked or enjoyed for its own sake.

3. For most workers the functions of work are primarily instrumental—making a living—and secondarily incidental—avoiding boredom and keeping in touch with other people. By comparison, those aspects of work that we have called internally motivating or self-rewarding are seldom mentioned. Many workers have some freedom on the job to choose methods of work and make individual decisions, and most feel that they have some say over what happens to them on the job. But the experience of self expression in the work itself is rare, and the experience of joining one's efforts with those of others to achieve a goal of social importance is rarest of all.

The data tell us that alienation is neither unitary nor categorical; the attachment of workers to work is dimensional—or rather, multidimensional. The current measures on some of those dimensions show a pattern of external motivation under reasonable conditions of effort and sociability—neither alienation nor engagement.

SYSTEM NORMS AND VALUES

We shall return now to a consideration of values from a system instead of an individual point of view. We shall describe the functions of system values and specify some of the patterns of ideological beliefs that motivate members.

Social systems, as the patterned interdependent activities of human beings, are characterized by *roles*, which differentiate one position from another; they are characterized also by a set of *norms* and *values*, which integrate rather than differentiate; that is, they are shared by all (or many) of the members of the system. We shall use the terms *norms* and *values* to refer to the common beliefs of an evaluative type which constitute a coherent interrelated syndrome. System norms make explicit the forms of behavior appropriate for members of the system. System values or ideology provide a more elaborate and generalized justification both for appropriate behavior and for the activities and functions of the system. Norms and ideology shade into one another so that the distinction is one of emphasis rather than of uniqueness. Norms refer to the expected behavior sanctioned by the system and thus have a specific *ought* or *must* quality. In this they resemble roles. Values furnish rationale for the normative requirements. For a value to become a norm for a subsystem it must have an explicit formulation with specific reference to identifiable behavior of a systemically relevant character so that it can be enforced.

System norms and values (ideology) are a group product and may not be necessarily identical with the privately held values of a representative sample of the individuals involved in the system. They are the standards to which reference is made for judging acceptable and unacceptable behavior of relevance to the system. The supervisor in a factory may give workers instructions about a job. They may not like the directive but their criterion for accepting or not accepting it is based on the system norm of whether it is within the supervisor's area of jurisdiction as the legitimate voice of management.

System norms and ideology have the general function of tying people into the system so that they remain within it and carry out their role assignments. The more specific functions are twofold: (1) system norms and ideology furnish cognitive maps for members which facilitate their work in the system and their adjustment to it, (2) norms and ideology provide the moral or social justification for system activities both for members and for people formally outside the system.

Three Criteria for System Norms and Values

The participants in all social systems hold common beliefs and attitudes about some aspects of the system and its functioning. When these common beliefs are accompanied by the feeling that these ideas are the relevant and appropriate doctrine that specifies behavioral requirements for members of the group, they are termed *group norms* or *system norms*. In other words, three criteria define system norms: (1) there must be beliefs about appropriate and required behavior for group members as group members, (2) there must be objective or statistical commonality of such beliefs; not every member of the group must hold the same idea, but a majority of active members should be in agreement, (3) there must be an awareness by individuals that there is group support for a given belief.

To stipulate the degree to which each of these elements must be present in order to constitute a norm would be arbitrary; all three; however, are necessary to the definition. Thus where people have the same or similar beliefs and attitudes as a result of some ecological or demographic factor, such as occupation or geographical place of residence, they may still lack the feeling that there are such common and appropriate belief systems among people like themselves. (Elements 1 and 3 are lacking.) In such instances, where there is little consciousness of kind, we do not use the term *group norms* nor do we regard the grouping as a social organization. We speak rather of a public and its common attitudes. Advertisers and politicians often divide the nation into groups and publics, dealing with the publics as people of similar interests and trying to develop some consciousness of kind among them.

Similarly, we are not dealing with group norms where people hold differing beliefs even though each person may feel that his or her notions have group support. (Element 2 is lacking.) This is one of the most difficult of all conditions for the operation of any social system. People act on their own idiosyncratic beliefs as if there were a high degree of group support for them. If carried to a logical extreme, this would mean anarchy as each person plays the game according to his or her own rules. This condition is characteristically unstable and tends to be dispelled as individual actors come into collision. When the antagonists attempt to rally support, the objective amount of that support becomes visible to all. Conflict is almost inevitably clarifying.

There are also cases where group members may hold the same beliefs, be aware that the majority of their colleagues hold similar views, and yet regard these beliefs as inappropriate to their group membership. (Element 1 is lacking.) This can be found in some labor unions where most of the members are Democratic in political preference and are aware that this is the common preference of other union members but reject the notion that the union should take a stand on political matters.

We should also recognize the situation in which the great majority of individuals have the same conflict between their own beliefs of proper group behavior and their own estimate of group support. They may favor one course of action but feel that the great majority oppose it whereas, in fact, the majority agree with them. This is the classic phenomenon labeled pluralistic ignorance by F. H. Allport (see discussion in Katz and Schanck, 1938), and illustrated by the Andersen fairy tale of the king's imaginary garment which, of course, must be visible to others. Schanck (1932) confirmed the existence of pluralistic ignorance in his study of Elm Hollow, where he found a discrepancy between public and private attitudes of church members on such matters as card playing. The majority incorrectly thought they were the minority. Pluralistic ignorance is of particular significance in social organizations where the channels of communications are controlled from above and fictitious group norms therefore can be developed and fostered.

The reason for adding the dimension of objective consensus of common beliefs is our concern with the prediction of social behavior and system outcomes. The individual psychologist can be satisfied with the subjective conviction of a person that the group supports his or her beliefs. The social psychologist who is interested in the common directions of group behavior must also take into account the actual amount of support in the social environment for a given system of beliefs. For the facts are that personal convictions and group support do interact, and most people over time bring their private beliefs into line with some of the social realities constituted by the opinions of others. Otherwise they may have little opportunity to put their beliefs into practice, since the structure for social action is based on social systems that provide channels for certain forms of behavior and barriers for other forms.

Types of Values

The substantive justification of system behavior is essentially of two types. It consists basically of (1) transcendental, moral, or sacred values or (2) pragmatic values associated with functional outcomes. Both kinds may be involved in social relationships but many social systems give greater emphasis to one or the other. Values of the first type, with their emphasis on some sacred quality, tend to imbue a symbol with properties over and above those of the reality it represents. Or to put it more precisely, these symbolic values often have little objective reference and so can be utilized by organizational leadership to support various programs. The tendency is to overwork these values, to allow them to creep into many specific means for meeting organizational objectives rather than reserving them for the objectives themselves. When this happens, rigidities in organizational behavior occur. What was a means to an end becomes an end in itself and, as Merton (1957) points out, the system becomes encrusted with ritualism.

An example of the pervasive character of symbolic values can be seen in the elaboration of the doctrine of organizational loyalty. Loyalty is applied to three types of behavior. In the first place, members should maintain their membership and should not desert to some rival organization. What is treason for the national state is diluted in its implications for organizations where the enemy character of competing systems is less pronounced. For union members, however, and for factory workers in general, the scab or strikebreaker is guilty of moral turpitude. Loyalty, then, is fostered as a moral value to keep people within the organization. In the second place, it is invoked as a supporting doctrine for the official purposes of the organization. Such purposes are not open to question; anyone who challenges them is guilty of heresy. This means of protecting the official ideology is easier to invoke in religious and political organizations than in other types of organized groups. Finally, loyalty, like other sacred values, may be used to protect the specific means for the attainment of organizational goals so that any criticism of accepted procedures is interpreted as a criticism of the organization itself.

Organizations that have direct commerce with their environment and rely heavily on technology for turning out a product have a more pragmatic than sanctified ideology. They must meet the changing demands of their clientele and so cannot afford to be ritualistic about their procedures. American automobile companies were slow to respond to public needs in the field of transportation, but they finally met the threat of foreign competition with smaller cars. A technologically oriented organization has its rationalized purposes geared to the world of empirical fact rather than to transcendental value. Absolutistic beliefs, unquestioning loyalty, and the excommunication of heretics just do not fit into a value system of pragmatic operationalism. Even such a sacred cow as the prerogatives of management is difficult to assimilate to concepts of consultative management and cooperative team effort. The technological system creates experts who are heavily task oriented, who fly no flags, and who are completely bored by ideological considerations. As experts in technology, they move into positions of leadership and pin on the walls their credo, "Data win."

The Central Role
of Organizational Activities and
Functions in Determining System Norms and Values

Many studies in social psychology have demonstrated the power of the norms of the group over the individual (Newcomb, 1943). The rewards and sanctions that the group can use for conformity to its values and for deviance from its norms constitute a major source of compliance. Another is the gratification of affiliative needs through sharing beliefs and attitudes with others. A third and potent source of the strength of a system ideology is that it reflects and justifies the way of life of the group. Norms develop around the dominant ongoing functions of the social system. They give cognitive support and structure to the behavior in which people are engaged. People do not possess universal minds familiar with all possible beliefs and values in this world. Their ideas and attitudes derive in good part from the input of information from their daily activities. The world of the coal miner is different from that of the farmer, or the worker on an assembly line, or the nuclear research worker, or the diplomat in a foreign capital. The common behavior and interests of functional groups produce a common language, a common belief system, and a common way of thinking. In addition to this intellectual commonality there is a community interest in justifying and glorifying a common way of life. Group norms and ideology are influential in affecting the behavior of members not only because of conformity and affiliation needs but also because the ideology of the system gears into the very functions in which individuals are engaged and invests them with a significance and meaning they would not otherwise possess.

Organized groups differ in the types of tasks they perform and a key determinant of characteristic organizational norms is the type of activity in which the organization is involved. A major political party devotes its energies to getting its candidates elected to office and develops an important value system around the notion of winning elections. Every nominee proudly pledges to conduct a winning campaign;

every party official maintains a public belief in victory for his or her side until the last shred of hope is gone. Professional politicians will make all sorts of compromises to insure a majority vote at the polls, and the political novice who has the magic of capturing votes is slated for a rapid rise in the party structure. In like fashion, the functions of a specific business enterprise determine its value system. And the Marine Corps, as the group with the task of pulling the military chestnuts out of the fire, develops a code of iron discipline, courage, and toughness.

The strength of system norms is due partly to their freedom from idiosyncratic patterns of genetic motivation. They derive their support from the common ongoing activities of the system. The severity of toilet training in early childhood is less relevant for system norms than the tribulations and rewards of adult behavioral requirements. The scientist's support of the value of freedom of inquiry is a necessity for his or her mode of operation. Individuals may have different reasons for following the same course of action, but in the organizational setting the means for reaching a variety of individual goals are reduced to a very few pathways. It is not necessary, therefore, to find a miniature reflection of the ideology of the system in the individual motivational patterns of most members in order to have an effective set of group values.

System ideology arises as a justification of system functions and as a guide to its activities, as previously noted, but it can in some organizations be geared into general societal values based on common socialization practices. Health agencies can capitalize on the universal standards of promoting human welfare. At one time political institutions were able to use patriotism. Schools and colleges enjoy fairly wide acceptance of education as a significant value. Even where all people do not share the value orientation of a given organization there is a selective process through which some organizations and some individuals do find one another. This is less true of business and industrial enterprises so that they start with less value commitment on the part of their personnel than do voluntary associations. In fact the lack of value consensus among rank-and-file workers about what they are producing is one reason for early emphasis on a punishment-reward model in profit-making organizations.

There is, of course, some common ideology in a society into which all subsystems do gear, but how much this can furnish a basis for motivating behavior in any specific organization is an empirical question. In the United States all that has been established is that the divisiveness has not crystallized along class lines. Mann (1970) in a review of the research on the issue reports that traditional theories tend to overstate both the value consensus that exists across individuals and the value congruence within the individual. Mann writes:

Cohesion in liberal democracy depends rather on the lack of consistent commitment to general values of any sort and on the pragmatic acceptance by subordinate classes of their limited roles in society. (p. 423)

Equity as a Key Organizational Value

A pragmatic organizational value associated with its functioning is the doctrine of equity. This is the underlying rationale of Weber's principles of universalistic criteria and of rational authority. It is the rule of law, not of individuals. Individuals willingly follow rules that involve some effort or even sacrifice on their part if they apply to all members. Equity has to do with the fairness with which regulations are administered and it is only one step away from fairness of administration to the essential fairness of the rule itself.

In bureaucratic structures equity has replaced respect for tradition as a guiding principle. Its essential logic has pushed beyond attacking personal favoritism to rejecting institutional discrimination against groups with ascribed characteristics such as race and sex.

The morale problem for years to come for organizations in Western countries will be one of equity. The modern survey, to be maximally useful, will center more on problems of fairness of procedures, of payment, of promotion, and so forth than on conditions of work or the closeness of supervision per se.

A continuing organizational dilemma is the fairness of treatment for all as against the personalized consideration of the individual case. If management takes into account all the special circumstances for a given personality is it being fair to all the people involved? The old issue of *if and when* to make exceptions to rules has not been solved but has become more acute for the organization. Two different principles are involved. The one is the equity doctrine, which we have been emphasizing. The other is the principle of human need and goes beyond the inputs of the individuals of the system, to their unfortunate circumstances of poor physical or mental health or other deprivation. We help victims of disease, famine, flood or fire on the basis of their need, not on the basis of their contribution to society. These two philosophies are exemplified in different types of organizations. In the work organization equity is important and we look at what the individual produces. In many governmental programs, such as public welfare or Medicaid, the principle of need becomes overriding. But not all organizations limit themselves to a single principle and hybrid solutions occur, as in the case of worker's compensation when both equity and need are taken into consideration. People are often confused about the two principles, as in the case of college students applying for food stamps, or college faculty members drawing unemployment insurance for summer vacations, or employees taking sick leave when they are not ill. Another instance of the compromise solution can be seen in hospitals where organized medical treatment must follow equitable rules and yet the clinical practice of dealing with the individual patient cannot be ignored.

It follows that careful attention should be given to the type of institution and its problems to see which principle should apply. In a school system grades should not be awarded on the basis of need, as has been done when all students are promoted regardless of accomplishment. Nor is the principle of need the guide in a work organization where rewards can be geared to effective effort. The ill and the deprived can be taken care of outside the work system.

Where rules are set up for benefits earned by individuals, then the same criteria for assessing returns must be applied to all. When people have contributed to a benefit system they are concerned with fairness of treatment as contributors. The Social Security Administration has been evaluated more favorably on fairness of treatment than agencies administering welfare, or medical care, or employment services by the American public (Katz, Kahn, Gutek, and Barton, 1975). The reason in good part is the objective entitlement of all people to the same benefits based on clear criteria of ages and years of employment. It is not a matter of the subjective judgment of a government clerk or social worker.

Equal pay for equal work is an example of fairness for the employee, but it also implies unequal pay for unequal work. This is subject to the limitation, however, that differential pay should be tied to clearly discernible differences in amount and quality of work or service performed for the organization. If it is difficult to establish such differences in the perceptions of organization members it is doubtful whether rewards should vary. We are following Adams' principle of equity (see Chapter 11) that equity is achieved when the perceived inputs of the individual relative to outputs are compensated in the same fashion as for peers.

Four procedures thus can be helpful in dealing with the problem of equity in organization: (1) Moving toward equality of return for all members save where differences of reward can be tied to palpable differences in input. (2) Taking more systematic account of how the various levels in the system perceive the equity of its functioning. What seems fair at an upper echelon may be seen as grossly unequitable at a lower level. (3) Distinguishing between returns earned by service and treatment that relates to individual needs and problems. The person may need help that goes beyond objective entitlement. Often this is a matter of referral to other organizations but even where the person's own organization takes some responsibility it should not be confused with objective entitlement. Other criteria need to be established, such as the character and extent of the need. (4) Not attempting to handle all problems by specific rules. The clinician gives priority to the individual case and not to general rules. The administrator falls back on objective regulations that apply similarly to all members. The moment we legislate for individual need or for clinical treatment we may create as many problems as we solve.

The Norm of Reciprocity

In his famous studies of the Trobriand Islanders, Malinowski (1926) came to the conclusion that their social structure was based on the principle of reciprocity and mutual interdependence. A striking example of this principle of reciprocal rewarding relationships was the partnership between an island villager and a coastal fisherman. Each villager raising vegetables inland had a specific partner in the coastal village. Their many ceremonial and social relations comprised a superstructure for a basic exchange of gifts by which the fisherman was assured a supply of fresh vegetables and his farming partner a supply of fish. This same reciprocal principle, Malinowski found, pervaded all tribal life and could be considered the equivalent in social relationships of the symbiotic principle in biological relationships.

Homans (1958) and Gouldner (1960) have reinstated this concept of reciprocity in sociological thinking, and Gouldner has asserted that it is a universal norm. He believes it to be as universal and as important as the incest taboo and to be one of the principal components of all value systems. This norm in effect means that people should help those who have helped them and should not injure those who have helped them. Gouldner, moreover, feels that equivalence of return to both parties is not necessary in the operation of the principle. Berkowitz (1963) has generalized the notion still further by postulating a norm of obligation to those dependent on us regardless of the return we achieve. In Berkowitz's experiments, subjects helped an individual who could not carry out a task without their assistance even though no rewards were offered them. This norm of helpfulness derives from the socialization process and, though it has some force in its own right, is undoubtedly of enduring strength because it does receive a considerable amount of reinforcement in adult life from specific acts of reciprocity.

The norms of reciprocity and helpfulness are important factors in *role readiness* (Chapter 5) which is so essential to large-scale bureaucracy. We have given considerable attention in the preceding pages to the functionality of norms and values in various types of social systems. Here we are dealing with a general norm for all role systems that also is tied to a basic functional requirement. The essence of the social relationship, as Malinowski pointed out, is the give-and-take character of the social setting in which people are mutually dependent on one another.

■ SUMMARY ■

Reward and punishment theories need to be supplemented by an account of the internal dynamics of the reactive individual according to which organizational activities become rewarding in themselves and thus provide a free good to management. Three important sources of internal motivation are value expression, self-determination and self-expression, and affiliative expression.

Internalization of organizational goals means that individuals work for these goals since they express their own values. Often the goals of the subsystem are, or become, congruent with the objectives of the members. People achieve self-identity with their occupational identification or their system involvement.

Self-expression and self-determination within the organizational role make possible intrinsic job satisfaction. The basic conditions for such self-expression are the variety, responsibility, and challenge of the job as the research literature attests. Changing job design to provide for job enlargement and job enrichment has generally been accompanied by more intrinsic job satisfaction.

Affiliative expression takes account of ego-expansion to include significant others. The work group can be one instrument for meeting the need for belongingness. The group may become an extension of the individual when individuals can share psychological fields. In fact some of the psychology of the individual applies to the small unified group as all members cooperate in a common task.

Reference group identification can occur for organizations and occupations, based on early socialization and adult socialization. Measures of collective involvement are being attempted and promise to add to the armamentarium of the organizational researcher.

Alienation is the opposite of attachment to the system or to the job and can be thought of as an intrinsic meaninglessness. Hence it does not follow that individuals who are non-work oriented are alienated. They may be flexible in their life interests and just not attached to a particular job or work setting.

For values and norms to be systemic rather than individual, (1) they must have reference to appropriate and required behavior of group members, (2) they must be accepted by a majority of active members and (3) individuals must be aware of group support for a given belief. Organizational activities play a critical role in determining system norms and values. In bureaucratic structures equity is a key value since the same rules apply to all incumbents of a given position. It is also true that norms of reciprocity and helpfulness are critical in organized behavior, in that cooperative contributions to collective outcome are essential.

13

■ MOTIVATIONAL ■
■ PATTERNS AND PERFORMANCE ■

Practitioners and research workers in organizations turn to motivational theory for explanations of individual performance, adequate or inadequate, and for predictions of individual response to changing conditions and programs. Most motivational theories do not provide such explanation and prediction of human behavior in the organizational context. Theories based on needs do not tell us what needs will be salient for different people under different organizational conditions. Expectancy models leave valences and goals to be determined.

These deficiencies from the organizational view are not failures but lack of concern. Few motivational theorists have been interested in linking their central propositions to organizational conditions for motive arousal or to the organizational consequences of such arousal. Maslow and Herzberg are exceptional in dealing both with the ordering or sequential arousal of human motives and, to some extent, with their relationship to organizational life.

THE ORDERING OF MOTIVE PATTERNS

The Maslow Motive Hierarchy

The Maslow model (1943, 1954) assumes a hierarchy of human motives ranging from biological needs through security, love, and belongingness, to ego needs of self-esteem, self-development, and self-actualization. Basic to the theory is the thesis that the motives at the bottom of the hierarchy are imperative in their demands and, until those demands are met, make the higher order needs relatively ineffectual. Once these lower level needs are assured satisfaction, however, the higher level needs take over and become all-important. It would follow that one does not offer the hungry man ribands to stick in his coat. Some organizational consequences of the Maslow approach become apparent when we look at the changes in motive patterns in an affluent society like the United States. Extrinsic rewards such as pay, job security, fringe benefits, and conditions of work are no longer suffice; people, especially younger people, are demanding intrinsic job satisfactions as well. Careers that emphasize only instrumental gratifications, often long-deferred, are losing some of their attractiveness.

In many organizations today the dominant motives of members are the higher-order ego and social motives—particularly those for personal gratification, independence, self-expression, power, and self-actualization (Katz and Georgopoulos, 1971; Georgopoulos, 1970; Schein, 1965). Expressive needs and the pursuit of immediate and intrinsic rewards are competing with economic achievement motives in importance, both in the work situation and outside. Correspondingly, the dominant incentives and rewards required for member compliance, role performance, and organizational effectiveness are social and psychological rather than economic (Georgopoulos and Matejko, 1967; Herzberg, 1966; Likert, 1967). Even at the rank-and-file level, where economic motives are especially strong, there is growing concern on the part of unions for other than bread-and-butter issues, and contract negotiations often stall on matters of policy, control, and work rules rather than money. As a result of these shifts, there is pressure for a place in the decision-making structure of the system from all groups and members in organizations, and there is a growing need for meaningful participation in the affairs of the organization at all levels.

Nor is this shift in motive patterns restricted to the United States. In a survey of 700 Japanese labor and industrial leaders, respondents were asked to assess the degree of concern among workers about certain aspects of the job situation (Takezawa, 1976). Both sets of leaders agreed that wages and salaries would decline in importance in the coming year but job satisfaction would increase in salience. Management representatives predicted that a major labor issue in the future would be the quality of working life.

In the more affluent European countries the initial reaction to such developments in the national labor force was to import "guest workers" from less prosperous countries. To some extent there has also been a tendency to "export" undesirable jobs to countries where workers have fewer options. Multinational corporations can make such allocations with relative ease, and can have a product designed in one country, fabricated in another, and sold in a third. These practices complicate the problems of analysis, but the emphasis on job satisfaction continues to grow.

According to the Maslow theory, lower level needs could again become dominant if they were not met satisfactorily on some regular basis. An economic depression, for example, could reinstate the importance of biological drives and more people would again be interested in any job so long as it paid well enough to meet minimal living standards.

Thus the process of motivational escalation is not irreversible. Reversal, however, in a complex dynamic field is always something different from a simple return to a previous situation. The experience of need-fulfillment at higher levels would influence the response to subsequent reductions, despite the undeniable dominance of subsistence needs.

The Herzberg Two-Factor Theory

Related to the more comprehensive motivational theory of Maslow is the two-factor model of job satisfaction (Herzberg, 1966). The two-factor theory assumes that dissatisfaction and satisfaction are independent dimensions, and that the aspects of the job that produce dissatisfaction differ from those aspects that produce satisfaction. The satisfied worker is not a person in whom dissatisfaction is minimal, because satisfaction and dissatisfaction are evoked by different stimulus conditions. Dissatisfaction can be caused by such extrinsic factors as pay, supervision, working conditions, and company policies—so-called hygiene factors. But the removal of unsatisfactory extrinsic factors is not in itself satisfying or motivating. Satisfaction and motivation come from a different set of factors—meeting the needs for recognition, achievement, responsibility, and personal growth. Herzberg thus accepts Maslow's notion of lower and higher order needs but goes on to draw qualitative distinctions between the two, first as "dissatisfiers" and "satisfiers" and then as "hygienes" and "motivators."

The technique employed by Herzberg in testing his theory is to ask people to respond to this request: "Think of the time when you felt exceptionally good or exceptionally bad about your present job or any other job you have had. Tell me what happened." Most respondents give answers for the time they felt good as relating to the work itself, to achievement, to recognition, and responsibility. The responses for the time they felt bad have to do with working conditions, supervision, peer relations, and company policy. In 17 empirical studies the results were the same, and they included engineers and accountants in a utility industry, women in high-level positions, county agricultural extension workers, male hourly technicians, female assemblers, hospital nurses, skilled hospital employees, unskilled hospital employees, housekeeping workers, Finnish supervisors, and Hungarian engineers. On the other hand, a number of researchers have not been able to confirm the theory. For example, Dachler and Hulin (1969), in a study of 442 male and female white-collar workers in a Canadian company town, asked respondents to rate both importance and satisfaction for 21 environmental and job characteristics. Intrinsic aspects were not perceived as important only for satisfaction and extrinsic aspects only as important for dissatisfaction. "The more satisfied or dissatisfied a person is with a characteristic, the more important he is likely to perceive that characteristic" (p. 262).

When research results of a number of studies testing a theory are in disagreement, one needs to examine both the methods employed and the statement of the theory itself. The Herzberg supporters are vulnerable to the charge of artifactual findings, because different techniques for collecting data do not confirm their results. When people are asked to tell what comes to mind when they were feeling bad it is much easier for them to talk about external factors than about ego failures, and conversely their good feelings are more readily assigned to ego successes than to objective aspects of the job.

It is also true that the theory is stated in too extreme a form. It may be that lower level needs differ from higher level, as Maslow has suggested, but that hygienic factors are completely nonmotivating and intrinsic factors nonproductive of dissatisfaction is too far-fetched a proposition. Thus the two-factor hypothesis is too idealized a logical position to fit psychological complexities in the real world. Triandis (1967) has proposed a compromise for the Herzberg controversy in which he admits that there may be two mechanisms—one for maintenance needs and the other for motivation needs—but proposes that satisfaction and dissatisfaction may not be independent dimensions. Others (Schneider and Locke, 1971) have attempted to develop response categories that permit an empirical test of the unidimensionality or separateness of satisfaction and dissatisfaction. Locke (1976) presents a succinct review of this work and of the problems with the two-factor theory as Herzberg propounded it.

In short, the contribution of Herzberg's theory is to remind students of organizations to consider separately the level of needs of members, the degree to which they are met, and the organizational consequences of their being sated or thwarted.

Most theories of job satisfaction, including the two-factor hypothesis, are essentially weak as motivational models because they are concerned with internal states rather than with antecedent conditions and consequent outcomes. Herzberg goes so far as to ask what it is that people are satisfied or dissatisfied *with*, but he does not ask about the behavioral outcomes of satisfied or dissatisfied need states. Labeling the satisfaction responses "motivators" indicates the preferences of the investigator but neither establishes nor explains the facts of motivation.

Motivation includes a direction, a goal or an objective, and the arousal of one or more drives. Organizational theorists have not addressed themselves to the question of what it is that people are motivated toward; they have assumed that if workers are "motivated" in some general sense, productivity will automatically result. A worker, however, may be motivated toward a variety of goals. The same level of drive arousal in one case may be expressed toward quality of performance, in another toward criticism of supervision, and in a third toward a good record in attendance.

The complexities of motivation in organizations can be understood if we develop an analytic framework comprehensive enough to identify the major sources of variance and detailed enough to predict differences among different organizational units. The framework we propose calls for the formulation of answers to three types of analytic questions:

1. What are the *types of behavior required* for effective organizational functioning? From most of its members any organization will require not one but several patterns of behavior, and the motivational bases of these various behavioral patterns may differ.
2. What different *motivational patterns* are used and can be used to evoke the required behaviors in organizational settings? How do they differ in their logic and psychologic? We have addressed ourselves to these questions in the previous three chapters but we have not inquired into the differential consequences of the various motivational patterns for organizational functioning. A given motivational pattern may be very effective in bringing about one type of necessary behavior and completely ineffective in producing another.
3. What are the *conditions for eliciting a given motivational pattern* in an organizational setting? After we are able to identify the type of motivation we think most appropriate for producing a given behavioral outcome, we still need to know how this motive can be aroused or produced in the organization. We have attempted some analysis of arousal conditions in preceding chapters; we want now to relate these conditions to the main patterns of organizationally required behavior.

BEHAVIORAL REQUIREMENTS FOR ORGANIZATIONS

In Table 13-1 we listed the major types of activity that the organization must engender in its members if it is to survive.

First of all, enough people must be kept within the system to perform its essential functions. People must be induced to enter the system at a sufficiently rapid rate to counteract retirement and defection. They must also be induced to remain within the system. The optimum period of tenure will vary for different individuals and situations, but high turnover is almost always costly. Moreover, while people are members of a system they must validate their membership by regular attendance. Thus turnover and absenteeism are both measures of organizational effectiveness, albeit partial measures. People may, of course, be within the system physically but be psychological absentees. The child may be regular and punctual in school attendance and yet daydream in class. Assembly-line daydreams, sometimes assisted with alcohol or marijuana, are common. Tasks and organizations vary in their demands

---

TABLE 13-1 Patterns of Individual Behavior Required for Organizational Functioning and Effectiveness

---

1. Joining and staying in system
   (a) Recruitment
   (b) Low absenteeism
   (c) Low turnover
2. Dependable behavior: role performance in system
   (a) Meeting or exceeding quantitative standards of performance
   (b) Meeting or exceeding qualitative standards of performance
3. Innovative and spontaneous behavior: performance beyond role requirements for accomplishment of organizational functions
   (a) Cooperative activities with fellow members
   (b) Actions protective of system or subsystem
   (c) Creative suggestions for organizational improvement
   (d) Self-training for additional organizational responsibility
   (e) Creation of favorable climate for organization in the external environment

---

for vigilance and magnitude of engagement, but merely holding people physically within a system is never enough.

Secondly, there must be dependable activity. The great range of variable human behavior must be reduced to a limited number of predictable patterns. In other words, the assigned roles must be carried out in ways that meet some minimal level of quantity and quality. A common measure of productivity is the amount of work turned out within some stipulated period by an individual or by a group. Quality of performance is not as easily measured, and the problem is met by quality controls which set minimal standards for the pieces of work sampled. In general, the major content of the member's role is clearly set forth by organizational protocol, observable characteristics of the situation, and instructions of leaders. The worker on the assembly line, the nurse in the hospital, the teacher in the elementary school all know what their major job is. To do a lot of it and to do it well are the most conspicuous behavioral requirements of the organization. It may be, of course, that given role requirements are not well conceived or functionally related to organizational accomplishment. This is a problem in organizational structure that does not contradict the fact that some major role requirements are necessary.

A third and often neglected set of requirements includes those actions not specified by role prescriptions but which facilitate the accomplishment of organizational goals. The organizational need for actions of an innovative, relatively spontaneous sort is inevitable and unending. No organizational plan can foresee all contingencies within its own operations, can anticipate with perfect accuracy all environmental changes, or can control perfectly all human variability. The resources of people for innovation, for spontaneous cooperation, for protective and creative behavior are thus vital to organizational survival and effectiveness. An organization that depends solely on its blueprints of prescribed behavior is a very fragile social system.

The patterned activity that makes up an organization is so intrinsically cooperative and interrelated that it tends to resemble habitual behavior of which we are unaware. Within every work group in a factory, within any division in a government bureau, or within any department of a university are countless acts of cooperation without which the system would break down. We take these everyday acts for granted, and few of them are included in the formal role prescriptions for any job. One worker will point out to another that her machine is getting jammed, or will pass along some tool that a companion needs, or will borrow some bit of material he is short on. Men and women will come to the aid of a fellow who is in trouble. In most factories specialization develops around such informal giving of help. One person will be expert in first aid, another will be expert in machine diagnosis. We recognize the need for cooperative relationships by raising specific questions about a person's capacity for them when he or she is considered for a job. How well will this person relate to the others, play on the team, fit into the situation?

Another subcategory of behavior beyond the formal requirements of role has to do with the protection of the organization against disaster. There is nothing in the role prescriptions of workers that specifies that they be on the alert to save life and property in the organization. Yet the worker who goes out of his way to remove the boulder from the railway spur, or to secure a rampant piece of machinery, or even to disobey orders when they are obviously wrong and dangerous, is invaluable for the organization.

Acts beyond the line of duty also take the form of creative suggestions for improving methods of production or maintenance. Some organizations encourage their members to feed constructive suggestions into the system, but coming up with good ideas for the organization and presenting them to management is not the typical job of the worker. An organization that can stimulate its members to contribute ideas for organizational improvement is likely to be more effective, since people who are close to operating problems can often furnish informative suggestions about them that would not occur to those more distant. The system that does not have this stream of contributions from its members is not utilizing its potential resources effectively.

Still another subcategory of behavior beyond the call of duty includes the self-educative activities of members who learn to do their own jobs better and prepare to assume more responsible positions in the organization. There may be no requirement that people prepare themselves for better positions, but the organization whose members spend their own time to master knowledge and skills for more responsible jobs in the system has an additional resource for effective functioning.

Finally, members of an organization can contribute to its operations by helping to create a favorable climate for it in the community that surrounds the organization. Employees talk to friends, relatives, and acquaintances about the qualities of the company for which they work. A favorable climate helps in problems of recruitment and, sometimes, product disposal.

In short, for effective organizational functioning many members must be willing on occasion to do more than their job prescriptions specify. If members of the system were to follow the precise letter of job descriptions and organizational protocol, things would soon grind to a halt. Many acts of spontaneous cooperation and many anticipations of organizational objectives are required to make the system viable. The ritualistic bureaucracy becomes inefficient partly because the prescribed behavior of role requirements is virtually the only form of behavior that remains. Clerks react to cases that cross their desks on the basis of the rules provided for their disposition. Cases occur, however, that are too complex or too difficult to handle within the existing rules. Instead of making the extra effort to meet such problems, the bureaucratized clerk pushes the atypical cases to one side for the supervisor to look at in the weekly cleanup. In turn, the supervisor may accumulate a set of exceptional cases to be pushed into a drawer for future consideration with the head of the department. Memoranda are exchanged, precedents are invoked, and an already overspecified book of rules is enlarged yet again. The organization moves in a costly and inefficient way.

The foregoing categories and subcategories of behavior, though related, are not necessarily motivated by the same drives and needs. The motivational pattern that will attract and hold people to an organization is not necessarily the same as that which will lead to higher productivity. Nor are the motives that make for higher productivity invariably the same as those that sustain cooperative interrelationships in the interests of organizational accomplishment. Hence, when we speak about practices and procedures that will further the attainment of the organizational mission, we need to specify the type of behavioral requirement involved.

TYPES OF MOTIVATIONAL PATTERNS

It is profitable to consider our three motivational patterns (see Chapters 10, 11, and 12) as they affect organizational behavior.

Type A. Rule Enforcement

The first pattern is the acceptance of role prescriptions and of organizational directives because of their legitimacy. The group member obeys the rules because they stem from legitimate sources of authority and because they can be enforced by legal sanctions. This is the basic pattern of motivation in simple machine theory. Motivation bears no relation to the activity itself. Any rule or directive from the proper authority must be obeyed because it is the law of the nation, of the organization, or of the group.

Type B. External Rewards

Incentives can be linked to desired behaviors. Actions can become instrumental to achieving specific rewards. Four subtypes of such instrumental rewards are often employed in social systems. In the first place, rewards can be earned merely through membership in the system and increased through seniority in it. For example, government, industry, and educational institutions offer retirement pensions, sick leave, health examinations, and other fringe benefits. They furnish cost-of-living raises and other across-the-board wage increases. They may provide attractive working conditions and recreational facilities. Many of these benefits are available without differentiation to any member of the system; others are apportioned according to status or seniority. But they are all system benefits, rewarding a whole category of persons for staying in the system.

In addition to these general system rewards are the individual rewards of pay increases, promotion, and recognition accorded to people on the basis of individual merit. They may take the form of a piece-rate system in which each individual is paid according to the amount he or she produces. They may take the form of giving outstanding workers some priority with respect to promotion. Or a suggestion system may reward individuals in proportion to the value of their suggestions to the company.

Another form of instrumental motivation for group members derives from the approval they receive from their leaders. This category does not refer to the approval of the superior interpreted by the employee as a promise of promotion. It refers to the gratification a person may find in the praise of a powerful and respected figure. Such a person wants to do things which will insure continued approbation from his or her superior, even without the implication of upgrading and higher pay.

A similar type of individual reward is social approval of one's own group. The potency of the peer group in influencing behavior is a continuing source of surprise to parents. Social approval of the immediate work group motivates members toward organizational requirements, however, only to the extent that those requirements are congruent with the norms of the group. This type of motivation can facilitate or prevent attainment of organizational objectives, depending on the nature of the group norms.

The motivational sources for these patterns of instrumental activities are varied. We shall not attempt to push them back to some ultimate physiological cause. For our purposes it is enough to recognize that many human actions are the means to the satisfaction of utilitarian drives or ego needs, and are performed for no other reason. Between a need and its satisfaction may be interposed almost any behavioral demand. Fulfilling the behavioral requirement is made a condition for the satisfaction of the need. The behavioral requirement may be otherwise unrelated to need satisfaction and, except for the rewards placed upon it, might seldom occur.

Type C. Internalized Motivation

This motivational pattern refers both to intrinsic job satisfaction and to the internalization of the goals of the group or organization as part of the individual's own value system.

Self-expression and self-determination are the basis for *identification with the job*, that is, for satisfactions deriving directly from role performance. The scientist derives gratification from scientific inquiry, the musical composer from creating a symphony, the craftsman from the exercise of skill in a job well done.

Value expression and self-idealization lead to the *internalization of organizational goals*. The goals of the group become incorporated as part of the individual's value system or conception of self. As a result, satisfactions accrue to the person from the expression of attitudes and behavior reflecting his or her cherished beliefs and self-image. The reward is not so much a matter of social recognition or monetary advantage as of establishing one's self-identity, confirming one's notion of the sort of person one sees oneself to be, and expressing the values appropriate to this self-concept.

CONSEQUENCES OF DIFFERENT MOTIVATIONAL PATTERNS

The preceding analysis of the various types of behavior required for organizational effectiveness and the different motivational patterns available for energizing and directing such behavior strongly suggests that there will be costs and gains in emphasizing any single desired outcome. Maximizing dependable role performance may involve motivational conditions that inhibit spontaneous and innovative behavior. Attracting people to a system and holding them in it may not lead to a high level of productivity. We need to examine in detail the differential effects of the three patterns of motivation on organizational behavior, and to analyze the conditions most likely to arouse these patterns.

Legal Compliance and the Punishment Model

Organizational and legal controls will not be generally effective for attracting people into a system or holding them there, except in cases where recruitment and tenure can be legislated. Military service and attendance at school can be organizationally compelled because the apparatus of government and the acts of legislatures stand behind the organizational demand for compliance. Absenteeism can be reduced through legal rules in all organizations, but the legalistic control of absence may be reflected in a higher rate of turnover.

There is some evidence that clarity of rules is a condition of some importance in holding people in the system. If people know what to expect and are clear about the roles they fulfill they are more likely to remain in the system. Weitz (1956), Youngberg (1963), and Macedonia (1969) found that prior knowledge and understanding of role requirements was a significant factor in keeping people in the company. In these investigations the experimental groups received information through booklets and the control groups did not. In a more subjective study Lyons (1971) reported that staff nurses who perceived their role demands as clear were less likely to leave or think of leaving.

Emphasis on legal compliance can bring about acceptable levels of individual performance both in quantity and quality. The more routine the activity, the more likely this is to be true. Creativity is difficult if not impossible to legislate. Legality, moreover, needs the reinforcement of situational reminders. The time clock, the use of mechanical "speeds and feeds" beyond the control of the worker, and the occasional policing of rules and regulations are characteristic of the legal motif in organizations.

Emphasis on the legalities of organizational control tends in practice to mean that the minimal acceptable standard for quantity and quality of performance becomes the maximal standard. If it is legitimate and proper according to company and union standards to turn out 40 pieces on a machine, then there is no point in exceeding this standard. One cannot be more legal or proper than the norm, though there are degrees of nonconformity in failing to meet it. Of course, individuals may be motivated to exceed the norm for various rewards but not for the satisfaction of properly meeting the rules.

Another reason for the minimal standard becoming the maximum in practice is that an organization geared to rules and regulations can find the overachiever just as much a problem as the underachiever. The eager beaver who turns out more work than the minimal standard requires is a problem to boss and fellow workers alike. The boss has problems in speeding up materials to keep the enthusiast supplied or in explaining to higher management why all the jobs in the section should not be retimed.

Punishing ineffective performance can improve the quality of work, as a series of field experiments by Miller (1965) demonstrates. In one experiment different techniques were employed to cut down on the errors of operators in classifying muffle boxes according to bore size—specifically, persuasion, feedback, and censure. When reprimands and warnings were added to feedback, the number of lots rejected for misclassification dropped to zero and remained at zero for the concluding six weeks of the observation. In two related experiments performance involved a group of co-workers and again errors were significantly reduced by the imposition of penalties. Feedback of some kind is necessary to permit the correction of errors, but feedback in itself does not provide the motivation to make such corrections.

Finally, the legal basis of influencing people is notoriously deficient in affecting performance beyond the narrow role prescriptions for quantity and quality of work. What is not covered by rules is by definition not the responsibility of the organizational member. "Working to the rules" thus becomes the traditional revenge of the legally constrained work force.

The attempt is usually made to extend the rules to cover more and more of the behavior required for good overall organizational performance. But several considerations argue against such extension. Acts of creativity or spontaneous, mutual helpfulness cannot be legislated. Major role requirements will be obscured if the legal specifications become too numerous. Finally, building up the role of every member would entail some upgrading of even the lowliest positions and would run counter to the machine-theoretical basis of many hierarchical organizations.

Total institutions can rely heavily on legal compliance. They presumably control all or most of the lives of their members, and so can decree and order activities within their confines. As we approach the extremes of such total regulation in prisons and military outfits, we find the most elaborate and dynamic of informal systems, as if people compensated in the social life of the group for the suffocating control of the formal institution.

Extrinsic Rewards: System and Individual

The first logical extension of machine theory beyond rules and sanctions is the addition of rewards to motivate performance. It is important to distinguish between rewards administered in relation to individual effort and performance, and the system rewards that accrue to people by virtue of their membership in the system. In the former category are piece-rate incentives, promotion for outstanding performance, or any special recognition bestowed in acknowledgement of differential contributions to organizational functioning. The category of system rewards includes fringe benefits, recreational facilities, cost-of-living raises, across-the-board upgrading, job security, and pleasant working conditions.

Individual rewards properly administered help attract people to the system and hold them in it. A major factor in the effectiveness of such rewards is the extent to which they are competitive with individual reward systems in other organizations. Individual rewards can also be effective in motivating people to meet and exceed the quantitative and qualitative standards of role performance. This effectiveness is limited, however, when large numbers of people are performing identical tasks, so that superior individual performance threatens the rewards and security of the majority. In other words, differential individual rewards are difficult to apply effectively to masses of people doing the same work and sharing a common fate in a mass production organization. It is no accident that large organizations have moved in the direction of converting individual rewards into system rewards.

Individual rewards are also difficult to apply to contributions that go beyond the formal requirements of role. Spectacular instances of innovative behavior can be singled out for recognition, of course, and heroism beyond the call of duty can be decorated. But the everyday cooperative activities that keep an organization from falling apart are more difficult to recognize and reward. Creative suggestions for organizational improvement are sometimes encouraged through financial rewards. In general, however, singling out of individuals for their extra contributions to the cause is not the most effective and reliable means of evoking high motivation for the accomplishment of organizational objectives.

If rewards such as pay incentives are to work as they are intended they must meet three primary conditions, as we noted in Chapter 11: (1) They must be clearly perceived as large enough in amount to justify the additional effort required to obtain them. (2) They must be perceived as directly related to the required performance and follow directly on its accomplishment. (3) They must be perceived as equitable by the majority of system members, many of whom will not receive them. These conditions suggest some of the reasons why individual rewards can work so well in some situations and yet be so difficult for application in large organizations.

In terms of the first criterion many companies have attempted incentive pay without making the differential between increased effort and increased reward proportional from the point of view of the workers. If workers can double their pay by working at a considerably increased tempo, that is one thing. But if such increased expenditure means a possible 10 percent increase, that is another. Moreover, there is the tradition among workers, and it is not without some factual basis, that management cannot be relied upon to maintain a high rate of pay for those making considerably more than the standard and that their increased efforts will only result in their "being sweated." There is, then, the temporal dimension of whether the piece rates that seem attractive today will be maintained tomorrow if individual productivity increases substantially.

The issue here is not merely one of keeping the faith. Time and motion study has as its aim the equalization of effort under specified methods of work. Every increase in individual productivity therefore raises the question of whether the worker is really working "harder" in accordance with the specified methods, or is working "smarter" and has in effect changed the methods of work so that the job is less demanding. In the latter case, the logic of time study argues that the job should be retimed.

More significant, however, is the fact that a large-scale organization consists of many people engaging in similar and interdependent tasks. The work of any one is highly dependent on what others are doing. Hence individual piece rates are difficult to apply on any equitable basis. Group incentives are more logical, but as the size of the interdependent group grows, we move toward system rather than toward individual rewards. Moreover, in large-scale production enterprises the role performance is controlled by the tempo of the machines and their coordination. The speed of the worker on the assembly line is determined by the speed of the assembly line. An individual piece-rate just does not accord with the systemic nature of the coordinated collectivity. Differences of opinion about the amount of effort to be expended on the job are settled not on the floor of the factory but during the negotiations of the union and management about the manning of a particular operation. Heads of corporations may believe in the philosophy of individual enterprise, but when they deal with reward systems in their own organizations they become realists and accept the pragmatic notion of collective rewards.

Since there is such a high degree of collective interdependence among rank-and-file workers, attempts to use individual rewards are often perceived as inequitable. Informal norms develop to protect the group against efforts that are seen as divisive or exploitative. Differential rates for subsystems within the organization will be accepted much more than invidious distinctions within the same subgrouping. Hence promotion or upgrading may be the most potent type of individual reward. The employee is rewarded by being moved to a different category of workers on a better pay schedule. Some of the same problems apply, of course, to this type of reward. Since differential performance is difficult to assess in assembly-type operations, promotion is often based on such criteria as conformity to company requirements with respect to attendance and absenteeism, observance of rules, and seniority. None of these criteria is related to individual performance on the job. Moreover, promotion is greatly limited by the technical and professional education of the worker.

It is true, of course, that most organizations are not assembly-line operations, and even for those that are, the conditions described here do not apply to the upper echelons. A large corporation can follow a policy of high individual rewards to division managers based on the profits achieved by a given division. A university can increase the quantitative research productivity of its staff by making publication the essential criterion for promotion. In general, where assessment of individual performance is feasible and where the basis of the reward system is clear, instrumental individual rewards can play an important part in raising productivity.

System rewards differ from individual rewards in that they are not allocated on the basis of differential effort and performance but on the basis of membership in the system. The main basis for differential allocation of system rewards is seniority in the system. A higher pension for 30 years of service than for 20 years does not violate the principle of rewarding membership. Management often overlooks the distinction between individual and system rewards, and operates as if rewards administered across the board would produce the same effects as individual rewards.

System rewards are most effective for holding members within the organization. Since these rewards are often distributed on the basis of length of service, people will want to stay on to receive them. The limiting factor is competition with attractions in other systems. As the system increases its attractions, other things being equal, it should reduce its problems of turnover. In fact, it may sometimes have the problem of too little turnover, with many poorly motivated people staying on until retirement.

System rewards will not lead to work of higher quality or greater quantity than is required to stay in the organization. Since rewards are given equally to all members or differentially in terms of seniority, people are not motivated to do more than meet the standards for remaining in the system. It is sometimes assumed that the liking for the organization created by system rewards will generalize to greater productive effort. Such generalization of motivation may occur to a very limited extent, but it is not a reliable basis for the expectation of higher productivity. Management may expect gratitude from workers because it has added some special fringe benefit or some new recreational facility. Employees will be motivated to remain in an enterprise with such advantages, but are unlikely to express gratitude by working harder for the company.

Although system rewards maintain the level of productivity not much above the minimum required to stay in the system, there still may be large differences *between* systems with respect to the quantity and quality of production as a function of system rewards. An organization with substantially better wage rates and fringe benefits than its competitors may be able to set a higher level of performance as a minimal requirement for its workers and still hold its employees. System rewards can be related to the differential productivity of organizations as a whole though they are not effective in maximizing the potential contributions of the majority of individuals within an organization. They may account for differences in motivation between systems rather than for differences in motivation between individuals in the same system. They operate through their effects on the minimal standards for all people in the system. They act indirectly in that their effect is to make people want to stay in the organization; to do so people must be willing to accept the legitimately derived standards of role performance in that system. The direct mechanism for insuring performance is legal compliance, but the legal requirements of the organization will not hold members if demands are too great or rewards too meager in comparison to other organizations. The mediating variable in accounting for organizational differences based on system rewards is the relative attractiveness of the system for the individual compared to other systems accessible to him or her.

System rewards do little to motivate performance beyond the line of duty, with two possible exceptions. As people develop a liking for the attractions of the organization, they may be more likely to engage in cooperative relations with their fellows toward organizational goals. They may be more likely also to contribute to a favorable climate of opinion for the system in the external environment. It may be easier for a company to recruit personnel when employees have described it as a good place to work.

The effective use of system rewards requires their uniform application for all members of the system or for plausible major groupings within the system. If rewards are to be given by virtue of membership in the system, any allocation favoring some individuals over others is suspect. Management is frequently surprised by resentment over differential system rewards when there has been no resentment of differential individual rewards.

One public utility, for example, inaugurated an attractive retirement system for its employees before such fringe benefits were common. Its employees were objectively much better off because of the new benefits, and yet the most hated feature of the whole company was the retirement system. Employee complaints centered on two issues: years of employment in the company before the age of 30 did not count toward retirement pensions; and company officials, because of their higher salaries and correspondingly higher pensions, could retire on livable incomes. The employees felt intensely that, if they were being rewarded for service to the company, it was unfair to rule out years of service before age 30. The service of a man or woman who started to work for the company immediately after high school graduation was unrecognized for a dozen years. Moreover, workers felt that a lifetime of service to the company should enable them to retire on a livable income as it enabled company officials to do so. The company house organ devoted considerable space over a few years to showing how much the workers actually benefited from the plan, as in fact was the case. On the occasion of a companywide survey, this campaign was found to have had little effect. The most common complaint was still the patent unfairness of the retirement system.

The critical point is that system rewards have a logic of their own, a logic of citizenship rather than performance. Since they accrue to people by virtue of membership or length of service in an organization, they will be perceived as inequitable if they are not uniformly administered. The perception of the organization member is that all members are equal in their access to organizational benefits. Office employees will not be upset by differences in individual rewards that recognize differences in responsibility. However, if their organization gives them free meals in a cafeteria and sets aside a special dining room for executives, many of them will be upset. In our culture we accept individual differences in income but we do not readily accept differences in classes of citizenship. To be a member of an organization is to be a citizen in that community, and all citizens are equal in their membership rights. Universities that do not extend to research workers the same tenure rights and fringe benefits accorded to the teaching staff have a morale problem on their hands.

Research has frequently not discriminated between system and individual rewards, between intrinsic job satisfaction and satisfaction with aspects of the job other than work content, and even among behavioral outcomes. At a general level we know that high pay rates and bonuses make the system more attractive and so reduce turnover and absenteeism. In their review of such studies Porter and Steers (1973) found that satisfaction with pay and promotion were correlated with turnover in the expected direction in nine out of eleven investigations (see Table 13-2). Rewards can also influence absenteeism, as Lawler

TABLE 13-2 Studies of Relations Between Organization-wide Factors and Turnover and Absenteeism

Factor	Population	n	Type of With-drawal Studied	Relation to With-drawal
Satisfaction with pay and promotion				
Patchen (1960)	Oil refinery workers	487	Absenteeism	Negative
Friedlander and Walton (1964)	Scientists and engineers	82	Turnover	Negative
Knowles (1964)	Factory workers	56	Turnover	Negative
Saleh et al. (1965)	Nurses	263	Turnover	Negative
Bassett (1967)	Engineers	200	Turnover	Negative
Ronan (1967)	Administrative and professional personnel	91	Turnover	Negative
Hulin (1968)	Female clerical workers	298	Turnover	Negative
			Turnover (pay)	Zero
Dunnette et al.	Lower level managers	1020	Turnover (promotion)	Negative
Kraut	Computer salespeople	Varied	Turnover	Negative
Telly et al. (1971)	Factory workers	900	Turnover	Zero
Conference Board (1972)	Salespeople; management trainees	Varied	Turnover	Negative

From Porter and Steers, 1973, p. 157.

and Hackman (1969) demonstrated in an experimental field study of part-time janitorial employees. A plan to provide cash bonuses for regular attendance was developed participatively in three work groups and imposed upon two others. The plan worked well in reducing absenteeism for the groups that had participated in its formulation and less well for the groups not involved in its development. A follow-up study a year later (Schefler, Lawler, and Hackman, 1971) showed that where the plan remained in effect for the participating workers, absence rates remained low; where the plan had been dropped by management, absences increased. Although the investigators attributed the decreased absenteeism to both the cash bonus and its method of introduction, it is not clear as to how much of the result was a matter of the bonus as an extrinsic reward and how much a matter of ego motivation deriving from involvement in the bonus plan.

Increasing financial returns on a productivity-contingent basis can lead to more productivity, subject to the conditions already described. Locke and Bryan (1967) demonstrated that in well-controlled laboratory studies increasing the financial rewards increases productivity. Lawler (1968) found that subjects working on a piece rate system produced 20 percent more than subjects working on an hourly system. But in these experiments rewards are tied to individual performance whereas in industry the problem is how to create such ties without encountering the obstacles already described. Increasing wages as such is no guarantee of increased productivity but the company with a high pay rate is in a strong position in attracting and holding employees.

The linkage between performance and rewards can be studied through the individual's own evaluation of incentives and own perception of the instrumentality of given actions for attaining rewards. Georgopoulos, Mahoney, and Jones (1957) reported that workers who saw productivity as leading to high pay were more likely to be high producers. Although the measure of productivity was a self-report, subsequent studies using superiors' ratings and objective indices confirmed the finding (Spitzer, 1964; Porter and Lawler, 1968). And Schneider and Olson (1970) also present evidence from a study of hospitals that indicates that attitudes toward the importance of pay are related to performance, but only where good performance does actually lead to higher pay.

Whether the model of perceived instrumentality and valence of outcomes should be multiplicative, as Vroom has proposed (see Chapter 11) is not firmly established. On the negative side, Spitzer (1964) found that multiplying importance by expectancy did not increase the prediction to performance. But most studies do support the multiplicative hypothesis. For example, Galbraith and Cummings (1967) had 32 workers in a plant manufacturing heavy equipment rate the value of such rewards as pay, promotion, and recognition and, in addition, evaluate the importance of effective job performance for the attainment of these outcomes. Multiplying the two sets of ratings did predict to worker output, especially in the case of recognition by one's superior.

The research of Galbraith and Cummings (1967) suggests that approval from one's superior is, like pay, an extrinsic reward and must be tied to performance to be effective for increasing productivity. The use of approval by an organizational leader is thus subject to the same limitations as other forms of external reward. Leaders can avoid inequity and make their approval part of the system reward by speaking words of encouragement to every member meeting standards. Or they can single out for special approval the very few who perform above standard. In the former case, the leader may merely contribute to the feeling that this is a pleasant place to work. In the latter case, he or she may strengthen the motivation of a few "company" people and add to the resistance of the majority.

The actions of the leader in ministering to the dependency needs of followers may even develop a satisfying interpersonal relationship which has a negative effect on organizational performance. The dependent employee may gravitate to the officer who can give him or her some psychological assurance in coping with personal problems. The support of the parental figure, understandably enough, may not be given to the person who does the job well but to the dependent person, who needs it more. In turn, the superior may derive gratification from playing this supportive role. Both individuals profit from the relationship, but it may be so unrelated to the tasks to be performed that it merely subtracts from the productive time of both people. Kaye (1958) has provided data consistent with this interpretation.

Internalized Motivation

We have considered some of the evidence on conditions productive of internalized motivation in Chapter 12. Here it remains to link such arousal patterns to their organizational consequences. We will consider first the organizational consequences of intrinsic job satisfaction, then value expression, and finally shared psychological fields and group cohesiveness.

Self-Expression, Self-Determination and Intrinsic Job Satisfaction

Most of the research on job enlargement and job enrichment reports a rise in satisfaction from the content of the work itself—greater feelings of autonomy, of responsibility, of demonstrating one's worth (Chapter 12). When productivity has also been measured in job enrichment experiments, most of them have shown increases in productivity as well. The assumption is that the challenge of the job motivates people toward greater effort. The further assumption is often made that subjective states of being able to express oneself or show one's abilities mediate between the objective characteristics of the enriched job and the increased productivity of the worker. Finally it is assumed that questions directed at these feelings adequately and validly measure the subjective feeling state. Although more research is needed to support these assumptions conclusively, there is considerable backing for them as more and more evidence accumulates in this area of investigation.

Porter and Steers (1973) in their review of studies of job satisfaction report a high degree of agreement on the relationship of job satisfaction and turnover. Fifteen out of sixteen investigations found an association between low turnover and high job satisfaction (Table 13-3). Where absenteeism was also measured similar results were obtained—low absenteeism was correlated with high satisfaction.

Earlier we referred to the four experiments of Paul, Robertson, and Herzberg (1969) on job enrichment. In one laboratory of an industrial research department, technicians were given the opportunity to participate in planning projects, setting goals, and making fiscal decisions. The measure of performance was the evaluation of research reports and research minutes of experimental and control subjects by a panel of three managers not members of the department. Three such staff assessments were carried out during the course of a year and the only group showing consistent improvement was one of the experimental groups.

With a more objective performance criterion, an experiment on sales representatives (Paul, Robertson, and Herzberg, 1969) showed a more dramatic outcome. For the group with enriched jobs, the gain over the previous year, after allowing for the additional work of making decisions about calls and claims, was almost 19 percent, amounting to $300,000 in sales value. The control group, on the other hand, declined by 5 percent. During the same period the control group showed no change in job satisfaction, while the experimental group improved some 11 percent.

The third Paul-Robertson-Herzberg experimental program was conducted among design engineers, for whom there was no such hard performance criterion as was available for the salespeople. Nonetheless, senior managers felt that the many changes giving the engineers more autonomy had cumulated significantly and positively. There was no evidence of poor decisions, more time was given to technical development rather than routine tasks, and important problems were solved.

In their fourth study the same investigators introduced changes in

TABLE 13-3 Studies of Relation of Job Satisfaction to Turnover and Absenteeism

Investigator(s)	Population	n	Type of With-drawal Studied	Relation to Withdrawal
Weitz and Nuckols (1955)	Insurance agents	990	Turnover	Negative
Weitz (1956)	Insurance agents	474	Turnover	Negative
Talacchi (1960)	Departmental workers	NA	Turnover / Absenteeism	Zero / Negative
Youngberg (1963)	Insurance salespeople	NA	Turnover	Negative
Hulin (1966)	Female clerical workers	129	Turnover	Negative
Hulin (1968)	Female clerical workers	298	Turnover	Negative
Katzell (1968)	Student nurses	1852	Turnover	Negative
Mikes and Hulin (1968)	Office workers	660	Turnover	Negative
Dunnette et al.	Lower level managers	1020	Turnover	Negative
Macedonia (1969)	Military academy cadets	1160	Turnover	Negative
Taylor and Weiss (1969a, 1969b)	Retail store employees	475	Turnover	Negative
Kraut	Computer salespeople	Varied	Turnover	Negative
Wild (1970)	Female manual workers	236	Turnover / Turnover	Negative / Negative
Waters and Roach (1971)	Female clerical workers	160	Turnover / Absenteeism	Negative / Negative
Atchison and Lefferts (1972)	Air Force pilots	52	Turnover	Negative

Note. NA = not available.
Both Kraut, and Atchison and Lefferts found that an expressed intention to leave represented an even more accurate predictor of turnover than job satisfaction.
From Porter and Steers, 1973, p. 154.

the work roles of production supervisors and of engineering supervisors. Again in the experimental groups more autonomy was provided for training, recruiting, discipline, and contributing to organizational problems. A number of the supervisors given the opportunity did contribute their experience and expertise to long-standing organizational and technical difficulties. In three cases where financial assessment was possible, the estimated annual savings totaled more than $125,000. Moreover, the production supervisors improved markedly in their training of workers; the number of assistants unable to do the job of the person they assisted fell by 37 percent. The engineering supervisors also interacted effectively with union officials, and relations between these two groups had long been difficult.

Other case studies of job enlargement for the most part report that increased autonomy and responsibility not only lead to more satisfaction with the content of the work but to improvements in the quality of the work and to higher productivity (Davis and Taylor, 1972 and Davis and Cherns, 1975). Not every case provides hard data on productivity but where such figures are available the findings are consistently in the same direction. Often total labor costs go unmeasured but the evidence again suggests that with job enrichment less time has to be spent by management in supervisory control.

Value Expression

A motive pattern relating to intrinsic job satisfaction is value expression, which can be tied to organization goals as well as to the content of the work. People can derive feelings of gratification in working for a system whose values they have internalized or whose values coincide with their own. The dedicated party worker or the committed employee is likely to meet all three organizational requirements— staying in the system, doing excellent work, and performing innovative acts supportive of organizational policies. Since many motivational problems would be solved if organizations had such value consensus among their members, it is of interest that research and practice is in its infancy in exploring the matter. Almost no studies have attempted to measure the distribution of organizational values and their relationship to various types of performance.

Perhaps the closest approach is in studies of occupational identification and organizational commitment. But occupational identification transcends the particular organization and so would not predict to turnover or necessarily to innovative acts to advance the goals of one organization. The notion of an occupational identity or personality that influences the individual in ways other than those stipulated by the specific organization is an old one (Becker and Carper, 1956). It has been revived in recent years through attempts at its measurement, and

Hebden (1975) has selected three components of occupational identification in his empirical research on data processors: (1) Commitment to particular task or preference for jobs within and outside the present employing organization, (2) reference group choice or the group to which the respondent looked for the evaluation of his or her work, and (3) autonomy of the occupational group for setting its own standards. On all three components the programmers in data processing were more occupationally oriented than the system analysts. The system analysts were apparently more concerned with the broader functioning of the organization and the programmers were more tied to their specific tasks. The one group stressed an organizational criterion for selecting managers and the other group stressed a theoretical criterion.

Dubin (1956) broadened the approach to occupational identification in his concept of *central life interests*. His questionnaire, originally of 40, now of 32 items, "was designed to determine whether the job and work place were central interests of workers or whether other areas of their social experience were important to them" (p. 134). The basic technique was to pose a type of behavior and ask for the respondent's preference for the setting or locale of his or her actions. For example, some of the items in the questionnaire follow:

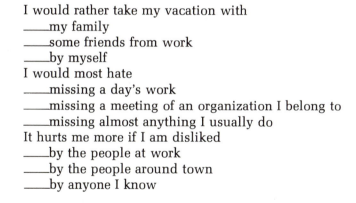

I would rather take my vacation with
_____my family
_____some friends from work
_____by myself
I would most hate
_____missing a day's work
_____missing a meeting of an organization I belong to
_____missing almost anything I usually do
It hurts me more if I am disliked
_____by the people at work
_____by the people around town
_____by anyone I know

From the many items a score could be assigned on the basis of job oriented versus non-job oriented responses. This measure has been used by a number of researchers to compare job status and occupation. In general, the empirical studies show that the lower the skill level and the responsibility of the position, the smaller the percentage of job-oriented central life interests—a set of findings consistent with the work on job satisfaction and occupation. For example, lumber workers studied by Ima (1962) had only 14 percent of their number with job-oriented scores. Similarly, long-distance truck drivers had only 12 percent with such scores (Latta, 1968) compared with 54 percent of industrial supervisors (Maurer, 1968), 41 percent of industrial specialists (Dubin and Goldman, 1972), 14 percent of British bank clerks (Parker, 1965), and 79 percent of nurses (Orzack, 1959).

The measure of central life interests includes more than occupational identification; it covers other aspects of the work situation, such as a congenial work group and a supportive and attractive organization. In fact Dubin, Champoux, and Porter (1975) found a strong relationship between job-oriented life interests and organizational commitment in a sample of 1,014 male and female blue-collar workers drawn from a bank and telephone company. Of the men with low organizational commitment only 14 percent were job-oriented, as compared to 65 percent of the highly committed group. Similarly the female clerical workers with low organizational commitment had 14 percent who were job-oriented, but with high commitment some 54 percent. The questionnaire measuring organizational commitment was a 15-item instrument developed by Porter and Smith (1970), based on their concept of commitment and described by Dubin et al. (1975) thus: "a highly committed person will indicate: (1) a strong desire to remain a member of a particular organization, (2) a willingness to exert high levels of effort on behalf of the organization, and (3) a definite belief in and acceptance of the values and goals of the organization" (Dubin, Champoux, and Porter, 1975, p. 414). The validity of the instrument is attested by its power in predicting turnover in a sample of managerial trainees over a 15 month period (Porter, Crampon, and Smith, 1976). The trainees who voluntarily left the company showed a definite decline in commitment prior to their departure.

Although both the Central Life Interests measure and the commitment questionnaire are useful for comparing different organizations and occupations, they are too global to answer questions about the dynamics of motivation with respect to systemic behavioral requirements. Thus they resemble the general measures of job satisfaction, and research has demonstrated that satisfaction with job content has to be differentiated from satisfactions with working conditions, supervision, and pay. What is needed in future research is methodological work that will compare the many measures already available to see to what extent they are tapping independent dimensions and to what extent they predict differentially to various outcomes. The work of Dubin, Champoux, and Porter (1975) in showing the relationship between organizational commitment and central life interests is a step in the right direction. It would be of interest, too, to separate out two of the concepts of the Porter-Smith scale of organizational commitment—a cognitive and a telic component. The first refers to the individual's acceptance of organizational values, the second to the amount of effort the individual is willing to exert to maintain the organizational system.

Shared Psychological Fields
and Group Cohesiveness

In our discussion of patterns of internalized motivation we emphasized the importance of the primary group, especially the potentiality of the group for providing the sense of task accomplishment and closure that is usually thought of only in individual terms. (See Chapter 12.) We called attention to the magnitude and unity of effort that can be motivated by attachment to the group. The great advantage of the cohesive group is that its members can find in group responsibility and group achievement satisfaction for their individual needs for self-expression and self-determination, as well as affiliation.

Research workers at the Tavistock Institute have been leaders in theory and experimentation involving the primary group as the motivational base for performance. Rice's (1958) experiment in a large Indian textile mill is a classic example of their approach and of the motivational power of the primary group. The preexperimental condition consisted of a highly specialized and fractionated division of labor, in which no worker nor group of workers could be identified with the task outcome; the output could be meaningfully described only as the result of their aggregative specialized roles. The experimental condition created groups of seven people, with each group responsible for specific looms—their maintenance, their servicing, their operation, and their output. There is division of labor within such groups, but each member of the group identifies with the group task and its accomplishment as well as with his or her own contribution to it. Increased motivation, increased performance, and increased satisfaction resulted in this case, as in many others. (See Chapter 20 for a more complete description of this and other Tavistock projects.) The discovery of the motivational power of the primary group, and of the fulfillment of individual needs through group achievement, is the greatest contribution of the "group dynamicists" and of the Tavistock research workers to organizational theory and practice. Its potential impact is no less than the discovery of the informal group by Elton Mayo and his colleagues. Organizational theory and practice has been slow to recognize the implications of these group phenomena, however, and only in recent years has the earlier work of Rice and Trist been extended.

One example of such extension is the research of Thorsrud (1976) and his Norwegian colleagues with "autonomous work groups" in factory settings. The emphasis on the primary group as the producing unit is also to be seen in the design of the Swedish "new factories." (The design and effects of this and other experiments are described in Chapter 20.)

Much remains to be learned about the limits of individual fulfillment through group accomplishment, and about the substitutability of shared outcomes for solitary ones. The potential formation of small cohesive work groups, engaged in tasks of meaningful size and with visible outcomes, seems a desirable objective in the design of production sequences and factories. The gains—psychological and material— would be substantial.

■ SUMMARY

Two popular models of motivation—the Maslow motive hierarchy and the Herzberg two-factor theory—are directed more at internal states than at behavioral outcomes. The Maslow theory holds that motives at the lower levels of the hierarchy such as biological drives are imperative in their demands and the higher order needs only became important when the lower needs are satisfied. Today organizations may have to satisfy more than bread-and-butter motives to motivate workers. The Herzberg model views satisfaction and dissatisfaction with job-related issues as independent dimensions. Dissatisfaction is caused by extrinsic factors such as pay or working conditions and satisfaction from ego-involved activities. According to this theory the removal of unsatisfactory extrinsic factors is not in itself motivating. Research suggests the model is oversimplified in its logical distinctions. What is needed is a more comprehensive framework for predicting the effectiveness of organizations in terms that specify the types of behavior required for organizational effectiveness, the different motive patterns that can evoke such behavior, and the organizational conditions that elicit these motive patterns.

Three categories of behavior are required to achieve high levels of organizational effectiveness. People must *join and remain* in the organization; they must *perform dependably* the roles assigned to them; and they must *engage in occasional innovative and cooperative behavior* beyond the requirements of the role but in the service of organizational objectives. More specific behaviors are described within each of these broad categories.

Three motive patterns are proposed as characteristic of organizations and as capable of producing the required behaviors in varying degrees. These are legal compliance, external rewards, and internalized motivation.

The complex sequences that link these and other mediating variables can be summarized for each of the three motive patterns as follows.

Legal compliance is evoked by the use of unambiguous symbols of authority, backed by the use or threatened use of penalties. It tends to produce performance at the minimum acceptable level, and to generate no particular willingness to remain in the organization when alternatives are available.

Instrumental satisfaction is evoked by the use of rewards, and is more strongly evoked as the rewards are immediate, constant, and adequate. The behavioral patterns produced by reliance on rewards vary according to these factors, and also depend heavily on whether the rewards are systemwide or tied more specifically to performance. In general, system rewards hold people in the system but do not necessarily encourage more than minimally acceptable performance and are ineffective for stimulating innovative behavior. Individual rewards for performance are difficult to apply in large-scale organizations but under the proper conditions of immediacy, constancy, and adequacy can lead to increased productive effort.

The *internalization of organizational goals* is at once the most effective of motive patterns and the most difficult to evoke within the limits of conventional organizational practice and policy. The extent of internalization depends on the character of the organizational goals themselves, and their congruence with the needs and values of the individual. It depends also on the extent to which the individual shares actively in the determination of organizational decisions and in the rewards which accrue to the organization. High internalization of organizational goals tends to result in low absence and turnover, high productivity, and maximal spontaneity and innovativeness in the service of those goals.

14

■ COMMUNICATION, FEEDBACK ■
■ PROCESSES, AND EVALUATION RESEARCH ■

The world we live in is basically a world of people. Most of our actions toward others and their actions toward us are communicative acts in whole or in part, whether or not they reach verbal expression. This is as true of behavior in organizations as in other contexts. We have said (Chapter 3) that human organizations are informational as well as energic systems, and that every organization must take in and utilize information. The intake and distribution of information are also energic processes, of course; acts of sending and receiving information demand energy for their accomplishment. Their energic demands, however, are negligible in comparison with their significance and implications as symbolic acts—as acts of communication and control.

When one walks from a factory to the adjoining head-house or office, the contrast is conspicuous. One goes from noise to quiet, from heavy electrical cables and steam pipes to slim telephone lines, from a machine-dominated to a people-dominated environment. One goes, in short, from a sector of the organization in which energic exchange is primary and information exchange secondary, to a sector where the priorities are reversed. The closer one gets to the organizational center of control and decision making, the more pronounced is the emphasis on information exchange.

COMMUNICATION: THE ESSENCE OF ORGANIZATIONS

In this sense, communication—the exchange of information and the transmission of meaning—is the very essence of a social system or an organization. The input of physical energy is dependent on information about it, and the input of human energy is made possible through communicative acts. Similarly the transformation of energy (the accomplishment of work) depends on communication between people in each organizational subsystem and on communication between subsystems. The product exported carries meaning as it meets needs and wants, and its use is further influenced by the advertising or public relations material about it. The amount of support that an organization receives from its social environment is also affected by the information that elite groups and wider publics have acquired about its goals, activities, and accomplishments.

Communication is thus a social process of the broadest relevance in the functioning of any group, organization, or society. It is possible to subsume under it such forms of social interaction as the exertion of influence, cooperation, social contagion or imitation, and leadership. We shall consider communication in this broad sense, with emphasis on the structural aspects of the information process in organizations, but with attention also to the motivational basis for transmitting and receiving messages.

It is a common assumption that many of our problems, individual and social, are the result of inadequate and faulty communication. As Newcomb (1947) points out, autistic hostility decreases communication and in turn decreased communication enhances autistic hostility. If we can only increase the flow of information, we are told, we can solve these problems. This assumption is found in our doctrine of universal education. It is fundamental in most campaigns of public relations and public enlightenment. Our democratic institutions, with their concern for freedom of speech and assembly, their rejection of censorship, and their acceptance of the principle of equal time for the arguments of opposing political parties, have extended the notion of competition in the marketplace to a free market for ideas. Truth will prevail if there is ready access to all the relevant information.

The glorification of a full and free information flow is a healthy step forward in intraorganizational problems as well as in the relations of an organization to the larger social system. It is, however, a gross oversimplification. Communication may reveal problems as well as eliminate them. A conflict in values, for example, may go unnoticed until communication is attempted. Communication may also have the effect, intended or unintended, of obscuring and confusing existing problems. The vogue enjoyed by the word *image* in recent years reflects in part an unattractive preoccupation with communication as a means of changing the perception of things without the expense and inconvenience of changing the things themselves. The television commercials, with their incessant and spurious assertion of new products and properties are the worst of numberless examples. In short, the advocacy of communication needs to be qualified with respect to the kind of information relevant to the solution of given problems and with respect to the nature of the communication process between individuals, between groups, and between subsystems.

Communication needs to be seen not as a process occurring between any sender of messages and any potential recipient, but in relation to the social system in which it occurs and the particular function it performs in that system. General principles of communication as a social-psychological process are fine; they set the limits within which we must operate. But they need to be supplemented by an analysis of the social system, so that they can be applied correctly to given situations.

The discovery of the crucial role of communication led to an enthusiastic advocacy of increased information as the solution to many organizational problems. More and better communication (especially more) was the slogan. Information to rank-and-file employees about company goals and policies was the doctrine; the means too often were stylized programs and house organs homogenized by the Flesch formula for basic English. Communication up the line to give top echelons a more accurate picture of the lower levels was a complementary emphasis.

Social Systems as Restricted Communication Networks

Although there were and are good outcomes of this simplistic approach, there are also weak, negligible, and negative outcomes. The blanket emphasis on more communication fails to take into account the functioning of an organization as a social system and the specific needs of the subsystems.

In the first place, as Thelen (1960) points out, an organized state of affairs, a social system, implies the restriction of communication among its members. If we take an unorganized group, say 60 people milling around at random in a large room, the number of potential channels of communication is $n(n - 1)/2$ or 1770. If, however, they are organized into a network of twelve combinations of five such that each person on a five-member team has one clearly defined role and is interdependent with four other people, the number of channels within the work group is reduced to *ten* in a completely interdependent condition or to *four* in a serial dependent position.

Without going into such complexities as task-relevant communication, the major point is clear. To move from an unorganized state to an organized state requires the introduction of constraints and restrictions to reduce diffuse and random communication to channels appropriate for the accomplishment of organizational objectives. It may require also the introduction of incentives to use those channels and use them appropriately, rather than leave them silent or use them for organizationally irrelevant purposes. Organizational development sometimes demands the creation of new communication channels. The very nature of a social system, however, implies a selectivity of channels and communicative acts—a mandate to avoid some and to utilize others.

In terms of information theory, unrestricted communication produces noise in the system. Without patterning, without pauses, without precision, there is sound but there is no music. Without structure, without spacing, without specifications, there is a Babel of tongues but there is no meaning.

The same basic problem of selectivity in communications can be considered in terms of Ashby's (1952) conceptual model. Thelen summarizes the Ashby contribution in these terms.[1]

[1]Mimeographed paper, 1960.

Any living system is an infinitely complex association of subsystems. The complex suprasystem has all the properties of a subsystem plus communication across the boundaries of subsystems. Ashby's brilliant treatment (1952) shows that stability of the suprasystem would take infinitely long to achieve *if* there were "full and rich communication" among the subsystems (because in effect all the variables of all the subsystems would have to be satisfied at once—a most unlikely event). If communication among subsystems is restricted or if they are temporarily isolated, then each subsystem achieves its own stability with minimum interference by the changing environment of other systems seeking *their* stability. With restricted communication, success can accumulate (from successive trials, for example), whereas in the single suprasystem, success is all-or-none. . . . Thus the way an overall system moves toward its equilibrium depends very much on the functional connectedness of its parts. Adaptation of the whole system makes use of two conditions: enough connectedness that operation of one subsystem can activate another so that the contributions of all can contribute to the whole; and enough separation of subsystems that some specialization of function is possible and such that "equilibrium" can be approached in the system as a whole. But no complex suprasystem would ever have equilibrium in all its subsystems at the same time. Each subsystem has the "power of veto" over equilibria in other subsystems, and under a variety of conditions one subsystem can dominant another.

Our loosely organized political system reflects the system requirements of restriction of full and free communication. Chaos in national decision making is avoided by the device of the two-party system. Instead of representing in clear fashion in Congress all the factional groups and subsystems within the nation, we go through a quadrennial process of successive agreements within the major parties, culminating in the nomination of a presidential candidate by each of them. This is in effect a restriction and channeling of the communication process. Once candidates are selected, the factional groups within each party tend to unite behind one ticket, and the amount of communication to the candidates is restricted. The rank-and-file voter neither communicates up the line nor receives much in the way of communication down the line except for the projected image of the candidate and the general image of the party.

Communication as a Two-Way Process
Communication basically means a process in which there is some predictable relation between the message transmitted and the message

received. A persuasive orator talking to an audience in a foreign language is not communicating. It is common practice, however, to omit or forget the recipient of the message and to ignore the operational measures that would indicate what, if any, message has actually been received. Many accounts of communication talk about characteristics of the message—its clarity, its content, its source, and its channels—and divorce the sending of information from its reception. Realistically, however, there is no communication without some indication that the intended receiver has been listening. In fact the accuracy of the communication process can only be checked by ascertaining what the listener has gotten out of the message. One analysis of empirical investigations of organization communications (Guetzkow, 1965) documents the common-sense notion that devices for verifying the content of messages as in feedback processes increase the accuracy of communication.

The interpersonal level has an enormous advantage over the organizational level in achieving accuracy of communication, although even individuals in face-to-face contact complain about communication problems. Marital difficulties and parent-child problems often are related to failures in communication. The mother complains that her words go unheeded and the child feels it can not talk to the ununderstanding parent. Nonetheless, in the face-to-face situation the person can ask an associate whether the message is clear and the associate can similarly ask if he or she has the appropriate meaning. What is imperative is some response, even at the elementary level of a shake of the head to indicate that one has heard the other.

For more complicated interchanges of meaning, restatement of the message by the second party can be helpful. One of the techniques of the group therapist is to ask the various parties involved what they thought the others were saying. In large organizations there is less opportunity than in small groups for getting signals from those down the line that they understand the new directive, that they know what is expected of them, or even that they have heard the order. What the superior intends as an order is often perceived by the subordinate as advice or information as Burns (1954) demonstrated in his study of a British firm. Departmental executives recorded systematically their interactions with others over a five week period and of the 165 messages recorded as specific directives by the head only 84 were similarly recorded by his deputy as instructions. Half the time what the manager regarded as an order was being received merely as information.

Ideally, there should be signs from all of those to whom the communication is addressed that they at least have received it and understand its directions. Certainly when we phone a person we expect the *Hello* response. In organizations, however, there is frequently a lack of automatic signaling about who is listening. And understanding of the rules, procedures, and policies of the system can show great gaps in spite of printed materials, house organs and official spokespersons. The small organization can utilize interpersonal channels more readily than the large organizations and thus can enjoy superiority to the larger system in the effectiveness of its communication processes. All organizations, however, must do more to utilize devices to insure that the sender of the message receives some reaction from the recipient about the communication.

The Coding Process

Individuals, groups, and organizations share a general characteristic that must be recognized as a major determinant of communication: the coding process. Any system that is the recipient of information, whether it be an individual or an organization, has a characteristic coding process, a limited set of coding categories to which it assimilates the information received. The nature of the system imposes omission, selection, refinement, elaboration, distortion, and transformation on the incoming communications. Just as the human eye selects and transforms light waves to which it is attuned to give perceptions of color and objects, so too does any system convert stimulation according to its own properties. It has been demonstrated that human beings bring with them into most situations sets of categories for judging the facts before them. Walter Lippmann (1922) called attention to the coding process years ago in the following famous passages. Even then he was merely putting into dramatic form what had been recognized by the ancient philosophers.

For the most part we do not first see, and then define, we define first and then see. In the great blooming, buzzing confusion of the outer world, we pick out what our culture has already defined for us, and we tend to perceive that which we have picked out in the form stereotyped for us by our culture. (p. 31)

What matters is the character of the stereotypes and the gullibility with which we employ them. And these in the end depend upon those inclusive patterns which constitute our philosophy of life. If in that philosophy we assume that the world is codified according to a code we possess, we are likely to make our reports of what is going on describe a world run by our code. (p. 90)

Most of us would deal with affairs through a rather haphazard and shifting assortment of stereotypes, if a comparatively few men in each generation were not constantly engaged in arranging, standardizing, and improving them into logical systems, known as the Laws of Political Economy, the Principles of Politics, and the like. (pp. 104–105)

Organizations, too, have their own coding systems that determine the amount and type of information they receive from the external world and the transformation of it according to their own systemic properties. The most general limitation is that the position people occupy in organizational space will determine their perception and interpretation of incoming information and their search for additional information. In other words, the structure and functions of a given subsystem will be reflected in the frame of reference and way of thinking of the role incumbents of that sector of organizational space. The different functions and dynamics of the production structure, the maintenance system, and the adaptive system (described in Chapter 4) imply that each of these subsystems will respond to the same intelligence input in different ways and that each will seek out particular information to meet its needs.

All members of an organization are affected by the fact that they occupy a common organizational space in contrast to those who are not members. By passing the boundary and becoming a functioning member of the organization, the person takes on some of the coding system of the organization since he or she accepts some of its norms and values, absorbs some of its subculture, and develops shared expectations and values with other members. The boundary condition is thus responsible for the dilemma that the person within the system cannot perceive things and communicate about them in the same way that an outsider would. If people are within a system, they see its operations differently than if they were on the outside looking in. It is extremely difficult to occupy different positions in social space without a resulting differential perception. Where boundary conditions are fluid and organizational members are very loosely confined within the system, as with people sent abroad to live among foreign nationals for some governmental agency, there will be limited tours of duty, alternation between foreign and domestic service, and careful debriefing sessions to insure that life outside the physical boundaries of the country has not imparted too much of the point of view of the outsider.

The Problem of Translation
across Subsystem Boundaries

Within an organization there are problems of clear communication across subsystems. The messages emanating in one part of the organization need translation if they are to be fully effective in other parts. In an earlier chapter, reference was made to Parsons' (1960) specific application of this principle to the chain of command. Instead of a unitary chain from the top to the bottom of an organization, Parsons pointed out that there are significant breaks between the institutional and managerial levels and again between the managerial and technical levels. Communications must be transmitted in general enough terms to permit modification within each of these levels. The same type of translation problem occurs between any pair of substructures having their own functions and their own coding schema. Without adequate translation across subsystem boundaries, communications can add to the noise in the system.

CHARACTERISTICS OF COMMUNICATION CIRCUITS

The major characteristics of communication networks that we shall consider are (1) the size of the loop, the amount of organizational space covered by given types of information, (2) the nature of the circuit, whether a simple repetitive pattern or a chain modification type, (3) the open or closed character of the circuit, (4) the efficiency of the circuit for its task, and (5) the fit between the circuit and the systemic function it serves.

Size of Loop

Communication circuits may embrace the entire system, may be restricted to a major subsystem, or may involve only a small unit within a subsystem. Some communication loops may be confined to officer personnel or even to top level echelons. A common organizational problem is the discrepancy between the size of given information loops as perceived by the ranking authorities and the size of the circuit which actually is found. Leaders characteristically overestimate the number of persons reached by their intended communications. Also, the larger the loop, the greater will be the problems of communication, particularly where the penetration of subsystem boundaries is involved.

Repetition versus Modification in the Circuit

A large information loop may reach many members of the system through a repetitive pattern of transmitters. For example, a directive may go down the line and be echoed at each level to the one below it. A different pattern of transmission is often used whereby a chain of command will pass along messages with appropriate translation at each level in the system. The same amount of organizational space is involved in both patterns, so that the size of the loop is the same, but the second pattern calls for some modification of the message. The first pattern has the advantages of simplicity and uniformity. Everyone is exposed to identical information. What is announced publicly topside is the same as what people hear from their own superior. Nonetheless, the simplicity of this system may be advantageous only for simple problems. For complex matters a directive repeated in uniform fashion is not necessarily uniform in its meaning across subsystems. It may need translation in different units to be effective.

Feedback or Closure Character

Although the flow of a communication pattern may have a dominant organizational direction (down the line, for example), there is a circular character to communicative acts. There is a reaction to the transmission that can furnish feedback to the transmitter, although it may only be the acknowledgment of the receipt of the message.

Closure of a set of communicative acts can vary from immediate fixed response of acknowledgment and acceptance of the initial message to reports of its inadequacy and attempts to alter its character. In the latter case, although the communication cycle has been completed through feedback about the faulty character of the original communication, the communication process is immediately reactivated. In a larger sense, closure has not been achieved for the organization by the first set of communicative acts. Thus, while almost all processes of communication are cyclical, with a return to the original transmitter, we can characterize some communication circuits as having more of a closed character for systemic functioning than others.

A closed communication loop would be one in which the cycle of transmission acts is not open to change once it has been initiated. In other words, no new information and no radical modifications in the process are provided for by the structural procedures. If the communication process is one of issuing directives and responding to the signal of mission accomplished, we have a closed circuit. The directive cannot be substantially modified. Rigid codes block out sources of information either by definition or practice. There is just no provision for admitting new information at various points in the transmission chain.

The Efficiency of Communication Nets

A related but somewhat different aspect of communication systems is the efficiency, which can be measured in terms of the number of communication links in a given network. In the beginning of our discussion of communication we pointed out that restriction in the communication process was part of the essential nature of social organizations. Experimental work has generally supported the hypothesis that the smaller the number of communication links in a group, the greater the efficiency of the group in task performance (Dubin, 1959). There are more links, for example, in the all-channel pattern than in the circle

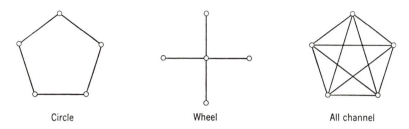

Figure 14-1 *Types of communication networks.*

pattern, and more links in the circle than in the wheel pattern (see Figure 14-1).

Using a sentence construction task, Heise and Miller (1951) found that a two-link system was more efficient than various three-link systems, as measured by the number of words spoken and the time taken to complete the task.

In an extension of Leavitt's earlier work (1951), Guetzkow and Simon (1955) used five-member groups in which the task was to discover which one of six symbols was held in common by all group members. The subjects were seated around a circular table, separated by five vertical partitions. They did not talk to one another, but communicated by passing messages through interconnecting slots. Each person was given a card with five symbols. The missing symbol was different for each subject. The experimenters employed three different networks of communication to which 56 groups were randomly assigned. In the circle net (see Figure 14-1) subjects could pass their messages to either or both of two neighbors. In the wheel net there is a key person to whom all four colleagues can communicate. In the all-channel pattern everyone can communicate with everyone else. Since messages must flow to some decision center for action and must flow back to the senders to inform them of the decision, the wheel provides a two-level hierarchy and the circle and all-channel nets a three-level hierarchy. In the circle, for example, two neighbors can send information to their opposite neighbors, who in turn relay this information with their own to the fifth member. That person can then send the solution back to the group, but three levels are involved in the process.

Leavitt (1951) had found the two-level hierarchy of the wheel to be the most efficient for task accomplishment. Guetzkow and Simon, however, reasoned that this superiority might well be due to the time it took a group to discover and use the optimal organizational pattern for its specific type of net, rather than to the patterns of the networks themselves. For example, a group assigned to the circle might spend considerable time in a more complex interaction than the optimal pattern described above. Hence, the experimenters provided a two-minute period between task trials for the groups to discover the best organizational pattern for their situation by allowing them to write messages to each other. The results confirmed the prediction of the experimenters. When groups in the all-channel or circle nets discovered the optimal organizational pattern, they were just as efficient as the wheel groups.

Nonetheless Dubin's basic hypothesis that the fewer the number of links in the communication network the greater the efficiency of the group still holds. Guetzkow and Simon have demonstrated that the group itself can restrict patterns even though given the opportunity to utilize a more time-consuming network. Other experimenters report similar findings. Cohen (1962) studied the performance of centralized and decentralized networks and found that the central-hub system was faster and led to fewer errors than the completely connected network. Shaw (1964) presents a similar picture with respect to performance indices. But the results of these experiments concerned with task-oriented communications should not be generalized to socioemotional or supportive types of communication. Groups in the completely connected networks have a higher overall member satisfaction with the job than those in the central-hub system. Cohen (1964) found that job satisfaction was correlated with centrality of role in communication and decision making. Although such responsibility was greatest for the central member in the wheel network, there was more participation for all group members in the decentralized system.

The demonstrated superiority in task performance of restricted networks in small groups does not take account of the complexities of interrelationships in a large organization. Cohen, Robinson, and Edwards (1969) in their ingenious experiments on organizational embeddedness have demonstrated that where there is some overlapping of members in functional subgroups, the same principles do not apply as in the small group. These investigators set up laboratory organizations of three functional subunits consisting of five members. Two of the five members who were involved in any subunit also belonged to another subunit. The organizations varied in degree of centralization and the best performance came from the less centralized systems. The researchers interpret their results thus:

> From these embeddedness findings one can conclude that in larger and more complex organizations the greater the opportunity to communicate among themselves, the less likely will members of a sub-group orient themselves externally. Despite the fact that centralized sub-groups develop centralized problem-solving systems (as found in isolated wheel networks), sub-group members in the embedded wheel deviated from the

kind of channel use that would be consistent with the formal and centralized internal channels of communication found in studies of isolated networks. Thus greater restrictions on communication are associated with tendencies to communicate to people outside that sub-group which can subvert the system that typically develops in a centralized network when it is in isolation. Thus centralized structures, which in isolation insure the emergence of certain kinds of centralized behavior, tend in the embeddedness design to be self-defeating: they produce behavior which circumvents the structure of the sub-group. (p. 219)

Going outside the immediate subgroup may run counter to the internal logic of the efficient subunit but can be functional rather than dysfunctional for the long-range effectiveness of the organization. Allen and Cohen (1969) studied the communication patterns in two research and development laboratories. They discovered that the persons who provided other members of the system with technical information were those who made greater use of individuals outside the organization or were greater readers of the literature.

In subsequent experiments Guetzkow and Dill (1957) found that groups seemed to prefer a minimum linkage system. Seventeen out of twenty groups that had started with a pattern permitting ten links had, by the end of twenty trials, cut this to four links. Pressures were generated within the groups themselves to move toward the simpler communication networks. The groups that did not follow this pattern, moreover, were less efficient in task accomplishment.

The Fit between the
Communication Circuit and Systemic Functioning

A circuit may be too large, involving irrelevant people, or too small, omitting key informants. One factor in information overload is the creation of many large communication loops so that people receive frequent messages that have little if anything to do with carrying out their organizational roles. Role incumbents are called on to decide what is functional and what is nonfunctional in the information they receive. Although they may make wise decisions, the time of decision making is taken from their own basic tasks.

A common dysfunctional arrangement in organizations is to have communication loops of disproportionate sizes with respect to message sending and message receiving. Top echelons issue directives for the whole organization, yet achieve closure from the acquiescence of their immediate subordinates. In other words, the loop involves all levels of the organization on the sending side but only the top two echelons on the receiving side.

Another lack of fit between the communication circuit and the functional needs of the system occurs when closed circuits are used for purposes other than the carrying out of directives in an emergency setting. With complex problems, where time is not highly critical, a communication loop that permits the introduction of new information at various points in the circuit can be highly adaptive. Yet the logic of the closed circuit is carried over into the inappropriate areas of information search. The questions for which information is sought are so formulated by some executives that they predetermine the answers to be supplied. The communication process returns upon itself. For example, a department head concerned about a recent productivity decline calls in division heads; he wants the problem explored, but it has been his experience, he informs them, that the lax practices of certain types of supervisors are the key factor in this sort of situation. The division heads report back after their exploration that he was indeed right, and they have taken the necessary steps to handle the problem. An open search for the causes of the productivity decline might have furnished a different answer.

DIRECTION OF COMMUNICATION FLOW

The communication processes within an organization can be studied with respect to the direction of information flow—namely, who communicates with whom. The direction of the flow can follow the authority pattern of hierarchical positions—*downward communication*—can move among peers at the same organizational level—*horizontal communication*—or can ascend the hierarchical level—*upward communication*.

Communication Down the Line

Communications from superior to subordinate are basically of five types:

1. Specific task directives: *job instructions*.
2. Information designed to produce understanding of the task and its relation to other organizational tasks: *job rationale*.
3. Information about organizational *procedures and practices*.
4. *Feedback* to the subordinate about his or her performance.
5. Information of an ideological character to inculcate a sense of mission: *indoctrination of goals*.

The first type of communication is generally given priority in industrial and military organizations and in hospitals. Instructions about the job are worked out with a great deal of specificity and are communicated to the role incumbent through direct orders from the superior, training sessions, training manuals, and written directives. The objective is to insure the reliable performance of every role incumbent in every position in the organization.

Less attention is given to the second type of information, designed to provide the worker with a full understanding of the job and of how it is geared to related jobs in the same subsystem. Many employees know what they are to do, but not why they are doing it, nor how the patterned activities in which they are involved accomplish a given objective. "Theirs not to reason why" is often the implicit, if not explicit, assumption of managerial philosophy. It is often assumed that an emphasis on information about full job understanding will conflict with strict allegiance to specific task instructions. If workers think they know a certain thing, they may attempt to do it in other than the specified fashion and the organizational leaders may not want to tolerate the variability of behavior this introduces into the system.

Information about organizational procedures completes the description of the role requirements of the organizational member. In addition to instructions about the job, he or she is also informed about other obligations and privileges as a member of the system, for example, about vacations, sick leave, rewards, and sanctions.

Feedback to individuals about how well they are doing in their jobs is often neglected or poorly handled, even in organizations in which the managerial philosophy calls for such evaluation. Where emphasis is placed on compliance to specific task directives, it is logical to expect that such compliance will be recognized and deviation penalized. This is necessary to insure that the system is working, and it is a matter of some motivational importance for the individual performer. Individuals frequently complain, however, that they do not know where they stand with their superiors. Often an employee is identified as a major problem for an organization so late in the game that poor performance or weak citizenship seem beyond remedy, and even transfer or discharge is difficult. There is belated recognition that there should have been an earlier review and discussion. Yet systematic procedures for rating and review of the work of employees by their superiors have not proved a panacea.

The reasons are not hard to find. The whole process of critical review is resented both by subordinate and superior as partaking of surveillance. The democratic values of the culture have permeated organizational members so that the superior sees him or herself as a leader, and not as a spy and disciplinarian. Subordinates in wanting to know how well they are doing, really want to have their merits recognized and to know how to develop their own talents more fully.

Another major reason for the unpopularity of supervisory appraisal is that many employees have little individual discretion in task accomplishment and little opportunity to excel. Both the company norms and the informal standards of the group set a uniform rate of accomplishment. The performance of workers is often so system-determined that there is little to be gained from evaluating workers as autonomous individuals. The occasional deviant does constitute a problem for the organization, particularly when the deviance is not formally recognized until it is too late. Nevertheless, such slips are probably less costly to the organization than a thorough surveillance system in which the individual does get early and systematic feedback on performance.

The fifth type of downward-directed information has as its objective the inculcation of organizational goals, either for the total system or a major subsystem. An important function of an organizational leader is to conceptualize the mission of the enterprise in an attractive and novel form. This can be done with particular effectiveness in organizations that are conspicuous for their contribution to societal welfare or for the hazardous character of their activities. For example, a police commissioner may describe the role of the police force as the work of professional officers engaged in a constructive program of community improvement.

Although organizational leaders are quick to recognize the importance of involving their followers in system goals, they are slow to utilize the most natural devices available to them in the form of job rationale. The second type of information in our listing, the understanding of one's role and how it relates to other roles, is a good bridge to involvement in organizational goals. If the psychiatric nurse in a hospital knows why she is to follow certain procedures with a patient and how this relates to the total therapy program for the patient, it is much easier for her to develop an ideological commitment to the hospital. This is one reason why some hospitals have developed the concept of the therapy team, which permits the doctor, nurse, and attendant to discuss the treatment program for given patients. On the other hand, if role incumbents receive information about job specifics without job understanding, it is difficult for them to see how their roles are related to the organizational objective and hence difficult for them to identify with the organizational mission.

Withholding information on the rationale of the job not only is prejudicial to ideological commitment of the member, but it also means that the organization must bear down heavily on the first type of information—specific instructions about the job. If workers do not understand fully why they should do a thing or how their job relates to the tasks of their fellow workers, then there must be sufficient redundancy in their task instructions so that they behave automatically and reliably in role performance. This type of problem was dramatically illustrated in the conflict about the information to be given to astronauts about their task in orbit. Some officials were in favor of reducing the astronaut's behavior to that of robots; others wanted to utilize the astronauts' intelligence by having them act on their understanding of the total situation. The result was a compromise.

The advantages of giving fuller information on job understanding are thus twofold: if people know the reasons for their assignment, this will often insure their carrying out the job more effectively; and if they have an understanding of what their job is about in relation to their subsystem, they are more likely to identify with organizational goals.

Size of the Loop
and Downward Communication

The size of the communication loop is an interesting variable in processing information down the line, and has implications for organizational morale and effectiveness. In general the rank-and-file member gets task instructions from those immediately above. The loop covers very little of the organizational structure. Upper echelons neither know what the specific task directives are, nor would acquiring such knowledge be an appropriate way for them to spend time and energy. In industry the methods department may have worked out the standard procedures for a job, but these are transmitted to the employee by the immediate boss. On the other hand, communications about the goals of the organization in theory cover a loop as large as the organization itself. Rank-and-file members, however, may in practice be minimally touched by this loop. Their degree of effective inclusion within it depends primarily on how they are tied into the organization. If they are tied in on the basis of being paid for a routine performance, information about the goals and policies of the larger structure will be of no interest to them.

The size of the loop is also important in terms of understanding the message. Communications from the top addressed to all organizational members are often too general in character and too remote from the limited daily experiences of the individual to convey their intended meaning. To be effective, messages about organizational policy need to be translated at critical levels as they move down the line, that is, translated into the specific meanings they have for given sectors of the structure. Katz and Lazarsfeld (1955) demonstrated a two-step process in the flow of communication in a community in which opinion leaders affected by the mass media in turn influenced the rank and file. Within organizations, however, not enough attention has been given to this problem of translation. Communications down the line must be converted to the coding systems of the substructures if they are to register and have impact.

A partial substitute for translation is the ability of some organizational leaders to develop confidence and liking for themselves as personalities among the rank and file. Their position on a policy issue will be accepted not because it is understood, but because people trust them and love them. This is more characteristic of political leadership than leadership in nonpolitical organizations.

The translation problem is related to the fit between the communication cycle and the functional requirements of the organization. The information loop about how a job is to be done should have the immediate supervisor as the key communicant. This does not necessarily mean that a worker should get all job directives from a single boss, but it does mean that additional bosses should be introduced only if they have an expertness about a clearly demarcated function. The research worker, in addition to listening to the project director, can also listen with profit to the sampling and statistical expert. Where the functional lines are fuzzy, the rule of a single boss has much to be said for it.

Transmitting information down the line may partake of a closed-circuit character if there is little opportunity for clarification of directives from above. Two things occur when directives remain limited and unclear because people down the line have no way of getting a fuller explanation. People will give minimal compliance so as to be apparently observing the letter of the law, or they will test out in actual behavior their own ideas of what can be done. If there is inadequate feedback up the line, this behavioral testing out can produce real deviations in organizational practice. Such deviations can run from constructive actions in support of organizational objectives to actions crippling and destructive to the organization.

Horizontal Communication

Organizations face one of their most difficult problems in procedures and practices concerned with lateral communication, that is, communication between people at the same hierarchical level. The machine model would be highly restrictive of lateral communication. A role incumbent would receive almost all instructions from the person immediately above, and would deal with associates only for task coordination specified by rules. Although such a plan neglects the need for socioemotional support among peers, it is still true that unrestricted communication of a horizontal character can detract from maximum efficiency. What are the conditions under which lateral communication is desirable?

We shall start with the proposition that some types of lateral communication are critical for effective system functioning. Many tasks cannot be so completely specified as to rule out coordination between peers in the work process. The teamwork by which a varsity team beats an alumni group of greater prowess has many parallels in other organizations. (In fact, there is something to be said for not mechanizing coordination devices for a group task unless the whole process can be mechanized.)

Communication among peers, in addition to providing task coordination, also furnishes emotional and social support to the individual. The mutual understanding of colleagues is one reason for the power of the peer group. Experimental findings are clear and convincing about the importance of socioemotional support for people in both unorganized and organized groups. Psychological forces always push people toward communication with peers; people in the same boat share the same problems. *Hence, if there are no problems of task coordination left to a group of peers, the content of their communication can take forms that are irrelevant to or destructive of organizational functioning.* Informal student groups sometimes devote their team efforts to pranks and stunts or even to harassing the administration and faculty.

The size of the communication circuit and its appropriateness to the function of the subsystem are important considerations for horizontal communication. By and large the nature and extent of exchanges among people at the same level should be related to the objectives of the various subsystems in which they are involved, with primary focus on their own major task. Thus, there are real disadvantages in lateral communication that cuts across functional lines and that nevertheless attempts to be highly specific. For example, if divisions with differentiated functions are part of a department, the communication between peers in different divisions should be on departmental problems and not on divisional matters. Peer communication on divisional matters can better be conducted within divisional boundaries.

Horizontal communication implies a closed circuit in that it satisfies people's needs to know from their own kind without taking into account other levels in the organization. In hierarchical structures it can mean that people overvalue peer communication with a neglect of those below them. Cabots talk only to Cabots, and vice-presidents only to vice-presidents. It is interesting to observe how often organizational leaders, when going outside their own structures for information, will seek their own status level, that is, their counterparts in other organizations. Sometimes, however, the really critical information is at levels below them.

It is important to look at lateral communication in terms of the control function in organizations. Horizontal communication, if in operation at various levels in an organization, is a real check on the power of the top leaders. The more authoritarian and hierarchical the system, the more information is a secret property of select groups, and the more it can be utilized to control and punish people at lower levels. In such a system there is little horizontal communication across levels of equal rank. The department chief knows about ten division heads and their respective divisions, but each one of them knows only about his or her own division. Hence the department chief is in a powerful position to manipulate them.

The simple paradigm of vertical funneling up the line with no horizontal flow of information is a fundamental basis of social control in most social systems. As systems move toward greater authoritarian structure, they exert more and more control over any flow of horizontal information. This is done by abolishing institutional forms of free communication among equals and by instilling suspicion of informers, so that people will be restricted in their communication even to friends. Without such communication there can be a great deal of unrest without organized revolt. People cannot organize cooperative efforts when they cannot communicate with one another.

Totalitarian regimes have shown ingenuity in their use of techniques to restrict and direct the flow of information. By blocking out the channels of horizontal communication and other sources of information, they have made their people dependent solely on communication from above. This channeling works to strengthen the hierarchical structure, but in modern society it is impossible to maintain such tight control of the communication processes over time.

Communication Upward

Communication up the line takes many forms. It can be reduced, however, to what people say (1) about themselves, their performance, and their problems, (2) about others and their problems, (3) about organizational practices and policies, and (4) about what needs to be done and how it can be done. Thus, subordinates can report to their boss about what they have done, what those under them have done, what peers have done, what they think needs to be done, their problems and the problems of their unit, and about matters of organizational practice and policy. They can seek clarification about general goals and specific directives. They may under certain circumstances bypass their own superior and report directly to a higher level. Or they can utilize the suggestion system of the company (an approved institutional method of bypassing). Grievance procedures represent another institutional pattern of getting problems referred to a higher level. In addition, systematic feedback and research may develop as formal processes in the system. These constitute such an important form of communication about organizational functioning that they are considered in a separate section of this chapter.

The basic problem in upward communication is the nature of the hierarchical administrative structure. The first role requirement of people in executive and supervisory positions is to direct, coordinate, and control the people below them. They themselves are less in the habit of listening to their subordinates than in telling them. The subordinates also fall into this role pattern and expect to listen to their bosses rather than be listened to. Thus, in an average sized community hospital Hage (1974) found that the steeper the status pyramid the greater the inhibition of upward communication.

Moreover, information fed up the line is often utilized for control purposes. Hence, there are great constraints on free upward communication. The boss is not likely to be given information by subordinates that will lead to decisions affecting them adversely. It is not only that they tell the boss what he or she wants to hear, but what they want the boss to know. In a study of upward communication Read (1962) reported less accuracy for subordinates with strong upward mobility aspirations than for those less ambitious. People do want to get certain information up the line, but generally they are afraid of presenting it to the most relevant person or in the most objective form. Full and objective reporting might be penalized by the supervisor or regarded as espionage by peers. The subordinate communicating with the superior sets greater store by his or her communication than does the superior receiving it and also believes it results in greater attitude change than actually occurs (Tenenbaum, 1970). To these difficulties must be added the fact that full and objective reporting is difficult, regardless of the organizational situation; no individual is an objective observer of his or her own performance and problems.

For all these reasons the upward flow of communication in organizations is not noted for spontaneous and full expression, despite attempts to institutionalize the process of feedback up the line. Suggestions for improvement of work procedures and company practices are also limited in quantity and quality in most organizations. The more top-heavy the organizational structure and the more control is exercised through pressure and sanctions, the less adequate will be the flow of information up the line. It is not a matter of changing the communication habits of individuals, but of changing the organizational conditions responsible for them.

The typical upward communication loop is small and terminates with the immediate supervisor. He or she may transmit some of the information to the next higher level, but generally in a modified form. The open-door policy of some high-level officers extends the theoretical size of the circuit to include all levels below them. It generally contributes more to the self-image of the officer as an understanding, democratic person, however, than to adequacy of information exchange. The closed nature of the upward circuits has already been indicated and resides both in the restricted communication passed upward and in the limited codes of the recipients.

Obstacles to vertical communication occur in both industrial organizations and democratic structures. Labor unions, in which the membership possesses the formal power to elect officers and command referenda on basic issues, manifest striking gaps in understanding between top echelons and local leaders closer to the rank and file.

ASYMMETRY OF COMMUNICATION NEEDS
AND COMMUNICATION FLOW

There are no studies of the distinctive types of communication that characteristically flow horizontally, upward, or downward in organizations, although such research is much needed. The information requirements of superior and subordinate are not symmetrical. What the superior wants to know is often not what the subordinate wants to tell; what the subordinate wants to know is not necessarily the message the superior wants to send. The greater the conflict between the communication needs of these two hierarchically situated senders and recipients of information, the more likely is an increase in lateral communication. Among peers there will be greater complementarity of information needs. Where a supervisor finds little reception from a superior, he or she will readily turn to fellow supervisors to talk about problems. Horizontal exchange can be an escape valve for frustration in communicating upward and downward; and sometimes it can operate to accomplish some of the essential business of the organization.

Another type of communication flow, thus far not considered, is crisscrossing, in which a subordinate in one unit talks to the boss of another unit or vice versa. Again, this process is furthered by blockages in communication up and down the line. A department head perceived as a sympathetic person may be sought out by people in other departments as an audience for their problems because they feel they cannot talk to their own department head.

In their review of communication studies in organization, Porter and Roberts (1976) cite several investigations showing that for managers about two-thirds of their communication time is spent on vertical messages (to superiors or superordinates) and about one-third on horizontal communications. In his hospital study Hage (1974) found that as specialization increased there was a greater increase in horizontal than in vertical communication, especially cross-departmental. This finding should be tested, however, for a less professionalized system than a hospital.

INFORMAL COMMUNICATION: THE GRAPEVINE

Formal communication patterns are always supplemented by informal interchanges since the organization places people with common problems in close association with one another. Not only is it natural for them to discuss matters of mutual concern, but even the closest monitoring of their conversations as in custodial institutions will not prevent them from developing an informal communication network. The grapevine has these advantages over the formal pattern: (1) It is a more spontaneous form of expression and hence is more intrinsically gratifying. (2) On certain topics where official censorship and filtering take place it can be more informative. (3) It can sometimes be more rapid than official channels. For example, the writers recall an automobile factory in which the foremen were the last to learn about the contract negotiations between management and the union. The foremen got the official account in a memo from the company but by that time the same information spread by word of mouth from union stewards throughout the plant.

It would be logical to assume that informal communication in organizations follows the principles of the rumor process in general—namely, an increase in grapevine activity with a decrease in formal communication. This does occur in extreme cases, as in the armed forces during wartime where official secrecy makes the military a giant rumor factory. Nonetheless, empirical investigations of normal situations in organizations suggest a positive rather than a negative relationship between formal and informal communication. Davis (1953), in his study of a moderately sized firm producing leather goods, found that where there was an effective official set of messages there was also an active grapevine and similarly where the official channels were not operating there was a lack of informal interchange as well. Hage (1974) also reports positive correlations between scheduled and unscheduled communications in hospital and welfare organizations—for example, frequency of committee meetings and workers conferring with other workers ($r = .42$), and supervisors with other supervisors ($r = .76$) and supervisors with their workers ($r = .58$). Increases in unscheduled communication occurred more for horizontal and crisscross flows between departments than for intradepartmental patterns.

INFORMATION OVERLOAD

Causes of Overload

To view social systems as restricted networks of communication, and as networks that treat communication very selectively even in accepted channels, implies the possibility of information overload—of communication input greater than the organization or certain of its components can handle. In Chapter 6 we called attention to the need for coordination of the many specialized activities in a complex organization, and to the consequent combining of numerous subsystem roles in single offices. The person holding such an office, as a member of multiple subsystems, receives information input from all of them. Incumbents of roles at major intersecting cycles of organizations are often so deluged by the requests reaching them that they respond only to two types of messages—telegrams and long-distance telephone calls. Programmed handling of some types of input with little intervention on the part of the officer reduces overload so long as the programmed solutions are not outmoded by environmental changes and new inputs of information.

In physical networks the limitations of the communication system with respect to overloading and underloading are readily recognized by the concept of channel capacity. Social systems also exist in a space-time manifold and are also subject to limitations of their communication capacity. The coordination of many cycles of interrelated behavior is necessarily geared to a time schedule. Any given act must be stipulated not only with respect to its adjacencies to other acts in space, but also with respect to its duration and its precedence, simultaneity, or succession to other acts. Temporal planning in the interests of efficiency allows little or no free time in the organization for handling unanticipated information. The receipt, assessment, and transformation of information is geared into the productive process and follows a corresponding time schedule. Even if some decision makers are freed from direct production responsibilities, they still must make their decisions within a limited time period.

Coordination of activity according to a time schedule, however, encounters the difficulty that social organizations do not exist in a constant social environment. Their potential sources of supply may diminish and require additional search or may change in character and require additional selective processes. The markets for their products may grow or decline. To maintain the same proportion of the market may require increased effort. The organizational structure, however, is geared to certain assumed constancies of production input, throughput, and output. Fluctuations overload the system at some point. Decreased output and volume of work, it is true, will create conditions of underload for some units in the organization. For the upper echelons, however, the decline in inputs means more information seeking both within and without the organization. New inputs have to be found or cuts have to be made in the organizational structure.

Change is not limited to the production system and its adjuncts of procurement and disposal. The maintenance inputs of people to staff the organization and to assume its many roles are necessary to keep the system viable. Here again inputs are not a constant. The labor market fluctuates and personnel attrition takes place at differential rates. Moreover, the values and requirements of personnel change with changes in the culture and subcultures in which they live. Any departure from an assumed normal level of operation creates problems of overload for certain echelons within the system. A threatened strike may mean that more demands are made on the production manager and his or her lieutenants so that they must attend both to production and maintenance problems. An actual strike may give this same group a holiday but may overload top management with other problems.

In summary, since organizational activity must be geared to certain constancies in a time schedule, changed inputs create a condition of overload in one or more of the organizational subsystems.

Inconsistencies in the environment of organizations are largely of human origin, a consequence of our organized search for knowledge and our technological exploitation of this knowledge. We have developed sources of new input that provide a constantly changing environment for social systems. In Miller's terms (1960), information input overload is a product of the technology and science of our times. Every year over 1,200,000 articles appear in 60,000 books and 100,000 research reports. Scientific and technical publications have doubled in size in the United States approximately every twenty years since 1800.

Miller's Analysis of Reactions to Overload

The responses to information input overload have been classified by Miller (1960) into the following seven categories: (1) omission, failing to process some of the information; (2) error, processing information incorrectly; (3) queuing, delaying during periods of peak load in the hope of catching up during lulls; (4) filtering, neglecting to process certain types of information, according to some scheme of priorities; (5) approximation, or cutting categories of discrimination (a blanket and nonprecise way of responding); (6) employing multiple channels, using parallel channels, as in decentralization; and (7) escaping from the task.

The Miller classification of responses to overload is useful but it treats all seven types of responses as mechanisms of adjustment. In applying this classification to social organizations, however, there are definite advantages in distinguishing between adaptive and maladaptive mechanisms for the functioning of the system. The use of one or more of these types of response will have consequences for organizational functioning and may result in changes in function and structure.

In differentiating between adaptive and maladaptive ways of responding we shall follow the distinction, commonly employed in individual psychology, between coping and defensive mechanisms. Coping or adaptive mechanisms are concerned with solving the problems that the individual encounters. Defensive mechanisms protect the individual from breakdown but do not solve the problem. Denial, for example, is the defense mechanism by which individuals ignore the objective facts and in so doing protect themselves from intolerable anxiety. In similar fashion, the failure to process information may keep a social system from total breakdown, but it is still not the optimal way to handle the problem of overload. Keeping the system functioning even at a low level of efficiency may be considered an adjustive outcome, as Miller does, but there is still the need to examine both the dysfunctional and the coping aspects of the process. Even a "successful" coping response can be evaluated in terms of the duration of the solution, the amount of organizational space to which the solution applies, and the cost to the organization of arriving at and implementing the solution. The shorter the duration, the more limited the area of application, and the greater the cost to the organization, the more dysfunctional do we consider the response.

Both omission and error are dysfunctional types of response to overload. Omission by definition denies information to the organization, and it characteristically does so on an irrational basis. Specifically, omission or failure to process information tends to be selective in terms of the ease with which input can be assimilated, rather than in terms of its importance for the organization. Failure to process critical inputs can magnify the problems with which the organization is sooner or later forced to deal. The grievance case that is not processed because of its ambiguities may be taken to court, and the precedent established there may permit thousands of workers to file suit. Such an actual instance in a large railroad company cost the company millions of dollars because of the failure to process the difficult case early in the game.

Error is also maladaptive by definition, and more or less costly to the organization. The cost often may be minimal, but devices are necessary to check against errors of potential seriousness. One common source of serious error in processing information is the tendency to reverse the meaning of the message. Under certain circumstances, it is easy to omit the *not* in a communication or to add it when it should not be there, and so change the meaning completely. One mechanism in thought association is contrast; we group together concepts at either end of a continuum, like sink or swim, failure or success. This conceptual affinity of opposites results in disastrous errors of the reversal type.

Queuing or delaying the processing of information can be either dysfunctional or adaptive. If the queuing is invoked merely to serve the ease of operation of the individual receiver, it is likely to be dysfunctional. But if it is utilized under circumstances of real overload and with equally realistic anticipation of a future lull, it can be adaptive.

Similarly, filtering or the selective receiving of information can be adaptive if it is set by priorities assigned by the organization and based on an assessment of organizational needs. But without thoughtfully established guidelines, filtering is likely to be maladaptive. People are apt to process the familiar elements in a message, which they readily understand and which do not constitute major problems for them. Under time pressures the parts of the communication difficult to decode are neglected for the more easily assimilated parts, even though the former may be more critical for the organization. In general, approximation or cutting of categories under conditions of overload would be dysfunctional. There are situations, however, in which the exchange of quality for quantity is justifiable and realistic. Escape from the task is by definition dysfunctional.

Finally, the use of multiple channels is in many instances highly adaptive in terms of organizational efficiency and effectiveness. Its inclusion in Miller's list suggests that he is in fact using two different criteria in talking about response to overload. On the one hand, he is referring to the inability of a given system with given capacities to handle overload (as when a nerve fibre cannot respond to continuous input in excess of its frequency rate, i.e., during its refractory period), and on the other hand, he is including system mechanisms that have been developed for handling overload and now are system structures in themselves.

Decentralization, which Miller cites as an example of multiple channels, is not so much the spontaneous dividing up of messages among parallel channels at times of overflow as it is the deliberate restructuring of an organization to handle overload. In the same manner, queuing and filtering can become institutionalized as devices for handling overload. In chain department stores, the priority drilled into clerks is to take the customers' money and make change first, and then meet the other demands of the task. To the extent that these institutionalized devices handle the problem, we no longer should speak of information overload save as a causal condition of changes in organizational structures.

A very different approach to problems of overload is to reverse the usual stance of seeking new mechanisms for handling overload and to seek instead ways of reducing the input. This is, of course, extremely difficult with respect to the external environment. Most organizations cannot control the environmental demands that are made on them, except by eliminating some function of their own. To take an obvious but unlikely example, an automobile dealer might solve his agency's traffic and parking problems by eliminating certain of its repair and service functions, but this would be an expensive and risk-laden approach to the problem of overload. *Within* organizations, however, the planned reduction of input is a more promising possiblity.

Part of the overload within organizations is created by the various subsystems and the various hierarchical levels inundating one another with information. The premise, as already noted, is the more communication between levels and units the better. What is often needed, however, is a method for cutting down on the output of information and restricting its flow. Some organizations restrict interoffice memoranda to a single page. The accessibility of all members of the organization to messages at any time during the working day is a technological triumph that has its drawbacks. Research, writing, the pondering of executive decisions, and other phases of creative work require uninterrupted blocks of time. The organization needs to put as much effort into protecting these activities from interruption as it does in facilitating communication where it is functionally required.

Although external demands usually cannot be curtailed at their source, organizations can be more protective of the many roles that their members assume within the interlocking structures of our bureaucratic society. Since universities are now concerned with research as well as teaching, with community and national service as well as maintaining ties with alumni, staff members of universities are subject to an increasing variety of demands as they take on new roles. The same process occurs in other growing organizations.

In his study of a university library, Meier (1961) analyzed the changes that occurred as a result of the increasing demand for books. He noted, among other processes: (1) the setting of priorities, such as giving precedence to the request of a faculty member over that of an undergraduate; (2) destruction of lowest priorities as the queue builds in size (wastebasket policy for communications), the library no longer attempting to preserve everything printed; (3) establishing active files, first the reserve desk and then the closed reserve; (4) creating branch facilities or decentralization; (5) encouraging intermediaries or utilizing extraorganizational channels such as publicizing availability of paperback editions in nearby bookstores; (6) creating a mobile personnel reserve, that is, training people in a variety of skills so that they can be shifted about as the pressures demand; and (7) reducing standards of performance to give legitimacy to actual lowering of performance and thus maintaining morale. Meier (1961) generalizes further about the organizational effects of overload as follows:

> The structural effects of being tested up to or even beyond the
> long run capacity for completing transactions can be expressed

in various forms. *Spatially,* the institution becomes decentralized, functionally differentiated in its various branches and *outliers,* develops a complex boundary for the receipt of messages, and evolves a strong headquarters unit. *Economically,* it accumulates deferred maintenance and generally transforms capital assets into a network of interdependencies with individuals and other institutions whose resources can be drawn upon in an emergency. *Status* within the institution depends much more upon functional effectiveness than upon official rank. As a *decision system* it is more complex and adaptive, having developed many alternative sets of rules during the test which can be reapplied as soon as the need arises. The *value* structure is permanently changed because operating at capacity has revealed the importance of conserving resources which were not otherwise scarce. Considered as a *network* of positions and relations, the institution develops a greater variety of relations, adds more positions, and greatly increases the centrality of some positions. Overload causes the destruction of relations more rapidly than they can be rebuilt through experience and instruction (internal communications). (pp. 55–56)

INFORMATION AND RESEARCH STRUCTURES

Organizations cannot rely on communication processes that develop naturally both for internal coordination and feedback from the external world. Hence, formal structures are devised to protect against the idiosyncratic perceptions and systematic biases of people in different subsystems, as well as to increase the total amount of relevant information. These structures make explicit the search process, the coding categories to be employed, and the procedures for processing and interpreting information according to these categories. Three types of informational procedures can be distinguished: (1) direct operational feedback, (2) operational research, and (3) systemic research. Operational feedback is basically a process of immediate routine control; systemic research, to use the distinctions employed by Rubenstein and Haberstroh (1960), is a process of delayed evaluation. Operational research is a mixture of these two processes.

Operational Feedback

Operational feedback is systematic information getting that is closely tied to the ongoing functions of the organization and is sometimes an integral part of those functions. For example, the number of units turned out by any division of an organization and the number of units marketed are necessary items of record keeping for everyday operations. Earlier, reference was made to the regulatory mechanisms that distinguish organizations from primitive groups (Chapter 4). These regulatory devices are based on built-in intelligence circuits that are parts of the operating mechanism itself or are close adjuncts to the mechanism. Information provided in this fashion can be readily systematized so that its reporting follows standard rules and includes detailed specifications about elements of time and quality. It is readily converted into terms of cost accounting and can be compared in many respects with similar figures of competing companies. In most organizations direct operational feedback is available for the performance of the total organization and for its major subsystems. It is frequently not informative about the performance of work groups or of individuals, and it does not deal with the effectiveness of social-psychological practices of the organization in carrying out its mission, for example, the value of given types of leadership procedures, of morale-building practices, or of training programs.

Operational feedback is thus the basis for regulation and control in an organization and is related to the power and authority structure of the system. When organizational theorists discuss problems of control, they generally are not dealing with issues of the locus of power or of policy formulation but with the mechanics of regulation. It is possible for both a democratically run organization and an authoritarian system to employ some of the same feedback mechanisms in the interests of regulation and coordination.

Porter, Lawler, and Hackman (1975) have addressed themselves to the question of how efficiency is to be achieved through control devices. They specify four basic elements as critical:

1. Standards or specified objectives
2. Monitoring devices to measure current performance of individuals, group, or system
3. Comparing devices to check on how close performance is to stated objectives
4. Action devices to bring deviations from standards into line.

Experimentation on the use of control devices, such as ongoing feedback systems, now includes participation of employees both in devising and operating the system. In fact Nadler, Mirvis, and Cammann (1976) specify as one principle for effective feedback that "all measures included in the system should be designed or at least reviewed by the people who will have to use the information" (p. 65). Their experimental findings in a midwestern bank are consistent with this assumption. Research on control devices such as budgets, financial reports, and feedback on performance show that these "management tools" can be functional for helping subordinates identify and solve task problems but dysfunctional as a basis for reward allocation (Camman, 1976). Employees responded defensively when they believed the control system was used to determine their pay.

The major function of operational feedback is to provide routine control over operations. It is thus similar to the negative feedback of the servo-mechanism that keeps the subsystem on course. This type of control information involves relatively short loops in the communication system. Information is generated by the operating unit involved and the backflow of information is directly to that unit. It follows that this type of operational feedback is a continuous rather than a delayed process. It is a form of routine control that permits decisions without lengthy consideration of a variety of inputs. The latter process involves a delayed evaluation (Rubenstein and Haberstroh, 1960).

Information feedback of the operational type develops as the natural extension of energic feedback (Katz, 1975). It thus comes first in those organizations where there is a direct relationship between input-output transactions: for example, so many units sold, so much raw material purchased. Organizations that do not have direct energic transactions with their supporting publics such as government agencies, universities, or prisons, have been slow to develop information subsystems about their own operations.

Direct operational feedback is limited to reporting of current operations. It is not concerned with an assessment of trends in the external environment nor with a detailed analysis of the functioning of subsystems or the total system. It is less a search for new information than a utilization of existing operational records. For this utilization, little additional organizational structure is required beyond existing managerial, production, and maintenance structures. A small unit is sometimes attached to the managerial structure to study the company records in relation to the records of competitors, but for the most part we are dealing with information-processing that is built into the ongoing operations.

The major limitations of this type of intelligence have already been noted: its coding categories are restricted to existing practices, and hence can report how well they may be working but not the reasons for their success or failure. The impact of environmental change may be felt by the organization, but the nature of such change is not revealed by direct operational feedback. The basic determinants of organizational functioning are hardly touched by the knowledge such feedback supplies. Nevertheless, this is still the basic institutional form of information on which many organizations rely. They will supplement it in various ways; that is, through the insight, observations, and wisdom of people in leadership positions; through the use of consultants; or even through an occasional special investigation or research project.

Though these supplementary means of intelligence gathering may prove of great value in critical situations, they do not provide an organization with a reliable means for getting adequate information about its prospects for survival and effectiveness in a changing world. So long as the coding categories and information processing are confined to the regulatory mechanisms of ongoing operations, there is a closed circuit informational system—a circuit, moreover, whose circular enclosure covers a small area of the relevant universe.

Operational Research

Organizations in a changing world develop adaptive structures, and within these structures may be housed departments of research and development. The most common type of intelligence activity that takes on an institutionalized form is operational research. It actively institutes search for new information and it seeks explanations as well as descriptions, but its focus is on two targets: the improvement of specific products, and the improvement of methods for turning them out. It is technologically oriented, and its achievements are in depth, not breadth. Operational research examines various problems in the production system and supplies information on the basis of which efficiencies can be effected. It supplements the inadequate descriptive function of operational feedback and logically derives from this more central organizational process.

The great limitation of operational research is that it deals so sparingly with the problems of the managerial structure, the maintenance structure, and the institutional relations with the larger environment. Since these structures are based on human interaction rather than on the technological transformation of materials, they are not seen as affecting productivity in a measurable way. When operational research ventures into the field of human relationships, it deals more with ecological patternings and with personnel measures than with the social structure of the organization. It is concerned with the improvement of technical operations and not with the relations of the organization to the external social world.

The coding categories of operational research provide a circuit of information that has no ready way of dealing with intelligence of a nontechnological type; for example, the causes of such events as workers threatening to strike, the legislature in the state increasing its taxes on local business, consumers boycotting a certain type of product, the production department at loggerheads with the sales department, or the personnel department having problems with the line production people about personnel procedures. In other words, the information loops of operational research, though larger than those of operational feedback, do not embrace the organization as it functions in its environment. Though there is more evaluation than in immediate routine control, the questions raised and the answers sought by such research are largely in terms of control.

Systemic Research

Organizations can and do extend their information resources by moving toward systemic research. Systemic research, like operational research, seeks new information, but its target is the functioning of the total system in relation to its changing environment. The objectives of systemic research include study of environmental trends, long-term organizational functioning, the nature of organizational structure, the interrelationship of the subsystems within the total system, and the impact of the organization on its environment. Where operational research concentrates on improving technical aspects of production, systemic research explores the organizational changes that technical improvement would produce, including both the intended and the usually unanticipated consequences of the technical change.

Stated in these sweeping terms, systemic research seems Utopian in organizations with limited financial resources and with limited, fallible human beings to initiate and carry out such research. The concept, however, is critical and of great practical importance. In some organizations the thinking of top leaders is systemic; they utilize whatever intelligence is available about the present and future relationship of their system to its environment, and they initiate research to guide them on central problems. For example, some companies with foreign holdings and foreign markets have economists and political experts on their staffs to study the development of the European common market, social forces in the developing African nations, and similar problems. The approach here is systemic even though the program of research to support it is tiny in relation to the firm's needs and resources. Another device of systemic research is the occasional study by a concern of its institutional relations with society, for example, the corporate image held by various sectors of the public or the public response to corporate bigness. Sometimes the organization may ask its own research unit to ascertain how a training program for supervisors is affecting the whole organization.

Various compromises are attempted by organizational leaders to provide some degree of systemic intelligence without an adequate allocation of resources and manpower to this function. Research units are set up to bring together and analyze data already available from other sources, such as governmental agencies, other companies, and university institutes. Outside consultants are hired not only for expert opinion, but for their knowledge of what is happening in the research world. These compromises may be of considerable value in giving top leadership guidance in their decision making. The greatest weakness in using them is the reliance on data gathered in another context and sometimes for a different purpose. The specific determinants of the organization's own problems may be slighted, and the existing data may not dig deep enough into causes.

Organizations will also attempt the compromise of using market research in place of more systematic investigation of the relationship of the organization to its environment. Although market research is concerned with consumer demand, which is an important aspect of system survival, its characteristic frame of reference comes from operational feedback. The search for new data will not go much beyond the sales figures of the organization. Additional surveys may pick up consumers' reactions to a form of packaging or the more obvious properties of the product. Thorough studies of the basic psychology of the consumer, with adequate samples, field experiments, and continuing panels, are the exception rather than the rule.

Systemic research then is limited by three factors. The first is the amount of resources available to an organization to carry on a continuing research operation concerned with systemic variables. The second factor is the conception of management held by the top leaders of an organization. If they do not think in system terms, or if they think in system terms only when confronted with disaster, then the coding of whatever systemic information is available will be fragmentary and inadequate. In our discussion of leadership (Chapter 16) we call attention to the importance of *systemic perspective* for the leader who is an innovator and creater of policy. The third factor that encourages or limits systemic research is the jolting of the organization as it pursues its course in the environment. A series of reverses in which successive *satisficing* moves have been only temporarily ameliorative may lead to a more *optimizing search*.

THE ORGANIZATIONAL LOCUS
OF INFORMATIONAL SUBSYSTEMS

Informational processes can have their primary locus at any level in the organization or in any one of its substructures. Operational feedback is received first by the appropriate operating unit and then filtered up the line as overall summaries of operations at each level to the managerial level just above. Thus, the head of each production unit knows the number of pieces turned out by his or her unit at the end of a given time period. The superintendent of production has summary figures for all the units reporting to him or her, and again makes a summary for the echelons above.

Since this kind of feedback is tied closely to actual operations, little distortion is possible over time, though some filtering may result in an oversimplified picture at top levels. The units with poor records may not be pinpointed in average figures covering all units. Interpretations of these figures may be supplied by the heads of units or divisions, but such interpretations tend to be coded by their transmitters as favorable to their own way of operating. If the productivity of a department is below expectations for a given month, the department head's explanations are not likely to include poor management. He or she may assert that the materials were not up to par or absenteeism due to illness was great. But the major distortion is probably not the defensive explanation; it is the selective bias of each unit head, who will utilize as a basis of judgment the specific frame of reference of the operations in which he or she is daily involved.

Operational research is generally geared into some part of the production system. Its reports, however, can go beyond the production system to top management. Since the changes its information may suggest for organizational functioning require some degree of acceptance by the production structure, there is some advantage to tying operational research closely to the operations under investigation. A common procedure is to have the group conducting the operational research report to one level higher than the specific operation being researched. This helps to protect its results from being ignored.

Information, however, that has direct relevance for system functioning, as in all cases of systemic research, should be reported to top management. This is even true of market research, which is often placed very low in the sales structure. The locus of market research thus does not provide the organization with information about the success of its product. Rather, it supplies the sales department with ideas for promotional campaigns. What may be necessary for organizational success is an actual change in product. This cannot be achieved through a research unit serving the sales department, since the function of the sales department is to sell what is being produced, and not to tell the production people what to produce. The information of the market research unit follows the general principle of being coded by the sales department as sales information, and it fails to be coded with its proper implications for the production structure.

Another common failing is to assign to a given substructure whose primary function is noninformational the secondary mission of providing information about the relations of the organization with the external world. The primary task determines the types of information that will be received and its mode of processing. For example, the State

Department has traditionally utilized its diplomatic personnel abroad to report on the political, economic, social, and psychological conditions of the foreign country. In their primary roles as diplomats, State Department personnel move in very limited circles; they meet primarily with their counterparts in the diplomatic corps of that nation. They are not necessarily expert in the subject about which information is sought; they seldom have training or knowledge of research procedures; and their major motivation is to carry out their function in the implementation of State Department policy. It is no wonder then that we have been consistently misinformed about the structures of foreign countries and the prevailing currents within them. Reliance on the impressions of exclusive upper-class informants, refugees from disaffected elements, amd émigrés from dispossessed groups, has aggravated the problem. A reverse situation occurred in the Cuban fiasco in which the Central Intelligence Agency, supposedly an information structure, became absorbed in overthrowing the Castro regime rather than in obtaining accurate information about it. In both cases, however, we are dealing with closed intelligence circuits that are not open to relevant information.

Two points are involved in the above examples. One concerns the necessity of an information subsystem with its own staff to carry on its own function and develop its own norms, standards, and expertness. The other concerns the place in the system to which intelligence should be reported.

The first problem has so far been presented as if there were only one answer. When information concerning the system as a whole and its relations to its environment is involved, there are genuine advantages in a subsystem that has this information gathering as its major responsibility. This can mean that specialized expertness is made possible, that the coding limitations of an irrelevant function are obviated, and that standards of accurate prediction and valid assessment develop as in a scientific research organization.

These advantages do not inevitably follow. The major values of the system still operate to affect the subsystem; directives of top management control the freedom of the subsystem and may indicate receptivity to only certain types of information. Cigarette manufacturers, for example, could set up a research agency reporting to top management with the task of investigating the relationship of cigarette smoking to lung cancer, heart disease, and related health problems. They could hire competent researchers (although perhaps not top scientists) with an adequate budget to pursue a research program. It is not likely, however, that the researchers would furnish top management unambiguous reports on the injurious effects of the use of tobacco and recommendations that the company change its goals and turn to the use of nicotine as a poison against insects or some such alternative.

To avoid the corruption of information by the system of which it is a part, it is necessary to guarantee to the researcher within an organization some of the same freedoms he or she would enjoy in a university setting. Some of the big electric and utility companies have actually done this in the natural sciences, and the resulting discoveries have more than justified the policy. With the exception of one or two token units, no industrial concern has ever done this in the social sciences even though it is in this area that management needs information most desperately. One type of freedom absolutely essential for such research is that the directives of top management do not pose specific questions they want answered. General problem areas can be indicated, but once the lines of inquiry are restricted in particularistic fashion, we are back to a closed system of intelligence. Answers are easily predetermined by the questions asked, especially when these questions originate at the top of a power structure. This applies both to an intelligence system that is conducting basic research and to one that is gathering information at a more descriptive level. A narrow definition of the mission of an information-gathering agency means that the answers it furnishes will also be extremely limited and frequently erroneous.

Another means by which an organization can avoid corrupting or being corrupted by its own information service is the astute use of multiple channels as check procedures. Multiple channels, if based on the same sources of information, can merely duplicate error. But they can be set up so as to utilize various sources of information and process it in similar enough fashion to produce a consistent or instructively inconsistent picture for decision makers.

The problem of the latitude to be permitted to an intelligence operation is an extremely difficult one for top management. On the one hand, the organization needs useful information, and if it gives researchers a completely free hand, the relevance of their findings for organizational functioning is not insured. To this rational consideration is added the irrational fear of the incomprehensible techniques and language of a suspect group of "longhairs." On the other hand, there is not much advantage to management in setting up an intelligence agency if it merely reflects management's coding processes.

The critical question is whether the task of the intelligence or research unit is system research or operational research. If the former is the case, then management has to be able to tolerate the differences in values, methods, and approach of specialists in information gathering. In fact, these differences are among the major reasons for hiring specialists. Some restriction on their activities can nevertheless be imposed in terms of the general objectives assigned to them. And even if no specific and immediate answers are demanded, over time the information agency must provide some useful information to the organization or forfeit its right to organizational support. An important factor working toward organizational control of information specialists (and often working too well) is the natural tendency for specialists to take on the coloration of the system and behave too much as conforming members rather than as objective outsiders.

Outside research agencies are occasionally called in to provide the types of information that organizational leaders think cannot be readily supplied by their own personnel. The more research-oriented outside agencies will seek to obtain a broader definition of the problem than management generally presents. In other words, the tendency of organizational leaders is to narrow the problem to the visible and troublesome symptoms, whereas adequate intelligence about it has to probe into the causes. The process of redefining the problem for management is often easier for the outside group than for the captive agency.

The question of the optimal place for reporting the results of systemic research becomes complicated in large organizations. Though top echelons should be the recipients of information about the functioning of the total system, it is difficult for them to find the time to take adequate note of it, let alone absorb it and give it some weight in their decisions. Hence, there is generally more relevant information in an organization than its top leaders utilize. Several changes are necessary in organizational structure to achieve reform in this respect. One is the elevation of the information agency in status, so that the head not only reports to top levels but also can command a hearing when staff members believe they have some vital intelligence. The second is the perfecting of translation mechanisms, so that critical pieces of information can be transmitted up the line in the information agency itself and finally to the top echelons of the organization. A third is the restructuring of the top jobs to reduce the component of routine administration; this will not guarantee the acquisition and use of systemic information, but it will have a powerful facilitating effect.

EVALUATION RESEARCH

How do complex organizations really function? Do they achieve their stated purposes? What unintended consequences do they have? How much accountability should there be for government programs or for private organizations affecting societal welfare? To attempt to answer these questions a new focus of research interest has become popular—namely, evaluation research. This movement has not proceeded systematically according to the theoretical framework just presented of operational feedback, operational research, and systemic research but has cut across such distinctions and in uneven fashion has attacked a variety of practical problems.

Gurel (1976) traces the rapid development of program evaluation in federal agencies to the emphasis on rationalized decision making in the Department of Defense. Gurel informs us:

> These emphases were subsequently formalized throughout the federal government by the (then) Budget Bureau's October 1965 Bulletin #66-3 requiring agencies to supplement the Planning Programming and Budget system, an essential element of which was the requirement that program effectiveness and efficiency be evaluated in cost-benefit terms. While the specifics of the Bureau of the Budget directive became obscured under the Nixon administration, the pressures for institutionalizing program evaluation have, if anything, increased. Given ever-present shortages of funds available for human services, continued pressures for intensified evaluation of public service programs are almost a certainty." (p. 11)

As early as 1966 Gross suggested a social systems accounting model for the nation-state as critical for national planning and the measurement of social change. It could provide, Gross wrote, "a conceptual and informational basis for economically scanning the array of all possible kinds of relevant data and selecting those that are more relevant under specific circumstances" (1966, p. 262). A similar shifting of framework from a single organization to the social system as a whole is found in the social indicators movement.[2] Campbell and Converse (1972) called attention to the need for systematic accounting at the national level of the psychological state of the people in terms of their satisfactions, frustrations, aspirations, and values. Subsequently, with Rodgers (Campbell, Converse, and Rodgers, 1976) they report an empirical survey of the quality of American life covering such areas as satisfactions with community, neighborhood, housing, recreation, job, and family for various ethnic, sex, and social class groupings. A companion volume (Andrews and Withey, 1976) similarly depicts the evidence on quality of life from a trend series of studies and ties satisfaction to such domains of life experience as marriage, family, neighborhood, friendships, housework, job, health.

---

[2]Social indicator research has a long history, although under other labels, as in the social trends investigations sponsored by the Hoover administration, but there is no denying its mushroom growth in recent years. Wilcox and his colleagues brought out an annotated bibliography in 1972 of indicator studies that includes hundreds of titles. Moreover, the overwhelming majority of the studies included were published since 1965.

The emphasis on social referents in studies of quality of life is elaborated by Rossi (1972) in developing his concept of community indicators. He proposes that we tie people's evaluation of their experiences to the community as a relevant social system. Hence, we should examine individuals' interest and involvement in local events, the residential locality as a reference group, the perception of a locality as a collectivity by its residents, their affective involvement in this collectivity, and the social climate of the locality. The use of such psychological measures as Rossi proposes for the community could be extended to other social systems such as work organizations, unions, political parties, and occupational groupings.

Evaluations of public programs have often been ad hoc efforts. They have not been built into the operating structure of the administrative agency and thus do not provide feedback of a continuing nature. Because they are scattered, piecemeal, and practical in character, they also do not contribute significantly to a cumulative body of social science knowledge. R. Schiller (1973), after a review of empirical studies in the field of welfare dependency, concludes that their findings have done little to change policies and practices of welfare agencies and have been inadequately reported in scientific journals and have not been integrated into the social sciences. He goes on to say:

> Indeed the gap between public perspectives and welfare realities is staggering. As a consequence it appears that many features of recent and pending welfare reform are likely to provide little satisfaction to either the dependent poor or the taxpayer." (1973, p. 28)

Most of the attempts at evaluation research have been concerned with a limited objective, for example, the efficiency of a specific program, and so are operational rather than systemic in character. Other efforts are even more narrow and attempt operational feedback as in various "body counts"—the number of cases opened, the number of cases closed, the number of clients handled, the recidivism rate, and so on. Efficiency is frequently measured by the evaluation of the ratio of benefits to costs, and the costs and benefits that can be easily calculated are the ones that are calculated. Short-range economic factors are favored over long-term societal considerations. An illustration is available in the Borus, Brennan, and Rosen (1974) cost-benefit analysis of the Neighborhood Youth Corps. In this study, the money earned in subsequent jobs was one criterion of success. Hence, training men rather than women would give the program a better rating, since men and women still do not receive equal pay for equal work. A cost-benefit analysis often tends to favor the status-quo and even to encourage some restriction of function. A program may be most cost beneficial when it handles those people with the fewest problems—those in less need of training, counseling, money, or whatever services the agency dispenses. The agency could thus be favorably evaluated because it has not addressed itself to its basic problems.

Another method of specifying criteria for service evaluation is the value-added approach. The amount of value added to the individual as a result of an encounter with a particular agency can eliminate the conservatizing trend of traditional cost-benefit analysis. But there are difficulties in dealing with indirect and long-range outcomes and there are "repair" programs, as in the case of hospital and medical benefits, where values are not always added.

Although client evaluation is often dismissed as an inadequate and subjective criterion, the responses of the people being helped constitute a useful measure. Measures of general satisfaction are subject to response biases of various sorts but detailed reactions to the specifics of their experience are generally more valid accounts. If a client had to contact several offices before finding the right one, if he or she had to stand in line over an hour, if the official made no effort to understand the case, if the problem was not solved to the client's satisfaction and so on, we have significant information about the functioning of an agency even though it comes from the people being served. Such data become more valuable if there are comparative figures from the clients of other offices, and even more valuable when they can be tied to some known characteristics of specific agencies. Even where such validation is difficult if not impossible on some aspects of agency functioning, the ultimate criterion can be the satisfaction of the consumer. If an overwhelming majority of clients report that one agency is very fair in its treatment and another agency shows favoritism, this psychological fact can not be dismissed because it is psychological.

Operational research utilizing client evaluation has yet to be exploited for its full utility. Welfare programs are among the most common services studied. In a survey of 52 empirical studies about welfare Schiller reported evidence to disprove five common assumptions about welfare reform measures based on data concerning recipients. The first assumption is that there is a qualitative difference between the working poor and the nonworking poor. Schiller notes, along with Rein (1972) and Meyers and McIntyre (1969), that work and welfare often supplement each other. The second assumption is that welfare recipients need a special stimulus to seek employment, and the third assumption is that lack of child-care facilities is keeping large numbers of AFDC mothers from the work force. Schiller pointed out that the work ethic is evident in welfare recipients, that lack of jobs or family responsibilities, rather than lack of motivation, keeps welfare recipients from working. He also argues that instituting child-care facilities is no guarantee that substantial numbers of mothers will enter the labor force since many mothers perceive child-care facilities to be less adequate than home care. This is associated with the fourth assumption, that jobs are available. Schiller notes that "empirical studies suggest that there is a tremendous gap between public expectations and labor market realities" (1973). The fifth assumption is that welfare dependency is harmful to recipients and their families. Schiller provides some evidence supporting the contention that poverty rather than dependency is deleterious to welfare recipients and their families. Meyers and McIntyre's data (1969), however, suggest an effect of dependency on self-esteem over and above the effect of poverty. Schiller concludes that there are significant gaps in information about welfare and the relationship of welfare to work.

Government services are widely utilized by the American public (Katz, Gutek, Kahn, and Barton, 1975). Their nationwide survey showed that it was not just small segments of the population with special problems who sought government help. Some 58 percent of the sample reported contact with at least one of seven types of public agencies: workmen's compensation, employment services, unemployment insurance, welfare, hospital, and medical care, job training, and retirement benefits. Underutilization of some services was marked with 30 percent needing job training compared to 9 percent who had received it. It is not only the needy and poor who avail themselves of government services but the eligible and knowledgeable people who seek unemployment insurance, workmen's compensation, and retirement benefits.

Evaluation studies have generally been concerned with measures of efficiency and immediate effectiveness but occasionally some questions do enter of longer range or systemic effects. Thus, in their comprehensive survey of the consequences of welfare policies based on interviews with 11,632 recipients and questionnaires from 1,069 case workers, Meyers and McIntyre (1969) also inquired about problems of alienation, powerlessness, political participation, employment potential, and self-esteem. Powerlessness had the highest correlation with maximum benefits paid but it was only $-.26$. Self-esteem was positively related to the fact of employment.

In their nationwide survey Katz, Gutek, Kahn, and Barton (1975) also raised system questions about agency functioning that went beyond immediate impact to confidence in national political leadership, stereotypes about bureaucracy, interpersonal trust, and symbolic nationalism. The study lacked a longitudinal design and so did not permit causal analysis but there were significant relationships between confidence in national leadership and stereotypes about bureaucracy and between interpersonal trust and bureaucratic stereotypes. The results, moreover, clearly indicated that the American people have two cognitive levels in their evaluation of governmental organizations: a pragmatic or specific frame of reference and an ideological or general frame. The same people who found public agencies prompt, efficient, and fair in their own specific encounters held stereotypes about government bureaucracy in general of a contrasting character. The more remote and general the target the greater was the negative evaluation. Although the government official they had contacted was seen as helpful, intelligent, and effective, the people running the government in Washington were viewed as incompetent and untrustworthy. Positive experiences with a particular office did not increase the evaluation of public bureaucracy in general, but specific negative experience lowered the general evaluation. This is reminiscent of the facts of organizational life in nongovernmental systems. It is easier to lose support by a particular action than to gain it. Research is needed in private organizations to ascertain whether these two orientations are found in the same people: namely, a positive frame of reference for pragmatic questions and a negative frame for more ideological issues. The same dual character of cognitive structure has been reported by Free and Cantril (1967) who refer to their results in a survey of attitudes toward political issues as schizophrenic in nature with respondents ideologically conservative but operationally liberal.

The explanation for the different frames of reference of the same individual can be more at the system than the personality level. He or she may be closely involved with a specific system such as the social security program and also tied to the national political system. The person's evaluations of the two systems may differ, even though they are both public or governmental, because in demands made and services rendered they are different systems.[3]

Evaluation research implies no new methodology beyond the known techniques of experiments, quasi-experiments and field studies but the difficulties of such evaluation call for more careful application and implementation of known procedures. In their excellent review of

---

[3]Gutek (1975) analyzed the data from *Bureaucratic Encounters* to test a related hypothesis—namely, that involvement in six social systems (economic, occupational, educational, family, political, and social welfare) would relate to various dimensions of system support. The evidence in its support was weak but no attempt could be made because of the limitations of the data to ascertain whether people were differentially involved in special service systems as against the larger political system. The theory and research of F. H. Allport (1967) have demonstrated the usefulness of measuring both the potency of involvement in a structure and the relevance of an attitude or action to such an involvement for predicting behavior.

field tests of fertility planning projects, Hilton and Lumsdaine (1975) make these technical recommendations, among others:

(1) More attention should be given in field comparisons to use of proper randomization and to closer relation of error estimates to the actual manner of sampling.

(2) Consideration should be given to establishing a representative population of subunits (geographical radio coverage areas, towns, counties, school districts, etc.) for the experimental study of new programs before they are used nationwide over a long period of time.

(3) Accordingly, in most experiments on major programs, experimental treatments must be assigned to intact population units or groups (cities, districts, etc.) rather than randomized among *individuals*.

(4) The most valid analysis for a group-assignment experiment requires using groups, *not* individuals, as the unit of analysis for estimating chance variability or experimental error in determining the reliability or so-called "significance" of treatment differences or program impacts.

(5) Particularly in the absence of an equivalent (random) control group, time series data are of considerable importance in interpreting changes in criterion indices that take place after the initiation of the experimental program treatment—for example, to allow for a preexperimental declining trend from which further decline (after the experimental treatment begins) is to be anticipated, *even if* the experimental treatment were ineffective.

In discussing general problems of feedback information Rosenthal and Weiss (1966) point out that it is especially critical in four circumstances: (1) where organizations are embarking on new programs; (2) where these activities require justification to outside groups (3) where crisis situations threaten the organization, and (4) when they find themselves in complex and unpredictable (or turbulent) environments. These authors also suggest from their study of the National Aeronautics and Space Agency (NASA) that feedback is necessary or desirable both from groups in direct and indirect functional relationships. Those with a direct functional tie would include (a) the specific public or clients being served, (b) superordinate groups, such as sponsors or regulatory agencies, (c) coordinate groups that can facilitate or inhibit organizational operations such as professional associations and citizens' groups, and (d) the supportive environment such as educational institutions for training personnel or the financial community.

Rosenthal and Weiss (1966) also make an interesting distinction between two types of effects on nonfunctionally related groups and individuals—primary and secondary. People not doing business with the organization can still be directly affected, as when landlords in a college town lose tenants with the opening of new university dormitories. There are also secondary less direct effects, as when a business corporation can unwittingly contribute to collective welfare psychology by turning their own organization into a welfare state for its salaried personnel. Second order effects are generally not considered highly relevant for feedback studies for the single organization. When we are dealing with the social system as a whole, however, they are of central importance.

▆ SUMMARY ▆

Human organizations are informational as well as energic systems, and both the exchange of energy and the exchange of information must be considered in order to understand the functioning of organizations. Information exchange is itself energic, of course, but its energic aspects are of minor significance compared to its symbolic aspects. In other words, information transmission is significant for what it implies, triggers, or controls. In general, the closer one gets to the center of organizational control and decision making, the greater the emphasis on information exchange and transmittal.

The importance of information processes to organizational functioning does not imply, however, a simple relationship between amount of communication and organizational effectiveness. The advocacy of communication as a desideratum of organization needs to be qualified with respect to the kind of information required for the solution of given problems, and with respect to the nature of the communication process between individuals, groups, and subsystems of organization. Indeed, social systems can be defined as *restricted* communication networks; unrestricted communication implies noise and inefficiency.

Every organization thus must solve the problem of what pattern of communication shall be instituted, what information shall be directed to what offices. One issue in establishing such a pattern is information overload. There are limits to the amount of communication that can be received, coded, and effectively handled by any individual. The tendency to overload certain executive offices with communications is strong, and the responses of individuals to information overload are often maladaptive. Miller has identified seven categories of response to information overload, each of which can be assessed in terms of its adaptive or maladaptive implications for the individual and the organization. These categories include omission, error, queuing, filtering, approximation, multiple channels, and escape.

Five dimensions are proposed for characterizing communications circuits in organizations:

1. The size of the loop; that is, the amount of organizational space encompassed by the communication circuit
2. The nature of the circuit
3. The openness of the circuit; that is, the extent to which messages can be modified once the communication process has been initiated
4. The efficiency of the circuit for task completion; that is, the speed and accuracy with which the circuit permits the completion of specified tasks
5. The goodness of fit between the circuit and its systemic function.

Further distinctions are made between communications in a hierarchical organization directed upward, those directed downward, and those directed horizontally. Each of these directions implies characteristic content in messages.

Informal communication supplements formal communication patterns and research shows that the more communication of a formal type, the more communication of an informal type. Unlike the rumor process in a crisis situation in which the grapevine flourishes with lack of information, the normal organizational pattern is a positive correlation between the amount of activity in formal and informal networks.

The chapter concludes with a discussion of formal communication devices, such as operational feedback, operations research, and systemic research. Operational feedback is used for purposes of regulation. Control devices such as budgets, financial reports, and performance measures provide information on organizational functioning. Operational research gets built into such indicators to furnish additional information about efficiency and effectiveness. It tends to be limited to the coding categories of the technological system. Systemic research extends its search in time and space to gather information about the interrelationships of subsystems, the impact of the organization on its environment, and environmental change.

Evaluation research, another term for assessing the function of organizations, can be either systemic in character, as in some of the work on social indicators, or operational, as in the determination of the efficiency of specific agencies. The need for evaluation research is especially salient for public agencies that have no feedback from the marketplace. The hypothesis is offered that communication and information subsystems are often located disadvantageously in organizations, both in terms of accessibility to top leaders and in terms of contamination of the information-getting process.

15
■ POLICY FORMULATION ■
■ AND DECISION MAKING ■

OUTLINE

Policy Making Defined by Three Dimensions
    Policy Making versus Administration
    Types of Policy Change

In What Sense Do Organizations Have Goals?
    The Cyert-March Model of the Firm
        The Concept of Organizational Slack

Central Questions for Policy Making with Regard to Substantive Goals
    Expediency and Organizational Objectives
    Broadening of Organizational Goals

The Decision-Making Process
    Immediate Pressures
    Identification and Analysis of the Problem
    Search for Solutions
    Anticipation of Consequences of Alternative Solutions

Rationality and Organizational Decision Making
    Bounded Rationality (March and Simon)
    Disjointed Incrementalism

Factors Affecting Decision Making
    Organizational Context and Its Constraints
        Precedent
        Division of Labor
        Entrenched Position of Specialized Elites
        Environmental Constraints
        Time Pressures
        Organizational Climate and Values
    Psychological Aspects of the Thought Process
        Determination of Thought by Position in Social Space
        Identification with Outside Reference Groups
        Reinforcement through the In-group
        Projection of Attitudes and Values
        Global or Undifferentiated Thinking
        Dichotomized Thinking
        Cognitive Nearsightedness
        Oversimplified Notions of Causation
        Statistical Models versus Clinical Judgment

Factors in Decision Making: Personality Determinants
 Ideology versus Power Orientation
 Emotionality versus Objectivity
 Creativity versus Common Sense
 Action Orientation versus Contemplation
Group Factors in Decision Making: The Janis Concept of Groupthink

Policy Making as the Development of General Procedures and Strategies

Combining Scientific Decisions and Value Judgments:
The Hammond-Adelman Method
Coordination Through Planning and Through Feedback
The Development of Objective Criteria for Decision Making
Coordination for Tomorrow: The Problem of Planning

Summary

Organizational policies are abstractions or generalizations about organizational behavior, at a level .that involves the structure of the organization. This definition is in contrast to the notion that policies are behavior itself, or that they are official statements regardless of their relation to organizational structure and behavior.

As abstractions about organizational behavior, policy statements may be either prospective or retrospective. If the latter, we are dealing merely with a process of recognition; the pattern was there but was not previously stated or formally acknowledged. The more interesting process, however, and the one around which this chapter is constructed, is policy *making:* prospective generalizations about what organizational behavior shall be, at a level implying changes in organizational structure. Such prospective statements of policy comprise a category of decisions: those decisions within an organization that affect the structure of the organization. Policy making is therefore an aspect of organizational change—the decision aspect. Policy making is also the decision aspect of that level of leadership which involves the alteration, origination, or elimination of organizational structure.

POLICY MAKING DEFINED
BY THREE DIMENSIONS

Decision making can be considered in terms of three basic dimensions: the level of generality or abstraction of the decision; the amount of internal and external organizational space affected by the decision; and the length of time for which the decision will hold. For example, suppose that the manager of a manufacturing plant announces that "every employee is to punch in at 8:30 a.m., without exception, and for the duration of operations in this plant." This is a policy that is low on the dimension of abstraction, but extremely high on the dimensions of time and internal organizational space. On the other hand, consider the following statement of a dean to the members of the faculty. "Our policy is to contribute our very best to facilitate student self-development." This policy is abstract and general, both with respect to the principle being enunciated and the means for its implementation.

The combination of these three dimensions enables us to distinguish among (1) policy making as the formulation of substantive goals and objectives, (2) policy making as the formulation of procedures and devices for achieving goals and evaluating performance, (3) routine administration, or the application of existing policies to ongoing operations, and (4) residual, ad hoc decisions affecting organizational space without temporal implications beyond the immediate event.

The first two categories of decision making are clearly in the area of policy formulation and represent the major content of this chapter.

The third category, routine administration, is not policy determination in any sense of the term; it includes the many small decisions that implement existing policies by prescribed means. The residual class of ad hoc decisions represents policy only in a negative sense. Decisions without acknowledged implications for the future imply a lack of continuity in organizational direction; they are policy making only in the sense that the organization has no policy. The warning cliche, "don't take this as a precedent," is the hallmark of a policy-shy management. That most organizational decisions have precedent value nevertheless, reflects a need for policy that is inherent in the nature of organizations.

The formulation of organizational goals would be represented by substantial positive positions on all three dimensions of decision making; such positions, in fact, are the criteria for classifying actions in this category of policy determination. The goal-formulating decisions of members of the executive or the legislative system must be general enough to transcend the specific case; they must hold over time for many cases; and they must affect a substantial part of organizational space or structure.

The mere announcement of an official that the policy of the organization will be thus and so is not in itself proof of policy making. To take a hypothetical case, it is possible for the president of a company to issue a pious statement that the policy of the company does not countenance discriminatory hiring practices. But this statement may have no effect on the operations of the company, and many other actions of the management of the company may be supportive of such practices. On the other hand, if the statement is not merely a public relations matter but does affect the activities of organizational members as they function in their roles, it can be regarded as a policy-making statement. A borderline case would be a conscious and explicit formulation of objectives that attempts no shift in operations but merely a recognition of current practices as official policy. If this formulation has no effect on the system apart from satisfying the needs of some officials for cognitive neatness, it would not be policy making. If, on the other hand, the conscious recognition of some current operation as expressing an organizational goal leads to structural changes to reinforce this mode of operation, the act of recognition would fall in the area of policy making.

Policy Making versus Administration

Policy making, however, is not only the product of deliberate consideration of long-run problems facing the organization. Policy is also created by day-to-day decisions, often made on an ad hoc basis and often made by administrators rather than by designated policy makers. The criterion again is whether systemic change in the organization has been produced by a cumulation of administrative decisions, even though their makers were not consciously trying to determine policy. Political theorists from Woodrow Wilson (1887) on have created a false distinction between policy making and administration because they have restricted policy making to deliberate attempts at decision making by the formal groups assigned such functions. This definition implies that policy must be sought in the pronouncements of a legislature or head executive, in contrast to the decisions of people in administrative positions. This legalistic approach has confused the issue and diverted attention from the facts of organizational life.

The real distinction between policy making and administration is not to be found in the formal separation of functions nor in the official titles of positions, but in the significance of decisions for organizational structure and functioning. The president of an organization may concentrate on routine administration while administrative assistants make policy. Actually, of course, in most organizations, there is some correlation between policy making and position in the hierarchy. The relationship is so imperfect, however, that some political scientists have tended to reject the distinction between policy making and administration completely.

Friedrich (1940) came to the conclusion that the policy-administration dichotomy had become "a fetish, a stereotype in the minds of theorists and practitioners alike." And Gulick (1937) suggested that modern theory should be concerned not "with the division of policy and administration but with the division between policy veto on the one side and policy planning and execution on the other." The fact that government, like other social structures, does not conform too well to the organizational blueprint, however, does not relieve us of the need for distinguishing decisions of a high level of generality with consequences extended in organizational space and time from decisions which are highly specific and have no effect upon organizational structure. Expectations about policy change are often unfulfilled. For example, a change in political control of a city, a state, or even the nation may create expectations of policy changes of a sweeping sort. Often, however, no novelty in the functioning of the system can be detected as a result of the political change. Government employees who entered the civil service more than a generation ago may not have changed their role performance radically through many successive administrations. They themselves will observe with satisfaction that while their departmental heads come and go, they go on forever.

Types of Policy Change

The consideration of organizational goals by policy makers may sharpen and clarify organizational purposes and exclude irrelevant activities, add new objectives, shift priorities among objectives, or shift the mission of the organization.

The last alternative is the least likely of these possibilities. Many policy decisions come about to clarify the main organizational mission, or to achieve consistency between it and subgoals that have developed in the organizational structure. Subparts of the organization may have developed too far on a logic of their own, and the system moves to redress the imbalance in its functioning. For example, a university finds that its program of competitive intercollegiate athletics has achieved a degree of professionalism that is in blatant conflict with its educational objectives. It is faced with a policy decision of reaffirming its basic mission and bringing athletics into line, or having its goals altered by the deviant subsystem. Or a labor union is faced with policy decisions about the elimination of racketeering in some of its locals. Imbalances within an organization may not in themselves compel a policy decision. Persistent imbalance leads, however, to external difficulties which do precipitate organizational action.

IN WHAT SENSE DO ORGANIZATIONS HAVE GOALS?

In accepting the concept of organizational goals we can easily be misled by teleological fictions presented by organizational leaders. The organization is a social system and the consciously expressed intent of some of its members is not to be confused with the functioning of the system. Hence, when officials announce a change in policy to embrace new objectives, we should look at the actual systemic changes taking place rather than accepting the statement at face value. We should follow such a procedure not because there may be insincerity in official pronouncements, but because the functioning of a system is not necessarily given in the statements of its leaders no matter how sincere they may be.

Changes in organizational objectives as stated by officials, however, provide a good starting point for determining whether changes in the system have taken place. We must recognize here the implications of a general social-psychological law. People act first and then rationalize their actions, but over time they acquire understanding of how and why certain behavior has been successful. This understanding is then systematically exploited through deliberate and conscious planning.

There is a danger, nevertheless, in applying the language developed for the psychology of the individual to describe the functioning of a social system. When we speak of organizational goals, organizational choice, organizational learning and decision making, we must restrict our reference to certain leaders or subgroups and not regard the organization as a person. If we do not we will oversimplify organizational behavior and miss the inconsistencies, the discontinuities, and irregularities in the operations of the organization. If we look at the organization as a superperson, we exaggerate the parallel character of people acting in concert to achieve a collective outcome and omit the interactions and continuing compromises of conflicting groups within the system. Policies are the outcome of organizational infighting, mutual concessions, and coalition formation. The decision of the organization to add a new plant in a new setting is the end result of many smaller decisions and complex interactions among its members. We forget that division of labor applies to decision making as well as to routine work. Specific subgroups and individuals have responsibilities and will make limited decisions, many of them ad hoc in nature. The organizational problem is to bring comprehensive, ultimate criteria to aid in their integration, and here there is no organizational equivalent of the single unitary nervous system of the individual. Hence all sorts of inconsistencies and compromises are used so that inaction will not paralyze the system.

The Cyert-March Model of the Firm

Cyert and March (1963) have been leaders in developing a behavioral approach to problems of decision making within business organizations. They view the organization as a coalition of individuals, some of them organized as subcoalitions. For some decisions the coalition may be stable with respect to personnel; for other decisions the personnel may shift. The operational goals of the various coalition groups are not in agreement. The salespeople have a different preference ordering of objectives than the production or the research teams, and hourly workers a different preferential ranking than salaried employees. Only when the goals are stated in ambiguous and nonoperational terms can they elicit widespread agreement. Moreover, organizational goals often take on the character of aspiration levels rather than imperatives to maximize or minimize outcomes, as Blau (1955) has demonstrated in his study of a governmental agency (see page 486). Hence it is unwise to look for organizational goals as a clear, consistent, and widely accepted set of collective objectives. Instead, organizations are characterized by a continuous bargaining-learning process that has irregular and even inconsistent outcomes.

Cyert and March point out three determinants in the formation of the goals of a coalition:

1. The bargaining process by which the composition and general terms of the coalition are fixed;

2. The internal organizational process of control by which the objectives are stabilized and elaborated;

3. The process of adjustment to experience by which coalition agreements are altered in response to environmental change. (1963, p. 29)

Coalition formation occurs through side payments, as in political bodies, not necessarily in the form of cash but through personal favors, promises, and policy commitments of various sorts. The winning coalition has booty to share but it is not a fixed amount and hence conventional game theory is not useful for dealing with the problems of coalition formation. A good deal of the bargaining that goes on is not economic in nature but political, and has to do with policy commitments. Organizational objectives are the outcome of the process and side payments are a central part of the process. Economic theories of marginal cost do not apply because the policy concessions made by some members of the coalition can be made without any monetary loss.

The objectives that result have three characteristics. First, they may be imperfectly rationalized and not necessarily consistent with existing policies. Second, they are sometimes formulated not as absolute goals but as levels of aspiration. Third, in some cases they lack operational specification and so can appeal to opposing subgroups.

Policy is not as changeable, however, as a continuing bargaining process would suggest. Internal controls give stability because of the precedent-setting character of past decisions and because of budgetary constraints in the allocation of resources. Decisions are made within the context of previous bargaining outcomes. Dominant coalitions may remain dominant.

In spite of stability achieved through internal controls, experiences in a changing world affect the constancy of organizational objectives. Cyert and March assume that organizational leaders are more concerned with attainable goals than with maximizing returns and so use aspiration level theory in proposing that "(1) in a steady state, aspiration level exceeds achievement by a small amount, (2) where achievement increases at an increasing rate, aspiration level will exhibit short-run lags behind achievement, and (3) where achievement decreases, aspiration level will be above achievement." These propositions can be tested at the organizational level but the extension of research from the laboratory has not moved appreciably beyond the work of Zander (1971) with small groups. In their one attempt at an application to organizations, Zander and Newcomb (1967) found that the Community Chest does not follow the individual pattern of downward shifts in levels of aspiration after failure.

The central thesis of Cyert and March is that organizational policies often reflect competing and sometimes incompatible goals which represent given subgroups within the organization. The inconsistency is handled by sequential attention to goals, so that today's behavior may well reflect different priorities from yesterday's actions. Thus Cyert and March have brought to the economic firm the political model in which successful leadership swings in a leftist direction today and in a rightist direction tomorrow to hold the support of most of the constituents.

The Cyert and March approach to decision making has been followed by Allison (1971) in developing a model for understanding the resolution of the Cuban missile crisis. Allison shows how the traditional approach of the single rational actor fails to take account of bureaucratic factors involved in either Russian withdrawal of missiles before American dismantling of Turkish missile bases or the American choice of a blockade as a weapon. The many subsystems comprising the national governments in both countries with their fractionated power pulled and tugged in the direction of various alternatives until final decisions were reached.

The Concept of Organizational Slack

Another contribution of Cyert and March is their development of the concept of organizational slack. Slack refers to the excess in resources the organization is committing over what would be required to hold its members and its clientele. It may be paying higher wages to workers than the going rate; its dividends to stockholders may be higher than necessary to keep the firm well capitalized; its services for its top officials may be more than adequate as inducements to hold them; its prices to its consumers lower than the market demands. Organizational slack provides a reserve or cushion for the system. In times of strain or recession the system can survive by making internal adjustments that take up the slack. Its resources makes the organization less vulnerable to environmental uncertainty.

All this is obvious in the case of economic slack, but it is less clear for underutilized psychological resources. For example, if titles and honors, which cost little, are lavishly disposed, does this create organizational slack and does a more restrictive policy with respect to such honorific rewards reduce slack? Intrinsic job satisfaction is still more difficult to understand as an indicator of organizational slack. Does an organization use up slack when jobs become less interesting, as it would by paying lower wages? In principle, any internal organizational resource, economic or psychological, beyond what is needed for current operations constitutes organizational slack. It seems to us, however, that the concept of slack is better adapted to economic exchange, in which one party offers inducements that represent a cost to it in return for services that represent a benefit.

Cyert and March have used their theory of the firm to construct computer models of organizational behavior. There is, however, a great gap between their general conceptual framework and the detailed mathematical paradigms they present. It remains for future students of the firm to work out the operational measures of the social psychological concepts they have formulated. Mathematics and computers will not take the place of such social psychological research.

CENTRAL QUESTIONS FOR POLICY MAKING WITH REGARD TO SUBSTANTIVE GOALS

Organizations that must formulate substantive goals are sooner or later confronted with two types of critical questions: (1) clarity and consistency of objectives versus the pressures of expediency, and (2) broadening of goals versus the narrow self-interest of the organization.

Expediency and Organizational Objectives

Organizations face the problem of adjusting to environmental change without losing their basic character and distinctive contributions and capabilities. On the one hand, if the objectives around which the structure has been built are adhered to strictly in spite of environmental change, there may be losses in input or even threats to survival. On the other hand, if the goals are modified over time, there is the risk of eventual defeat in carrying out the original mission of the organization. Decisions that compromise the principles upon which the organization is based may cause it to lose its distinctive character, its members, and its clientele. (The Social Democratic Party in Germany, for example, furnished very weak opposition to the Nazis. It had so often followed the dictates of expediency that its members no longer knew what their principles were and when they should take a stand in their support.)

On the other hand, in a dynamic world an organization cannot maintain its goals in uncompromising purity without the risk of becoming ineffective or even extinct. The American scene has had a radical political party which has maintained a pure Marxian position over the last 70 years or more—the Socialist Labor Party. It would not compromise its stand by advocating political reforms such as social security legislation, because it was interested in changing the capitalist system and not in repairing its inequities. Hence, the Socialist Labor Party has remained a doctrinaire group of no consequence in American politics. The Catholic Church, with its unparalleled depth and breadth of experience, has combined idealism and realism in its policy making. Its leaders have been opportunistic when they saw real gains, but they have also insisted on the preservation of ideological convictions about basic goals. The present ecumenical movement is only the most recent example of such flexibility.

Since any organization must survive in order to carry out its basic functions, survival becomes a salient goal for organizational decision makers. We have described in Chapter 4 the dynamic forces generated by maintenance structures that have as their implicit, and sometimes explicit, goal the survival of present organizational forms. For many administrators and officials, concern with the preservation of the bureaucracy assumes primary significance. Indeed, the term bureaucracy is often used, not in the Weberian sense, but in the sense of an officialdom absorbed only in the preservation of its own structure and in the ease of its own operation. When bureaucratic survival becomes paramount, there is an abdication of policy making with respect to the substantive goals of the organization. And paradoxically, this form of concentration on survival leads readily to organizational disaster.

Another issue in the definition and maintenance of organizational goals concerns multiplicity as against singleness of purpose. The labor union that attempts to combine political action with its established economic activities may become a stronger organization if it succeeds, but to succeed as a multiple-purpose organization is a difficult task. The success of Samuel Gompers in organizing skilled workers in the early days of American unionism, when more radical leaders were failing, can be attributed in part to the simplicity and consistency of his objective. He preached pure and simple trade unionism, the organization of skilled workers to achieve a better economic bargain for themselves. There was no militant ideology of social change, no political objective save a personal rewarding of friends and a punishing of enemies at the polls. The American Federation of Labor was a business union striving for a good business bargain and not concerned with broad social objectives. The success of the A.F. of L. was due in part to its ideological compatibility with the larger patterns of American society, but in part also to its singleness of purpose and simplicity of organizational objective.

Broadening of Organizational Goals

A radically different question about the formulation of organizational goals has to do with their breadth, their relation to societal welfare. This issue is characteristically bypassed in behavioral science because it is so heavily laden with value judgments. Yet the sociologist or social psychologist who accepts the policies of the organization as *givens* is merely accepting the value judgments of the immediate social environment and is less objective than if he or she had explored the problem more thoroughly. A study of the relationship between the ideological goals of an organizational system, the motivation of its members, and the effectiveness of its functioning can yield valuable knowledge about the nature of the undertaking. For example, an organization devoted to public welfare, such as the American Cancer Society or the Red Cross, has special motivations on which it can draw. In contrast, an essential requirement of a business enterprise is to make profit; otherwise it cannot stay in business. To this extent its goal is narrowly defined as protecting and furthering the interest of one group, its owners.

Although there are many instances of the survival of narrow-interest organizations concerned solely with the making of profit, the general trend has been for business officials to broaden their policies to take account of some aspects of the public interest. The private enterprise of classical economics has been modified by the collectivistic ideology which grows naturally out of the common interests of an interdependent society. Private business will dip into its profits to make donations to charities, will contribute to foundations in the public interest, will make substantial grants to education and the support of research. And the higher its profits, the more it must by law pay out in taxes to the support of collective and national purposes.

The general trend in organizations as they grow is toward a broadening of their social goals. In his study of a federal agency for law enforcement, Blau (1955) reported a succession of goals through which officials moved in extending the limited directives of their original mission. In opposition to the thesis of Michels (1949) that bureaucratic personnel become obsessed with administrative detail, Blau proposed the hypothesis that "internal bureaucratic conditions, except in atypical cases where insecurity prevails, generate increasing concern with objectives that formerly appeared Utopian." Expressions of concern for societal welfare, even if initially rationalization, can contribute to actual changes in policy. Our political state and our political parties are beginning to include as first-class citizens people of all religions and all skin colors. To their theological goal of the doctrinal salvation of the individual, many churches have added the objective of improving social conditions in the here and now. Churches of all denominations have been prominent in recent efforts to achieve racial equality in education, housing, economic opportunity, and civil rights throughout the United States.

The recognition of some responsibility for the national welfare by the church or business enterprise is an illustration of the general principle that organizations obtain their legitimation through their acceptance of the values of the larger society. The interdependence of an advanced technological society increases the significance of cooperation toward common goals. The overriding values of such a society will therefore be reflected in the policy formulation of many organizations and subsystems.

THE DECISION MAKING-PROCESS

Organizational decisions of a policy-making character, although they may be more complex than decisions made outside organizations, are still made by individuals. Organizational procedures are set up to guard against the more common errors of individual judgment, and the latest development of this sort is the programming of the decision process for electronic computers. An adequate model for understanding policy making must start with the individual and the many types of fallibility, but it must also take account of the collective situation in which executives function.

We shall follow the classical account of Dewey (1910) in describing four stages in the process of problem solution, and shall relate these stages to the way in which individuals function in an organizational context. We can distinguish among (1) immediate pressures on the decision maker (Dewey's old felt difficulty), (2) the analysis of the type of problem and its basic dimensions, (3) the search for alternative solutions, and (4) the consideration of the consequences of alternative solutions, including the anticipation of various types of postdecisional conflict and the final choice.

These stages in the process of reaching a decision are affected by (a) the nature of the problem, (b) the organizational context, (c) the basic personality characteristics of the policy maker, and (d) the cognitive limitations of human beings stemming both from situational and personality factors.

Not all policy decisions involve all four stages in any thoroughgoing sense. Immediate pressures may result in an immediate solution with little analysis of the problem, no search for alternative solutions, and little attempt to weigh the consequences. Or the analysis stage may be short-circuited and a great deal of attention conferred on the anticipation of certain possible types of consequences.

Immediate Pressures

The immediate forces that induce the felt difficulty may stem from the executive's own encounter with the problem, from the requests of others in the organization, of from demands made by individuals or groups outside the organization. The immediate pressures not only call attention to a problem; in many instances they also suggest a strategy of solution or even a specific solution. Thus the executive is confronted with demands that vary from "something has to be done" to "unless the salaries of our electronic engineers can be raised by 30 percent, we will lose at least half of these employees."

Some of these pressures will develop as it becomes known that management is considering a change in policy. As executives discuss the situation within and without the organization, they may find themselves committed, or urged to become committed, to some of the views generated in these discussions. The strength of these pressures depends on the power and influence of the group pushing for a given solution, the unanimity within the group, the clarity of their proposal, and often the degree of immediate personal contact. The lieutenants surrounding the executive may exert more influence than a powerful group of stockholders more remote in time and place.

Immediate pressures often seem so overriding to executives that they will accept some hasty solution and bypass a thorough analysis of the problem and a careful weighing of the likely major consequences of their action. The objective circumstances may be of such an emergency nature that decisive actions must be embarked upon immediately. Often, however, specific organizational pressures and personality considerations are responsible for decisions being reached without an adequate analysis of the problem or an intelligent assessment of the consequences. And action may give momentary relief to the decision maker whether or not it really solves the problem. Sometimes the urgency is induced by the perception that hostile outside forces can be halted by organizational anticipation of their direction.

In general, organizations develop policies and procedures for change which are designed to guard against such short-circuiting of the process of problem solution. Nevertheless, immediate pressures can lead to bypassing the necessary stages in problem solution, either through the creation of a feeling of urgency or through the heavy weighting given a particular course of action by the forces creating the pressure.

Identification and Analysis of the Problem

The immediate pressures experienced by executives are not necessarily synonymous with the basic problem confronting the organization. The identification of the nature of the problem and an analysis of its dimensions may call for a different solution than that dictated by the immediate pressure. In an older period of our industrial history, management in many companies reacted to the threat of unionism by attempts to smash unions. The problem was identified in terms of the immediate pressures, namely the move by union leaders to organize a given plant. The basic problem of the need of workers for first-class citizenship in a structure affecting their lives was not recognized. The direct attempts to solve the problem by expelling the organizers, by force if necessary, and intimidating the workers were successful in some instances. By and large, however, efforts directed at such symptoms probably stimulated rather than hampered the growth of unionism in a democratic society.

One basic element in the analysis of difficulties confronting the decision maker has been suggested by Anatol Rapoport (1960), who distinguishes between *problems* and *dilemmas*. The problem can be solved in the frame of reference suggested by its nature, by past precedents for dealing with it, or by the application of existing policy. A dilemma, on the other hand, is not soluble within the assumptions explicitly or implicitly contained in its presentation; it requires reformulation. Many mechanical puzzles or trick problems are dilemmas in this sense of the word. If we approach a puzzle with all our customary preconceptions about the nature of the problem, we can never solve it. We must abandon our habitual set and find a new way of looking at the puzzle. Policy makers in organizations encounter similar situations. While many organizational difficulties are problems of the variety that can be solved in their own terms of reference, other difficulties call for innovation in the very formulation of the problem.

The facts of organizational life often preclude the recognition of dilemmas and their requirements for a radical restructuring of the very basis of the problem. Decision makers at lower levels in the organization often lack the power to reformulate the problem. It comes to them with the givens of previous policy decisions which they must accept. At top levels in the organization, there are also constraints on the recognition of dilemmas and the development of innovative solutions. These constraints may come from the public upon which the organization depends or from other structures with which it is interdependent.

The organizational context is by definition a set of restrictions for focusing attention on certain content areas and for narrowing the cognitive style to certain types of procedures. This is the inherent constraint. To call a social structure organized means that the degrees of freedom in the situation have been limited. Hence organizations often suffer from the failure to recognize the dilemma character of a situation and from blind persistence in sticking to terms of reference on the basis of which the problem is insoluble. Just as a person can persist in the same series of fruitless manipulations in trying to solve a mechanical puzzle, so too can management try a series of related efforts that are doomed to failure because the problem as conceived is insoluble.

For example, management may persevere in attempting to get a kind of dedication from its hourly employees that logically is to be expected only from first-class citizens in the organization. Managers may hope to do away with group norms restricting productivity or to imbue workers with a sense of organizational mission. They will try new communication methods; they will single out certain employees for rewards; they will give supervisors courses in human relations. But none of these approaches goes outside the conventional managerial frame of reference, the conception of employees as hourly workers without tenure or prospects for major advancement, participating in the labor but not in the legislation of organizational life. Nor has management seriously considered what might be done to bring hourly workers into first-class citizenship in the organization. In addition to the situational constraints that prevent the decision maker from breaking out of the customary framework for the analysis of such problems, there are more personal reasons for staying with the conventional assumptions.

The failure to distinguish between problems and dilemmas can take a curious reverse form. Under certain circumstances some executives try to find an outlet for their creativity and innovative ability by turning problems into dilemmas. Many problems easily solved in their own terms of reference are reformulated to admit of novel solutions. Novelty and originality become values in their own right, whether or not they are appropriate to the organizational problem. Some executives are bored by routine solutions to routine problems, and their frustrated artistic creativity finds outlet in change for the sake of change, which is then rationalized as having virtue because "it keeps the animals stirred up."

To aid in the analysis of problems and dilemmas, the organization develops resources in its research and planning departments and in its intelligence operations. Both the basic data and the interpretations of their organizational implications are fed to top policy makers by operational intelligence or by the research staff. Operational intelligence alone can be a weak informational support because of the vested interests that develop in the substructure. Hence it needs to be checked by staff research and by outside experts. The executive in a complex organization must utilize more than one system of information so that he or she will not become a captive of one sector of the organization.

Search for Solutions

The identification of a difficulty as a dilemma or as a problem will determine the type of search conducted for an appropriate solution. If there is recognition of the dilemma character of the situation facing the organization, then the search will be directed in an imaginative fashion toward many conceivable answers. If the difficulty is more problemlike in character, the dictates of organizational precedent and policy will determine the direction and limits of the search.

In general the search for a solution begins at the specific level of past precedent and may stop there if a satisfactory answer is found. If not, the search goes on to a more general level of existing policy, and perhaps to the most general statement of organizational purpose. In other words, the search proceeds on the principle of conservation of organizational and individual energy. Old policies will be redefined and sharpened before attempts are made to change them or to develop new policy.

In the search process one of the first lines of inquiry is directed at the experience of other organizations with the same type of problem. A university president or dean will turn to the solutions reached by the leading universities in the country. The perplexed industrial executive will attempt to find out how executives in other companies are handling similar problems. Political parties will copy each other's techniques, especially when they seem successful. In the absence of more thorough research on the organization's own problems, it is natural to look to the experience of others. Policy makers can of course be betrayed by slavish imitation of more illustrious organizations. They can fail to account for the differences between their own situation and that of their model, and so misapply a solution. This is another way in which the emotional and intellectual attributes of leaders affect organizational decisions.

Anticipation of Consequences
of Alternative Solutions

The policy maker facing a decision, pressured by colleagues and by outside interests, and influenced by the staff analysis and their suggested solutions still must weigh the probable costs and gains of alternative courses of action. For the policy maker who is close to the operational problems of the organization, the first consideration will be the ease or difficulty of getting a new plan to function. *Will it work* is often the policy maker's first question, and this question does not mean: *Is this the best solution*, nor even, *is this a highly desirable solution*, but *can we put it into acceptable operation easily?* Considerations of the practical problems of implementing a plan, including the difficulties it may raise for the decision maker, may arise even before its potential value as a solution is weighed. Many good ideas may fail to get an adequate hearing because the obstacles to their implementation raise questions about their practicality.

The logical model of a four-stage process in reaching a decision, in which analysis of the problem and identification of alternative solutions precede a consideration of consequences for the organization, does not fit the actual sequence of many organizational decisions. Short-circuiting of various types may occur, including the dismissal of solutions without regard to their intrinsic merits, because they involve difficulties for administrators and hence are ruled impractical. Excellent long-run plans for the solution of organizational problems may be summarily dismissed on trivial grounds. If the merits of the plan as a solution are considered fully and found to be outstanding, means usually can be found for its practical implementation.

Considerations of practicality can also be underestimated, of course. The policy makers of some organizations are so remote from everyday operations that they make decisions in terms of desirable goals with little regard for their translation into practical operation. Top management may adopt a new safety plan for reducing accidents in its factories with no consideration for the psychological acceptance of the cumbersome equipment to be worn by workers or the troublesome routines to be followed. They find subsequently that, in spite of the cost of the program, there has been no appreciable reduction in accidents.

This then is one of the dilemmas of large-scale organizations. On the one hand, policy decisions cannot be made purely on the basis of their theoretical desirability. Such a tendency may occur when decision makers are at a great distance, in terms of experience and psychological understanding, from the area in which their decisions are to apply. Human intelligence and insight are not so godlike that they can divorce desirable ends from the concrete experiences for achieving them. On the other hand, the administrators closest to a problem are likely to overestimate the practical difficulties that loom large in their everyday mode of functioning. Their frequent answer to any radical plan for policy change or structural reorganization is to point out that the eggs are already scrambled. They argue that we are not starting *de novo* with the possibility of imposing a new blueprint for the organization. We are dealing with long-established patterns and must act within this framework. This view leads to defeatism with respect to desirable policy change.

One solution to this organizational problem may be to bring together the top decision maker concerned with long-range objectives and the middle or lower level administrators with practical experience relevant to the alternative under consideration. This solution seems so simple and so obvious to the naive outsider that students of organizations have a difficult time in explaining why the complexities of organizational life so often prevent problem-solving activities across hierarchical lines.

Where the probability of success is fair and the gains for the organization outweigh the costs only slightly, the crucial factor in an executive decision may be the executive's own potential gains and losses. Policy makers are human; it is difficult for them to divorce their own fate from the fate of the organization, and there is more than a grain of truth in their equating of individual and organizational interests. The power and rewards of the executive grow as the organization prospers. Both personal and organizational factors enter into the judgmental process, and they tend to become fused. The legal doctrine of conflict of interest has been developed precisely because individuals do not easily divorce their own interests from those of the organization. The personal interests of the official cannot be relied on to dictate the same type of decision as the interests of the organization. Any analytic scheme for identifying the forces involved in decision-making must take into account the ambitions and motives of individuals for their own careers as well as their perceptions of systemic outcomes for the organization.

The consideration of the consequences of alternative solutions may be very restricted or may range widely through the sectors of organizational space and into the extraorganizational environment. Immediate pressures from outside may lead to a neglect of the probable effects of a course of action on the internal structure. And the converse is also true. Side effects and long-range consequences may be difficult to assess. For example, the introduction of automation may have the direct consequences of increasing organizational efficiency and creating problems in the employment of displaced workers, and these effects may be carefully considered before the automation program is launched. The problems of moving to shift work because of the need to keep the expensive automated plant operating 24 hours a day are also likely to be foreseen. Consequences less direct and less likely to be foreseen might include problems of overproduction and the need for entering into industrywide agreements to alleviate it.

The executive will often be profoundly affected by anticipation of the many postdecisional conflicts that a policy action may engender. Janis (1959) has outlined a schematic balance sheet for dealing with the various factors affecting decisional conflicts. He calls attention to the utilitarian gains and losses, the social approval and disapproval, and the self-approval or disapproval the decision maker may anticipate. These factors are affected by the conscious goals, the preconscious affective charge, and the unconscious charge which they have for the decision maker. Wholly rationalistic models of human behavior are inadequate for describing policy making, in part because the executive's rational assessment of the objective merits of a proposal may be affected by emotional forebodings about postdecisional conflicts.

The objective and complete assessment of probable consequences of a policy decision can be aided by research on a pretest of the contemplated change, on the resistance or readiness to change of various affected groups, or on some of the assumptions underlying the proposed change. The effective use of research for such purposes requires a commitment to long-range planning on the part of top management.

RATIONALITY AND ORGANIZATIONAL DECISION MAKING

Bounded Rationality (March and Simon)

It is apparent that the evaluation process in reaching a decision on an organizational problem is not readily reduced to the total and simplistic rationality of the economic man. March and Simon (1958) have employed instead the concept of a bounded rationality or *the cognitive limits of rationality,* and have written cogently about the realities of organizational decision making in these terms. There are always limitations with respect to knowledge of alternative courses of action, of the relative utility of these alternatives, and of the consequences of these courses of action. March and Simon reject the older model of rationality because it does not examine its own crucial premises.

> The organizational and social environment in which the decision maker finds himself determines what consequences he will anticipate, what ones he will not; what alternatives he will consider, what ones he will ignore. In a theory of organization these variables cannot be treated as unexplained independent factors, but must themselves be determined and predicted by the theory.... Choice is always exercised with respect to a limited, approximate, simplified "model" of the real situation ... the chooser's ... "definition of the situation." (p. 130)

The complexities of the problems facing organizations are so great that the executive as a limited human being must attempt to deal with matters by simplifying the dimensions of the problem and the possible alternatives. The executive will seek to retain the major features of a problem without all of its complexities.

> The simplifications have a number of characteristic features: (1) Optimizing is replaced by satisficing—the requirement that satisfactory levels of the criterion variables be attained. (2) Alternatives of action and consequences of action are discovered sequentially through search processes. (3) Repertories of action programs are developed by organizations and individuals, and these serve as the alternatives of choice in recurrent situations.

(4) Each specific action program deals with a restricted range of situations and a restricted range of consequences. (5) Each action program is capable of being executed in semi-independence of the others—they are only loosely coupled together. (p. 169)

In other words, executives deal with problems in piecemeal fashion; they tend to handle one thing at a time, and they tend to follow an established repertory of programs for dealing with immediate problems. They do not consider all possibilities of problem solution because it is of the very nature of organizations to set limits beyond which rational alternatives cannot go. The organization represents the walls of the maze and, by and large, organizational decisions have to do with solving maze problems, not reconstructing the maze walls.

March and Simon carry their concept of bounded rationality into decisions of planning and innovation. They point out, for example, that theories of rational choice tend to ignore the distinction between deciding to continue existing programs and deciding to initiate new ones, and that such theories are particularly weak with respect to innovation. Rational theory might well predict more innovative change than actually occurs, because it would expect innovations to be adopted whenever their costs and organizational return compared favorably with those of present operations. Yet the chances are that this rational optimization is less likely than the maintenance of existing operations so long as they yield a satisfactory return.

These authors suggest also that the rational process followed by organizations in a search for programs to achieve organizational goals is not one of objective logic but of limited psycho-logic. Attention will be given first to the variables under control of the decision maker or the organization, and if this attempt is unsuccessful, then to variables not under organizational control. If this does not work, the criteria for a successful program will be reexamined with the possibility of relaxing them so that a satisfactory program can emerge. In other words, the ease of the administrator is an important consideration, and the assumption is that people will move toward a thorough and full exploration of all possibilities in terms of successive efforts from a series of frustrations. They will not usually move to a new stage of search and appraisal if they can work out some satisfactory adjustment at a prior stage. Objective rationality would call for full evaluation of all possibilities, limited only by the objective organizational costs of the search. Psychological rationality means the acceptance of the most immediate and painless solution.

Devices are built into organizations to facilitate the rational solution of problems in spite of personal limitations. These devices may not work perfectly nor do they necessarily work in all situations. Moreover, they entail certain recognized and unrecognized costs. Nonetheless, they help in the prevention of error and they avoid risks as the organization plays "percentage ball."

Specific procedures and general programs have been developed in many organizations to counter immediate pressures in problem solving, to insure more penetrating analysis of problems, to increase the search for alternative courses of action, and to assess more adequately the utility functions of such alternative courses. Automation and the use of computers will strengthen this development. Thus far the contribution of the computer is most easily appreciated in the fields of memory and of complex calculation. The fallibilities of human memory are well known and they often affect decision making. The computer has a perfect memory not only for specific items of information stored within it, but for the weights assigned to these items in relation to their significance for outcomes. It can perform in fantastically rapid fashion complex computations about courses of action and, for certain types of problems, can actually test alternative solutions in experimental settings.

The process of casting organizational problems into the language of the computer is itself an exercise in the direction of rationality. The creation of a decision-making program requires that one be very clear about the variables and parameters to be taken into account, the sequence or priority with which different criteria of decision making are to be invoked, and the process of inference by which decisions are to be made. The procedure requires the elimination of undefined terms, and builds in complete stability from one decision-making situation to another. In short, *if* the essential data and procedures for decision making can be programmed, many of the erratic and fallible elements in organizational decisions are eliminated.

Adelman, Stewart, and Hammond (1975) describe a case study in which computer graphics technology and input-output analysis in their pictorial and statistical presentation revealed the exact nature and extent of the cognitive differences of policy makers. The clarification led to an understanding and subsequent reassessment of the differences in the policies recommended.

Disjointed Incrementalism

A similar approach to the "satisficing" conception of March and Simon is the incrementalism stressed by Braybrooke and Lindblom (1963). These authors point out that decisions tend to be incremental. Instead of a clearly formulated set of goals and a comprehensive program for their achievement, policy makers make small, incremental changes in response to immediate pressures.

Our program for the aged is not a program at all; it is not a comprehensively considered and coordinated policy. Rather, it consists of Old Age and Survivors' Insurance, special provisions for the aged under the income tax law, old age-assistance provided through the cooperation of state and federal government, and county and municipal provision for the needy aged. . . . It has been developed—and goes on developing—as a sequence of decisions. . . . (1963, p. 72).

Moreover, in attacking an important problem area the prevailing strategy is one of disjointed incrementalism—the fragmentation of decision making among many centers in imperfect communication with one another.

Schoettle (1968) has listed the eight interrelated attributes of the Braybrooke and Lindblom incremental theory as follows:

1. Choices are made in a given political universe, at the margin of the status quo.
2. A restricted variety of policy alternatives is considered, and these alternatives are incremental, or small, changes in the status quo.
3. A restricted number of consequences are considered for any given policy.
4. Adjustments are made in the objectives of policy in order to conform to given means of policy, implying a reciprocal relationship between ends and means.
5. Problems are reconstructed, or transformed, in the course of exploring relevant data.
6. Analysis and evaluation occur sequentially, with the result that policy consists of a long chain of amended choices.
7. Analysis and evaluation are oriented toward remedying a negatively perceived situation, rather than toward reaching a preconceived goal.
8. Analysis and evaluation are undertaken throughout society, that is, the locus of these activities is fragmented or disjointed.

In budget-making a given bureau or department in times of prosperity will get a small percentage increase and in recession periods a small percentage decrease. In other words, instead of scrutinizing the budget as a whole in relation to priorities and accomplishments of the many subunits, the practice of administrators is to impose some increment or decrement across the board. Ease of administration governs decision making rather than genuine problem solving. It would take long and arduous study to evaluate achievement and to determine priorities. Moreover, it is politically more feasible to impose a percentage increment or decrement on all units than to drop one completely or drastically penalize it. People may grumble but they accept the uniform treatment more readily than differential treatment. Studies by Wildavsky (1964) furnish empirical support for incrementalism in governmental budget decisions.

FACTORS AFFECTING DECISION MAKING

Three factors can be identified as general determinants of the decision-making process. First, the organizational context and its constraints narrow and channel both the substantive policies considered and the procedures for formulating them. Second, psychological aspects of the thought process affect the character of decisions. Even though the computer is utilized to control human error (and the computer does not forget), programs are still written by fallible humans. Finally, the personalities of leaders, though also constrained by computers, play a role in policy formation.

Organizational Context and Its Constraints

The wide range of possible decision outcomes is narrowed in institutional settings in predictable ways and organizational constraints are basic determinants. Six types of organizational constraints should be noted: (1) the legal character of rational authority with the emphasis on precedent, (2) the division of labor, which limits the emphases of subsystems to given functions, (3) the entrenched position of different kinds of specialized expertise, (4) environmental constraints imposed by the demands of constituents, the actions of competing organizations, and the abundance or scarcity of resources, (5) the time pressures for decision making, and (6) the organizational climate or value orientation associated with the system, which can include all of the above factors.

Precedent

Rational authority calls for an internal consistency to provide a basis of dependability and accountability. Legal precedent is a ready device to insure predictability. The logic of following rules makes decision makers mindful of precedent. Moreover, organizational practices have to be brought into line with court decisions and so the precedents shift from the subsystem to the larger system. Courts of law become the first resort of aggrieved citizens and organizations increase their legal staffs and the protection of following precedent becomes as important as problem solution.

Division of Labor

The division of labor has far-reaching consequences for policy formulation. Each subsystem will have its own set of norms and values built up around its primary function. It will set different priorities and use different criteria for its recommendations about policy. National policy on foreign aid is a clear example of conflict and competition between governmental bodies. Four committees consider the presidential program on foreign aid: two substantive committees: the Senate Foreign Relations Committee, the House Committee on Foreign Affairs and two "money" committees or the appropriations committees of both houses. The substantive committees generally are made up of senators and representatives with an intrinsic interest in foreign affairs and they evaluate proposals for foreign aid in the framework of American foreign policy. The appropriations committees are more concerned with total government expenditures and generally recommend smaller outlays for foreign aid than do the substantive committees. The Appropriations Committee gives more attention to information from the General Accounting Office than does the Foreign Relations Committee, (for example, facts about tangible results of expenditures for given projects; Geiger and Hansen, 1968).

The top of the organizational structure should ideally reflect the balanced composite wisdom of the system but practically it consists of specialists who have difficulty communicating with one another or administrative generalists who lack depth of knowledge about many problems. There is often a fractionation of responsibility so that it is difficult to know who is in charge. But the top decision-making group is limited by the values and expertise of the subsystem in which they have been trained; for example, the engineering point of view of the former head of the production department will vary from the market orientation of the former head of sales. The administrative generalist is not as system-grounded as he or she might be and often has the approach of the accountant. In other words, the division of labor in the organization has been more successful in creating specialists than in producing integrators and coordinators at the system level.

Entrenched Position of Specialized Elites

A further constraint on organizational decision making is the entrenched position of the specialized elites with respect to policies related to their expertise. Their detailed knowledge can be given undue weight because other individuals, however highly placed, lack the specific information to counter the given expert. Besides, there is a reciprocal courtesy of not challenging others in their field and not being challenged by others in one's own area of competence. In the Bay of Pigs episode both President Kennedy and Arthur Schlesinger (1965), in spite of their own misgivings, deferred to the CIA and the Joint Chiefs of Staff—the supposedly knowledgeable people about Cuba and the military possibilities of invasion. Janis (1972) in his analysis of this and similar blunders in decision making explains the process as one of groupthink, in which irrational processes take over much as they do for the abnormal personality. Although groupthink accounts for some of the dynamics of these situations it does not give adequate attention to the organizational constraints built into the policy-making system.

The specialized elites guard their prerogatives in decision making by the doctrine of secrecy. Information relevant to their decisions is not available to other than the professional in-group and so their policies cannot be readily challenged. The extreme form of this practice can be seen in the making of foreign policy in which certain cautions have to be exercised to keep information from the enemy. But Karas (1974) has pointed out that there is a cost in secrecy through constriction in the organization learning process. In his words, "The wall of executive secrecy, however, doubly insulates the foreign policy bureaucracy from ... correctives. Secrecy not only encourages policy makers to screen out external messages, but it prevents the outside specialists from obtaining the information which would permit *them* to form more cogent opinions about some foreign policy matters (and incidentally, thus restrains full competition in the public marketplace of ideas)" p. 165.

Environmental Constraints

In Chapter 5 we dealt at length with environmental constraints and though our focus here is on organizational variables, the interaction between organization and environment cannot be ignored. The technological surround becomes critical for an enterprise in a competitive market. External turbulence can be reacted to differentially depending on organizational slack but it places definite pressures on policy makers. The nature of the dependence on clientele and constituents will vary but in our political system Congressional policy makers are sensitive to the needs of organized subgroups in their own districts. For example, Rundquist and Griffith (1974) document the parochial constraint on foreign policy making by noting the military expenditures between 1952 and 1972 received by states with Congressional representatives in a key position to affect appropriations. They found that states where representatives or senators served on the House and Senate Armed Services Committees and Appropriations Subcommittees on Defense and Military Construction obtained, on the average, an increase of $25.2 million for each $1 billion of additional procurement expenses as against only $6.4 million for the states without membership on these committees. These figures suggest that foreign policy determination is indirectly affected by local interest groups.

The pressures of economic forces on government is an old chapter in political history and the thesis of an industrial-military complex is still being debated. Although neither extreme proponents or opponents of this concept have emerged victorious, Kolko (1969) has cited some interesting evidence about the closeness of the business and military elites. He maintains that key business leaders pass in and out of bureaucratic posts in the Defense Department, staying long enough to influence policy and then returning to business. Business careers become the aspiration of many military leaders. In 1959 the 72 largest suppliers alone employed 1,426 retired officers, 251 of them of general or flag rank.

This "revolving door" between government and business has also been documented by a Common Cause study of Knejer, Gettings, and Conway (1976). These investigators found that five of six commissioners appointed to the Federal Trade Commission during 1971–1975 came from companies regulated by the Commission, and all five who left during that period assumed positions with such companies. The report also shows that 1,406 Defense Department officers and employees left the Defense Department to work for defense contractors and some 379 of them took jobs with contractors with whom they had dealt while in office or who were under their jurisdiction. So long as the revolving door operates so smoothly, the boundaries between industry and government are difficult to draw with precision.

Time Pressures

An overriding variable in much organizational decision making is the restricted time for the many stages of policy formation. Answers may be required before information can be adequately analyzed or even collected. Executive groups, moreover, are deluged with immediate, compelling problems and are not set up to explore matters of long-range strategy. A common device to deal with this dilemma is to establish a separate planning and policy board in addition to the executive council for handling the day-to-day decisions. Although there are benefits in this arrangement there are difficulties in coordinating the two bodies in that the policy group may function at too remote a distance from actual problems and the executive group may not want to give up its planning function.

Organizational Climate and Values

Finally, organizational decisions are not only made in a social context to which all the above factors contribute but also are affected by certain dominant values—namely the values justifying the major functions of the system. In a profit-making enterprise research unrelated to maintaining or increasing profits is not supported. In a research organization the highest prestige attaches to scientific discovery and breakthroughs. In his discussion of educational policy making by Congressional committees, Halperin (1976) called attention to the political ethos in which these committees have operated. The pro-education orientation of Congress as a whole and the specific world view of the subcommittees produced authorizations for federal spending and massive and complex omnibus bills. This is what the committees were set up to do. "In post secondary education alone," Halperin states, "according to a Library of Congress survey there are 369 separate programs or authorities." Halperin continues:

> With a political culture stressing output, quantity, it is understandable that a "friendly competitiveness" characterizes the members and staffs of the three House education subcommittees as each vies to report out legislation in its areas of jurisdiction. The unwritten rule seems to be: each subcommittee is entitled to report out one or more major bills each year. If the elementary-secondary education subcommittee gets a bill out, then the post-secondary subcommittee has its "turn." Everybody wins; nobody loses. Furthermore, when the House Committee on Education and Labor reports an education bill to the floor of the House of Representatives, it passes, usually overwhelmingly, and generally becomes the law of the land.

It would follow, then, that the information search by policy makers is not for all the relevant and valid information possible but for data that will be useful to implement their own basic values.

Psychological Aspects of the Thought Process
A discussion of the cognitive limits of rationality would be incomplete without a more specific description of the psychological factors that determine the nature of the thought process. The human mind, though an amazingly complex apparatus for problem solving, operates according to known principles that make for fallible judgments. Nine such principles are discussed in the following pages.

Determination of Thought by Position in
Social Space
It is a truism that we all stand somewhere in social space and time, and that our standards for judgment are accordingly affected. The ethnocentrism of the "unugly American" is paralleled by the ethnocentrism of the citizens of every nation.

Sherif (1936) has used the term community centrism to refer to more limited effects of social space, the effects of the norms of subgroups in a culture on values and frames of reference of group members. Similarly we need to take account of the system centrism of the members of any social organization; their position in organizational space will affect their knowledge, their experiences, their attitudes, and their judgments. Such determination of thinking applies both to the information and knowledge people possess, and to their standards of judgment for evaluating that information. We are all affected by national, class, and organization centrism to some degree; organizational leaders are particularly prone to system centrism, a tendency to evaluate everything from the frame of reference of their own organizational milieu. Drucker (1946) writes of this problem as follows:

> The executive of a big business affects society by every one of his moves and is affected by it. Yet he inevitably lives in an artificial environment and almost as isolated as if he were in a monastery. This isolation is necessary. The executive of a big corporation—like the executive of any big organization—is too busy to see people except on business. . . . His contacts of people outside of business tend to be limited to people of the same set, if not to people working for the same organization. The demand that there be no competing outside interest and loyalty applies to the corporation executive as it does to the army officer. Hence, executive life not only breeds a parochialism of the imagination comparable to the "military mind" but places a considerable premium on it.
>
> In our present-day society this isolation is emphasized far beyond the necessary. It is, for instance, made practically impossible for the corporation executive to find out anything about the ideas, concerns, approach and mentality of labor in his frequent contacts with union leaders—or for union leaders to find out anything about management and managers. For those two never meet except as antagonists trying to defeat each other. (p. 81)

The system centrism of the executive is prominent in his choice of subordinates and successors. As a result, the managements of some organizations come to resemble themselves more and more closely, a form of inbreeding that is likely to sap the vitality of the organization rather than to increase it.

Identification With Outside Reference Groups

Executives not only follow the norms of the organizational family; they are also affected by outside groups with which they identify. Such groups tend to be at the executive's own level of power and status, or somewhat above it. The information and values of these outside groups are given more weight than similar inputs from groups of lower status and power. The parochialism described above refers primarily to cognitive limitations due to the executive's way of life. The process of identification refers to emotional ties with groups of the same or superior power to which he or she turns and may defer. There is rational justification for giving full consideration to power groups, since they may be helpful to the organization. The irrational element enters when they are consulted even though they have little to contribute in the way of knowledge or of other help, and when more lowly groups with relevant knowledge are ignored.

In setting up programs for our various international policies, the State Department has often ignored the people with field experience abroad, both in its own staff and in other organizations. Instead it has organized conferences of top industrialists, university presidents, and other key leaders apparently chosen more for position than for relevant experience and expertise. Many poor organizational decisions are made on the basis of overweighting information from powerful and illustrious sources irrelevant to the problem. It is a truism that organizational leaders frequently make important policy decisions without obtaining relevant information from within the organization.

Reinforcement Through the In-Group

The tendency toward selective perception through identification with reference groups is exaggerated by the very nature of organized group meetings. People are placed together in organizational space and play similar roles. Hence they reinforce one another in maintaining a common frame of reference toward problems. March and Simon (1958) describe this process as follows:

> Within the organizational unit there is reinforcement through the *content of in-group communication*. Such communication affects the *focus of information* and thereby increases subgoal persistence. The vast bulk of our knowledge of fact is not gained through direct perception but through the second-hand, third-hand, and nth-hand reports of the perceptions of others, transmitted through the channels of social communication. Since these perceptions have already been filtered by one or more communicators, most of whom have frames of reference similar to our own, the reports are generally consonant with the filtered reports of our own perceptions, and serve to reinforce the latter. In organizations, two principal types of in-groups are of significance in filtering: in-groups with members in a particular organizational unit, and in-groups with members in a common profession. Hence, we may distinguish *organizational* identifica-

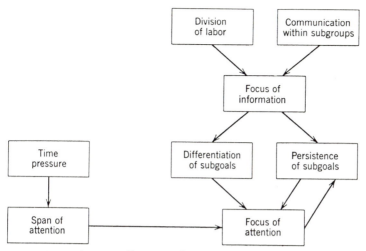

Figure 15-1 *Some factors affecting selective attention to subgoals.*
(From Organizations, James G. March and Herbert A. Simon, New York: Wiley,
1958, p. 154.)

tions and *professional* identifications. There are others, of
course, but empirically these appear to be the most significant.

Finally, there is reinforcement through selective exposure to
environmental stimuli. The *division of labor in the organization*
affects the information that various members receive. This differentiation of information contributes to the differentiation of
subgoals. Thus perceptions of the environment are biased even
before they experience the filtering action of the frame of reference of the perceiver. Salesmen live in an environment of customers; company treasurers in an environment of bankers; each
sees a quite distinct part of the world [Dearborn and Simon,
1958; pp. 152–153).

Division of labor and the restricted communication within subgroups narrows the focus of the information received. This leads to
differentiation and persistence of subgoals, with a resultant narrowing
of the focus of attention. Time pressures also contribute to restricting
the focus of attention (Figure 15-1).

Projection of Attitudes and Values
Reciprocal to the process of identification is that of projection. In
the former case, people see themselves as similar to those of greater
prestige and power; in the latter, they see others as similar to themselves. Projection is the attribution to others of our own feelings and
beliefs. The term is often used to describe the defense mechanism by

which we project our own unrecognized faults and *id* impulses on to other people, in whom we can then attack these undesirable qualities. We are referring here, however, not to the unconscious mechanism for dealing with internal conflict but to the tendency to see other people as sharing our ideas and values.

When decision makers are not confronted directly by realities and objective research data are not introduced, they will often assume that groups within their own organization or outside their organization share the same values as they do. Heads of many industrial enterprises have often been surprised by the success of unionization among their own employees. They could see why unions might gain a footing in other companies, but, after all, they had treated their own workers very well and could see no reason for such employee defection. What they did not appreciate was that workers did not share their frame of reference about good treatment nor their beliefs about company objectives and policies. Attributing to others our own attitudes operates most freely in the absence of factual information about the psychology of other groups.

Global or Undifferentiated Thinking

Instead of grasping the many differentiations in the world about us, we move toward a simplified cognitive structuring of external realities. We tend to see other groups and other peoples as homogeneous entities.

The more remote the group in terms of psychological contact, the more we tend to regard it as an undifferentiated entity. We think of Russia as a communist nation and do not recognize the differentiations within that structure of its various ethnic groups and occupational groups, or the differences between party members and nonparty members.

Dichotomized Thinking

Another common form of simplification in human thought is to view the world in terms of opposing categories (good and evil, black and white, good guys and bad guys). The oversimplified dichotomy of free enterprise versus collectivism has led many of our industrial leaders to contradictory actions. Some of their decisions reflect their interdependence with other industrial structures; in other decisions they are moved by appeals to free enterprise which deny any collective or cooperative action. Our dichotomies of East versus West and communism versus democracy have long been resented by the leaders of nations who see themselves as belonging in neither camp. They are eastern in geography but not in alliance with China or Russia, and politically they belong in neither the communist nor the democratic group.

Political leaders are especially vulnerable to such simplifications. They have to deal with the dichotomous aspects of social reality; the creation of issues that can be reduced to a for-and-against choice is their stock in trade. Moreover, they win or lose at the polls on an all-or-nothing basis. Yet many of the problems with which they deal are multidimensional and involve a continuum of positions. Having talked in dichotomous terms, these leaders become prisoners of their own propaganda.

Cognitive Nearsightedness

People characteristically respond to the immediate, the visible, and the palpable and neglect the dimensions of the problem that are more remote in time and place. A concrete demonstration means more than the presentation of the scientific principles on which it is based. The spatial and temporal frame of reference of human beings is limited. The immediate situation looms greater than problematic events several months removed. This immediacy has many advantages but it militates against a long-run, intelligent course of conduct. Successful organizational policy requires a larger frame of reference both spatially and temporally than comes readily to most people. This human limitation results in the overweighting of immediate pressures in organizational decision making. Moreover, leaders who can free themselves from cognitive myopia must face the further problem of persuading shorter-sighted colleagues to support the implications of their vision.

Oversimplified Notions of Causation

In the analysis of organizational problems and in the assessment of alternative courses of action, decision makers must guard against the common fallible notions of causation. We tend to be animistic and to attribute causes to personal agencies. We tend to accept the exciting event as the major cause. We are given to faculty thinking or the tendency to attribute the cause of an observed action to a faculty for that activity on the part of the actor. Faculty thinking is thus a form of tautology which consists essentially of using a name or synonym to account for the process observed (as we think we have an explanation for a disease if we can find a name for it). We are frequently guilty also of linear thinking, in which we see only a one-way sequence of cause and effect, whereas we are really dealing with a cycle in which cause and effect are mutually interacting.

Most of these errors are forms of nondialectical thinking about the causal process. The dialectical approach of modern physics has departed from the class thinking of Aristotle, with its attribution of cause to the class of properties of which the object is an example, and with its assumption of simple and constant correlations between factors. The modern scientific approach is to view causation as an aspect of a mutually interacting field of forces. A given factor is not a constant but is influenced by the pattern in which it is found. The events in a field of forces are thus determined both by the elements in the field and by the structure of the field, that is, the transformation of those elements resulting from their relationship.

Many problems of industrial management are incorrectly analyzed as a result of oversimplified notions of causation. The problem of informal restrictions of productivity is one example. The linear, simple-cause approach may attribute the restrictive standards to the work of a few agitators; a more sophisticated but still Aristotelian type of thinking will relate them to irrational fears of workers stemming from past and outmoded management practices of cutting rates. A more complex view, which sees such standards as a viable compromise between top management demands and worker needs, accepted by workers, by stewards, and by supervisors in immediate charge of operations, is rarely presented in the councils of management.

Statistical Models Versus Clinical Judgment

The last four factors (global thinking, tendency to dichotomize, cognitive nearsightedness, and oversimplified attribution of causation) point to the imperfections of the human mind as an information processing apparatus. We often neglect cognitive limitations, Dawes (1975) reminds us, and ascribe errors in human judgment to motivational factors such as wishful thinking. But Dawes contends that we may be using emotional predisposition as an explanation for faulty conclusions when the difficulty may be one of cognitive functioning. Dysfunction is accounted for in motivational terms as if human cognition in itself was perfect. Predictions about patient response to treatment, recidivism, and academic success show the superiority of statistically based judgments over assessment based on clinical intuition. But could not clinical judgment contribute to the accuracy of statistical evaluation which perhaps provided just a floor for prediction? Dawes goes on to say:

> The floor turned out to be a ceiling. In the early fifties Meehl (1954) reviewed approximately 20 studies in which actuarial methods were pitted against the judgment of the clinician; in all the actuarial method won the contest or the two methods tied. Since the publication of Meehl's book there has been a plethora of additional studies.... But Meehl (1965) was able to con-

clude . . . that there was only a single example in the literature showing clinical judgment to be superior. (pp. 3–4)

Even this single example has been challenged (Goldberg, 1968).

Errors of the opposite kind are possible, of course. One can imagine a mindless addiction to formula-derived decisions, in which the relevance and validity of the quantified variables are accepted uncritically and mistakenly. It should go without saying that a relevant experiential judgment is better than an irrelevant quantification. The force of Meehl's research, however, is that errors are more often made by neglecting data and relying too much on clinical judgment and conventional wisdom.

The actuarial or statistical model is a combination of measures reflecting some set of scores on specified measures. Clinical judgment is the holistic appraisal of the expert in which the elements entering into the prediction are not quantified. It is like the old problem of coding qualitative materials—how much should coders be allowed to use global judgments for overall ratings and how much should they be tied to specific codes, the scores which the computer will later combine? The issue of specification and statistical combination versus global judgment is of direct relevance to decision making in organizations. Policy makers will often use statistical data but will process it in their heads, together with other information, and will emerge with what is essentially a clinical judgment. The chances are that their experiential wisdom will not give as good an appraisal as an actuarial model. No insurance company would allow its assessment of mortality rates to be based on clinical judgment as against computer estimates. Although the insurance company has the advantage of dealing with readily quantifiable facts, the push for other organizations should be to quantify relevant data and experiment with statistical models for decision making.

Factors in Decision Making: Personality Determinants

In addition to the general cognitive limitations of human thinking, organizational decisions are affected by deep-seated orientations of personality, those attributes that individual decision makers bring with them because they are what they are.

The personality determinants of decision making are overplayed by psychoanalysts and underplayed by social determinists. The psychoanalytic approach neglects the field in which the leader operates, the component of rationality in his or her thinking, and the fact that different substantive decisions can express the same personality need. Social determinists overlook the differing patterns within a broad trend of social events which a given personality can effect. Without the personality of Adolph Hitler the Weimar republic in Germany would in all probability have been replaced by a military autocracy, but the excesses of the Hitler regime might well have been avoided. Historians tell us that Stalin's paranoid character led to excesses in his repressive policies not called for by the objective insecurity of the Soviet regime (Nove, 1964; Tucker, 1965). In the beginning Soviet Russia faced external threat and the need for internal restructuring to provide a viable economy. Stalin's actions were initially directed at these difficulties but his perception of Russia's needs was readily identified with his own need for personal power. Consequently, he turned his attention from the preservation of the revolution to the liquidation of fellow Bolsheviks who might threaten his own domination. Thus systemic forces set the stage for Stalin's dictatorial role, but his reign of terror was less a response to system needs than a function of his own paranoid personality.

Social psychologists have asserted consistently that characteristics of personality act in combination with situational factors to cause behavior. Lewin's summary statement that behavior is a function of personality and environment has been reiterated almost to the point of banality. Like many worthy principles, however, this one has been honored in speech and neglected in deed.

Among the more important personality dimensions of policy makers that may affect their decisions are: (1) their orientation to power versus their ideological orientation, (2) their emotionality versus their objectivity, (3) their creativity versus their conventional common sense, and (4) their action orientation versus their contemplative qualities.

Ideology Versus Power Orientation

The extremes of this dimension are represented by the fanatic and the broker. The fanatic has internalized the ideology of the organization so thoroughly that he or she is constitutionally incapable of compromise. Any deviation from organizational objectives is seen as treason. Social movements are much more likely to have leaders of this type than are established formal organizations. The broker can work skillfully within different organizational frameworks. He or she is the politician less concerned with the platform of the party as a statement of compelling ideals for which to work, and more given to the practical realities of getting elected and staying in power. The broker could serve either political party, and it is an accident or a pragmatic choice that he or she represents one rather than the other.

Few organizational leaders are pure types, either crusading warriors for their ideas or power-actuated political manipulators. Most decision makers represent combinations of these value orientations, and often view practical compromises to achieve power as a way of achieving their ideological goals. How much they salvage of their ideology after they take office, and how much they can rationalize any behavior that promises personal success are the significant questions to ask.

An organization dominated by power-driven leaders will find its policy decisions moving in the direction of the survival and aggrandizement of those leaders rather than toward its healthy development. There may be times when the power interests of leaders and the organizational welfare coincide, but this coincidence is often short-lived. The question to be answered is how permanent are the contributions of the leader to the organization; what is left for the structure when the leader has moved on.

A company may have a remarkable executive whose brilliant rise in the company structure is accompanied by new organizational developments which are part of a personal empire. The executive moves on to a larger rival organization and leaves behind nothing of substantial benefit to the organization. The correlation between the motivational orientation of leaders and their organizational contribution is less than perfect, but it is positive. The educators who have left a permanent effect upon their institutions, such as Eliot and the elective system at Harvard, Wilson and the preceptorial system at Princeton, Hutchins and the great-books approach at Chicago, have all been people with definite ideological orientations.

Emotionality Versus Objectivity

As Janis (1959) points out, two types of emotionality may affect organizational leaders and the objectivity of their judgments. One is the load of preconscious affectivity, the emotional impulses that can move into the conscious sphere; the other stems from deeper defensive needs of which the individual has no awareness. The second would consist both of chronic emotional biases and of momentary emotional impulses.

Janis cites a number of decisions of President Truman that were apparently based on his immediate, conscious emotional arousal; for example, when he dismissed General MacArthur in part because he became angered by a MacArthur press release in open defiance of administration policy. Defensive needs are weaknesses in basic character structure that threaten the ego to the extent that they are not consciously recognized by the person but nevertheless overdetermine behavior. Time after time in World War II Hitler made military decisions reflecting his need for the strength of a superman. Armies, though outflanked, were never to withdraw but were to fight to the death. The Germans suffered unnecessary losses on the Russian front, in Egypt, and finally on the western front because decisions were made not only on the basis of objective military strategy and tactics, but also on the basis of Hitler's unconscious needs to avoid any display of weakness.

Defensive needs can operate at any stage of the problem-solving process. They can block out or distort the analysis of the problem, or the assessment of consequences, or they can overweigh a given type of solution. Experimentation has demonstrated the intervention of defense mechanisms even in the perception of incoming information. Threatening and unpleasant facts are often denied, ignored, or distorted. Organizational executives whose defensiveness results in their avoiding certain types of unpleasant information may be reinforced in their blindness by subordinates who keep such facts from them.

One great weakness in an autocratic structure is that defense mechanisms among its top leaders will receive institutional support rather than correction. Subordinates protect their own positions by screening facts to accord with the emotional biases of the chief. The whole institutional environment may become modified to confirm the pathological tendencies of the people on the top. The realities of the immediate social environment are ordinarily a good check on fictitious views of the universe and delusional systems. But in the autocratic organization so modified, social realities now reinforce fictions, false perceptions, and erroneous beliefs. Criteria for the evaluation of organizational performance will be avoided under these circumstances, because they threaten the present comfortable way of life of the authorities by intruding with objective facts. Its leaders become incapable of changing policy, and unless these leaders can be replaced, the organization faces disaster. Any organization that is unable to adapt to environmental forces will be destroyed by them. Even democratic organizations are not wholly exempt from such problems. They do, however, have the advantages of internal criticism and of provision for orderly change of leaders after a specified term.

Creativity Versus Common Sense

People differ not only in general intelligence (Spearman's g factor), but in two rather contrasting types of ability. Some individuals are gifted in originality; they are able to see new relationships and to impose new structure on old facts. Others may have marked ability in making common-sense judgments requiring the assessment of many relevant factors and accurate prediction of likely outcomes. Although not logically antithetical, these two abilities do not often occur in the same person. The innovative person, by virtue of enthusiasm, originality, and creativity, does not examine the flow of ideas with searching criticism. Such an attitude would inhibit creativity. On the other hand, the person seeking to make a balanced judgment and concerned with giving the appropriate weight to competing plausible notions is unlikely to produce a new solution. Occasionally, the two abilities are combined in a person who can move from a phase of creativity to a phase of criticism.

In general, organizational policy making is in the hands of those who show good judgment, rather than creative people. The executive of good judgment can take on subordinates to perform the innovative function. The creative executive can supplement that talent by hiring people who have good sense but the executive must still make final judgment. It is understandable, then, that the most original minds in any organization are rarely found in top executive positions. The complexities of organizational life with its many conflicting demands on executives mean that critical and judgmental abilities are the essential requirement at this level.

Action Orientation Versus Contemplation

Another personality characteristic relevant to organizational functioning is the capacity for action, the ability to act on judgments. Many people have excellent ideas; not nearly as many translate their ideas or even their decisions into the required implementing actions. Most of us make that translation and write what the group dynamicists have called the action paragraph, only under the compulsion of the situation. As a result the opportunity for action is sometimes lost entirely.

German generals had plotted to overthrow Hitler long before the outbreak of World War II. Hitler was successful, however, in getting rid of the men of action, and the rest lacked that decisive quality of personality so necessary for a successful coup. Hitler himself possessed this quality of immediately moving to decisive action, and it contributed heavily to his meteoric rise and to the early success of German arms. While others talked and debated or reached intellectual decisions, Hitler acted. Moreover, his pace of action was always ahead of his opponents' gait. Information was often available to his enemies in advance of his moves, but it did not seem to help them. The Norwegian government knew of the impending invasion but moved with incredible slowness compared to the pace of the German attack.

Group Factors and Decision Making:
The Janis Concept of Groupthink

We have called attention to the Janis concept of groupthink in dealing with the mutual reinforcement of members of the in-group, but the power of the face-to-face group to affect and perpetuate policy is so great as to merit further exploration. Even the presence of others is enough to influence the individual's expression of perceptual judgments and to report falsely on personal experience, as Asch (1952) has demonstrated. A cohesive group of individuals sharing a common fate exerts even greater pressures toward conformity. Janis selected a number of fiascoes in foreign policy decisions including the Bay of Pigs, the Korean Conflict, and the escalation of the Vietnam War and found it difficult to account for the blunders of the policy makers on the basis of their intellectual and personality characteristics. They were highly qualified people in training and experience and selected for their intelligence and competence. Moreover, they included people of liberal and humanitarian values.

Janis sees the answer to this puzzle in the exaggeration of irrational tendencies through processes of groupthink. Specifically, he believes, six defects in decision making occurred. (1) Early group discussion was limited to too few alternative courses of action. The decision to launch planned air strikes against North Vietnam, according to a Defense Department study quoted by Janis (p. 102), "seems to have resulted as much from lack of alternative proposals as from any compelling logic in their favor." (2) Once launched upon a course of action, the group members do not reexamine their original assessment of its gains, costs, and consequences. (3) They fail to take a second hard look at alternative policies. (4) They neglect to utilize information from experts relevant to alternative courses of action. (5) Group members are selective in the information and opinion they do use and are very partial to that which supports their original position. (6) They give little consideration to the realistic implementation of their policy and do not provide for the usual difficulties in the execution of even *well-laid* plans such as bureaucratic inertia or political opposition. There is a lack of contingency planning for setbacks.

It is Janis's thesis that while individuals also suffer from similar weaknesses in judgment, the group setting can magnify rather than correct such tendencies. There is an illusion of invulnerability about risky actions in that if there is unanimity in the group it is perceived by its members as extending widely beyond the group. There is, in fact, an illusion of unanimity within the group in that serious dissent does not surface once the official line becomes apparent. Silence is assumed to give consent.

Although Janis is correct in his contention that policy outcomes could not have been predicted by looking at the personal characteristics of the decision makers, it is not obvious that group processes in the face-to-face group account fully for the errors in decision making. Mistakes can be traced to system variables as well as groupthink processes. For example, the Bay of Pigs decision shows the dominance of the CIA in the foreign policy structure at the time. The plan to invade Cuba was a logical output from a subsystem concerned with espionage, manipulation, and intervention. Such espionage substructures tend to acquire unusual power in national systems. President Kennedy in later problems was on his guard against the advice of the CIA. While groupthink was involved in the fiascoes Janis describes, a more complete explanation would include system variables as well.

POLICY MAKING AS THE DEVELOPMENT OF GENERAL PROCEDURES AND STRATEGIES

In addition to substantive decisions about the nature of objectives, policy is also made by decisions about the general procedures for attaining objectives. Whereas decisions about organizational goals meet clearly the policy-making criteria of generality and spatial and temporal effects, decisions about procedures can vary from questions of what the constitutional rules should be to a question of revising some detail in the method of time and motion study. We are concerned here with the former type of procedural decision, decisions about the general strategy for attaining organizational goals. Once a strategy has been adopted, it can be applied to problems as a routine matter of administration. But setting up new procedures or changing existing ones are matters of policy.

By procedures we do not refer to the role prescriptions which specify how each person is expected to do the job. We refer to the general rules or strategies that commit the organization to follow one path toward achieving its goals and not another, rules according to which it handles external problems, and meets internal ones, and assesses its progress.

For example, two hospitals may have the same objectives of patient care; yet one may be committed to the open-hospital strategy of maximum freedom for patients and for teams of staff members of differing occupational and professional status, while the other may follow the traditional rules of medical hierarchy. Two industrial enterprises may have the same objectives of producing cars and making profits; yet one may decentralize its divisions, while the other follows a procedure of heavy control from the top of the organizational structure. As a matter of policy, one company may handle the adjudication of internal conflicts through the immediate intervention of top management; another may attempt to have such conflicts worked out at lower levels, with the conflicting parties deeply involved in the solution of difficulties. One organization may have developed clear criteria for the evaluation of performance which become the guidelines to everyday decisions about operations and personnel; another may have as its criterion of performance only the occasional protest from some articulate member of its public.

Procedural decisions thus vary in generality from those that affect the basic structure of the organization to those that provide rules for the solution of very minor conflicts. At the most general level, procedural decisions constitute policy with respect to where and how various types of policy decisions should be made in the organization.

Combining Scientific Decisions and Value Judgments: The Hammond-Adelman Method

We have called attention to the proven superiority of a statistical model summarizing independent specific measures over global clinical judgment. A general issue in organizational policy formulation is the extent to which such models should be the accepted procedures to employ in decision making. A common objection to their use is that they do not apply to the area of value judgment, that they are limited to supplying information for scientific and technical decisions. Hence it has been proposed that an adversary system with a science court be set up with science advocates for opposing positions. Kantrowitz (1971) and Hammond and Adelman (1976) point out, however, that adversary procedures emphasize winning rather than correctly assessing the facts, and they have proposed a method for applying a scientific approach both to technical issues and to social judgments.

They have applied this to the practical problems facing a community pressured by its police forces to adopt a different form of hand gun ammunition—namely a hollow-point bullet that flattens on impact. The suggested change was opposed by minority groups and the American Civil Liberties Union. The proponents claimed that the hollow-point bullet had greater stopping effectiveness, inflicted less injury, and was less likely to ricochet and hurt bystanders than the solid bullet. The opponents challenged these contentions. As action researchers Hammond and Adelman cut through the controversy by first dividing the problem into technical questions and issues of social value. Ballistic experts were asked to consider 80 bullets on the criteria of injury, stopping effectiveness, and threat to bystanders on the basis of such criteria as weight, muzzle velocity, and kinetic energy. Social judgments were made by policy makers and community representatives not on the technical factors such as muzzle velocity but on the acceptability to the community of injury, stopping effectiveness, and threat associated with various hypothetical bullets. The two sets of judgments—the technical and the socially evaluative—were then combined in a formula that gave equal weights to the three criteria and to the technical and social judgments. A bullet was found that met the criteria as established by the formula that had greater stopping effectiveness than those currently in use but was less apt to cause injury than the bullet proposed by the police force. It was accepted by the city council and by all other concerned parties.

Hammond and Adelman advocate this method for making decisions in controversial matters not because it is flawless but because it makes public and explicit both procedures and standards of judgment. Hence it allows for subsequent improvement and for the building of cumulative knowledge. It takes a great deal of the discussion of the problem out of the area of controversy and into the area of fact-finding. The value judgments are still made by the appropriate group of policy makers but they base them on the specified criteria and they externalize some of the intuitive aspect of judgment. The use of this method would call for more fact-finding, more turning to objective criteria, and more quantification and specification for value judgments. Methodologically it is a breakthrough for the problems of policy makers but its merit does not guarantee its wide adoption.

Coordination Through Planning and Through Feedback

A basic procedural strategy concerns the proper mix of coordination through planning and coordination through feedback. March and Simon (1958) point out that the activities of the system can be organized according to established schedules or according to the transmission of new information as in feedback. No organization can survive if it attempts coordination solely on the one basis. The environment does not furnish sufficient constancy for the routine following of prearranged programming but the essence of organized effort requires planning. The football coach goes into a contest with a game plan but makes adjustments as the game proceeds and there is feedback about what is taking place on the field. In general the more turbulent the environment, the more planning has to be supplemented with feedback. Often the test of an organization is its resilience in adapting to difficulties when plans do not work out well.

The advantages of planning are many. A program can be set in operation and maintained with little effort of the hierarchical chain of command. Individual errors are reduced. Moreover, it is possible to program some patterns of work to allow for correction through feedback, but there is the limitation that all types of feedback cannot be anticipated. March and Simon (1958) call attention to the problems of adaptation in noting that organizations can have a repertory of plans for different contingencies and can even have a computerized procedure for selecting the appropriate program from its repertory. The military has developed contingent programs with more detailed elaboration than most organized systems.

Additional distinctions concerning coordination mechanisms that break down feedback into finer categories have been made by organizational theorists. Thompson (1967) calls attention to a personal mode and a group mode for coordination through feedback in which the new information is handled through the individual or through the group. Within the personal mode the pattern can be vertical or horizontal. It is also possible, as Lawrence and Lorsch (1967) point out, to have a designated expediter who coordinates activities involving people over whom he or she has no formal authority. For the group mode the mechanism can be either scheduled or unscheduled meetings (Hage et al; 1971). The research of Van DeVen and Delbecq (1976) suggests the usefulness of distinguishing various types of coordination mechanisms. In their study of 16 district offices and administrative headquarters of a large state employment security agency they found that an increase in unit size was accompanied by an increase in planned coordination and an increase in vertical communication (though smaller), whereas horizontal channels did not vary as unit size changed. They also reported that task interdependence was related to an overall greater use of all coordination mechanisms.

The Development of Objective Criteria
for Decision Making

Procedures or strategies can emphasize the development and use of criteria for the evaluation of organizational functioning and success. Or, the strategy of the organization may be to give little attention to assessment and to throw all its energies into the self-fulfilling prophecy. For example, a manufacturing concern may not explore the psychological market for a new product but may rely instead on creating such a market through a huge advertising campaign. In general, however, the trend is toward the development and utilization of yardsticks for the measurement of performance and progress toward organizational goals.

March and Simon (1958) have distinguished between *operational* and *nonoperational* organizational goals. The distinction is based on whether means of testing actions can be employed to choose between alternative courses of action with respect to an objective. Thus the goal of promoting the general welfare is nonoperational and can be related to specific actions only through the intervention of subgoals. Subgoals are often substituted for the more general goals of an enterprise in order to gain the advantages of operationality. In general, restricted objectives and subgoals lend themselves more readily to the employment of operational criteria in making decisions. March and Simon argue further that where there are shared operational goals, differences about the course of conduct are more likely to be resolved by rational, analytic processes. Where the shared goals are not operational (or where the operational subgoals are not shared), differences are more likely to be adjusted through a qualitatively different process, that of bargaining. In other words, if shared goals are operational, the problem of differential perceptions of the optimal course of action has a logical solution. If the goals are nonoperational, there is no logical and testable answer to such differences of judgment. The probable outcome is therefore a compromise based on concessions and trading, and more attuned to achieving internal harmony than organizational objectives.

Although there is a trend in technological society toward making organizational goals operational, there is some counteracting of this tendency because of organizational growth. As an organization increases in size and complexity, the goals of the overall system become increasingly difficult to operationalize, even if the goals of the subsystem remain operational. This is a basic argument in favor of decentralization; it gives autonomy to organizational units in which goal operationalization is possible. In fact, decentralization takes advantage of one important criterion by which the goals of business organizations are made operational—the yardstick of the marketplace. The effectiveness of a division, which is often difficult to assess within the total system, is readily measured if it must compete for its share of the market.

The yardsticks for measuring performance and progress toward organizational goals are measures of feedback from organizational transactions with the environment or from cycles of internal operations. Assessment of organizational functioning can be built around any of the major import-export relations of the organization with its environment. Its exports to the environment (product or service, image in the outside world, ideological output, by-products, and others) are all capable of measurement. In fact, however, only the assessment of product sales compared to other organizations, the yardstick of the marketplace, has been widely used.

Criteria of internal functioning can also be developed for the different substructures within the organization. The less the dissension and conflict within the organization, the better job the maintenance structure is doing. The more numerous the new ideas and the better their quality, the better job the research and development groups are doing. A more general criterion of internal functioning is the development of capable leaders to solve the difficult problem of managerial succession.

Finally, cost accounting is commonly employed to give some measure of the total input of energy in relation to output. Although theoretically a good approximation to energic exchange, the practical difficulties of accurate, reliable, and adequate cost accounting are such that it needs to be combined with other devices for the evaluation of performance of the various substructures within the organization.

Profitability and growth are two additional indicators of overall organizational success that are widely used. Both these measures are complex outcomes of many interacting factors, including properties of the organization and of its immediate environment. They are feedback of a kind, but the feedback loop is so long and the information reflects so many causes that they are less than satisfactory as criteria for organizational functioning. The company whose profits plunge is in trouble, but management still requires measures of internal and external functioning which will indicate the nature and locus of the trouble. Rate of growth is still more complicated and ambiguous in meaning.

Coordination for Tomorrow:
The Problem of Planning

A basic issue of strategy for large organizations in modern industrial societies concerns their policy with respect to planning. Industrialized societies are dynamic in character. Once past a critical point in the accumulation of scientific knowledge, technology grows at an ever accelerating pace. Through its development, luxuries not available to royalty a century ago have become necessities for American society. Moreover, technology moves in many directions: toward improving the material way of life, toward conquering disease and extending the span of life, toward the conquest of space, and toward unbelievably efficient devices for the destruction of the human race.

The rapidity of change and the diverse potential uses of technology put a premium on the anticipation and direction of these changes through systematic planning. Any organization that does not have a four-, or five-, or ten-year plan is risking destruction or a series of continuing crises in its operations. In his description of one of the largest and most successful of industrial corporations, Drucker (1946) writes, "Of all the functions of central management, this responsibility to think ahead is perhaps the most important. . ."

The generic policy decision in organizations with respect to planning has to do with the extent to which there will be programming for innovation. At one extreme would be the policy of leaving to top management the task of coping with problems as they arise. At the other extreme would be systematic institutionalization of the planning process. March and Simon (1958) contend that under the former policy the rate of innovation would be more sensitive to environmental changes, but that the average rate of innovation would be higher under a policy of institutionalization of innovation given a relatively stable environment.

Programmed planning can be implemented through two auxiliary or staff functions, one to develop specific alternative courses of action for anticipated changes in the environment, the other to gather intelligence about environmental changes and reactions to organizational programs. Both these functions are generally combined in a single staff group, to the great neglect of the intelligence function. Guesswork replaces exact knowledge of environmental trends.

The planless extreme is currently illustrated by many municipalities that did not plan for zoning, traffic, water, and sewage services. They are now paying the price for the old policy of day-to-day opportunism.

Policy decisions concerning general procedures can profoundly affect planning possibilities and planning decisions. Our governmental structure at the local, county, state, and national levels is geared to operating on a fiscal budget for a single year. No governmental agency can legally make commitments beyond a 12-month period. Congress is elected on a two-year basis and no congress can make fiscal decisions legally binding on its successors. Informal arrangements have helped to bypass these restrictions on planning, but public accountability in terms of yearly budgets is a severe handicap to planning policy.

We have called attention to the dilemma of modern organizations in facing increasingly turbulent environments. On the one hand turbulence by definition makes long-range planning difficult; on the other hand such planning becomes the only effective way of dealing with turbulence. Few organizational theorists have seriously addressed themselves to the problem, but Michael's thoughtful treatment (1973) depicts the basic issues related to coordination of the future. Michael believes we lack a social technology for national planning, that there are no ready-made solutions for important societal tasks, and that the crying necessity is the acceptance of the concept of long-range social planning as a process. First, social science itself must change to improve its understanding of societal dynamics. Second, it is necessary to introduce the requirements of learning to deal with long-range social problems into organizations so that their structures can be continuously redesigned for this purpose. Third, it is important to make organizational boundaries more permeable so that organizations learn to incorporate members of the environment into their midst and learn from them. In short, as Michael puts it:

> We shall have to extend the societal learning process to learn *as a society* how to learn in the situation that makes long-range social planning necessary. But, much more so than in the past, we shall have to be self-consciously committed to the learning process and to the learning experience as such. (p. 283)

He summarizes his suggestions in the following terms:

> Changing toward long range social planning would require that people working in organizations, and in the social and natural environment linked to them, find it rewarding to learn how to do these things:
> 1. Live with and acknowledge great uncertainty.
> 2. Embrace error.
> 3. Seek and accept the ethical responsibility and the conflict-laden interpersonal circumstances that attend goal-setting.
> 4. Evaluate the present in the light of anticipated futures, and commit themselves to actions in the present intended to meet such long-range anticipations.
> 5. Live with role stress and forego the satisfactions of stable, on-the-job, social group relationships.
> 6. Be open to changes in commitments and direction, as suggested by changes in the conjectured pictures of the future and evaluation of ongoing activities. (pp. 218–282)

SUMMARY

An organizational policy is an abstraction or generalization about organizational behavior, at a level that has structural implications for the organization. Such generalizations can be made retrospectively, as recognitions of existing practice; the more interesting process, however, is policy *making*, the making of general statements of what organizational behavior shall be. The making of policy in this sense is at once a category of decision making, an aspect of organizational change, and perhaps the most significant expression of leadership.

Organizational decisions can be characterized on three dimensions: level of generality or abstraction, amount of organizational space affected, and duration. Two major categories of policy making are proposed, based on these dimensions: the formulation of organizational goals and objectives, and the formulation of strategies and procedures for achieving and assessing progress toward such goals.

To equate the organization to the individual in the pursuit of goals is to neglect the complexities of decision making in which coalitions and subcoalitions within the system strive for a variety of objectives. The result of their competitive strivings, conflicts, and compromises is a series of actions but not necessarily a consistently formulated or clearly stated set of goals.

The formulation of organizational goals includes sharpening and clarifying present organizational purposes, adding new objectives or relinquishing old ones, shifting priorities among objectives, and altering the major mission of the organization. Examples of all these policy-making activities are considered. Least in evidence are major shifts in organizational mission, which are opposed by all the stability-seeking machinery of the organization itself.

That form of policy making which deals with strategy and the assessment of performance in relation to accepted goals involves somewhat different activities. These include the development of criteria for decision making, and the development of feedback measures that provide information about the adequacy of present organizational functioning. Feedback measures in principle can be constructed around any internal organizational process and around any continuing transaction between an organization and its environment. In practice these potentialities for guiding data are little developed. Only cost accounting, sales, profitability, and growth are in general use as feedback mechanisms established and maintained as matters of policy. The limitations of these devices are considered, particularly under conditions of rapid and continuing technological change.

To define policy making as a category of decision making raises very general questions about how decisions are made, what situational factors affect the making of them, and what inherent limitations in rational decision processes are implied by the nature of human beings as decision makers. The latter sections of the chapter deal with these issues. Decision making is described in terms of four stages, in accordance with the schema first proposed by John Dewey. In sequence these include immediate pressure or felt difficulty experienced by the decision maker, analysis of the presenting problem and its basic dimensions, search for alternative solutions, and consideration of the consequences of these alternatives.

In any specific instance movement through these stages and the decisional outcome itself will be affected by the nature of the problem, the organizational context, the personality characteristics of the decision makers, and the cognitive limitations of human beings. These include the determination of thought processes by position in social space, identification with outside reference groups, projection of one's own values and attitudes, the tendency toward undifferentiated or dichotomized thinking and toward cognitive nearsightedness, and the reliance on oversimplified notions of causality.

A number of these limitations are summed up in the March and Simon concept of bounded rationality in which reaching a *satisficing* rather than *optimizing* outcome is the rule. Problems are simplified; a restricted set of alternative solutions is considered, alternatives of actions are discovered sequentially and not as a planned program, and each specific action deals with a restricted range of situations and of consequences. The disjointed incrementalism of Braybrooke and Lindblom is a similar conception and has been applied to governmental decision making.

Not only do motivational factors interfere with rational determination of policy but cognitive processes themselves are fallible. Actuarial prediction is almost always superior to clinical judgment and an actuarial model should be very useful in organizational decision making.

Janis has theorized that individual weaknesses in judgment are exaggerated through processes of *groupthink*. The reinforcement and conformity in the in-group make it difficult to reexamine the original assessment of gains, costs, and consequences.

The chapter concludes with a review of objective criteria for policy formulation and a discussion of coordination through planning versus coordination through feedback.

16
■■ LEADERSHIP ■■■■■■■■■■■■■■■■■■■■■■■■

The concept of leadership has an ambiguous status in organizational practice, as it does in organizational theory. In practice, management appears to be of two minds about the exercise of leadership. Many jobs are so specified in content and method that within very broad limits differences among individuals become irrelevant, and acts of leadership are regarded as gratuitous at best, and at worst insubordinate. Nevertheless, management typically responds to instances of organizational success by rewarding the formal leader, and to instances of organizational failure by blaming the person so designated. There is an almost universal assumption that even a small subpart of an organization can operate successfully only if some person has been formally designated as leader. Difficult assignments are often awarded with the injunction to "make it work," a kind of implicit recognition that something more than the formal prescriptions of organization is required for the system to function successfully. Managerial practice acknowledges to some extent the needs of the organizational system for continuing creative elaboration, revision, and improvisation; and management expects every member of the organization to exercise such creativity on occasion—some more than others, according to their position in the structure.

GENERAL APPROACHES

The recent popular trend has been to abandon the hero image of leadership, the notion of noble or superior qualities of intellect, character, and personality. The anti-hero has emerged and the pendulum has swung to considering the abnormal and even pathological qualities of leaders. We explore the curious quirks of character that lead political figures to gross errors of omission and even grosser errors of commission. The emphasis has shifted from explaining wise decisions to accounting for the irrational actions of leaders. How did Truman come to decide to drop the atomic bomb not once but twice? Why did President Kennedy go along with the Bay of Pigs policy? Why did Nixon not burn the incriminating tapes? We turn to the groupthink of Janis to account for irrationality of leadership. But it is still necessary to recognize the positive actions of leaders and so the concept of charisma is invoked to explain good decisions but even more to explain why people accept the poor decisions of leaders.

"Great-Man" School versus
Cultural Determinism

Among social scientists who emphasize the concept of leadership there is no close agreement on conceptual definition or even on the theoretical significance of leadership processes. On the one hand, the "great man" school views history as the study of biography. The Protestant reformation is the story of Luther, of Calvin, and of Zwingli; the French revolution, the story of Voltaire, Robespierre, Danton, and Napoleon; and our own period, the tale of Hitler, Roosevelt, Churchill, Stalin, Gandhi, Mao, DeGaulle, and Tito. On the other hand, the cultural determinists see history in terms of social patterns relatively unaffected by the intervention of leaders. In the recent past several writers have acknowledged this unsatisfactory state of affairs and have attempted to make sense of the differences by proposing some schema or paradigm that encompasses both viewpoints (Gibb, 1954; Bass, 1960; Stogdill, 1974; Cartwright, 1965; Tannenbaum, Weschler, and Massarik, 1961, and Hollander and Julian, 1969.)

Leadership appears in social science literature with three main meanings: as the attribute of a position, as the characteristic of a person, and as a category of behavior. To be a superior is to occupy a position of leadership, and to be company president is to occupy a position of greater leadership. Yet it may be said that a certain supervisor exercises considerable leadership, and that the presidents of some companies exercise very little. Moreover, leadership is a relational concept implying two terms: The influencing agent and the persons influenced. Without followers there can be no leader. Hence, leadership conceived of as an ability is a slippery concept, since it depends too much on properties of the situation and of the people to be "led." If the powerfully leading suvervisor were catapulted into the president's office, would his or her leadership abilities still be manifest? And if the supervisor could not lead as president, what would have become of his or her leadership abilities?

One common approach to the definition of leadership is to equate it with the differential exertion of influence. Thus we would not speak of a leader in a group of people all of whom were equally effective or ineffective in influencing one another in all areas of the group's functioning. Even where one individual has more effect on peers than another, we do not ordinarily speak of leadership if the effect derives almost entirely from a position in the social structure rather than from special utilization of that position. The sergeant who passes along the order "forward march" when the whole company is on the move is close to the zero end of the continuum of leadership. The same sergeant, however, in charge of a platoon in combat may deploy them effectively and energize them to hold their position against odds. The sergeant's behavior would then fall far toward the positive end of the leadership continuum. This is not to equate leadership with the exertion of influence at the informal level (which would rule out acts of institutional leadership). We maintain that leadership does occur in formal structures, and indeed that every act of influence on a matter of organizational relevance is in some degree an act of leadership. To the extent that such influential acts are prescribed for certain positions in the organization, even the routine functioning of the role system involves acts of leadership.

Leadership as Influential Increment

When we think of leadership in contrast to routine role performance, however, we become particularly interested in the kinds of individual behavior that go beyond required performance and realize more fully the potential of a given position for organizational influence. In other words, *we consider the essence of organizational leadership to be the influential increment over and above mechanical compliance with the routine directives of the organization.* Such an influential increment derives from the fact that human beings rather than computers are in positions of authority and power.

With respect to the legitimate power of office and the rewards and sanctions that go with it, all supervisors at a given level in the hierarchy are created equal. They do not, however, remain equal. Some of them are much more knowledgeable about the technical aspects of production than others; some have a better understanding of people, and the character traits of some are more acceptable to superiors and subordinates. French and Raven (1960) have suggested five types of power: legitimate power, reward power, punishment power, referent power, and expert power. (Referent power refers to influence based on liking or identification with another person.)

The organization does provide equal legitimate power to all supervisors at the same level and the same access to the use of organizational rewards and punishments. But one supervisor may utilize his or her legitimate power in appropriate and telling ways to maximize his or her influence in the structure, whereas another may fail conspicuously to use the organizational structure to get the job done. Such differences are cryptically summarized (and exaggerated) in the old dictum, "You can't delegate power." Moreover, both the particular utilization of legitimate power and the actions of the supervisor outside the use of formal power have a marked effect on his or her referent power, that is, influence based on affection and respect.

A person's expertise in technical matters and in organizational lore also provides increased acceptance of his or her suggestions and directives. Neither referent power nor expert power can be readily conferred by the organization and yet both are important in getting organizational work done. Even the appropriate use of legitimate power cannot be spelled out in the organization rule book for the higher and more complex officer positions. Detail, contingencies, and ramifications make such efforts self-defeating.

The concept of influential increment has relevance for organizational effectiveness in several ways. First, expert and referent power, to the extent that they develop within a group, represent additions to the power available from the organizationally given stock of rewards and punishments and from the legitimizing acceptance of organizational policies. There is literally an increase in the total amount of control that such a group can exert over its members, and this has been shown to be a persistent factor in increased organizational performance (Tannenbaum, 1962).

Secondly, expert and referent power can be substituted for other bases of power. As substitutes for power based on punishment especially, expert and referent power are relatively free of unintended and undesirable organizational consequences. Individuals who comply for fear of punishment long for the day when they can escape or overpower their superior. People who comply for external rewards are likely to ponder how they can obtain the rewards without the circuitous and strenuous business of compliance. Even legitimate power, if unaccompanied by referent and expert power may produce a sullen and grudging performance. To the extent that referent and expert power are substitutable for, or can be added to these other bases, they offer clear organizational advantages. The whole human relations emphasis in organizational leadership can be thought of as an attempt to promote referent power in addition to, and to some extent instead of, power based on rewards, punishments, and the acceptance of organizational law. Likert's (1961) *new patterns,* McGregor's (1960) *theory Y,* and Argyris's (1962) *interpersonal competence* have this emphasis in common.

Finally, referent and expert power represent potential additions to total organizational control and effectiveness because they are available to all members of the organization. They depend much more on personal and group properties than on the formal definition of organizational roles. They can be used by peers as well as by supervisors and formal leaders. Peer influence has been shown in many situations to be more readily accepted than influence from organizational superiors, and as such has a unique contribution to make to organizational effectiveness.

The hypothesis of influential increment through the use of referent and expert power was tested by Student (1966, 1968) in his study of 48 work groups in an appliance factory. This investigation used hard measures of the performance of groups, namely average earnings, unexcused absences, turnover, safety (percentage of injuries in the work group), and percentage of suggestions submitted. In addition ratings by management of supply costs, scrap costs, maintenance costs, indirect costs, performance against schedule, and quality of work were obtained. The perceptions of workers were taken as indicators of the type of influence exerted by supervisors. A correlational analysis (Table 16-1) shows that for the performance measures legitimate power has no significant relationships with any of the criteria. Coercive power does little better with one significant correlation (suggestions submitted) but with a number of negative, though low correlations, with some of the other criteria. Reward power is similarly not a consistent factor making for good performance. It helps on supply costs but is negatively related to average earnings. Expert power is somewhat better with two significant positive correlations and a general pattern of positive correlations. Referent power tops the list with four significant positive correlations. Incremental influence based on a combination of referent and expert power is also positively related to the criteria but with only two significant correlations.

Partialling out reward, coercive and legitimate power decreases the strength of both referent and expert power. Nevertheless the combination of these latter two forms in the measure of incremental influence accounts for positive effects over and above that due to the use of rewards, coercion, or legitimacy. These findings do not mean that legitimate, coercive, or reward power can be omitted completely from the supervisor's repertoire of influence practices. It means that what differentiates the very effective supervisor from colleagues is the ability to use more than a formal role in relating to people.

The Need for Leadership

We may ask why an organization, once it has attained maturity, has any requirement for leaders, leadership, and influential increments. Does not the exertion of influence in the organization automatically flow from its structural properties rather than from the particular people who happen to be the role incumbents in the officer echelons? Why will the organizational system not roll on unchanged and unchanging in social space?

There are several answers to this question, including the necessary imperfections and incompleteness of the organization as a formal, abstract design; the changing external conditions under which every organization must operate; the changing internal state of the organization produced by separate dynamics of the several substructures of the organization; and finally, the special characteristics of human beings as occupants of organizational positions and fillers of organizational roles.

The Incompleteness of Organizational Design

The characteristic incompleteness and imperfection of organizational design is obvious whenever the organization chart and charter or

TABLE 16-1 Relationships Between Production Performance Measures and Supervisory Power

Production Performance Measure	SUBORDINATE WORK-GROUP'S MEAN PERCEPTION OF THE SUPERVISOR'S					
	Incremental Influence	Referent Power	Expert Power	Reward Power	Coercive Power	Legitimate Power
Indirect cost performance	.27*	.40[c]	.10	.15	.22	.00
Maintenance cost performance[a]	.12	.00	.18	-.20	-.30[b]	.10
Supply cost performance	.31*	.21	.32[b]	.31[b]	.08	.08
Scrap cost performance	.25	.33[b]	.13	.26	.12	.06
Performance vs. schedule	-.11	.05	-.21	-.06	.04	-.05
Quality	.36*	.32[b]	.31[b]	.13	-.08	.11
Average earnings	.01	.00	.01	-.40[c]	-.22	.05
Suggestions submitted	.28*	.36*	.14	.09	.40[c]	.10

Note.—Group means, $N = 40$.
[a] Mean for 29 groups used as measure for mean of remaining 11 groups.
[b] $p < .05$, one-tailed.
[c] $p < .01$, one-tailed.
From Kurt Student, 1968, p. 192.

the written policies of the organization are compared with the ongoing cycles of behavior that define the pattern of the "real" organization. For one thing, the actual behavior is infinitely more complex, inclusive, and variable than the plan. Everyone knows this. The new worker, after receiving from the personnel division the official version of a job and the policies which will affect his or her life, is brought to the group with which he or she will be working. The worker's first concern is to learn from the other members of the group how "things are really done," the unwritten but all-important facts of organizational life.

Another, and equally familiar, evidence of the insufficiency of the formal organizational plan is provided by a form of legal insubordination and sabotage which is occasionally employed by organization members. It consists merely in following the letter of organizational law, doing what is formally stipulated, but no more nor less. The jokes and comedies which present this theme in the military and in industry are numberless, and no audience misunderstands them.

Thus the secretary who has been ordered not to interrupt the boss dutifully refrains from announcing the arrival of an important visitor. The machine operator who has instructions to leave maintenance to the engineering staff continues to run an expensive and rapidly deteriorating piece of equipment. A transport-workers union, forbidden to strike, brings traffic to a state of near-disaster by following all instructions "on the books," regardless of their irrelevance or redundancy. Rules are by definition generalizations of some degree, and generalizations inevitably involve data reduction. The concrete case always needs something of interpretation and adaptation, embellishment or thoughtful omission.

Leadership as a Boundary Function

A specific aspect of the incompleteness of organization design can be found in the relationships between subsystems and in the relationship of the system to its environment. The articulation of parts or of the whole with its surround is not necessarily specified in the programmed arrangements. Leadership emerges as individuals take charge of relating a unit or subsystem to the external structure or environment. Where no formal role has been designated for a leader, an informal one arises especially for those at juncture points in the system (Herbst, 1962). Leadership is a boundary function, Rice (1963) contends, and is located at the borders where there is a break between parts of the system. The greater the break the more leeway there is for acts of leadership, as in the case of supervisors who are caught in the gap between management and workers. Rice (1963) concludes as follows:

> In general, if leadership is a boundary function, the relationship between a leader and his followers will depend to a major

extent on the leader's capacity to manage the relationships between the external and internal environments in a way that will
allow his followers to perform their primary task. (p. 210)

Changing Environmental Conditions

A second source of the organizational requirement for leadership
stems from the openness of the organization as a system, and from the
fact that it functions in a changing environment. Every open system is
affected by the environment in which it functions and with which it
engages in energic exchange. Since this environment is subject to
technological, legal, cultural, climatic, and many other kinds of
change, the organization is characteristically confronted with demands
that it change, too, in order to maintain its relationship with the environment or establish a new one on the terms now available. Thus a
systemic state or environmental relationship that was optimal initially
may become inefficient or completely unfeasible. The history of organizations (and of nations) is littered with the corpses of enterprises
that failed to respond appropriately to the demands of the environment
for change.

Many aspects of the relationship of organization to environment
are well represented in Lewin's (1951) concept of quasi-stationary
equilibrium. It is consistent with Lewin's exposition of such equilibria
that environmental fluctuations of certain kinds and amplitudes are
handled by the organization without any change in the organization
itself as a system. It absorbs and adjusts to the external change and
returns to the previous level of equilibrium. When an environmental
change exceeds this amplitude, the organization may nevertheless adjust to it, but it will undergo systemic change itself in the process and a
new level of equilibrium will be established with the environment. It is
adaptation of such scale that demands invention and creativity beyond
the performance of role requirements; it requires leadership of a high
order.

The Internal Dynamics of Organization

A third source of developing organizational imbalance and consequent need for system change stems from the internal dynamics of
organizations as systems. At the level of the organization as a whole,
one of the most important tendencies is the growth dynamic. Organizations as open systems show characteristic striving to insure survival by
extending their sovereignty over those parts of the outside world that
impinge on them. Those who have the greatest stake in the organization seek to secure it as a system. Yet this effort, paradoxically enough,
leads to demands for organizational change. When an organization
extends its control over the environment, new functions are added
within the organization itself; new complexities of structure are created

to provide for these functions; new needs for coordination with existing structures arise, and new policies must be invented.

At the level of organizational substructures, the internal tendency toward imbalance (and recovery) can also be observed. We have noted earlier the different dynamics of the several subsystems that make up the organization as a whole. (See Chapter 4.) For example, the efficiency dynamic of the production structure is in some opposition to the characteristic attempts of the maintenance structure to bind members into the organization and prevent them from leaving. A characteristic observation by production people is that the people in the personnel department would "give away the front gate" if they were not prevented from doing so by wiser heads, that is, by members of a substructure dedicated to a different organizational subgoal and permeated by a different dynamic (immediate efficiency in the productive process).

The result of such internal differences and organizational tendencies is not merely a continuing need for coordination and adjudication. It is persisting organizational change, internally and in relation to the environment, and a consequent need for additional complementary changes, in order to achieve a new balance and working structure.

The Nature of Human Membership in Organizations

A fourth and final reason why organizations, once launched, do not continue to spin unmodified in social space lies in the nature of human membership in organizations. The energic cycles that constitute organizational life are not free-floating, but of human origin and human embodiment. The organization is an open system with respect to its human maintenance aspects as well as to its production inputs. From this fact stem several characteristics of organizations, all of which militate against the maintenance of equilibrium without structural modification.

Only people can be members of an organization, but people are not only members of organizations, and above all not members of only one organization. Human membership in an organization is segmental in nature; it involves only a part of the person. Other activities and affiliations fill other hours, make demands on energies, gratify needs. These extraorganizational and other-organizational aspects of a person's life affect behavior of the person in the organization, and changes in these aspects of life produce changes in his or her behavior on the job. If such changes disrupt the organizational patterns of required behavior, they will necessitate some kind of complementary and adaptive change within the organization (modifications in rewards, penalties, and work content, for example).

We can also view the requirements for organizational change introduced by members of the organization in terms of individual change and development. People mature, age, and otherwise assimilate the continuing experience of living. In so doing they undergo changes in the pattern and intensity of their needs, motives, and characteristic responses. Each such change has organizational ramifications and represents a kind of extraorganizational source of demand that cannot be wholly predicted from organizational properties.

Closely related to such changes is the inevitable wearing out of the human part. Every organization member must be replaced at some time, and every replacement brings to the organizational role his or her unique experience and personality. Despite attempts to define organizational roles in such a way as to minimize the effects of turnover and replacement, these effects persist. Especially in the complex, demanding, and maximally influential roles in organization will the formal prescriptions necessarily stop short of the needed behavior and the unique attributes of the person effect ramifying organizational changes.

When the president of a large company retires and a successor is about to be named, what interest is generated over the specialty from which the new executive will come! This is a rational concern, a recognition that a former salesperson will have a concept of the job and of the organization different from that of a former engineer or accountant. In some degree every event of departure and replacement has its effects and requires adaptation on the part of the organization as well as the person who accedes to office. The process is uniquely important when there is a change in the head of state, as the national and international attention to such an event attests.

For all these reasons (systemic incompleteness of the formal organization, changing external conditions, the diverse dynamics of organizational subsystems, and the segmental nature of organizational membership) the organization functions under the continuing necessity of motivating the behavior required of its human members. Tools, machinery, equipment, the nonhuman components of organization, share with the human components a kind of mortality. They too wear out and must be replaced. But their specifications render them truly interchangeable; mass production was impossible until this condition was achieved. The processes of teaching and learning the organizational role, of mutual accommodation, and the property of performing only when motivated are peculiarly human. Much of leadership has to do with these processes and properties.

THE NATURE OF ORGANIZATIONAL LEADERSHIP: THREE BASIC PATTERNS

A consideration of the nature of organizational functioning clearly shows the sources of demand for leadership practices and the degrees of freedom for their exercise. In fact, organizational leadership, like other cases of the exertion of influence in complex social settings, is always a combined function of social structural factors and of the particular characteristics of the individuals making up the structure. And yet, social psychological literature is only beginning to take account of the operation of leadership processis in the real world, namely, within social systems (Fiedler, 1967 and Vroom, 1976).

Three basic types of leadership behavior occur in organizational settings: (1) the introduction of structural change, or policy formulation, (2) the interpolation of structure, that is, piecing out the incompleteness of existing formal structure, or improvisation, and (3) the use of structure formally provided to keep the organization in motion and in effective operation, or administration.

The origination of structure, or the initiation of structural change,[1] is the most challenging of all organizational tasks and rarely occurs without strong pressures outside the organization. Changes in market and competition can necessitate such changes. Selznick (1957) describes well the conversion of the Ford organization from the Model T to the Model A. This organizational change was a grudging and delayed response to a disastrous decline in sales. Retooling was extensive; whole factory interiors were altered as the huge single-purpose machines of the Model T era were removed. Turnover was tremendous; the conversion required 18 months and cost (in 1927) $100,000,000. In Selznick's view, the changes in human organization continued for a decade and a half, and only during the period of World War II did the Ford Company complete a reorganization in depth. Such changes in the formal structure of organization, the addition or elimination of major departments and the like, are easily observed.

Less apparent, and continuous rather than occasional, is the piecing out or interpolation of the existing formal structure. Every statement of organizational policy is by definition general and every problem is in some aspects unique. As a result, the formal structure of organization must be continuously and creatively embellished or pieced out. Every supervisor functions within the limits of formal policy, but within these limits he or she adds and improvises. For example, sergeants in the United States Army are notorious for their skill in developing their own structures for supplementing, bypassing, or cut-

---

[1]The Ohio State leadership studies (Fleishman, Harris, and Burtt, 1955) use the concept of *initiation of structures* in a different sense than that employed here. Their use applies to supervisory behavior that is task-oriented in contrast to *consideration* or behavior that is psychologically supportive. They do not deal with organizational structure in their concept of initiating structure but with the tendency of the supervisor to give directives to subordinates about the task to be performed. In our framework this would more often refer to the use of existing structure than to the creation of new structures.

ting through bureaucratic procedures for getting a job done. Such improvisation of structure is a second organizational means for preventing systemic failure.

Third, there is the use of already existing structure, the response of the organization as a system to some potential disruption that has been so fully foreseen that the corrective mechanisms and procedures are prescribed and built into the organization. Such acts are often seen as so institutionalized as to require little if any leadership. Nevertheless, existing organizational devices can be employed with varying degrees of frequency and intensity, with degrees of consistency and inconsistency, and with degrees of appropriateness to differing situations. Such differential uses of available organizational means will have consequences for the behavior and attitudes of rank-and-file members relevant to organizational functioning and thus constitute acts of leadership.

PATTERNS OF ORGANIZATIONAL LEADERSHIP AND HIERARCHICAL POSITION

The distribution of leadership acts is by no means random. Some positions (offices) are defined very largely in terms of expectations involving such influential acts. The presidency of a company is an example, and so is the office of first-level supervisor. The exercise of leadership by persons who occupy such positions is facilitated by the organizational resources (rewards, punishments) that are made available to them, and above all by the power of legitimacy, the implicit contract that each member makes to accept influence in prescribed matters from designated "leaders." The distribution of information in organizations follows a similar pattern, so that positions designated formally as offices of leadership receive information that increases the expertise of the occupants relative to those they are expected to lead.

There is a relationship between the three patterns of leadership we have described and the hierarchical levels of positions in the organization. Except in democratically constituted systems, only the top echelons of line and staff officers are really in a position to introduce changes in structure. The piecing out of structure is found most often in the intermediate levels of the organization. And the lowest supervisory level has open to it mainly the exercise of leadership by the skillful use of existing structure. In other words, the degree of freedom to supplement existing structure is not as great at the lowest officer level as it is at the second and third levels of command. And the freedom to originate, eliminate, and change organizational structure is not as extensive at the intermediate as at the top levels. It is true, of course, that the top level can exercise all three patterns of leadership, so that as we ascend the hierarchy we find more types of action available to the officer groups.

The exercise of these three patterns of organizational leadership also calls for different cognitive styles, different degrees and types of knowledge, and different affective characteristics. Hence the leadership skills appropriate to one level of the organization may be irrelevant or even dysfunctional at another level. The consistent and equitable employment of devices characteristic of the good administrator at the lowest level may be of little use to the policy maker at the top level.

This observation is congruent with the existing literature on personal factors associated with leadership. Personality traits related to leadership in one situation will not necessarily be predictive of leadership in other situations (Stogdill, 1948; Fiedler, 1967; Vroom, 1976). Important beginnings in the specific application of the relational approach have been made in the contingency theory of Fiedler (see pages 565–567). We shall turn, then, to a more careful examination of the cognitive and affective requirements of the three patterns of organizational leadership (see Figure 16-1).

COGNITIVE AND AFFECTIVE REQUIREMENTS OF THE THREE PATTERNS OF ORGANIZATIONAL LEADERSHIP

In general, our attempt to show some of the differences between the cognitive orientation and the affective style of the leader is congruent with the experimental findings that the two basic dimensions of the leader-follower relationship are task direction and socio-emotional supportiveness. In studying groups without formal leaders, Bales (1958) found that these two functions of progress toward the task goal and social support for members of the group invariably appeared, sometimes in the person of a single leader, but more often in separate people. Carter (1949, 1950, 1951) and other experimenters have confirmed these results. Moreover, Fiedler's (1958) enigmatic finding that the socially distant leader is more effective is readily understandable if his research investigations are scrutinized in terms of these two dimensions. In organized groups his task-directed and socially distant leaders were influential provided that the supportive function was handled by other means or through other leaders. In describing the methods of leadership associated with our three basic patterns, we shall examine first the cognitive or more task-oriented skill requirements, and second the appropriate affective orientation of the leader in relation to followers.

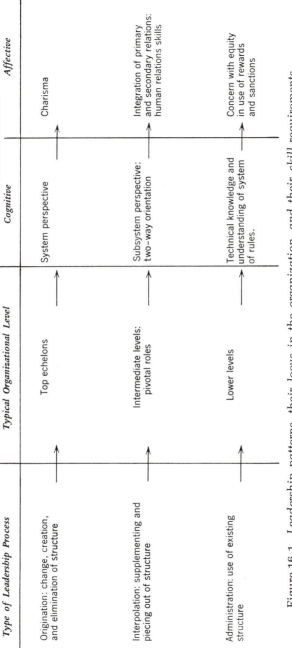

Figure 16-1 *Leadership patterns, their locus in the organization, and their skill requirements.*

Origination: Change, Creation, and Elimination of Structure

The major cognitive requirement for the origination or modification of organizational structure is *systemic perspective* and the major affective requirement is *charisma.*

Systemic Perspective

We have in mind two aspects of systemic perspective. One of these is external perspective, and has to do primarily with the complex which we may call organization-in-environment. This environment is made up in part of other organizations (agencies of government, competing organizations, labor unions, and the like) and in part of individual persons. Everyone who has lived the organizational life has experienced the differences among individuals in their ability to see, conceptualize, appraise, predict, and understand the demands and opportunities posed to the organization by its environment. Yet the intellective aspect of leadership has been neglected in research. Persuasiveness, warmth, and interpersonal skills are frequently urged as the essentials of leadership, but to what end? If a leader is seriously mistaken about the systemic requirements of the organization or the demands of its environment, his or her interpersonal abilities may become organizational liabilities. To be wrong and influential is organizationally worse than being merely wrong. It is better to be wrong and beloved than wrong and hated to boot, but interpersonal skill and organizational perspective are different attributes of leadership and largely independent of each other.

External perspective is thus in part a sensitivity to environmental demands, to the requirements that the organization must meet in order to maintain a state of equilibrium with its environment. In part external perspective involves a sensitivity to environmental opportunities, to the possibilities of achieving a more advantageous relationship with the environment. Finally, external perspective requires sensitivity to trends and changes in the environment, which is characteristically in a state of movement both with respect to the demands it makes on organizations and the opportunities it affords to them.

To some extent, then, external perspective is a matter of obtaining information about the organizational environment. At least as important, however, is the understanding of environmental factors, the successful relating of facts in the environment to facts about the organization. This process in turn permits forecasting the probable effects of different courses of action and consequent choosing among them. The importance of external perspective increases as one ascends the hierarchy of organization. Mann (1964), whose trilogy of technical, interpersonal, and conceptual skills emphasizes some of the same points as our discussion of system perspective, has proposed that in the upper managerial levels the conceptual abilities of the manager considerably overshadow in importance technical skills and skills in human relations. This has also been the emphasis in decision theory (Cyert and March, 1963) with respect to the systematic and quantitative assessment of variables affecting judgment.

In most organizations a review of the important executive decisions of any year makes immediately apparent the importance of external perspective. The decision to merge or to resist merger, to make a major change in location or to maintain a present position, to launch an entirely new line of products or to stay with the traditional items, to be the first with a new manufacturing process or to wait until others attempt it—these are the kinds of issues that demand the greatest understanding of the environment on the part of management. They are also the kinds of issues that will make the difference between successful and unsuccessful competition, between growth and stagnation, survival and failure. Lack of such perspective has led once successful companies to persist in the production of conventional washing machines when the whole market was about to become automatic, or to persist in the use of slow and elegant letterpress printing when the techniques of photo-offset were about to create entire new markets. A striking example of a failure to adapt on an industrywide national scale is the Swiss watch industry. It almost missed the transition from a mechanical to an electronic basis and has been desperately trying to catch up in recent years.

It is, of course, easy to speak of the organization in relation to its environment when such appraisals are made in retrospect. The test of external perspective is the ability to make appraisals on a predictive basis. This predictive test cannot be rejected by the leadership of any organization. To reject it is to fail it, and in the long run every leadership group is judged by the criterion of external perspective.

The concept of internal system perspective is analogous in many ways to the notion of external perspective. Every organization, itself a system, consists in turn of subsystems. These subsystems have different needs, and the people in them manifest characteristically different kinds of strivings. It is an unavoidable function of leadership to attempt to integrate and harmonize these subsystem differences; indeed, coordination and control of subsystems are essential functions of the managerial subsystem as described in Chapter 3. To perform these functions successfully requires constant awareness and perceptiveness of the changing requirements of the subsystems and their populations.

Consider, for example, the production structure and the ancillary structures of a typical business organization (sales, engineering, personnel, and others). It is inherent in the conditions of the private market and in the division of labor represented within the organization that these subsystems shall have somewhat different needs and goals. Thus the manufacturing division judges a product design very largely on the efficiencies of production it permits. The sales division, on the other hand, is in direct touch with the consuming public and will be more concerned with meeting the preferences of consumers than with conforming to production requirements about which its members are likely to be very little informed. For the management which must integrate the different strivings of these and other subsystems, interpersonal skills are useful, but somewhat more than interpersonal skills is required. The management will be more effective if it understands the dynamics, needs, and potential of these subsystems, and if it can express that understanding in terms of organizational structure. Interpersonal abilities may help management to get the appropriate data into its hands, but this function is additional to and separable from internal perspective on the nature of the system.

When internal strain threatens the integrity of an organization, as in the case of universities during the sixties, leaders have difficulty in maintaining systemic perspective on their problems. Accommodation of conflicting interests of subsystems is important but it can lead to concessions to the most demanding groups to be followed by concessions to their competitors. The leader becomes the target of influence rather than the agent of influence as each side mobilizes its forces for the next round of the struggle to gain more than in the last round. Blau (1964) has pointed out that leadership derives from the exchange process in which the leader acquires political capital by doing something for subordinates. But when concessions are won by exerting pressure on the leader, subordinates feel no obligation toward the leader but rather heighten the search for points of weakness in the leader's personality or position. As leaders play the role of the mediator or referee they lose referent power and, like umpires, their character is impugned, their ability is disparaged, and even their eyesight is questioned. To maintain perspective calls for the capacity to make empirical adjustments without compromising basic principles.

The leader with systemic perspective about the internal functioning and the external relations of the organization understands the nature of the symbols and values both of the larger organization and of its subsystems. Many of these symbolic values are associated with sacred prerogatives such as the right to manage in industry or academic freedom within a university. Effective leadership takes account of these symbols and avoids their arousal when dealing with issues internal to the organization. Threats to symbolic values can lead to bitter conflict between parts of the organization. Hence the wise course is to deal with the practical realities and skirt the symbolic issues. The organizational statesman avoids ideological struggles within the system, except as a last resort. Such conflicts are not only divisive, but are difficult to mediate and lasting in their effects. Issues of practical interest can be handled more readily through compromise and negotiation. This avoidance of symbolic struggle, however, refers only to feuds within the organization. The values of the system may be involved effectively in mobilizing the structure against the outside world.

Among theorists of leadership, the importance of systemic perspective, external and internal, has been best recognized and explicated by Selznick (1957). It is at the heart of his distinction between institutional leadership and mere administrative efficiency.

For Selznick, the institutional leader is the unique possessor of system perspective, and it is this quality which distinguishes him or her from the leader who is merely an interpersonal adept. Institutional leaders are concerned with policies as well as with persons; they are concerned with content as well as with process. They are concerned, as Selznick puts it, with the dynamic adaptation of the total organization to its own internal strivings and to its external pressures. There may be only two or three decisions in the course of a year that demand perspective on this level, but Selznick argues that they are crucial, and that their quality is quite independent of the human relations skills of the manager and of the psychological glamor that he or she may possess. These are decisions which insure the survival of the organization and avoid unintended corruption of organizational aims. Management that is unable to rise to the challenge of such decisions retreats either to technology or to the uninformed practice of human relations. By contrast, Selznick argues, the leadership that deals successfully with the dynamic adaptation of the total organization to internal striving and external pressures is alone truly creative. It is, in his terms, "beyond efficiency." Such leadership is characterized by "an institutional embodiment of purpose, by a clear definition of organizational mission, and by the adaptation of organizational policy to take into account the achievement of that mission in the context of the conditions presented by the environment and by the internal life of the organization."

The Subordination of Structure

One measure of systemic perspective is the ability of the management to act on such perspective, to change the organizational clientele, its own personnel, or its policy if the demands of the environment require these things. In terms of the three basic functions of leadership that we described earlier—the use, interpolation, and origination of structure—the emphasis of effective leadership is away from the unvarying use of existing structure and toward the origination of structure. Such leadership manifests the ability to change in response to external demands for change. To put it another way, the subordination of structure means that leaders assert freedom from the requirements of existing structure; they propose to use structure for the achievement of organizational goals, rather than to be used by it. Thus they can change existing structures either in the social or technical systems. Technology as well as social arrangements can be subordinated to system objectives.

Perhaps the outstanding example of the subordination of structure in our time was provided by Franklin Delano Roosevelt. His creation of new agencies of government produced an alphabet of bureaucracy and became a joke in the hands of his friends and enemies. The central truth, however, was that the government was taking on new functions, especially during the early years of the New Deal, and that it had an overwhelming mandate to do so. To have attempted the accomplishment of these functions entirely within existing structures of government would have been extremely difficult, given the background and ideologies of the old-line government agencies. It was far wiser to permit the old-line agencies to remain in their mausoleums while new agencies of government, lodged in temporary quarters of all sorts, got on with the new and crucial jobs.

We are not advocating the subordination of structure as an unvarying good in the practice of leadership. We are asserting that one mark of effective leadership is the ability to subordinate structure when situational requirements are clear and popular support is adequate. The subordination of structure, in other words, is the behavior that flows reasonably from an adequate attainment of system perspective.

The importance of what we have called subordination of structure—a willingness to interpolate, alter, and originate structure—can be highlighted by imagining an organization led by people with the complete inability to make structures subordinate to the needs and mission of the organization. Such a leadership group would be destined forever to use the structure of the organization only as they had inherited it. The inability to alter and originate structure is perhaps an inconspicuous disease of leadership. Indeed, on most days the failure to subordinate structure to organizational needs would be superficially unobservable, and the leadership group might appear competent and blameless. Nevertheless, in the long run the disease is absolutely and certainly fatal to organizations.

An example of subordination of structure is the refusal of the top leader to be scheduled into deadlines of decision making by the established time patterns of organizational machinery. These constraints, though ordinarily essential, can in critical situations give the executive too little time to consider adequately alternative possible solutions. Unrelenting time pressure is what many high-ranking officials in government regard as their most trying experience. The political scientist Neustad (1960) has described this aspect of the presidency and has pointed out how Franklin D. Roosevelt became the master of the self-created deadline. Neustad writes:

> Not only did he [Roosevelt] keep his organizations overlapping and divide authority among them, but he also tended to put men of clashing temperaments, outlooks, ideas in charge of them. Competitive personalities mixed with competing jurisdictions was Roosevelt's formula for putting pressure on himself, for making his subordinates push up to him the choices they could not take for themselves. It also made them advertise their punches; their quarrels provided him not only heat but information. Administrative competition gave him two rewards. He got the choices and due notice, both.
> As a result he also got that treasure for a President, time to defer decision. By and large, his built-in competitions forced the choices to him early, or at least made him aware that they were coming. He, not others, then disposed of time to seek and to apply his own perspective. (1960, pp. 157–158)

As with other aspects of effective leadership, the importance of the ability to subordinate structure varies with the echelon of leadership. It is of particular importance at the apex of the organization. It varies also with the stability of the organizational environment and with the stage of the organization in its total life cycle. During periods of rapid environmental change or rapid development of the organization itself, the ability to modify and originate structure is of the greatest importance. During times of environmental stability and organizational maturity, the requirements for structural subordination will be minimal.

Charisma

Even the top organizational leader, who possesses legitimate power and controls rewards and sanctions, can mobilize more support for policies if he or she can generate charisma, that magical aura with which people sometimes endow their leaders (Weber, 1947). Charisma derives from people's emotional needs and from the dramatic events associated with the exercise of leadership. The critical period of a war and the dependence of people on their military leaders is productive of charisma. In less strenuous times bold and imaginative acts of leadership help to create a charismatic image of the leader.

Charisma is not the objective assessment by followers of the leader's ability to meet their specific needs. It is a means by which people abdicate responsibility for any consistent, tough-minded evaluation of the outcome of specific policies. They put their trust in their leader, who will somehow manage to take care of things. Charisma requires some psychological distance between leader and follower. Immediate superiors exist in the work-a-day world of constant objective feedback and evaluation. They are very human and very fallible, and immediate subordinates cannot build an aura of magic about them. Day-to-day intimacy destroys illusion. But the leader in the top echelons of an organization is sufficiently distant from the membership to make a simplified and magical image possible. Thus between the upper echelons of a system and its rank-and-file membership there may develop an emotional tie that is not accessible to the lower echelons of supervision.

The formulation of policy and the origination of structure represent the kind of leadership acts most appropriate to charismatic leadership. The great majority of people are not in a position to evaluate proposals for major organizational change in any detail. They may or may not want to see social changes, and they may be sound in their judgment of overall goals, but they will not often be knowledgeable about specific programs to attain these goals. Hence they will turn to the great leader whose character, strength, and skill give assurance that the problem will be solved.

This charismatic idealizing of the remote general in contrast to the realistic evaluation of the top sergeant does not mean that the top leader has only to emphasize distance from followers in order to achieve charisma. On the contrary, to achieve maximum emotional identification the leader must have what Brown (1936) called membership character in the group being led. The leader must be like followers in some readily perceptible ways so that a common bond can be formed.

Two criteria can be employed to produce operational measures of charisma: (1) the degree of emotional arousal among followers and (2) the global character of the leader's power as perceived by followers (Katz 1973). People feel intensely about the charismatic leader and they do not have a discriminating image of his or her strengths and weaknesses. Moreover, the hypothesis can be ventured that in a democratic society charisma has a negative as well as a positive side in that there will be those who hate as well as those who love the great leader. We might expect a well-defined U curve of affectivity with few persons assuming neutral positions in the case of the charismatic leader.

What, then, leads to such high emotion and such exaggerated beliefs about a leader? Two kinds of interpersonal relations are covered by the global concept of charisma. (1) Leaders may supply a wishful symbolic solution to the internal conflicts of followers in their persons or programs as in the mysticism of some religious and political leaders.

(2) The ability of the individual in realistically appraising people's conscious needs and formulating a clear program for achieving them may generate emotional excitement about the leader.

McFarland (1969) presents a similar interpretation to our first type of charisma in his account of Biblical history. He writes:

> Thus in times of value strain, a charismatic hero may appear whose psychological processes are paralleled by his public actions perhaps in a widely appealing resolution of a personality identity crisis that provides the critical decisions and values for a new social identity, thereby leading to social change through the establishment of new social structures infused with new ideology. (p. 175)

Similarly L. W. Pye (1961) uses Erikson's description of identity crisis (1958) as the key to the understanding of charismatic leadership in the political development of the emerging nations. The tribal bond and community ties lose their strength as old customs lose their meaning. People seek a new collective identity. The leader who articulates a new integration can become a symbol of national liberation.

The second type of charisma develops around the program of the leader as it is responsive to basic needs rather than around symbolic resolution of conflict. It is exemplified by the appeal of Franklin Roosevelt to the American working classes as he proposed plans for dealing with unemployment and social welfare.

Interpolation: Supplementing and Piecing Out of Structure

Origination of organizational structure refers to policy changes directly affecting formal structure. Interpolation or piecing out of structure refers to the development of ways and means for implementing existing policies and reaching existing organizational goals. As we leave the first line of supervision and move into the intermediate level of a hierarchy, we find that managerial roles often prescribe objectives without specifying every detail of the route to the objectives. Even where there is considerable prescription of the means, alternative courses are sometimes possible.

The critical task of the intermediate levels of management is to piece out the organizational structure, or guide subordinates to do so, in ways which optimize organizational functioning. On the cognitive side this involves some degree of internal system perspective, specifically technical know-how about tasks of the relevant subsystems and knowledge of their relationships with immediately adjacent subsystems. In terms of affective orientation, the basic requirement is the ability to integrate primary and secondary relationships. This type of orientation has been associated with human relations skills. The difficulty with the human relations concept, however, is that it is frequently used without reference to an organizational context. It does require some skill in human relations for a supervisor to become a parental figure for some employees, and such a relationship can be therapeutic in part for both parties. These facts do not in themselves imply organizational value; the relationship may be irrelevant for organizational functioning or may even impair organizational effectiveness. In referring to human relations skills we shall assume an organizational context and organizational goals and shall be mainly concerned with the integration of primary and secondary patterns, personal relationships and role-prescribed relationships.

Subsystem Perspective:
Two-Way Orientation of Leader

The middle ranges of management, to develop supplementary structure successfully, must face two ways in the organization. They must understand how those above them are likely to act because of their organizational position and how those below them are similarly motivated and limited by their placement in organizational space.

The area of freedom open to the middle management operator is neither as broad as superiors sometimes define it, nor as narrow as they view it when something goes wrong. The operator must understand the functioning of the subsystem and its contribution to the larger organization, so that he or she can work out the appropriate degrees of freedom for operations. If the division is counted on to raise productivity and the productivity does increase, the manager is not likely to meet with much censuring from above even if he or she pieces out existing structure in new and unconventional ways. Another important criterion in setting the degrees of freedom for middle management is the avoidance of organizational embarrassment with the outside world. This criterion is more difficult of assessment and generally has lower priority than getting results. A football coach is likely to be more concerned with winning games than with the possible unfavorable image of the university arising from overzealous recruiting practices or questionable procedures for keeping the team eligible.

In addition to assessing the area in which superiors will permit movement, middle managers must face toward the people below them. They must depend on subordinates for the efficient accomplishment of the subsystem task, and modifications in structure must be acceptable to subordinates. The echelons above may not inquire into tough and repressive measures, for example, but astute middle level officers will realize that such procedures are better for tightening existing organizational structure than for elaboration and improvisation. If they seek the productive advantages of reform rather than the tightening of controls, they need the ingenuity and sustained extra effort of those below them. Such behavior is not easily elicited by external pressure but flows from internalized motivations.

Another aspect of the two-way role of middle managers is their function of representing the needs of the people below them to superiors. In the first Michigan study of the Detroit Edison Company, Pelz (1951) found that supervisors following good human relations practices had no better morale and motivation in their units than supervisors following less desirable practices. When Pelz examined the supervisors in terms of their effectiveness in representing their men up the line, and controlled on this factor, then the anticipated correlation between worker morale and good supervisory relations was clear. The person in the middle, to be effective, must realize that he or she is in the middle and must relate effectively in both directions. Likert (1961) has emphasized the significance of this principle and has made it one of the foundation stones of his theory of management. According to this theory, every member of the organization, except at the very highest and lowest levels, should act as a linking pin between two levels of the organizational structure.

Subsequent research has raised questions about the generality of the Pelz findings about the critical importance of upward influence of the supervisor for the morale of workers. Wager (1965) examined both leadership style of supportiveness and hierarchical influence as they affected the attitudes of followers in eight areas: identification with the total organization, perceived solidarity of the work group, attractiveness of members of the work unit, job autonomy, promotional opportunity, lay-off equity, general work satisfaction, and intent to stay with the organization. Leadership style was measured by questions asked of employees about their supervisor's understanding of their problems, skill at handling people, clarity in letting them know what was expected of them, and so forth. Supervisory influence was measured by employee rating on how much an immediate supervisor could affect his or her superior. The upward influence of the supervisor was positively correlated with positive attitudes in most of the areas investigated but not as much so as the psychological supportiveness of the leader. Wager concludes that the greater the upward influence of the supervisor as perceived by the employee the more effective were the supervisor's human relations skills in improving morale; but he cautions that the differentials in effectiveness of differing degrees of skill for high and low upward influence are small. There are suggestions in Wager's research as to reasons for his not replicating all of the Pelz findings. For one thing Pelz did not ask about whether supervisors could influence superiors but whether they actually did go to bat for subordinates. On the issue of promotional opportunity, which is closer to the older research, Wager reports a similar relationship, namely, that for low influence supervisors the more supportive the leadership style, the less favorable are the attitudes of workers. For another thing, Wager was studying white collar workers (some 1,063 of them) and he himself states:

> "the hierarchical influence of lower level supervisors in the organization may be less important to this white-collar population because they identify the power to modify unsatisfactory working conditions at higher levels in the organization. These higher level orientations suggest that their immediate superiors may be perceived to be less crucial figures to these white-collar employees generally than they are to other types and levels of employees. . . . (p. 398)

Our observations about the intermediate levels of management have been made in part by other writers about the first level supervisor, the "man in the middle" between the officers and the workers. Often, however, in large organizations the real "men in the middle" stand higher in the organizational structure. The first level supervisor in many firms has too restricted an area of freedom to supplement structure or to deal effectively with superiors. We are directing our analysis to the levels in the organization where the emphasis in role definition is on objectives rather than on the means for accomplishing objectives—in Morse's terms, the pivotal organizational roles (1956). In some companies, of course, this will take us to first level supervisors.

The Representative Function

The two-way orientation of the leader can be seen clearly in political systems as the representative function in which elected officials must achieve some compromise between demands of constituents and the requirements of the system. They must make as strong a case as they can for their clientele and yet adjust to social realities so that they do not become ineffective. In meeting these essential requirements they may sacrifice their own beliefs and values about desirable policy, and their role may become that of the lawyer representing a client. In fact political leadership seems to favor the role of the lawyer more than that of the ideologue. The facts are that in Western democracies political leaders are frequently drawn from the ranks of the legal profession. The causal process is complex but lawyers do outnumber the members of any other profession in the parliaments of European democracies, in the

American Congress, or among governors of states in the United States (Blondel, 1963; Milbrath, 1965).

Not only is the representative function an acknowledged aspect of our political system, it also applies to nonpolitical organizations such as business enterprises, universities, and labor unions as indicated above. They are not that apolitical. If the leader is to perform a representative function the question arises as to whether he or she should not be elected directly by his constituents rather than appointed. Julian, Hollander, and Regula (1969) have investigated one aspect of this problem experimentally, namely endorsement of the elected compared to the appointed leader under conditions of success and failure and perceived high and low competence. The results of their laboratory study showed that electing leaders rather than making them more secure with followers makes them more vulnerable to censure. There were greater expectations for the elected person than for the appointed person. If appointed leaders achieved success they were favorably evaluated even if their competence was questioned. The elected leader had to be both competent and successful to be endorsed. It should be noted that the three factors of election—appointment, competence-incompetence, success-failure—were manipulated independently in the research design.

Integration of Primary and Secondary Relationships

The essence of good human relations practices in an organizational context is the integration of primary and secondary relationships, and the integration of the primary group with the larger secondary structure. Where such integration occurs, the norms of the work group are congruent with the norms of the organization, the paths for organizational success are the paths for individual achievement, and the organizational requirements are in themselves productive of member satisfaction, rather than an indirect means to such satisfaction. Obviously these achievements have little to do with such superficialities as calling workers by their first names or remembering the birthdays of their children. Let us define more closely what we mean by primary and secondary relations and consider their significance in organizational life.

Secondary relations in an organization are those interpersonal transactions required by organizational role. For example, the division of labor in most organizations makes the creation of the organizational product a highly coordinated, sequential business. The polisher in a washing machine factory cannot proceed with her task until the grinder has smoothed the aluminum casting and handed it on. The grinder must wait for the shake-out man, who knocks off some of the larger protuberances and disposes of the debris of molding and casting.

For each pair of roles so related, there are formal prescriptions in terms of which the interdependence is defined. This is equally true for formal leaders (supervisors, managers, and the like) and the people under their supervision. The relationship is defined by the prescriptions of the supervisory role and each complementary subordinate role. Typically the job description of the supervisory role will state the content areas in which the supervisor is to have jurisdiction over the subordinate, the activities which he or she will supervise, and the means (rewards and sanctions) by which his or her legitimate authority may be enhanced. The subordinate is given complementary information; the supervisor's legitimate rights appear as the subordinate's obligations. Such secondary relationships are in large part the stuff of which formal organizations are constructed; the properties of each office are defined in part in terms of obligations, expectations, and rights in respect to other offices. These relationships tend to be rational when viewed in the frame of reference of the defining organizational cycle of input-transformation-output and the intended organizational product.

Secondary relationships tend also to be universalistic rather than particularistic. The organizational presumption is that any occupant of a given office will be treated like all others who might occupy that office or similar ones. The military here, as in so many other respects, epitomizes the bureaucratic characteristic: salute the uniform, not the man. The supervisor who violates the universalistic aspect of role relations in organizations is accused of playing favorites, or worse. As for the subordinate whose behavior toward the supervisor becomes particularistic, there is a whole vocabulary of terms by which colleagues characterize the person, the behavior, and the relation to the supervisor.

Perhaps the most telling property of the secondary relationship is its alleged affect-free quality. The common assumption of organizational theory is that the role relationships in organizations imply no fear or delight in interdependence, no pleasure in giving rewards, no hatred in receiving punishment. In institutional society this aspect of human relationships is carried to extremes. Executioners are not required or expected to feel for the criminal either hatred or sympathy. Their job is to pull the switch.

The providing of help is no less transformed. We create roles and even entire social agencies to provide economic assistance, without any implication of affective bonds between helpers and helped, nor among those engaged in the common task of providing assistance. It must be said that the perfection of organizational role-taking as rationalistic, universalistic, and affect-free is more to be found in organizational theory than in organizational practice, and fortunately so. Nevertheless, practice and theory agree in this area to some extent. It follows from this definition of the secondary role relationship that the motivation for engaging in such relationships must be largely instrumental (for example, to earn wages) and not primarily intrinsic to the relationship. Indeed, the development of personally meaningful relationships in the work situation (significantly designated "informal") is a kind of triumph over bureaucratic requirements.

Primary relationships involve direct face-to-face interaction rather than remote organizational connections. They tend to be person-specific (particularistic) rather than universalistic, and they are affectively connected rather than rationalistically role-related. The relationships within families or among friends provide examples of what we mean by primary. In such cases the motivation to sustain the relationship is largely intrinsic to the activities jointly engaged in and the personal satisfactions derived therefrom.

The dichotomy between primary and secondary relationships, however, is a conceptual distinction which though useful is less than clear in the life situation. All roles are in some degree segmental, asking only for parts of people (part of their time, part of their skills, part of their interests). But people, despite their ability to compartmentalize and despite the schizoid character of modern life, are not essentially segmental. In a physical sense the segment of the person corresponding to a job role cannot report for organizational duty. The whole person is either present or absent, and with the physical self necessarily arrive all that person's psychological properties, potentialities, and uniquenesses. Organizations (as systems of rational-legal authority) operate specifically by controlling and reducing that variability of human behavior which directly expresses idiosyncratic motives and needs.

The inherent conflict between individual needs and organizational requirements is handled in part by emphasizing the separation of the requirements of organizational roles from the nonrole motives of affective, moral, or other origin. The vocabulary of bureaucracy is rich with the disavowals of primary motives in secondary relationships. "Nothing personal, but. . . ." "I am sorry to have to do this, but. . . ." "Business is business." "I have my job to do too, you know." The common meaning of these and similar expressions is: your primary needs are about to be disregarded. As we have said, the separation of primary from secondary relationships works in part. Some people even resent in organizational life the invoking of values which they would approve outside. Outside the organization, for example, we do not necessarily consider it immoral that a people should be given some special financial assistance simply because they need it, nor that we should behave differently toward people according to the affection which we bear toward them.

Even in formal organizational roles, however, people respond affectively to support and approval, as they do to punishment and restriction. Their behavior in role therefore is always a mix of role-determined and other-determined characteristics. We have already noted that a persistent characteristic of effective leadership is the use of referent power, a kind of power that depends on a bond of liking and respect (primary relationship) and is not a role-given characteristic.

There is ample evidence also that informal relationships in the work situation may be powerful enough to enhance greatly the performance of the organization or to impede substantially its ability to accomplish the formal mission. The classic and perhaps the first quantitative demonstration of this phenomenon was provided by Roethlisberger and Dickson (1939) in the course of experiments at the Western Electric Company. They found systematic, group-determined restriction of individual production in the manufacture of telephone equipment, a type of finding that has often been corroborated in the subsequent research literature. (Coch and French, 1948; French and Zander, 1949; Dubin, 1951; Viteles, 1953; Whyte, 1955; Argyris, 1957).

Roethlisberger and his colleagues also discovered at Western Electric an outstanding example of informal group structure acting to enhance production. Under a variety of physical circumstances the experimental groups at the Hawthorne Plant showed increases in productivity that were at first baffling but were ultimately interpreted as an experimental side-effect deriving from improved interpersonal relations.[2] In the years since the Hawthorne experiments a long line of research has added to the evidence that group solidarity and loyalty is sometimes associated with productivity and effectiveness. (Katz and Kahn, 1952; Merton and Lazarsfeld, 1950; Argyris, 1957).

Moreover, several studies have been conducted that bring into the same schema and situation both kinds of group effects—enhancement and impedance of larger organizational goals. Seashore's (1954) research demonstrates that the most direct and consistent effect of group cohesiveness (attraction of the individual to the group) is on the *variance* of the behavior of members, rather than on the energic or productive level of that behavior. Members in cohesive groups adhere more closely to group norms, and other factors (the behavior of leaders, the structure of rewards, and the degree of supportiveness in the organi-

---

[2]For a discussion of the so-called Hawthorne effect see Chapter 18 on organizational change.

zation as a whole) determine whether those group norms will exceed, equal, or fall below the formal production demands of the organization. Similar findings are reported by Zaleznik (1958) and his colleagues.

The conclusion urged on us is that the most effective leader in a pivotal organizational role is not the perfect bureaucrat (rational, role-actuated, heedless of primary bonds), but rather the successful integrator of primary and secondary relationships in the organizational situation. This means not only that the successful leader mediates and tempers the organizational requirements to the needs of persons, he or she does so in ways that are not organizationally damaging and, indeed, are organization-enhancing. Such leaders promote group loyalty and personal ties. They demonstrate care for persons as persons. They rely on referent power rather than on the power of legitimacy and sanctions alone. They encourage the development of positive identification with the organization and create among peers and subordinates a degree of personal commitment and identification. They do these things by developing a relationship with others in the organization in which they introduce what might be termed primary variations on the secondary requirements of organization. Within limits these leaders adapt their own interpersonal style to the needs of other persons. In so doing, they generate among members of the group a resultant strength of motivation for the achievement of group and organizational goals which more than compensates for occasional bureaucratic irregularities. The secondary role requirements remain the dominant figure in the behavior of leaders, but they appear on a background of, and are embellished by, an attention to primary interpersonal considerations. According to Kahn (1964) and his colleagues, when people are asked how they themselves would like to be treated by those above them in the hierarchy, they reply in terms consistent with the pattern of primary-secondary integration, rather than in the impersonal language of secondary relationships.

The motivational effects of such an integration of primary and secondary relationships tie into the patterns important in leading a person to enter an organization, remain in it, and perform satisfactorily the requirements of the role to which he or she has been assigned (Chapter 13). One of these patterns has to do with acceptance of legitimate authority and fear of sanctions. Another stems from the fact that the performance of the organizational role is instrumental to need gratification in the life of the person both inside and outside the organization.

Still other possibilities for motivating a person to membership and role performance depend on the satisfactions inherent in the performance of the task itself. Traditional theories of organization, with their emphasis on external rewards and control, and their relative disregard for informal interpersonal relations and for the intrinsically rewarding properties of the job, represent a clear and restricted emphasis on the first two of these motivational patterns. More recently, the literature of management has paid some attention to the intrinsically satisfying aspects of the job, although this attention has for the most part taken a perverse form. The perversion consists in making an ideology of the importance and psychological rewardingness of work, rather than considering what definition of the job might make it directly experienced as satisfying and rewarding. Concern with image has been greater than concern with structural reality. There has been a more realistic attempt to correct the situation in the movement concerned with the redesign of jobs to make for job enrichment in both the vertical and horizontal expansion of work roles.

The most effective formal leaders bridge the gap between primary and secondary relationships in many ways, and in so doing enhance all three of the motive patterns described above. With respect to the instrumentality of the job for other groups and affiliations, effective leaders are positive and accepting. In dealing with subordinates they acknowledge these primary relations to which the job is secondary. They manifest interest in subordinates' off-the-job life, without insisting on information that they have not earned.

With respect to the instrumentality of the job for gratifying social needs in the work situation, effective supervisors are accepting and constructive. They regard the value of the group to each individual as a potential asset rather than a bureaucratic irrelevancy or a threat to authority. As a result, they devote a good deal of effort to creating a cohesive work group, a group in which each member finds the fact of membership rewarding. They permit, encourage, and may even model informal interaction. They use task-relevant decisions as opportunities to build the group. In short, they deviate from the bureaucratic ideal by endowing the relationships in the work group with a primary quality, making them valuable and valued for themselves.

This is admittedly a difficult feat within a conventional bureaucratic structure, since it implies some conflict with the depersonalized, affect-free ideal of the bureaucratic relationship. The conflict, however, is more with the petty requirements of organizational life than with the overall goals of organizational effectiveness, and many leaders manage a tolerable compromise. The human-relations fraud, of course, is the bureaucrat who professes primary concerns for members of the group without feeling for them and without any willingness to acknowledge their modifying claims on bureaucratic protocol.

Finally, effective pivotal leaders make the task requirements themselves more satisfying by permitting greater autonomy and influence by members of the group. This constitutes a revision in some degree of the requirements themselves. In all these ways the effective leader merges the secondary aspects of organizational life with the primary qualities of "chosen" interpersonal relationships. The construction of cohesive, close, informal relationships built around the achievement of organizational goals adds materially to worker motivation and organizational effectiveness.

Administration: Use of Existing Structure

In discussing the initiation of structure and the piecing out of structure we have emphasized major acts of organizational leadership, attempts to meet challenges to organizational functioning and survival. Much more common, particularly as we move down the organizational hierarchy, are those lesser acts of leadership that use existing organizational devices and follow established organizational rules.

Routine directives and routine compliance fall near the zero point on the continuum of leadership, but for the most part they meet the definition; they involve influence on matters of organizational relevance. Only when the influence attempt is completely ineffective, or redundant because compliance is forthcoming anyway, does administration lose all its leadership properties. Moreover, the utilization of existing rules and regulations for exercising influence is never wholly mechanical; it can be judged in terms of consistency and appropriateness. Administration is the least of the levels of leadership, but administration can be sloppy or efficient, helpful or saturated with officiousness.

Technical Know-How

Because such distinctions are possible, the concept of influential increment is appropriate with respect to administration, as it is to those levels of leadership which we have called interpolation and origination of structure. The use of legitimate structure to produce an influential increment depends on the supervisor's technical knowledge of the tasks, understanding of the rules, and concern with fairness, consistency, and equity in their application. Technical know-how and understanding of the legal system are primarily cognitive attributes; concern with equity is an affective orientation.

Knowledge of the technical aspects of the job to be done enables administrators to make judicious use of the personnel and resources under their command. Part of their responsibility is to see that their people have an adequate flow of materials, proper tools for doing the work, and appropriate directives on how to apply their energies. In a study of railroad section gangs, Katz, Maccoby, Gurin, and Floor (1951) found that the foremen whose work groups were superior in productivity were the foremen with greater technical competence in the relevant task. They supplied expert technical direction to the work of the group. A later study in heavy industry (Kahn and Katz, 1960) corroborated this finding, as do the studies in power plants done by Mann and Hoffman (1960).

Equity and Rule Enforcement

In addition to technical skills the administrator must also understand the system of rules and be concerned with the effects of their application. The strength of a legal system depends in practice on two factors: (1) equity or the use of rewards and penalties in a clear, consistent, fair manner and (2) a reasonable consideration of the law in terms of spirit as well as letter.

Equity in the application of rules does not mean that the rules themselves must be completely equitable; it does mean that it is not the individual as an individual who is rewarded or penalized. Suppose that a rule of seniority accords extra vacation to employees after five years in the organization. The rule may seem inequitable from some points of view because one person may have put in five years of outstanding service and another person five years of marginal performance. Nevertheless, once such rules exist, they must be applied consistently, so that people will know where they stand and what they can expect. Personal favoritism and prejudice of superiors thus will not affect their fortunes. Moreover, even where the rules do not provide specifically for equity with respect to a given treatment, the good administrator acts in accordance with this principle. A new employee may be brought in at a high salary because of the competitive labor market. The administrator must then fight for higher salaries for older employees of equal competence.

The importance of adherence to rules as a matter of equity is borne out by the research of Kahn (1964c) and his colleagues on role conflict. In a study of six industrial organizations they found extremely widespread convictions that each member of the organization "should obey the rules of his organization and follow orders. . . . He should treat other members of the organization according to generally acceptable standards (universalistically), rather than according to their individual relationship to him (particularistically)." These convictions were particularly strong among people of supervisory responsibility and long tenure. Moreover, in those situations in which the norms of rule orientation and universalism were relatively weak, role conflict and job-related tensions were almost twice as prevalent.

The second requirement for the successful use of structure concerns a contextual rather than a literal interpretation of rules. Administrative decisions should take into account not only the sentence in the book but the context in which it appears. The meaning of the rule is furnished by the larger framework, which often includes rule relevance to organizational functioning. Literal interpretations lead to ritualism and officiousness. Traffic officers in crowded urban centers, for example, cannot afford such practices. They have to keep traffic moving and to do so they must be less concerned with minor, irrelevant infractions of the traffic code than with positive directives to avoid traffic snarls.

TWO IMPORTANT FUNCTIONS OF LEADERSHIP: TASK DIRECTION AND PSYCHOLOGICAL SUPPORTIVENESS

A basic distinction made in this volume concerns maintenance and production functions of social systems, between holding the group together as an organized group and getting it to perform at acceptable levels. In Chapter 3 we pointed out the necessity for taking account of maintenance inputs as well as production inputs and called attention to Cattell's use of the concepts of maintenance synergy and productive synergy (1951) as referring to the energy required to keep the group together and the energy required to get the job done. We have already called attention to the work of Bales (1958) and Bales and Slater (1955) in empirically verifying these two group functions and in showing that experimental groups without formal leaders soon develop task leaders concerned with the production process and socio-emotional leaders concerned with furnishing social support for group members. Occasionally the same individual will combine the two functions but, generally, the task-oriented leader is not socially supportive and vice versa. What is essential, however, is that both functions be carried out for groups to maintain cohesion and to perform effectively.

The interesting fact is that industrial psychologists have tended to overlook the necessity of both the socio-emotional and the production functions of leadership. The human relations approach, as developed in the work of McGregor and Argyris, has emphasized the supportive aspects of leadership and has assumed that increasing this type of influence will automatically increase performance. But the early research of Fiedler (1958) has shown that the socially distant leader often has a more effectively performing group than the socially close leader. The first interpretation of these findings was that it is more important for the leader to be task-oriented and uninvolved with subordinates. But closer scrutiny of the Fiedler work on the distance between the head and workers reveals that in addition to the production-directed leader there was a socially supportive leader at another level in the system. Where both functions were adequately in motion the groups did well. This led Fiedler to a more theoretical analysis of group functions in which he developed his contingency theory of leadership presently to be discussed.

The many and frequently inconsistent findings of the Ohio leadership studies are also accounted for by a theoretical framework that recognizes the importance of both maintenance and production functions. These studies were grounded in an empirical approach to leadership in which separate scales were developed to measure *initiation of structure* (basically task orientation) and *consideration* (basically socio-emotional support). "A good deal of the research that has grown out of the human relations movement" observes Tannenbaum (1977), "has employed measures that are conceptually akin (if not operationally identical) to consideration and initiation of structure— e.g., supportive vs. punitive supervision, employee vs. production centered supervision, general vs. close supervision. . . "

Since it is commonly assumed that there is only one leader in a social system, much of this research was directed at finding out whether the leader was primarily task-oriented or socially supportive and then looking at the performance and satisfaction of subordinates. Since any social system must embody both processes this empirical approach with its either-or assumption predictably led to conflicting results. Adherents of the Ohio school have accordingly remedied their atomistic point of view. The volume of work with the Ohio scales measuring leadership justifies a closer examination of the research associated with interaction of structure and consideration (Stogdill and Coons, 1957).

The scale measuring consideration is appropriately labeled and reflects the socially supportive activities of the leader as studied in morale research. The eight sample items which follow give the flavor of the dimension under investigation:

CONSIDERATION

He does personal favors for group members.

He refuses to explain his actions. (Reverse scoring)

He backs up members of the group.

He acts without consulting the group. (Reverse scoring)

He treats all members of the group as his equals.

He is friendly and approachable.

He demands more than we can do. (Reverse scoring)

He rejects suggestions for changes. (Reverse scoring)

Thus consideration is defined as reflecting "the extent to which an individual is likely to have job relationships characterized by mutual trust, respect for subordinates' ideas, and consideration for their feelings" (Fleishman and Peters, 1962). Initiation of structure is not, however, as clearly labeled and deals with what is generally known as the task orientation or production centeredness of the leader as the following sample items indicate.

INITIATING STRUCTURE

He schedules the work to be done.

He maintains definite standards of performance.

He emphasizes the meeting of deadlines.

He encourages the use of uniform procedures.

He lets group members know what is expected of them.

He sees to it that the work of the group is coordinated.

He encourages overtime work.

He offers new approaches to problems.

The definition of the scale is consistent with these items, "the extent to which an individual is likely to define and structure his role and those of his subordinates toward goal attainment" (Fleishman and Peters, 1962). The difficulty is with the term *initiating structure*, for most of the items in the scale have to do with the use of existing structure. Most organizational positions of leadership, except those at the top, supply the structure that people who occupy those positions can use whether or not they do so effectively, but this is a different skill than the ability to improvise and create structure as we have previously noted. The failure to distinguish between the use and creation of structure limits the usefulness of the Ohio State scales. It is also true that *consideration* is not a unitary dimension. At least two components can be distinguished, namely, warmth and friendliness toward associates and a willingness to stand up for them in organizational struggles. A significant but neglected study of relevance is the investigation of Pelz (1951) of the employees in a large public utility cited on page 549. Pelz found that the supervisors perceived to be reliable and effective fighters for their subordinates had work groups of higher morale than supervisors who merely had a friendly smile or kind word.

The Ohio State scales have seen some revision and their psychometric properties have been examined by Schriesheim and Kerr (1974). These investigators report that the scales show acceptable reliability with respect to internal consistency and, in the case of one version, the Leader Opinion Questionnaire, acceptable test-retest reliability. But on content validity three of the four versions are unacceptable and both their construct and predictive validity are unknown qualities. Schriesheim and Kerr conclude, however, that despite the shortcomings of the scales some consistent patterns of findings have begun to emerge. An early review of the use of these scales (Korman, 1960) was less optimistic. Korman reported methodological difficulties, ambiguous findings, and a lack of specification of contingent variables.

The review of Kerr and Schriesheim (1974) is much more hopeful of cumulative knowledge and finds a number of studies that explore moderating variables affecting the relationship between leadership behavior and subordinate performance. Kerr and Schriesheim, moreover, call attention to the interesting question of the direction of causality between the behavior of the leader and the behavior of the follower. They cite two experimental studies and four field studies (see Table 16-2) that are directed at measuring the change in one set of variables after a change in the other. These studies demonstrate that we are dealing with a circular pattern of causality, as in many social event series. A poorly performing worker may encourage directive behavior from the supervisor and in turn a closely supervised employee can suffer in motivation to perform. Which comes first, the chicken or the egg, is scarcely the appropriate inquiry when we have mutually reinforcing processes. What is appropriate is the query of under what conditions the circle can be broken through, for example, can the poor performance be raised by some combination of task direction and of social support? Research in the future should deal with the problem of such systemic self-reinforcing cycles but to date the problem has been only lightly touched in the linear thinking prevalent in the conventional approach.

It is widely recognized that cross-sectional correlational studies are limited with respect to causal inference, but conventional uses of experimental design and of cross-lagged correlations also fail to illuminate fully these mutually reinforcing systemic processes. A well-designed experiment may establish one direction of causal flow, but that fact does not exclude the reciprocal process—although it is usually

TABLE 16-2 Studies Attempting to Establish Causality by Using Longitudinal or Experimental Designs

Study	Methodology	Major Findings
Longitudinal Cummins, 1972	LOQ forms were administered prior to ratings of performance, while ratings of Consideration and Initiating Structure were taken simultaneously with ratings of performance	Leader-member relations moderated relationships between LOQ attitude scores (particularly for Initiating Structure) and work group performance.
Greene, 1973	Employed cross-lagged panel correlational techniques and dynamic correlational analysis. Collected LBDQ and performance data from managers and subordinates, on three occasions, each approximately one month apart	Subordinate performance was found to cause both leader Consideration and leader Structure. Consideration was found to cause subordinate satisfaction, but no significant relationships were discovered between Structure and satisfaction.
Experimental Dawson et al., 1972	Consideration and Initiating Structure (measured by the SBD questionnaire) were experimentally manipulated by teachers	Both Consideration and Initiating Structure produced positive effects upon the productivity of work group (student) members.
Lowin and Craig, 1968	Experimentally varied the performance of subordinates, and observed effects upon subsequent leader behavior	High-performing confederates evoked high-Consideration low-Initiating Structure behavior, while low performers generated low Consideration and high Structure.
Lowin et al., 1969	Manipulation of Consideration and Initiating Structure by writing "scripts" for supervisors, using phrases taken from the SBD form	Level of Consideration did not affect perceived level of Structure, but perceived Structure level did affect perceptions of Consideration. Consideration affected productivity, quality, and job satisfaction, but no significant relationship was found between Structure and productivity.
Hand and Slocum, 1972	Employed "human relations" training to change Consideration scores (as measured by both the LOQ and SBD questionnaire)	Increased Consideration yielded significantly better performance (measured by superior ratings taken 18 months later).

From Kerr and Schriesheim, 1974, p. 562.

Note: LOQ = Leadership Opinion Questionnaire; LBDQ = Leader Behavior Description Questionnaire; SBD = Supervisory Behavior Description.

assumed to do so. Similarly, the usual interpretation of differences between cross-lagged correlations, namely, pairs of variables at two or more points in time, has been that the direction of causality runs exclusively as given by the larger of two "diagonal" correlations. There is no adequate substitute for experimentation in which the proposed intervention in an ongoing system of interacting variables is tested directly.

One small study of 54 respondents from 18 units of a national black service organization is suggestive in its use of consideration as a moderating variable. Schriesheim and Murphy (1976) found that supervisors giving more directions had lower performing subordinates when they were low in the use of consideration but higher performing subordinates when they were high in consideration. This is consistent with our generalization that both aspects of leadership are essential and it supports an earlier study of Fleishman and Harris (1962). The conclusion of the Fleishman-Harris investigation was that the task emphasis of the leader can be threatening when he or she is not considerate, but helpful when he or she is socially supportive.

Schriesheim and Murphy (1976) also investigated job stress and unit size in their work on the national black service organization as contingent conditions with respect to types of leadership behavior. They report that when people have anxieties about the job situation, task direction correlates positively with performance but where anxiety is low, task direction has a negative relationship to performance and consideration has a positive relationship. In other words, where people find the job stressful they do better when the leader takes more active responsibility for directing the task. The results are similar to those of Halpin (1954) and Fleishman, Harris, and Burt (1955). There was also some suggestive evidence in the Schriesheim and Murphy work in the black service organization that unit size acted in the same way as job stress. Consideration was more important in small than in large units in its relationship to performance.

Our central thesis that both socio-emotional and task leadership are necessary for effective organizational functioning has ample support in the history of research and theory on the problem. Likert (1961) has included supportive and task-oriented functions in his theory of management in having the superior provide high standards of performance together with strong psychological support. Halpin and Winer (1957), after examining some of the studies on initiation of structure and consideration, thought that effectiveness would result from a combination of both styles of leadership rather than an emphasis on only one. Blake and Mouton (1964) have similarly maintained that the key to organization success is a combination of concern for people and an interest in production.

It is of interest that the same conclusion was reached by Misumi and Tasaki (1965) as a result of their research. The first studies of Misumi (1960a, 1960b) showed that low producing groups were led by employee-centered supervisors and high producing groups by production-oriented supervisors. But a further examination of the situation revealed that in the high producing groups more than in the low producing groups the second-line supervisors were employee centered. In fact Misumi found that among 500 coal getters the low producing groups were likely to have first- and second-line supervisors who both were concerned only with production problems. As in Fiedler's work (1967) the relationship between productivity and task-oriented leaders was sustained by the socio-emotional function being carried by other levels of the organization. Misumi and Sharakashi (1966) put this proposition to experimental test by creating an organization in which subjects or workers counted holes in IBM cards under the guidance of other subjects designated as supervisors. The supervisory style of the leaders was experimentally manipulated and subjects assigned at random to work groups. Again the workers who were the most productive functioned in groups in which there was emphasis on human relations as well as on the task.

The Fiedler Contingency Theory
In his theoretical analysis and programmatic research Fiedler (1967) has given us the most comprehensive account of the determinants of leadership effectiveness. In his early work, as has been noted, he found instances of the importance of the task orientation of the leader but closer observation showed that the socio-emotional function was not lacking in productive groups. In a 15-year program of research, which included experiments and field studies in a variety of governmental and industrial settings, he broadened variables under investigation to cover three contingent conditions: structure of the task to be performed, the power position of the leader, and the relationship between leader and group members. He then examined the effects of his original variable of social distance on group performance under various combinations of these conditions. In all this would have called for studies of eight sets of conditions and Fiedler was successful in carrying out investivations in all but one combination of contingencies— namely for a well-structured task, with a poor power position of the leader and poor relations with group members.

Fiedler's measure of supportiveness of the leader is either the assumed similarity of opposites (ASo) or Least Preferred Co-worker (LPC). The ASo asks the subject to rate his or her most preferred co-worker and least preferred co-worker on a number of personality characteristics such as helpfulness and friendliness. The score is based on the averaged difference of these ratings and a high difference score indicates a low assumed similarity between opposites and reflects a nonsupportive orientation. The LPC is the score derived from the description of the least-preferred co-worker and is a component of ASo. The two measures are highly correlated and can be used interchangeably. Factor analysis of LPC scores and other personality measures (Bass et al., 1964) showed that low task orientation is associated with high LPC scores and that high LPC people are also higher in consideration of others.

The contingent variable of the leader-member relationship is basically a measure of the acceptance of the leader by subordinates and, in real life, groups can be operationalized by sociometric choices of group members and in laboratory groups by a group atmosphere rating by the leader. In a number of respects leader-member relations are less a moderating condition than another measure of the socio-emotional function of leadership. But task structure and the power position of the leader are organizationally determined and are valid contingencies. The following four scales from Shaw's system (1963) were taken to get an index of task structure:

1. *Decision verifiability.* The degree to which the correctness of the decision can be demonstrated.
2. *Goal clarity.* The degree to which the requirements of the task are clearly stated.
3. *Goal path multiplicity.* The degree to which the goal can be reached by a variety of procedures (reverse scoring).
4. *Solution specificity.* The degree to which there is more than one correct solution (reverse scoring).

Position power is another contingent condition and is provided by the organization for the leader's use as in the concept of legitimate power. It has to do with whether a leader can reward or punish members on his or her own accord, can recommend promotion and demotion, whether the group can depose the leader, whether he or she enjoys special or official rank and status in real life which sets him or her apart from group members, and so forth. In all some 18 items of this nature comprised the measure of position power.

Table 16-3 summarizes the results of some 63 studies by Fiedler and his associates and presents correlations between the leader's LPC score and group performance for seven combinations of contingent conditions. (The conditions are identified as "octants" in Table 16-3.) A high score on the Least Preferred Co-workers scale means low task orientation and high social supportiveness on the part of the leaders; a low LPC score means high task orientation and low supportiveness.

In three of the four situations in which the leaders are well accepted by the group (Octants I, II, III, and IV), the task-oriented

TABLE 16-3   Median Correlations Between Leader LPC and Group Performance in Various Octants

	Leader-Member Relations	Task Structure	Position Power	Median Correlation	Number of Relations Included in Median
Octant I	Good	Structured	Strong	−.52	8
Octant II	Good	Structured	Weak	−.58	3
Octant III	Good	Unstructured	Strong	−.33	12
Octant IV	Good	Unstructured	Weak	.47	10
Octant V	Moderate Poor	Structured	Strong	.42	6
Octant VI	Moderate Poor	Structured	Weak		0
Octant VII	Moderate Poor	Unstructured	Strong	.05	12
Octant VIII	Moderate Poor	Unstructured	Weak	−.43	12

From Fiedler, 1967, p. 142.

leaders do better than the socially supportive leaders. The exception is the combination of conditions in which the leaders lack position power and the task is unstructured (Octant IV). Here the socially supportive leaders achieve better results. Since position power and task structure are both lacking in this condition, the supportive leaders can make the most of their referent power.

In the four situations in which the leaders are not well accepted by the group (Octants V, VI, VII, and VIII), the supportive leader does better where he or she has strong position power and the task is structured (Octant V). When lack of acceptance by the group is combined with an unstructured task and weak position power, (Octant VIII), the task-oriented leader is more effective. Apparently this is a chaotic combination of conditions, and group members seize upon the one anchor—the structure provided by the directive leader.

Leadership itself may be a contingent condition for organizational change. We can reverse the emphasis in the Fiedler point of view and instead of searching for the situations that maximize a given type of leadership look for the leadership characteristics that can facilitate or impede system changes in response to environmental demand. Meyer (1975) has pointed out that strongly entrenched leadership can effectively resist external pressures. His study was based on data from 215 city, county, and state departments of finance, comptrollers' offices, and auditors' offices. These agencies were surveyed in 1966 and again in 1972.

Entrenched leadership was defined in terms of three characteristics: independence of authority, insularity of department heads, and turnover. When the heads were appointed by higher officials they were considered dependent as against those elected or appointed through civil service procedures. Insularity was measured by the amount of time spent in dealing directly with the head of the governmental unit. There was no relationship between environmental characteristics and structural variables such as number of levels of supervision for organizations with entrenched leadership. Moreover, the usual causal relationship between size and other organizational variables was attenuated. Structural characteristics tend to remain stable with stable leadership. The two surveys six years apart suggest a causal relationship between continuity of leadership and continuity of structure in that 1966 measures of leadership were related to 1972 structural characteristics. It is possible, of course, that leaders anticipating change could have left before the change occurred but the whole pattern of results is consistent with the above causal interpretation. Thus autonomy, or independence, as well as insularity, were related over time to continuity of structure.

Meyer's study is also of interest in that he deals with leadership as an organizational variable rather than a personality trait. Entrenched leadership is described in terms of the manner of appointment and the amount of contact with higher officials. In many studies there is no careful attempt to differentiate between leadership as a personality variable and as an organizational condition. The Fiedler program of research was especially valuable in considering system variables such as position power and task structure together with the basic style of the leader. Eagly's work (1970) revealed that Fiedler's measure of assumed similarity as a personality predisposition helps but does not insure appropriate role differentiation along task and supportive lines in leaderless groups. She set up 60 experimental, five-person groups, each with one low scoring LPC member, one high scoring, and three intermediate scoring LPC members. A group task was provided without formal structure. In 25 of the 60 groups role differentiation of the expected variety did not take place either because of the weakness of the LPC measure or because role differentiation is too complex a process to be fully predicted by knowing only a single personality characteristic. Informal groups do allow insight into other personality traits associated with punitive versus supportive leadership.

Hinton and Barrow (1976) simulated a production type organization and allowed leaders to use positive and negative economic reinforcements. The Cattell-Eber Sixteen Factor Personality Test (1964) was used to measure personality dimensions of supervisors. Those who were high in the use of rewards were more confident, more relaxed, more responsible, more careful, and more conventional, more enthusiastic and sentimental, and preferred to make their own decisions. Those who were relatively high in the use of negative sanctions were more suspicious, opinionated, more socially bold and uninhibited, careless in observing protocol, less truthful with themselves, but more conscientious and more likely to think in abstract terms.

PROBLEMS OF CONCENTRATION ON A SINGLE PATTERN OF LEADERSHIP

Because of the contradictory character of organizations, with their needs for rule enforcement and their needs for spontaneous and internally motivated actions in the interests of the organizational mission, there is a good deal of ambivalence about administration and administrators. On the one hand administrators are regarded as bureaucrats and administration as the uninteresting performance of household chores in contrast to policy making and creative leadership. Our own description of organizational leadership follows this line of thought. On the other hand, the administrative arts are sometimes glorified as the main forms of organizational control, and some top managers preoccupy themselves with administrative chores and eschew genuine policy making and origination of structure. Running a tight ship becomes more important than accomplishing a mission.

Either extreme may lead to the neglect of important organizational functions. If the emphasis on administration becomes the major concern of the top echelons, they may give too little time to critical issues of change, policy formulation, and planning. The increasing recognition of the organization as an open system carries with it an increasing understanding of this problem. But it is also possible to observe the neglect of the administrative function in organizations in which the top leaders spend almost all their time discussing policies and plans and are out of touch with the daily requirements of organizational life. Under such circumstances the household chores just may not get done, and appalling inefficiencies may characterize the system. It is true that man does not live by bread alone but it is also true that without bread he perishes. Organizations do not achieve greatness on the basis of their adequacy in handling daily administrative chores, but unless these are taken care of, the organization deteriorates. If there is no office space for the new professor, no research laboratory for the researcher, poor telephone service, and inadequate arrangements for assigning classrooms and duplicating reading lists, the university has increasing difficulty in holding together its staff of scholars and scientists. When administration is neglected, many people are forced into a grudging, costly, and inadequate effort to compensate for it. Alternatively, disregard for administration at higher levels in an organization may lead to the administrative function being carried out independently of policy making. Administration thus develops a rigidity and a life of its own which may have many dysfunctional elements for the larger system. Some rapidly growing universities illustrate well the first type of neglect; some governmental bureaucracies, the second.

The relative emphasis on the three forms of organizational leadership—origination, interpolation, and use of structure—should reflect the relationship of the system to its environment. An organization in a relatively stable environment with some assurance of inputs into the system will require less attention to changes in structure than an organization in a rapidly changing environment. Different patterns of leadership are also appropriate to different periods in organizational history. After a period of change an organization may require a period of stability, with consolidation of the changes and concomitant emphasis on the use of structure rather than further origination.

At any time, however, the relative importance of originating, interpolating, or using structure will be different for different echelons of organization, as we suggested earlier in this chapter. The recent work of Mann (1964), although it does not employ the conceptual scheme here proposed, is concerned with the different *skill-mix* which seems to be appropriate at different levels of organization and at different times in the organizational life cycle. Mann and his colleagues report, for example, that department heads in hospitals are satisfied or dissatisfied with their superiors primarily according to the superiors' coordinative and integrative abilities. The measures and descriptions of these abilities fit well our concepts of systemic perspective and origination of structure. People at lower levels in the organization, however, are more concerned with their supervisors' fairness and supportiveness and speak in terms that fall within our category of the equitable use of structure.

A study of an organization during a period of profound technological change (e.g., conversion of major clerical and billing operations to electronic data processing) shows, as one would expect, that the sharp differentiation of required *skill-mix* at different echelons is temporarily reduced, and that there is a heightened emphasis on systemic perspective and the origination of structure throughout the managerial structure. Mann suggests that during a period of major change this emphasis moves like a wave through the organization, beginning at the top and spreading rapidly downward as the top executives formulate objectives and policy changes and then expect the next echelon to make the complementary changes that will create a new organizational state of equilibrium.

Distribution of Leadership Function

Perhaps the most persistent and thoroughly demonstrated difference between successful and unsuccessful leadership at all three levels has to do with the distribution or sharing of the leadership function. We have defined leadership as the exertion of influence on organizationally relevant matters by any member of the organization. By and large, those organizations in which influential acts are widely shared are most effective. The reasons for this are in part motivational, having to do with implementation of decisions, and in part nonmotivational, having to do with the excellence of decisions.

The motivational argument is familiar. People have greater feelings of commitment to decisions in which they have a part, or in which they act autonomously. This has been demonstrated repeatedly in small-group research and in organizational studies. Less evidence is available for our second assertion—that the wide distribution of the leadership function is likely to improve the quality of decisions. The argument depends essentially on the notion that the group utilizing its informational and experiential resources most fully will be most effective. All the knowledge of the world within and outside the organization is not located in the formal chain of managerial command, much less at the upper end of that chain. Few indeed are the organizational disasters that occurred unforeseen—by someone. The sharing out of the leadership function means using more fully the resources of the organization. It means, incidentally, avoiding some of the crucial problems of overload that are so common in large-scale organizations, especially in the managerial structure.

There are many ways in which the distribution of the leadership function may be manifest. Even a broad categorization would distinguish among delegation, participative decision making, accessibility to influence, and communication of organizationally relevant information. In formal organizations of business and government all of these appear often as voluntary modifications in the formal structure of organization by some designated leader. The leader may change the official distribution of the leadership function by ceding directly to his or her subordinates duties for which he or she is formally responsible. This is what we mean literally by delegation, and the extent of delegation has proved to be one of the better predictors of productivity in organizations of many kinds.

Another way in which the formal leader of a group in a hierarchical organization may broaden the distribution of leadership is by including subordinates in making decisions affecting the group itself or the larger organization. Suppose that the manager of a trucking depot is told that an unusually heavy shipment of packages will arrive the following day, and that it must be given home delivery within one day thereafter. The drivers are paid on a complicated basis reflecting hours worked and rate of performance. If the manager insists on the completion of the extra work within the usual eight hours, the drivers will receive incentive pay; if the manager allows them extra hours of work, they will receive overtime pay. Because this decision is within the limits of the manager's formal authority, he or she has a choice: make it alone or involve the drivers in the decision and attempt some degree of joint decision-making. This is another area in which the evidence of studies of small groups and large organizations is generally consistent. We would confidently predict higher performance in those cases where the drivers were involved in the decision.

Less conspicuous than the formal delegation of leadership functions or the interpolation of group decision making is the voluntary openness of the supervisor to influence from subordinates. The leader may exercise legitimate powers in a way that permits neither questions nor suggestions from others in the group. For example, if the leader has been given the responsibility for determining the kinds of equipment required for a unit, he or she may not tolerate discussion of the wisdom of requisitions (nor listen to the suggestions of subordinates in such matters). Another supervisor may tolerate suggestions, discuss them, sometimes even act on them. Tannenbaum (1962) and others have shown that such accessibility to influence is consistently associated with higher performance at the group and organizational levels.

Perhaps the least way in which a formal leader initiates the distribution of the leadership function is by providing information to those in the group regarding resources, processes, problems, external demands, and the like. This principle is well understood and often given a kind of inverse demonstration: leaders who wish to keep their powers unshared covet information, permit exchange of information within the group only through themselves, and maintain subordinates without potential influence by keeping them without data on which to base a course of action or an influence attempt. It is perhaps more accurate to view the sharing of information by the formal leader as a preliminary to the distribution of the leadership function rather than as constituting in itself any functional change. Again, the empirical evidence relating increased communication from formal leaders to increased performance within groups is substantial and consistent.

VALUES AND MOTIVES OF MANAGERS

Cultural differences in the philosophy and motives of managers have implications for the understanding of leadership processes. The values expressed by those in positions of authority are generally more idealistic than their practices but they often anticipate future trends in managerial style. Tannenbaum (1977) in his review of the literature on cross-national comparisons in organizational psychology finds that there is general support across countries for the concepts of consultation and participation with more unevenness of endorsement of democratic involvement among the developing than among the developed nations. Tannenbaum and Cooke (1977), after examining studies in communist, socialist, and capitalist society, also report that there is widespread approval of participative decision making. In an extensive investigation of 3,641 managers in 14 countries Haire, Ghiselli, and Porter (1966) found that in all cultures there was a tendency to regard democratic methods as the best methods of leadership. At the same time the majority of managers had little faith that the average individual has the capacity for initiative and leadership. This discrepancy suggests that executives were more progressive in ideology than in practice.

Managers were also asked about need satisfaction in the Haire, Ghiselli, and Porter survey. Across all countries two needs stand out as unsatisfied—the need for autonomy and for self-actualization. High expectations were particularly noticeable in the developing countries of Argentina, Chile, and India, and in two Latin-European countries (Spain and Italy). The investigators conclude that there is a common motivational core in all business cultures and that to recruit the ablest leaders in the future business will have to offer greater opportunities for self-determination and self-realization.

We would expect differences in attitudes between management levels on the basis of the different functions appropriate to hierarchical position but the findings of the Haire-Ghiselli-Porter study are equivocal in this respect. In the United States upper management expresses a more authoritarian philosophy than middle management, whereas in England the higher the level of a manager's position the greater the tendency to adopt a participatory democratic attitude. Less puzzling were the results on need satisfaction with upper managers expressing greater fulfillment of their needs for autonomy, self-actualization, and esteem than lower level management.

A dramatic demonstration of the relation between organizational values and leadership motivation can be found in the study of Andrews (1967) of two industrial firms in Mexico. The one firm was relatively modern and progressive and emphasized accomplishment. The second firm was more traditionally oriented and reflected the feudal values of an earlier period. The executives in the two enterprises had been tested for their need for power and achievement two to four years before Andrews examined their rate of advancement. In the more

TABLE 16-4 Correlations, Biserial (rb) and Pearsonian (r), in Traditional and Modern Firms Between Motive Score (*n* Ach and *n* Pow) and Three Measures of Advancement (Job Level, Frequency of Promotion, Frequency of Raises)

Motive	JOB LEVEL: I OR II		PROMOTED YES OR NO		NUMBER OF RAISES	
	N	rb	N	rb	N	r
Modern Firm						
n Ach	26	$+.64^c$	24	$+.43^c$	21	$+.36^a$
n Pow	26	$-.39^b$	24	$+.11$	21	$-.20$
Traditional Firm						
n Ach	30	$-.37^b$	30	0.00	No data available	
n Pow	30	$+.38^b$	30	$+.34^b$		

[a] $p < .10$ (one-tailed test)
[b] $p < .05$ (one-tailed test)
[c] $p < .01$ (one-tailed test)
Adapted from Andrews, 1967, p. 166.

modern firm he found a significant positive correlation between need for achievement and actual promotion but no such relationship between need for power and advancement. Similarly, in the more traditionally oriented firm he found a positive correlation between the power motive and promotion but no relation between need achievement and promotion (see Table 16-4). This accords with McClelland's thesis (1961) that the significant motivational syndrome for leadership in a technological society is need achievement rather than power. The people moving up the ladder in the Mexican firm where productivity was a central value were not power driven but achievement oriented.

■ **SUMMARY** ■

In the description of organizations, no word is more often used than leadership, and perhaps no word is used with such varied meanings. Leadership is sometimes used as if it were an attribute of personality, sometimes as if it were a characteristic of certain positions, and sometimes as an attribute of behavior. The last of these seems to us to offer distinct conceptual advantages, and we define leadership in behavioral terms as *any act of influence on a matter of organizational relevance*.

This definition of leadership includes many routine acts of supervision; the essence of leadership, however, has to do with *influential increment* which goes beyond routine and taps bases of power beyond those that are organizationally decreed. These include *referent power*, which depends on personal liking between leader and follower, and *expert power*, which depends on the knowledge and ability of the leader. In contrast to these are the organizationally given powers of reward, punishment, and legitimate authority.

One may question the need for leadership so defined, and ask why an organization properly designated for its purpose will not function adequately without acts of leadership. The answer lies in four inescapable facts of organizational life: necessary incompleteness of organizational design, changing environmental conditions, internal dynamics of organization, and the nature of human membership in organizations.

No organizational chart and no book of policies and procedures can specify every act and prescribe for every contingency encountered in a complex organization. To attempt such specification merely produces an array of instructions so ponderous that they are ignored for the sake of transacting the business of the organization. Moreover, even if such specifications could be provided, they would soon be out of date. Organizations are open systems and exist in ever-changing environments. Each change in the environment implies a demand for change within the organization. To some extent such demands are foreseeable and the appropriate responses can be programmed; to some extent they require leadership beyond such responses. Additional factors that mitigate against organizational stability and create a continuing need for leadership are the uneven development and different dynamics of the several organizational subsystems, and the segmental nature of human membership in organizations.

To analyze leadership behavior, we propose three categories or levels of leadership acts, differentiated in terms of their effects on organizational structure: the *origination of structure,* or policy formulation; the *interpolation of structure,* or the piecing out of policies to meet immediate problems; and the *use of structure,* or the routine administration of applying prescribed remedies for predicted problems. Each of these categories of leadership behavior is characteristically encountered at a different organizational level, and each requires for successful use a different cognitive style, different kinds of knowledge, and different affective characteristics.

Industrial psychologists have often overlooked the necessity of two functions of leadership, the socio-emotional or supportive aspect and the production-oriented aspect. Some of the conflicting research findings as in the Ohio work on consideration and initiation or in Fiedler's early studies are understandable when both aspects are taken into account as contributing to organizational effectiveness. Fiedler has further analyzed group functions and situational variables in his contingency model of leadership.

Values and motives of managers have been studied in different cultures and there is agreement that in business cultures both achievement and democratic practices are emphasized. Nevertheless while democratic methods are regarded as superior to authoritarian procedures, practice lags beyind ideology.

Finally, no pattern of leadership is appropriate for all phases of organizational life. There is evidence, however, that the broad sharing of leadership functions contributes to organizational effectiveness under almost all circumstances.

17
■ WORK AND HEALTH ■

The open-system approach to human organizations seems to invite oversimplification. The brief litany of input-transformation-output is recited; examples are given in terms of raw materials, manufacture, and sales, and the rest is ignored. The great societal dialectic is acknowledged in the abstract—we create social institutions and are in turn created by them—but ignored at the level of individuals and organizations.

As some modest documentation of this general point, consider the subject of work and health, the effects of jobs on the people who do them. The 1965 *Handbook of Organizations* (March) contains 28 chapters, none of which deals with this issue, nor is there a single health entry in the index of that handbook. The same can be said of the Dubin (1976) *Handbook of Work, Organization, and Society*. Its companion volume, *The Handbook of Industrial and Organizational Psychology* (Dunnette, 1976) also shows no indexed references to health or illness, although it does contain a chapter on stress and performance (McGrath, 1976). Textbooks and books of readings confirm this pattern. The well-being and illness of individuals are not ordinarily regarded as organizational outcomes, even in part.

The central proposition of this chapter, on the other hand, is that the demands and opportunities, the stresses and supports of organizational work roles affect the health of the individuals who enact those roles. We consider their health, physical and mental, to be a complex outcome determined in part by properties of the organizations in which they work and the positions they occupy in those organizations. Such effects are thus part of the organizational output. They are usually among the "unintended" effects of organizational life, however, or at least they stand low in the list of organizational priorities. Partly for that reason, such effects are seldom measured, seldom counted, and almost never included in the major accounting procedures of organizations. Moreover, the effects of organizations on their members are less easily observed than the main organizational throughput; organizational effects on individuals merge with other effects, environmental and genetic, present and past.

Accidents and physical illnesses conspicuously distinctive to particular occupations are exceptions to these general observations. Folk wisdom and experience identified certain occupational diseases long before more systematic data became available. The phrase "mad as a hatter" came into the language before we knew the effects of mercury, which was used in felting, on the central nervous system. And so it has been with other occupations and diseases—the "black lung" of coal miners and the melancholia of sailors among them. In more recent years the documentation of such occupational hazards has become extensive (*Health and Work in America,* 1975); the first general legislation for occupational health and safety in the United States has been enacted, and some research has been initiated on more subtle occupational effects—physical and mental, immediate and delayed, even in some cases positive as well as negative. In this chapter we will propose a model in terms of which such findings may be reviewed, and will then attempt such a review.

PROBLEMS IN THE STUDY OF WORK AND HEALTH

Imagine an organization well-established and ongoing, taking in materials and various forms of energy, altering their shape and other properties in ways that increase their utility, and selling the product in a competitive retail market of consumers. These cycles of activity are performed by people who must be attracted and retained as members of the organization and motivated to enact the interdependent roles that in combination produce these organizational outcomes. The efficiency and success of the organization as a system can be measured in various ways, as we have suggested (Chapter 8).

That pattern of recurrent systemic behavior is familiar from our earliest chapters. But now let us take into account the complex phenomenon of partial inclusion, to which we referred in Chapter 3. That concept reminds us that people have lives, activities, goals, and intentions outside the organization. We can think of the individual in terms analogous to those of the organization. The individual is also an ongoing system, with criteria of well-being and requirements for continuing life quite separate from those of the organization. Some such individual requirements are beyond argument—air, water, food, and sleep in appropriate quantities. Social and psychological requirements are less well established, as are the criteria of social and psychological well-being.

In general, we are more agreed on indicators of individual malfunction than optimal function, symptoms of illness rather than health. And we are more agreed on the indicators and categories of physical illness than mental. The Freudian definition of well-being as the ability to work, love, and play has been operationalized and extended in various ways but the very number of such efforts indicates lack of agreement.[1] There is some convergence, nevertheless, around the Freudian functions, around the idea of freedom from distressing symptoms (gastric discomfort, inability to sleep, etc.), around verdicality of percep-

---

[1] Among the more recent discussions of mental health, happiness, and well-being are those of Maslow, 1954; Jahoda, 1958; Gurin, Veroff, and Feld, 1960; French and Kahn, 1962; Cantril, 1965; Bradburn and Caplovitz, 1965; Bradburn, 1969; Campbell, Converse, and Rodgers, 1976.

tion, and around positive affect toward self and toward life. These criteria of individual well-being, objective and subjective, are quite separate from the criteria of organizational effectiveness.

The enactment of an organizational role by an individual can thus be thought of as an intersection and partial overlap of two separate systems, the person-system and the organization-system. The overlap occurs in certain cycles of behavior (the enactment of the organizational role) that are shared in time and space—indeed, are identical—for the person and organization. The behaviors themselves are part of the ongoing life of the individual and of the organization; they define in part both systems.

We are accustomed to studying the extent to which these shared or overlapping cycles contribute to efficiency, productivity, growth, and other criteria of organizational effectiveness. Has the individual performed his or her role with the energy, skill, regularity, and judgment that are sufficient for the continuing success of the organization? It is equally appropriate to ask the complementary questions: Does the enactment of the organizational role enhance or reduce the well-being of the individual? Does it enlarge or diminish the person's valued skills and abilities? Does it increase or restrict the person's opportunity and capacity for other valued role enactments?

These questions are difficult to answer; in fact only fragments of answers are available. The complications involve the (1) confounding of properties of the person and of the work role, (2) confounding of the effects of the work role with those of other roles, (3) evaluation of the benefits of the work role in comparison to its individual costs or disutility, and (4) the difficulty of establishing a frame of reference for assessing both the positive and negative effects of the work role. We will consider each of these briefly.

Suppose, as an example of the confounding of person-properties and role-properties, that a worker complains of various psychosomatic symptoms; is the job too stressful or the person too fragile? In one sense the question is unanswerable; the immediate causal factors are person-in-organization events, not either alone. For pragmatic purposes, however, the question must be answered, and answers are usually given in comparative terms: Do other people who perform similar jobs do so without such symptoms? And is the person in question plagued by such symptoms when he or she performs other roles, work and non-work? The general judgment about the stresses of jobs, therefore, are made in terms of a reasonable population of job holders.

The confounding of job-effects with the effects of other experiences, past and present, is equally difficult. People enact many roles, and each role imposes its stresses and offers its rewards. If the individual shows signs of strain, who can say which role is responsible?

When we ask about the effects of the work role, we single it out as the active agent and in effect disregard or hold constant the effects of other roles. We could with equal rationality have treated any other of the individual's roles as focal in this sense.

Indeed, the major activity that was undertaken by the management of the Western Electric Company following the famous Hawthorne experiments (Roethlisberger and Dickson, 1939) was a massive interviewing program that proceeded on the assumption that off-the-job events were interfering with on-the-job performance. We do not find the data persuasive, but they illustrate the fact that the work role may be viewed both as affected and affecting in relation to other roles. Consider the following (Cass and Zimmer, 1975):

> For example, an interviewer talked with Joe Brown, who complained about conditions in the shop, the drafts, smoke, and fumes.... Then he talked about his brother, who had recently died of pneumonia.... the complaints were really an indication of his pre-occupations about his health.
>
> Another employee complained that his piece rates were too low. As he continued to talk, he related that his wife was in the hospital, and that he was worried about his doctor bills. In effect the complaint about piece rate is an expression of his concern about his ability to pay his bills.
>
> Another employee complained of his boss being a bully.... As the talk turned to his past experiences, he talked about his father, an overbearing, domineering man whose authority could not be questioned. Gradually the interviewer could see that the employee's dissatisfaction was rooted somewhere in his attitude toward authority, developed during early childhood. (pp. 293–294)

The problem of costs and benefits to the person who takes the work role is perhaps more a value judgment than a scientific question, but it reminds us of a basic fact about work and work organizations. Such organizations were not invented primarily for the direct gratification or edification of their members. The intended benefits are in the main indirect; work is essentially instrumental. The job takes the worker away from the family and probably prevents at least for some hours the performance of other more expressive activities. But the job, or rather its material rewards, sustains the family and pays the costs of engaging in various hobbies and recreations. At what point is the cost-benefit ratio unfair, unnecessarily harsh, or otherwise inappropriate?

Last in this list of complications surrounding the effects of work on the worker is the problem of frame of reference. When we call a job hazardous or boring or isolating, there is always an implied comparison. Life has no zero point on any such dimensions, and few known optima. Should the hazardousness of a job be rated in comparison to some average for work situations, or to the best of work situations, or to the most likely alternative non-work activity? Answers are possible, but we believe that they are unavoidably arbitrary, as the available data will show.

APPROACHES TO STUDYING THE EFFECTS OF WORK

As social psychologists of organization, we can set some limits to such questions and some criteria for satisfactory answers to them. First, we are interested primarily in the social-psychological aspects of work; architecture and technology and toxicology are not of themselves our subjects of inquiry, although they have social-psychological effects. Such effects concern us, even if their causes must be described in the vocabulary of other disciplines. Similarly, social-psychological attributes of work are of interest to us, even if their effects are physiological or political, for example. Thus, the relationship of duration of the work cycle on a job to boredom on the part of the worker would be within our area of interest, and so would the relationship of boredom to blood pressure (if any).

Several kinds of comparisons have been used to investigate such relationships. The most common (and least satisfactory) is a comparison of different sets of individuals engaged in differing tasks, with an attempt to explain observed differences in health in terms of the differing jobs. Such analyses present obvious and difficult problems of self-selection. Do bureaucrats acquire bureaucratic personalities because of their work, or are people of such characteristics attracted to and selected for bureaucratic positions?

Such problems of interpretation are eased when comparisons can be made of the same individuals in two or more different work situations. What happens, for example, when people are promoted, or move to jobs of different technology or organizational characteristics? A special instance of such longitudinal comparisons involves changes into and out of work roles. Are there, for example, predictable consequences to the movement from non-work to work roles (student or homemaker to employed worker)? And from work to non-work, either voluntary or involuntary?

Finally, we can study the effects of jobs by looking at substantial numbers of people engaged in the same job (occupation) and attempting to discover uniformities, although this gives in itself only a weak basis for inference.

All of these, of course, are methodological observations; they do not in themselves say anything about the theories, hypotheses, or models in service of which such comparisons might be made. A number of such models have been proposed for the study of stress (Scott and Howard, 1970), but almost none of them emphasizes the work role. An exception is McGrath's (1976) model, which is concerned primarily with the performance of tasks in the organizational context. The model consists of a postulated causal sequence in which four elements (objective situation, perceived situation, response selection, and behavior) are linked by four processes (the appraisal process, the decision process, the performance process, and the outcome process (See Dunnette, 1976, p. 1356.)

The ISR Model

The McGrath model has much in common with that proposed by French and Kahn (1962) and elaborated by them and their colleagues in the course of subsequent research (Kahn, French, and Cobb, 1974). The purpose of the latter model (Figure 17-1) is to provide a framework for research on the effects of the work role on health, and it serves that purpose for a continuing series of investigations at the Institute for Social Research of the University of Michigan (ISR).

The ISR model is extremely broad when presented in these terms; it is in fact a set of conceptual categories rather than the representation of a theory. It becomes both more restrictive and more informative as concepts are introduced into the several categories (boxes) and hypotheses are proposed (arrows). Thus, hypotheses of the A → B category have to do with the effects of the objective work environment on the psychological work environment (the work environment as the individual experiences it). For example, people whose jobs require them to engage in transactions across the organizational boundary (a fact in their objective work environment) more often report that they are subjected to incompatible demands on the job (a fact in their psychological environment).

Hypotheses of the B → C category relate facts in the psychological environment to the immediate responses that are invoked in the person. For example, the perception that one is subject to persistent conflicting demands on the job is associated with feelings of tension. The C → D category deals with the effect of such responses on criteria of health and illness. The relationship of sustained job tension to coronary heart disease (perhaps more arguable with respect to the empirical evidence) illustrates the C → D category.

Finally, the three categories of hypotheses just described must be qualified by an additional class, represented by the vertical arrows in Figure 17-1. This class of hypotheses states that relationships between

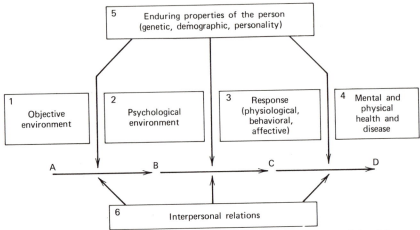

Figure 17-1   ISR model: the social environment and mental health.

objective and psychological environment, between psychological environment and response, and between response and health or illness are modified by enduring properties of the individual and by interpersonal relations. For example, the extent to which a person experiences tension on being exposed to role conflict depends very much on the personality characteristic of flexibility-rigidity; people who are flexible rather than rigid respond with greater tension to the experience of role conflict. On the other hand, supportive relations with others seem to buffer some of the relationships between the demands of the work role and the consequences for the individual. For example, French (1974) found in a study of a government agency that quantitative work load was related to diastolic blood pressure ($r = .33$), but only among those employees who had poor relationships with their supervisors. In similar fashion, other properties of the person and his or her interpersonal relations act as conditioning or modifying variables in the causal sequence that leads from the work role to health or illness.

Given this framework, we can define an adequate explanatory sequence. It would consist of a chain of hypotheses beginning with some characteristic of the objective work environment, ending with some criterion of health, specifying the intervening variables in the psychological environment and in the immediate responses of the individual, and stating the ways in which this causal linkage is modified by the differing characteristics of individuals and their interpersonal relations. Such a causal chain might be called a theme, and a set of such themes, logically related, would constitute a theory of work and health.

No one could claim that such a matured theory yet exists, much less that its components have been subjected to empirical test. The framework serves to remind us, however, of one form that such a theory might take. It reminds us also of the cumulative meaning of such empirical fragments as are presently available to us regarding the social-psychological aspects of work and health.

OCCUPATION, INDUSTRY, AND CLASS OF WORKER

One aggregation of findings that link work and health is the differential incidence of certain diseases and disabilities among workers in different industries, occupations, or "classes" (that is, private industry, government, and self-employment). For the social psychologist, such findings often fail to specify the causal factors within these labor force categories and they omit the intervening explanatory structure. They are nevertheless a useful point at which to begin an empirical summary of things known about work and health.

If one uses the eight major industrial categories developed by the Bureau of the Census (agriculture, mining, construction, manufacturing, transportation and public utilities, wholesale and retail trade, finance and real estate, and service), the gross amount of reported disability from all causes is surprisingly narrow in range. Days of restricted activity per person per year range from 10.3 to 12.8; days of work loss range from 4.7 to 6.3; and days of bed disability (in nonagricultural industries) from 3.6 to 4.2 (*Health and Work in America*, 1975). The reasons for disability, however, show a plausible pattern of occupational and industrial differences; farm workers have the highest proportion of musculoskeletal disability and white-collar workers are highest in cardiovascular disability, for example (Haber, 1971).

Disabilities categorized as nervous or mental were about 8.3 percent of all disabilities, and the range was narrow (7.2 to 9.9 percent) across the occupational categories of white-collar workers, blue-collar workers, farm workers, and craftspeople, and blue-collar supervisors. Severe disability, however, was most common among workers whose complaints were "mental or nervous," especially in the case of blue-collar workers. Almost three out of four blue-collar workers with such problems were rated severely disabled (unable to work regularly); the proportion of severe disability among all workers disabled for any reason is only one in four (Haber, 1971). The pattern for accidents also reflects the hazards of blue-collar jobs and the industries—manufacturing and construction—in which they are concentrated (*Health and Work in America*, 1975). The magnitude of these differences, for injury and illness combined, is shown in Figure 17-2.

A great deal of information has been accumulated for the purpose of specifying in more detail the categories of physical illness associated

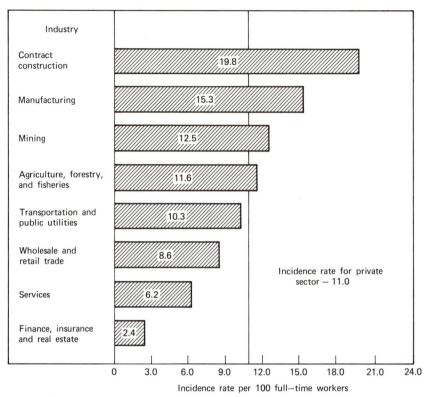

Figure 17-2 *Injury and illness incidence rates, by industry division, United States, 1973. (From Bureau of Labor Statistics, U.S. Department of Labor, unpublished data, 1973.)*

with different occupations and industries and identifying the physical substances and modes of exposure that account for such associations. The collection, interpretation, and use of such information is central to a number of professions other than sociology and psychology. It is known, for example, that fatality rates attributable to certain kinds of chemical exposure are extremely high. Asbestos workers have about five times the "normal" expected rate of fatal lung cancer, and the ratio of actual to expected deaths increases with years of exposure (Selikoff and Hammond, 1975). Twelve percent of all working miners and 21 percent of nonworking miners showed X-ray findings of pneumoconiosis (Leinhart et al., 1969). Abnormal births—infants with congenital abnormalities—appear to be about twice as frequent among women workers exposed to anesthetic gases in operating rooms as among similar workers not so exposed (*Anesthesiology*, 1974). Meat-wrappers using polyvinyl chloride wrapping materials and price labels have distinctive respiratory and related symptoms (69 percent) and characteristic weekend and vacation remissions (77 percent; Bardand, 1973).

Since the passage of the Occupational Safety and Health Act in 1970, there has been a rapid establishment of standards in the United States for the use of these and other materials. At least 25 such standards were set in the period 1972–1975, for stressors ranging from the commonplace to the exotic—from heat and noise to beryllium and toluene diisocyanate. Neither the research workers who have discovered these occupational hazards nor the people who promulgate ways of protecting workers against them believe that the problems are thereby solved. Indeed, it could be argued that the problems move from the domain of toxicology and traditional occupational medicine to the domain of organizational theory, persuasion, and the introduction of change. Thus, some steps have been taken with respect to physical hazards of work, but similar steps have not yet been taken with respect to social psychological stresses and consequences. For example, the summary chart book, *Health and Work in America,* 1975, does not include such stresses. And even more rare is any mention of the work outcomes that contribute directly to the well-being of the individual—the use of valued skills and abilities, for example, and the opportunity to add to such personal attributes.

Like the studies of work and physical health, much of the research that links work to mental health categorizes work roles in terms of occupation, industry, or class of worker. Hollingshead and Redlich (1958) were concerned mainly with social class and its consequences for mental illness; the characteristics of jobs at different class levels are more inferred than measured. Their findings included the increased incidence of mental illness in successively less advantaged social classes, and the tendency toward different patterns or diagnoses between classes, with schizophrenia conspicuously more often given as the diagnosis of mental illness among people in the lower socioeconomic classes.

Srole and his colleagues (1962), studying patterns of mental health and illness in the central area of New York City, also used occupation and social class as their major independent variables. Their data show the familiar association between social class and mental impairment, the latter measured in terms of a six-category scale ranging from Well (no symptoms) to Incapacitated. The resultant "Sick-Well ratios" increase steadily in successively lower socioeconomic categories, from 46 in the top category to 470 in the sixth and lowest, a tenfold difference. Moreover, these effects are exacerbated by downward mobility. The sons of professional and executive fathers who did not themselves enter such occupations show 20 times the symptoms (sick-well ratio) of sons who followed their fathers into these advantaged occupations.

STUDIES OF WORK

Quinn and his colleagues (1973, 1974) have done research that provides more recent data along similar lines and has the advantage of being based on successive nationwide samples. It also has the characteristic limitation of such representative data-sets; it is based wholly on self-report. The data not only include issues of safety and health, but also some 18 other aspects of working conditions that have been the subject of government action, legislation, and labor negotiation, and are therefore of continuing concern to the United States Department of Labor. These areas include, in addition to health and safety, income and income loss, hours and schedules of work, discrimination (for reasons of race, sex, or age), transportation to and from work, employment service and referral, and union relations with their members.

With respect to most of these issues, the data (1969–1973) show considerable stability. Health and safety at work are among the problems most often cited; about 40 percent of all workers describe themselves as having problems in this area, and about half of those consider them to be serious ("sizable" or "great"). The related problem of unpleasant physical conditions was mentioned with similar frequency, as were problems of transportation, inconvenient or excessive hours of work, and inadequate fringe benefits. All other problems were mentioned less often, although about one worker in five reported inadequate family income as a problem, and for most of those who reported it at all, the problem was serious. Several other problems showed this pattern; they were reported by only a small proportion of workers, but they were serious for most of those who were affected at all. Problems with union management and democracy, with employment agencies, with racial discrimination, and with assigned (garnisheed) wages affected fewer than one worker in ten, but in every instance the problem was serious for a majority of those affected.

Only about one worker in ten reported no problem in any of the 19 areas of specific inquiry, and the overall average number of problems mentioned was three. As expected, more problems were mentioned by wage-and-salaried workers than by those self-employed, more by blue-collar than by white-collar workers, and more by operatives (machine workers) than by those in any other occupation. Moreover, this general finding of disadvantage of blue-collar, industrial, and service jobs summarizes a pattern of almost unbroken specific disadvantages. Exposure to physical dangers and unhealthy conditions, for example, is twice as common among uneducated workers (less than eight grades) as among those with college degrees, and more than twice as common among blue-collar workers (craftspeople, machine operatives, transport operators) as among professionals, administrators, and salespeople. The pattern holds for work-related illnesses and injury, and is exacerbated in regard to such economic matters as wages and employment security. Unsteady employment is essentially a problem of certain occupations and industries. It is reported by only 1–3 percent of white-collar workers in government, finance, insurance, and real estate; but it is reported by 40 percent of construction workers, 20 percent of miners, and more than 20 percent of unskilled laborers regardless of industry.

Complaints of unpleasant conditions at work are less concentrated, and so are complaints about transportation and traffic. The flight to the suburbs imposes costs on those who move as well as those who do not. In general, however, the pattern of advantage and disadvantage is consistent rather than compensatory; disadvantaged jobs are consistently disadvantaged.

Moreover, it appears that the overall quality of working conditions shows considerable stability in time—at least for the period (1969–1973) for which comparable data are available. Reported problems increased in some specific areas and decreased in others. Increases occurred (or increased sensitivity led to more frequent reporting of difficulties) with scheduled hours of work, with transportation, with fringe benefits, with union democracy and management, and with discrimination on the basis of sex. The model we have proposed (Figure 17-1) leads us to look for patterns of response—affective, behavioral, and physiological—that reflect the differences in occupational and industrial categories that we have now reviewed. With respect to affect, feelings of satisfaction or dissatisfaction about work, those expectations are fulfilled. Overall job satisfaction, as measured by Quinn and his colleagues (1974) varies among occupational groups from −42 to +27, with machine operatives and laborers at the bottom of that range and professionals and managers at the top. The pattern is particularly sharp with respect to the content of the job (challenge), and is not at all apparent for some other facets, especially satisfaction with one's co-workers.

The same pattern extends to life satisfactions. These varied from −24 to +23, again with machine operatives at the bottom of that range and professionals at the top. It does not, however, extend to most measures of on-the-job behavior that were available: self-reported lateness to work, absence from work, and intention to quit. It is plausible that these behaviors are under the control of organizational rules and penalties for tardiness and absence, and that decisions to quit or remain depend more on the labor market and the vested interest in the job than on satisfaction with it. Only the behavior of making or withholding suggestions for changes to the employer revives the familiar occupational pattern, and with a plausible and ironic reversal. The groups who described their jobs as having the most problems and themselves as being least satisfied nevertheless made fewest suggestions to their employers—laborers and operatives at the bottom of the frequency distribution, professionals and managers at the top.

The apparent influence of the work experience on general satisfaction with life is to be expected for both intrinsic and instrumental reasons. It is not plausible that the perceptions and the affective and physiological responses evoked at work should vanish without trace at the moment each day when the work role is relinquished. Moreover, regardless of the individual's success in compartmentalization of that kind, the material rewards and penalties of the job carry over into non-work life. Other factors than work shape life satisfactions, of course (Quinn and Shepard, 1974; Campbell, Converse, and Rodgers, 1976). People come to terms with life, and express increasing satisfaction (not happiness) as they age—except with respect to the domain of health. Education that includes at least a college degree seems to have effects not wholly accounted for by the attainment of better jobs. And race shows a pattern of difference that is not merely occupational; blacks are less satisfied with their jobs and with their lives than whites are, although only 15 percent of blacks reported that they were discriminated against on their present jobs.

These relationships must be seen, however, against a background of two more general tendencies: the fact that satisfactions (or dissatisfactions) with different aspects of life are intercorrelated, and the fact that satisfaction with work is a strong predictor of the others. As Campbell, Converse, and Rodgers (1976) put it in their study of the quality of American life:

> all of the measures of domain satisfaction, including work, are positively intercorrelated. Specifically, those who express high levels of satisfaction with their jobs are more likely than those who are less satisfied to express high levels of satisfaction with other life domains. The correlations are highest for the financial domains, nonworking activities, family life, and friendships, but are positive for all of the domains included in this study.
>
> Expressed job satisfaction is also related to how satisfied a person says he is with his life as a whole. . . . Job satisfaction explains about one-fifth of the variance in the Index of Well-Being, and is one of the most important predictors of that index (p. 317).

The relationship of work to mental health begins to emerge in such findings.

Jobs lower in status, rewards, and tending toward simple and re-petitive activities are associated with lesser satisfaction at work, more symptoms of depression, and lesser satisfaction with life. Whether they are associated with increased mental illness is uncertain, but they are certainly associated with different patterns of diagnosed illness (especially higher incidence of schizophrenia).

The active causal factors that account for such differences are not yet clear; the social-psychological equivalent of toxicology and traditional occupational medicine is perhaps in the making, but it is not yet made. McLean (1974), Levi (1975), and others have identified occupational mental health as an area of medicine and psychiatry, but that is more by way of setting the task than alleging its accomplishment. Studies like those of Quinn and his colleagues (1974) illuminate the nature of work and the work experience as reported by those who do it, but leave us with questions about the objective properties of work situations and their effects on health as those effects might be assessed by physicians, psychiatrists, and by the evidence of the laboratory. Studies like those of Selye (1956, 1971), tell us a great deal about the physiology of stress but little about the ways and the extent to which stress is induced in real-life work situations. The specific linkage of work, stress, and health has only begun to be made.

STRESS AND STRAIN: LABORATORY EXPERIMENTS

Research on work and health can be regarded as following two main strategies of explanation and design. One, exemplified by the research just described, deals with large populations and attempts to partition them in ways that permit at least tentative inferences about the work-health relationship. Such statistical analysis may proceed by categorizing the population according to some characteristic of the job—for example, occupation—and then looking for corresponding differences in criteria of health or indicators that hint at such criteria. Analysis may also begin with the dependent variable, and look for job differences across groups of respondents that have reported differences in symptoms or health behavior.

A different strategy, less wide-ranging and descriptive but often more powerful in the identification of causal sequences, usually begins with a particular hypothesis and tries to test it. This approach is less likely to rely on self-report and is more likely to use a variety of measurement methods. It is therefore more often done in the laboratory than in the field, and thus uses as independent variables not jobs but stimulus conditions that can be manipulated in the laboratory. Such conditions may have been chosen to imitate the world of work, or they may have been chosen for their place in some hypothesis having no obvious relevance to work.

McGrath (1970, 1976) has summarized these experimental studies in terms of three broad stimulus-categories: those involving the manipulation of some intrinsic task content, those involving the social-psychological conditions under which the experimental task is carried out, and those involving physical conditions or consequences of the experimental task. These three categories and the most frequent sub-categories are listed below:

> Task content: riskiness of decisions, difficulty of task, time pressure for task completion, dullness and repetitiveness of task.

> Social-psychological conditions: threat of evaluation, task failure, interpersonal disagreement, role disadvantages (conflict, ambiguity, low status), and vicarious exposure to these and other stressful experiences (films, staged incidents, etc.).

> Physical conditions: electric shock, injection or puncture, sleep deprivation, auditory or visual distraction, environmental restriction (sensory deprivation, limitation of movement, space limitation, etc.), drugs, and visual or vicarious exposure to any of these stimuli.

The most general result of this laboratory work has been to demonstrate relationships between a considerable number of stressful conditions and an equally impressive number of responses indicative of strain, both for animals and for human subjects. The design of these experiments often involves confounding of task content, social-psychological conditions, and physical conditions or penalties; we will summarize them, however, according to what seems to be the main significance of the findings for work and health:

Task Content

The physical demand of experimental tasks produces physiological signs of strain (elevated heart rate, elevated systolic blood pressure, increased secretion of adrenaline and noradrenaline) only if the physical demand is heavy or if it is perceived as heavy (Frankenhaeuser, 1971). Mental tasks (e.g., mental arithmetic) have also been shown to evoke physiological strain, at least when the tasks are performed under distracting conditions. These have included recorded workshop noise (Frankenhaeuser, 1971), flickering light (Raab, 1968), and other irritating factors presumably of the kinds encountered at work (Fran-

kenhaeuser and Patkai, 1964). All these experiments involved characteristically brief periods of task performance, but Levi (1972) conducted
one experiment in which subjects (army officers and corporals) engaged in a simulated electronic firing of rifles against moving targets
for a period of 72 hours. There was a marked decrement in performance
and a marked increase in physiological indicators of strain (adrenaline
and protein-bound iodine), together with considerable subjective distress, as time went on.

Social-Psychological Conditions

Physiological signs of strain have been evoked experimentally by
embarrassing interrogation (Hamburg, 1962), by the anticipation of uncomfortable or annoying situations (Berman and Goodall, 1960), and by
the anticipation of tasks characterized by uncertainty of success or
penalty (Frankenhaeuser, 1971).

Physical Conditions, Real and Vicarious

Much of the research on physical conditions as stressors has been
done on animals, for reasons of ethics, and the extrapolation to human
beings in general and the work role in particular remains uncertain.
Nevertheless, it is worth remembering that acute increases in blood
pressure and other symptoms of strain have been produced in laboratory animals by means of long-lasting noise, crowding, conflicting
messages of stimulation and inhibition, and physical bumps or blows
(Brod, 1971).

A few of the animal experiments on stress seem to have closer
relevance to the stresses of work. One such series dealt with the differences between stresses taken singly and in combination (Dean,
1966). Rats were subjected separately to conditions of heat (115 degrees
Fahrenheit), altitude, and random vibration, and also to combinations
of these conditions. Animal deaths under the separate conditions varied from 0 to 7.5 percent, but heat and vibration in combination caused
a 65 percent death rate, and altitude and vibration had similar results.
The significance of the experiment lies in the fact that work situations
often produce stresses in combination, while the canons of experimental research are usually interpreted to mean that stimuli should be
studied one at a time.

Another line of animal experimentation that seems important for
understanding the work role has been concerned with the imposition of
punishment (electric shock) under various task-relevant circumstances,
in an effort to discover to what extent the punishment itself is the
source of strain and to what extent the task-related circumstances of its
imposition. Some findings (Corson, 1971) suggest that unavoidable
stress, insoluble problems, and inescapable punishment causes most

strain (heart rate, respiration rate, and temperature in dogs). Other experiments, including those of the widely publicized "executive monkeys," seem to argue that strain is maximized when the punishment can be avoided by the performance of a strenuous task and when the subject has "responsibility" for avoiding punishment both to self and to a visible other.

Rioch (1971) altered the usual procedure of stress experiments with animals in a way that seems to capture the particular stress of responsibility for the well-being of others. His experiments involved pairs of monkeys, visible to each other, engaged in a recurring six-hour "task" situation. During the "work" period, a shock was scheduled for application at regular intervals, sometimes as brief as 20 seconds. Each monkey had access to a lever, and one of the levers was "preventive"; if it were pressed, the shock was avoided, not only for the monkey that pressed the preventive lever but for the other monkey as well: hence the term "executive" for the animal whose behavior permitted or prevented that punishing shock. The design of the experiment insured that the exposure of both animals to the electric shock would be identical; they escaped or were punished together, but only one of them—the executive—could prevent the shock. All of the "executive" monkeys died of gastrointestinal lesions in periods varying from nine to 48 days; none of the equally shocked nonexecutive monkeys died, and none showed gastrointestinal pathology.

Human experiments on the stresses of physical conditions have for the most part involved extreme or exotic situations of uncertain relevance to most work roles: sensory deprivation (summarized by Clemedson, 1971), overstimulation, centrifuge rides (Frankenhaeuser, 1971), medical procedures of a strenuous kind, parachute jumping, and the like (Sarason and Spielberger, 1976).

Extreme sensory deprivation and isolation (Hebb, 1958) was rated "unbearable" by subjects after three or four days. Within that period they showed tension, sleeplessness, personality changes, reduced intellectual performance, and feelings of "depersonalization"; all of these symptoms quickly disappeared when subjects were no longer isolated and inactive. The symptoms were evoked by experimental conditions that involved no restraint of movement except for remaining in the small isolation room; moreover, subjects took their meals outside these rooms.

Frankenhaeuser (1971) reported increases of adrenaline and noradrenaline under more moderate conditions of understimulation—the requirement to press a button in response to an irregular signal under conditions of isolation from others. The signs of strain increased when the task was made more complex—the matching of responses by buttons and pedals to multiple signals. This combination of specialized overload and general understimulation (lack of opportunity for interaction with others, limitation of activities to a small but demanding repertoire) is suggestive of many work roles, white-collar and blue-collar, in advanced technologies.

A few experiments have been done that attempt the simulation of work roles under realistic conditions. Levi (1972) had groups of subjects sort ball bearings according to small differences in size. The task was simple, monotonous, routine, and demanded neither much learning nor much skill. On the other hand, it was not an easy task; mistakes were easy to make and there was the constant necessity of making decisions. Moreover, there were time pressures to complete the job, critical observations about the performance, variations in light, and a background of recorded workshop noise. The task required about two hours of such work. It produced subjective ratings of unpleasantness and physiological changes of increased heart rate and blood pressure, increased secretion of adrenaline and noradrenaline, and increased concentrations of triglycerides and free fatty acids in the blood plasma. The experimenter comments that "it is tempting to speculate about the effects of the socio-economic or other real-life stressors, which may be repeated over months and years and surely may represent a threat to the individual far exceeding that implied in our laboratory situation" (Levi, 1972, pp. 91–105).

STRESS AND STRAIN: FIELD STUDIES

Real-life settings do not partition stress into task, social-psychological, and physical categories. Studies of stress in such settings tend to involve contrasts between groups with very different life experiences, responses of groups to extreme situations of many kinds, and responses to crises. Such studies are consistent in showing signs of strain, physiological and psychological, as a concomitant or consequence of active threat or relative disadvantage. It is not equally clear, however, what the causal sequence has been.

Group comparisons have been made of soldiers and civilians, and of front-line versus noncombatant soldiers, interpreted as showing the physiological effects of physical danger. Comparisons between racial groups in the United States (black and white), showing higher incidence of hypertension among blacks, have been interpreted as reflecting differences in social status (Brod, 1971). Studies of extreme situations have been made on populations of prisoners (Cunningham, 1962), on communities confronted by natural disasters or the disasters of war, and on populations of various sizes between these examples. Haas and Drabek (1970) cite more than 300 such studies, and the criterion variables are many—performance decrements, personality changes, physiological signs of strain. But similar effects have been reported in studies of everyday events: driving an automobile (Bellet, Roman, and Kostis, 1969), flying as a passenger in an airplane (Raab and Kimura, 1971), being admitted to a hospital (Raab, 1966), taking an academic examination (Bogdonoff, et al., 1960), and others. The implication seems to be that any event that requires a response of coping or adaptation is likely to evoke some indication of strain. Holmes and Rahe (1967) have taken exactly this view, and treat all such events as stressors, regardless of whether they are sought or unsought, and experienced as positive or negative. Thus their 42-item Schedule of Recent Experiences (SRE) includes the death of one's spouse, the purchase of a new car, marriage, and losing one's job. Only the element of situational change and therefore change-demand seems common throughout the list.

Such findings make ambiguous the results of various studies of migratory changes that involved the taking up of the work roles characteristic of industrial societies. Studies of this kind have shown blood pressure elevation on the part of Chinese immigrants to the United States, similar increases on the part of African black immigrants to the United States, and among immigrants from remote Pacific islands to Europe (Brod, 1971). One can ask whether the stress consisted mainly in the migration or in the subsequent industrial life style. Some indication in favor of the latter hypothesis comes from the complementary finding of reduced blood pressure on the part of American immigrants to China before World War II. Moreover, recent studies of nonindustrial societies report little relationship of blood pressure to age, in contrast to the increase that has come to be called normal in industrialized countries.

The effects of urban life, abrupt change, industrial employment, and relative loss of status are confounded beyond extrication in these studies. Some attempt at isolating the effects of status or status-incongruence has been made in research comparing the occupations, residences, and socioeconomic status of fathers and sons. The industrially employed sons of fathers not so employed show higher than expected sickness rates from all causes combined; similar results were obtained for the urban sons of rural fathers (Tyroler and Cassel, 1964). Increased incidence of coronary heart disease has been observed in a number of such father-son shifts—occupational, residential, and socioeconomic (Syme et al., 1964, 1965).

In an effort to identify more clearly the stressor variables in work, some investigators have selected occupations for reasons of some a priori characteristic or comparison. Such studies have not, however, usually included any independent measure of the assumed stressor. Russek (1962) confirmed predicted ordering of hypertension and coronary heart disease within three professions—medicine, dentistry, and law. For medicine, the ordering increased from dermatologists to pathologists, and then to anesthesiologists and general practitioners; for dentistry the incidence of these diseases was successively higher among the following groups: periodontists, orthodontists, oral surgeons, and general practitioners. For law the ordering was patent law, other specialties, trial law, and general legal practice. Similar occupational contrasts in blood pressure have been found in Poland, for miners and laborers (high) compared to teachers and bank clerks (low) (Rozwadowska-Dowzenko et al., 1956), and elevated blood pressures have been reported for other occupational groups who must be responsive to many people under continuous time pressure—telephone operators at a large exchange (Mjasnikov, 1961), taxi drivers (Hamr, 1956). London bus drivers and conductors (Raffle, 1959) fully exposed to metropolitan traffic showed more sick absence, more absence due to functional nervous disorders, and more due to illnesses of the stomach and duodenum than did bus drivers and conductors selected from the same pool but assigned to more protected jobs.

In short, there is an abundance of evidence that people in different occupations show plausible differences in physiological and psychological strain. There is very little evidence, however, regarding the reasons for these differences. The clusters of plausible explanatory factors have yet to be disaggregated. Such differentiation is proceeding, however, in part by means of field experiments, more often by means of multivariate analysis and improved measurement of underlying occupational characteristics.

DIFFERENTIATION OF
OCCUPATIONAL STRESSORS

Our model of stress in the work role (Figure 17-1) emphasized a causal sequence that begins with objective properties or facts about specific work roles and moves successively to the perceptions of those facts by the persons enacting the roles, the immediate responses (behavioral, physiological, and affective) of those persons, and the longer run consequences for their health. The model further stipulates that such causal sequences will be modified by the enduring properties of the individuals involved (their backgrounds, personalities, needs, abilities, and the like) and by the interpersonal context in which the occupational role is enacted. The empirical research that we have just reviewed did not fulfill the model—nor did the various research workers have such intentions. They were, of course, making their own explorations, testing their own hypotheses, and thinking in terms of their own models.

The work of French, Kahn, Caplan, and their colleagues, however, has attempted to develop and test this model of stress in the work role, and the work of Gardell, Frankenhaeuser, and their colleagues (1976) in Sweden has proceeded along similar lines. We will review the results of this research with respect to the identification of specific stressors in the work role, the individual differences in responding to those stresses, and the place of interpersonal support in facilitating the management of work-related stress.

Conflict, Ambiguity, and Overload

The concept of stress (stressor in Selye's terminology) is global, and any research on stress must be more specific. The work at Michigan began with role conflict, which was measured in terms of the wishes of the individual members of 53 role sets in industry (Kahn et al., 1964). Conflicts or discrepancies between their wishes and the behavior of the focal person were shown to have negative effects (correlations) on that person's feelings about the job and the people associated with it. Subsequent research demonstrated that often the effective stress was overload (Sales, 1969). Sales' research showed that the earlier indexes of role conflict consisted of at least two subscales, one of which measured conflict as such (incompatible role expectations). The other subscale measured overload—the perception that one is being asked to do more than time permits, although the required activities themselves are neither intrinsically incompatible or beyond one's abilities. People often experienced such overload as a conflict between quality and quantity, given the constraints of time. Coping could consist of doing less than was expected, doing less well than was expected, or taking more time than was expected; the constraints of quantity, quality, and time could not be met simultaneously. Such overload in the work role has been shown to produce signs of physiological as well as psychological strain.

Caplan (1971) measured overload objectively (visitors, telephone calls, work interruptions) and subjectively, and found both objective and subjective overload to be related to heart rate and serum cholesterol among employees of a government agency. There is some evidence that overload should itself be differentiated, and that quantitative overload (having too much work to do) has different effects from qualitative overload (having work that is too difficult to do). Both generate tension, but administrators appear to be more sensitive to quantitative overload and professors to qualitative overload (French, Tupper, and Mueller, 1965). There is some evidence also that overload tends to be underestimated by the person who is subjected to it, as if a sort of defensive distortion were being employed (Kraut, 1965).

Cobb (1973) has undertaken research on a special form of workload, responsibility, and still more specifically, responsibility for persons as compared to things. He notes that both such responsibilities are associated with cigarette consumption, and that responsibility for the future of others is associated with diastolic blood pressure and cholesterol level. Among the government employees who took part in this research, however, these findings hold only for those who showed "Type A" personality characteristics—an impatient, work-seeking, hard-driving life style first described by Friedman and Rosenman (1959). Cobb also interprets in terms of heavy responsibility for other persons a number of other findings which show occupational associations with disease. These include the high frequency of ulcer among physicians (Doll and Jones, 1951); the high rate of coronary heart disease among anesthesiologists and general practitioners as compared to dermatologists and pathologists (Russek, 1960); and the earlier British finding (Morris et al., 1952) that myocardial infarcts were twice as common among general practitioners as among other physicians in the same age range (40 to 60 years).

Responsible positions in industry show a similar gross pattern, but without any clear isolation of responsibility as the relevant stressor. Supervisors and executives in England have more ulcer disease than the people they supervise (Doll and Jones, 1951); foremen and assistant foremen in Holland have more peptic ulcers than workers under their supervision (Vertin, 1954). Similar results are reported elsewhere in Europe (Pflanz et al., 1956; Gosling, 1958) and in the United States (Cobb, 1973). In one large data set (4,325 air traffic controllers compared to 8,435 second-class airmen), the inference of responsibility is particularly compelling. Hypertension is four times more common among the air traffic controllers, and diabetes and peptic ulcer more than twice as common. Moreover, all three diseases show earlier dates (ages) of onset, and two of them (hypertension and peptic ulcer) show a "traffic effect"—that is, they are more common among traffic controllers assigned to the busier airports.

Overload and Underutilization

The stresses of ambiguity, responsibility for others, and the necessity of choosing between conflicting demands are very real and they have real effects. They are not, however, the most prevalent of job stresses. Many jobs present problems of underutilization rather than qualitative overload; they use few of the worker's skills and abilities (although they may make heavy demands on those few). Gardell (1976) reports a series of field studies investigating such problems in manufacturing, pulp and paper, and sawmill industries in Sweden. In manufacturing jobs, subjective ratings of monotony were related to low self-esteem, low life-satisfaction, and to frequency of nervous complaints and symptoms. In the pulp and paper industry, subjective ratings of autonomy were related to positive scores on the same criteria. In the sawmills, jobs were rated objectively on such dimensions as duration of operating cycle, restriction of posture and movement, demand for sustained vigilance, constraint of work method and pace, and restriction of communication (noise). Workers in jobs rated negatively (disadvantaged) in such respects reflected these ratings in their own perceptions, which were associated with physical and mental exhaustion at the end of the work day, worry about job-related health risks, and relatively high rates of absence attributed to gastrointestinal distress and other physical symptoms.

Two cross-section surveys, one in Sweden (Bohlinder-Ohlstrom, 1971) and one in Denmark (Svane et al., 1974), confirmed this pattern of results. Jobs judged independently as constrained in pace and method tended to be perceived as stressful and monotonous by those who worked at them, and those workers tended also to be more subject to nervous complaints and symptoms, depression, and insomnia. A comparison of extreme groups (hectic pace/low autonomy versus moderate pace/high autonomy) shows such symptoms to be about four times more frequent in the former group.

A more intensive study was conducted by Gardell and his colleagues (Gardell, 1976) within sawmills and lumber-trimming plants. Three categories of jobs were selected for study, a "risk" group and two control or comparison groups. The risk group consisted of jobs with extremely short operating cycles (usually less than 10 seconds), total dependence on machines (saws, edgers, trimmers, etc.) for determining the work pace, sustained positional and postural constraint, and a need for unremitting attentiveness. The first control group included jobs in the same factories but not subject to the same control by machines; these jobs were also less skilled than those in the risk group. The second control group consisted of maintenance workers, whose jobs are high in skill and autonomy. Other factors are comparable across jobs—age, sex, seniority, and (with exceptions) hours of work and methods of pay.

The results show a sharp and consistent pattern of perceived stress, negative affect, and symptoms of strain in the risk group compared to the other two groups. Consistent with that pattern is the higher rate of absence, both general and stress-attributed. Workers in this group also showed lower patterns of off-the-job participation in organizations, and even their participation in union activity was quite low. These findings are summarized in Table 17-1.

Physiological stress reactions were also measured for men in these groups, by means of the amount of adrenaline and noradrenaline in the urine. The results of this analysis are presented in Figure 17-3, which

TABLE 17-1 Job Comparisons in the Sawmill Industry (Sweden): Responses to Objective Stress (Monotony, Lack of Autonomy) (Percentages)

	RISK GROUP	CONTROL GROUP	
		I	II
Workers' perceptions of job			
Very monotonous	43	0	8
Hectic work pace	36	10	0
Work prevents social contact	43	0	0
Workers' affective responses			
Loath to go to work	50	0	0
Physically weary after work	36	10	0
Mentally weary after work	43	10	0
Worried about health risks	29	10	0
Physiological responses			
Elevated blood pressure	14	10	0
Headache	36	0	20
Nervous complaints	36	0	0
Gastric ulcer/catarrh	50	50	30
Back ailments	43	10	20
Behavioral responses			
Malaise attributed to work	57	20	25
30 or more days absent[a]	29	0	0
One or more absences (stress)[a]	43	0	0

[a]Absences, for all causes combined and for reasons of work stress, refer to the twelve months preceding the research.
From Gardell, 1976.

shows significant differences between the risk group and the combined control group, both in level and in pattern during the work day. The secretion of adrenaline and noradrenaline has been used extensively in laboratory research to measure physiological responses to a variety of stimuli regarded as stressful (Frankenhaeuser, 1971), and its reliability and validity are well established. In the present research, a base value was computed for each individual while "at rest." Readings at four times during the work day are shown averaged as percentages of these base values, and the bar charts represent the group averages for the work day.

The overall stress effect of the work day is shown by the bars, which indicate that the risk group has a secretion rate during the work day that is about 150 percent of its rate at rest, while the average secretion rate of the control group at work is little higher than its rate at rest. The pattern of difference during the work day is even more impressive, and is congruent with the subjective reports of the two groups.

The control group begins the day with a secretion rate only a little

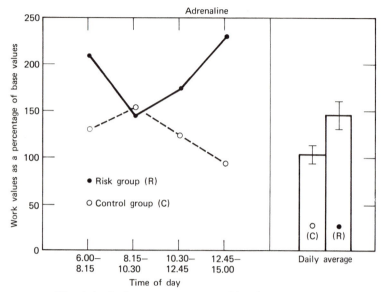

Figure 17-3 *Physiological stress as measured by excretion of adrenaline and noradrenaline. (From Gardell, 1976.)*

above resting levels, peaks early, and "winds down" gradually to an end-of-day reading slightly below rest level. By contrast, workers in the risk group show considerable anticipatory stress at the beginning of the work day and, after a midmorning reduction to rest level, become increasingly stressed, so that their peak reading (more than twice their own base level) occurs at the very end of the work day. This pattern of catecholamine secretion fits their statements of reluctance and anxiety about going to work and their avoidance of social activities after work. As one of them said, "It takes at least a few hours to get all that work rhythm and noise out of your system and before you even feel up to . . . (being) with the family."

SOCIAL SUPPORT AND THE STRESS OF WORK

The relationship of various stressors in the work situation to various indicators of strain is impressive but irregular. Partly to explain such irregularities, and partly for the pragmatic purpose of discovering natural "buffers" against stress, recent research has investigated the extent to which social support may moderate the impact of stress on individuals. Definitions of social support are not agreed on, but the core idea is the communication of positive affect—liking, trust, and respect—by significant other people in one's life. Kahn and Quinn (1976) have included affirmation of one's beliefs and perceptions, and certain kinds of direct assistance. There is disagreement also about the inclusion of reciprocity, the idea that a supportive relationship implies the giving as well as the receiving of support.

In spite of definitional differences, there is a persuasive pattern in the empirical research, especially with respect to the buffering effect of social support during stressful episodes. Cobb (1976) has provided a useful review, which includes evidence from research on various kinds of stressful events and associated strains. The relationship between stress and strain was reduced in the presence of social support, in all of the following situations:

Situational changes and pregnancy complications
(Nuckolls et al., 1971)

Hospitalization (children) and psychological reactions
(Jessner et al., 1952)

Surgery (adult) and speed of recovery (Egbert et al., 1964)

Tuberculosis and success of sanitorium treatment
(Holmes et al., 1961)

Severe life stresses and affective disorder (Brown et al., 1975)

Job loss and arthritis symptoms (Gore, 1973)

Job loss and cholesterol elevation (Cobb, 1974)

Job stress and escapist drinking (Quinn, 1973)

French and his colleagues, working with white-collar employees in a government agency (French, 1976) found that social support from one's peers, supervisor, and subordinates conditions (reduces) the effects of job stress (especially quantitative work load) on serum cortisol, blood pressure, glucose levels in the blood, and number of cigarettes smoked.

The next step has been taken in using a social support framework for on-the-job therapy. In a cooperative union-management venture Weiner, Akabas, and Sommer (1973) have engaged members of the work group as participants in helping fellow workers with their problems. Instead of pulling people out of their jobs, the program kept them on as workers with assists from their colleagues. This unusual delivery of health services involving the work group had marked success in maintaining individuals as functioning members of the organization.

Much remains to be learned about the moderating effects of social support in the work situation, but the evidence thus far argues for its inclusion in studies of work and health. Moreover, it may be only one of a number of interpersonal factors that moderate life stresses, as our model (Figure 17-1) proposes.

STRESS, STRAIN, AND PERSONALITY

The idea that individuals differ in their ways of handling stress and in their ability to do so without damage is very old. It is simple in the abstract but complex in actuality because the issue is not general tolerance or intolerance for stress, but specific responses to specific stressors. President Truman's often-quoted advice that people who can't stand heat should stay out of the kitchen has a metaphoric appeal, but it is more easily quoted than applied.

For one thing, individual tolerance for stress does not generalize across all stresses. Tolerance for isolation and for information input overload, for example, would seem to require rather different resources of personality. The nature and extent of such differences has not been much explored. Secondly, it appears that many attributes of personality may be implicated in an individual's response to a single kind of stress. For example, individual strain in reaction to role conflict was reduced by such personality traits as rigidity, extroversion, and lack of emotional sensitivity (Kahn et al., 1964). Diastolic blood pressure was associated with executive responsibility for the futures of other people, but only for executives who scored high on one or more of the "Type A" personality dimensions—involved striving, persistence, leadership, and positive attitude toward pressure (Friedman, Rosenman, and Carroll, 1958; Sales, 1969; Cobb, 1973).

Research workers in neurophysiology have long been concerned with the issue of specificity and nonspecificity in stress reactions, and Selye (1971) defines stress as the *nonspecific* response of the body to any demand made upon it—that is, a phylogenetically ancient preparation for physical activity, fight or flight. Even so general a definition, however, leaves the question of what elements in the environment (characteristics of the work role, for example) evoke this generalized response. Selye's answer to that question is that every physical and psychosocial factor can act as a stressor, depending on the amount of it. The implication is that for any environmental stimulus or demand, there is a continuum ranging from deprivation to excess as defined in terms of human needs and capacities. At some point between these extremes, the demands and opportunities of the situation would coincide with the abilities and needs of the person. Stress in Selye's sense (strain in ours) would be minimized at the midpoint between these extremes. Levi (1972) presents the model as shown in Figure 17-4.

The symmetry of the figure is schematic rather than repre-

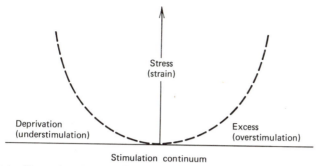

Stress
(strain)

Deprivation
(understimulation)

Excess
(overstimulation)

Stimulation continuum

Figure 17-4   *Stress (strain) in relation to stimulus strength. (After Levi, 1972.)*

sentational in a precise sense. It suggests that some function of this general shape would describe the response of a "normal" population of individuals to any environmental stimulus or demand. Individual differences might be manifested in a number of ways. People certainly differ, for example, in the point of minimal strain for any given variable; unbearable deprivation of company for one person may be welcome solitude for another. People may differ also in the shape of the curve as it would be generated by their own responses to some variable stimulus; a person may be much more able to tolerate the presence of crowds than their absence, for example. The exploration of such differences is an empirical problem; their prediction a problem for personality theory and physiology.

French, Rodgers, and Cobb (1974) have developed a model that defines stress on any given dimension as lack of fit between the needs or abilities of the individual on the one hand and the supplies or demands of the environment on the other. In order to measure goodness-of-fit between person and environment (work role), the relevant property of the work role and of the person must be measured in the same terms. When they are so measured, the size of the discrepancy indicates the degree of fit. Their model does not specify the symmetrical curve of the Selye model, but leaves open the possibility that the shape of the curve may vary for different dimensions, and may be either linear or curvilinear. It seems unlikely, for example, that being paid "more than one needs" would produce strains comparable to those of being paid "less than one needs."

French (1973) and his colleagues tested this model with a population of about 200 men in government employment. Curvilinear relationships were obtained between role ambiguity-clarity and two self-reported strains (symptoms of depression and job-related threat), and between opportunity for participation and the same strains. All four curves showed the lowest strain where goodness of fit between the role and the person was perfect—for example, where the person's job provided the amount of participation that he had said he wanted, neither more nor less. Most of the relationships between person-role fit and indicators of strain, however, were linear, as if "too much of a good thing" (or too little of a bad one) were a contradiction in terms. The issue is worth further exploration, and seems likely to provide insight into the design of jobs beyond that available from measures of job satisfaction alone. In short, research to date on problems of stress at work is agreed on the importance of personality and other individual attributes as modifying the relationship between specific stresses and responses. Agreement remains to be developed regarding the most adequate way of taking such attributes into account in theory and practice.

WORK, NONWORK, AND HEALTH

The concept of goodness-of-fit and the research findings showing that stimulus deprivation can be as stressful as overload are important for those who study the effects of work. Without such reminders the identification of stressors at work could be interpreted as a simplistic argument for nonwork. To the contrary, every study of work deprivation seems to show that it is a more stressful condition than work. The effect of retirement is itself unclear at this point. When they were given the chance in real life, more Detroit auto workers chose early retirement than almost anyone predicted, even though the choice involved reduced pensions. On the other hand, many retired people are unhappy with the lack of required or regularized activity.

The issue seems to be one of replacement, in part. That is, if something of value is to be taken away, what substitute (or improvement) will replace it? The second issue, of course, is how to build into presently disadvantaged occupations those characteristics that make work a valued experience, and how to get rid of some of the social-psychological stressors.

AN ATTEMPT AT INTEGRATION

A recent research project (Caplan et al., 1975) has made an unusual effort to study simultaneously a number of questions addressed in this chapter, from occupational differences to goodness-of-fit. A sample of approximately 2,000 employed men was chosen from 23 widely assorted occupations, exclusive of those known for hazardousness and toxic risk. Self-reported data were obtained on occupational characteristics, symptoms, and health behavior from the entire sample. For a substantial subsample (approximately 400), physiological data were also obtained (blood pressure, pulse rate, and two blood samples). The analysis of these data represents an attempt to investigate all of the major categories of relationships prescribed by the model. The findings are as follows:

1. There are gross differences among occupations with respect to the presence (self-reported) of factors known as stressors from laboratory and field research.
2. These differences can be partitioned to a considerable extent in terms of four occupational clusters—blue-collar unskilled, blue-collar skilled, white-collar nonprofessional, and white-collar professional.
3. When occupations are so ordered, they are ordered also with respect to participation in decisions, social support, certainty (versus ambiguity) about the future, complexity, and freedom from quantitative overload and unwanted overtime.
4. Exposure to the stressful end of these dimensions is associated with negative affective responses, especially boredom and dissatisfaction with the work role.
5. These negative reactions to the job are in turn associated with more general negative affects—feelings of depression, irritation, and anxiety. These in turn are associated with somatic symptoms.
6. Occupations that are conspicuously advantaged with respect to the social-psychological descriptors of content also show some expected health patterns. For example, scientists have lower blood pressure than other occupational groups, and professors fewer respiratory and cardiovascular illnesses (visits to physicians).
7. The predictive power of the social-psychological descriptors of work roles is enhanced when goodness-of-fit with the needs of the individual is taken into account—for example, unwanted overtime, less task complexity than preferred, underutilization of (perceived) skills and abilities.
8. The effects of many job stresses on the persons exposed to them—that is, the relationship between stress and strain—appears to be buffered or moderated by the presence of social support, the sense that one is part of a network of people who communicate, understand, and help each other.

The description of occupations in terms of quantitative social-psychological variables is by no means complete. Multiple correlations obtained in the preceding research are of the order of .7 for the prediction of job-related affect (boredom, work-load dissatisfaction, and overall dissatisfaction); these predict the more general effects of irritation and depressive symptoms with about the same power, and these in turn predict somewhat less well to somatic symptoms.

Occupation, to the social-psychologist, is in a sense a surrogate variable, and descriptors of a more specific kind are wanted. But such descriptors are not yet able to account for all occupational differences, nor would occupation become an obsolete concept even if they could do so. Work is offered in packages, not as separate variables, and occupations denote those packages or work roles. Understanding of work must therefore take occupational differences into account, and the improvement of work roles must take place within occupations.

■ SUMMARY ■

Let us return to the model with which we begin (Figure 17-1), and consider the extent to which it has been illuminating and illuminated. Two aspects of that model are particularly important for this process: (1) the basic causal sequence that leads from *objective factors* in the work environment to *subjective factors* (work as perceived), from those perceptions to *responses* (psychological, physiological, and behavioral), and from those responses to *indicators of health or illness:* and (2) the modification or conditioning of that sequence by properties of the person (physique, personality, background) and of the interpersonal context (social support, etc.)

With those aspects in mind, we can summarize the research evidence in order of its presentation. First, evidence links occupation (and class of worker) to health. Most social-psychological stressors and their negative consequences for well-being are concentrated in occupations of lower status. Certain forms of overload and responsibility for persons are exceptional in this respect. Physical hazards and toxic exposures, while sometimes completely specific to certain jobs, also are more prevalent in low-status, blue-collar occupations.

Second, laboratory research has identified many stressors—social-psychological, physical, and task-intrinsic. The replication of such research under ongoing organizational conditions has begun (Gardell, 1976, for example), but much remains to be done.

Third, some social-psychological stressors have been assessed in real-life organizations and their psychological and physiological effects have been demonstrated, at least in part.

Among such stressors are role conflict, role ambiguity, overload, responsibility for persons and for things, lack of autonomy, and monotony. Field studies of stress have been conducted for the most part on small and concentrated populations, but more representative samples (Caplan et al., 1975, for example) have begun to come into use.

Fourth, we know that relationships between stress and strain are not uniform. Individuals differ in their tolerance for different kinds of stresses and in their ways of handling them. It seems likely also that the effects of stress at work are moderated or conditioned by other interpersonal resources available to the individual, or at least by the interpersonal context in which the stress is experienced.

The studies of stress in the laboratory, in selected field situations, and on representative population samples are complementary. In combination they have begun to illuminate both the epidemiology of stress and the causal relationships between specific stresses and strains.

18
■ CONFLICT

OUTLINE

The fact of conflict—of being somehow involved with opposing forces—must surely be among the most common of human experiences. We recognize conflict in the opposition of wishes within ourselves, in the clashes between others whom we observe, and in the struggles against those we ourselves oppose. And, according to our temperament and experience, we seek it or avoid it, fear it or enjoy it, call it sickness or call it life.

Social science has been no less ambivalent. Incompatible motives within the person, incompatible aims between competing organizations, incompatible interests among different social classes were much emphasized in earlier theories of human action (Freud, Marx, and the classical economists, for example). There followed a period of what now seems substantial underemphasis, both of the pervasiveness of conflict and of its possible functions.

About 1950, however, there began to appear a stream of publications calling attention to the importance of conflict for understanding human behavior, criticizing its neglect, and proposing researchable questions about it. A group of social scientists committed to the study of conflict as a social process founded the *Journal of Conflict Resolution* in 1957 at the University of Michigan and, shortly thereafter, a center for research on the same subject. Several major books on conflict appeared within a few years of each other (Coser, 1956; Dahrendorf, 1959; Rapoport, 1960; Boulding, 1962). Since that time, the empirical study of conflict has grown steadily, although much of that growth has involved small experiments within the framework of game theory, especially two-person, zero-sum games.

The applicability of such research to organizational behavior is neither easy nor certain, and still less certain is the answer to Boulding's (1962) question: "Is there a general phenomenon of conflict, and therefore a general theory of conflict, that applies in all these areas?" Boulding answered his own question in the affirmative and attempted to provide such a general theory. We are inclined to a more qualified response. There is indeed a general category of phenomena that share certain common characteristics and can reasonably be called conflict. But the differentiating characteristics of conflict at different phenomenal levels are of sufficient importance to require separate conceptual and theoretical specification. The conflicts of individuals and groups, organizations, and nation-states require explanations that take account of their emergent differences as well as their similarities. Our efforts are concentrated on the explanation of conflict at the organizational level, where the parties at conflict are either total organizations or relatively autonomous subunits of organizations. We begin with an attempt to describe conflict in terms that have general applicability, and then proceed to develop a model that is specific to organizational conflict.

The remainder of the chapter examines the evidence for the major elements of this model.

THE DEFINITION OF CONFLICT

Like so many other organizational terms—effectiveness or leadership, for example—conflict has both a colloquial meaning and a discouragingly long list of specific definitions. The list includes at least four rather different usages of the term: (1) *antecedent conditions* to some overt struggle (for example, scarcity of resources); (2) *affective states* (for example, tension or hostility); (3) *cognitive states* (for example, the perception that some other person or entity acts against one's interests); and (4) *conflictful behavior,* verbal or non verbal, ranging from passive resistance to active aggression (Pondy, 1967).

Our definition of conflict belongs to the last of these four categories, although the preceding categories are interesting and relevant. If two business firms are engaged in a price war, or a business and labor union are engaged in a strike, it is those actions that constitute conflict as we understand it. Whether a particular instance of such conflict is characterized by real or imagined differences of interest, by great anger or lack of it, by a hostile act or a misunderstood gesture of friendship are appropriate questions to understanding the conflict but not to defining it; it is defined by the collision of actors.

Two systems (persons, groups, organizations, nations) are in conflict when they interact directly in such a way that the actions of one tend to prevent or compel some outcome against the resistance of the other. This definition is comfortably close to the colloquial meaning of conflict and true to the Latin origin of the word (strike together), although neither of these facts contributes to its scientific utility. More to the point, the definition makes conflict a matter of observable behavior, a kind of behavior characterized by systems at many levels. It also serves to distinguish conflict from such related phenomena as incompatibilities ("conflicts") of interest, unfavorable or unflattering opinions, and separate seeking after the same scarce resource or unique outcome. Moreover, the definition distinguishes conflict from non-conflictual influence and persuasion; conflict requires direct resistance as well as a direct attempt at influence or injury.

Competition and Conflict

Like conflict, competition involves two or more systems, individual or social, engaged in activities that are in some sense incompatible; the successful completion of one precludes the successful completion of the other. By our definitions, however, competition itself involves no direct action of one party to interfere with the ongoing actions of the other. Should such interference and resistance occur, the competition would have become conflict. The distinction is familiar enough in sport. Track events are competitive rather than conflictful. For example, each pole vaulter attempts to go higher than the other competitors for the record, but their efforts are separate in time and the major competitors need not even be in the same place to compete for some titles. On the other hand, opponents in football or tennis or chess act directly against each other, and the success of one person or team depends to a large extent on successful interference with the activities of the other.

We have encountered exactly this distinction in the discussion of organizational environments (Chapter 5). Even in a placid-randomized environment, two systems dependent on the same scarce inputs may be said to compete, and in placid-clustered environments the competition becomes more explicit; superior knowledge improves the prospects for survival. In the disturbed-reactive environment, competition is heightened and conflict begins. As Emery and Trist (1965) describe it:

> ... the existence of a number of similar organizations now becomes the dominant characteristic of the environmental field. Each organization does not simply have to take account of the others when they meet at random, but has also to consider that what it knows can also be known by the others. The part of the environment to which it wishes to move itself in the long run is also the part to which the others seek to move. Knowing this, each will wish to *improve its own chances by hindering the others*, and each will know that the others must not only wish to do likewise, but also know that each knows this. (p. 25)

And although Emery and Trist do not define conflict in terms of "improving one's own chances by hindering the others," their explication of the organization in a disturbed-reactive environment fulfills our definition well:

> ... The new element is that of deciding which of someone else's possible tactics one wishes to take place, while ensuring that others of them do not. An operation consists of a campaign involving a planned series of tactical initiatives, calculated reactions by others, and counter-actions.

We can thus distinguish among three commonly used concepts— *conflict of interest*, by which we mean incompatible needs or preferences; *competition*, by which we mean incompatible activities with respect to some objective; and *conflict*, by which we mean incompati-

ble interactions. This is quite consistent with Coser's (1956, 1958) definition of social conflict as a ."struggle... in which the aims of the
conflicting parties are not only to gain the desired values but also to
neutralize, injure, or eliminate their rivals (1958, pp. 232–236)." Conflict, then, is a particular kind of interaction, marked by efforts at hindering, compelling, or injuring and by resistance or retaliation against
those efforts.

CONFLICT AS PROCESS

To define conflict as a particular kind of interacting behavior (hindering, compelling, injuring against resistance) implies that it can best
be understood as a process. Such acts do not occur without reason and
they seldom occur singly. Nor is the process sustained indefinitely; it
begins with some attempted action against and a concomitant attempt
at resistance, and it has an observable duration and conclusion. The
conflict process, in other words, can be thought of as consisting of a
series of episodes, each with its beginning and ending.

Any of several endings is possible. The initial attempt at compulsion or interference may be abandoned, the resistance may cease, some
compromise pattern of activity may be agreed on that offers partial
satisfaction to each of the contesting parties, or some wholly creative
outcome may be devised that changes the initial terms of reference and
renders the incompatible compatible. Regardless of the outcome—
victory, defeat, compromise, or new solution—the conflicting behaviors reduce or cease and an episode of conflict may be said to have
ended.

There may be other conflict episodes, of course, on the same issues
and between the same protagonists, and when we speak of a conflict
relationship we imply a series of such episodes or conflict cycles. It
should be possible, then, to identify such episodes and the more specific behaviors that comprise them when we observe organizational
life; they form a special subset of the ongoing events of that life. This
does not imply, however, that elements of that set belong only to it; acts
of conflict may also be acts of leadership, of control, or of innovation
and change, for example. To put it another way, the topic of conflict
cuts across many other issues in organizational theory and research,
and the meaning of conflict becomes clearer as we examine these inter-
sections.

Some continuing struggle for existence is implied in the definition
of organizations as open systems, systems that tend to "run down" and
to lose the qualities that differentiate them from their environments.
They maintain themselves and their boundaries only by means of continuing advantageous interaction processes for resources (time, space,

materials, energy, etc.) that are almost always scarce in some sense and frequently contested. The consequent emergence of conflict seems unavoidable, given this view of organization and environment; it is the forms and magnitudes and modes of resolution that are at issue.

The potentiality for conflict inherent in mere maintenance of the organizational system is heightened by the bureaucratic tendency we have called the maximization principle. Whether this is an inevitable concomitant of bureaucratic organizations, or a dynamic that can be subordinated to maintenance and equilibrium as external conditions require, remains to be seen. The forces toward maximization are certainly present, however, and they imply conflict. To the extent that the organization drives toward expansion, the conflict is likely to be external; to the extent that it decides against expansion, the conflicts are likely to be internal. The rationale for creating supranational organizations is in part to relocate national conflicts within the new organizational boundaries and to provide within those boundaries modes of resolution less disastrous than military action. (See Chapter 4 for discussion of the maximization principle, and Chapter 5 for more extended discussion of system properties and environmental relationships.)

Indeed, the internal structure of organizations can be seen as a complex set of arrangements, many of which have conflict as an unintended outcome and some of which have the prevention or management of conflict as their primary purpose. To some extent the division of labor itself creates subsystems with distinctive interests and aims, and yet with the unavoidable need to reconcile and coordinate in order to create a common output. The situation includes conflict of interest and competition for scarce resources by definition; conflict itself begins as soon as the representatives of one subsystem act to prevent or handicap the efforts of another, or speak to disparage its claims.

Still more productive of conflict, of course, is the vertical or hierarchical dimension of organizational life, although this is also the major means for the prevention and adjudication of conflict in conventional bureaucratic organizations. The organizational hierarchy is essentially a gradient of power and authority, concerned with the allocation of resources, the setting of performance commitments, the assignment of activities to roles, and the prevention or adjudication of differences. The scale of these concerns increases as one ascends the hierarchy, and the immediacy of surveillance and decision making decreases. These activities are in some respects conflict-preventing and conflict-limiting, and are so intended. On the other hand, leaders of organizations often encourage competition among individuals and subunits in order to energize them and improve their performance. Such competition readily escalates to conflict and many managements are continually engaged in reducing some of the resulting conflicts while unintentionally preparing the ground for others.

Perhaps more important for the prevalence of intraorganizational conflict is the fact that acts of hierarchical authority almost inevitably involve the prevention of behavior and the frustration of efforts at lesser levels; some naysaying cannot be avoided. To the extent that the hierarchy of authority has less legitimacy than the term implies and less than overwhelming power of other kinds, the hierarchical decisions are likely to be contested by those whom they disadvantage.

Moreover, the hierarchy of management in conventional organizations is almost always a hierarchy of reward and privilege as well. To the extent that pay, job security, fringe benefits, flexibility in hours and movement, opportunity for conversation, and the like are differentiated on a vertical basis, the organization tends to consist of two or more social classes, and important lines of potential conflict are thus defined. Further potentialities for conflict are inherent in the nature of organizational membership. To say that people are only *partially included* in an organization, or that a person's role in an organization is only one of an array of roles enacted by that individual means that perfect congruence among role expectations is highly improbable. Incompatible demands mean role conflict for the individual, as we have seen (Chapter 7). To the extent that the individual acts to modify those expectations or fails to fulfill them, he or she makes change demands on others and may well be led into conflict with them.

In short, every aspect of organizational life that creates order and coordination of effort must overcome other tendencies to action, and in that fact lies the potentiality for conflict. Organizational roles prescribe one set of behaviors out of a very large repertoire, and in prescribing necessarily proscribe as well. Rewards and incentives are necessary inducements to membership and performance, but consensus about their allocation is almost unattainable, and conflict about it increases with their attractiveness. Authority is a conflict-reducing invention, but its exercise implies submission to influence, which is almost never perfect. Organizational change is necessary for survival, but an organization with no internal resistance to change would be no organization at all; it would move in any direction and in response to any suggestion. Change and the resistance to change, however, mean conflict.

Such tendencies toward conflict, prominent within organizations, are exacerbated in interorganizational life. The common bonds of membership, the partial identification with overall systemic success, the sharing of a fate that depends at least on the survival of the enterprise are all factors that tend to contain intraorganizational conflict but are less relevant in the interorganizational situation. Yet here potential conflicts may be contained by supraorganizational forces—normative and statutory. Civil and criminal law sets some limits on interorganizational conflict behavior, and regulatory agencies set others.

Moreover, organizations in conflict are also likely to be cooperating in some respects. A union and management may be at conflict over wage demands, but they are also engaged in a collaborative process of wage determination. Charles Horton Cooley (1918) said long ago that "the more one thinks of it, the more he will see that conflict and cooperation are not separable things, but phases of one process which always involves something of both." (p. 39) The problem then becomes not the elimination of conflict but its understanding and regulation.

A MODEL OF CONFLICT

Social scientists have sometimes been accused of "boxology," a malady manifested by the irresistible urge to reduce complex phenomena to diagrams consisting of small boxes and connecting arrows. This accusation, whether or not generally true, applies to the literature of conflict and the models it contains. A more serious problem for our purposes, however, is that most models of conflict are abstracted from organizational reality. One of the exceptions is that of Thomas (1976), and we have used it in developing our own.

Let us begin by considering two organizations as the systems or parties at conflict, and then proceed to specify the categories of variables necessary to understand the conflict process and its outcomes.

1. *Organizational properties.* Experience argues that organizations differ in their tendencies to engage in conflict even when the external risks and incentives are not different. The conflict-relevant properties of organizations have not been well-established, but several possibilities seem worth investigation.

   We would begin by looking for conflict-prone organizational structures. An organization that has established some special substructure to conduct conflicts is more likely to engage in them. The means are at hand; other organizational units can "delegate" to the specialists conflicts that they might otherwise have felt it necessary to resolve earlier. Moreover, when conflict-conducting roles are created, the people assigned to them are conflict-prone. An organization that creates strong-arm squads or espionage units will have a different conflict history from one that puts the same investment into experts in arbitration and mediation.

   Organizational ideologies about conflict also differ, as union-management relations and intercompany relations clearly indicate. It is likely that the conflict-relevant aspects of organizational ideology originate at or near the top, and that norms about seeking or avoiding open conflict move gradually through the organization.

Finally, there are organizational properties that are likely to be conflict-generating even though they have no explicit ideological content. For example, an organization that is growing more rapidly than the supply and demand properties of its environment must alter its growth pattern or maintain it at the expense of its competitors. Competition under such circumstances may move toward conflict.

2. *Conflict of interest.* This is an emergent concept. A conflict of interest exists when two or more organizations (units) exhibit incompatible properties. Substantive areas of conflict of interest require specification, as does the extent of the conflict of interest in each area—that is, the extent to which the successful performance (goal attainment) of one organization precludes that of the other. In game theory, these characteristics are usually presented as a "pay-off matrix." Both objective conflict of interest (independently assessed) and subjective conflict of interest (perceived by the actors in the situation) are relevant for the prediction of conflict behavior.

3. *Role expectations.* To talk of organizations in conflict is accurate in a sense, but not all members of conflicting organizations are interacting across the organizational boundaries. On the contrary, organizations at conflict are represented by relatively small numbers of people in certain boundary positions. Those people do interact across the organizational boundaries, and their behavior is particularly important in determining the outcome of the conflict. Their behavior is not spontaneous, however; to a large extent it is role behavior, determined by the role expectations of people in the organizations from which the boundary persons come and to which they return.

Diplomats, labor negotiators, soldiers, and other organizational representatives in conflict situations are always, in this respect, instructed delegates. They are also subject to the unique set of influences and expectations generated by the conflict interaction itself. Adams' (1976) discussion of the stresses associated with boundary roles has a special relevance for those most difficult boundary positions. Other properties of roles and role-sending as described in Chapter 7 are applicable to the conflict situation.

4. *Personality and predisposition.* The behavior of people in any role reflects in part their individual characteristics of background and personality. Those characteristics influence the role

expectations themselves, the expectations as perceived by the individual, and the consequent behavior (Chapter 7). The importance of such predispositional factors increases with the autonomy of the role and the distance of its enactment from the role set. These tendencies may be offset in the conflict situation by the peculiar visibility of the people at the conflict boundary and of the outcome of the conflict, if not the process itself. Conflict roles also legitimize aggressive and hostile behavior (especially in the eyes of the constituencies) that would not be tolerated in other circumstances. It is plausible that selection processes for such roles (and self-selection as well) bring to them people who find such behavior acceptable or even rewarding. Every organization has the problem of excluding from such roles people who cannot be depended on to manage their own aggressive tendencies.

5. *External norms, rules, and procedures.* Conflicts between organizations are subject to a number of constraints external to the conflicting organizations themselves. Some of these are legal; the usual civil and criminal proscriptions apply to conflict situations, and special statutes may also apply. The Wagner Act and the Taft-Hartley Act are only two of a long line of legislative attempts to regulate labor-management conflict in the United States. Forms of presentation, timing and postponement, "cooling-off" periods, conditions under which mediation or arbitration by third parties may be offered or compelled are set by law or executive ruling, presumably in terms that represent the interests of the larger system or society of which the conflicting organizations are elements.

In addition to these constraints or assistances, there may be less formal norms and values that are strongly held in the larger society and therefore define the allowable forms and outcomes of conflict. The contesting organizations may even agree in advance on their interpretation of these external factors and on supplements to them.

6. *Interaction.* This term refers to the behavior of those people who are enacting the organizational conflict, and it is predicted and explained by the preceding five sets of variables. The interaction of parties at conflict, however, is a process in its own right and it generates dynamics of its own. Their behavior at any moment is determined in part by the preceding exchange, and those before it, and so on to the beginning of the process or the end of discernible effects.

These six sets of variables and their major relationships are shown in Figure 18-1, for two conflicting organizational units (*A* and *B*), each

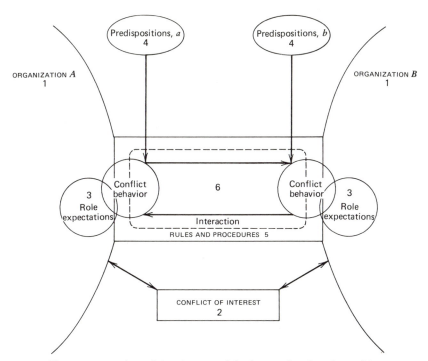

Figure 18-1 *A multivariate model of organizational conflict.*

represented by a single individual (a and b). The remaining sections of this chapter consider the major evidence and hypotheses for each of the six sets thus identified.

Organizational Properties

Many characteristics of organizations and organizational environments can be offered as plausible factors in the determination of conflict, but few such hypotheses have been investigated. Certain loci of intraorganizational conflict, however, are very familiar: line versus staff, sales versus manufacturing, and points of resource allocation among relatively autonomous organizational units (Blake, Shepard, and Mouton, 1964).

Lawrence and Lorsch (1967) found that differentiation among departments increased the amount of conflict among them with respect to time, funds, and other chronically scarce resources. This is consistent with the earlier finding by Collins and Guetzkow (1964) that time pressure increased conflict in decision-making conferences, and the finding by Cyert and March (1963) that organizational "slack" of any kind tends to reduce interdepartmental conflict by reducing the required tightness of interdependence and coordination.

There is also some evidence for "conflict proneness" as an aspect of organizational climate or ideology. Thomas (1976) predicts some tendency toward intraorganizational consistency in handling conflicts, based on the finding that supervisors who emphasize peace and cooperation tend to evoke such behavior from their subordinates. Multiorganizational research to identify conflict-prone and conflict-managing organizations is much needed. In many ways the classic experiment on organizational conflict to date remains Sherif's (1958) Robbers Cave experiment, in which conflict between groups of boys at a summer camp was induced by the emphasis on differences and competitive activities, and was subsequently resolved by the creation of superordinate goals—the posing of situations in which members of both groups could get what they wanted (money for a movie, truck repair to enable a trip to the city, etc.) only through cooperative effort. The experimental manipulations were complex, involving the introduction of new goals and a consequent reduction in conflict of interest, and one may question the ethics if not the effectiveness of the initial induction of conflict between the groups. The relevant fact for our present purposes, however, is the extent to which intergroup conflict was created by emphasizing incompatibilities of interest between groups.

Blake, Shepard, and Mouton (1964) report similar conflict dynamics in more than 150 groups of executives engaged in a training program; the attainment of superordinate goals (except for understanding the conflict process itself) was not a part of their design, however. Their training design typically involved two groups of about 20 executives, with most of the activities concentrated within the groups. Each group developed a kind of competitive curiosity about the other—its rate of progress, its learning, and the like. These feelings intensified greatly when the experimenters announced an intergroup competitive exercise, the two competing "products" to be evaluated by a panel of judges at a public ceremony, with appropriate recognition of the winning group. Matters of communication or secrecy between groups, truth or falsehood, espionage or disregard were left to the decision of the groups themselves. The evaluation of the group products, however, was to take place only after representatives of each group had explained the virtues of their own group product and rebutted the claims of the other group.

The scenario from that point on was almost unvarying for the 150 groups: the unquestioning acceptance of the conflictful frame of reference, the intragroup emphasis on winning rather than on learning or on maximizing quality of product, the increase of tension, the closing of ranks and consolidation of leadership, the suppression of deviant ideas within groups, the deprecation of the other group, and the enhancement of one's own. When the two group products were made available for the inspection of all participants, the conflict became open, with verbal attacks and counterattacks, minimizing commonalities of the two products and disregard of integrative possibilities. Representatives from each group were scheduled to present and explain its product at a meeting of all participants and judges. Group instructions to these representatives were quasi-military: attack and win; don't concede anything. The representatives of the two groups thus did not have much opportunity to develop a group culture of their own of negotiation and compromise. They were under the eyes of members of their own group who might regard conciliatory moves as disloyal.

After the judges' decision, members of the winning group lionized their representative, congratulated each other, and showed little disposition to learn from the experience. Nor did they exhibit any empathy for the losers. The losing group, on the other hand, was typically unhappy, concerned with understanding the defeat, and much more likely to learn from it. The losers were also likely, however, to put considerable energy into blaming and scape-goating, partly directed at their opponents and the judges, but partly at their representative.

This series of training experiments by Blake and his colleagues can be considered as multiple replications of the Sherif (1958) experiment. They illustrate well the functional and dysfunctional elements in conflict: the energizing and the distortion, the increased motivation to attain a group goal, and the displacement of that goal from solving a problem to beating an opponent. The Blake experiments also illustrate the power of organizational arrangements—even in a simulated situation—to shape human behavior, the behavior of persons with wide experience no less than that of pre-adolescent children. Finally, these exercises must be taken as reminders of the ease with which conflict behavior can be evoked in our culture.

Conflict of Interest

By conflict of interest we mean incompatible needs or preferences regarding some action. Deutsch (1973) uses the concept of *contrient interdependence* to describe this state of affairs, thus reminding us that conflict requires interdependence; indifference does not motivate conflict behavior. In the case of organizations, we would begin by looking for conflict of interest in connection with the three major organizational processes: resource getting, throughput, and appropriate disposal of output. For example, two organizations or organizational subunits may depend on the same scarce resources or materials, may utilize the same production facilities and staff, or may compete for the limited dollars of the same clientele or funding source.

Under such circumstances either may act to block or otherwise interfere with the activities of the other, or both may engage in such conflict behavior. The overt conflict, however, need not occur at the point of the essential incompatibility. Two organizations manufacturing the same type of product may have arrived independently at the goal of doubling their share of the market. The goals are incompatible and, more specifically, the incompatibility involves the "sharing" of a limited market or clientele. The overt conflict, however, might take the form of one trying to prevent the other from obtaining needed inputs.

Schmidt and Kochan (1972) review a number of studies illustrating different loci of initial incompatibility and subsequent conflict. They propose the hypothesis that the likelihood of overt conflict between organizational units is a function of three variables: the incompatibility of their goals, the interdependence of their activities, and the extent to which they share the same resources. The locus of the overt conflict might presumably be chosen for reasons of strategy, left to chance, or might develop out of competitive activities in the area of incompatibility.

Trist and Bamforth's classic study of coal mining (1951) illustrates technologically determined conflicts of interest and the loci of the resulting overt conflicts. In the short-wall technology there was competition between mining teams, sometimes consisting of only six workers on three shifts, for maximizing the team earnings (incompatible goals). Moreover, the teams used a common supply of tubs in which to convey the coal (shared resources). If one team held more tubs than it needed, another was likely to have fewer than it needed. Conflict between teams occurred mainly around the sharp practices of their "trammers" in obtaining and holding the team's supply of tubs.

The conversion to the more mechanized methods that Trist and Bamforth call "conventional longwall" involved the specialization of function by shift, with the first shift cutting into the coal face, the second shift shoveling the coal into the conveyor, and the third shift advancing the coal face and enlarging the gateways. Further task specialization occurred within shifts, and pay was individually computed. There was conflict of interest between shifts with respect to maximizing pay, and overt conflicts developed at the points of interdependence—between the "gummers" and "fillers," for example. The gummers could and did interfere with the fillers' ability to do their job. When the gummers left some of the gummings (thus maximizing their own productivity as computed for payroll purposes), they created increased difficulty for the fillers, who were then unable to meet their production goals. Some of the gains subsequently shown by the composite longwall method as an alternative organizational form can be explained by the avoidance of such intraorganizational conflict.

The interdependence of the three shifts in the conventional longwall technology was not an unadulterated conflict of interest. In some respects the interests of the three shifts converged: the second shift could not shovel more coal than the first shift had cut; the third shift could not advance the coal face beyond the area that had been cut and cleared, and so on. The shifts were thus dependent on each other in positive as well as negative ways; the volume of work done by each shift not only set its own pay but also defined the pay opportunity for the next shift.

Deutsch (1973) uses the concept of *promotive interdependence* to describe such relationships, in contrast to the *contrient interdependence* that constitutes pure conflict of interest. In conflict experiments, the two can be presented in pure form; in organizations they are likely to be mingled. Sales and manufacturing departments are often in conflict, for example, and they are characteristically interdependent in both promotive and contrient ways. Each depends on the other; sales can sell only what has been manufactured and manufacturing can continue only if the products are sold. On the other hand, the work of selling is made easier if delivery is immediate, prices are low, and product specifications are flexible; the work of manufacture by most processes is made easier and more profitable if delivery schedules can be made flexible, prices are set well above costs, and product variations are limited. Thus, the potential for conflict is high, at least under conventional forms of organization.

Dutton and Walton (1966) describe such a conflict, between a production department emphasizing the goals of efficiency and cost control, and a sales department emphasizing the quality of service and the building of sales volume. The blocking or interference was mutual, and took the form of distorting or withholding information. Production staff would claim not to have certain materials available, in order to prevent sales staff from making product or delivery commitments opposed by the production group. Sales would withhold information that might have facilitated cost control in the productive process.

The evidence for conflicts of interest and conflict behavior between organizational units is voluminous but for the most part neither experimental nor quantitative. Certain issues and loci of conflict predominate, among them resource allocation (Walton and McKersie, 1965), matters of jurisdiction between departments (White, 1961; Seiler, 1963), autonomy and control between supervisors and those supervised (Argyris, 1964), and, at the individual level, questions of status and its rewards. Measures of magnitude of conflicts of interest are much needed.

Laboratory experiments with conflict, while limited in many ways, have been able to vary systematically both the absolute and the relative conflict of interest between persons, and to measure the effects of such variations on their behavior within the terms of the experiments. The absolute magnitude of a conflict of interest is measured in terms of the size of the stakes, the total amount a party may gain or lose, in units of dollars, prestige, or other quantities. The relative conflict of interest is a ratio, the unit gain to one party for each unit loss to the other. This ratio is thus a measure of the "zero sumness" of a game; it is +1.00 for a completely zero-sum situation and −1.00 for a completely cooperative situation in which no conflict of interest exists.

Rapoport and his colleagues (1965) conducted a series of conflict experiments in which each party was given the opportunity to make a choice that maximized their joint reward or maximized self-reward at the expense of the other. The experimenters refer to these as cooperative and defecting choices. As the experimental series proceeded, they systematically increased the reward for "defecting"—that is, taking advantage of a person who had made a cooperative choice. Rank-order correlations between conflict of interest and conflict behavior, so defined, were .86 in two-person games and .78 in three-person games. No other predictor exhibited such power. Solomon (Deutsch, 1971) showed a similar pattern in reverse; experimental subjects became increasingly trusting in their moves as the payoff matrix was modified to make it clear that one gained little or nothing by acting against the other.

Experiments in which either the relative or the absolute conflict of interest was varied separately show that each has potent effects. Gumpert, Deutsch, and Epstein (1969) kept the matrix pattern (relative conflict of interest) constant in a series of experimental games, but increased the stakes (absolute conflict of interest) successively from zero (no money) to one cent, five cents, ten cents, and one dollar per trial. Cooperation decreased steadily as stakes increased over twenty trials. Similar results are reported for other laboratory exercises (Deutsch, Canavan, and Rubin, 1971). The inference seems clear: conflict of interest makes conflict behavior rational in some terms of reference, and therefore makes it more probable.

Role Expectations

The behavior of individuals in organizational conflicts is essentially role behavior, a fact that makes generalizations from two-person laboratory games problematical and prediction from personality characteristics alone even more dubious. In addition to the processes of role-sending and receiving already described for organizational life in general and boundary roles in particular, two properties of conflict roles deserve mention.

1. The role-set within the parent organization is likely to be large and varied, and to include persons well up in the organizational hierarchy. Conflict roles are important, symbolically and prag-

matically, and their role-sets can be expected to reflect their significance.

2. The conflict role involves complex phenomena of representation and constituency. The person in such a role can be thought of as subject to the expectations of two role-sets (or two discrete parts of a single set), one inside his or her own organization and the other in the opposing organization. Something similar could be said of all boundary positions, but in conflict roles the two sets of expectations are oppositional by definition. To the extent that third parties and publics enter into the situation, the role expectations of the protagonists become still more complex.

Most conflicts within and between organizations are enacted by individuals who come from some organizational sector (department, division, subsystem, etc.) and who represent it—either officially or in the sense that their behavior will be subsequently reviewed and evaluated by others in their sector. Such representatives often find themselves engaged in two conflicts—one with their antagonists and another with their constituents, who have their own ideas about how the former conflict should be conducted.

During a prolonged conflict, the dynamics of such constituent groups both support and constrain the representative, further complicating the requirements of the role. The closing of ranks, the increased unity of purpose, the strengthening of hierarchy and leadership during periods of conflict have been often observed. Representatives are thus assured of the group's support, but at the same time new conditions and incentives are added, to win and win on the group's terms. The constraints are often informal (Festinger et al., 1950), but they may also take the form of explicit instructions to the representative and a requirement that any resolution of the conflict be subject to ratification (Megginson and Gullett, 1970).

Evidence for the direction of such group pressures is consistent: they stimulate "win-or-lose" tactics and reduce the tendency to compromise or "problem solve." In a series of laboratory experiments with male college students, Brown (1968) found that even a silent audience of significant peers evoked a strong motive on the part of antagonists to "save face." When the audience indicated to either antagonist that he had lost face, that person's subsequent behavior tended to be aggressive even when the risks and costs of aggression made such behavior unwise.

These results of Brown from a conflict game (the Deutsch and Krauss game that sets two truck operators in conflict over the use of a common one-way stretch of road) involved only small monetary stakes and brief simulations of organizational life. Research in organizational settings (Walton and McKersie, 1965; Stern and Pearse, 1968) also shows a tendency for constituent groups to want their representatives to report victory, not mere problem solving. Stern and Pearse (1968) suggest that this tendency could be eliminated by providing opportunity for constituents to be exposed to the pressures and alternatives in the conflict situation. The facts of organizational life make it difficult and costly to provide such opportunities even when people are convinced of their importance. Open meetings on issues at conflict, wider access to the records of such meetings, rotation of people in conflict-representing roles may be useful, but the many difficulties are inherent in the conflict roles themselves.

Behavioral Predispositions

Popular explanations of conflict behavior exemplify a kind of Aristotelian logic: two parties are observed to be in conflict, and their conflictful behavior is ascribed to the bellicose natures of one or both. The research on conflict gives some small support for such explanations, but the weight of the evidence is counterintuitive: situational factors of several kinds are more important predictors of conflict than are individual predispositions.

Berkowitz (1962) offers some experimental evidence that individuals develop characteristic hierarchies of response, which come into action successively as required to attain some goal. Blake and Mouton (1964) assume that parties to a conflict situation approach it with some dominant style or orientation, and a back-up style in case of initial failure. The "win-lose orientation" is hypothesized to be a major determinant of conflict behavior. Walton and McKersie (1965) argue that this orientation leads parties to define problems in zero-sum terms when other definitions are at least equally true to the presenting facts.

Some evidence for such effects has been found in organizational settings. Stagner (1962) showed that labor relations at the plant level bore a modest relationship to personality characteristics of managers and union stewards, especially their needs for power and dominance. In the same study, the tendency of managers and stewards to behave accommodatively was related to their needs for affiliation, a finding replicated by Bass and Dunteman (1963). Moreover, individual differences in response to conflict—for example, the tendency to experience aggression as satisfying—are well established (Berkowitz 1962).

Personality traits that lead to constructive approaches to conflict have been suggested but little researched. They include optimism, which is hypothesized to make the individual more willing to search for integrative solutions to conflict (Blake, Shepard, and Mouton, 1964), and lack of egocentricity, which is presumed to facilitate taking the role of the other and thus getting to the issues underlying a conflict (Follett, 1941; Deutsch, 1969; Walton, 1969).

The emphasis of these investigators on predispositions does not imply a belief in some genetic imperative, territorial or otherwise. Most of them would agree with the statement made long ago by May and Doob (1937) that "human beings by original nature strive for goals, but striving with others (cooperation) or against others (competition) are learned forms of behavior (p. 23)." The issue that remains, however, is to what extent such behaviors are "learned for life" (and therefore difficult to modify), and to what extent learned for specific situations (and therefore responsive to changes in organizational properties or conflict of interest).

Quantitative research on individual predisposing characteristics has shown very modest results, both in the laboratory and elsewhere. In a series of laboratory experiments, Bartos (in Swingle, 1970) computed correlations between demographic characteristics and toughness in a bargaining game. Zero-order correlations in a population of 784 subjects ranged from .04 to .09, and various personality measures yielded no stronger relationships. Rapoport and Chammah (1965) approached the question of individual differences in a different way; they computed correlations between players in many trials of the same game (the Prisoner's Dilemma). Interplayer correlations ranged from .9 upward when the rules of the game and the payoff matrix were held constant. We endorse their conclusion:

> This result suggests that the interactions between the members of pairs rather than inherent propensities of individuals to cooperate are the dominant factors in determining performance of a repeated PD (Prisoner's Dilemma) game.... Whatever effect individual propensities may have on the performance of an individual is masked by the interaction effect. (1965, p. 832)

Extensive reviews of personality measures in relation to the behavior of laboratory subjects in conflict games (Terhune, 1970; Deutsch, 1971) show a spotty and inconsistent pattern. There is greater consistency to the finding that situational factors tend to reduce personality effects, and that strong situational factors tend to eliminate personality differences in conflict behavior. Terhune (1968; Terhune and Firestone, 1967) has showed this pattern clearly in a series of laboratory experiments. In one-trial games with modest payoff differences, some personality effects were found. Subjects high on the need for power tried to deceive their opponents; those high on the need for achievement were more likely to be cooperative for the sake of maximizing the joint payoff. But as the initial expectations of subjects were structured (by instruction or previous trials) and as the temptation to double-cross the other party was increased (by experimental setting of the payoff matrix), personality effects were obliterated.

Rules and Procedures

Perhaps the most important fact about conflicts within and between organizations is that they are limited—by statute, common law, and a variety of intraorganizational arrangements. Some of these limitations are formal and are devised specifically for the purpose of containing or adjudicating conflict. Others are informal and seem to develop without verbalization. For example, the necessity for future interaction curtails the exploitation of one party by another even in the brief games of the laboratory (Marlow, Gergen, and Doob, 1966).

Within organizations there are additional conflict-limiting properties. The hierarchical order at each level tends to be more interested in the product of lower levels than in their intramural conflicts. If a deadlock between sales and manufacturing threatens to stop production, both lose. They are in a condition of common membership and fate as well as a condition of conflict. Both the presence of norm-representing third parties (Wells, 1967) and the fact of common membership among parties to a conflict (Wilson, Chun, and Katanyi, 1965) have been shown to limit conflict behavior in the laboratory.

Deutsch (1973) reports a series of experiments in which limiting factors were varied systematically. The experimental task was the Acme-Bolt Truck Game, first proposed by Deutsch and Krauss (1962), in which two experimental subjects attempt in successive trials to move their electronic "trucks" from a pair of fixed starting points to a pair of destinations. Each has two possible routes, one exclusive but circuitous, the other direct but unavoidably and competitively shared. Either can block the other, but payoff to each is for completed trips. Figure 18-2 shows the experimental arrangement.

Without changes in the game itself or in the amount and method of payoff, Deutsch and his colleagues varied the following conditions: instructions to behave cooperatively (maximize joint payoff), individualistically (maximize own payoff), or competitively (maximize difference between own payoff and that of opponent); possibility of communication before acting, necessity of acting simultaneously with one's opponent, possibility of reversing one's announced intentions, and the size of the task (ten-trial versus one-trial sequences).

All of these manipulations have their organizational counterparts, and have conflict-limiting effects, as measured by the proportion of "cooperative" choices (taking turns going through the one-way stretch of road, or setting up some other decision rule). By far the most powerful effect, however, was the initial instruction, one version of which

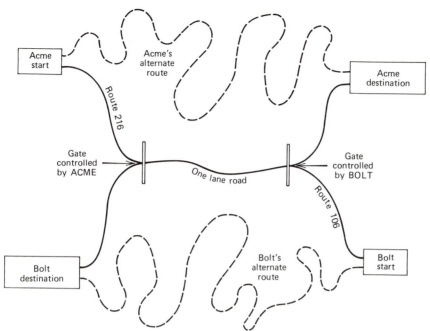

Figure 18-2   *The Acme-Bolt truck game. (From Deutsch, 1973, p. 219.)*

stressed cooperation and concern with the welfare of one's partner, a second emphasized maximizing own winnings, and a third maximizing own winnings and beating one's partner.

The results of these experiments are presented in Table 18-1. Under every experimental condition (six in all) the cooperative orientation results in significantly more cooperative choices than do either the individualistic or competitive orientations, and within every condition except B and F the individualistic orientation results in more cooperative choices than the competitive orientation. A comparison of the cooperative orientation across different experimental conditions show no significant results. For the individualistic orientation, however, communication and "reversibility" increase the percentage of cooperative choices; for the competitive orientation, only "reversibility" has this effect.

In subsequent experiments, Deutsch and his colleagues measured the relative payoff to the participants under three somewhat more extreme sets of instructions, identified as social problem solving, individualistic, and "chicken," the last named for the dangerous game apparently invented by adolescent boys in the United States. The rules of "chicken" are simple but lethal: two drivers approach each other at high speed while keeping the highway center-line between the wheels

TABLE 18-1 Percentage of Cooperative Choices by Individuals and by Pairs for Different Motivational Orientations and Different Experimental Conditions

Condition	N	Individuals Who Chose Cooperatively	Pairs in Which Both Chose	
			Cooperatively	Noncooperatively
No Communication,				
Simultaneous Choice				
Cooperative	46	89.1	82.6	4.3
Individualistic	78	35.9	12.8	41.0
Competitive	32	12.5	6.3	81.3
No Communication,				
Nonsimultaneous Choice				
Cooperative	48	79.3	73.9	17.4
Individualistic	48	18.8	4.2	62.5
Competitive	30	16.7	6.7	73.3
Communication,				
Simultaneous Choice				
Cooperative	32	96.9	93.8	
Individualistic	34	70.6	58.8	17.6
Competitive	48	29.2	16.7	58.3
Communication,				
Nonsimultaneous Choice				
Cooperative	32	84.4	81.3	12.5
Individualistic	42	52.4	38.1	33.3
Competitive	44	34.1	27.3	59.1
Reversibility				
Cooperative	74	94.6	94.6	5.4
Individualistic	70	77.1	77.1	22.9
Competitive	62	36.1	36.1	63.9
Ten Trials,				
No Communication,				
Simultaneous Choice				
Cooperative	34	70.9	55.5	15.0
Individualistic	34	35.6	13.5	43.2
Competitive	42	25.3	3.9	52.9

From Deutsch, 1973, p. 186.

of their cars. The first to swerve is the "chicken," and the other is declared the winner.

As Figure 18-3 shows, the competitive (chicken) orientation, once entered on, has its own dynamics. There is some evidence of early learning, but it does not persist and at no time do the contestants attain the break-even point. It is interesting that the individualistic and problem-solving orientations, while they may produce different reward

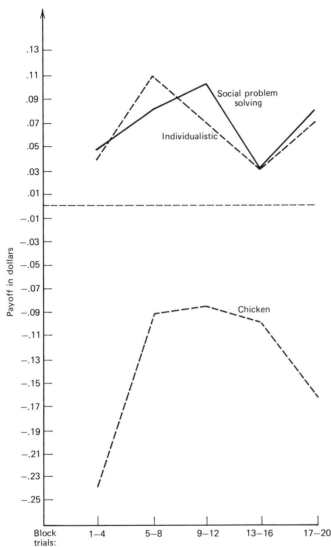

Figure 18-3 *Mean joint payoff for the Acme-Bolt truck game. (From Deutsch, 1973, p. 300.)*

allocations, show about the same total payoff. In other experiments with the same game, both the individualistic and the competitive subjects exhibited deteriorating cooperation over successive trials. Deutsch suggests that once the hope or expectation of cooperation has been disconfirmed, participants are "out of phase" and have difficulty attaining cooperation again despite the material rewards of doing so.

Experimental studies of games show that even young children, ages 5 to 8½ years, systematically take other's outcomes as well as the task setting into account in making choices (McClintock and Moskowtiz, 1976). In a coordinative setting cooperative choices dominated and in a conflict setting competitive responses were the rule. In an individualistic setting children did forego own gain for maximization of reward relative to others. Gaming situations often involve mixed motive patterns and whether the motive is absolute gain, relative gain or competition, cooperation, or altriusm depends both on the external setting and the individual's predispositions.

Interaction

The last of the determinants of conflict behavior specified by our model is the interaction process itself. There is an obvious problem of circularity in demonstrating this effect, but the data are compelling. Engaging in conflict behavior with another human being is a process that generates dynamic forces in its own right.

One of the best-established findings about conflict interaction is the tendency toward similar or reciprocal behaviors. and the consequent escalation of the conflict process. Actions evoke similar reactions (Deutsch 1949): tactics between opponents become congruent even if they were not initially so (Rapoport and Chammah 1965); consistently competitive behavior evokes a competitive response even from cooperatively oriented persons (Kelley and Stahelski 1970). Even specific tactics—attempts at forcing, avoidance, and the like—show this tendency toward congruence in the course of a conflict (Thomas and Walton, 1971).

For many reasons, the response of meeting conflict with no less than equal conflict leads to escalation. Such behavior is not merely, as Richardson (1960) suggested, ". . . what people would do if they did not stop to think." The aim of winning becomes a goal in itself, supplementing or even supplanting the original conflict of interest. This is a very personal matter. Sermat (1967) ran two series of experiments, one in which experimental subjects played against a machine that was programmed to respond exactly as the subject had acted toward it, and another in which experimental subjects played against opponents who were in fact experimental confederates and had been instructed to behave with exact reciprocity.

When playing against the machine, people "learned" to act cooperatively to maximize their total payoff, even when by so doing the machine won an even larger sum. When the opponent was a person the effect was reversed. In the "machine-opponent series," at the end of 30 trials the subjects were 90 percent "cooperative;" in the "personal-opponent series" they were aggressive in about the same proportion, even though they reduced their own payoff by so behaving. The attempt was to make sure that one's opponent did not "win," rather than to maximize one's own payoff. The concentration was on the relationship between own score and opponent's rather than on the amount of one's own gains.

The experiment was replicated with military staff members as subjects. One is reminded of the reported statement of Dean Rusk, then Secretary of State, to John Scali of the American Broadcasting Company, who was about to tell the American public the outcome of the Kennedy-Kruschev exchange regarding the placement of Soviet missiles in Cuba: "Remember when you report this that, eyeball to eyeball, they blinked first."

Concomitant with such conflict behaviors are changes in processes of thought and perception respecting oneself and one's own group in contrast to that of one's opponent. Cognitive processes are simplified, so that virtues are seen increasingly to reside on one side of the conflict and vices on the other. Hostility and distrust are thus justified, and they in turn justify coercive tactics (Raven and Kruglanski, 1970). Communications are reduced, enabling the development and maintenance of what Newcomb (1947) vividly described as autistic hostility. Acts of conflict continue, however, without other forms of communication.

The syndrome of escalating conflict is described in remarkably similar terms, regardless of whether the observations were done in the laboratory (Osgood, 1961; Deutsch, 1966), in training situations for managers (Blake and Mouton, 1961), in labor negotiations (Stagner and Rosen, 1965), or in a boys' camp (Sherif, 1961). Moreover, the escalation process not only intensifies conflict over the original issues; it proliferates to other issues, either because hostility reinvokes them or because they offer some tactical advantage. Such spread has been demonstrated experimentally in labor-management simulations (Bass, 1966) and in the classroom (Kelly, 1966). The deepening and broadening of the conflict, if unchecked, thus culminates in a perceived need to end the relationship—that is, to buy or sell elsewhere, make other friends, abolish a union, eliminate or absorb a competitor, fire or drive away an employee, and in short to annihilate an opponent.

All actions during a conflict process need not be direct behaviors against the opponent, of course. There may be conciliatory behaviors as well, and there may be threats and promises of varying degrees of aggressive or conciliatory content. Unconditional and unexplained conciliatory or cooperative behavior seems to lead to exploitation, at least in the laboratory situation. Several sets of investigators have reported this pattern, in terms that suggest that they would have preferred the data otherwise. Shure, Meeker, and Hansford (1965) introduced a number of experimental variations intended to induce reciprocal conciliation. These included advance communication of the intent to make a cooperative move, explanation of a special basis of personal conviction (Quakerism) as the reason for acting pacifically, and introduction of visible electric shock (simulated) as a heightened example of aggressive power held in restraint. None of these altered the tendency for opponents to exploit the gains of unconditional cooperation. Solomon (1960) had reported similar results; opponents are pleased by unconditional benevolence, puzzled by it, and take advantage of it. Explanation in terms of religious conviction or other principles relieves the puzzlement but does not alter the exploitation.

In short, persistent aggression evokes reciprocal aggression, and persistent and unconditional compliance evokes much the same aggressive pattern. The question arises as to what behavioral initiative has more conflict-limiting effects, once the process of interaction has begun. Experimental research has explored the effects of three such initiatives, which can be labelled threats, promises, and conditional cooperation.

Threats are statements that one will make some specific aggressive action unless one's opponent complies with a specific request (to do something or refrain from doing something). The experimental evidence on the effects of threats is discouraging. In a real estate game, Hornstein (1965) found that all pairs of experimental subjects reached agreement and thus maximized their payoff provided that neither threatened nor aggressed. If threats were introduced, the proportion of pairs attaining agreement dropped to about half, and if threats and aggressive moves were introduced, only one pair in 12 reached agreement. Most of the attempts to make threats more effective have involved increasing their potential damaging effect, the visible power of the threatener to impose the threatened damage, and the certainty that the threat will be carried through unless the demands are met. To some extent, these efforts interfere with each other. Long before he became Secretary of State, Henry Kissinger (1961) recognized this tendency for threats to lose credibility as they increased in magnitude: "The greater the power, the greater the inhibitions against using it, except in the most dire emergencies; therefore a reduced probability (risk) that any encroachment will justify its use.... The smaller the risks, the more likely they are to be accepted."

Efforts to make threats credible and therefore effective have taken the form of trying to convince an opponent that they will be carried through. The dictionary of "brinkmanship" is full of such tactics—the "doctrine of the last clear chance" (Schelling, 1960) and the tactic of "locking in," for example. Locking in simply means putting oneself in a situation where the threatened behavior cannot be avoided except by the opponent's compliance. Failure to comply evokes the threatened behavior; the threatener *cannot* withhold it and the opponent sees that it cannot be withheld. One driver in a game of chicken locks the steering wheel in place and raises his or her arms for the opponent to see.

Schelling (1960) discusses a number of such tactics under the general heading of the "rationality of irrationality." (One is tempted to reverse the nouns in that phrase.) Deutsch (1973) and his colleagues introduced the locking-in tactic to the Acme-Bolt truck game; either contestant could lock his or her truck in gear so that it could not be stopped or reversed during the trial and that fact was visible to the opponent. Joint payoff was maximized when both contestants could "lock in," apparently because both tended not to do so if they knew the opponent had the same power. But the somber fact is that collisions occurred whenever the lock was available, unilateral or bilateral.

Promises, like threats, are conditional statements about future behavior; unlike threats, the behavior in question is positive. In the truck game, a typical promise was "I'll let you through first this time, if you let me through first next time." Promises are demonstrably more effective than threats in those experiments where both have been studied (Deutsch and Solomon, 1959; Deutsch, 1960 and 1961; Cheney, Harford, and Solomon, 1971; Lewicki, 1971).

Still more effective, however, is conditional cooperation (Sermat, 1964; Swingle, 1970) or conditional benevolence (Solomon, 1960). This is essentially an initiative that goes one step beyond a conditional promise; a cooperative move is made and at the same time a reciprocal act of cooperation is requested. If there is a cooperative response, it in turn is responded to, and the dynamics of de-escalation and cooperation are under way. If the cooperative initiative is met with aggression, however, the aggression is reciprocated. Nevertheless, in a further trial, the cooperative initiative is again taken, on the same conditional basis. One is reminded of Osgood's (1959) proposal for the reduction of international tensions.

The affective reactions of opponents are consistent with the relative effectiveness of these several tactics. Promisers are regarded as wiser and more reasonable and likable than threateners, and conditionally benevolent opponents are liked better than unconditionally benevolent. The unconditionally malevolent, plausibly enough, are liked least. Within the boundaries of a group or an organization, collaborative and accommodative behavior appears to be more highly valued than aggressive competition or outright avoidance of conflict. Managers who make initiating moves of cooperation are rated more favorably by their subordinates (Burke, 1970) and are considered more promotable (Dutton and Walton, 1966).

GAMES OF CONFLICT

Conflicts of interest and conflict behavior have been studied more in the laboratory than in organizational life, and more through games of conflict than any other design. The assumptions of such experiments make extrapolation to organizational reality difficult and risky, but their clarification of some issues in conflicts of interest makes them important. As Rapoport says, "the limited relevance of game theory to a theory of behavior of real players should be apparent. However, this relevance, though limited, is not nil..." (1970, p. 2). Three contributions of these experiments seem important for understanding organizational conflict:

> The quantitative representation of specific patterns and magnitudes of conflicts of interest through payoff matrices

> The demonstration that different payoff matrices have predictably different effects on conflict behavior, including failures to resolve conflict, and resolutions that consistently benefit one party more than another

> The demonstration that a stable resolution may maximize return neither to individual parties nor to the contestants in combination.

The Tragedy of the Commons

Hardin's (1968) eloquently described "tragedy of the commons" presents a conflict problem at the village level, and treats it as the prototype for the major problems of human survival—nuclear warfare, population control, natural resources, energy, pollution among them:

> The tragedy of the commons develops in this way. Picture a pasture open to all. It is to be expected that each herdsman will try to keep as many cattle as possible on the commons. Such an arrangement may work reasonably satisfactorily for centuries because tribal wars, poaching, and disease keep the numbers of both man and beast well below the carrying capacity of the land. Finally, however, comes the day of reckoning, that is, the day when the long-desired goal of social stability becomes a reality. At this point, the inherent logic of the commons remorselessly generates tragedy.

> As a rational being, each herdsman seeks to maximize his gain. Explicitly or implicitly, more or less consciously, he asks, "What

is the utility *to me* of adding one more animal to my herd?"
This utility has one negative and one positive component.

1) The positive component is a function of the increment of one
animal. Since the herdsman receives all the proceeds from the
sale of the additional animal, the positive utility is nearly +1.

2) The negative component is a function of the additional overgrazing created by one more animal. Since, however, the effects
of overgrazing are shared by all herdsmen, the negative utility
for any particular decision-making herdsman is only a fraction of
−1.

Adding together the component partial utilities, the rational
herdsman concludes that the only sensible course for him to
pursue is to add another animal to his herd. And another; and
another.... But this is the conclusion reached by each and every
rational herdsman sharing a commons. Therein is the tragedy.
Each man is locked into a system that compels him to increase
his herd without limit—in a world that is limited. Ruin is the
destination toward which all men rush, each pursuing his own
best interest in a society that believes in the freedom of the
commons. Freedom in a commons brings ruin to all.

Such conflicts of mixed motives or perverse dynamics have something
to teach us about relationships within and between organizations. National decisions to increase or reduce armaments have been conceptualized in these terms (Fisher, 1964; McNeil, 1965), and they seem
relevant to any organizational situation in which there is a mutually
beneficial outcome but it is attainable only if each party can trust the
other or if both are influenced by some third party, external constraint,
or altruistic value.

Three general points can be made:

1. The vigorous pursuit of self-interest, rationally and in accordance with the "rules of the game," may be self-defeating, either
directly (the prisoner's dilemma) or indirectly (the tragedy of the
commons). Adam Smith's invisible hand, in other words, is sometimes sinister. We need to identify the game before choosing the
strategy.

2. The dynamics of some games constitute paradoxes or dilemmas, not merely problems. That is, a satisfactory outcome can be
attained only by going beyond the terms of reference in which
the problem is initially presented. So long as the choice of

strategy is defined as a problem in identifying one's immediate self-interest, neither the prisoner's dilemma nor the tragedy of the commons can be resolved.

3. Such problems are inherent in organizational life because they derive from the processes of differentiation and integration in terms of which systems and subsystems are defined. The survival of an organization (and even more, its growth) requires the importation of energy through continuous advantageous transactions with systems in its environment. The dynamic within the organization is not only for survival, but for growth. The needs of the larger system sometimes coincide with the expression of this organizational dynamic and sometimes do not, as problems of pollution and monopoly pricing remind us.

Similar problems of differentiation and integration occur within organizations, although the integrative mechanisms are more conspicuous and more successful. The differentiation of organizations into subsystems is required for efficiency but it inevitably creates differential interests and dynamics as well as a division of labor. Subsystem success at the expense of the larger organization is a continuing hazard. When differentiation in rewards and perquisites is added to functional differentiation, the problems of integration become more difficult.

EFFECTS OF CONFLICT

To ask the effects of conflict is to pose a question too general to answer, and therefore to invite others: what kind of conflict, how great in magnitude and duration, effects on what? Our theoretical view is that for any system certain kinds and levels of conflict will be optimal for certain criteria—maximization of output, adaptation to environmental change, long-term survival. Neither the theoretical nor the empirical work has been done to specify those optima, however. Our opinion, in the absence of such data, is that most organizations show levels of conflict considerably above the optimum.

Some data support this view. Collaborative initiatives in a group are reported to enhance feelings of well-being and self-actualization among members (Aram, 1971). Lawrence and Lorsch (1967) found that interunit collaboration within an organization was positively associated with organizational performance, whereas conflict between units was negatively related to the performance of the organization as a whole. This relationship held for the three organizations included in their research. Blau (1955) reported a similar finding in government agencies, but proposed that the negative relationship between competitive behavior and performance would be expected to hold only in situations where the group norms were for cooperation.

On the other hand, Hoffman and Maier (1961) found that experimental groups with heterogeneous members and consequent "conflicts" of interest and opinion produced better solutions to standardized sets of problems. Pelz and Andrews (1966) made a similar interpretation of the fact that scientists who were exposed to discussion with differently oriented colleagues tended to be more productive. Hall (1971), summing up such research and a good deal of his own, stated that "conflict, effectively managed, is a necessary condition for creativity."

Many others have made similar points about the positive effects of limited or controlled conflict—as leading to the discovery of new and better organizational arrangements (Follett, 1941), as necessary for progress (Van Doorn, 1966), as directing managerial attention to needed changes (Litterer, 1966), as bringing a dynamic situation into a better state of congruence with the facts of power (Coser, 1956), as effecting a search for better means of conflict reduction (March and Simon, 1958; Litterer, 1966). A similarly wide range of speculative benefits has been proposed at the individual level, with the assumption that people require certain levels of stimulation and the continuing experience of tension-generation and reduction, within limits, in order to function well and with satisfaction (Allport, 1953; Hunt, 1963; Driver and Streufert, 1964). Deutsch (1971) speaks more specifically of conflict as a stimulus to interest and curiosity, to the full use of individual capacities, and as a welcomed means for testing and assessing one's abilities.

These assertions are more judgmental than demonstrated. They have in common not only their assertion of positive effects, but also the view that conflict must be somehow limited or contained if the positive effects are to outweigh the negative or even to be realized at all. Such limits raise the issue of conflict management, both as in its preventive sense, through organizational design, and in its more conventional sense of limits and remedies applied during the period of active conflict itself.

CONFLICT MANAGEMENT

Approaches to managing, limiting, and resolving conflict—or preventing it altogether—can be thought of in terms of their method, immediate target, and the sequence of assumed and desired effects. A change approach to conflict management could thus take as its immediate target any of the six elements identified in our structural model of conflict. In fact, the literature of conflict management has not developed in these terms and the programs to manage conflict tend to have multiple targets and unspecified assumptions. Our reinvoking of the model is therefore a matter of theoretical preference rather than expository convenience.

Organizational Properties

Organizations differ in their tolerance for conflict and in their ways of handling it. That assertion is perhaps sufficiently apparent not to require documentation, but only a few comparative studies have in fact been done. One of them (Walton et al., 1966) involved the relationships between sales and production divisions, two traditional parties to subsystem conflict, in six organizations. The study showed substantial variance in mode of conflict management, from collaborative to persistently conflictful. Blake and Mouton (1964) had reported a similar range among smaller organizational subunits, and Litwin and Stringer (1968) at the level of organizations themselves.

Research on conflict resolution, however, has emphasized the phenomena of interaction at group and individual levels, and there is little evidence regarding what formal properties of organizations are associated with successful conflict management, internally or externally. Two exceptions are the approach of Likert and Likert (1976), which treats conflict management as one of the derivative advantages of participative organizational structure ("System 4"), and that of Walton and his colleagues (1966), whose model of lateral relationships in organizations includes structural variables.

The Likerts' view is that the supportive interpersonal style and the structure of overlapping groups that are the central characteristics of System 4 organizations are also the basis for superior management of conflict. To these they would add the criterion that a conflict shall be deemed resolved only when the parties to it are all satisfied. They propose that resolution requires an emphasis on integrative goals, a de-emphasis of status, and the use of consensus rather than majority rule. Moreover, to the extent that the relevant groups are not already connected by means of overlapping vertical and lateral membership, such structural changes must be initiated. Examples of the resulting complex matrix structures are given at organizational (industry, school systems) and at community levels. Measurement and feedback, with appropriate third-party coaching and consultation, are proposed as the means of bringing about such structural and interpersonal changes. No data on the conflict-reducing effects of such programs are presented, however.

Walton's approach to conflict management emphasizes lateral relationships in organizations, which he assesses in the terms summarized

TABLE 18-2   Components and Characteristics of Contrasting Types of Lateral Relationships

Component of Relationship	TYPE OF LATERAL RELATIONSHIP	
	Integrative	Distributive
Form of joint decision process between units	Problem solving: Free exchange of information. Conscientious accuracy of information transmitted.	Bargaining: Careful rationing of information. Deliberate distortion of information.
Structure of interaction and interunit decision framework	Flexible, informal, and open.	Rigid, formal, and circumscribed.
Attitudes toward other unit	Positive attitudes: trust, friendliness, inclusion of other unit.	Negative attitudes: suspicion, hostility, disassociation from other unit.

From Walton, Dutton, and Fitch, p. 445. (1966)

in Table 18-2. A study of six plants of the Peerless Company (Walton, Dutton, and Fitch, 1966) shows rank-order intercorrelations of .54 to .94 between the structural variables and the decision-making process. Rigid, formal, and circumscribed structural arrangements between groups were associated with restriction and distortion of information by each group in its dealings with the other. Conflicts were resolved, if at all, by bargaining rather than joint problem solving. Attitudes of suspicion and hostility were consistent with the structural pattern. Walton and his colleagues concluded that an intervention to change the formal structure within which the groups interacted would in turn induce change toward more problem solving and less bargaining or open conflict.

No such intervention was reported for the six-plant study, but a later study (Walton, 1967) provided a successful example. A "country director" in the U.S. Department of State in Washington reduced interagency conflict by means of a new lateral structure—a voluntary monthly meeting of representatives from a dozen agencies. Representatives had in common their concern with the country in question; they differed in specialized knowledge and agency function. Meetings were informal, with emphasis on sharing information, encouraging the discussion of differing views, and building trust and liking among members of the group. The initiator and chairman modelled and encouraged such behavior. The reported results included improved problem solving and conflict resolution among the agencies represented.

These examples must be taken as suggestive rather than conclusive with respect to the improvement of the organizational capacity to manage conflict. Longitudinal studies in a number of organizations, in which specific structural changes can be seen in relation to quantitative measures of conflict, are much needed.

Conflict of Interest

Sherif's experiment in a boys' camp, instructive in many respects, provides evidence also on the resolution of conflict by changing the incentive structure or, as he put it, introducing important superordinate goals that could be attained only through joint effort of the previously conflicting groups (Sherif et al., 1961). Stage 3 of that experiment included three such tasks—repairing the camp water supply, raising funds for a camp-wide expedition to a town where a popular movie was playing, and getting a broken-down truck under way. These experiences in goal-induced joint activity converted conflict to friendly interaction. Mere social contact (attending films, eating together, watching fireworks) did not have the same conflict-reducing effects.

The logic of reducing conflict by reducing or eliminating the situational incentives to it and rewards from it is unobjectionable in principle but difficult in practice, and the introduction of superordinate goals is still more difficult. Blake and his colleagues (1965) argue that the imposition of superordinate goals is not enough, that education in problem solving and improved interpersonal skills are necessary as well. Moreover, most organizational conflicts are probably mixed-motive situations, with incentives both to conflict and to conflict resolution.

Where the power to change incentive structure (conflict of interest) is at hand, however, it provides an important means for reducing conflict. The much-researched prisoner's dilemma (Rapoport, 1967) literally disappears if each contestant is allowed to alter his or her choice after learning the choice of the other. There may be few cases of organizational conflict in which the initial conflict of interest can be made to vanish merely by changing a procedural formality, but the finding is instructive, nevertheless. Reducing conflict of interest, where it can be done, is a method of primary prevention, with all the advantages and appeals of preventive medicine.

Role Expectations

We have noted earlier ways in which pressures from constituent groups intensify conflict behavior. There are social pressures to limit conflict, however, and they are particularly visible within the boundaries of an organization or group, where most members are likely to share the concern that conflicts shall not escalate to the point of system break and organizational damage. Such normative pressures to keep conflicts within limits have been remarked by Blau (1955), who noted the group practice of punishing overcompetitive and conflict-prone members, and many others. Blake and his colleagues (1964) report such systematic playing down of differences between various organizational subsystems—headquarters versus field units, superordinate versus subordinate units, and interdepartmental peer units.

Such pressures may prevent conflict resolution and the confrontation of issues, however, as well as avoid some crisis of conflict. If the costs of conflict are high and the parties doubt their ability to resolve their differences, intraorganizational pressures to avoid open conflict are likely to be strong. The unspoken assumption is that the system can't stand conflict.

Role expectations, as our model indicates, are immediate determinants of conflict behavior, and changing them is therefore almost certain to change behavior. Bringing about changes in the structure of conflict roles, however, is likely to require prior changes in organizational policies and properties. Such approaches to conflict management were discussed under "organizational properties."

Behavioral Predispositions

Changing the predispositions of individuals with respect to conflict suggests great difficulties and long processes of re-education or restructuring of personality. There is some evidence, however, that very brief instructions, or explanations, or training experiences may alter the initial behavior of individuals in conflict situations—or at least in the conflict situation to which the instruction pertains directly. Krauss and Deutsch (1966) attained substantial increases in cooperative behavior and joint payoff in the Acme-Bolt truck game simply by providing a short "tutored communication" before the game began, in which subjects were advised to begin by making "a fair proposal," with fair defined as a proposal that would seem fair "to you if you were she."

It can be argued that the circumstances were peculiarly favorable for compliance to such tutoring. The experiments were brief; the stakes were not high enough to affect the lives of the subjects in significant ways, and the experiments took place under the aegis of the employer. Participants in these experiments were all women employees of the Bell Telephone Laboratories, aged 18 to 32 years.

Nevertheless, the results have been replicated, at least in general terms. Blake and his colleagues (Blake, Shepard, and Mouton, 1964) report similar results in three companies, although the data on conflict reduction are more impressionistic than quantitative, and the training process involved at least one week of intensive group exercises and individual instruction. Participants were instructed in specific approaches to conflict management, for example, being sure that one understands the opposition point of view well enough to state it to the satisfaction of one's opponents, acquiring skill in building on areas of agreement, and re-examining disagreements jointly so that a consensual statement of the issues at conflict can be made.

To argue that the predispositions of participants in these exercises were changed in an enduring way goes beyond the data. A more conservative interpretation would be that the initial predispositions of the participants were modified by the creation of a new situation and a new set of role expectations, to which the participants responded as students to an instructor. As with other instruction, the carry-over to other situations and later times then becomes an empirical question. Only the demonstration of such transfer of conflict-managing behavior would justify the claim that individual predispositions or personality characteristics had been changed.

Rules and Procedures

Rules and procedures are inherent in organizational life, formal and informal, and they are much implicated in organizational conflict. The can create and heighten conflict, or prevent and reduce it. No other generalization about rules and conflict should be attempted out of context, except about their prevalence. Dunlop (1958) described the relationships between management, government, and labor as conflict and cooperation within a "web of rules," and Dubin (1957) pointed out that where formal rules end, informal rules have developed to the degree that they constitute the "common law of the plant."

Decision rules, to the extent that they cover cases unambiguously and are accepted by those affected, prevent conflict by making issues unarguable. If the union contract includes a clause that vacation days will be accrued at a fixed rate for each month of work, conflicts about vacation accrual are greatly reduced. They are not eliminated, of course, but moved from daily contests over individual cases to annual negotiations about the contract, a change in locus that has disadvantages as well as advantages; settling many issues at one time may be more difficult than settling them as they arise.

Perhaps more important to the reduction of conflict is that rules change the basis of power away from threat and coercion, and toward legitimacy (Thibaut and Kelley, 1959). Moreover, a negative rule-based decision evokes less hostility than an identical decision imposed on most other bases. For these and other reasons, points of recurring conflict in organizations tend to produce rules to cover them in future situations, and the more sensitive areas are particularly likely to become rule-laden (Thibaut and Kelley, 1959).

Even successful rules have side effects, however; their benefits have costs. They may acquire an aura of moral obligation, and be followed with a fanaticism that defeats or dilutes their original purpose. The merits of cases may be disregarded in favor of the legalistic issue of the rule and its applicability. The active and contentious process of problem solving may be neglected. The rules themselves may proliferate to the point of relative or absolute diminishing returns, a tendency that Merton (1957) identified long ago as intrinsic to bureaucratic organizations. Worse than side effects of appropriate rules, of course, is the enactment of inappropriate, conflict-heightening rules. The following four dimensions are offered as examples of subjects often covered by rules. They are stated as dimensions to remind us that the effects could be either to heighten or reduce conflict, depending on the appropriateness of the stipulation:

Length of interval between contacts of conflicting parties

Separation or combination of issues at conflict

Formality of presentation and decision

Representation of parties at conflict

Conceptualization and statement of issues

Meeting only at prescribed intervals allows time for cooling off and attending to matters other than the subject of conflict, but long intervals make for the development of stereotypes and the accumulation of issues. Settling many issues at once has the sound of efficiency but may make settlements more difficult. Fisher (1964) has proposed the "fractionation of conflict" as an important principle in international relations, and Patten (1970) argues that multiple issues lead to "horse-trading" rather than problem solving.

Formal requirements for presentation of issues by special representatives limit the forms of conflict and the numbers of people involved. But they have been shown in some circumstances to reduce the amount of problem solving and to involve specialists at conflict rather than specialists in knowledge of the issues (Lawrence and Lorsch, 1967).

Some of the reported successes in conflict reduction have involved rules and procedures along one or more of these dimensions. Continuing rather than intermittent contact between union and management has reportedly led to improved relations and more rapid settlement of grievances (Lesieur and Puckett, 1969). McKersie (1964) cites the case of the International Harvester Company, in which grievance rules were instituted stipulating that all grievances would be handled immediately, by the people directly involved, and without written records of the initial discussion. Only if these procedures were unsuccessful were more formal steps to be taken. Blake et al. (1964) describe similar rapid disposition of conflicts by small standing committees (problem-solving teams) of union and management.

Rules regarding the statement or presentation of issues at conflict usually pertain to formalities rather than conceptualization. Walton and McKersie (1965), however, illustrate the possibility of a rule requiring an "integrative" rather than a "distributive" statement of the matter. For example, a sales department may press for quick delivery in order to get and hold customers, while a production department may argue for "long runs" to keep costs down. The integrative rule would put the question somewhat along the following lines: How can we furnish quick delivery without sacrificing productive efficiency? The key idea is that the issue must be stated in terms that satisfy both parties to the conflict.

ROLE OF "THIRD PARTIES" IN CONFLICT RESOLUTION

Third parties may enter into conflicts in several broad role categories—as possessors of superior power to impose a settlement (arbitrators, judges, superiors in an organizational hierarchy); as reconcilers of disparate interests (mediators, consultants); and as expert assistants to one or the other party at conflict (attorneys, consultants, paid representatives). Performance in all these roles is more art than science, however, and evaluative studies of third-party interventions are rare.

Most intraorganizational conflicts are in fact settled by arbitration, with the arbitrator being the person in the hierarchy to whom the contesting parties both report (Scott, 1965). An early study by Blake and Mouton (1961) showed less satisfaction with arbitrated decisions than with those settled by principals, but there is of course a strong likelihood that conflicts that go to arbitration are more difficult and inflamed. Stagner and Rosen (1965) reported a similar tendency toward dissatisfaction with arbitrated conflicts between labor and management, and a tendency for unions to ignore decisions that they considered unfair.

Several social scientists experienced in the role of third-party consultation have described a process of two or more stages, the first of which involves the deliberate intensification of conflict and the second its reduction. Thus, Schmidt and Tannenbaum (1969) speak of sharpening issues before attempting resolution, and Walton (1969) speaks of a differentiation phase as preceding a phase of integration. At its best, this initial period represents the surfacing and making accessible of matters that can then be worked at. At its worst, one can imagine something analogous to iatrogenic illness, in which the physician "cures" a complaint that he or she has in fact created.

The many solutions and ideologies that attempt to deal with organizational conflict constitute three major sets. One appeals to the individual, and asks that conscience or altruism or at least longsightedness shall prevail over the immediate dynamics of the payoff matrix and the conflict. In effect, this approach proposes to solve an organizational conflict by making it an intraindividual conflict. It also presents us with the problem of inculcating the values that are supposed to triumph in such transposed conflicts.

The second solution to conflicts in which the invisible hand seems to produce unacceptable results is to impose constraints from the next higher system level. This is the usual solution within organizations, where many resources are shared but almost none is available for private exploitation (common in Hardin's sense of the term); indeed, the constraints often are carried to the point of unnecessary interference with the subsystem operations. Such constraints may be best accepted and perhaps most appropriately devised when they are enacted by the people who will be affected by them, either through direct or indirect participation. The constraint then has the character that Hardin calls "mutual coercion mutually agreed upon," and that social psychologists recognize as participation.

The third solution to problems of conflict begins with conflict of interest, and alters the reward pattern. Not all transactions between organizations and organizational subsystems are conflictful, fortunately, and not all conflicts are characterized by perverse dynamics. Boulding calls these happier encounters games of cooperation rather than conflict. Like the introduction of constraints, such alterations of conflict of interest are likely to require intervention from a systemic level that includes the parties at conflict. The creation of such systems (and their utilization where they already exist) is the primary task in conflict resolution.

In spite of theoretical differences, there is a certain agreement among social scientists about the kinds of things that can be done by third parties to assist in conflict management, once a conflict has arisen. Some of these involve the development and improvement of rules: clarity, equity, adequacy of promulgation, visibility of violation, rewards for adherence. Others involve assistance within an existing structure of rules: help in identifying issues, in setting the circumstances for confrontation of issues, in correcting distortions of fact, setting norms for interaction, and in making settlements acceptable to the parties at conflict.

◼ SUMMARY ◼

We have defined conflict as the direct interaction of two or more parties (persons, groups, organizations, nations) such that the actions of one tend to prevent or compel some outcome against the resistance of the other. Conflict is thus behavioral, observable, and marked by attempts at hindering, compelling, or injuring, and by resistance or retaliation to such attempts. Such behaviors do not constitute a unique set in organizational life; an act of conflict can also be an act of leadership, control, or change, for example. A model of conflict behavior is proposed that incorporates six categories of variables as predictors of conflict within or between organizational systems:

1. Organizational properties of the interacting units—including size, hierarchical structure, ideology, needs for resources and for the absorption of output, growth rate, and other dynamic tendencies
2. Conflict of interest—interactional incompatibilities in organizational properties
3. Role expectations—organizational prescriptions and proscriptions to boundary positions directly involved in conflict
4. Personality and other predispositions of persons occupying conflict-relevant boundary positions
5. External conflict-regulating norms, rules, and procedures
6. Previous conflict interaction, including immediately preceding acts

Empirical evidence is reviewed within each of these categories. For example, conflict within organizations appears to be increased by internal differentiation, time pressure, tightness of scheduled interdependence and coordination. Frequent loci of conflict include line versus staff, and sales versus manufacturing. Incompatible interests (conflicts of interest) tend to produce actual conflict, although the locus of the conflict behavior may not be the same as that of the conflicting interests.

Conflicts of interest are discussed as combinations of promotive and contrient interdependence and specific examples are given from mining and manufacturing. Laboratory experiments show conflict of interest to be the single strongest predictor of conflict behavior, with both relative and absolute magnitudes of conflict of interest having effects. The inference is that conflict of interest makes conflict behavior rational in some sense, and therefore more probable.

Role expectations for boundary positions in organizational conflict are analyzed in terms of the complexity of the role-set and the problems of representing a constituency not directly exposed to the conflict but to some extent controlling the behavior of those who are. The internal dynamics of such constituent groups during conflict are seen as urging uncompromising behavior by the representatives.

Personality and other predisposing factors have been shown to have some importance in extraorganizational contexts, but they show only weak and irregular effects on organizational conflict, presumably because their influence is obliterated by situational and organizational factors.

Virtually all organizational conflicts take place within some set of rules and procedures—organizational, statutory, or otherwise prescribed. Common membership and acceptance of such rules tend to limit the forms and duration of conflict. Examples include the required presence of third parties, authoritative instruction to the parties at conflict, and communication before action is taken.

Evidence for the dynamics of conflict interaction shows that actions evoke similar reactions, and that the process of action and reaction tends to escalate the conflict. Conflict interaction has also been shown to involve perceptual and cognitive simplifications, in which opponents are seen as evil and supporters as virtuous. Such views justify more aggressive behavior.

Conflict-reducing behavior has been less studied. The evidence suggests that unconditional submissive behavior is not effective, that conditional promises are more effective than threats, and that conditional cooperation (repeated cooperative initiatives with requests for cooperation but readiness to reciprocate aggression) is most effective. Approaches to conflict management are further analyzed in terms of the six categories of variables specified in the conflict model.

19

■ ORGANIZATIONAL CHANGE ■

OUTLINE

Theories of change presuppose a great deal, and technologies of change require even more. An explanation of system changes assumes some considerable knowledge already in hand—the major properties and functions of the system, its structure, and its characteristic inputs and outputs. A theory of change then builds on such information to describe the ways in which system changes occur: what altered inputs or environmental circumstances, for example, will have what effects on system properties and output. If empirical work has kept pace with theory, we will be able to measure such circumstances and system properties at any given time and thus test and improve our hypotheses about system change.

Ambitious as such accomplishments may seem, technologies of change require even more. They require that we shall be able to produce at will and at tolerable costs of time and effort, changes of desired kinds and amounts. And they assume that values and goals exist that make some system states preferable to others and therefore imply the changes to be sought. Technologies of change then consist of the tools for producing such changes, and the procedures for using those tools.

In the process of inventing the rules and tools of change for any given category of systems, there usually occurs a good deal of differentiation; different kinds of changes are described in terms of separate theories and are the subject of separate technologies. We are unlikely, for example, to encounter a general theory of change in individuals. Instead there are theories that deal with intrinsic, genetically programmed changes (growth, maturation, and aging); theories that deal with specific categories of inputs and their effects (nutrition, toxicology); theories specific to various pathological processes (bacterial and viral invasion, carcinogenic agents); and there are theories organized around more general ideas of perfection and perfectability (socialization, education, and psychotherapy).

The fact that organizational change is still regarded as a fit subject for some single theory and kind of intervention suggests a modest state of achievement rather than any intrinsic simplicity in the subject matter. A great deal of differentiation will be needed before some integrated theory and technology of organizational change will emerge.

The lines of that differentiation are not yet apparent. There is at present a kind of competition among different theories and technologies of organizational change, but they are best described as scattered rather than differentiated. The nomenclature is familiar—Theory X versus Theory Y, System 1 versus System 4, 1-1 versus 9-9 managers, T-groups and laboratory training, job enlargement and job enrichment, survey-guided development, and on through an ever-growing, ever-changing vocabulary.[1]

---

[1]Systems 1 and 4 are opposed models proposed by Likert (1967) as bad and good modes of operation based in part on research findings from a variety of settings. The

The attempt to describe and compare this array of theoretical ideas and approaches to organizational change is less a process of discovery and mapping than one of invention and assignment. We must choose the dimensions we consider important for understanding organizational change, and then describe the various approaches to change in terms of those dimensions, hoping in the process to illuminate rather than conceal their similarities and differences.

DIMENSIONS OF COMPARISON

At the minimum, a technology for organizational change should deal with three questions: What is the present state of the organization? What is the preferred state? By what means is it proposed to move from the present to the preferred state? Those questions suggest the following properties as a basis for comparing approaches to organizational change: point of entry, initial state of the system, preferred state, method of change, primary target, hypothesized linkage between primary target and preferred end-state, method of assessing change.

Point of entry refers to the origin of the change attempt. If, as so often happens, an outside consultant is brought into the organization to lead or facilitate certain change programs, who invites the consultant? If a new program for training first-level supervision in conflict management is launched internally, who decreed the launching?

Initial state of the system is important for two reasons; it is the base-line against which any subsequent change must be measured and it is likely to explain in part the reasons for seeking change. People attempt to change things when they are dissatisfied or uncomfortable with them as they are. The initial state of the system helps us locate and understand the motivation for change.

Some approaches to organizational change—Likert's (1967) and Blake's (1969) for example—include an assessment of the initial state of the system on certain variables as part of the change technology. The managers whose behavior will define change or the lack of it both give and receive information about the initial state of the organization, in-

---

favorable extremes on the following dimensions constitute *System 4* and the unfavorable extremes *System 1*:

    (a) Supportiveness and openness of leaders
    (b) Character of motivational forces
    (c) Nature of communicative process
    (d) Involvement of subordinates in decision making
    (e) Character of goal setting
    (f) Use of feedback

1, 1 and 9, 9 managers are distinctions based on the grid organizational development program developed by Blake and Mouton (1969). The 1, 1 style reflects low concern for both people and productivity; the 1, 9 style high concern for people and low concern for production; 9, 1 style high concern for production and low concern for people; and 9, 9 high concern for both people and productivity.

cluding their own behavior, using standardized questionnaires or rating scales. Other approaches use less quantitative methods of initial assessment for similar purposes; Beckhard (1969) describes "confrontation meetings," for example. And many approaches to organizational change make no assessment of the initial situation, either for purposes of motivating the people involved or modifying the change effort itself.

The importance of the initial state of the system for change processes has been demonstrated in the research of Peterson and his colleagues (1978) in their study of attempts by dominantly white colleges to increase black enrollment. These investigators found internal predisposing factors in colleges achieving substantial increases in black students. Two significant internal factors were: a president who was a strong proponent of the shift and on-campus demonstrations by white students in favor of increased black enrollment. When pressures for organizational change are wholly external, institutions seek ways of resisting or neutralizing the external demands.

Preferred state of the system gives the goals of change and the standards against which a change attempt will be measured. Some theoretical approaches to organizational change include explicit descriptions of preferred or ideal states. The major thesis of McGregor's (1960) book was the superiority of Theory Y principles as a basis for understanding and influencing human behavior in organizations, and therefore as a basis for management. Likert (1961) is equally explicit about the greater productivity and satisfaction that accrue from organizations with System 4 characteristics, and the main emphasis of organizational development by means of the managerial grid (Blake and Mouton, 1969) is the effort to attain 9,9 managerial behavior, a superior pattern characterized by simultaneous and maximum concern for "people and productivity."

Method of change refers to the specific behaviors or activities by means of which organizational change is to be induced. Giving lectures on work simplification is a method, and so is psychoanalysis (if undertaken for the purpose of organizational change). Sensitivity training (T-groups) is a method and so is the Scanlon Plan (with its specific components of profit-sharing, worker representation, and the like). The method refers to what is actually done; naming a method does not suffice.

Primary target identifies the subsystem or echelon or specific position to which the method of change is immediately directed. In many cases the method stipulates the primary target. "Start at the top" is common advice among practitioners of organizational change. Survey-guided development (Hausser, Pecorella, and Wissler, 1975) as developed at the Institute for Social Research (Michigan) uses a somewhat more flexible decision rule: "deciding how high in the organization one must go depends upon the level at which people have some real power and control over what happens below them in the organization" (p. 15). Most methods of organizational change have a preferred target, explicit or implicit, although practitioners are likely to show some adaptability to local opportunities and resistances. We propose to locate the primary target of a change effort in terms of the organizational subsystem to which it is addressed, the level or echelon in the hierarchy, and the aspect of organizational structure or behavior with which it deals. For example, the AT&T program of job enrichment (Ford, 1973) was aimed at a part of the production subsystem, concentrated on nonsupervisory employees, and involved the division of labor (role prescriptions).

Hypothesized linkage from the activities involving the primary target to the intended changes in the state of the organization may be long or short, well-substantiated or unsubstantiated, infallible or improbable. Every technology of change, however, involves some such linkage. The change method (input) itself is generally not identical with the preferred state it is supposed to bring about.

If a survey of the organization is supposed to initiate a process of change that moves the organization toward the System 4 profile of supervisory behavior and employee attitudes, what is the sequence that occurs between survey and behavior change and change in attitude? If psychotherapeutic intervention with a company president is to lead to an ultimate increase in productivity and profit, how is this to occur?

Assessment of change is the last characteristic in terms of which we will compare approaches to organizational change. Methods of organizational change and the users of those methods differ in their emphasis on assessment. Ideally, we would like to know the extent to which a given attempt at organizational change altered the primary target in the intended ways, and the extent to which those alterations had the effects predicted by the hypothesized linkage. For example, did the company-wide T-group training really increase the self-awareness of the participants, their sensitivity to the reactions of others, and their understanding of group processes? If so, were there more general improvements in interpersonal relations throughout the organization, greater liking and respect, greater willingness to express feelings and accept such expression from others? And if such changes occurred, were they followed by changes in more conventional criteria of organizational success—reduced absence and turnover, increased productivity, and the like?

The assessment of organizational responses to change efforts is not unique in asking questions of this kind. They are questions familiar to every experimentalist: Did the independent variable really move? And if it did, did its movement have the predicted effects?

Not all theories and technologies of organizational change deal explicitly with these six dimensions, of course. Some normative theories urge organizational change without any explicit discussion of method; McGregor's *Human Side of Enterprise* is an example. Some theories of change are intentionally content-free, and avoid the normative specification of a preferred state. Lippitt, Watson, and Westley (1958) offer such a theory of planned change in organizations and communities, although they are by no means unconcerned about social outcomes. Rogers and Shoemaker (1971) provide another example. Their interest is in the diffusion of innovations, and the home-canning of food and the use of marijuana are equally appropriate to their purpose.

Moreover, some studies that have become prominent in the literature of organizational change were not primarily studies of change at all. They were undertaken to test some substantive hypothesis or to compare two different organizational forms. Whether the method of doing so constituted a practical technology of organizational change was of secondary concern or none at all. Our emphasis, however, is on methods of creating change in organizations, and we compare different methods in terms of the dimensions just described.

INDIVIDUAL APPROACHES TO ORGANIZATIONAL CHANGE

Attempts to change organizations by changing individuals have a long history of theoretical inadequacy and practical failure. Both stem from a disregard of the systemic properties of organizations and from the confusion of individual changes with modification in organizational variables. That confusion is due in part to the lack of precise concepts for distinguishing between behavior determined largely by the prescriptions of structured roles within a system and behavior determined more directly by personality needs and values. The behavior of people in organizations is still the behavior of individuals, but it has a different set of determinants than behavior outside organizational roles.

Let us examine the individual approach to organizational change in more detail. Its essential weakness can be labelled the *psychological fallacy*, the concentration on individuals without regard to the situational factors that shape their behavior. The logic of individual approaches to organizational change asserts that since organizations are made up of individuals, we can change an organization by changing its members. This is not an impossible proposition, which perhaps accounts for its durability, but it is a great oversimplification. It does not deal directly with the aspects of behavior that are to be changed and the expectations and incentives that evoke those behaviors.

Changing an organization solely in individual terms involves an impressive and discouraging series of assumptions, usually unspecified. They include, at the very least, the assumptions:

That the individual can be provided with new insight or knowledge or attribute of personality

That these will produce some altered pattern of motivation with respect to the organizational role

That these insights and motivations will persist even when the individual leaves the special circumstances in which they were acquired and returns to his or her accustomed role in the organization

That they will be adapted as necessary to that role (or it to them); that coworkers will be persuaded to accept the changes in behavior that confront them

That they will be persuaded to make complementary changes in their own expectations and behavior.

Moreover, if the newly acquired insights and motives imply behaviors that go beyond the present policies, authority structure, or division of labor of the organization, the individual approach to change leaves the task of changing those things to the individual. The task of organizational change, in short, is delegated. The major forms of individually based change are information giving, training, counseling and psychotherapy, selection, and removal.

The phrase "changing individuals" can be read two ways, especially in the context of organizational change. It can refer to bringing about change in the behavior patterns (and perhaps attitudes, values, and perceptions) of certain persons, or it can refer to the replacement of individuals in organizational roles. The latter meaning is discussed in terms of the usual categories of administrative action—selection, placement, and termination. These actions involve a variety of problems—of prediction, power, and restraints on power. They have nevertheless some considerable strengths as modes of organizational change. The new person moves into an "old" situation, of course, but unburdened by its past. The person-situation interaction is new, and the prospects for organizational change correspondingly better. They are limited, of course, by the strength and rigidity of the situational requirements, which are likely to prevent change at positions low in the hierarchy and technology dominated, but to allow it for positions of power.

Information

The use of information to bring about organizational change, especially change in performance of existing roles, is very common. It is usually used within the line organization, often by persons highly placed in the organization, and the information flow is characteristically downward. There may be expert consultation, internal or external, in the preparation and presentation of the message. The impetus for the information giving is typically some official dissatisfaction with continuing performance indicators (profit, volume of production, cost of service) or some specific event that is interpreted as potentially dangerous (a rumored strike, an unexpected loss to a competitor, a sudden increase in unexplained absence). Whether such information giving has any success in changing the organization depends first of all on whether there was lack of information to begin with. That top management would prefer regular attendance to Monday-and-Friday absenteeism will not be news to the rank and file, nor are the reasons for that executive preference likely to be new. Yet making clear what changes are wanted and giving the rationale for desired changes are the functions that information can perform in a program of organizational change.

These functions have their uses, but they are supplementary and supportive to other methods; the motivation to change must come in other ways. The exception, of course, is the case in which ambiguity or lack of information has been the obstacle to appropriate performance. People are then likely to accept suggestions that clarify matters and offer a sense that things are under control.

Training

Training is so general a word that it should be immediately qualified. We use it here in its conventional sense, as a combination of information giving and skill practice. Such training is widespread, and is offered both within organizations and by specialized agencies outside them. Training programs are of many kinds, and are specialized both occupationally and hierarchically. New foremen or other first-line supervisors are likely to attend an on-the-job course in supervisory skills and responsibilities, for example, and similar opportunities are given to people in other positions. Such training has more to do with organizational stability than change. It is an experience in socialization, either for a role now held or for one aspired to. The content of the training, intended or unintended, teaches "how we do things here," not how to change them.

The dilemma of training individuals to change wisely the framework within which they were trained is, of course, one of the great riddles of human institutions, and there is no evidence that the usual forms of organizational training have solved it. Van Maanen (1976) reviews the evidence on training and socialization in organizations and concludes that "while organizations differ regarding the expressive content of their training programs, all organizations at least require that the new member demonstrate the 'proper attitude.' "

Counseling, Psychotherapy, and Personality Changes

The failure of information and training to alter individual behavior raises the question of approaches that "go deeper." The logic of psychotherapeutic approaches to changing behavior begins with the assumption that the behavior in question expresses deep-lying values, motives, or other attributes of personality. If therapeutic insight alters these, changes in behavior will follow.

Gordon Allport (1945, 1946, 1954) suggested that giving people insight into the psychological dynamics of prejudice toward other races and nations might be an effective way of restructuring their attitudes. Katz, Sarnoff, and McClintock (1956) demonstrated that prejudices toward blacks could be changed momentarily by information, but that more lasting change resulted from giving people insight into their own motivation about prejudice. A number of industrial organizations have utilized consulting firms for therapeutic counseling of middle management personnel, sometimes selecting certain individuals as problem cases, sometimes offering the therapeutic facility to any manager who wished to take advantage of it. No comprehensive evaluation of such approaches to organizational change has been made. Our expectation would be that the effects of therapy, even where beneficial to the individual, would be negligible for the organization in most cases.

The problem, as we have already implied, is the long and doubtful route that leads from individual therapy to social change. The patient is first removed from the social situation in which his or her usual behavior is reinforced. In isolation from organization associates, the patient learns to relate to the therapist, and thereafter to colleagues. Since there have been no corresponding changes in them, the subject encounters a series of shocks in presenting the new personality to the old colleagues. It is a task to maintain the personality change itself, let alone reshape the organization in its image. Such changes would, after all, be tertiary effects: the primary target of psychotherapy is the personality of the individual, and the secondary task is the restructuring of the individual's relationships with others.

Three exceptions to this negative view should be specified: the case of people seriously ill, the case of people who hold positions of rare organizational power, and the case of individual therapy used as the first stage of a two-stage sociotherapeutic process. People with serious neurotic problems or with psychotic illness impede organizational functioning. Successful therapy relieves the impediment and in this sense improves the organization as well as the individual. The paranoiac who was too fearful and suspicious to engage in the normal exchange and task-oriented cooperation of organizational life may, after therapy, be integrated into the work group.

There is also the occasional case in which personality conversion is achieved in the individual who is either the most powerful figure in the organization or who is close to the top in power position. Here, of course, the change achieved through individual therapy may have reverberations in the organization as a whole. Since such a person is in a position to introduce legitimized change in the organization through utilizing its authority structure, any real changes in his or her personality can have important organizational consequences. This is especially true in small organizations, where the other social forces maintaining a steady state are less imposing in their weight.

The third circumstance in which therapy seems to contribute to organizational change is illustrated in some of the Tavistock cases. Menzies (1960) describes the extreme levels of anxiety and defensive behavior that she encountered in some key members of the nursing staff in a hospital. She argues that organizational changes were not feasible until "emotional ground-clearing" was done. Sofer (1972) reports similar experiences in industry and in a technical college, and argues the importance of individual therapeutic intervention in combination with other means:

> ... while its immediate purpose may be to cope with psychological tensions, this has been done not for its own sake but in the pursuit of more radical aims involving structural alterations. (p. 396)

Psychotherapy is not the only way of approaching personality change, although it is certainly the best known and the most widely used. McClelland (1962, 1963) has argued that achievement motivation (nAch) leads to managerial success in individual cases and to national affluence in the aggregate. Although he regards this motive pattern as embedded in cultures and transmitted through child-rearing practices, he has proposed that the need to achieve can be heightened in adults, with consequent organizational improvements. Some experimental work along these lines has been done in India. The published data, however, are meager and unencouraging.

Selection and Placement

These two functions may constitute the oldest area of applied psychology, and they have been the subject of highly sophisticated methodological work. Selection tests were described by Cattell (1890) in the late nineteenth century. Munsterberg's (1913) tests for the selection of street-car motormen are still cited in histories of psychology. The Otis "intelligence" tests, transformed to the Army Alpha and Beta forms, were used on a massive scale for the screening and placement of soldiers in World War I. The techniques have been steadily developed, and comprehensive treatments of test construction, validation, and utilization are available (Cronbach and Gleser, 1965; Guion, 1976).

The purpose of such tests is to discriminate among individuals in terms that will predict their subsequent performance in organizations, sometimes in a specific job. In recent years their use has been challenged in the courts—*Myart v. Motorola*—on the grounds that they are often discriminatory in another sense of the word, specifically forbidden by the 1964 Civil Rights Act (French, 1965). Regardless of the long-term effects of this controversy, we believe that selection tests tend to be conservative regarding organizational change. The conservatism is inherent in the criterion problem, which is almost always success in the organization as it is. It can be argued that the organization that uses such tests meticulously comes to resemble itself more and more closely—not to change in any more profound sense. It is possible, of course, to choose a different criterion and thus to bring in a set of potential organization-changers rather than persons likely to succeed in the organization as is, but the instances of systematic use of selection tests for organizational change must be few.

One such instance was described by Argyris (1954). The selection procedures of a bank were seen by its top management to have become dysfunctional for precisely the reasons we have just discussed. Individuals were being selected who fitted well the profile of successful well-regarded junior managers in that bank—quiet, noncompetitive, deferential, conservative. The decision of top management to recruit more self-assertive and venturesome managers was taken in order to change the organization, in response to changing business patterns and opportunities in its own environment. Moreover, the recruiting program had the intended effects, although it appears also to have had the unintended effect of creating a sustained conflict between the new and the old recruits (Porter, Lawler, and Hackman, 1975).

This study is rare, if not unique; other such descriptions of selection testing for organizational change are not available. The principle of selection for change is observable, however, in specific instances, without the formal procedures of testing. Especially in the selection of top executives or the election of organization presidents, the choice may reflect dissatisfaction and the hope for organizational change. Wise choices at high levels may well fulfill such hopes, not so much because the selection process constitutes organizational change as because it leads to change. The task of change has been delegated to the newly selected leaders, and awaits them.

Termination

The classic action for unsuccessful performance in an organizational role is removal from it. In most organizations, decisions for retention or removal are hierarchical; they are made from above. Such decisions are little studied, and the reasons given for dismissal are typically cloudy, perhaps in order to avoid the addition of insult to injury. As a result, it is difficult to distinguish externally compelled reductions in force from internal decisions based on performance.

It seems likely, however, that the systematic use of termination to produce other kinds of organizational change is uncommon. It is nevertheless potentially potent. Termination is the obverse of selection, and the rate at which people leave an organization often sets the pace for selection. A new generation, selected on change-inducing criteria, cannot take power until others have relinquished it. And until that transfer of power has occurred, the potential changes are unlikely to be enacted.

In this respect, the various protections of individuals against arbitrary dismissal—union contracts, academic tenure, legal statute, and organizational common law—are conservative. Such guarantees were themselves expressive of social change when they were attained, and they continue to be expressive of important social values. Their intraorganizational effects, however, are toward stability rather than change.

Behavior Modification in Organizations

The work of B. F. Skinner and his followers, usually identified as operant conditioning or behavior modification, developed in the framework and tradition of individual psychology. It was characterized by a great deal of laboratory experimentation on animal and human subjects, and a marked disregard for organizational phenomena. Skinner's theory is essentially a theory of individual behavior, based on the proposition that all organisms tend to repeat behaviors that are rewarded and to inhibit (stop, conceal, alter) behaviors that are punished.

Stated in those terms, the Skinnerian approach is of no special organizational interest. Most organizations utilize a variety of rewards and punishments, from promotion to dismissal and from praise to reprimand. These are administered on the assumption, justified or not, that they will affect future behavior. It could be argued therefore that hierarchical organizations already accept the Skinnerian dictum that behavior is determined by its consequences, and attempt to shape individual behavior by rewards and punishments. To the extent that this is true, a Skinnerian description of organizational life might be more distinctive in its vocabulary than in its ideas.

In recent years, however, a number of people have proposed organizational applications of operant conditioning, calling it organizational behavior modification (O. B. Mod., for short), and a number of case studies have now been completed. Moreover, Skinner himself has for many years been concerned with social applications of operant conditioning—first as fiction (*Walden II*, 1948), then in the proposed design of experimental communities (1968), and most recently in the area of organizational change (1973).

The organizational cases thus far on record have several elements in common besides their Skinnerian theoretical base. Their point of entry into the organization is high, at least high enough so that the schedule of reinforcing rewards or punishments can be established. That schedule has usually been set on a hierarchical basis, with those in positions of formal authority using their control over resources to set performance-contingent rewards and punishments for people lower in the hierarchy. The initial state of the system seems to be regarded as irrelevant except that its performance is less than desired by those who initiate the change experiment and set the reinforcement schedule. The common method is to analyze in detail the specific individual behaviors that are to be increased or decreased, and then to set the specific rewards or punishments that will be administered following the "emission" of these behaviors by the subject individuals. The target is individual behavior in the work situation; if supraindividual effects are expected, the presumption is that they come about through aggregation of changed individual behaviors.

Luthans and Kreitner (1975) provide a detailed model for creating a change program along these lines. They emphasize the importance of reducing the desired performance to "observable and countable" events (behaviors), measuring the frequency with which the individual is engaging in these behaviors, establishing a set of rewards (and perhaps punishments) that will be administered contingent on the person's performance (or lack of performance) of the desired behaviors, giving the individual continuing information about his or her performance, administering rewards and punishments according to the contingency schedule, and evaluating the changes in individual behavior.

One of the most successful applications of the Skinnerian approach is the case of an air freight company reported in Organizational Dynamics ("At Emery Air Freight," 1973). The company's purpose was to increase profit, and the project began with an analysis of those individual behaviors that had the greatest impact on profitability. It then proceded through the sequence of steps described above. For example, the efficient utilization of air-freight containers was found to be crucial to profit, but a performance audit showed that containers were shipped at only 45 percent of their capacity. A program was initiated that required each dockworker to keep a tally of the proportion of container capacity actually utilized (self-maintained feedback) and each supervisor to reinforce positively all instances of utilization at or near capacity. A supervisors' workbook was provided, with specifications of more than 150 reinforcements, from a smile and a nod of encouragement to "Let me buy you a coffee." Performance in container utilization went from 45 percent to more than 90 percent, with savings in excess of $2,000,000 over a three year period.

A more complex creation of situational settings and contingent rewards is described by Cohen and Filipczak (1971). They conducted a field experiment in the rehabilitation of teen-age delinquent boys whose crimes ranged from auto theft and housebreaking to rape and homocide. Forty-one of these young men, all of whom had been committed to the National Training School for Boys in Washington, D.C., were placed in a separate experimental "living and learning environment," designed in accordance with Skinnerian principles.

Their base-line situation in the new environment was equivalent to the usual arrangements at the Training School—dormitory sleeping arrangements, crowded common rooms, limited but adequate diet, and few recreational alternatives. Their reinforcement schedule, however, made it possible for them to have private bedrooms, private offices or studies, a wide choice of foods, and various other advantages. These rewards were obtainable only through purchase with local "currency," and the currency could be earned only through academic test performance. Learning or, more precisely, the demonstration through test scores of things learned, was the behavior to be reinforced. The short-term results are impressive; within six months, 90 percent of the young men showed the equivalent of four years of academic growth in at least one subject. Scores on the Army Revised Beta test (IQ) went from a mean of 92 to a mean of 108 during a four-month period.

Many issues, pragmatic and ethical, have been raised about such experiments (Argyris, 1971; Whyte, 1972). We believe that the major issues have to do with the exclusively individualistic emphasis of the performance analyses and reinforcement schedules, and the assumption of unilateral authority to set such schedules. The wish to name the game, to choose and define it rather than merely to play it, is distinctively human and the trend in human organizations is toward recognition of that fact. Applications of behavior modification to organizations thus far do not recognize it, nor do they deal with organizations as social systems.

Behavior modification is thus in danger of becoming a new Taylorism, which assumes that the organization is controlled by a rule-enforcing hierarchy, that the tasks of individuals have been hierarchically set, and that the remaining problem is to evoke high individual performance under these circumstances. As the O.B. Mod. enthusiasts come increasingly to confront the efforts of human subjects to define their own contingency schedules, the limitations and potentialities of the Skinnerian approach in organizations will become clearer. For *organizational* change, the crucial question may be one that has not been made explicit in the experiments conducted to date: How must conventional *organizations* be changed in order to evoke greater effort and commitment from their members?

GROUP APPROACHES
TO ORGANIZATIONAL CHANGE

Group approaches to organizational change are of many kinds, but they have in common the use of the group as a means of increasing learning and heightening commitment to things learned. For purposes of organizational change, the most important distinction involves the primary target and therefore the hypothesized linkage to the organization. When groups are made up of individuals unrelated to each other by organizational role and membership, the primary target is necessarily the individual, and the application of things learned to organizational problems involves all the attenuating elements already discussed. In comparison to individual approaches, the advantages of such groups for inducing organizational change will depend entirely on the quality and strength of the initial learning experience (unless, of course, the group is to have a continuing existence of its own and thus to become a kind of organization in its own right).

Groups may also be made up of people who are members of the same organization and who may occupy closely related positions in the organization. Under these circumstances, the primary target of change may be the group itself and the relationships among its members. The social distance between the learning experiences in such groups and their utilization for organizational change is correspondingly less. The prospects for organizational change are in this respect greater, although the intrusion of authority relationships and other organizational formalities into the learning situation may limit what can be done in the group itself. The resultant dilemma in the composition of groups for organizational change is discussed later. Let us begin, however, by reviewing the evidence for the power of groups to change individual attitudes and behavior.

Influence of Organizational Groups

Kurt Lewin and his followers were the first to demonstrate systematically the superiority of the group method over the usual informational approach in modifying individual behavior. Most of the group experimentation in this tradition has dealt with ad hoc assemblages that were not embedded in organizations and had no post-experimental life of their own. Their product and the measure of their effectiveness was the sum of individual changes—cognitive, attitudinal, and behavioral. Other experiments, however, have used the group method under conditions closer to the organizational context. Bavelas (Lewin, 1947), for example, tackled the difficult problem of changing the informal norms of a work group regarding productivity. Employees in a garment factory were given the problem of their production standards for group discussion and decision. Two other groups used as control groups also had discussion but were under no constraint to come up with a group decision about a solution. The group that reached a decision about production goals was the only one to increase its productivity.

Coch and French (1948), also working in the Lewinian tradition, employed the method of group discussion to gain acceptance for changes in work methods in the garment factory where Bavelas had conducted his action research. A change in work methods generally meets with resistance among workers, who feel threatened by it. It tends to be accompanied by lowered morale, a decline in productivity persisting beyond a reasonable period for relearning, and an increase in turnover. In the factory in question, turnover was significantly higher among operators whose jobs were changed than among those who continued in the old pattern. Moreover, experienced operators not only showed a decline in productivity during the period of learning their modified assignments, but they took much longer to learn these assignments than newly hired workers.

In the Coch and French experiment a control group of employees was introduced to the job changes in the conventional manner. They were informed in a group meeting of what was now required of them, what the new piece rates would be, how they had been arrived at, and why the company had to institute these changes to meet competitive conditions. A question and answer period followed the announcement. Two experimental treatments involved three other groups of workers. In one treatment, the workers were given the problem facing the company, invited to discuss it, and after they had reached agreement about the need for change, were asked to name the workers who would first be given special training. The last provision was especially important because the work of these selected operators during relearning would be the basis for the new piece rates. Workers are always concerned that new time standards should not be set by the performance of the fastest in the group and in this experimental situation they had control over the problem. In the second experimental treatment, the participation technique was pushed even further, and all members of the two experimental groups were involved in the training for the revised job assignments.

It should be added that the initial presentation of the problem to the experimental groups was much more dramatic than to the control group. Two garments were shown to the workers, one of which sold for 100 percent more than the other. Each group was asked to indicate which garment was cheaper but could not do so. This demonstration effectively shared with the group the need to reduce production costs. The members reached a general agreement that a savings could be effected by removing the "frills" from the garment without affecting individual efficiency ratings. It can be argued that such a dramatic demonstration gave a genuine advantage to the experimental group discussion method without being an intrinsic part of it. It is an open question whether the demonstration would have been as effective in the control group, where the company spokesman would have picked a few representatives of the group to decide which was the better garment. The main point is that the experimental treatment moved in the direction of group participation and the control treatment did not.

At any rate, the results of the treatment were spectacular, even though the number of workers was small. The control group showed hardly any improvement over its earlier efficiency ratings after the change and displayed marked hostility toward management and its representatives. Moreover, 17 percent of this group left the company within the first forty days. The groups in the first experimental treatment demonstrated quick relearning; they were back at their prechange level within fourteen days and showed some improvement thereafter. The groups in the second experimental treatment relearned even more quickly, were back at their prechange level after the second day, and went on to show a 14 percent improvement over that level. (Even a return to the old level of 60 units a day with the improved work methods represented a great gain for the company.) Under both participation treatments, morale was high, with only a single act of aggression against a supervisor under this regime and with much evidence of cooperation. And not a single employee in the experimental groups quit during the forty days of the experimental observation. It is not surprising that this action experiment has been so widely quoted, in spite of the small number of cases.

Coch and French (1948) also ran a second experiment in which they reassigned the members of the control group to new jobs after thirty-two days of the older treatment. This time the workers were introduced to their new jobs through group participation. They responded as the other experimental groups had done, with rapid relearning, an increase in productivity, and a modification from their previous pattern of hostility to one of cooperation.

The dramatic results of the Coch-French experiment were not replicated, however, when French and some Scandinavian colleagues (1957) attempted a similar experiment in the footwear department of a

Norwegian factory. Again the problem was one of getting workers to accept changes in work methods with as much organizational effectiveness as possible. Two groups were subjected to the experimental treatment of group discussion and decision about allocation of articles to be produced, length of training, division of labor, and assignment of jobs within groups. Three groups were given the experimental treatment of participation only with respect to the allocation of articles, and four groups in the control condition did not participate in any of these four types of decisions. Though more members of the experimental than of the control groups felt that they had had greater influence over the change in work methods than in previous years, there were no significant differences in production as a result of the participation procedures. All groups kept fairly close to the standard level of production, although the two experimental groups participating in all four types of decisions reached this standard more quickly than other groups.

The failure of the group-decision method to raise productivity in the Norwegian experiment is explained by the investigators as the weakness of the experimental manipulations and the factor of the legitimate expectations of the Norwegian worker. The manipulations were weak in that they dealt with allocation of articles and of workers rather than production standards and piece rates. The workers were not manipulated because they already had the power to set the production rate, and their union representatives had the right to bargain about the piece rate. The legitimate expectations of the Norwegian workers were that their participation in such issues would be mediated through their elected union representatives and not through the intervention of a research team.

In short, the Norwegian experiment emphasizes a central fact about group discussion in the organizational context: the effect of the discussion on the group norms and behavior is strongly conditioned by the larger organizational structure, and by the expectations and power that reside in that structure.

The power of a group to influence its members in the organizational context depends on the significance of the issues with which it is permitted to deal and its freedom and authority to act on those issues. One basis for the efficacy of group discussion is the involvement of people, the degree to which they can work out problems of importance to themselves and make decisions about their own fate. Workers are not generally as involved in making higher profits for management as they are in their own problems of making a living, achieving job security, and doing interesting work under good working conditions. The group discussion method, to be successful with hourly employees, must offer something of importance to them for decision making. Unless the area of freedom in the organization gives them some scope, the method may be ineffective or may actually boomerang. To be asked to invest time and energy in discussing trivial matters, while important issues are forbidden, can be infuriating.

Besides the major factor of influence in significant decisions, there are other factors that account for the effectiveness of group process. Discussion and decision about problems of importance invoke powerful individual forces of self-expression and self-determination. Not only are people discussing important matters, but each individual is given a chance to express his or her own views and to persuade others. Ideas that come from the outside, even if significant for personal welfare, are not as satisfying as the expression of a person's own ideas on the problem.

Sensitivity Training:
The Technology of the Peer Group

The early experiments on group processes by Lewin and his associates developed rather quickly a form of education variously labelled sensitivity training, T-groups, and laboratory method. Research on group effects and decisions continued, of course, but a specific use of the peer group for individual and organizational change was invented and propagated.

The first clear use of this method took place in Bethel, Maine, during the summer of 1947, under the auspices of an organization created for the purpose, the National Training Laboratory for Group Development. Leland Bradford, the long-time director of the National Training Laboratories (NTL for short) has collaborated with others prominent in that development to describe the basic T-group method, its history, and its offspring (Benne, Bradford, Gibb, and Lippitt, 1975).

The prototypical T-group is an *ad hoc* assembly of individuals who meet together, initially as strangers, away from their usual roles and responsibilities. They enter the group as peers, unrepresentative of their group memberships, and move quickly into an exploration of group processes and leadership. The frustrations in dropping their usual role supports and ingrained organizational techniques lead to a reexamination of methods of participating in groups and influencing other people.

Each T-group (training group), consists of approximately ten to sixteen people, including one or two trainers. The group is scheduled for one or two meetings each day over a period of about one week. The meetings typically last for an hour and a half or two hours.

Each group begins without agenda, structure, division of labor, or rules of procedure. The people in each group are strangers to each other, brought together only by the common goal of learning more about themselves, the impact they have on others, and the ways in which groups can become effective instruments for meeting the needs of their members. The absence of the usual props of officers agenda, and Robert's Rules of Order creates an initial vacuum that is often quite uncomfortable. As the members struggle to fill this vacuum with meaningful activity and relationships, the trainer attempts to observe problems of communication, attempted seizures of power, misunderstandings, and other phenomena of interpersonal life. The trainer communicates these observations to the group, whose members gradually begin to attend to such matters themselves and to check the accuracy of their own observations by describing them and asking for corroboration or correction from others. By this method (which is difficult to describe but often exciting and rewarding to experience) the members of the group attain increased sensitivity to their own behavior, the actions of others, and the nature of group development. Group members often emerge with a restructuring of their values about people and about their operations in group settings.

A T-group in this original form is a peculiarly self-contained series of events. It has its beginning of strangeness and uncertainty, its mid-period of self-discovery and insight into group development, and its end. The end, in spite of various efforts to anticipate the problems of re-entry and to rehearse the uses to which group-acquired insights will be put, is characteristically sad. It is as if members understood, better than they knew, the magnitude of what has come to be called "the carry-over problem."

The nature of that problem and its magnitude depend, of course, on what one considers to be the purpose of the T-group experience, and therefore what should be carried over. These questions are answered differently by the various agencies that offer such training and the individuals who elect it or are sent to receive it. For many of them, perhaps most, sensitivity training is a form of individual development, and the appropriate criteria of success would include increases in self-acceptance, empathy, ability to express warmth, and the like. In the hundreds of quantitative research studies that have been done on T-groups (Gibb, 1975), these are the kinds of criteria used most frequently. Effects are overwhelmingly positive, as measured by self-report at the end of the group experience. About one-third of such studies included data for periods ranging from one week to six months after training. The data show that changes, where they have occurred at all, tend to persist, as measured by self-report. Longer range follow-up, including self-reported and independent measures, is much needed. The evidence to date, however, is encouraging at the level of individual experience.

T-groups in Organizations

Of the ten million people estimated to have some variant of sensitivity training (Benne, 1975), a substantial proportion entered into it with the sponsorship of some organization, more often than not an organization in which they were employed. For them and for the organization to which they returned, it is appropriate to evaluate the training experience in terms of subsequent changes in individual role performance and in the organization as a whole. In doing so, we must distinguish two rather different strategies of organizational change via sensitivity training—a strategy based on individual effects and their diffusion, and a strategy based on group effects. We must distinguish also between the use of T-groups as the primary means of organizational change and their incorporation in programs using several methods simultaneously.

The simplest, grandest, and most optimistic of assumptions about T-groups was that they would transform human institutions and human life. Individual changes in insight, interpersonal skills, and values would occur and persist; as the proportion of individuals so changed increased in any organization, their new orientation and abilities would transform the organization itself. Such hopes are the stuff of every evangelical dream, and they are rarely fulfilled. In this case they are not. Individual changes in attitudes occur often, as we have seen. Moreover, they are sometimes accompanied by changes in individual behavior in the back-home organizational situation. Increased sensitivity to others, greater openness in communication, and increased flexibility in role behavior have been cited in several reviews of research on T-groups (Campbell and Dunnette, 1968; Buchanan, 1969; House, 1967). Such effects are by no means certain, however; Bowers (1973), in the single most comprehensive evaluation of the organizational effects of T-groups per se, found no significant changes in 23 organizations.

Moreover, even organizations that carried sensitivity training to a point of near-saturation in their supervisory and managerial populations showed no subsequent changes that could be considered transforming; products and priorities, managerial authority and reward allocation seemed quite unaffected. As Gibb (1975) concludes in a generally sympathetic review, there is a "growing impression that this simple approach is minimally effective." Many plausible reasons for this conclusion can be proposed, and have been (Strauss, 1976; Beer, 1976): individual differences in the people trained, in the trainers and the purposes stressed in the training, differences in the receptivity of the back-home situation. Two explanations have had a major continuing influence on the current development of T-groups, however: the hypothesis that sensitivity training is not enough but should be used in combination with other approaches to organizational change, and the hypothesis that the individual is not the appropriate carrier of the effects of sensitivity training. The first of these explanations, which we consider very important, is discussed later, with other combinations and convergences in organizational change. The second involves the use of sensitivity training as a group approach to organizational change, and is relevant here.

The primary target of change in a T-group of strangers is necessarily the individual. The group has no previous or subsequent existence, and the insights of its brief life must be carried by individuals. The weakness of this model for purposes of organizational change was recognized early, and led to a gradual change in primary target. Stranger groups were followed or replaced by "cousin groups," people from the same organization but not reporting to the same supervisor. These in turn were followed by "family groups," in which a manager and the people immediately reporting to him or her constitute the T-group.

Such family groups represent a trade-off solution to the carryover problem. The group members can remind and reinforce each other in continuing the lessons of sensitivity training in the home situation. Moreover, within the limits of their organizational autonomy, they can make such changes as they agree on during the T-group sessions or thereafter. In these respects the T-group becomes a group method of organizational change—not only because the training experience occurred in a group but because the group (as well as its individual members) is the medium of implementation.

The problem, of course, is that the facts of group life carry over equally well in both directions, wanted and unwanted. The "family" T-group can carry its new insights, internal relations, and decisions back to the organization. But it has in its own sessions had to deal with the carryover of authority relationships, old interpersonal habits, rewards and penalties that are among the facts of organizational life.

Comparative research is almost nonexistent, but the many judgmental appraisals and the few data suggest that the tradeoff favors the family groups (Morton and Wight, 1964; Kuriloff and Atkins, 1966). Beer (1976) concludes that "while unfreezing and learning effects are likely to be greater in stranger groups because of the relative safety of this environment, refreezing of behavior and transfer of learning to the back-home environment are likely to be greater in cousin and family groups" (p. 942). It is nevertheless an uneasy tradeoff. Oshry and Harrison (1966) stated it well: "The uniqueness of the T-group lies in its apparent disdain for back home and its almost exclusive focus on the immediacy of current experience." To strangers that may come naturally; for members of the same organizational family, it requires an act of faith.

Surveys and Feedback in Organizations

Surveys of individual attitudes and perceptions have become commonplace in large organizations. Data are collected, usually by means of written questionnaires, and the results are summarized in some fashion, qualitative or quantitative. Such studies can be compared to other standardized forms of information input to organizations, and are perhaps more like the occasional studies of markets than the continuing flow of data on costs and productivity, absence, and turnover. Standardized surveys had a considerable vogue as instruments of organizational change in their own right, but problems of utilization (analogous to the carryover problem in sensitivity training) became increasingly apparent. Many surveys were launched without any plans for their use, other than the distribution of the report to those members of management on the list for other assessments of the overall condition of the organization. The target thus became those individuals, and the impact of the survey as an instrument of change depended on their individual receptivity to change, readiness and insight in interpreting the findings, and power to act on their interpretations. The results were disappointing.

Survey Feedback and Organizational Families

To make the survey an effective form of feedback for organizational change Floyd Mann (1951, 1957) and his colleagues at the Michigan Survey Research Center developed a plan for group discussion of survey results by appropriate "organizational families." Mann's approach was first used in a fairly large company in which there had been a thorough survey by questionnaire and interview of all officers and workers. The concept of the organizational family refers to a supervisor at any hierarchical level and the employees reporting directly to him or her. Any supervisor thus would have membership in two organizational families: the group he or she supervises and the group in which he or she is one of several coordinate supervisors of a "family" reporting to the same person. Thus, the concept of organizational family takes account of the linking of subgroups in an organizational structure through the dual membership of individuals at all levels of supervision.

The hierarchical character of an enterprise is further recognized by starting the feedback process with the top organizational family, for example the president and the vice-presidents. The next series of feedback discussions might include each vice-president and the department heads who report to him or her. Starting at the top of the structure means that the serious examination of survey results is sanctioned or legitimized by the executive system. Every supervisory officer who calls a meeting of immediate subordinates has already been through a comparable discussion session with his or her coordinate officers and their chief.

The feedback material prepared for each session by the research team is, moreover, of special relevance for the particular organizational family into which it is introduced. The branch chief meeting with his or her department heads will be given companywide totals of employee ideas and feelings about all issues as well as branch totals, but, in addition, the branch totals will be broken down for the departments represented at the meeting. Thus, at the meeting the participants can see how their branch compares with the company as a whole as well as the strong and weak points of the departments within the branch. In turn, when the department head meets with his or her supervisors, they will have before them data to show how their department compares with the branch of which it is a part and how the sections within the department, manned by the supervisors present, compare with one another. In general then each organizational family is presented feedback about its own problems in detail and comparative information about the company as a whole or the larger part of the company to which it belongs.

For example, in one company studied by Mann, the top echelons of one department could immediately see that they compared very unfavorably with the company as a whole on certain aspects of employee morale. A much higher percentage of workers in that department than in the rest of the company had thought about quitting their jobs during the past year and were apparently waiting for the first good opportunity to leave; identification with the company was much lower in that department and dissatisfaction with supervision was higher. These findings brought home forcibly to the departmental officers and to their superiors what they had long been aware of to some degree, namely that top management had at times considered the department as expendable, its services always replaceable by contractual arrangements with outside firms. That company policy had affected rank-and-file employees so deeply was, however, something of a surprise.

The presentation of survey findings to the various organizational families sometimes brought new problems to light. More often it gave an objective and factual basis to problems that had either been brushed aside or dealt with by some opinionated gesture. Not only had vague reports about the perceptions and feelings of employees been reduced to facts and figures, but comparisons could be made among similar groups and the findings could be related to possible causal factors. In this objective atmosphere questions could be raised about the data, many of which could be answered by further analysis of the same data. And this was the emphasis of the feedback procedure—group discussion of facts and figures in a task-oriented atmosphere where people were seeking to analyse the problem, identify possible causes as objectively as possible, and agree on possible solutions. The reason for utilizing organizational families and presenting to them the relevant data about their operations thus becomes clear. The members of a specific organizational family have been involved in these very problems, already know a good deal about them, and know what questions should be asked to dig deeper into the available data for answers. Moreover, the group members are the immediate agents for implementing any policy changes with respect to problems at their own level. If they understand the causes, have been involved in a discussion of solutions, and perhaps have proposed the new policy, they will be more effective agents for achieving change.

The feedback technique, utilizing group discussion and group involvement in this fashion has the great advantage of working within the existing organizational structure. Each organizational family can act directly on those issues within its realm of authority, and can send its supervisor as emissary to the next level of management with requests beyond its own power. The effectiveness of this type of feedback program, especially when the measures are repeated at intervals, was demonstrated initially in the accounting departments of a large public utility in which the interval between surveys was 18 months (Mann, 1957):

> Two measures of change were employed: a comparison of answers to sixty-one indentical questions which had been asked in the previous surveys and a comparison of answers to seventeen questions dealing with changes perceived by the workers since the 1950 survey. In the experimental group (comprising four departments), a fourth of the sixty-one items showed relative mean positive changes, significant at the .05 level or better; the change for another 57 per cent of the items was also positive in direction, but not statistically significant. Major positive changes occurred in the experimental groups in how employees felt about (1) the kind of work they do (job interest, importance, and level of reponsibility); (2) their supervisor (his ability to handle people, give recognition, direct their work, and represent them in handling complaints); (3) their progress in the company; and (4) their group's ability to get the job done. The seventeen perceived-change items were designed specifically to measure changes in the areas where we expect the greatest shift in per-

ceptions. Fifteen of these showed that a significantly higher proportion of employees in the experimental than in the control departments felt that change had occurred. More employees in the experimental department saw changes in: (1) how well the supervisors in their department got along together; (2) how often supervisors held meetings; (3) how effective these meetings were; (4) how much their supervisor understood the way employees looked at and felt about things, etc. These findings indicate the extent to which the feedback's effectiveness lay in increasing understanding and communication as well as changing supervisory behavior. (pp. 161–162)

Similar results were obtained in an unusually ambitious study by Bowers (1973) and his colleagues, involving 23 organizations and approximately 14,000 people. The survey feedback process showed effects on most of 16 indexes of organizational climate, leadership, group process, and satisfaction. Moreover, there was some evidence of diffusion to groups that had not participated directly in the feedback process during the one-year period between measurements.[2]

Lippitt, Watson, and Westley (1958), in their incisive analysis of planned change, pointed out long ago the problems raised by interdependence among the subparts of a system with respect to change processes. Change in one subpart can generate forces in other parts to produce related modifications, but interdependence can also mean that more sources of resistance are mobilized against any alteration of established procedures. Hence, these authors emphasized the need for defining the unit in the organization appropriate to the change attempted:

If the subpart is too small to cope with a given problem, it will be unable to change because of resistance originating outside the subpart, coming either from the larger systems in which it is embedded or from parallel systems to which it is related. If the unit is too large and includes semiautonomous subsystems which are not directly involved in the change process, it may be unable to change because of resistance originating within the system. On the other hand, if the size of the unit selected as a

[2]The Navy in its Human Resources Management Program, recognizing the need to compete with civilian manpower in an all-volunteer Navy, ordered all its units to be surveyed and the results fed back to appropriate organizational sectors (Bowers, 1975). Such a massive program employing consultants of various levels of training meant that the ideal model of Mann was approximated very unevenly in the many units of the Navy. Institute of Social Research workers who followed the feedback procedures believe that even with the weaknesses of the crash program the Navy has shown in two years the same progress in organizational development that it took private industry some 15 years to achieve.

client system is appropriate for a particular change objective and if several subparts of this system all become committeed to achieving the same objective, the motivation and energy available to the system for working on change will be intensified by the interdependence and interaction among the subparts. (p. 77)

CHANGING ORGANIZATIONAL VARIABLES

Social scientists become involved in problems of organizational change as theorists of change (Lippitt, Watson, and Westley, 1958; Havelock, 1972, for example), as consultants, and as experimentalists (Evan, 1971). As theorists of "planned change," they have usually emphasized a point of entry well up in the hierarchical structure, a primary target either of individuals or small groups, and a method in which information transfer dominates. As experimenters in organizational change, social scientists show the same pattern of emphasis and avoidance, not only because of their theoretical preferences but also, one may suppose, because of their lack of power and resources. As consultants, social scientists have entered into problems of organizational change in the special context of helping the formal leaders of an organization do more successfully what they wanted to do. Consultation has also tended to avoid major changes in structure and to emphasize the improvement of productivity and related criteria through individual and small-group methods.

These generalizations, necessarily gross, invite the remarking of exceptions, and many individual exceptions could be noted. The most important categorical exception, however, is that of sociologists. They have been much concerned with organizational structure, but they seldom conduct experiments that involve structural changes in organizations and they seldom serve as consultants to organizational parties. As a result, the emphasis on structural change can be seen in sociological theories, but it is not equally visible in the empirical literature of sociology or in the professional experience of sociologists.

The world of affairs, in all these respects, offers a considerable contrast to that of social science. Structural changes in organizations are frequent and various. Organizations are changed in size, in number of echelons, in scheduled times of operation, in distribution of authority, in allocation of rewards, in choice of technology, and in many other properties of formal structure. Moreover, attempts to change organizations by dealing directly with such properties are not limited to those in power; such attempts are made both by present leaders and by those who wish either to replace or constrain them.

The common element is direct change in the role structure of the organizations—the adding or eliminating of roles, or the alteration of formal expectations associated with them. Such change sometimes comes about by executive order, as when two companies merge and large sectors are reorganized or even eliminated. It can come about from revolution from within, as when young reformers capture a state or local political organization, oust the old guard from control, and reorganize the functioning of the political party. Systemic change can come about from pressures from without, as when the government orders the reorganization of an industrial empire that has achieved something of a monopolistic position in a given field of enterprise. Or the outside pressure can be the power of a labor union, which moves in on some of the old management functions of employee discipline, lay-off, and dismissal. In these examples, roles are changed; power is reallocated; requirements and perquisites of office are altered. In short, the structural properties of organization become the primary target of change.

Such changes do not make interpersonal processes and individual motives irrelevant. Formal change may be promulgated, but it remains to be enacted, legitimated, learned, and in some degree internalized. Not all changes are feasible, therefore, although history has made all too clear the range of behavior that can be induced and maintained in the organizational context. Perhaps the most important difference between the direct manipulation of organizational variables and the several approaches to organizational change that we have already considered involves the primary target and the hypothesized linkage between it and the desired end state. Direct systemic change begins by changing the situation in which members of organizations work—the demands or the rewards, the authority or the required response to authority, the size or nature of the task itself, the access to information, the meetings to which invitations are given, the decisions on which votes are taken, and the like. The hypothesized sequence leads from such structural changes to changes in the behavior of the people who experience them, and thus to ramifying changes in the state and output of the organization, and in the long run to enduring changes in the individuals themselves.

At this level of generality, many social scientists would find the sequence plausible. The issues become more apparent and the difficulties greater, both for theory and for the pragmatic purpose of organizational design, when we attempt to specify the particular systemic change, the sequence of ramifying effects, and the "end effect" on the functioning of the organization. For example, Herzberg's "two-factor" theory predicts that job enrichment (increasing the complexity of monotonous and repetitive tasks) will increase worker motivation and thus improve quality, productivity, and attendance. The same theory tells us that improvements in working conditions and general increases in wages will not have similar effects on motivation and behavior. In terms of this specificity, hypotheses about systemic change become testable.

Other approaches to organizational change do not exclude such structural alterations, but they appear (if at all) at later points in the hypothesized linkage between intervention and end effect. An enthusiast for sensitivity training might predict, for example, that the interpersonal openness and authenticity generated in such groups would gradually make itself felt in the work situation, that the discussions of work problems and arrangements would begin to reflect more accurately the needs and aspirations of organization members, and that formal or structural changes might then occur as an expression of such individual and interpersonal changes. The data have not been kind to this set of assumptions, but they can be made specific and testable.

The number of well-documented instances in which organizational change of the direct systemic kind was introduced and its effects measured is not large. In 1964, Seashore noted that "few people have had any direct experiences in conducting field experiments with complex organizations." In 1967, Barnes called the field experiment "one of the most promising but underutilized methods for the study and measurement of organizational change." In 1971, Evan, in a preface to his book on "organizational experiments," explained that "relatively few field experiments have as yet been performed. . . ." Such statements are unfortunately not yet obsolete, although the number of organizational experiments is growing and so is the proportion of them that involves direct systemic change. The task force assigned by the then Secretary of the Department of Health, Education, and Welfare to review the effects of work on the well-being of workers (*Work in America*, 1973) found 34 "case studies in the humanization of work," all of which involved some structural alteration in the work situation, and most of which involved quantitative evaluation of the effects of the change. Major experiments are now under way in a number of countries, sparked by growing interest in such slogans as humanization of work and industrial democracy. Research and the application of research both benefit from that interest, but their needs are in some respects divergent. The manipulation of a single organizational variable may provide the clearest test of a hypothesis, but the simultaneous or sequential manipulation of several variables may increase the probability of getting a wanted result. The social scientist who wants the power and reality of experiments in ongoing organizations is likely to pay a price in loss of experimental control. As a result, the change experiments that have been conducted in organizations cannot be sorted neatly in terms of the independent variable manipulated and the means of manipulation. More than one variable is likely to have been changed and more than one means is almost certain to have been used to change it.

Four substantive categories of change experimentation seem worth distinguishing, nevertheless: participation and authority, rewards and incentives, division of labor and task definition, and goodness of fit between the social and technical aspects of the organization. For each of these target areas of systemic change, we will describe the kinds of experiments that have been conducted and give one or two examples in more detail.

Authority, Participation, and the Distribution of Power

Participation is one of the more durable concepts in organizational research, and an equally durable catch-word in research application. As a single word, it has only a very general meaning—take part; but in what is one to take part, and in what degree, and how? The usual answers to those questions in participation-oriented theories of organization are that each person is to take part in those decisions that affect his or her role in the organization, that such participation is to begin with matters that are local and immediate, and extend toward matters of larger and more remote organizational policy. Participation in the localized and immediate decisions is to be done directly, usually in a group of those persons similarly affected. Theorists and advocates differ on the matter of extending this process to organization-wide matters and on the means, representative or otherwise, by which such extension is feasible.

The underlying hypothesis is that participation is typically low in conventional bureaucratic organizations, that increasing it will cause increases in satisfaction and motivation to meet the organizational goals, and that there may also be gains in the wisdom of the decisions made on a participatory basis.

Increasing participation is thus what Leavitt (1965) calls a procedure of power-equalization, although it may increase the total amount of influence brought to bear on the individual as well. Moreover, many approaches to organizational change include participation as a secondary or incidental target. It is implied in sensitivity training and included in most survey instruments. The supposed sequence of events would lead from the insights of the T-group or the survey to changed individual behaviors and interpersonal relationships, and perhaps eventually to formal changes in authority and the locus of decision making.

Participation can also be increased (or decreased) by direct intervention in organizational structure, as the following three experiments illustrate. Their chronological order, conveniently enough, also serves to order them in terms of organizational scope; the clerical experiment (Morse and Reimer, 1956) involved four parallel divisions of a large department; the Banner study (Bowers and Seashore, 1963) was conducted in a separate geographical unit of a large corporation, and the Weldon study (Marrow, Bowers, and Seashore, 1967; Seashore and Bowers, 1970) involved the acquisition of an entire company.

The Clerical Experiment

This experiment (Morse and Reimer, 1956) was in many respects a first. It undertook field experimentation on a large scale in an ongoing organization; it included an ambitious and sustained program of measurement; it incorporated comparisons of contrasting experimental treatments; it was designed around a direct and deliberate attempt to change an organizational variable. The organizational variable selected for modification involved the authority structure of the system, or more specifically the degree of organizational decision making at various levels in the company. The experimenters, following the theorizing of F. H. Allport, conceptualized this variable as the degree of *axiality*, since organizations can be described as having an *axis* of control and regulation of their processes extending from the person or persons in the highest authority position down to the rank-and-file members of the organization.

In this experiment the objective was to change the role structure with respect to decision making and its accompanying activities so that the lower hierarchical levels in the structure would have more power and responsibility for carrying on the work of the organization. The essential idea was that all the advantages of small group democracy are lost in an organization in which the group has virtually no power to make decisions of any importance. Unless a given person or group in the legitimized authority structure is assigned responsibility for decision making, all the training of individuals or of small groups to utilize group process and group decision is likely to be transitory or even abortive in its outcome.

Hence the experimenters worked with the top echelons in the company to attain a legitimized change in organizational structure, so that the rank-and-file employees would be given the authority and responsibility for carrying out not only their own previous assignment but also the previous functions of the first-line supervisors. The first-line supervisors were to give up their previous decision making for the people under them and were to take over the running of the division. In turn, the division managers gave up their former divisional responsibilities and were made responsible for the department. This left the department head without a major function and so he was asked to assume some of the executive vice-president's duties of coordination between the production department in question and the methods and personnel departments.

In other words, axiality, or the degree of control and regulation of the activities of the organization, cannot be changed at one level without affecting the whole organization. In fact, this is characteristic of any systemic property. If we are really dealing with an organizational or system variable, its manipulation will involve the entire organization. Direct change of organizational characteristics is regarded as inherently difficult to bring off because it means changing so much, and, of course, this is correct. What is overlooked, however, is that modification of major organizational processes by working with less relevant variables is infinitely more difficult to attain, even though working with such variables may entail less effort on the part of the change agent.

Individual or group change applies only to specific points in organizational space and is more likely to be vitiated by the enduring systemic properties than to change them. The point of entry in the clerical experiment was thus high in the organizational structure; the active support of the relevant vice-president and the sanction of the president were necessary to initiate the proposed change. The preferred state—a locus of authority lower in the hierarchical structure—was explicit and intrinsic to the experiment. The primary target of change was the authority structure itself, and thus the prescriptions for all the roles in that structure. To enact this change, however, a variety of procedures was employed.

First in sequence was the persuasion of the executive vice-president and assistants of the desirability of the change. Part of the persuasion was accomplished through group sessions of the vice-president's own staff and the research team, part through the presentation of findings from a previous survey in the company, the implications of which supported downward delegation.

A second procedure was the use of group discussion at various levels in the organization to prepare the employees for the anticipated change. This method of preparation also included the training of supervisors for their new roles.

The third procedure was the official introduction of the change as the new policy of the company, in a presentation by the executive vice-president to the employees. In other words, the change was legitimized as new role requirements by the proper authority structure. Finally, group discussion and decision making was the mode of operation by which the rank-and-file employees and first-line supervisors implemented the new program.

Some nine months were spend in preparation for the experimental changes, including the early meetings for securing the approval of top management. The experiment itself ran for a year, with before and after measurements of productivity and morale. In all, four parallel divisions of one department were involved. Two of the divisions were assigned to the experimental treatment described above. The other two were placed in a change program that also involved manipulation of the axiality variable, but in the direction of tighter control and increased regulation from the upper echelons. In a field experiment the classical notion of a control group that operates as usual is not sufficient, since the experimental group has the advantage of special treatment no matter what the treatment. Accordingly, the design in this experiment called for the two opposed experimental treatments, to control for the effects of special attention. The divisions in the two programs were matched in productivity on the basis of their performance during the previous year. The program of downward delegation was called the *Autonomy Program*; the program of tighter control from above the *Hierarchically Controlled Program*. In the latter program of hierarchical control, decisions formerly made by first-line supervisors and by division heads were now made at the departmental level.

Some 33 supervisors and 204 nonsupervisory employees constituted the four divisions in the two programs. Each division processed contractual forms and had separate sections dealing with lapses, cash surrenders, new business, and the like. The volume or work accomplished by a given section was not under its control, and thus productivity was measured by the number of employees required to complete a given volume of work. Increased productivity thus could be achieved only by out-placing some of the clerks, or not replacing those who left of their own accord. Decreased productivity would result from calling in extra workers (or floaters, in the company's terminology).

The experimental manipulations were successful in creating two different social subsystems for the two sets of divisions. In the Autonomy Program the clerical work groups did in fact make a variety of group decisions on matters of importance to them, such as recess periods, the handling of tardiness, work methods, and work processes.

In the Hierarchically Controlled Program, on the other hand, the employees were less involved than before in the regulation and control of their own activities. It was hypothesized that the Autonomy Program would show gains, relative to the Hierarchical Program and its own base-line scores, in (1) self-actualization, (2) satisfaction with supervision, (3) liking for working for the company, (4) job satisfaction and (5) liking for the program. Correspondingly it was predicted that there would be a decrease in favorable attitudes in these areas in the Hierarchically Controlled Program. It was also hypothesized that over time there would be an increase in productivity in the Autonomy Program and a decrease in productivity in the Hierarchically Controlled Program.

Most of these predictions were fulfilled. Self-actualization increased in the Autonomy Program and decreased in the Hierarchical Program. Relationships with supervisors (assistant managers and division managers) improved significantly in the Autonomy Program and deteriorated in the other. Attraction to the company followed the same pattern. Differences in the attitudes of the clerks toward the programs to which they had been assigned were particularly marked. Clerks in the Autonomy Program felt that they were gaining a great deal from it, wanted it to last indefinitely, and did not like the other program. Clerks in the Hierarchical Program felt that the company was gaining from it, wanted it to end immediately, and expressed a liking for the other program.

The experimental results were less clear-cut with respect to intrinsic job satisfaction and productivity. As predicted, there was a significant decrease in job satisfaction in the Hierarchical Program, but there was no significant change in the Autonomy Program. To what extent this reflected the dominance of the technology, which did not change, and to what extent the rising aspirations of clerks in the autonmous condition could not be determined.

Both experimental groups showed significant increases in productivity, about 20 percent in the Autonomy Program and 25 percent in the Hierarchical Program. These results are related to the difficulties of achieving a productivity gain in the democratic group. Productivity was measured by hours required to handle the volume of work within a given time period. There were just two ways of increasing productivity: using few or no floaters and cutting down on the number of regular workers. Rejecting colleagues was difficult for the democratic group, especially as it gained in cohesion in sharing responsibilities.

Likert (1961) proposed that the high-producing behavior of the Hierarchical Program was unstable, and that a longer time span was necessary to show its instability and its full costs. We are inclined to believe that strong hierarchical control is indeed one means of evoking high productivity, although it also evokes a number of negative side effects, some of which are apparent in the attitudinal data. Others were apparent in the turnover pattern and in the negative comments at exit interview. Productivity measures that included the costs of turnover and replacement would have been more appropriate for the purpose of the study, as would a work situation in which individuals and groups could increase or decrease their output by means other than exporting or importing members. Moreover, the clerical employees who participated in this experiment, almost all of whom were young women only recently graduated from high school, may have been less work-involved and more docile than the labor force at large. Some of these problems are illuminated in the Banner experiment (Seashore and Bowers, 1963).

The Banner Experiment

This experiment was an attempt to serve two purposes, one scientific and the other pragmatic, and its strengths and weaknesses derive largely from this combination. The scientific purpose was to test the effects of movement from conventional management to that described by Likert (1961) as System 4. The pragmatic purpose was to help an existing management deal with a new and difficult economic situation by increasing organizational performance.

The Banner Company was one of the largest manufacturers of packaging materials in the United States, although not large by the standards of other manufacturing industries. It consisted of two plants, in turn organized into departments. The total number of employees was about 800. Management within each plant included foremen, department supervisors, and a plant superintendent. Management of manufacturing as a whole included two levels above the plant superintendents and several staff and service units. About 70 percent of the non-supervisory employees were men, with an average age of 32 years and an average length of service slightly more than three years. There was an independent union. The company had a long history as independent and directed by its founders, but in more recent years it had become a division of a large diversified corporation located in another city.

Seen in retrospect, the development of the company shows several differentiated periods—an initial period of moderate but steady growth, a decade during which volume more than quadrupled, and a period of intense competition and economic difficulty. The entire sequence reflects market conditions much more than company-initiated change. The study developed when the vice-president of the firm, concerned about the company's market position and intrigued by things he had heard about new approaches to management, got in touch with the research group (Survey Research Center, University of Michigan). After considerable discussion with him and his immediate staff, an experimental design was agreed on that called for introducing change simultaneously with respect to five independent variables:

1. Amount of emphasis on the work group as an organizational unit
2. Amount of supportive behavior by supervisors
3. Amount of decision making by employees

TABLE 19-1 Main Variables in the Experimental Design

Independent Variables (Variables to be Deliberately Altered)	Dependent Variables (Criteria of Effectiveness)
Increase in emphasis on the work group as a functioning unit of the organization: Supervisors' use of group approach Employees' perception of belonging to a team that works together	Increase in employee satisfaction re: Foreman Company as a whole Work group Working conditions Pay Job security Promotion opportunity
Increase in amount of supportive behavior by supervisors and peers: Supervisory support (achievement) Supervisory support (affiliation) Peer support (achievement) Peer support (affiliation)	Increase in productivity rate: Machine efficiency as percent of standard
Increase in participation by employees in decision-making processes: Amount of employee influence on what goes on in department Extent to which supervisor accepts influence from employees	Decrease in waste rate: Waste cost as percent of processes material cost
Increase in amount of interaction and influence among work group members: Peer influence among employees Peer productivity pressure Peer waste—reduction pressure Increase the linking of groups through overlapping membership	Decrease in absence rates: Instances of absence Days absent Late arrivals Early departures

From Seashore and Bowers, 1963, p. 19.

4. Amount of interaction and influence within work groups
5. Linking of groups through overlapping membership (The experimenters regarded this as a means of producing the above changes rather than as a change in its own right.)

Dependent variables included satisfaction, productivity, waste, and absence. The first of these was to be measured before the experimental changes were introduced and after the experiment. The others were measured continuously by the company. These variables are summarized in Table 19-1.

The manipulation of five independent variables of course raises problems of confounding. On the other hand, they constitute a single syndrome and are derived from a single theory. Moreover, the needs of the organization were to maximize effects, and "starting strong" is not a bad experimental strategy. Differentiation could come later.

The targets of change were thus multiple, with the first two independent variables emphasizing interpersonal changes, expecially by supervisors, and the other three variables involving structural changes, especially regarding authority and influence. Methods of change were also multiple, and included changes in formal policies to help legitimate the manipulations and eliminate policies incompatible with them; changes in the formal structure of work groups, to attain clarity of membership and overlapping structure; lectures, coaching, and counseling to facilitate the cognitive and behavioral changes called for in the experimental design. One full-time member of the research staff served as "change-agent."

The experiment continued for 30 months, with continuing measurement of the performance criteria and three measurements of the other variables. Three phases of work occurred during this period: Phase I began immediately after the pre-experimental measures had been taken, was concentrated in one of the five departments, and lasted five months. Phase II included two additional departments and lasted 16 months. Phase III can be regarded as a period of consolidation; the research staff, including its change agent, withdrew and the experimental changes became part of the ongoing management of the company. During Phase I, the experimental departments showed dramatic improvements in machine efficiency and in the reduction of waste; of the five other departments, three showed losses and two small gains. The more important comparisons, however, are between the three experimental and the two control departments over the entire 30-month period. These comparisons include the pre-experimental differences between the two sets of departments, the post-experimental differences between them, and the changes in each relative to its own pre-experimental measures. Before the experiment, the control departments were superior to the experimental departments on all independent variables (11 measures). At the end of the experimental period, these initial differences had been reversed in all but one instance. The experimental departments showed the intended direction of change on all but one measure, with the amount of change highly significant on six of the measures. The independent variables clearly moved.

The predictions regarding the dependent variables were met in varying degree. With respect to employee satisfactions, the experimental departments, which were initially like the control departments except for satisfaction with pay, ended the 30-month period superior to the control departments on all but one dimension. It is interesting and conspicuously difficult for the theory, however, that the experimental

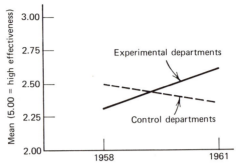

Figure 19-1 *Change in independent variables 1958–1961 (9 scalable only).*
(From Bowers and Seashore, 1971, p. 199.)

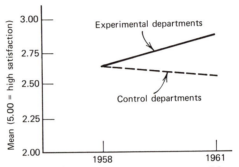

Figure 19-2 *Change in satisfactions 1958–1961 (7 variables combined). (From*
Bowers and Seashore, 1971, p. 199.)

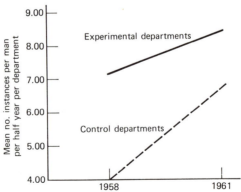

Figure 19-3 *Change in instances of absence 1958–1961 (instances absent,*
leaving early, late arrival combined). (From Bowers and Seashore, 1971, p.
199.)

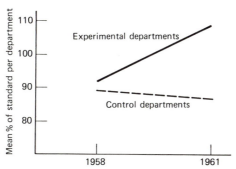

Figure 19-4 *Change in machine efficiency 1958–1961. (From Bowers and Seashore, 1971, p. 199.)*

departments showed no significant increase in satisfaction with the work group. Machine efficiency (the efficiency with which machines are used) increased in the experimental units and decreased in the control units. Waste performance improved, but the data were available on only a plant-wide basis, so this improvement cannot properly be attributed to the experimental treatment. These results, combined for the independent variables and for each of the three sets of dependent variables, are presented graphically in Figures 19-1, 19-2, 19-3, and 19-4.

The Banner experiment can be considered a success and, despite differences in theoretical origins, an extension of the work of the clerical experiment already described. The limitations of the Banner study are partly intrinsic to the design (the combination of independent variables, the testing of organization-level hypotheses in suborganizational units), and partly the result of operational problems that emerged during the experiment itself. The latter include the self-selection of the second and third experimental departments, the number of other changes that took place during the experimental period, and the impossibility of getting hard criterion measures for all variables at the departmental level. Some of these limitations were successfully avoided in the Weldon experiment, which involved the same investigators.

The Weldon Experiment

The Weldon experiment was built around a company acquisition, routine in some respects and remarkable in others. Acquisitions by purchase are routine, and this was an acquisition by one company of another competing company of about the same size, age, product line, and technology. There were, however, marked differences between the management philosophies and systems of the two organizations. Harwood, the acquiring company, had a 30-year commitment to participative management, social science application, and measurement. It had been the site of the experiments by Coch and French (1948) described earlier and its chairman, Alfred Marrow, was himself a prominent psychologist. The Weldon company, also about 30 years old and employing about 1000 people, was conventional and authoritarian in its management practices. Harwood was organized by the Amalgamated Clothing Workers; at the time of the acquisition, the same union had recently lost an election at Weldon, after a long and mutually costly campaign.

Differences in performance were impressive. In the year of acquisition (1962), Harwood showed a 17 percent return on invested capital, Weldon a loss of about equal magnitude; average production at Harwood was six percent above the time-study base, at Weldon 11 percent below; worker earnings were significantly higher at Harwood; turnover and absence at Harwood were half the Weldon rate.

The differences in managerial philosophy and style would almost certainly have created strain between the Harwood and Weldon groups sooner or later; the poor performance of the Weldon plant called for immediate action. As Marrow said, "These findings gave us no choice. To protect our investment in Weldon, we had to find ways to get better utilization of the human resources" (Marrow et al., 1967, p. 65).

The Harwood management therefore undertook a program of organizational change, the immediate purpose of which was to bring Weldon to resemble Harwood in structure and managerial practice. The expectation was that Weldon would then come to resemble its new parent in worker perceptions and attitudes, union-management relations, and performance. The change effort was to include the Weldon management itself, the Harwood management, and an assortment of social science consultants and technical experts. Measurements of managerial behavior and employee attitudes were to be taken before the change program began, after it concluded, and perhaps at other intervals. Productivity, absence, turnover, and fiscal performances were measured routinely.

These plans were carried through. The result is a quantitatively documented case study in organizational change, more or less experimental in form, nearly unique in scope, and important both for its substantive findings and for the methodology of change. In terms of research design, the Weldon study presents some serious inferential problems, the first of which was almost unavoidable and the second of which reflects the compromise of pragmatic and scientific aims. The first problem involves the basis on which change is to be inferred. No real "control" was feasible; there was not a second Weldon and there were compelling reasons to make the change effort organization-wide. Therefore change must be inferred on two bases—comparison of data for Weldon before and after the change program, and comparison of Weldon with Harwood at the same points in time.

The second problem involves the attribution of causality for observed changes in performance and even for intervening attitudinal variables. While the main emphasis of the change program can properly be described as an effort to move the managerial system of Weldon, in Likert's terminology, from System 1 toward System 4, that is from "authoritative" toward "participative" organizational structure and behavior, other changes were instituted at the same time. Some of these were technical, and included modifications in work flow and in the physical arrangements for shipping. Some involved reward allocation, and especially introduction of incentive pay to the cutting and shipping departments. Some involved selection and training, which were improved, and the termination of a few persistent absentees. Moreover, during the two-year period of the change program, a contract was peacefully negotiated with the Amalgamated Clothing Workers Union and a new federal minimum wage was established.

It is impossible to rule out the possible effects of these changes in technology, pay, and personnel procedures. Having identified the authority structure (loci of influence and decision making) as the main target of change, however, we can (1) describe the means used to create change in these aspects of organization, (2) observe the concomitant changes in other organizational and interpersonal variables, and (3) evaluate the outcomes in terms of performance.

(1) The changes in authority structure and decision making were initiated with a self-conscious process of modelling by the consultants and the representatives of the new owners. The top Weldon managers were then asked to participate in a program of training in which "laboratory method" (T-groups) played a major part. The composition of these groups followed the pattern of "organizational families"; each group consisted of a manager and the people in immediately subordinate positions. The initial training sessions were of several days' duration, and took place off the job. They were followed by on-the-job attempts to use the new skills and insights to solve specific problems as they arose. Consultant help and coaching was available during this process.

This form of training was repeated for the top managerial group and extended to others. Meanwhile, joint problem-solving meetings were held by work groups and their immediate supervisors, in their usual places of work and on the shop floor. Engineers as well as line managers were included in such meetings, each in the appropriate

TABLE 19-2   Management System Used—or Desired—in the Weldon Plant as Revealed by Means for Period Shown

	USED				DESIRED	
	PRIOR TO 1962				EARLY 1964	
As seen by:	Form A $\overline{\text{M}}$	Systems 1–4 Score	Form A $\overline{\text{M}}$	Systems 1–4 Score	Form A $\overline{\text{M}}$	Systems 1–4 Score
Upper management	3.25	(1.37)	9.40	(3.01)	13.56	(4.12)
Supervisors	4.50	(1.70)	9.99	(3.16)	13.37	(4.06)
Assistant supervisors	6.27	(2.17)	10.38	(3.27)	13.36	(4.06)

Management System Used—or Desired—in the Harwood Plant

	USED		DESIRED	
	EARLY 1964			
As seen by:	Form A $\overline{\text{M}}$	Systems 1–4 Score	Form A $\overline{\text{M}}$	Systems 1–4 Score
Upper management	11.66	(3.61)	13.92	(4.21)
Supervisors	11.77	(3.64)	13.24	(4.03)
Assistant supervisors	11.30	(3.51)	14.02	(4.24)

From Likert, 1967, p. 36.

organizational family. The bulk of this effort took place during one 12-month period, but significant activity took place during the period of more than two years between the two major surveys.

(2) Changes in authority patterns and related managerial behaviors were measured by means of 43 scales developed by Likert and his colleagues for distinguishing management systems ranging from authoritarian (System 1) to participative (System 4). Each scale was presented as a horizontal line marked with 15 subdivisions, so that raw scores run from 1 (authoritarian or least participative) to 15 (most participative). These 43 scales represent six substantive areas— motivations, communications, interactions, decision making, goal setting, and control—and an inspection of the items suggests that all but the first are in the primary target area of change at Weldon.

Changes in these characteristics, as seen by three managerial levels, are presented in Table 19-2. That table shows data for Weldon as perceived before the change program (1962), after the change program (1964), and as ideal or desired (196?). Similar data are shown for the

TABLE 19-3   Indicators of Organization Efficiency in Production, Harwood and Weldon, 1962 and 1964

Area of Performance	Year	Weldon	Harwood
Return on capital invested	1962	−15%	+17%
	1964	+17	+21
Make-up pay	1962	12	2
	1964	4	2
Production efficiency	1962	−11	6
	1964	+14	16
Earnings above minimum	1962	None	17
(Piece rate and other	1964	16	22
incentive employees only)			
Operator turnover rates	1962	10	3/4
(monthly basis)	1964	4	3/4
Absences from work (daily rate,	1962	6	3
production employees only)	1964	3	3

From Marrow, Bowers, and Seashore, 1967, p. 147.

Harwood plant, for purposes of comparison. All data are shown as means of raw scores and (for convenience) as converted to a scale of 1 to 4 to correspond with Likert's designation of management systems. These data reflect significant change toward the desired pattern of management in every one of the six substantive areas, and they show also a considerable convergence in the perceptions of the three managerial levels.

Worker responses are consistent in direction with those of management, but the trends are less sharp. Attitudes toward the job, the compensations system, and the company all become more positive during the two-year period, and the perceived effort invested in the job increases during the same period. In all these respects, Weldon comes to resemble Harwood more closely. Only in attitude toward fellow employees is there no similar convergence; both plants show slight gains.

The pattern of significant gain at Weldon and increasing similarity between the two plants is particularly clear in the six major criterion variables (Table 19-3), four of which are specifically economic and two of which (absence and turnover at the operator level) are behavioral measures of attraction to company and job. Hourly earnings increased by 26 percent during this time.

The Weldon experiment is unusual in one further respect; the research workers involved in the experiment were able to obtain an additional data set in 1969, five years after the "termination" of the experiment as such. The data show further movement toward the System 4 pattern in all six of the relevant substantive areas (Figure 19-5).

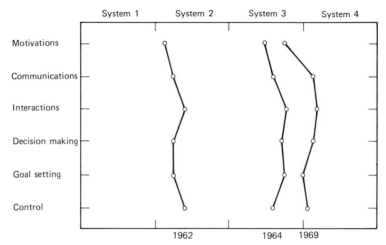

Figure 19-5 *Change in profile of organizational characteristics. (From Seashore and Bowers, 1970, p. 231.)*

These findings are extremely important because they bear on a subject of which little is known—the durability of planned organizational change. Indeed, little is known about the variable of time as it enters into attempts at planned change. In principle, any manipulation of an organizational variable will have its ramifying effects throughout the system during some ascertainable period of time, the amount of time depending on the specific manipulation and on the properties of the system.

The specification of these parameters is yet to be achieved. Meanwhile, questions arise as to whether a particular experiment was continued long enough to attain a new stability (for example, the clerical experiment, p. 683), or whether an attained experimental change will persist. The homeostatic tendencies of systems are well known, and many state changes are in fact brief, and are followed by a return to the previous equilibrium. Since field experiments are rare in organizations, it goes without saying that long-lasting experiments and continuing or repeated measures are rarer still. The scientific value of the Weldon experiment was greatly enhanced by the addition of the 1969 data, five years post-experimental.

On balance, the Harwood-Weldon experiment is an important success. It is also a confounded success. Authority patterns changed; workers' perceptions and attitudes became more positive, management came into greater agreement with the System 4 pattern. Performance improved dramatically. Indications are that workers, management, union, and owners are all better off in terms of their own criteria. These changes, however, came about after a manifold program of planned change. The primary target can be identified as the authority structure, as we have done, but others might make different identifications. Moreover, the secondary targets were numerous and the methods of change equally so. These issues are debatable. The fact of planned and attained and persisting change is beyond debate.

Rewards and Reward Allocation

Work is largely an instrumental activity, rewarded in industrialized societies by money and in others by barter or direct share in the product. In societies that have a money economy, money becomes an almost universal reinforcer, and is so recognized. Labor negotiations are more concentrated on wages than any other issue, and governments stand or fall on the basis of their policies regarding wages and prices. Nevertheless, there has been little organizational research and almost no field experimentation in which the allocation of monetary rewards was the primary target of change.

No one can be certain of the reasons for this, but we believe that they reflect the importance of money rather than its lack of importance or inability to motivate. Leaders of organizations have been generally less willing to experiment with tangibles than with intangible variables, and economic rewards are uniquely tangible. Social scientists have lacked the power and resources to experiment with the reward structure of organizations, and they have been docile about such issues. Our inclusion of this topic among the strategies and experiments of organizational change, therefore, is less to report research than to state the conviction that increasing instrumental rewards will, other things being equal, tend to bind present members more closely to an organization and attract new ones. Moreover, if the increased rewards are made contingent on performance, they will tend to evoke such performance, subject of course to a number of well-demonstrated counterforces— boredom and fatigue, physical and mental limits, and the fear of subsequent disadvantage (unrewarded speed-up, for example).

Research on the effects of pay in organizations has been well-reviewed by Opsahl and Dunnette (1966), Lawler (1971), and by Belcher and Atchison (1976). This research, some of it based on organizational surveys and some on laboratory experiments, provides a good deal of information on the importance of monetary rewards, on the additional importance of perceived equity in their allocation, and on the reward system as a reflection of managerial philosophy and of technology. Least evidence is available on the issue that interests us most in the context of organizational change: Can the reward structure be effectively used as the primary target of more general organizational change?

Profit Sharing

There is suggestive evidence, static and correlational, that performance-contingent rewards of significant amounts motivate increased effort at work. The top executives of 1100 companies listed on the New York Stock Exchange in 1970 received amounts equal to about 50 percent of their base pay as bonuses for production, and firms that used such bonus plans were more profitable than those that did not (Brindisi, 1971). More general profit-sharing plans show some relationship to company success, but the term profit sharing is applied to a variety of reward systems and the data are correspondingly ambiguous. A few profit-sharing plans have been attended by remarkable and prolonged organizational success, but the process of adoption and organizational change has not been documented. The Lincoln Electric Company, which manufactures welding equipment, is probably the outstanding example. Employees currently receive more than double their base pay as a result of profit-sharing and through a system of combined profit-sharing and incentive pay (Fein, 1976).

The Scanlon Plan

The Scanlon Plan is in several important respects an exception to what we have said about rewards and organizational change. It is a program of organizational change in which pay and participation—the reward structure and the authority structure—are the primary targets. It has been used in more or less comparable form in a substantial number of organizations; and the process of change has been studied in several such cases (Lesieur and Puckett, 1968, 1969).

The Scanlon Plan is a set of management principles, a set of structural arrangements that embody them, and a procedure for enacting and maintaining those arrangements. McGregor (1959) called it "a philosophy of management." A matured Scanlon Plan would include a set of related production committees, from the shop floor to the total organization. Within each department, the members of these committees would have been elected by the workers, and a representative (usually the supervisor) appointed by management. The departmental committees meet once a month or more often, review every suggestion submitted by individual workers or by the union, and make immediate decisions respecting jobs or methods or departmental functions, within certain limits of cost and without affecting other departments. More costly or interdepartmental changes are referred to company-wide committees, similarly elected and constituted.

So described, the Scanlon Plan is the embodiment of many a manager's dream: the entire work force involved in a sustained effort to increase productivity and reduce waste. The problem, of course, is how an organization can be moved to such effort and what motivates its continuation. The answer, in spite of the important ideological aspects of the plan, seems to be money; changes in the reward system are part of the initial agreement between company and union. The union contract guarantees that there will be no reduction in pay below the base levels, and the Plan involves a commitment to share the results of any gains in productivity that come about because of the Plan.

The first task of the company-wide committee is to agree on the basis on which such gains will be computed and the resultant revenues shared. Scanlon's original proposal was that all direct gains should go to the workers, and that management and stockholders would get the benefit of the indirect gains (more intensive use of plant and equipment, etc.). Fein (1976) has criticized these arrangements, not on the basis of equity but for operational difficulty in making such determinations and for their tendency to become increasingly invalid through successive changes in product line and technology.

The Scanlon Plan is unique in its emphasis on the reward system as the primary target in organizational change. The point of entry is also unusual, in stipulating that the plan requires the presence of a labor union as one of the contracting parties, and that the initial agreement to enact the plan include both management and union. The initial state of the organization is unspecified, except that a base productivity period must be agreed to for the purpose of computing subsequent productivity gains. The preferred or end-state is explicit in the plan, so far as the committee structure is concerned. The goals of increased productivity and revenues are specified only in comparative terms.

The primary target of change is thus the reward structure or perhaps the reward structure and the authority structure in combination, since the initial agreement between company and union commits both organizations to a particular form of profit-sharing and to the structure of production committees. It seems appropriate to say that the financial incentives motivate the effort of workers to improve methods and performance; the production committees offer the formal arrangements for doing these things. Ramifying changes in organizational climate, supervision, and interpersonal relations stem from these initial alterations in reward and authority.

The most recent comprehensive review of Scanlon Plans in operation (Lesieur and Puckett, 1968) shows 180 companies using the plan in close approximation to its original form and perhaps another 500 using variations of that form. There have been failures in installing the plan, some of which have been described, although the total number is not known. But experience with the plan now extends over 40 years, and permits some conclusions.

The Scanlon Plan works. Many companies use it, with wages increased at least 25 percent above union contract by the resultant productivity gains. Frost, Wakeley, and Rhu (1974) have reviewed six recent studies of the Scanlon Plan and they report favorable outcomes when the Plan is fully implemented. A central role in its implementation was the use of participative democratic management, which was correlated with the retention of the Plan and with attitudes toward it. The largest American corporations are not among the Scanlon Plan companies, and many managements seem unwilling to accept the stringent commitment to profitsharing and the authority of the elected production committees that together form the core of the plan. It stands as the clearest example of organizational change through changes in the allocation of extrinsic rewards.

Division of Labor
as the Primary Target of Change

Among the possible primary targets in organizational change is the division of labor itself. Approaching the accomplishment of organizational change in this way is structural, of course. Moreover, it implies change in the technology (tools used, "rules" for using them, and persons or roles specified for their use) as well as the social structure. Such change is near the core of organizational life; it begins by making formal changes in roles as they relate to the organizational throughput. These changes can be initiated very modestly or on a very ambitious scale, both in terms of the amount of organizational space (number of roles) involved and in terms of the extent of the change within those roles. For convenience, we will make only a dichotomous differentiation, in order to distinguish between changes in the division of labor that are limited and role-specific (job enlargement or enrichment) and those that are organization-wide or include some coherent suborganizational unit (plant or department, for example). We will reserve the term sociotechnical change for the latter case, although we recognize that many programs of job enlargement are informed by the principle of improving the goodness-of-fit between the social and technical aspects of organization.

Job Enlargement and Job Enrichment

Job enlargement is at the minimum an addition of activities to an existing work role. Such changes are enacted on the assumption that the fractionation of jobs has in many cases gone beyond the point of contributing to productivity and far beyond the point of contributing to satisfaction. Such changes are usually enacted by management, which in conventional organizations has the authority to define task content. Further distinctions are sometimes made, depending on the nature of the activities added. As we have noted in Chapter 12, Herzberg (1968) stresses the distinction between mere enlargement and enrichment, reserving the latter term for the addition of activities that make the work more interesting and intrinsically motivating. Such additions he calls "vertical job loading," in contrast to the addition of equally simplistic and controlled activities, which he calls "horizontal job loading."

The documented instances of job enlargement or enrichment are now sufficiently numerous in the United States. Great Britain, Sweden, and other countries so that some generalization seems safe. Such changes are feasible; they have usually generated improvements in quantity and quality of performance. The extent to which they generate ramifying changes throughout the organization depends on the magnitude and locus of the initial interventions. There seems to be no necessary organization-wide consequence. Relevant accounts of such projects have been given by Herzberg (1968), Ford (1973), Davis and Cherns (1975), and Tausky and Parke (1976).

Sociotechnical Approaches to Organizational Change

When organizational structure is taken as the primary target in organizational change, the process may begin with any aspect of structure. Emery and Trist (1960) and their colleagues at the Tavistock Institute originated an approach that took account of two major aspects of organizational structure, the social and technical. Rice (1958) put it as follows:

> The concept of a socio-technical system arose from the consideration that any production system requires both a technological organization—equipment and process layout—and a work organization relating to each other those who carry out the necessary tasks. The technological demands place limits on the type of work organization possible, but a work organization has social and psychological properties of its own that are independent of technology ....(p. 4)

Even if the technology is taken as given, which the Tavistock group tended to do especially in its early sociotechnical studies, alternative social-psychological arrangements are usually possible within the technical requirements of the machines and tools for getting the task done. Yet one social-psychological structure may be far superior to another, both for member satisfaction and productivity. Two questions of goodness of fit are thus raised: the fit between the social and the technical aspects of an organization, and the fit between the resulting sociotechnical structure and the human characteristics of the people who enter it.

The Tavistock studies assumed three major needs for which people sought gratification in the work situation: (1) closure or a sense of completion in finishing a meaningful unit of work, (2) some control over their task activities by those engaged in the task, and (3) satisfactory relationships with those performing related tasks. Three further assumptions were made about the composition of work groups, stated as factors conducive to group stability and harmony: (4) homogeneity of skill levels within the group, (4) homogeneity of prestige and status, and (4) individual choice in group membership.

The importance of meaningfulness, autonomy, and good relationships with others in the work situation has already been discussed (Chapter 13). The Tavistock research was original in emphasizing the primary work group as the unit within which task-meaning and autonomy might be attained. The completion of a whole task by an individual is of course difficult to achieve in many types of industry, but the feeling of completing a meaningful cycle of activities can be provided by the group assignment in such situations.

If two or more people are given a common task, the psychological satisfaction of task completion carries over to their joint activities. One member may achieve closure through the activities of another or may be stimulated to complete a task begun by another. This is possible, of course, only if they share in some perceptible fashion a meaningful task. In similar fashion, the need for autonomy can find genuine expression at the group as well as the individual level. Not every person has to make all the decisions about his or her work in order to experience a feeling of autonomy and self-determination. If a person's immediate work group has a significant degree of decision making, this can satisfy individual needs to a considerable extent. Moreover, the sharing of decisions may save the individual from being overwhelmed with responsibilities.

THE TRIST STUDIES OF BRITISH COAL MINES.   Among the earliest of the Tavistock projects to embody the sociotechnical approach were the studies of Trist and Bamforth (1951) on problems of technological change in the mining of coal. The production side of coal mining includes three basic operations: (1) the winning of the coal by hand or machine from the coal face, (2) the loading and transportaion of the coal from the face, and (3) the supportive and preparatory activities of advancing the roof supports and of bringing up the conveyor system as the mining cuts deeper into the coal face. The early organization of these technical operations in many British mines was a simple system of small, self-contained units working independently. For example, in some pits the primary work group would consist of six men, two to a shift. Each man would be a complete miner, that is, would have all the skills for carrying out the three types of operations described above. The two men working during the day would go through that part of the cycle of activities that the work demanded. The two men who succeeded them on the next shift would take up the task at whatever stage in the cycle their predecessors had left it, and so on through the three shifts. All six men would be on the same paynote, that is, they would be paid the same wages, with the amount based on the productivity of the six-man group. The composition of the group was based on self-selection, with men selecting their own mates. Any primary work group tended, therefore, to have six men fairly equal in overall performance. The earnings and performance of different mate or marrow groups, however, varied greatly, with differences of two hundred and three hundred percent between the most productive and least productive of them. Each work group enforced its own standards of production and had considerable autonomy in its task. This simple system of working had advantages in mines in which irregularities of coal seams put a premium on the adaptability of work groups. Each team could set its own work pace as the conditions required, and each worker as a complete miner could adapt to the changing situation. Moreover, there were many psychological advantages in the system. Workers gained satisfaction from being engaged in meaningful cycles of activity, in having considerable autonomy and variety of work, and in being part of a group of their own choosing.

This traditional method of single place working was replaced in Britain by the longwall method of mining, partly because of the introduction of the face conveyor. This technical change in the coal mining process was accompanied by a reorganization of jobs and of work relationships. The model was the machine theory of the mass production industries. Division of labor in which each worker was limited to a single task replaced the integrated task and complete miner of single place working. The three basic types of operations were separated, so that the first shift had the task of cutting into the coal face, the second shift the task of shoveling the coal into the conveyor, and the third shift the task of advancing the face and enlarging the gateways. Moreover, within each of these phases there was further job specialization. When mechanical cutters were used in the first phase, five different work roles were specified. In place of the single work group of the older system six or more task groups were established. Although the longwall technology clearly required some modification of the older social system of single place working, the kind of job fractionation introduced and the neglect of the motivational forces of the primary work group were mistakes of the first order.

The justification for job fractionation is the economy in training a worker to exercise only a single skill, and the greater efficiency of the person performing a single operation over the person performing a number of functions. But the skills that were separated out for specialization in the longwall system were not of such complexity or variety that their combined performance by a single worker prevented the attainment of a high level of efficiency.

A further difficulty with the conventional longwall method was its failure to maintain the natural or spontaneous coordination of the work cycle that had existed prior to its introduction. Formerly each work group of six men had carried through all three phases of the mining operation, had taken joint responsibility for the amount of coal turned out, and had been paid accordingly. The longwell method organized work groups around task specialties, and each specialty had its own pay rate. Since miners were no longer paid according to the amount of coal turned out by their own group, pay rates for each main task and its related subtasks became subject to negotiation. The result was a long list of itemized prices to cover all subtasks and related activities.

Finally, the miners found the fractionation of their jobs distasteful. Under the old system there was variety and challenge in their work. They much preferred being multi-skilled complete miners to being hewers or cutters or fillers.

A COMPARISON OF TWO DIFFERENT SOCIAL SYSTEMS FOR DEALING WITH THE SAME TECHNICAL PROBLEMS OF PRODUCTION: THE CONVENTIONAL LONGWALL VERSUS THE COMPOSITE LONGWALL SYSTEMS. The Tavistock researchers found that not all pits had moved to the conventional longwall method with its job specialization and machine theory applications. Especially in pits in which coal was found in short faces, the traditions of the single place system had sometimes been carried over into the new technology, with its new face conveyors and its new cutters. A comparison was therefore possible between two pits, one of which had taken over the conventional longwall method and the other of which had adapted the older social structure to the new technology. This adaptation was called the composite longwall system.

THE COMPOSITE LONGWALL SYSTEM. The composite method of the single working place originally had involved groups of six men, two on each of three shifts, with each group of six carrying major responsibility for completing the three basic phases of the production cycle. The adaptation of this system to longwall operation in the pit under observation involved 41 men, divided among three shifts. The requirement of additional skills for handling the new machines was met, not by tieing each worker to a specific job, but by the movement of the team from one task to another as the work demanded. Not all men were necessarily rotated through all the specialized tasks required by the new machines. There was still, however, variety in the work in that all men were rotated through a number of different jobs.

The composite work method applied to longwall mining thus restored the continuity of task effort so lacking in the conventional system. In the composite system little external coordination of activity is required because the men move naturally from one task to the next as part of the requirements of their overall role. There is no lag between phases and no group conflict over the difficulties created by one group for the succeeding group.

The cohesiveness of the composite group stems from several sources. The group selects its own members and so the marrow, or mate, relationships traditional in British coal mining are preserved. This is an especially important factor for difficult and hazardous occupations. Moreover, the group assumes responsibility both for the overall task and for the allocation of members to the various jobs. It provides not only for ready job rotation but for shift rotation as well.

Finally, the method of payment recognizes and increases the interdependence of the group members. Their monetary rewards are tied directly to their performance. To the base rate of payment is added incentive pay based on the productivity of the group. This pooling of earnings does not require that each member draw exactly this same pay. The basic assumption, however, is that every miner in the group is a multiskilled worker, interchangeable with his mates according to the requirements of the unfolding task, and hence entitled to the same reward. In short, the composite longwall system mobilizes the social-psychological forces of the immediate work group for maintaining a high level of production. Moreover, it saved management the cost of an external system of coordination and of the bickering each payday over payments for the itemized list of subtasks.

The observations of the Tavistock researchers on the functioning of the two longwall systems and their theoretical analysis of the superiority of the composite system were put to test by a factual comparison of the two systems in operation. Two panels of 41 workers each were studied, one panel organized on the conventional longwall pattern, the other according to the composite method. Although the panels were in different pits, the conditions of work were basically the same—both coal faces were in the same seam; the geological conditions were very much alike; similar haulage systems were employed; and the same cutting technology was used.

One measure of the effectiveness of group functioning is the rate of absenteeism, both voluntary and involuntary. In this respect, differences between the conventional and the composite systems were striking; total absence rates in the conventional panel are two and a half times as great as in composite panels, and voluntary absence is ten times as great. The productivity measures also implied clearly the superiority of the composite to the conventional method. Production was much more regular in the composite system. As Trist says,

> ... the conventional longwall with conditions quite normal ran for only twelve weeks before it lost a cut, and during these twelve weeks it needed reinforcement to enable it to complete its cycles. The composite longwall, on the other hand, ran for sixty-five weeks before it lost a cut, and never needed any reinforcement. (p. 125)

Productivity as measured by output per man-shift was 3.5 tons for the conventional longwall, which was very close to the national norm; for the composite system it was 5.3 tons. When allowances were made for possible differences in seam sections and other factors, the composite system was found to be operating at 95 percent of its potential and the conventional system to be operating at 78 percent of its potential. Finally, a measure of organizational effectiveness must go beyond output per worker and include such other costs as supervision. The greater need for external coordination in the conventional longwall method necessitated the assignment of a supervisor not required by the composite system. Not only were the 41 men in the composite panel turning out more work than the conventional panel, but they were doing it without costing management the salary of a supervisor.

The Tavistock research team extended its investigation to the sociotechnical systems emerging in other British coal fields with the introduction of new technology. For example, they compared two composite longwalls that varied in the degree to which the ideal of the composite system was approximated. One embodied all the features of the composite system, the other only some of them. This latter longwall system was organized as two face teams. Each worker was assigned one main task, supplemented by occasional involvement in other work roles. There was little movement of workers from one task group to another, and responsibility for each given task was on an individual rather than a group basis. The other longwall group resembled much more closely the composite system described earlier, with multitask jobs, rotation of work, and free movement of workers within the panel. Both the modified and the composite systems operated in the same seam, under similar technical conditions, and with workers very much alike in qualifications and experience. Again the "pure" composite panel was definitely superior to the modified composite panel; it had a lower absence rate, a lower accident rate, higher productivity, and a more successful regulation of cycle progress.

The research team was not able to work directly with top management, government, and union officials to introduce a change program in the industry as a whole. They worked at the local level in those mines where local officials were willing to have research conducted and were interested in research outcomes. In some cases the research findings and the concepts of the researchers had an effect on the ongoing change process. The availability of new machines had plunged the coal fields into a process of technological change, and the way was partly open to seek the most appropriate change in the accompanying social-psychological system. Nevertheless, the thrust of the Tavistock group toward developing the best fit between the technological system and the social system met with only partial success. Its efforts were limited by its inability to gain entry to the top-power circles in the industry, the difficulty of communicating the research results to groups who had not themselves been involved in the experimental comparisons, and the threat to the larger social system of the implications of a thorough rational reform.

RICE'S STUDIES OF INDIAN TEXTILE MILLS. The impact of a behavioral science approach, with its emphasis on adequate theory and hardheaded experimental findings, should not be discounted. An inroad was made in the British mining industry, and the follow-up studies of Rice (1958), another Tavistock researcher, in the calico mills of India attest to the validity of their conceptualization of a productive organization as a sociotechnical system in which effective performance depends on the adequacy of both the social and the technical structure, and on their articulation. Rice's action research was conducted in a single company with two textile mills in Ahmedabad, employing some 8000 workers as of December, 1955. The research was undertaken at the invitation of the chairman of the mills. The consultant-client relationship was unusually broad, in that Rice as the representative of Tavistock was not committed to specific projects that management might want. Moreover, the company agreed that any of its workers or officers might discuss in private with the investigators any problems about their work, their roles, or their relationships. The general objective of the project was to help in the solution of social and psychological problems arising from changes in methods of work and managerial practice.

The first major problem of the research team had to do with the failure of the introduction of automatic looms to improve productivity. Although the morale of workers appeared good, and the supervisors and workers seemed to get along well, neither the quantity nor the quality of cloth was higher than that woven on the old nonautomatic looms. Observation of the work process revealed that twelve different occupational roles had been assigned individual workers to assure continuous operation of the looms. The twelve job roles were: *battery fillers* to keep the batteries full of new bobbins, *weavers* to keep the machines in operation by mending broken warp threads and the like, *cloth carriers* to cut and remove the finished cloth from the machines, *smash hands* to deal with such major entanglements as the breaking of a large number of warp threads at the same time, *gater* to remove exhausted beams and gate in new ones, *jobbers* and *assistant jobbers* to adjust, tune, and maintain the looms, an *oiler* to keep all moving parts oiled, a *feeler-motion filter* to maintain the automatic device for ejecting empty bobbins, a *humidification fitter* to keep the plant at the humidity level necessary for the yarn to hold up in the weaving process, a *bobbin carrier* to remove empty bobbins, and a *sweeper* to remove the fluff from the shed and to clean under the looms during gating. In all, 29 men were distributed over these roles for the operation of 224 automatic looms.

With the exception of the jobbers and assistant jobbers who did comprise a group, the 29 workers constituted an aggregate of individuals with a confused pattern of interrelationships. Although the three smash hands served the eight weavers, the priorities of the eight weavers for their services had not been clearly established. Similar ambiguities in relationships existed among the other types of workers. Moreover, the task demands varied in that the thickness of the yarn for the different types of cloth changed the work load differentially for the various types of workers. A weaver might drop from operating 32 looms to 24 if given finer yarn because there would be more frequent warp breaks. On the other hand, a change to yarn of a higher count would increase the number of looms serviced by battery fillers and gaters, because the greater quantity of finer yarn wound on bobbins and beams would last longer. No rigid specifications could therefore be set down for the timing of the interdependent activities of the workers, nor did the technical system with its job fractionation and individual role responsibility encourage any internal group structure making for cooperation. Moreover, there was no psychological reward in the accomplishment of a whole task either by the individual alone or by his participation in the group.

If productivity was to be raised to take advantage of the new automatic looms, management faced two alternative courses of action. One was to retain the new sociotechnical system and police it with more supervisors. The other was to reorganize it to provide internal group structure related to task accomplishment. The first alternative would add to personnel costs and would risk resistance by the workers to more external controls. "The workers would not only continue to experience the discomfort of their unstructured confusion but would feel further coerced and policed."

The researchers therefore proposed to management, after further study of the problem, a reorganization by which a group of workers would be responsible for a group of looms, with some sharing of the previously fractioned job assignments and with an overall group leader. Management accepted the proposal and planned to introduce it in one section of the weaving shed through a series of group meetings and discussions with successive levels of supervision, and finally with workers. There was such spontaneous acceptance of the plan, however, that the supervisors and workers immediately took over the scheme and proceeded to implement it. Through a process of mutual choice the workers formed four groups of seven men each, four in the weaving subgroup and three in the gating and maintenance subgroup. Moreover, they agreed to take over the ancillary services previously allocated to workers performing only a particular service.

By and large the history of the effects of the experimental plan is an amazing success story. This does not mean that all problems were automatically solved, that quantity and quality of production continuously soared, and that no new problems confronted management or workers. The amount of cloth woven did rise sharply during the first eleven days for the reorganized groups, fell during the next three days, then rose again and remained at a high level for four months, regressed to the preexperimental levels for two months, but then recovered and maintained its high rate for the next year and a half. For the two years and three months of measurement, productivity averaged some 95 percent of potential, as compared to 80 percent before the experimental reorganization. Quality of production, measured in terms of amount of damaged cloth, improved remarkably over the course of the 27 month period. In the first few days of the experiment damage actually rose, but it fell from 32 percent in the preexperimental period to about 25 percent during the next fifteen moths, 20 percent for the six months thereafter, and to about 15 percent for the final six months of the experiment. The ups and downs in quantity and quality indicate that difficulties did arise in the new system and that they were resolved successfully by an alert management working with employees motivated to maintain the new system. Some of the adjustments required to make the new system work at high levels of performance were: allowing adequate time for the training of new workers, providing spare workers for increased stoppage rates with increased speed of production, keeping a group on the same type of yarn as long as possible, and confining experimental sorts (or types of yarn) to whole groups rather than spreading them over all groups. The success of the experimental program led to its extension to the entire weaving shed, a change that the workers under the old system themselves pressed for.

In spite of the great difference in culture between India and western societies, the same psychological findings in worker motivation are apparent. When people have a meaningful task and have membership in a satisfactory primary work group organized meaningfully for task accomplishment, they work harder and are more satisfied with their work. In other experiments in the same calico mills, the sociotechnical system for nonautomatic looms was changed by integrating workers into a group with responsibility for performing a whole task on a group of looms. Efficiency was improved and the new system spread to other sheds in the plant using nonautomatic looms. Although the cost of the original experimental shed was 13 percent higher than other sheds because of higher worker earnings, the output was 21 percent higher and the number of damages 59 percent less.

■ SUMMARY ■

A theory of system change requires understanding of the structure and functioning of the ongoing system. The change theory then goes further and describes how altered inputs or internal developments or contextual changes of different kinds will change the system under study. A technology of change, which some theories of change attempt to include, goes still further; it describes ways in which desired systemic changes can be brought about.

An adequate technology of organizational change should therefore include at least the following specifications: point of entry into the organization, initial state of the organization (acceptable range and means of assessment), preferred state, method of bringing about change, primary target of change effort, linkage from primary target to preferred end state (and evidence for it), method of assessing system change. Current approaches to bringing about change in human organizations vary in the extent to which they include these specifications, and in their demonstrated effects in achieving change. Three major approaches are distinguished, on the basis of the primary target: individual, group, and organizational or structural. More detailed approaches are described within each of of these categories.

Individual approaches. Attempts to change organizations by changing individuals involve many assumptions—that imparting some counsel or information will change the individual, that the individual will therefore behave differently in the organizational context, that the members of the person's role set will accept these changes and modify their own behavior in complementary ways, and that all this can either be done without changing the formal policies and structure of the organization or that ramifying changes in structure and policy will take place. Information programs, training programs, counseling and psychotherapy all share these assumptions, and all are extremely limited as methods of organizational change. Selection and termination can also be regarded as individual approaches to organizational change. They are in some ways more powerful than other individual approaches; they are also less concerned with the well-being of the individual, at least as they are often used. Perhaps for this reason, they are increasingly limited by societal values about the rights of individuals to their jobs.

Group approaches to organizational change. The power of peer groups to change the behavior of their members has been well demonstrated. Various group approaches to organizational change (ad hoc peer groups, organizational groups or "families," and sensitivity training groups) all make use of this demonstrated power, with modest success. The dilemma of such approaches is that the power of the group to change its own members depends partly on its freedom from considerations of status and external sanctions, but the power of the group to bring about change in the larger organization involves exactly those considerations. Survey feedback is another group approach, in which the anonymous survey technique is used to generate data about the immediate organizational situation that might otherwise be unknown or withheld. The discussion of such data in organizational groups appears to produce measurable change, especially in combination with coaching and counselling.

Changing organizational variables. The direct manipulation of organizational (structural) variables is a more powerful approach to producing enduring systemic change. Several specific examples are presented, differing in the aspect of organizational structure that they take as the primary target:

> The authority structure (distribution of power; participation in decision-making)
> The reward structure (amount of pay; method of determining pay)
> The division of labor (job enlargement and enrichment).

Three examples of organizational change beginning with the authority structure are described—the clerical experiment, the Banner experiment, and the Weldon experiment. The Scanlon Plan is analyzed as a major example of organizational change that begins with the reallocation of material rewards. Job enrichment as practiced in a number of organizations and countries is presented as an approach that takes the division of labor as its primary target. The early sociotechnical experiments of Rice and Trist are also described as approaches to organizational change that emphasize the division of labor as primary.

ORGANIZATIONAL CHANGE:
CONVERGENCES AND COMBINATIONS

The social sciences, one way and another, have been greatly concerned with organizational change. Historians recount it, sociologists propose theories to explain it, and anthropologists search out enclaves untouched by it. Psychologists, more than most of their colleagues in other disciplines perhaps, have been involved in attempts at creating and measuring organizational change. These attempts, as we have seen, have utilized different methods, sought various targets, and made diverse assumptions about the ramifying effects of the initial intervention. In most of these attempts at change, psychologists have been in the role of consultants to management. Evaluative studies are, perhaps for that reason, much less frequent than change efforts. Nevertheless, enough experimentation and evaluation has been done to document some successes and bring to light some failures.

RESISTANCE TO CHANGE

The weakness of many attempts at organizational modification highlights the built-in resistances in ongoing structures. Six sources of resistance can be noted.

1. Enduring systems are overdetermined in that they have more than one mechanism to produce stability. For example, they select personnel to meet role requirements, train them to fill specific roles, and socialize them with sanctions and rewards to carry out prescribed patterns. Thus, when it comes to change, organizations show defenses in depth.
2. There is an error of local determinism in assuming that one piece of a system can be changed without affecting the rest of the structure. The larger system can nullify local changes. The relationship of the part to the whole is developed in the last section of this chapter.
3. There is both an individual and a group inertia in that established ways have the ease of habits and require little new adjustment. Even when single individuals might change some behaviors they encounter the difficulty of little modification in the complementary and reciprocal activities of others.
4. Changes in organizational patterns may threaten the expertise of specialized groups. For example, job enlargement for rank-and-file workers can mean an invasion of some of the tasks of skilled specialists.
5. Changes in organizational patterns can threaten the established power relationships in the system. If some decisions are to be made down the line, for example, then managerial personnel may fear intrusions of their own authority.

6. Finally, changes may threaten those groups in the system that profit from the present allocation of resources and rewards. This applies not only to vertical strata of worker and supervisor but also to horizontal divisions of function.

These built-in resistances had much to do with the fate of attempted reforms in the administrative-management section of the U.S. Department of State in the 1960s and 1970s as reported in the case study of Warwick (1975). In July 1965 the Deputy Undersecretary introduced a major reorganization of a threefold character: (1) a reduction of hierarchical layers through management by programs, (2) increased autonomy of decision making through management by objectives, and (3) a decentralization of some functions to regional and functional bureaus. Although gains in efficiency were achieved during the first two years, the old system reasserted itself over time. Suspicion of possible empire building by the undersecretary, the nervousness of higher officials about flagrant departures from traditional management practices, the negative attitudes of Congressional committees and the fears of untrained personnel about new techniques all contributed to difficulties in the new program. With a new undersecretary not sympathetic to its rationale the reform collapsed. Nevertheless some elements did survive in less hierarchical layering and less administrative personnel. Warwick (1975) concludes:

> Almost any significant change in executive bureaucracy touches the interests and self-definitions not only of employees involved, but also of related congressional committees, constituency groups, and interested publics. To treat a reorganization solely as an intra-agency matter is to overlook the fundamental values and assumptions undergirding the U.S. government. (p. 205)

The difficulties of organizational change are generally not appreciated because of the selective reporting of successful attempts relative to unsuccessful attempts. In fact, journals and publishers do not care for negative results and investigators are not eager to publicize their failures. Mirvis and Berg (1977) have taken the unique step of editing a volume on *Failures in Organization Development and Change* in which they present case studies and analyses of efforts that have not succeeded. They cover failures in achieving entry, failures in implementing the influence attempts, failures in affecting the dependent variable, the lack of sustained change, and the lack of diffusion. The emphasis in the Mirvis-Berg analysis, however, is on the positive side—namely, what can be learned from these unsuccessful experiments and how the proportion of successes can be increased.

THE SOCIOTECHNICAL APPROACH

In our judgment, experiments involving the direct change of organizational variables have accounted for more than their share of the successes. Moreover, these structurally oriented experiments, despite their variety, show certain similarities and convergences. They tend to use several methods of inducing change, even when one target structure and one method are regarded as primary. They also illustrate, and sometimes include in their experimental designs, the interdependence of organizational substructures. In the Scanlon Plan experiments, for example, we see that formal changes in the allocation of rewards motivate the enactment of a changed division of labor, and that changes in the division of labor alter the relationships of authority and legitimize the discussions of reward allocation.

The emphasis on some aspect of organizational structure as the primary target, the use of several methods of change in combination, and the inclusion of extrinsic rewards and technology among the areas of change contrast sharply with earlier social science approaches. These were marked (and handicapped) by a kind of methodological addiction—for example, to sensitivity training or unelaborated survey feedback or executive therapy. They were marked no less by a set of substantive aversions or taboos—for example, avoiding any major challenge to the existing upper structure of authority, the allocation of material rewards, or the division of labor, especially as given by the existing technology of the organization.

The sociotechnical approach to organizational change has made a major contribution in its inclusion of such factors. That approach takes as its target a complex emergent variable: goodness of fit between the social and the technical aspects of organization, and by extension between those aspects of organization and the needs and abilities of individuals. The distinction between the social and technical aspects of human organizations, while it involves some danger that the unity of the organization as a single sociotechnical system may be forgotten, is extremely important. It reminds social scientists of areas of previous neglect. It implies that theory and research on organizational change must take account of both social and technological facts. And it implies that goodness of sociotechnical fit can be improved by changing any element of organizational structure, social or technical.

The distinction between social and technical aspects of organizations can be thought of in spatial terms: how much of the organization is included in the target area of change and how much excluded from it? A common way of thinking about organizational space, of course, is in terms of jobs or roles. In these terms we can distinguish three discrete magnitudes, any one of which can be taken as the primary target for organizational change: the job (or some category of jobs), the work group, and the organization as a whole. In combination these identify six broad possibilities for characterizing attempts at organizational change:

Organizational Units	SYSTEM ASPECTS	
	Social	Technical
Job (role)	1	4
Work group	2	5
Organization	3	6

For example, the abolition of the assembly line in the Medfield plant of the Corning Glass Company was primarily a work-group change in technology (Cell 5), although other aspects of structure were also involved. The enlargement of the job of stockholder correspondent at the American Telephone and Telegraph Company was primarily a social change in the division of labor; the tools and machinery, which are less conspicuous in the office than in the factory, remained unchanged. The AT & T example would thus fit in Cell 1 of the 6-cell schema; it was the individual jobs that were changed. The clerical experiment of Morse and Reimer (pp. 683–687) was primarily an organizational change because it involved the authority structure of large departments although the content of individual jobs was also changed as a result of the autonomous and hierarchical treatments.

In principle, goodness of sociotechnical fit could be improved by direct change in any of these six categories. In practice the early sociotechnical experiments, while ahead of their time in bringing technological and social considerations into the same framework, concentrated their change efforts on social aspects of organization, especially at the group level (Cell 2). Rice's work in the calico mills of India, for example, accepted the new looms as they stood, as Trist and Bamforth's work assumed the acceptance of the newer mining machinery as it stood. The problem of sociotechnical fit then became one of discovering or inventing a work-group structure that used the new technology but met more of the psychological needs of workers.

THE NORWEGIAN EXPERIMENTS

More recent developments, especially in Norway and Sweden, have made possible experiments that are organization-wide and that involve attempts to maximize sociotechnical fit by changes in the technology itself as well as in the social structure through which it is operated. The Norwegian experience has been described by Thorsrud and his colleagues (Thorsrud, Sørensen, and Gustavsen, 1976). Conditions for the program of their Work Research Institute were from the outset unusually favorable. National organizations of labor and management invited and sponsored jointly a program of field experiments in "industrial democracy" (Emery and Thorsrud, 1969; Thorsrud and Emery, 1969).

> ... the Industrial Democracy Program (I.D.) aimed primarily at the development and testing of *alternative organizational forms and their impacts on employee participation* on different job levels. Major emphasis was placed on the concrete conditions for personal participation, including technological factors structuring the tasks, the work roles, and the wider organizational environment of workers. A project within the program could not be limited only to the level of the workers, since major changes in any work system cannot be sustained without correlative changes eventually at all levels of the organization. (Thorsrud, Sorensen, and Gustavsen, 1976, p. 422.)

The program was seen as a large-scale collaborative effort between researchers and researched. The Trade Union Council and the Employers' Association, which shared the initial costs of the program until the Norwegian government added its sponsorship, created the Joint Research Committee, which in turn had broad governing power over the goals and assumptions of the program. Agreement was reached regarding the major psychological needs of individuals at work (assuming that wages, hours, safety, security, and the like would be covered by union agreement, at least with respect to acceptable minima). Six individual needs were identified to serve as guides for the experimental work:

1. Challenge and variety
2. Opportunity for continued learning
3. Area of personal decision making and responsibility
4. Social support and recognition
5. Meaningful relation of work to social life
6. Relation of present job to future career

A similar set of postulates was drawn up for the organization as a system. These, adapted from Emery (1969) and Thorsrud et al. (1976) can be summarized as follows:

1. The goals or purposes of an organization can be understood as a continuing attempt to maintain a steady state of interdependence with its environment by which its potential energy or capacity for work is maximized.
2. An organization can achieve such a state only by maintaining constancy of direction and an acceptable rate of progress toward it.
3. Because internal and external change occurs continually, there is a continuing need to match the actual and potential capacities of the organization to the actual and potential requirements of the environment.
4. The primary task of management therefore involves the boundary conditions of the enterprise.
5. The accomplishment of a steady state requires self-regulation—regulation by the constituent parts of the system. Members must therefore be committed to its attainment and be able to adapt their behavior to move toward it.
6. Organizational parts and individual members must therefore have substantial autonomy and selective interdependence.

Beginning in 1964 and continuing to the present time, a number of organizational experiments have been conducted with all the experimental sites chosen by the national committee. The first four of these experiments included a wire-drawing mill, a paper and pulp plant, a metal fabrication plant, and a fertilizer plant. We describe each of these experiments briefly, and then consider their combined significance.

Wire-drawing Mill

The wire-drawing mill was part of a larger steel manufacturing operation. It involved the batch processing of wire, organized on a "one man–one machine" basis. Unpredictable variations in raw materials caused similar variations in task difficulty and in piece-rate earnings. Mutual help was impossible. Individual job-allocation was changed to group work, in which allocation was made to each group of about six men. Each group was responsible for a set of machines or benches, and job rotation was instituted within groups. Pay was changed to fixed base rates, with a bonus based on the output of the group. Feedback of results was made to the group; technical changes were made to facilitate group control of production. Maintenance and repair service was on call from the group, and an effort was made to redefine the duties of the foreman to external (departmental) matters.

Workers involved in the experiment preferred the new system, and reported increases in job interest, variety, and group involvement. They also increased productivity by about 20 to 25 percent, with commensurate increases in earnings. Resulting issues of equity arose, and management and union were unwilling to extend the experimental changes.

Paper and Pulp Plant

This was a traditional firm, engaged in chemical processing of wood pulp, and under financial pressure to increase efficiency. Production was organized on a batch basis, but with round-the-clock operation. Roles were specialized, with differential base rates and bonuses, and coordination was a function of technical and supervisory staff.

Experimental changes established work groups with considerable autonomy. Production standards, input-output measurements, and decentralization of maintenance and technical service were coordinated to these groups. The bonus system was modified accordingly, and guarantees of pay and manpower were given. Training for the multiple roles within groups was initiated. Supervision was redefined in terms external to the groups.

After an initial period of rapid change, with improvements in yield and quality, strong opposition developed among foremen. There was a year of stagnation, followed by the initiation of a new project and some apparent diffusion throughout the company and to other organizations.

Metal Fabrication Plant

This was a small plant (100 employees), manufacturing a variety of sheet-metal products. The experimental changes were begun in one department of 30 workers doing semiskilled and unskilled jobs on a piece-rate basis. The experimental changes established groups of 10 workers. Each group was responsible for its production, and operators were trained to perform a variety of the required operations. Each group, through a "contact person," coordinated its operations as necessary with the others. Maintenance and technical services were decentralized to the group level, with some attendant technical changes. Wages were changed from piece rate to a fixed base rate and a departmentally based bonus; pay thus reflected the success of the groups at internal management and at coordination.

Productivity increased 20 percent during the initial experimental period of ten weeks, and increased an additional 10 percent during each of the two following years. Quality control improved; turnover and absence were below average for the industry and region. Employee attitudes were strongly positive. Earnings were increased in proportion to the gains in productivity. Some problems of relations with management and union arose, but the experimental system was extended (with no conventional supervision) to a new and larger plant.

The Fertilizer Plant

This was the first of several plant-wide experiments conducted within the same company, a large manufacturer of chemicals. The experimental changes were numerous and involved the managerial structure as well as nonsupervisory levels. Specialized individual roles were reorganized into partly autonomous work groups, with job levels based on competence in broad areas of operations. The wage system was changed to fixed base rates and a plant-wide bonus based on improvements in quality and reduction of waste-pollution. Housekeeping and maintenance were decentralized to the work groups. Formal changes in management policy were made; for example, the first national contract was signed guaranteeing the opportunity for continuous learning to all workers. Attitudes of production workers toward the changes were positive. Regularity of production increased, and costs were significantly reduced. Some skilled workers, however, and many supervisors and managers opposed the changes, and a two-year period of stagnation followed the experiment. Thereafter, a further program was begun to establish alternative roles for lower and middle management.

Convergences in the Norwegian Experiments

The Norwegian program is unusual in a number of respects, beginning with its broad sponsorship. The experiments are unusual also in the number and range of structural variables that have been directly altered. These have typically included enlargement of individual work roles, creation or strengthening of work groups through increased authority and autonomy, changes in the reward structure to provide a base wage and a performance bonus for group or departmental accomplishment, and some adjustment of technological arrangements (information, maintenance, and the like) to fit the new social structure.

The results of the experiments are favorable with respect to worker responses and productivity. They are mixed regarding the responses of technical and managerial staff. Diffusion has been encouraging but by no means general or uninterrupted. It seems likely that the resistance of people whose own roles are threatened by such experimental changes can be constructively dealt with only through their inclusion in the process of change and organizational redesign. Finally, the Norwegian experiments, ambitious as they are, have involved social changes in work arrangements even more than technological ones; changes in the technical aspect of the "sociotechnical" organizations have been fewer and less profound. The reasons for this are obvious—the existing factories and machines cannot be greatly changed without great expense. Even more important, existing technologies are available, by definition; alternative technologies require development and testing.

NEW FACTORIES: THE SWEDISH EXPERIMENTS

The difficulty and expense of modifying large machine installations suggests that the greatest opportunities for maximizing sociotechnical goodness of fit occur when new plants are being planned. Exactly that point of view has informed the establishment of what the Swedish Employers' Confederation (1975) has called "the New Factories." These are by no means limited to Sweden, although several of the best-known and deservedly famous examples are in that country—the Saab-Scania plant at Sodertalje and the Volvo plant at Kalmar among them. Both plants are engaged in manufacturing processes for which the assembly line has been considered economically essential (engine assembly and auto assembly) and both are operating without such lines.

The Saab Engine Plant

Saab-Scania, a very large Swedish corporation, is a group of companies manufacturing automobiles, aircraft, and heavy trucks. The Scania Division at Sodertalje, a short distance south of Stockholm, manufactures trucks and automobile engines; it employs about 5000 men and women. Experiments to improve the quality of the work experience and solve some problems of efficiency and costs began in 1969, initiated jointly by management and trade unions. Management was concerned about high turnover (about 70 percent annually), high rates of absence, and difficulties in recruitment. Workers and unions were showing an increasing interest in participation, consultation, and direct and continuing influence of the worker over the job. There was a widely shared belief that the ideas of workers were not often utilized and a hope that greater utilization would contribute to improved operations and greater feelings of responsibility.

Overall guidance of the experiments, including their design and evaluation, was assigned to a group of about 20 people, led by the technical director of the company and including representatives of all functional units and all employee organizations. This group of 20 was called the reference group, a label that has nothing to do with the use of the concept in social psychological theory. Specific changes in work units, however, were to be initiated or discussed by the employees directly involved (production groups), and by groups that also included supervisors and engineers (development groups). The resulting structure of overlapping groups is reminiscent of Likert's system of representation, adapted for the specific purpose of experimental change. The early stage of the experimental work involved only two work groups and a development group, all in the truck plant. The possibilities for change were severely limited by the existing assembly-line technology. Nevertheless, the hope was that some improvements could be made, that a satisfactory group structure for experimental innovation could be created, and that things learned in these circumstances could be applied in the design of a new engine factory, planned for 1972.

Despite some difficulties, the first experimental stage must be considered successful on all these counts. Between 1969 and 1972, unplanned stoppages dropped from 6 to 2 percent of total time, extra work and adjustment needed to correct omissions and errors in the finished products dropped by one-third, and turnover on the chassis line dropped from 70 percent annually to 20 or less. (Other parts of the plant also showed decreases in turnover, from 40 percent to 20 percent, during the same period.) The production and development groups proliferated during the same period, to about 130 and 60 respectively.

The second and major stage of the Saab experimental program was the development of an alternative to the assembly line in the new engine factory. The decision to build a "new" factory—actually a new interior layout in existing buildings—had been made in 1969. The product was to be a new Saab engine, originally of British manufacture. Data on required capital investment, costs and time requirements of production, and the like were available from the British experience. Equipment for conventional assembly of the engine, using a timed and driven assembly line with individual work stations, was readily available. Production requirements, estimated at 110,000 engines annually, were well within the capacity of such equipment.

Between the time of that decision and the commissioning of the new engine factory in the autumn of 1972, the workers, unions, and management at Saab had acquired the experience of the earlier experimental efforts and established the structure of production and development groups. In addition, the Swedish Employers' Confederation and the Swedish Confederation of Trade Unions had concluded an agreement on "work rationalisation" that expressed their joint commitment to increasing the quality of the work experience.

To the groups working on the design of the new factory, this meant reducing the extent to which the individual worker was required to remain at a particular position and perform at a particular pace, increasing the worker's opportunity to acquire additional skills, and making it possible for assembly workers (as individuals or in small groups) to influence the distribution of work and the allocation of tasks. Management had the additional goals of wanting a work organization more flexible than the conventional assembly line, and therefore more able to adjust to changes in specifications and demand. The assembly line was not categorically ruled out, but "if possible, it was desired to replace the assembly line by something else."

Therein lay the major challenge to the project development group. As Norstedt and Agurén (1973, p. 11) put it:

> It is no coincidence that the assembly line has become so common in the world's car factories. When consideration has to be given to limitations regarding costs, utilisation of space, handling, processing of materials and throughput times, a continuous means of production employing mechanised handling is the natural and indeed the only solution. This has subsequently given rise to a limited number of technical detail solutions which are used the world over.

The project development group included three workers, one supervisor, one assembly instructor, and the company doctor, although many others were involved in the process of generating and evaluating alternatives. The group reduced the technical problems to six basic issues, and attempted to specify the major alternatives for each, shown in Figure 20-1.

The reduction of the assembly problem to these specific alternatives, the evaluation of their relative advantages and disadvantages, and the decision among them was the work of months. The choices were for *group assembly* of engines, with each primary group (10 people or less) having responsibility for building an entire engine; an *undriven system* of control, with each group accepting engine blocks and sending out completed engines when it was ready to do so; the *engines were to be moved to the materials;* the *fitters (workers) were to* "*accompany the engine*," rather than stay next to a supply of material or parts to be added to the engine as it passed their stations; the *materials were to be supplied in bulk by truck* to the work groups, and the engines would be moved to and from the work groups *by conveyor.*

Several arrangements were considered to meet these specifications, varying in cost, originality, and approximation to the objectives. If we think of them as alternatives to the conventional assembly line, the proposal that departed least from that model was the introduction of buffer stocks, supplies of materials that would permit a group of workers doing some related operations to vary their speed without imposing the same variations on all subsequent positions on the line. This would be a limited form of group assembly, as illustrated in Figure 20-2, but the limitations would be more conspicuous than the group characteristics. The line would still be driven, and the duration cycle of

Alternative techniques	
Assembly	
	□ assembly line
	□ group assembly
	□ individual assembly
Control	
	□ driven system
	□ undriven system
Flow	
	□ material moved to engine
	□ engine moved to material
Workplace	
	□ fitter accompanies engine
	□ fitter accompanies material
Supply of material	
	□ supply in bulk
	□ material for one engine
	□ material for series of engines
Transport system	
	□ handling by truck
	□ handling by conveyor
	□ supply by means of chutes from stores on the mezzanine level
	□ minimum handling by assembly in stores

Figure 20-1. *Analysis of engine assembly problem, project development group, Saab-Scania. (From Norstedt and Aguren, 1973, p. 34.).*

each worker's job would be determined by the speed of the line. If the production schedule called for one engine per minute to come off the line, no worker's job could have a cycle of more than one minute.

Precisely for these reasons the project development group and the others to which it was linked were not satisfied with the "buffer stock solution." They wanted more independent groups of production workers, with each group assembling a complete engine. The implication was for parallel groups. Such groups could be readily visualized, but the problems of supplying them with materials and removing their completed work efficiently were formidable. The principle of parallel groups, assembling complete engines under "undriven" conditions, was accepted (Figure 20-3). The problem then became one of inventing a system of materials transportation for such groups that would be reasonably efficient, as compared to the transport efficiency of the single linear assembly line.

Stated in its initial terms, even this derivative problem had all the properties of a dilemma—how to retain a *mechanically paced and*

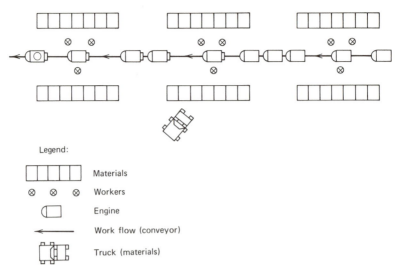

Legend:

| | Materials
⊗ ⊗ ⊗ Workers
⊏⊐ Engine
⟵ Work flow (conveyor)
Truck (materials)

Figure 20-2. *Assembly line with buffer stocks. (From Norstedt and Aguren, 1973, p. 35.)*

driven conveyor for transporting engines, and at the same time provide for parallel, relatively autonomous, *self-paced groups*, building complete engines. The problem is indeed insoluble if one also makes the usual assumption that the workers' pace and the conveyor pace must be closely coupled and interdependent, as when workers are located in linear fashion along the two sides of the conveying line. The solution arrived at by the Saab development group was to locate the work groups transversely to the conveyor line, on which they would place engines when completed, and to arrange for the delivery of parts and materials by truck to each group in a way that did not interfere with this mechanical conveyance (Figure 20-4).

That system of engine assembly has been running since late in 1972. It is no longer considered an experiment by the Saab management, the unions, or the workers, none of whom think it would be either possible or desirable to return to conventional methods. The following more specific conclusions seem warranted:

1. By the conventional criteria of management, the system is a success. Quantity of production is within the expectations (worker minutes per engine) of conventional assembly methods. Absence and turnover, which were special problems in the assembly operation, are now no higher than in other worker categories.

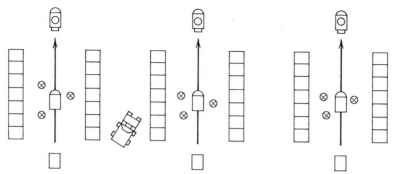

Figure 20-3. *Assembly by parallel groups. (From Norstedt and Aguren, 1973, p. 37.)*

2. The system is also successful in terms of the intrinsic content of the jobs and the relative autonomy of work groups. The work cycle on a conventional assembly line for this engine, assuming an annual production of something over 100,000, would have been less than two minutes; the cycle in the present system can be as high as 30 minutes, depending on the decision of the group. Each bay or parallel workshop has positions (space and tools) for ten workers, and each group is responsible for building complete engines. The allocation of tasks is decided by the group; each worker may build engines independently, all workers may divide the task, or subgroups may form. Job rotation may be introduced or not, by group decision. In practice, the preference seems to be for subgroups of two or three to work together, although preferences vary between groups and need not remain the same for any one group. Moreover, the flexibility of the system means that variations in market demand can be met by transferring some workers to other tasks; a bay can operate with one worker, ten, or any number between.

3. The subjective aspects of the Saab experiment are not adequately documented. A survey in 1976 (*Kilometeren*, December 1976) showed generally positive descriptive findings, but no basis of comparison with the earlier assembly-line condition or with more conventional parts of the Saab-Scania operations. To this problem must be added the tendency of people to shift their frame of reference and standard of comparison as their situation improves. Employee responses were most positive with respect to the social and physical conditions of work; 90 percent judged their contacts with fellow workers good; 80 percent were satisfied with their hours of work, and 72 percent

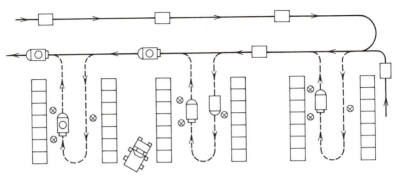

Figure 20-4. *Parallel groups and mechanical conveyance. (From Norstedt and Aguren, 1973, p. 37.)*

liked the physical milieu. They were somewhat less positive about the work itself, but more neutral than dissatisfied. About 50 percent thought the required speed of work was not a problem, and about 14 percent thought it was. About 50 percent thought their work was not hard, and about 20 percent thought it was. Forty-three percent said their work was interesting—a higher percentage than would be found among American assembly-line workers—but 27 percent said the work was not interesting.

4. Changes of this kind require investment, in many senses of that word. The system of parallel workshops requires more space than the conventional assembly line. The method of conveying engines and materials was more costly to install, in part because the layout and equipment for conventional assembly systems are ready-made. To these costs must be added the time of the committees that labored to invent and create the new system. Extension of the same aims and principles to other operations and other employing organizations would require similar effort, investment, and creativity.

The Saab engine-plant experiment was modest in size, but not in significance. It is an important instance of union and management collaboration to improve the quality of the work experience. It is also an important instance of planned organizational change, albeit the planners were members of the organization rather than "change agents." Most significant, perhaps, is the solution of a sociotechnical problem by modifying the technical as well as the social aspects of organization.

The Volvo Plant at Kalmar

The construction and staffing of the Volvo plant at Kalmar, in southeastern Sweden, in 1974 can be considered an experiment in organizational change only by using the words experiment and change rather loosely; there was no control group, no measurable "before" condition, and many variables were manipulated at once. It is nevertheless a development of importance for understanding organizations and change, and it has stirred great interest. A factory of substantial size for the final assembly of automobiles on a mass basis (capacity 60,000 per year on two shifts) was constructed without a conventional assembly line. It is unlikely that a similar event had occurred since Ford initiated large-scale assembly-line methods in Highland Park, Michigan, 60 years earlier.

The Volvo experiment resembles the Saab experiment in many respects. It took place in the same industry and in the same country and culture. It put the same emphasis on job content and autonomous groups. It encountered the same necessity to alter technology to achieve social objectives. And it was accomplished primarily by union, management, and staff groups working collaboratively, rather than by external change agents. There was a more conspicuous use of social science than of social scientists.

The Kalmar experiment differed from Saab in scale, in the opportunity to design a factory from the beginning, and in the extent of subsequent evaluation. Management and employees jointly requested the Rationalization Council, itself a creature of the Swedish Employers' Confederation and the Swedish Trade Union Confederation, to evaluate the operation of the Kalmar plant. The resulting monograph (Agurén, Hansson, and Karlsson, 1976) brings together production data, economic comparisons, and survey responses.

Plans for the new plant were described by the corporation president in terms that stressed social objectives:

> ... to organize automobile production in such a way that employees can find meaning and satisfaction in their work ... (to) give employees the opportunity to work in groups, to communicate freely, to shift among work assignments, to vary their pace, to identify themselves with the product, to be conscious of responsibility for quality, and to influence their own work environment. (Pehr Gyllenhammar, quoted in Agurén, Hansson, and Karlsson, 1976, p. 5)

That statement can be understood best in the context of Swedish life and the technology of the company at the time. The production process had been increasingly mechanized, machine-paced, and specialized over a twenty-year period. Work flow and total volume had increased steadily, and work cycles had been correspondingly shortened. Such technological tendencies had begun to be much discussed and criticized in the latter 1960s, and unions had begun to demand increased influence over such conditions of work. Nonverbal indicators emphasized these points; turnover and absence rates were high, especially in assembly operations, and recruiting was difficult. The hope was that the new factory, by redefining the conditions of work, would solve such problems "without any sacrifice of efficiency or results."

The broad objectives quoted above were interpreted as implying a sociotechnical system in which an identifiable product would be built by small groups or teams, each with its own workshop, each accountable for its own quality of work, each deciding its own internal division of labor and, insofar as possible, its own working methods and work pace. As with the Saab-Scania experiment, a project group was established to develop specific proposals and a larger reference group to provide general guidance and evaluation. The project group included foremen, production technicians, and architects. The reference group included direct representation of all relevant trade unions. Engineers, behavioral scientists, and other specialists were called by these two groups as needed. The results of earlier discussions in conventional settings (Volvo Torslanda plant) and of employee surveys in such settings were available to these groups. Their work, and the factory design that it produced, illustrate the meaning of the term sociotechnical when its two components are given near-equal weight.

The task at Kalmar is the final assembly of passenger automobiles, about 30,000 per year per shift. The work force (day shift) numbers about 600—30 work teams of 15 to 20 persons each. These teams are considered the primary producing units, and the shape of the factory reflects that fact; it is a set of centrally joined hexagonal wings. Each work team has its own work area, usually located along one outer wall of one of the hexagonal units. The exterior walls are glazed and the storage facilities are located at the center of the building, so that the view is open from each work area. The several work areas also have their own entrances and accommodations—"changing" room, sauna, carpeted coffee room with heating and refrigeration.

The task for a team is typically the completion and installation of a major subassembly—the steering gear or the electrical system, for example. Each automobile chassis begins its progression by being placed on an electrically driven platform or carrier, on which it remains throughout the process of assembly. The carrier moves from one team area to the next, and the chassis it carries gradually accumulates the successive subassemblies for which each team is responsible. The carrier permits the chassis to be elevated or rotated 90 degrees on its side, so that the team can select the position most comfortable for its work.

The movement of each carrier from one team to the next is guided by electrical tracks buried in the floor and timed by a central computer at a pace negotiated by union and management. In these respects there is some resemblance to the conventional assembly line, with each team of 15 or 20 workers becoming a miniature assembly line. There are, however, a number of differences that in combination are more significant than the similarities. The carriers have manually operated controls that can override the computer-scheduled pace; each team area has buffer positions that permit the team to vary its pace, either to "work ahead" or catch up; and each team can decide its internal allocation of tasks.

The most prevalent choice is for straight-line assembly within a team, which means that workers operate in pairs, one worker on each side of the car. Such a pair does the complete "team" task for a car, moving with the car through the several positions in the work area. When the pair of workers finish with the car and it moves to the outgoing position, they go back to the incoming position in their team area and begin work on another car, usually switching sides at the same time. The other pairs of workers that make up their team are working in the same way, two to a car. The work cycle time ranges from 16 to 40 minutes, depending on these choices and on the number of carrier positions in the work area—about ten times the typical assembly cycle. (The cycle for conventional assembly methods varies from less than one minute to approximately two minutes.) This process is illustrated in Figure 20-5.

An alternative method of work within the same technological constraints is dock assembly, in which each carrier position in a team's area becomes the territory of a particular subgroup. Each incoming car on its carrier then goes to one of these subgroup positions and remains there, while the subgroup of several workers completes the total team task for that car. Supervision for both straight-line and dock assembly is thin by conventional standards—one supervisor for two or three adjacent work areas (30 to 60 workers). Feedback on quality (quantity is obvious to the team) was planned to be continuously available to each team through a system of closed-circuit television with screens in each work area. In practice, while feedback is specific to each team, worker preference has been for personal communication, and most feedback is therefore verbal.

The representation and influence of workers outside their immediate group (team of 15 to 20) involves three structures. There is the conventional path of successive levels of supervision. There are the employee unions—one for "metal workers," one for salaried or office

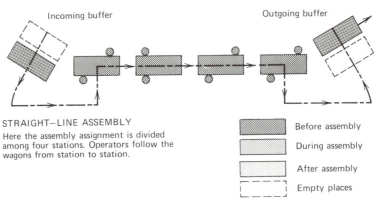

Figure 20-5. *Straight-line assembly within a work team (Kalmar Plant, Volvo).* *(From Aguren, Kaarlsson, and Hansson, 1976, p. 11.)*

workers, and one for foremen and supervisors—all three of which are represented in the plant-wide works council. And there are the functional councils—two for production, two for materials, one for quality, one for industrial engineering, and one for personnel and finance. Only the functional councils are an innovation at Kalmar; the overall works council is required by national agreement between the Employers' Confederation and the Trades Union Confederation, for all companies with more than 50 employees.

The research evaluation of the Kalmar factory by the Rationalization Council was done by a group of five—one representative from the Volvo company, one from the major union, two secretaries similarly representative, and one outside research specialist who served as chairman. Their investigation was made during 1976, after the plant had been in operation about two years. Data sources included the fiscal and production records of the company and approximately 100 interviews. Respondents were not randomly selected; most of them were members of one or another of the six "functional councils," which include representatives selected by the work teams, supervisors, engineers, and managers. A "control group" of 20 randomly selected employees was also interviewed, and found not to differ in response pattern from the larger set of respondents. The research report can be seen as dealing with four main questions: physical environment, team organization, worker influence, and organizational effectiveness.

1. *Physical environment.* The planning group had set out to make the Kalmar plant a superior workplace in a physical sense. Among the special features were acoustically baffled ceilings to bring the average noise level to 65 decibels, large exterior windows, lifting and tilting devices on the car carriers to make working positions comfortable,

TABLE 20-1   Worker Attitudes Toward Physical Conditions (Kalmar Plant, Volvo)

	WORKERS (judging the work environment in their team area)		WHITE-COLLAR EMPLOYEES (judging the plant's work environment as a whole)	
The table shows how many (number and percentage) of all workers (69) and white-collar employees (33) interviewed are satisfied with different factors in the work environment	No.	%	No.	%
Physical heaviness	57	83	30	98
Working positions	38	55	23	70
Noise	55	80	32	97
Lighting	59	86	31	94
Large windows/view	49	71	27	82
Climate, air pollution	34	49	25	76
Labeling and safety warnings on chemicals, solvents, etc.	40	58	27	82
Personnel facilities	49	71	30	91
Accident risks	56	81	30	91
Medical care	66	96	32	97
Safety	59	86	32	97
Working areas and workplaces	57	83	31	94

From Agurén, Hansson, and Karlsson, 1976, p. 34.

coffee-rooms and showers at each work area. The interview data indicate that the effort to create a comfortable working environment was generally successful; almost 80 percent of the blue-collar workers and more than 90 percent of the white-collar employees expressed overall satisfaction. Their specific responses to twelve aspects of the physical environment are summarized in Table 20-1.

Some of the points of dissatisfaction suggest rising standards of evaluation rather than objective failures in design. For example, the chassis lifting and tilting devices work, but some installation tasks are still difficult; the large windows are welcome, but they make it more difficult to balance the air conditioning system; moreover, some groups are better located than others with respect to the outdoor views and the coffee and relaxation areas.

2. *Team organization.* The Kalmar plant was built around the concept of work teams, producing units of 15 to 20 workers performing a meaningful group task under conditions of substantial autonomy. The

TABLE 20-2   Worker Perceptions and Attitudes Regarding Work Procedures (Kalmar Plant, Volvo)

	ASSEMBLY WORKERS		ALL WORKERS	
How many engaging in these forms of work?	No.[a]	%	No.	%
"Practice teamwork"	26	93	60	87
"Job-switching practiced in the team"	25	89	52	75
"Work ahead for extra breaks"	16	57	36	52

	ASSEMBLY WORKERS		ALL WORKERS	
Opinions of those engaging in teamwork, job-switching, and working ahead?	No.	%[b]	No.	%
"Like teamwork"	24	92	55	93
"Like job-switching"	24	96	50	96
"Like working ahead"	14	88	28	78

[a]Of the 102 persons interviewed, 69 were workers and 33 white-collar employees. Of the 69 workers, 28 were in assembly jobs.
[b]Percentage of workers practicing the forms of work.
From Agurén, Hansson, and Karlsson, 1976, p. 18.

functioning of these teams is a crucial issue in evaluating the Kalmar experiment, and in most respects they function well. They formed as clear social groups, their group properties encouraged by the physical territory and task assigned to each, and expressed in terms of group decisions. Some of these relate to the work itself—switching jobs within the group, providing assistance to group members, working ahead of schedule to increase the length of rest periods. Other group decisions involve the use of space, care of the group common rooms (coffee, showers, sauna), or the playing of recorded music in the team area. And occasionally there is a decision, initiated either by an individual member or the group, that someone should transfer to another group. The group also seems to be influential in designating one of its members as the team leader, a designation made formally by management. The team leader speaks for the team and receives information about team performance but has no formal hierarchical power over team members.

Most teams report and overwhelmingly approve the formation of subgroups around the work requirements, mutual assistance within and between such subgroups, and regularized switching of jobs among team members. Working ahead of schedule is less general, although

TABLE 20-3   Worker Perceptions and Attitudes Regarding Opportunities for Direct Influence (Kalmar Plant, Volvo)

Opportunities for direct influence on the work itself?	ASSEMBLY WORKERS		ALL WORKERS		WHITE-COLLAR EMPLOYEES	
	No.	%	No.	%	No.	%
"Yes, considerable"	7	25	25	36	21	64
"Yes, though small"	14	50	28	41	10	30
"No, scarcely any"	7	25	9	13	1	3
"No, none"	—	—	2	3	—	—
No reply	—	—	5	7	1	3
TOTAL	28	100	69	100	33	100
Would like greater opportunities	23	82	48	70	16	48

From Agurén, Hansson and Karlsson, 1976, p. 26.

most teams do it and workers in those teams like doing it. Team tasks vary in the opportunity they offer to work ahead of schedule, and all teams are limited in doing so by the number of buffer positions between teams. The importance of the teams is reflected also in the rarity of transfers. Workers who want experience in tasks outside their team area can become members of a pool assigned as needed to replace absentees; joining and leaving the pool are voluntary acts by the individual workers. Table 20-2 summarizes worker responses regarding several aspects of teamwork and their feelings about them.

3. *Worker influence.* Observation of the work teams at the Kalmar plant gives the impression of dominant team influence on the allocation of tasks; substantial influence on method, but constraint by product specifications and tool design; less influence on work pace, since only the buffer positions provide flexibility; and no direct influence on the product to be produced by the team. The buffer system seems to provide less flexibility than had been intended, although the entire system is far more flexible and worker-influenced than conventional assembly methods. Worker responses suggest some agreement with these observations, but a wish for considerably more influence than the present system allows. This preference is strongest among assembly workers and least strong among office workers, a pattern familiar in other industries and other countries. These data are presented in Table 20-3.

Worker perceptions and attitudes about opportunities for indirect influence are less favorable. The teams elect directly their representatives to the functional councils, but they are not agreed as to the role of

TABLE 20-4 Worker Perceptions and Attitudes Regarding Indirect Influence (Kalmar Plant, Volvo)

Opportunities for influence through discussion groups, functional council and union?	ASSEMBLY WORKERS		ALL WORKERS		WHITE-COLLAR EMPLOYEES	
	No.	%	No.	%	No.	%
"Yes, considerable"	10	36	25	36	13	40
"Yes, though small"	14	50	32	47	10	30
"No, scarcely any"	2	7	7	10	3	9
"No, none"	—	—	2	3	2	6
No reply	2	7	3	4	5	15
TOTAL	28	100	69	100	33	100
Would like greater opportunities	22	79	49	71	8	24

From Agurén, Karlsson, and Hansson, 1976, p. 26.

these councils—discussion and communication, advice, decision making—nor with the relationship of the councils to the official functions of the unions. Nor do workers feel generally well informed by their representatives. These data are summarized in Table 20-4.

4. *Organizational effectiveness.* The research group made a careful evaluation of costs and quality in the Kalmar plant, taking as their basis of comparison the conventional facility of the same company in Torslanda (Gothenburg). They conclude that efficiency is as good or better at the Kalmar facility. Direct assembly times—worker hours per car—are unchanged. This equality reflects the fact that the Kalmar plant, although its method of conveyance (battery powered carriers) is more time-consuming than the driven assembly line, has attained a higher utilization of its "potential" capacity (96 percent). There is less "down time" at Kalmar. Indirect costs per car are somewhat higher at Kalmar, but this is said to result from the single-shift operation.

There are fewer white-collar employees at Kalmar, and fewer supervisors. The assignment of work, training of new workers, handling of materials, and monitoring of work quality is largely done within the work teams. Absence and turnover are less at Kalmar than at Torslanda. Absence rates in 1976 were 14 percent and 19 percent respectively; turnover rates were 16 and 21 percent. The company expects that the Kalmar facility will accommodate to product changes more easily, but that remains to be seen. It is estimated that the Kalmar facility cost 10 percent more to construct than a conventional plant of like capacity, a fact that probably reflects the costs of innovation rather than intrinsic design.

Finally, the two plants can be compared with respect to quality, which appears to be the same. The responsibility for quality has been shifted substantially to the workers at Kalmar, and they want it that way, but this has not had the expected effect of increasing quality overall. What further changes would enable the Kalmar system to improve quality is not clear—more team control over materials, more use of "adjusters" (workers with special quality-oriented functions within teams), better feedback to teams, or less working ahead to increase free time. Quality at Kalmar is satisfactory by the Torslanda standards, which are high, but quality control has not become obsolete at Kalmar.

The conclusions we reached regarding the Saab engine factory apply as well to the Kalmar plant:

1. By the conventional criteria of quantity, quality, and costs, the new plant is acceptable; it equals conventional assembly methods. In addition, some of the traditional problems of assembly work—absence and turnover—are reduced.
2. The new system is successful in changing the intrinsic content of assembly work. Work cycles, at 16 to 40 minutes, are about ten times longer than in conventional methods. Task allocation, division of labor, job rotation, and related decisions are made within each work group of 15 to 20 persons. White-collar and supervisory staff are reduced.
3. Worker perceptions generally reflect these objective data. Workers are favorable to the new system but sensitive to its limitations, especially with respect to local determination of work pace. No significant preference for conventional methods is found among workers, unions, or management.

Convergences in the Swedish Experiments

The Saab and Volvo experiments are the best known and best documented of the Swedish efforts at work improvement, but they are not isolated examples. At least seven such "new factories" and 500 experiments within plants are noted in Lindholm's (1975) discussion of job reform in Sweden. These explorations in organizational change are not only numerous but multifaceted; they involve changes in the work cycle, in patterns of decision making, in the structure and function of work groups, and in systems of pay.

The Swedish experiments have taken place in a social context that has been strongly positive—supporting, encouraging, at times demanding changes in the organization of work and almost always prompt to legitimize those changes. The general context includes a tradition of labor-management harmony and trade union strength, with 95 percent of blue-collar workers and 75 percent of office workers belonging to unions. Technology is relatively advanced; political practice is democratic, and public interest in the content of work has been growing.

Some of the key events in the development of work reform are as follows:

1971   Swedish Confederation of Trades Unions endorses principle of "company democracy," reversing its 1961 decision that unions should stay out of managerial functions.

1972   Union and employers' confederations conclude a national "rationalization agreement," stating that four goals are to be given equal weight—increased productivity, increased satisfaction, better working environment, and job security.

1973   National legislation establishing worker representation on company boards of directors (two voting positions or more). National legislation limiting employers' power to dismiss employees.

1974   National law giving employees' safety representatives the power to shut down any work operation judged unsafe.

1975   Agreement between employer and union confederations that works councils (representative bodies of labor and management required by previous agreement in all companies employing 50 or more than 50 persons) shall have the right to examine the company's books, with outside assistance if the workers' representatives request it.

How long this complex and dynamic process of intraorganizational experimentation, union-management agreement, legislative sanction, and popular support will continue is difficult to predict. For the 1970s, however, Sweden provides a unique example of significant and spreading work reform, and of sociotechnical change.

JOB DESIGN AND ORGANIZATIONAL CHANGE

Advocates and practitioners of job enrichment differ in their concern for larger questions of organizational design, and in the extent to which they see job enlargement or enrichment as a strategy for large-scale organizational change. Herzberg's (1968) review of his own approach to job enrichment stressed its limited applicability—"not all jobs can be enriched, nor do all jobs need to be enriched—" but suggested some prospects for diffusion—"job enrichment will not be a one-time proposition, but a continuous management function." Davis, on the other hand, regarded job design as a means of general organizational change. Job design and sociotechnical approaches to organizational change he considered two terms for the same thing; the terminological differences were mere accidents of national vocabulary (Davis, 1966). It is therefore fair perhaps, and it is in any case instructive, to evaluate efforts at job design (also called enlargement, enrichment, and work structuring) as forms of *organizational* change. To the usual test of internal validity—were the intended experimental changes induced and did they have the predicted effects on those directly involved—we thus add three other questions: Did the changes in the design of certain jobs persist over time? Did they ramify and diffuse? Did they involve organizational changes of other kinds?

Social science efforts at creating organizational change, as we have seen, have in the past shown two great weaknesses—avoidance of technostructural issues and concentration on variables at the group or individual rather than the organizational level. Job design, which directly involves the division of labor and at least some aspects of technology, corrects the first of these weaknesses; it does not speak directly to the second. Moreover, the evidence is that job design per se—changing a few jobs experimentally—does not create enduring organizational change. Under most conditions, such job changes neither endure nor ramify, even when they are locally successful in increasing worker satisfaction and at least equalling the performance of conventional arrangements.

A full inventory of job design experiments and their subsequent history is not available, although a few summaries have been attempted (Ford, 1969; Maher, 1971; Alderfer, 1976). Most published accounts end with the announcement of brief and local successes. The experience of some companies, however, although unpublished is available in greater detail. The experience of a Dutch manufacturer of electrical and electronic products is particularly enlightening because it extends over a period of 15 years (1961 to 1976) and includes some 60 projects in job enlargement and enrichment. The conclusion is that job enrichment does not in itself lead to larger and enduring organizational changes:

> After the remarkable first pilot projects a "thousand experimental flowers" began to flourish. Successes were achieved at the micro level. Unfortunately, most of the experimental projects became isolated from daily organizational practice. Sooner or later they died a quiet death in an unchanged organizational environment. (den Hertog and de Vries, 1977)

Those early projects in what came to be called "work structuring" included instances of quantitative job enlargement, qualitative job enrichment, and job rotation. In some of them, group assembly of complete products or subproducts replaced conventional assembly lines, although on a very small scale and without the support provided at Saab or Volvo. The most publicized of these experiments involved the assembly of portable television sets by small, semiautonomous groups. Groups of seven workers were given the responsibility for internal allocation of work, quality control, and related functions. This arrangement can be compared with a lesser experimental change in which a conventional assembly line was formed into five subgroups (minilines) with buffer stocks between groups. These three contrasting methods for assembling television sets are summarized in Table 20-5, elements of which are taken from van Vliet (1970) and den Hertog and de Vries (1977).

Both the modified assembly line and the group assembly experiments were successful in themselves. Performance under the modified assembly-line conditions improved, waiting (down) time reduced by 55 percent, time spent in balancing (trying to equalize the time demands of individual positions) was reduced, and the number of faulty assemblies decreased. At the same time workers reported themselves as more free to determine their own pace, having less experience of tension, and being more satisfied with their jobs. The experiment in assembly by semiautonomous groups showed lower costs than a conventional assembly line producing the same television set. In addition, workers in these groups reported that they were more satisfied with their work, no longer considered the old situation acceptable, and wanted more of the participation and autonomy that they had begun to experience.

By these indicators the experiments were successful, but they did not persist nor were they extended to other operations or locations. The reasons for this failure of the work structuring experiments to generate larger organizational change were not investigated systematically, but some clues were suggested in the course of a subsequent conference of staff and management called to consider past problems and the prospects for reviving the experimental activities. Worker enthusiasm for the changes and for their extension was not seen as an unmitigated blessing. Line managers were concerned with the implied threats to their own authority and functions, which some of them saw as encroached upon both by the workers and by the staff experts who devised the experiments. There were references to the "hobby club," complaints that "talking all day long about half-baked ideas" got "no real business" transacted, and assertions that the experiments were not part of the "real production culture."

In addition to these psychological barriers to diffusion or continuation of the experimental work, there were technical problems. Changes

TABLE 20-5 Job Characteristics Under Three Methods of Television Assembly

Job Characteristics	Conventional Assembly Line	Modified Assembly Line (miniline)	Semiautonomous Groups
Job cycle	1½ minutes	3–4 minutes	20 minutes
Pacing	Driven belt between individual positions	Timed movement between groups, buffer stocks	Complete assembly within groups
Group size	100+ (total line)	25–30	7
Number of groups	1	5	2
Quality control	Inspectors at end of line	Inspector in each group	Merged with assembly function
Job consultation	None specified	None specified	1½ hours, at two-week intervals
Other elements added	—	—	Ordering of material; allocation of work

in the content of nonsupervisory jobs required changes in the handling of materials, in the layout of space and equipment, in tools, in machinery, and perhaps in product design. As the investigators put it, there was a need to attend to the "structural conditions for work structuring"—from tools and conveyors to staff-line relationships. Moreover, the amount of organizational space and resources involved in such changes required the sanction and even the commitment of top management. It was easier to declare a local experiment successful and forget it.

In the company under discussion, considerable effort has been made to deal with such problems, and there are signs that some renewal and diffusion of the experiments has occurred. Assembly lines of more than 100 positions and job cycles of three minutes used to be common. Present lines have no more than 24 positions and job cycles of at least 15 minutes. Moreover, motor-driven lines have been modified to include some method of control by the workers themselves. Those who have been most involved in moving the experiments in job design from small, brief, and isolated episodes to "standard practice" are encouraged, but see the construction of new factories as presenting both special opportunities and special tests for the present organizational commitment.

The experience of this large, multiplant company with job enrichment (enlargement, design, work structuring) illustrates the potential convergence of such activities with organizationwide sociotechnical change. That convergence also implies the answer to a query posed by Robert Ford (1971), who has worked on job enrichment in the American Telephone and Telegraph Company:

> What does it take to successfully introduce the concepts of job enrichment throughout an organization, especially a very large one? A perfectly honest answer to my own question would have to be: 'I don't know; I haven't seen it done yet by anyone.' (Ford, in Maher (ed.), 1971, p. 211)

The early efforts at job enlargement proceeded as if the jobs to be changed were so isolated that their enlargement or enrichment would have no significant effects on other positions. Such effects were not specifically denied, but they were not thought through. It is now obvious that the enrichment of many jobs at the rank-and-file level will require many other organizational changes, but exactly what changes is much less obvious. At least three lines of ramifications should be considered: horizontal, vertical, and "temporal."

The horizontal implication is clear; as we enlarge jobs in a functional sense, we end up with fewer functional specialties. Some of those specialties—inspection, for example, or job set-up or maintenance—represent prized positions. Another line of ramification is vertical. As responsibility for performance or planning or pacing or quality or coordination is built into nonsupervisory jobs, it is "built out" of certain staff and supervisory and managerial positions. The shape of the organization is changed; it becomes flatter and its parts more autonomous. We believe that the implication, contrary to some management-reassuring predictions, is a reduction in management—less managing and fewer managers. This permits economies for the organization and relief of the overburdened manager, not to mention the oversupervised worker, but it also threatens the elimination of some of the more interesting and better-rewarded positions. It is therefore unlikely to be popular with the incumbents.

Finally, there are those ramifications that we have called temporal, but could as well be called technical. They have to do with the fact that the physical and technical aspects of organization not only constrain the possibilities for job design, but also in a sense precede job design. Factory buildings are designed and constructed, machine tools are built and contracted for long before workers assume their roles. To the extent that the content of those roles is to be unconventional by present standards, the temporal chain of decisions affected grows long. In short, job design implies organizational design. This is an outcome inevitable if we think of organizations as open systems, or indeed as systems at all. The magnitude of the job changes themselves, the structural interconnectedness of the organization, and the contextual support or opposition will determine how far and how strongly the ramifications will run.

LEGISLATION AND REPRESENTATION

The difficulties of diffusion encountered by the proponents of job enrichment, even after clear local successes, illustrate some central truths about social systems—especially the selective receptivity (and unreceptivity) to data and the strength of the homeostatic tendency to preserve the existing character of the system. The success of a job-enrichment experiment in one department is an interesting datum for other departments and organizations, but data alone are seldom enough to induce qualitative organizational change. Information in itself does not automatically overcome long-established stereotypes, create new skills, or eradicate conflicts of interest. Molecular solutions do not simply multiply and so take care of molar problems. The slogan of organizational change "from the bottom up" has a democratic ring, but it is a weak approach to change in hierarchical organizations where local innovations are vulnerable to veto at each ascending point in the hierarchy. A strategy for the general adoption of job enrichment should take account of the concerns of staff specialists and supervisors that their special contributions and rewards are threatened, the difficulty of learning new staff and supervisory roles, and the importance of hierarchical and contextual support for the organizational changes.

It does not follow of course that some general pronouncement from the organizational or national summit will suffice to create organizational change. Such generalities exemplify the complementary error in strategies of change. They give change within organizations a kind of sanction but neither specification nor statutory force. The laws requiring minority representation of workers on corporate boards go a step beyond generalities. They impose change at the corporate level and they give legitimacy and encouragement to developments at other organizational levels. They do not make such developments unnecessary. The presence of two workers' representatives on a board making decisions about organizational structure, technological acquisitions, and resource allocation has its own importance, but it is the substance of those decisions that determines the content and rewards of work.

Nevertheless, the various national laws and programs providing for the representation of workers on corporation boards must be included among the important facts of contemporary organizational life. In western Europe, where such developments have been most pronounced, they are considered part of a more general trend toward "industrial democracy." National differences in content and terminology are substantial—co-determination in Germany, reform of the enterprise in France, and industrial democracy in Scandinavia—but the similarities are unmistakable. A considerable literature, more ideological than empirical, has accumulated about these developments, and two recent summaries are available (Vanek, 1975; *Annals*, 1977). In addition, the Yugoslav experience with workers' councils and self-management under much more comprehensive legislation has been extensively studied (*Participation and Self-Management*, 6 volumes, 1972–73). At least three general conclusions for organizational change can be drawn from these different national experiences with legislated worker involvement in corporate decisions: (1) Worker representation on corporate boards has pragmatic and symbolic importance. (2) The formal involvement of workers in corporate decision making not only alters the traditional functions of management but also those of labor unions. (3) Such legislation has had its greatest impact on organizational life when it has been combined with intraorganizational programs.

1. The immediate significance of worker representation on company boards is the creation of new rights and opportunities for employees; the meaning of citizenship in the organization is expanded

(Windmuller, 1977). At the very least, the worker representatives have access to information on fiscal affairs, production, and other matters traditionally regarded as exclusive to management. The extent to which such information may be legally shared with workers and union officers varies in different countries, and the linkage between workers and their representatives varies between companies as well. The facts of information access, however, have been redefined.

Membership on corporate boards also confers on workers' representatives the right to be heard. This may remain a right little exercised, but it may be used to good effect and it is likely to be if the law stipulates that workers' representatives shall be present in significant numbers and shall have the vote. They can then enter directly and influentially into corporate deliberations that would otherwise be closed to them, and they can speak in the board room on subjects that they could otherwise discuss only in union meetings or public forums. Windmuller (1977) lists as examples the location of plants, the opening or closing of entire operations, the purchase of major equipment, the determination of wage and salary policies, and other such matters. Where the number of worker representatives is large enough to affect corporate decisions directly, representation takes on additional meaning; a basic change in the distribution of power occurs.

2. The formal involvement of workers' representatives in corporate decision making implies a participatory model of organizational life, whereas the tradition of collective bargaining emphasizes the separateness of unions from management and persisting conflicts of interest between labor and management. The problems of unions in adapting to the formal participatory model are epitomized in the British slogan that "you can't sit on both sides of the bargaining table" (Sturmthal, 1977).

The core issue is whether the new role of union or worker representatives on management boards compromises the traditional union functions of independent criticism, bargaining, and defense of workers against arbitrary managerial actions. It can be argued that board membership does not weaken these union functions, but merely relocates some of the controversial discussions—from the bargaining table to the board room. Such relocation, however, would seem to imply local rather than industry-wide decisions, which unions have generally opposed.

It is also possible that unions and managements may, through their common board memberships, resolve their differences at the expense of the consumer and the general public. This special kind of syndicalist threat has been made an explicit issue in the United Kingdom (Sturmthal, 1977). And in the United States, the traditional union view has been that collective bargaining is the "American form of industrial democracy" (Derber, 1970, 1977). Some union officials have expressed interest in ways of improving the quality of the work experience as well as its rewards. No major commitment to the principle of worker representation has been made, however.

3. Legislated representation at the board level is not a substitute for shop-floor participation, job security, or interesting work. Legislation can facilitate such developments, however, and help to legitimize them, and they in turn can lead to legislation. The interaction of developments at these several levels is best seen in the Scandinavian countries (Schiller, 1977). In Norway, for example, the Trade Union Confederation proposed in 1963 and 1965 that the development of industrial democracy should proceed simultaneously along three lines: expanded consultation among employers, shop stewards, and plant committees; education of workers to prepare them for participation; and changes in company organization to enable workers to take part in decision making. Work along the first two lines was well advanced before acts of Parliament in 1972, 1974, and 1975 established corporate assemblies for all companies employing more than 200 persons. These assemblies must have at least 12 members, two thirds of whom are elected by shareholders and one-third by employees. In Sweden, on the other hand, legislation at the national level seems to have preceded developments at the level of the enterprise.

In short, the movement toward legislated worker representation in the conduct of enterprise is both a significant force for future organizational change and a reflection of changes that have already occurred at the organizational level. An employing organization is a system that exists in a larger social context, and that context includes both labor unions and legislative bodies. Organizational change can be extended or contained, accelerated or retarded, demanded or denied by these contextual agencies.

The problems of sustaining change and of diffusion are especially critical when modifications of organizational practices are attempted in another culture or in experiments in developing nations. Baumgartel and Jeanpierre (1972) studied the effects of 17 training programs offered in three training units in India. Two hundred and forty manager-respondents, a random sample of past participants of these programs, were questioned about their experiences and observations about the adoption of new techniques. The investigators concluded: "if management training centers in the national setting wish to accelerate the rates of adoption of advanced technologies in the companies they serve, they must assume the responsibility for major organizational development programs in addition to conventional management training. Only as these client companies develop climates favorable to innovation and change will the society obtain the maximum pay-off for its investment in the management training movement." p. 693

This is not merely to say that everything is connected to everything else, from the individual job to the nation-state and beyond. Organizations are characterized (at least in those countries for which we have data) by considerable autonomy and control over resources. Change at the organizational level is therefore often feasible without substantial effects on other organizations or substantial support from them. The plant-wide experiments described earlier in this chapter illustrate the degrees of freedom at the organizational level. On the other hand, major changes in some subpart of an organization typically take root and grow only if sanction and encouragement, material and symbolic, are given at the organizational level.

Change at any point and level in a social system constitutes a change-demand on surrounding structures, but the strength and urgency of the demand depend on the particular properties and relationships of those structures. Within those limits, the leading subsystem may be at the national level (legislative) or at the level of the enterprise (union and management), but the tendency is toward congruence. Within a multiorganizational society, there are many paths toward a given congruent pattern.

■ SUMMARY

This chapter reviews recent experiments in the design of organizations and analyzes their commonalities and differences. The commonalities include an emphasis on some aspect of organizational structure as the primary target, the use of several methods of change in combination, and the inclusion of extrinsic rewards as a potential area of change. Furthermore, they tend to be organization-wide or plant-wide in scope and to involve changes in technology as well as adaptations to it.

Four such experiments are cited from the work of Thorsrud and his colleagues in Norway—in a wire-drawing mill, a pulp and paper plant, a metal-fabricating factory, and a fertilizer plant. Six individual needs were taken as a basis for the experimental changes: challenge and variety, continued learning, decision making and responsibility, social support and recognition, meaningful relationship of work to social life, and of present job to future career.

Changes in these experiments included the creation of small, semiautonomous groups and the allocation of work to these groups. Technical and maintenance services were made available to the groups at their request. Members of the groups were trained for the performance of all roles in the group, and job rotation was introduced or encouraged. Wages were changed to a combination of fixed base and group bonus (plant-wide in the fertilizer plant). Measures of experimental effect were not identical in all four experiments, but gains in productivity of the order of 20–25 percent were common and gains in satisfaction were recorded in the three experiments for which such data were collected.

Of the many Swedish experiments in organizational design, two are presented in detail—one at the Saab-Scania engine plant, the other at the Volvo Kalmar plant. Both are remarkable for the modification of conventional technology to satisfy human needs more fully. The Saab experiment was initiated jointly by management and the trade unions. Management was concerned with relatively high rates of absence and turnover; the unions wanted increased participation and autonomy. The major experiment involved the assembly of engines, and introduced four major changes—from conventional line assembly to semiautonomous groups of about 10 workers; from a mechanically driven to an undriven, worker paced procedure; from highly fractionated jobs to complete assembly by group, subgroup, or individual; from fixed assignments to rotation or reallocation as group members choose. The results are clearly successful. The work cycle changed from less than 2 minutes to more than 30, if the group so chooses. The system is highly flexible, and adapts easily to market changes. Workers are consistently positive toward the new system, and productivity equals conventional assembly methods.

The Kalmar experiment is similar to that at Saab, but on a larger scale. It involved the construction of an entire new plant and addressed the more difficult task of inventing an alternative technology for the final assembly of passenger automobiles. The assembly line was not used; instead, the task of assembly is accomplished by teams of 15–20 workers, located in bays or workshops. The pace of assembly is computer-controlled, but there are buffer positions between groups to allow some group autonomy regarding work pace. Work allocation within groups is done by group members; work cycles therefore vary. The range is from 16 to 40 minutes, about ten times conventional assembly methods. Information about quality and related matters is fed back to the groups, which are also represented in functional councils for plant-wide decisions.

Experimental results are positive. Satisfaction is relatively high. The teams operate as social groups and their members like it that way. Organizational performance compares satisfactorily with a conventional plant doing equivalent work. The experimental plant has fewer supervisors, fewer white-collar workers, and fewer work interruptions.

These ambitious experiments are compared with a number of others, in which the job rather than the plant was taken as the primary target. The evidence suggests that diffusion of the job-oriented experiments throughout the organizations in which they are conducted is unlikely without additional and direct intervention at the organizational level. Without such support, experiments in job design more often die out than diffuse, even when local results are positive. A complementary point is made regarding formal systems of worker representation on policymaking boards. Such representation, usually to a small number of positions, does not substitute for or necessarily lead to changes on the shop floor. The Saab and Volvo experiments involved technological change, change in job content, emphasis on semiautonomous groups, along with formal representation on company councils. Trade union activity strongly supported these developments, as did national legislation. The combination seems to have provided a mass and momentum that made for success, at least within the limits of these experiments.

21
■ CONCLUSION ■

OUTLINE

Organizations and Open-System Theory: a Summary
The Nature of Open-System Theory
An Open-System Approach to Organizational Theory
Types of Structure as Functional Subsystems
Organizational Models
Processes of Organization
Organizational Effectiveness
Organizational Change

Dilemmas of an Organizational Society
The Issue of Job Design
The Issue of System Design
The Issue of Participation
The Issue of System Contributions
The Issue of Change and Resistance to Change
The Issue of Social Equity

In this book we have attempted to apply and extend open-system theory to human organizations. In making this attempt we have confronted the following questions:

What is open-system theory?
How can it be made a theory of human organizations?
How does an open-system theory of organizations deepen our understanding of organizational problems and processes—communication and influence, policy-making and leadership, effectiveness and change?

We intend this last chapter as a brief summary of our answers to these questions, which have been discussed at greater length throughout the book. We intend it also as a statement of a few of the chief dilemmas of organization that await solution, and which in solution will shape the future.

ORGANIZATIONS AND OPEN-SYSTEM THEORY: A SUMMARY

The Nature of Open-System Theory

In some respects open-system theory is not a theory at all; it does not pretend to the specific sequences of cause and effect, the specific hypotheses and tests of hypotheses that are the basic elements of theory. Open-system theory is rather a framework, a meta-theory, a model in the broadest sense of that overused term. Open-system theory is an approach and a conceptual language for understanding and describing many kinds and levels of phenomena. It is used to describe and explain the behavior of electronic equipment, living organisms, and combinations of organisms. The open-system approach and the major concepts of open-system theory are applicable to any dynamic recurring process, any cyclical pattern of events that occurs in some larger context.

Such a recurrent pattern of events, differentiated from but dependent on the larger stream of life in which it occurs and recurs, constitutes an open system. All such systems involve the flow of energy from the environment through the system itself and back into the environment. They involve not only a flow of energy but a transformation of it, an alteration in energic form. That transformation can be regarded as the goal of a given system; it is in any case one of its defining characteristics.

The functioning of any open system thus consists of recurrent cycles of input, transformation, and output. Of these three basic systemic processes, input and output are transactions involving the system and some sectors of its immediate environment; transformation or through-put is a process contained within the system itself. The transactions by which agencies in the environment accept the systemic product usually are linked to the transactions by which new inputs are made available to the system. To locate a system, to specify its functions and to understand them, therefore, requires that this cyclical ener-gic process be identified and traced. An open system is located by its boundaries for the selective reception of inputs (a coding process) and for its typical transmission of outputs. It is further characterized by such properties as negentropy to counteract the tendency of all systems to run down; feedback or responsiveness to information provided by its own functioning; homeostasis, the tendency to maintain a steady state; equifinality or the use of different patterns to produce the same effect; differentiation, that is, the tendency toward elaboration of structure; and coordination or integration of parts.

An Open-System Approach
to Organizational Theory

Some advocates of the open-system approach believe that a single theory can comprehend all levels of life. For the general-system theorists this is an article of faith. Our view is that theoretical progress can best be made by attempting instead to adapt the open-system model to each genotypic category of phenomena to which it is to be applied, adding specification to the meta-theoretical framework in order to maximize its explanatory power for the population category under study. The end result, if such efforts were successful, would be a set of open-system theories, each specific to a genotypic level of phenomena and all linked by certain shared concepts and assumptions. We have attempted such a theory for human organizations.

For human organizations, as for other open systems, the basic sys-temic processes are energic and involve the flow, transformation, and exchange of energy. Human organizations have unique properties, however, that distinguish them from other categories of open systems. Perhaps the most basic of these unique properties is the absence of structure in the usual sense of the term—an identifiable, enduring, physical anatomy that is observable at rest as in motion and which in motion generates and performs those activities that comprise the sys-temic function. The human organization lacks structure in this anatom-ical sense; its land and buildings are trappings; its members come and go. Yet it has structure; membership is not accidental and the behavior of members is not random.

We have argued that the resolution of this paradox lies in the patterns of the events of organizational life themselves. The events are structured, and the forms they assume have dynamic properties. Social organizations as contrived systems are sets of such patterned behavioral events. They consist of such events and have no anatomical structure analogous to that of physical and biological systems. In the most generic sense the structure of a social organization is contained in its various functions. In small subsystems the functions may be directly observable in the human activities involved; in larger sectors of organizational activity the overall patterns and functions are also inferred from observable events, but less directly.

This primary structural-functional quality of human organizations is closely linked to others that can be derived from it. The fact that organizational structure is created and maintained only as the members of the organization interact in an ordered way suggests a high degree of openness, a persistent and inherent vulnerability to forces in the organizational environment. It suggests also a continuing necessity to maintain the organizational structure against such forces or to adapt it to them. Much of the theorizing and empirical work about organizations has assumed explicitly or implicitly a closed system, in which the inputs into the system are regarded as constants. The open-system approach reminds us that organizational inputs are neither constant nor guaranteed. A human organization endures only so long as people are induced to provide those inputs, including membership and role performance.

One way of giving theoretical recognition to these organizational characteristics is to distinguish between the energic flow that goes into procuring, transforming, and exporting the organizational product, and, on the other hand, the energic flow that goes into overcoming the centrifugal and permeable qualities inherent in the unique function-structure of the human organization. We have done so by proposing an essential dichotomy between production inputs and maintenance inputs. Production inputs are the materials and energies directly related to the throughput or the work that comprises the activity of the organization in turning out a product. Maintenance inputs are the energic and informational contributions necessary to hold the people in the system and persuade them to carry out their activities as members of the system. No social organization can exist without its members habitually accepting their expected activities, possessing the knowledge and skill needed for the performance of those activities, and having the motivation to engage in that performance.

Another theoretical problem in the treatment of organizations as open systems arises from the characteristics just described. How can this function-as-structure system of influenced, motivated, interdependent events be described and conceptualized? Moreover, how can it be conceptualized in terms not only meaningful at the systemic level but with meaning as well for the individual processes of cognition and motivation that create the system? Our answer to these questions depends on the concept of role and on role theory.

The set of activities required of an individual occupying a particular position in an organization constitutes a role. The requirements of a role may be obvious to an individual because of his or her understanding of the surrounding technology and larger organizational task. Whether or not that is the case, the requirements will be communicated by those other members of the organization who depend on that person's role behavior in order to meet the requirements of their own jobs. The entire organization can thus be viewed as consisting of roles or clusters of activities expected of individuals, and of role sets or overlapping groups, each consisting of persons who hold such expectations for a given individual. At one level of conceptualization, then, the organization is a structure of roles.

This is not to say that the particular array of roles that gives form to an organization is constant. Though role systems and subsystems can be abstracted from their human carriers for anthropological or historical study, a full understanding of them must be predicated on the continuing motivational and cognitive processes that keep (or fail to keep) the individuals performing their roles.

In the early chapters we have attempted some specification of the subsystems that arise to give continuity to and to provide developmental opportunities for the organization. The most generalized description of the various substructures at a social-psychological level, however, is that of the role system. A role system is a set of functionally specific, interrelated behaviors generated by interdependent tasks. The enactment of roles always consists of individual behaviors, but the behaviors are primarily defined by the system requirements and do not necessarily express the personality of the individual in significant ways. The forces that maintain the role system are the task demands, the shared values, and the observance of rules. Organizations may have developed historically out of primitive groupings in which these first two forces were dominant, but they grow by formal elaboration of the third factor of rule enforcement. The formulation of rules and the sanctions of rewards and punishments constitute the authority structure of an organization. Although the maintenance of authority involves sanctions, it is also supported by the nature of the task demands and, in varying degree, by the shared values of organization members. The norms of an organization tend to be supportive of its role structure. The most generic of organizational norms is legitimacy—acceptance of the rules of the particular organizational game because of a more general belief that there must be rules. The values of the organization are a justification and idealization of its functions. Increasingly in contemporary organizations the values emphasize an ethic from below based on social experience rather than an ethic from above deriving its force from special competence or divine revelation. Legitimacy in many organizations thus takes on the pragmatic meaning of observing traffic rules rather than obeying a moral imperative.

Types of Structure as Functional Subsystems

As organizations develop the various functions of carrying on the work of the system, insuring maintenance of the structure, obtaining environmental support, adapting to environmental change, and of coordinating and controlling activities, they become differentiated into appropriate subsystems. Thus, the technical or productive subsystem grows around the major type of work that gets done. The maintenance subsystem insures the survival of organizational forms through the socialization of new members and the use of penalties and rewards in rule enforcement. Production-supportive functions of procurement and disposal are directed at transactions with agencies in the external environment.

These boundary transactions also include the critical task of connecting and orienting the organization to the larger society in a more general sense—that is, legitimizing the functions and demands of the organization in relation to that society. Changes in the societal context of the organization constitute change-demands and opportunities for the organization; interpreting and responding to such external events in terms of research and planning are the functions of the adaptive subsystem. Finally cutting across all subsystems is the managerial structure that adjudicates conflicts within the organization and coordinates the activities of the subsystems both in relation to one another and to the external world.

To some extent, each subsystem has its own norms, its own set of coding categories, and its own dynamic. The people in the boundary subsystems are moved by the dynamic of securing environmental support and of adapting to change, and face out toward the external world; the production and maintenance people face in upon the organization and develop different values. The dynamics of the organization as a whole emphasize survival, growth, and maximization.

The maximization dynamic requires a reformulation of the principle of equilibrium for bureaucratic organizations; the equilibrium sought is not static but involves growth and expansion. The proficiency dynamic of the production system leads to increased volume of throughputs; to insure continued inputs the supportive subsystems attempt to control or ingest more environmental space; the adaptive subsystems move toward adjustments which place the organization in a position of advantage. Finally, bureaucratic structures are role systems in which an overall organizational task has been divided and allocated to individual positions. There is a tendency in such organizations to solve new problems by creating new roles, a tendency that contributes therefore to continuing expansion and growth.

The functional relationships among organizational components are continuingly being altered by such processes of growth and elaboration, which occur unevenly in different subsystems, and they are also altered by external events. The formal equilibrium of parts is thus also dynamic, and is redefined at intervals to accommodate or anticipate such changes.

Organizations differ, of course, in many respects. We have suggested a basic typology that characterizes them according to their function for the larger society. Those functions we have identified by shifting to the societal level the categories used to describe the subsystems of organizations. Thus, from the point of view of the larger society, the productive or technical function is carried out by economic organizations, the managerial function by political structures and penal institutions, the maintenance function by agencies of socialization and rehabilitation (schools, churches, hospitals), and the adaptive function by research organizations and universities.

Organizational Models

Since Weber's account of bureaucracy there has been a profusion of organizational models utilizing Weberian characteristics but often seizing on some specific set of issues to the exclusion of others. Frequently these theories clash with one another. Thus, the value consensus in the Parsons approach is challenged by the conflict theories of Marx and Dahrendorf. The machine-like paradigms of Taylor and Gulick are countered by organic conceptions like the aggregation model of Janowitz or the temporary system of Bennis and Slater. The human relations approach tries to reduce the constraints of structural theory to problems of interpersonal relations as in the writings of McGregor and others. Likert's System 4 does seek structural modifications to allow for the effective utilization of principles of human relations but the changes are not revolutionary. The Chinese model attacks partial inclusion as the *sine qua non* of organizations, but in spite of its goal of the organization as a community, relies heavily on hierarchical principles. The sociotechnical system of Trist and Emery seeks the optimal combination of technical and social subsystems in carrying out organizational tasks. Etzioni focuses on ways for producing compliance.

Most of the theoretical models have centered about one of three motivational patterns: compliance with rules—the power model; responsiveness to external incentives—the reward model; or internalized motivation—the value consensus model. Each of these patterns is elaborated in separate chapters with respect to its assumptions and contingent conditions.

Processes of Organization

In human organizations the processes of energy transformation operate at two levels, the direct and the symbolic—the utilization or modification of energy as such (steam, electricity, muscle) and the use of energy as information exchange, especially among members of the organization. These interpersonal transactions we have treated in several ways—as communication, influence, leadership, and as conflict.

At the most general level we have discussed communication with respect to the ways in which information flows through an organization, including the restrictions of the flow. Here the concern is with such problems as closed circuits, the direction of the flow, information overload, and the utilization of feedback.

At a more intermediate level of generality we have considered interaction in terms of influence. To a large extent the expected activities in terms of which individual roles are defined are expressed as communicative acts of an influential character. The role prescriptions specify the persons from whom one is to accept influence and expect role-related communications, as well as the persons over whom one is expected to exert such influence and to whom such information is to be provided. The authority structure of an organization is nothing more than the pattern of such legitimized and influential communicative acts.

At a more specific level we have dealt with problems of leadership as differential acts of influence, differential in the sense that some individuals contribute much more to the outcome of the social process than others. Within the organizational framework the exercise of authority contributes heavily to influence process. Nonetheless, the fact remains that individuals in the same authority positions differ in the increments of power they exert. Indeed, we have asserted that the essence of leadership consists in the expansion of influence to such other bases as expertise and personal liking. Leadership is most effective when it is based on these modes of influence as well as or instead of the organizational forces of legitimacy and the associated stock of rewards and punishments.

Like other phenomena of organization, leadership can be viewed at the systemic level as well as the interpersonal. In systemic terms we have distinguished three categories of leadership acts—those that involve alterations in organizational structure, those that involve minor extensions or interpolations of structure to fit particular cases, and those that involve merely the application of existing structural provisions.

Our discussion of policymaking is built around the same basic concepts. Policy is defined as an abstraction or generalization about organizational behavior, at a level that has implications for organizational structure. A proposed policy describes some set of transactions that will be required for some or all organization members. It is thus a set of multiple role prescriptions, and it is also the highest of the three forms of leadership that we have proposed (acts involving changes in organizational structure). As a policy is carried out, it is expressed by means of influential and communicative acts.

Conflict within and between organizations is defined as a particular category of behavior in which two or more parties (organizations or subsystems) attempt to block, damage, or incapacitate each other. Most conflict behavior of individuals in organizational contexts is role behavior and is therefore determined to a considerable extent by processes of role-sending and receiving within the organization. The dynamics of interorganizational conflict are analyzed in terms of such internal processes, the conflict-regulating rules and procedures of the larger society, and the dynamics of the conflict interaction itself. Organizations contain built-in conflicts of interest of two types: *vertical*, or differences in rewards and power of various levels in the hierarchy, and *horizontal*, or differences between competing functional groups.

Organizational Effectiveness

The concept of organizational effectiveness is treated in terms of the same basic processes of communication, influence, and energic exchange. A distinction is made between organizational effectiveness as an inclusive measure of the ongoing state of the organization in relation to its environment, and organizational efficiency as one component of effectiveness. Efficiency is defined in terms of the energic ratio of organizational output to input. An organization is most efficient when, without any incapacitation of its resources over time, all of its inputs emerge as product. As increasing proportions of organizational input are utilized to maintain and energize the organization itself, and are therefore absorbed rather than transformed into product, the organization becomes less efficient.

Organizational effectiveness is a more inclusive and elusive concept. At the organizational level it can be defined as maximization of return to the organization by all means for some specific period of time. If the time period is long, the tendency toward maximization must be constrained to insure continuing inputs, absorption of outputs, and acceptance by the larger society. At the societal level, the effectiveness of a particular organization is given by the costs and benefits associated with its continuing functions.

At the individual level, organizational effectiveness is discussed in terms of three generic requirements—joining and remaining in the organization, performing dependably the assigned activities, and engaging in occasional innovative and cooperative behavior in the service of organizational objectives. The motive patterns for maximizing these three requirements are not the same, nor will the same conditions necessarily arouse all of these motive patterns. Organizations thus face the problem of what mix of conditions they seek to create for what sectors of the organization in order to achieve given types of effectiveness.

The relationship between the organization and its individual members is analyzed both in terms of the induced contributions of members to organizational effectiveness and in terms of the consequences of organizational membership for individual health and well-being. The health and well-being of organization members is thus regarded in part as an organizational output. The role properties that maximize individual well-being—challenge, autonomy, variety, opportunity for social interaction, task closure and meaningfulness, and material rewards—are considered in relation to the requirements of organizational life, both requirements intrinsic to organization as such and requirements imposed by conventional bureaucratic or technological assumptions.

Organizational Change

Different approaches to organizational change are analyzed in terms of seven characteristics: point of entry, initial state of the system as assumed or measured, preferred state of the system, method of change, primary target, hypothesized linkage between the primary target and the preferred state for the system as a whole, and method of assessing changes. Three basic categories of change are considered, according to their primary target: the individual, the group, or some property of the organizational structure itself. Individual approaches include information programs, counseling, selection, and termination. Group approaches include sensitivity training in its various forms, and survey feedback. The direct change of organizational variables includes as primary targets the authority structure, the reward structure, and the division of labor. Field experiments involving such changes in several countries are described.

DILEMMAS OF AN ORGANIZATIONAL SOCIETY

The characteristic properties of bureaucratic structures, which we have just summarized, are responsible for many of the benefits of contemporary industrial society and for some of its major dilemmas. In the first place, the maximization dynamic, with its push toward organizational growth and efficiency, has on the one hand made possible a richer material life, and on the other has created organizations that are neither sufficiently committed to the general welfare nor easily constrained to its requirements. The tendency to maximize has also created organizations of great size—multinational and conglomerate, private and public. In combination these outcomes raise fears of a society in which the nonorganizational sectors of life are shrinking and the organizational sectors fusing into a single comprehensive set of role requirements.

Such fears, realistic or not, are fed by a second organizational trend in modern society: the extension of formal role systems to deal with problems traditionally handled by individuals, families, friendship and neighborhood groupings, and other less formal structures. This tendency can be seen as another kind of maximization, in which organizations grow (or new ones arise) by taking on qualitatively different functions rather than increasing the volume of existing activities. The advantages of such developments are some efficiencies in the delivery of services and perhaps the establishment of effective minima that can be provided to all. The disadvantages are some impoverishment of personal relations, loss of self-identity, and weakening of the nonorganizational elements in society. The emergence of old-age homes and old-age care as an industry in the United States in recent years illustrates both the advantages and disadvantages of such developments.

In the third place, the pragmatism of bureaucratic organizations has economic advantages and moral disadvantages. The test of organizational success is the acceptance of the product, preferably on terms that leave a fiscal surplus. The test of individual success is contributing to that outcome by diligent role behavior, doing things that are expected. Empirical outcomes are the measure. Moral and ethical standards enter as constraints, and are often opposed or ignored for that reason. Corruption and bribery are not new, but the moral puzzlement of people caught at them may be.

Finally, the size, complexity, specialization, and technological sophistication of large-scale organizations makes the meaningful involvement of the rank and file in decision making increasingly difficult at the same time that it becomes increasingly urgent. The larger the organization, the greater the distance from the shop floor to the conventional centers of decision making. The more fractionated the roles, the fewer members will grasp the organizational mission. The more sophisticated the technology, the greater the danger of a sort of technocratic tyranny, in which tunnel vision takes over where societal perspective is needed.

We have called these organizational properties dilemmas because of the mix of intended and unintended outcomes that they generate.

The characteristic combination of wanted and unwanted organizational consequences has become very clear in recent years as the limits of the earth itself to renew and sustain life are approached. For example, improved technology and organization for catching and processing fish quickly exceeds the rate of reproduction, so that improvement in short-term effectiveness and output brings longer-term losses both organizational and societal. The organizational ability in affluent countries to provide private automotive transportation to most citizens manifestly exceeds the long-term possibility of fueling the vehicles, providing space for their movement and storage in urban areas, and breathing the air which they have breathed.

One can imagine the human race engaged in a kind of Faustian exchange with its own organizational creations, in which material aspirations are realized but on unendurable terms. A more constructive use of imagination, however, is to redefine the problems of human organization in terms amenable to solution. Rapoport (1960) defines dilemmas as problems that cannot be solved in the terms in which they are initially presented, the implication being that solution may be possible if the terms of reference are changed. Let us conclude by attempting to state six issues of contemporary organizational life in terms that admit the possibility of successful action: job design, system design, participation, system contributions, change and resistance to change, and social equity.

The Issue of Job Design

The disaggregation of the organizational task into individual roles involves many variables and allows many solutions, so many that it is to some extent an art form or an expression of cultural preferences rather than merely a technical exercise. The variables involved in determining the optimal content of organizational roles are most visible in organizations that turn out some tangible product, but they are applicable to other organizations as well. Schools and hospitals, political parties, and government agencies no less than factories must accomplish a division of labor in order to accomplish anything.

The division of labor must answer implicitly or explicitly the questions of job design: how much monotony or variety, simplicity or difficulty, physical demand or comfort, supervision or autonomy, external pacing or individual preference, method-prescription or individual choice? The optimal answers to these questions will depend on the criteria of optimization, the population for whom those criteria are to be optimized, and the kind of organization for which the answers are sought.

By any of these criteria, however, the evidence favors the enlargement and enrichment of rank-and-file organizational roles. Short-term organizational efficiency is perhaps the most restrictive criterion: how much salable product in exchange for a given input cost? Even in these terms the fractionation of roles and rigidity of role prescriptions appears to have gone beyond the point of optimization (Chapter 19). One can speculate on the reasons for an ideology of efficiency going beyond its own criterion. To some extent the game of fractionation may develop its own dynamic and provide its own satisfactions; simplification becomes an end in itself. Moreover, to the extent that work simplification leads to the complete elimination of human labor, it may be justified as a developmental stage if not in other terms.

It also appears that conventional job design itself suffers from the effects of fractionation, especially in accounting. Fractionated jobs may decrease acts of spontaneous support for organizational goals, increase absence rates or add to turnover and therefore to the costs of labor, recruitment, and training. These costs, however, are not accounted in ways that influence job design. Jobs are typically designed to cost criteria that assume the worker's presence. Absence and turnover may be caused in part by the decisions of the production subsystem, but the duty and cost of combatting them are more likely to appear in the supportive or maintenance subsystems.

A further issue in the redesign of jobs is the competence and training of the designers. Industrial engineers are not well prepared to design jobs to social-psychological criteria; their education has been far too specialized for them to feel comfortable or competent with such notions. Nor are social scientists well prepared to respond to the technical aspects of job design. The design of jobs is a sociotechnical task, but the curricula of higher education are not sociotechnical.

The enrichment of jobs can be thought of as an incremental process, and we may then ask how far the process should go. The criterion of short-term cost efficiency gives one answer, which is significantly beyond present industrial practice. Other criteria—job satisfaction, self-actualization, or overall societal well-being, for example—give other and more change-demanding answers.

The first step, enriching jobs to the point of increasing *total* costs to the enterprise, would be highly significant, as the experience of numerous organizations has demonstrated. The additional step of changing accounting practices so that they assess those costs realistically and allocate them to their sources would change the motivational context within which managers and job designers work. The third step of modifying the curricula of universities and technical schools would increase the competence of job designers to meet the enriched demands of their own jobs.

Job enlargement encounters special problems in organizations distributing benefits, such as the Social Security Administration. The roles of service personnel can not be increased to allow for autonomy for the individual in decisions about dispensation of gratuities. In the interest of equity such decisions have to be constrained by rules of objective entitlement. Hence the challenge is to provide some combination of tasks that will still assure uniform treatment to all clients entitled to given levels of benefits.

The Issue of System Design

The foregoing suggestions imply a fact that we have made explicit in another context (Chapter 20): job design as such is a limited strategy for the solution of organizational problems. At some point the properties of the larger organization prevent changes in job design or must themselves be changed. The issue of job design thus merges with the larger issue of organization or system design.

The design of organizations as human systems can be made to subsume all other organizational problems. We will emphasize the problem of coordination, and the closely related matters of size and participation. Conventional organizational design, like conventional administration, has tended to treat coordination as a benefit instead of a cost. It may be a benefit to the coordinators, whose complaints of overload are mitigated by the excitement and rewards of their coordinative tasks. It is an urgent necessity in organizations like the space agency (NASA), where the results of many scattered activities must be brought together at a particular time and place. Necessary or not, however, coordination is an economic cost to the enterprise, and more often than not a psychological cost to those whose activities are being coordinated, a process that inevitably involves control.

Coordination of organizational activities requires the acquisition and retention of performance information in some form, the retrieval of such information as appropriate, its use in making coordinative decisions, and the communication of those decisions as role expectations or policies. These processes of communication and information transfer have been accelerated almost beyond belief during the past century. Bennis (1970) cites increases of 10^2 in the speed of travel, 10^7 in communication of the spoken or written word, and 10^6 in data storage and retrieval. The last of these exponential numbers has been increasing so rapidly, however, that annual or semi-annual revisions of the estimate would be required for accuracy. The means of coordination have grown immensely.

The organizational investment in coordination has also grown, although perhaps not at an exponential rate. The use of air travel, long-distance telephone, closed-circuit television, and computer technology is coordinative in considerable part. The "walkie-talkie" radios and shirt-pocket paging devices round out the electronic assault on autonomy. The growth of coordinative positions in organizations has also been great, although comprehensive data to document their growth are not available. We suspect them to be the most rapidly growing stratum of organizational life—even in universities, where arguments for close coordination have only modest plausibility.

All these developments can be seen as attempts to answer a single question: How can we get more rapid and pervasive coordination in organizations? We propose as a major criterion of system design a complementary but neglected question: How can we design organizations that require less coordination?

One answer to that question has already been given: enlarge or enrich individual roles. When a single individual performs a number of related activities there is a kind of coordination going on, but it occurs in the mind of the individual and probably adds to the interest and satisfaction of the role. As roles are divided and redivided, especially along functional lines, the need for coordination between individuals increases. The workers at the Saab engine plant, any one of whom may assemble an entire engine instead of adding a part or two, need less "coordinating" than their counterparts on conventional assembly lines.

A second answer to the question of reducing the need for coordination is to increase "organizational slack." Buffer stocks, storage areas, small amounts of unscheduled or free time are all ways of making split-second coordination less necessary. The creation of slack resources is a cost, of course, but so is coordination. The Volvo plant at Kalmar uses buffer positions between work groups, as we have seen. The resulting method of assembly is somewhat less efficient than conventional assembly on paper but not in practice. The costs of building in slack resources are apparently no greater than the costs of coordinative failures ("down time") on the conventional line.

Galbraith (1973) calls these two approaches to organization design *information reduction strategies*, and contrasts them with two other strategies, one of which stresses lateral relations: direct coordination between interdependent groups without hierarchical intervention. It is not clear that this reduces the coordinative function, although it may reallocate it in ways that are more satisfying to those involved. Finally, there is what Galbraith calls the strategy of the vertical information system; such arrangements vary tremendously in sophistication and technology, but they are essentially means of hierarchical coordination, an organizational attribute we have proposed to minimize.

Schumacher's (1973) provocative argument that "small is beautiful" could be considered a fifth coordination-reducing strategy. The vision of small organizations, responsive to active memberships and communities, is attractive and in some respects persuasive. This approach would call for federated structures with considerable autonomy in their sub-parts, rather than a tightly centralized system. Such an organizational concept is so contrary to the organizational dynamics of growth and maximization that it is difficult to imagine its adoption except under greatly altered social conditions.

One may ask what the prospects and incentives may be for the more modest changes in job and organization design that we have proposed. We consider them good for several reasons. Organizations characterized by richer roles and less hierarchical coordination—more within roles and less between, so to speak—are not only competing successfully with conventional bureaucracies but seem to be avoiding some of the persistent problems of conventional organizations. A second factor that favors organizational redesign is the changing education of managers, who are in fact the major designers of organizations. Schools of business administration vary a great deal, but many of them have begun to question rather than preach the older organizational theories. Some carryover may be expected.

In northern Europe and Scandinavia, two other factors are active in urging the redesign of organizations—the demands of labor unions for improving the quality of the work experience and the intervention of government to the same purpose. Whether similar developments are imminent in the United States is unclear, and whether substantial changes in organization design will occur without them is in doubt. The interest of labor unions and government in issues of organization design is increasing, however, and the quality of the work experience is becoming more prominent as a possible criterion for such design.

The Issue of Participation

Participation is a familiar organizational issue, and one much misunderstood. Rank-and-file members often say that they want to participate more fully in organizational affairs, and organizational leaders often speak of participation as if it were some fringe benefit to be given or withheld. Conflict of interest is confounded by misunderstanding of what organizational participation means and how it is inherently related to other aspects of organizational life. Participation, strictly speaking, means simply engaging jointly with others in some set of activities. Managements almost universally urge some forms of organizational participation—regular attendance, punctuality, vigilance in the performance of assigned tasks, responsiveness to authority, and turning out work of substantial quality and quantity. When workers fail to "participate" sufficiently in these terms, management calls it lack of motivation. When the rank and file speak of participation, however, they are more likely to stress their competence and interest in other kinds of activities—information sharing, goal setting, allocating rewards, choosing among methods of work, and the like.

The issue of participation is thus an issue of allocating human resources to roles. It is an issue of the division of labor, functional and hierarchical, of job design, and of system design. Seen in these terms, we believe that the cardinal fact in bureaucratic organizations is underparticipation, underutilization of human resources, often aggravated by heavy demands for performance within a very narrow range of activities.

Some exclusion of organization members from organizational activities is implied in any structure of roles. A role structure not only serves to provide prescriptions but proscriptions as well; every activity that is prescribed for one category of positions is proscribed for others. If the maintenance engineer is to keep the machine in repair and the set-up expert is to prepare it for each new run, the machine operator is thereby informed—explicitly or implicitly—not to perform those tasks. But the operator, even if not formally expert, is in some degree a unique source of information about such matters. And so it is with the nurse and even the hospital patient in relation to the doctor in charge.

These are examples of small scale. In such cases, given some formal encouragement, coaching, and feedback, the individuals involved might well enlarge the participative process, improve the information base on which decisions are made, and increase the motivation of the workers who carry them out. When the decisions involve large-scale reallocation of resources and many potential participants, the case becomes more difficult.

To provide for the participation of rank-and-file members in all the decisions that affect them thus poses a real organizational dilemma. If the participative process is to be direct and is not to become overwhelmingly absorptive of time and energy, organizations must either be very small or so loosely coupled that small units are quite autonomous in most matters. If the process of participation in major decisions is to be indirect, the problem is to make it something better than formalism and to maintain strong ties between representatives and their constituencies.

Research, experience, and experimentation agree that participation in organizations can be increased substantially over conventional bureaucratic practice, with positive effects. The data also agree that the process of attaining such increases is not easy, that it implies changes beyond what most organization leaders are prepared to initiate spontaneously, and that some conventional positions of supervision and technical specialization are explicitly threatened by the participative process.

Difficult as they are, these problems are more easily solved than the question of what the participative base *should* be for different kinds of decisions. Rule-of-thumb answers have stressed the making of decisions by those who will be affected by them, or by those who have the information and experience to make them best, or even by those who "want to." Even if agreement could be reached on one of these decision rules, it would be difficult to apply. For example, *who* should make the decisions in a state university: the academic administration, the faculty, the students, the board of trustees, the state legislature, or the people of the state in direct referendum? And *how* shall the decisions be made?

Without attempting to answer such questions specifically for universities, we note the implication that at least four groups can be considered the relevant participants for a given decision:

> Organizational elites (owners, managers, formal leaders, specialists)
> Organizational membership at large
> Organizational clients (customers, users, direct beneficiaries)
> Members of the larger society (community, nation)

No statement about the prerogatives of these groups will hold for all decisions, all organizations, and all circumstances. We must search instead for the answers to component questions: As the role of any of these groups is increased for a given category of decisions, how is its role performance affected? How is its well-being (satisfaction, health, etc.) affected? How are the performance and well-being of other groups affected? How are the contributions of the organization to the larger society (products, by-products, waste and damage) affected?

The answers to these questions and to subdivisions of them, as research provides them, will deal partially with the larger issue of participation in human systems. They will leave an unavoidable and important residuum of value choices: decisions about participation are in part choices about the kind of society we wish to be and the kinds of individuals we wish to become.

The Issue of System Contributions

The issues of job design, system design, and participation thus assume and require criteria: design and participation for what? What are the criterion variables to be optimized?

The tendency in organizations and parts of organizations is to answer such questions too narrowly. The tendency toward organizational ethnocentrism is strong. A structure set up to carry out a given function tends to become concentrated around its own preservation and expansion, and usually around the protection and perpetuation of that function as the means of organizational preservation. But every organization can be thought of as having three essential functions rather than one: (a) the achievement of a given throughput, (b) the maintenance of effective relations with an immediate market or clientele, and (c) conformity or adaptation to the constraints and opportunities of the larger society.

For commercial organizations operating in a market economy, market behavior commands adaptation. It is less than a perfect mechanism, but it is powerful; no market-dependent producing system can go on for long turning out unsold products.

When market dynamics or other direct checks do not operate, however, the primary task of throughput may take over, and external needs and relationships may be virtually disregarded. This overconcentration on the aggrandizing performance of a narrow and fixed task is particularly characteristic of the authority structure (managerial subsystem), which often operates as if the immediate throughput of giving orders and invoking sanctions were its total function. If we take the organization as our frame of reference, however, the function of the authority structure is to provide predictability and coordination of performance. If order-giving fails to perform this function, the diligence of commanders and the frequency of memoranda are irrelevant or counterproductive. The traffic policeofficer in a crowded urban center who concentrates on the punitive exercise of power for minor infringements is not likely to keep the traffic moving, which is what other subsystems require. When people object to bureaucracy and bureaucrats, they are really protesting this tendency toward concentration on some narrow task with concomitant neglect of the supersystem. Different critics speak of this phenomenon in different terms; the television comedies show bureaucrats shuffling papers instead of solving problems; Parkinson made the unjustifiable expansion of administration nearly immortal as Parkinson's Law; more conventional academic critics write of administrative intensity.

The remedy is less obvious than the problem. It is easy to say that people in organizational subsystems should behave in accordance with the larger organizational mission, and that leaders of organizations should be as concerned with meeting the needs of the larger society as with the organizational throughput and return. But the immediate throughput is more directly linked to role performance, more measurable, more predictable, and less demanding of change.

The immediacy of the throughput as compared to the function that it will serve outside the unit in which it is produced is inherent. Librarians lend and receive books; teachers assign and correct lessons; nurses give out medicine. If the immediate throughput becomes an end in itself, the librarians become custodians of books, teachers custodians of children, nurses custodians of the sick. Reading, learning, and healing are the external needs that justify the support of libraries and schools and hospitals, but meeting those needs is more difficult to accomplish and to measure. Because the overall contributions of any system to the larger suprasystem—positive and negative—are difficult to assess and the measurement of immediate throughput is easy, we take the latter as a surrogate for the more important thing. In so doing, we feed the tendency we have called organizational ethnocentrism.

Perhaps another reason for the concentration on throughput and the relative neglect of meeting external needs is the discomfort of change. The market or client group is seldom an unchanging and uncritical receiver of organizational throughput. To concentrate on being responsive to changing needs and requirements means being prepared to learn new things, abandon familiar and perhaps satisfying ways of doing things. It is easier to concentrate on throughput and hope for the best, or even to invest heavily in persuading clients that the familiar throughput is what they really need and want after all.

The neglect of damaging or destructive effects is a related problem. The human race acquired the habit—in earlier times of small numbers, feeble technologies, and slow movement—of relying on natural extraorganizational processes to correct or compensate for the neglect of the overall systemic effects of human activity. Those times are past. Well-being and even survival require better attention to system outcomes, wanted and unwanted. The treatment of organizations as closed systems emphasizes the disregard of system products, once they have been exported. Open system theory is well-suited to improving the prediction of organizational outcomes, wanted and unwanted, and thus bringing them under control.

The Issue of Change and Resistance to Change

To call organizations open systems means to expect internal change in response to external events. It is usual to speak of resistance to changes we advocate, and to use other terms to characterize persistence in the face of change-demands that we oppose. Such opposition is common when the requirements of change are strenuous, at least from those on whom they fall most heavily.

Whatever the terminology, the issue of change and resistance to change must be counted among the inherent dilemmas of human organization. An organization that changed in response to every external signal would be no organization at all. The essential conditions of organizational life—recurrent cycles of behavior, predictability, internal coordination—would erode very quickly and the organization would lose the properties that differentiate it from its environment. On the other hand, an organization that responds to no such signals is also doomed. It will become irrelevant or worse, and the environment will refuse it the means of existence. The issue is what criteria shall shape an organization's selective acceptance of external change inputs? Will such inputs be accepted or rejected in terms of the needs and well-being of the suprasystem? If not, how can that criterion be made more significant in organizational decisions about change?

As the preceding discussion suggests, conventional bureaucratic organizations tend to be responsive to change demands and opportunities that maximize material returns and preserve existing patterns of hierarchical order and advantage. Other kinds of change inputs are more likely to be resisted. The emphasis of some authors on the rapidity of change in modern life is accurate in a technological sense, but neglects the powerful maintenance of established organizational patterns and character. Automobile companies may respond to (or create) changes in automotive style, but resist the societal need for alternative forms of transportation, or even for the reduction of poisonous automotive emissions. The postal service of the United States maintained its old-line civil-service style of operations even after it was formally removed from the government establishment. Within broad limits, the self-correcting mechanisms of bureaucratic organizations act to absorb the impact of external events and maintain the organization as it is. Defense in depth is the first rule; adaptation is never more than second.

To what extent these tendencies can be successfully decreased by the reduction of hierarchical prerogatives, the leveling of the steep gradients of reward, the limiting of tenure in elite and powerful positions, and the more extensive participation of relevant groups in decision making remains to be seen. A first step is to acknowledge the change-resistant aspects of bureaucracies. A second is to treat their modification as a researchable problem. Our prediction is that selective openness or resistance to change can be made a matter of system design rather than accident.

The Issue of Social Equity

The dilemma of social equity cuts across all of the preceding five issues—job design or system design for whose benefit, participation to whose satisfaction, evaluation of organizational contributions to what societal criteria, change-acceptance or resistance to what purpose? These can be regarded as problems in choosing the appropriate frame of reference for assessing organizational performance and attempting organizational change. The ancient question *cui bono* is not outmoded; we must decide for whose benefit we act or propose action.

Tracing the effects of organizational behavior more fully and predicting them more accurately will reduce the unintended consequences of human organizations, and in so doing improve greatly the prospects for survival. The question of equity, however, includes organizational purposes as well as accidents. Moreover, the question has dilemma properties. As Christian Bay (1958) has pointed out, what is functional for one group or set of individuals may be dysfunctional for others. Blau and Scott (1962) distinguish four major beneficiary groups that organizations serve, any one of which may be advantaged at some cost to the others: the owners or managers of the enterprise, the rank-and-file members, the customers or clients, and the public at large.

These groups only begin to establish a sufficient frame of reference for organizational decisions. The interests of owners and managers often diverge; stockholders may prefer higher dividends when managers urge the reinvestment of capital, for example. Under conditions of public ownership, the public at large are nominal owners but they are likely to be distant and inarticulate. Nor do their interests necessarily coincide with those of the managers or workers, both of whom may benefit from high prices at the expense of consumers and public.

After the relevant interest groups have been identified, the question arises as to how much any of them can be justifiably advantaged relative to the others, and what costs to any one group will be allowed for the comfort and satisfaction of others. The traditional hazards of coal mining and the risks of exposure in some chemical processes illustrate this aspect of the problem of social equity. Limited hazards, exposures, hours, and wages all deal with the issue of equity by putting constraints on the disadvantages that may be imposed on any group as conditions of work.

A further issue in frame of reference and social equity is time span. When the Dutch set out to create great areas of new farm land from the sea bottom, they were exchanging the labor of one generation for the benefit of those succeeding. The salty land, even after dikes and drainage, would take years to become fertile. The rapid consumption of irreplaceable resources makes exactly the reverse decision about social equity; the warmth and rapid travel and throwaway plastics for the present generation imply the probability of shortage, discomfort, and danger to those who come later. Some large lumber corporations claim to be replacing fully with new growth all the timber they cut, and some countries have enacted laws requiring that they do so. Such an organizational policy, other things permitting, could hold for perpetuity. The standard may be impossible of achievement but it illustrates an important point about organizational frames of reference: the criterion of social equity involves time perspective as well as distinctions among groups.

Finally, there are questions of equity at successive levels of human organization and aggregation—equity within the organization and its clientele, within the community, within the nation-state, and within the human society as a whole. The colonial system embodied different concepts of equity within the colonies and the parent country. Most nations, new and old, have rejected that frame of reference. They continue, however, to apply different standards of equity within their boundaries than across them, as the gross differences between the rich and poor nations of the world remind us.

There may be little agreement about a model for a just and productive society, and a comprehensive frame of reference for recognizing approximations to it. The increase of social equity, however, involves answers to three more specific questions:

How can concentrations of wealth and economic power be limited?

How can concentrations of political power be limited?

How can societies without concentrated economic and political power be productive and provide a good life for all?

In most countries that permit the private ownership of agriculture and industry, economic differences are very great. Some countries that call themselves socialist have introduced controls on this kind of economic power, but at the expense of greater accumulations of political power. The kibbutz communities of Israel have checked both types of concentration by allowing neither the ownership of capital nor the extended holding of political office. They have at the same time improved the living standards of their people and the land they occupy. Their way of life has been more admired than emulated, however, and the adaptation of their utopian standards to mass technological society brings us again to the dilemma of social equity and the means of its attainment. Those who study human organizations must address themselves to this dilemma.

BIBLIOGRAPHY

Adams, J. S. 1963(a). Toward an understanding of inequity. *Journal of Abnormal and Social Psychology, 67,* 422–436.

Adams, J. S. 1963(b). Wage inequities, productivity and work quality. *Industrial Relations, 3,* 9–16.

Adams, J. S. 1965. Injustice in social exchange. In Berkowitz, L. (ed.) *Advances in experimental social psychology.* New York: Academic Press. Vol. 2, 267–299.

Adams, J. S. 1976. The structure and dynamics of behavior in organizational boundary roles. In Dunnette, M. D. (ed.) *Handbook of industrial and organizational psychology.* Chicago: Rand McNally, 1175–1199.

Adams, J. S. and Jacobsen, P. R. 1964. Effects of wage inequities on work quality. *Journal of Abnormal and Social Psychology, 69,* 19–25.

Adelman, L., Stewart, T. R., and Hammond, K. R. 1975. A case history of the application of social judgment theory to policy formulation. *Policy Sciences, 6,* 137–159.

Agurén, S., Hansson, R., and Karlsson, K. G. 1976. *The impact of new design on work organization.* Stockholm: The Rationalization Council SAF-LO.

Alderfer, C. P. 1976. Change processes in organizations. In Dubin, R. (ed.) *Handbook of work, organization, and society.* Chicago: Rand McNally.

Allen, T. J. and Cohen, D. I. 1969. Information flow in research and development laboratories. *Administrative Science Quarterly, 14,* 12–19.

Allison, G.T. 1971. *Essence of decision: explaining the Cuban missile crisis.* Boston: Little, Brown.

Allport, F. H. 1933. *Institutional behavior.* Chapel Hill: University of North Carolina Press.

Allport, F. H. 1934. The J-curve hypothesis of conforming behavior. *Journal of Social Psychology, 5,* 141–183.

Allport, F. H. 1954. The structuring of events: outline of a general theory with applications to psychology. *Psychological Review, 61,* 281–303.

Allport, F. H. 1962. A structuronomic conception of behavior: individual and collective. I. Structural theory and the master problem of social psychology. *Journal of Abnormal and Social Psychology, 64,* 3–30.

Allport, F. H. 1967. A theory of enestruence (event structure theory): report of progress. *American Psychologist, 22,* 1–24.

Allport, G. W. 1945. Catharsis and the reduction of prejudice. *Journal of Social Issues, 1,* 1–8.

Allport, G. W. 1953. The trend in motivational theory. *American Journal of Orthopsychiatry, 23,* 107–119.

Allport, G. W. 1954. *The nature of prejudice.* Cambridge, Mass.: Addison-Wesley.

Allport, G. W. and Kramer, B. M. 1946. Some roots of prejudice. *Journal of Psychology, 22,* 9–39.

Almond, G. A. and Verba, S. 1965. *The civic culture: political attitudes and democracy in five nations.* Boston: Little, Brown.

American Public Health Association. November 1975. *Health and work in America: a chart-book.* (Available from the Superintendent of Documents) Washington, D.C.: U.S. Government Printing Office.

American Society of Anesthesiologists. 1974. Occupational disease among operating room personnel: a national study. *Anesthesiology*, 41, 4, 3–42.

Anderson, T. H. and Warkov, S. 1961. Organizational size and functional complexity: A study of administration in hospitals. *American Sociological Review*, 26, 23–28.

Andrews, F. M. and Withey, S. B. 1976. *Social indicators of well-being.* New York: Plenum.

Andrews, I. R. and Henry, M. M. 1963. Management attitudes toward pay. *Industrial Relations*, 3, 29–39.

Andrews, J. D. W. 1967. The achievement motive and advancement in two types of organizations. *Journal of Personality and Social Psychology*, 6, 163–169.

Annals, May 1977. Industrial democracy in international perspective. *The Annals of The American Academy of Political and Social Science.* Vol. 431.

Aram, J. D., Morgan, C. P., and Esbeck, E. B. 1971. Relation of collaborative interpersonal relationships to individual satisfaction and organizational performance. *Administrative Science Quarterly*, 16, 289–296.

Aranya, N. and Jacobson, D. 1975. An empirical study of theories of organizational and occupational commitment. *Journal of Social Psychology*, 97, 15–22.

Argyris, C. 1954. *Organization of a bank.* New Haven, Conn.: Labor and Management Center, Yale University.

Argyris, C. 1957. *Personality and organization.* New York: Harper.

Argyris, C. 1962. *Interpersonal competence and organizational effectiveness.* Homewood, Ill.: Irwin-Dorsey.

Argyris, C. 1964. *Integrating the individual and the organization.* New York: Wiley.

Argyris, C. 1971. *Management and organizational development.* New York: McGraw-Hill.

Argyris, C. 1971. Beyond freedom and dignity by B. F. Skinner, a review essay. *Harvard Educational Review*, Vol. 41, No. 4, 550–567.

Argyris, C. 1976. *Increasing leadership effectiveness.* New York: Wiley.

Asch, S. 1952. *Social psychology.* Englewood Cliffs, N.J.: Prentice-Hall.

Ashby, W. R. 1952. *Design for a brain.* New York: Wiley.

Astin, A. W. 1964. Distribution of students among higher educational institutions. *Journal of Educational Psychology*, 55, 276–287.

Atchison, T. J. and Lefferts, E. A. 1972. The prediction of turnover using Herzberg's job satisfaction technique. *Personnel Psychology*, 25, 53–64.

Atkinson, J. W. 1958. Toward experimental analysis of human motivation in terms of motives, expectancies and incentives. In Atkinson, J. W. (ed.) *Motives in fantasy, action and society.* Princeton, N.J.: Van Nostrand, 288–305.

Atkinson, J. W. 1964. *An introduction to motivation.* New York: Van Nostrand Reinhold.

Atkinson, J. W., Heyns, R. W. and Veroff, J. 1954. The effect of experimental arousal of the affiliation motive on thematic apperception. *Journal of Abnormal and Social Psychology, 49,* 405–410.

Baker, A. W. and Davis, R. C. 1954. *Ratios of staff to line employees and stages of differentiation of staff function.* Columbus: Ohio State University. Monograph No. 72.

Baker, B. 1954. Accuracy of social perceptions of psychopathic and nonpsychopathic prison inmates. Unpublished manuscript.

Baldamus, W. 1951. Type of work and motivation. *British Journal of Sociology, 2,* 44–58.

Bales, R. F. 1958. Task roles and social roles in problem-solving groups. In Maccoby, E., Newcomb, T. M., and Hartley, E. L. (eds.) *Readings in social psychology,* 3rd ed. New York: Holt, Rinehart and Winston, 437–447.

Bales, R. F. and Slater, P. E. 1955. Role differentiation in small decision making groups. In Parsons, T. and Bales, R. F. (eds.) *Family, socialization and interaction process.* New York: Free Press.

Bardand, E. J. 1973. Results of current investigations of disability among meatwrappers in the Portland Metropolitan area. University of Oregon Health Sciences Center.

Barker, R G. 1963. On the nature of the environment. *Journal of Social Issues, 19,* 17–38.

Barker, R. G. and Gump, P. V. 1964. *Big school, small school: high school size and student behavior.* Stanford, Calif.: Stanford University Press.

Barnard, C. 1938. *The functions of the executive.* Cambridge, Mass.: Harvard University Press.

Barnes, L. B. 1967. Organizational change and field experiment methods. In Vroom, V. H. (ed.) *Methods of organizational research.* Pittsburgh: University of Pittsburgh Press.

Barnett, A. D. and Vogel, E. F. 1967. *Cadres, bureaucracy and political power in Communist China.* New York: Columbia University Press.

Barnowe, J. T., Mangione, T. W., and Quinn, R. P. 1973. The relative importance of job facets as indicated by an empirically derived model of job satisfaction. In Quinn, R. P. and Mangione, T. W. (eds.) *The 1969–1970 survey of working conditions: chronicles of an unfinished enterprise.* Ann Arbor: Institute for Social Research, University of Michigan, 263–320.

Bass, A. R., Fiedler, F. E., and Krueger, S. March 1964. Personality correlates of assumed similarity (ASo) and related scores. Urbana, Ill.: Group Effectiveness Research Laboratory, (Mimeograph)

Bass, B. M. 1960. *Leadership, psychology, and organizational behavior.* New York: Harper.

Bass, B. M. and Dunteman, G. May 1963. Behavior in groups as a function of self, interaction, and task orientation. *Journal of Abnormal and Social Psychology, 66,* 419–428.

Bass, B. M. and Vaughn, J. A. 1966. *Training in industry: the management of learning.* Belmont, Calif.: Wadsworth.

Bassett, G. A. 1967. *A study of factors associated with turnover of exempt personnel.* Crotonville, N.Y.: Behavioral Research Service, General Electric Company.

Bauer, R. A. 1966 (ed.). *Social indicators.* Cambridge: Massachusetts Institute of Technology Press.

Baumgartel, H. and Jeanpierre, F. 1972. Applying new knowledge in the back-home setting: a study of Indian managers' adoptive efforts. *Journal of Applied Behavioral Science.* No. 6, 674–694.

Bay, C. 1958. *The structure of freedom.* Stanford, Calif.: Stanford University Press.

Becker, H. S. 1960. Notes on personal commitment. *American Journal of Sociology, 66,* 32–42.

Becker, H. S. and Carper, J. N. 1956. The development of identification with an occupation. *American Journal of Sociology, 61,* 289–298.

Beckhard, R. 1969. *Organizational development: strategies and models.* Reading, Mass.: Addison- Wesley.

Beer, M. 1976. The technology of organization development. In Dunnette, M. D. (ed.) *Handbook of industrial and organizational psychology.* Chicago: Rand McNally.

Belcher, D. W. and Atchison, T. J. 1976. Compensation for work. In Dubin, R. (ed.) *Handbook of work, organization, and society.* Chicago: Rand McNally.

Bell, H. M. 1937. *Youth tell their story.* Washington, D.C.: American Youth Commission.

Bellet, S., Roman, L., and Kostis, J. 1969. Effect of automobile driving on catecholamine and adrenocortical excretion. *American Journal of Cardiology, 24,* 365.

Bendix, R. 1956. *Work and authority in industry, ideologies of management in the course of industrialization.* New York: Wiley.

Benne, K. D. 1975. Conceptual and moral foundations of laboratory method. In Benne, K. D., Bradford, L. P., Gibb, J. R. and Lippitt, R. O. (eds.) *The laboratory method of changing and learning.* Palo Alto, Calif.: Science and Behavior Books.

Benne, K. D., Bradford, L. P., Gibb, J. R., and Lippitt, R. O. 1975. (eds.) *The Laboratory method of changing and learning.* Palo Alto, Calif.: Science and Behavior Books.

Bennett, E. B. 1955. Discussion, decision, commitment, and consensus in "group decision." *Human Relations, 8,* 251–273.

Bennis, W. G. 1966. *Changing organizations.* New York: McGraw-Hill.

Bennis, W. G. Fall 1970. An era of change: the consequences. *Midwest Research Institute Quarterly.*

Bennis, W. G. and Slater, P. E. 1968. *The temporary society.* New York: Harper and Row.

Berkowitz, L. 1962. *Aggression: a social psychological analysis.* New York: McGraw-Hill.

Berkowitz, L. 1963. Responsibility and dependency. *Journal of Abnormal and Social Psychology, 66,* 429–436.

Berlew, D. E. and Hall, D. T. 1966. The socialization of managers: effects of expectations on performance. *Administrative Science Quarterly, 11,* 207–223.

Berman, L. and Goodall, McC. 1960. Adrenaline, noradrenaline, and 3-methoxy-4-hydroxy-mandelic acid (MOMA) excretion following centrifugation and anticipation of centrifugation. *Federation Proceedings: Federation of American Societies for Experimental Biology, 19,* 154. Bethesda, Md. Cited by Raab, W. in Levi, L. (ed.) 1971. *Society, stress and disease,* Vol. I, *The Psycho-social environment and psychosomatic diseases.* London: Oxford University Press.

Bible, B. L. and Brown, E. J. 1963. Role consensus and satisfaction of extension advisory committee members. *Rural Sociology, 28,* 81–90.

Bible, B. L. and McComas, J. D. 1963. Role consensus and teacher effectiveness. *Social Forces, 42,* 225–233.

Biddle, B. J. and Thomas, E. J. (eds.) 1966. *Role theory: concepts and research.* New York: Wiley.

Blake, R. R. and Mouton, J. S. 1961. Reactions to intergroup competition under win-lose conditions. *Management Science, 7,* 420–435.

Blake, R. R. and Mouton, J. S. 1964. *The managerial grid.* Houston, Tex.: Gulf.

Blake, R. R. and Mouton, J. S. 1968. *Corporate excellence through grid organizational development.* Houston, Tex.: Gulf.

Blake, R. R. and Mouton, J. S. 1969. *Building a dynamic corporation through grid organization development.* Reading, Mass.: Addison-Wesley.

Blake, R. R., Shepard, H. A., and Mouton, J. S. 1964. *Managing intergroup conflict in industry.* Houston, Tex.: Gulf.

Blau, P. M. 1955. *The dynamics of bureaucracy.* Chicago: University of Chicago Press.

Blau, P. M. 1964. *Exchange and power in social life.* New York: Wiley.

Blau, P. M. 1970. A formal theory of differentiation in organizations. *American Sociological Review, 35,* 201–18.

Blau, P. M. and Schoenherr, R. A. 1971. *The structure of organizations.* New York: Basic Books.

Blau, P. M. and Scott, W. R. 1962. *Formal organizations.* San Francisco: Chandler.

Blauner, R. 1964. *Alienation and freedom: the factory worker and his industry.* Chicago: University of Chicago Press.

Blondel, J. 1963. *Voters, parties and leaders.* Hammondsworth, England: Penguin Books.

Blood, M. R. and Hulin, C. L. 1967. Alienation, environmental characteristics and worker responses. *Journal of Applied Psychology. 51,* 284–290.

Bogdonoff, M. D., Estes, E. H., Harlan, W. R., Trout, D. L., and Kirshner, N. 1960. Metabolic and cardiovascular changes during a state of acute central nervous system arousal. *Journal of Clinical Endocrinology, 20,* 1333.

Bohlinder, E. and Ohlstrom, B. 1971. *En enkatundersokning bland LO-medlemmarna rorande psykiska pafrestningar i arbetsmiljon.* Lund: Bokforlaget Prisma i samarbete med Landsorganisationen i Sverige.

Bond, B. W. 1956. The group-discussion-decision approach: an appraisal of its use in health education. *Dissertation Abstracts, 16,* 903–904.

Borre, O. and Katz, D. 1973. Party identification and its motivational base in a multiparty system: a study of the Danish general election of 1971. *Scandinavian Political Studies, 8,* 69–111.

Borus, M. E., Brennan, J. P., and Rosen, S. 1974. A benefit-cost analysis of neighborhood youth corps. In Hasenfeld, Y. and English, R. (eds.) *Human Service Organizations.* Ann Arbor: University of Michigan Press.

Boulding, K. 1953. Toward a general theory of growth. *Canadian Journal of Economic and Political Science, 19,* 326–340.

Boulding, K. E. 1956. General systems theory: the skeleton of science. *General Systems.* Yearbook of the Society for the Advancement of General System Theory, 1, 11–17.

Boulding, K. E. 1962. *Conflict and defense.* New York: Harper.

Bowers, D. G. January 1973. OD techniques and their results in 23 organizations: the Michigan ICL study. *Journal of Applied Behavioral Science, 9,* 21–43.

Bowers, D. G. 1975. *Navy manpower: values, practices and human resources requirements.* Ann Arbor, Mich.: Institute for Social Research, The University of Michigan.

Bowers, D. G. and Seashore, S. E. 1971. Changing the structure and functioning of an organization. In Evan, W. M. (ed.) *Organizational experiments: laboratory and field research.* New York: Harper & Row, 185–201.

Bradburn, N. M. 1969. *The structure of psychological well-being.* Chicago: Aldine.

Bradburn, N. M. and Caplovitz, D. 1965. *Reports on happiness.* Chicago: Aldine.

Bradford, L., Gibb, J., and Benne, K. (eds.) 1964. *T-group theory and laboratory method: innovation in re-education.* New York: Wiley.

Bradley, D. F. and Calvin, M. 1956. Behavior: imbalance in a network of chemical transformations. *General Systems.* Yearbook of the Society for the Advancement of General System Theory, 1, 56–65.

Braybrooke, D. and Lindblom, C. E. 1963. *A strategy of decision.* New York: The Free Press.

Brim, O. G. Jr. 1966. Socialization through the life cycle. In Brim, O. G., Jr. and Wheeler, S. (eds.) *Socialization after childhood.* New York: Wiley.

Brindisi, L. J., Jr. 1971. Survey of executive compensation. *World.* (Published by Peat, Marwick, Mitchell and Co.) 5, 53–56.

Brod, J. 1971. The influence of higher nervous processes induced by psychosocial environment on the development of essential hypertension. In Levi, L. (ed.) *Society, stress and disease,* (Vol. I). The psycho-social environment and psychosomatic diseases. London: Oxford University Press.

Brown, B. 1968. The effects of need to maintain face on interpersonal bargaining. *Journal of Experimental Social Psychology, 4,* 107–122.

Brown, W. 1960. *Exploration in management.* London: Heinemann.

Brown, G. W., Bhrolchain, M. N., and Harris, T. 1975. Social class and psychiatric disturbance among women in an urban population. *Sociology, 9,* 225–254.

Brummet, R. L., Flamholtz, E. G., and Pyle, W. C. 1968. Human resource measurement: a challenge for accountants. *The Accounting Review, 43,* 217–224.

Bryan, E. J. 1975. Work improvement and job enrichment: the case of Cummins Engine Co. In Davis, L. E. and Cherns, A. B. (eds.) *The quality of working life.* New York: Free Press. Vol. II, 315–329.

Buchanan, B. II. 1974. Building organizational commitment: the socialization of managers in work organizations. *Administrative Science Quarterly, 19,* 533–546.

Buchanan, P. C. 1969. Laboratory training and organization development. *Administrative Science Quarterly, 14,* 455–477.

Bullough, B. L. 1967. Alienation in the ghetto. *American Journal of Sociology, 72,* 469–478.

Burke, R. J. April 1970. Methods of managing superior-subordinate conflict: their effectiveness and consequences. *Canadian Journal of Behavioral Science, 2,* 124–135.

Burns, T. 1954. The direction of activity and communication in a departmental executive group. *Human Relations, 7,* 73–97.

Burns, T. and Stalker, G. M. 1961. *The management of innovation.* London: Tavistock.

Cahnman, W. J. and Heberle, R. (eds.) 1971. *Ferdinand Toennies on sociology: pure, applied and empirical: selected writings.* Chicago: University of Chicago Press.

Cammann, C. 1976. Effects of the use of control systems. *Accounting, Organizations and Society, 1,* 4, 301–313.

Campbell, A. and Converse, P. E. (eds.) 1972. *The human meaning of social change.* New York: Russell Sage Foundation.

Campbell, A., Converse, P. E., Miller, W. E., and Stokes, D. E. 1960. *The American voter.* New York: Wiley.

Campbell, A., Converse, P. E., and Rodgers, W. L. 1976. *The quality of American life.* New York: Russell Sage Foundation.

Campbell, J. F. 1971. *The foreign affairs fudge factory.* New York: Basic Books.

Campbell, J. P., Bownas, D. E., Peterson, M. G., and Dunnette, M. D. (eds.) 1974. *The measurement of organizational effectiveness: a review of relevant research and opinion.* San Diego: Navy Personnel Research and Development Center.

Campbell, J. P. and Dunnette, M. D. 1968. Effectiveness of T-group experiences in managerial training and development. *Psychological Bulletin, 70,* 73–104.

Cantril, H. 1965. *The pattern of human concerns.* New Brunswick, N.J.: Rutgers University Press.

Caplan, R. D. 1971. Organizational stress and individual strain: a socio-psychological study of risk factors in coronary heart disease among administrators, engineers, and scientists (doctoral dissertation, University of Michigan). *Dissertation Abstracts International,* 1972, *32,* 6706b–6707b (University Microfilms, 72-14822).

Caplan, R. D., Cobb, S., French, J. R. P., Jr., Harrison, R. D., and Pinneau, S. R., Jr. 1975. *Job demands and worker health: main effects and occupational differences.* Washington, D.C.: U.S. Government Printing Office.

Caplow, T. 1964. *Principles of organization.* New York: Harcourt Brace Jovanovich.

Carlson, E. R. 1956. Attitude change through modification of attitude structure. *Journal of Abnormal and Social Psychology, 52,* 256–261.

Carter, L., Haythorn, W., and Howell, M. 1950. A further investigation of the criteria of leadership. *Journal of Abnormal and Social Psychology, 45,* 350–358.

Carter, L., Haythorn, W., Shriver, B., and Lanzetta, J. 1951. The behavior of leaders and other group members. *Journal of Abnormal and Social Psychology, 46,* 589–595.

Carter, L. and Nixon, M. 1949. An investigation of the relationship between four criteria of leadership ability for three different tasks. *Journal of Psychology, 27,* 245–261.

Cartwright, D. 1949. Some principles of mass persuasion. *Human Relations, 2,* 253–267.

Cartwright, D. (ed.) 1959. *Studies in social power.* Ann Arbor, Mich.: Institute for Social Research.

Cartwright, D. 1965. Influence, leadership, and control. In March, J. D. (ed.) *Handbook of organizations.* Chicago: Rand McNally.

Cartwright, D. and Zander, A. (eds.) 1960. *Group dynamics: research and theory,* 2nd ed. Evanston, Ill.: Row, Peterson.

Cass, E. L. and Zimmer, F. G. 1975. *Man and work in society.* New York: Van Nostrand Reinhold.

Cattell, J. McK. 1890. Mental tests and measurements. *Mind, 15,* 373–380.

Cattell, R. B. 1951. New concepts for measuring leadership, in terms of group syntality. *Human Relations, 4,* 161–184.

Cattell, R. B. and Eber, H. W. 1964. *Handbook for the sixteen factor personality questionnaire.* Champaign, Ill.: Institute for Personality and Ability Testing.

Centers, R. and Bugental, D. E. 1966. Intrinsic and extrinsic job motivation among different segments of the working population. *Journal of Applied Psychology, 50,* 193–197.

Chapanis, A. 1970. Relevance of physiological and psychological criteria to man-machine systems: the present state of the art. *Ergonomics, 13,* 337–346.

Chapanis, A. 1976. Engineering psychology. In Dunnette, M. D. (ed.) *Handbook of industrial and organizational psychology.* Chicago: Rand McNally.

Cheney, J., Harford, T., and Solomon, L. Effects of communicating threats and promises upon the bargaining process. *Journal of Conflict Resolution, 16,* 99–107.

Child, J. 1973(a). Predicting and understanding organization structure. *Administrative Science Quarterly, 18,* 168–185.

Child, J. 1973(b). Parkinson's progress: accounting for the number of specialists in organization. *Administrative Science Quarterly, 18,* 328–348.

Clemedson, C. J. 1971. Physiological and psychological reactions in man during exposure to an extreme environment. In Levi, L. (ed.) *Society, stress and disease,* Vol. I, *The psycho-social environment and psychosomatic diseases.* London: Oxford University Press.

Cline, V. B. 1964. Interpersonal perception. In Maher, B. (ed.) *Progress in experimental personality research.* Vol. I. New York: Academic Press. 221–284.

Cline, V. B. and Richards, J. M., Jr. 1960. Accuracy of international perception: a general trait? *Journal of Abnormal and Social Psychology, 60,* 1–7.

Cobb, S. December 1973. Workload and coronary heart disease. *Proceedings, Social Statistics Section,* American Statistical Association.

Cobb, S. 1974. Physiological changes in men whose jobs were abolished. *Journal of Psychosomatic Research, 18,* 245–258.

Cobb, S. 1974. Role responsibility: the differentiation of a concept. In McLean, A. (ed.) *Occupational Stress.* Springfield, Ill.: Thomas.

Cobb, S. 1976. Social support as a moderator of life stress. *Psychosomatic Medicine,* Vol. 3, 5, 300–314.

Coch, L. and French, J. R. P., Jr. 1948. Overcoming resistance to change. *Human Relations, 1,* 512–533.

Cohen, A. M. 1962. Changing small group communication networks. *Administrative Science Quarterly, 6,* 443–462.

Cohen, A. M. 1964. Predicting organization in changed communication networks: III. *Journal of Psychology, 58,* 115–129.

Cohen, A. M., Robinson, E. L., and Edwards, J. L. 1969. Experiments in organizational embeddedness. *Administrative Science Quarterly, 14,* 208–221.

Cohen, A. R. 1959. Situational structure, self-esteem, and threat-oriented reactions to power. In Cartwright, D. (ed.) *Studies in social power.* Ann Arbor, Mich.: Institute for Social Research.

Cohen, E. 1954. *Human behavior in the concentration camp.* London: Jonathan Cape.

Cohen, H. L. and Filipczak, J. 1971. *A new learning environment.* San Francisco: Jossey-Bass.

Collins, B. E. and Guetzkow, H. 1964. *A social psychology of group processes for decision making.* New York: Wiley.

Conference Board. 1972. *Salesmen's turnover in early employment.* New York: The Conference Board.

Converse, P. E. 1969. Of time and partisan stability. *Comparative Political Studies II, 2.*

Converse, P. E. 1975. Public opinion and voting behavior. In Greenstein, F. and Polsby, N. W. (eds.) *Handbook of political science,* Vol. 4, Reading, Mass., Addison Wesley, 75–169.

Converse, P. E. 1976. *The dynamics of party shift: cohort analyzing party identification.* Beverly Hills, Calif.: Sage Publications.

Cooley, C. H. (rev. ed. 1922). *Human nature and the social order.* New York: Scribner.

Corson, S. A. 1971. Pavlovian and operant conditioning techniques in the study of psycho-social and biological relationships. In Levi, L. (ed.) *Society, stress and disease,* Vol. 1, *The psycho-social environment and psychosomatic diseases.* London: Oxford University Press, 7–21.

Coser, L. 1956. *The functions of social conflict.* New York: Free Press.

Cronbach, L. J. and Gleser, G. C. 1965. *Psychological tests and personal decisions.* (2nd ed.) Urbana: University of Illinois Press.

Crozier, M. 1965. *LeMonde des employés de bureau.* Paris: LeSeiul.

Cunningham, C. 1962. The effects of sensory impoverishment, confinement and sleep deprivation. *Journal of British Interplanetary Society, 17,* 311–313.

Cyert, R. M. and March, J. G. 1963. *A behavioral theory of the firm.* Englewood Cliffs, N.J.: Prentice-Hall.

Dachler, H. P. and Hulin, C. L. 1969. A reconsideration of the relationship between satisfaction and judged importance of environmental and job characteristics. *Organizational Behavior and Human Performance, 4,* 252–266.

Dahrendorf, R. 1958. Toward a theory of social conflict. *Journal of Conflict Resolution, 2,* 170–183.

Dahrendorf, R. 1959. *Class and class conflict in industrial society.* Stanford, Calif.: Stanford University Press.

Dai, B. 1955. A socio-psychiatric approach to personality organization. In Rose, A. (ed.) *Mental health and mental disorder.* New York: Norton, 314–324.

Danserau, F. Jr., Graen, G. and Haga, W. J. 1975. A vertical dyad linkage approach to leadership within formal organizations: a longitudinal investigation of the role-making process. *Organizational Behavior and Human Performance, 13,* 46–78.

Davis, K. 1953. Management communication and the grapevine. *Harvard Business Review, 31,* 43–49.

Davis, L. E. 1966. The design of jobs. *Industrial Relations, 6,* 1, 21–45.

Davis, L. E. 1976. Current developments in job design. In Warr, P. (ed.) *Personal goals and work design.* London: Wiley.

Davis, L. E. and Cherns, A. B. 1975. *The quality of working life,* Vols. 1 and 2. New York: Free Press.

Davis, L. E. and Taylor, J. C. (eds.) 1972. *Design of jobs: selected readings.* Harmondsworth, Middlesex, England: Penguin.

Dawes, R. M. April 1975. Shallow psychology. Paper presented at Eleventh Annual Carnegie Symposium on Cognition. Carnegie-Mellon University.

Dean, R. 1966. Human stress in space. *Science, 2,* 70.

Dearborn, D. C. and Simon, H. A. 1958. Selective perception: a note on the departmental identifications of executives. *Sociometry, 21,* 140–144.

Denhardt, R. B. 1970. Bureaucratic socialization and organizational accommodation. *Administrative Science Quarterly, 13,* 3, 441–450.

Derber, M. May 1977. Collective bargaining: the American approach to industrial democracy. *The Annals of the American Academy of Political and Social Science,* Vol. 431, 83–94.

Deutsch, M. 1949. A theory of cooperation and competition. *Human Relations, 2,* 129–152.

Deutsch, M. 1969. Conflicts: productive and destructive. *Journal of Social Issues, 25,* 7–41.

Deutsch, M. 1971. Toward an understanding of conflict. *International Journal of Group Tensions, 1,* 42–54.

Deutsch, M. 1973. *The resolution of conflict.* New Haven, Conn: Yale University Press.

Deutsch, M., Canavan, D., and Rubin J. 1969. The effects of size of conflict and sex of experimenter on interpersonal bargaining. *Journal of Experimental Social Psychology, 7,* 258–267.

Deutsch, M. and Krauss, R. M. 1962. Studies in interpersonal bargaining. *Journal of Conflict Resolution, 6,* 52–76.

Deutsch, M. and Solomon, L. 1959. Reactions to evaluations by others as influenced by self-evaluation. *Sociometry, 22,* 93–121.

Dewey, J. 1933. *How we think.* New York: D. C. Heath.

Doll, R. and Jones, F. A. 1951. Occupational factors in aetiology of gastric and duodenal ulcers. *Medical Research Council, Special Report Series, 276,* London: HMSO.

Dornbusch, S. 1955. The military academy as an assimilating institution. *Social Forces, 33,* 316–321.

Driver, M. J. and Streufert, S. 1964. The 'general incongruity adaptation level' (GIAL) hypothesis: An analysis and integration of cognitive approaches to motivation. Institute Paper No. 114, Institute for Research in the Behavioral, Economic, and Management Sciences, Krannert Graduate School of Industrial Administration, Lafayette, Ind.: Purdue University.

Drucker, P. F. 1946. *The concept of the corporation.* New York: John Day. Reprinted 1960, Boston: Beacon Press.

Dubin, R. 1951. *Human relations in administration.* Englewood Cliffs, N.J.: Prentice-Hall.

Dubin, R. 1956. Industrial workers' worlds: a study of the "central life interests" of industrial workers. *Social Problems, 3,* 131–142.

Dubin, R. June 1957. Industrial conflict and social welfare. *Journal of Conflict Resolution, 1,* 179–199.

Dubin, R. 1959. Stability of human organizations. In Haire, M. (ed.) *Modern organization theory.* New York: Wiley. 218–253.

Dubin, R. 1973. Work and non-work institutional perspectives. In Dunnette, M. D. (ed.) *Work and non-work in the year 2001,* 53–68. Monterey, Calif.: Brooks, Cole.

Dubin, R. (ed.) 1976. *Handbook of work, organization, and society.* Chicago: Rand McNally.

Dubin, R., Champoux, J. E., and Porter, L. W. 1975. Central life interests and organizational commitment of blue-collar and clerical workers. *Administrative Science Quarterly, 20,* 411–421.

Dubin, R. and Goldman, D. R. 1972. Central life interests of American middle managers and specialists. *Journal of Vocational Behavior, 2,* 133–141.

Dunlop, J. T. 1958. *Industrial relations systems.* New York: Holt, Rinehart and Winston.

Durkheim, E. 1947. *Division of labor in society.* New York: Free Press.

Dutton, J. M. and Walton, R. E. 1966. Interdepartmental conflict and cooperation: two contrasting studies. *Human Organization, 25,* 207–220.

Dunnette, M. D. (ed.) 1976. *Handbook of industrial and organizational psychology.* Chicago: Rand McNally.

Dunnette, M. D., Arvey, R., and Banas, P. 1969. Why do they leave? Cited by Porter and Steers. *Psychological Bulletin, 80,* 2, 153.

Eagly, A. H. 1970. Leadership style and role differentiation as determinants of group effectiveness. *Journal of Personnel, 38,* 509–524.

Easton, D. 1961. The analysis of political systems. In Macrides, R. C. and Brown, B. E. (eds.) *Comparative politics.* Homewood, Ill: Dorsey, 81–94.

Easton, D. 1965. *A systems analysis of political life.* New York: Wiley.

Edgren, J. and Rhenman, E. 1970. *Lon och effektivitet. Om loneadministration for produktionsarbete.* Stockholm: Svenska Arbetsgivareforeningen.

Egbert, L. D., Battit, G. E., Welch, C. E., and Bartlett, M. K. 1964. Reduction of post-operative pain by encouragement and instruction of patients. *New England Journal of Medicine, 270,* 825–827.

Emery, F. E. (ed.) 1969. *Systems thinking.* Harmondsworth, Middlesex, England: Penguin.

Emery, F. E. and Thorsrud, E. 1969. *Form and content of industrial democracy.* London: Tavistock (Published in Norway in 1964).

Emery, F. E. and Trist, E. L. 1960. Socio-technical systems. In *Management science models and techniques.* Vol. 2. London: Pergamon.

Emery, F. E. and Trist, E. L. 1965. The causal texture of organizational environments. *Human Relations, 18,* 21–32.

Emery, F. E. and Trist, E. L. 1973. *Toward a social ecology.* New York: Plenum.

Endler, N. S. 1966. Conformity as a function of different reinforcement schedules. *Journal of Personality and Social Psychology, 4,* 175–180.

Erasmus, C. J. 1961. *Man takes control.* Minneapolis: University of Minnesota Press.

Erikson, E. H. 1958. *Young man Luther: a study in psychoanalysis and history.* New York: Norton.

Etzioni, A. 1975. *A comparative analysis of complex organizations.* New York: Free Press, Rev. Ed. First edition, 1961.

Evan, W. M. 1966. The organization-set: toward a theory of interorganizational relations. In Thompson, J. D. (ed.) *Approaches to organizational design.* Pittsburgh: University of Pittsburgh Press.

Evan, W. M. (ed.) 1971. *Organizational experiments: laboratory and field research.* New York: Harper and Row.

Fein, M. 1976. Motivation for work. In Dubin, R. (ed.) *Handbook of work, organization, and society.* Chicago: Rand McNally.

Festinger, L., Schachter, S., and Back, K. 1950. *Social pressures in informal groups.* New York: Harper.

Fiedler, F. E. 1958. *Leader attitudes and group effectiveness.* Urbana: University of Illinois Press.

Fiedler, F. E. 1967. *A theory of leadership effectiveness.* New York: McGraw-Hill.

Fisher, R. 1964. Fractionating conflict. In Fisher, R. (ed.) *International conflict and behavioral science: The Craigville papers.* New York: Basic Books.

Fleishman, E. A. and Harris, E. F. 1962. Patterns of leadership behavior related to employee grievances and turnover. *Personnel Psychology, 15,* 43–56.

Fleishman, E. A., Harris, E. F., and Burtt, H. E. 1955. *Leadership and supervision in industry.* Research Monograph No. 33, Columbus: Ohio State University, Bureau of Educational Research.

Fleishman, E. A. and Peters, D. R. 1962. Interpersonal values, leadership attitudes and managerial success. *Personnel Psychology, 15,* 127–143.

Follett, M. P. 1941. In Metcalf, H. S. and Urwick, L. (eds.) *Dynamic administration: The collected papers of Mary Parker Follett.* New York: Harper and Row.

Ford, R. N. 1971. A prescription for job enrichment success. In Maher, J. R. (ed.) *New perspectives in job enrichment.* London: Van Nostrand Reinhold.

Ford, R. N. 1973. Job enrichment lessons from AT&T. *Harvard Business Review*, 51, 96–106.

Frankenhaeuser, M. 1971. Experimental approaches to the study of human behavior as related to neuro-endocrine functions. In Levi, L. (ed.) *Society, stress and disease*, Vol. I, *The psycho-social environment and psychosomatic diseases*. London: Oxford University Press, 22–35.

Frankenhaeuser, M. and Patkai, P. 1964. Inter-individual differences in catecholamine excretion during stress. *Scandinavian Journal of Psychology*, 6, 117–123.

Free, L. and Cantril, H. 1967. *Political beliefs of Americans*, New Brunswick, N.J.: Rutgers University Press.

Freeman, J. H. 1973. Environment, technology and the administrative intensity of manufacturing organizations. *American Sociological Review*, 38, 750–763.

French, J. R. P., Jr., 1974. Person-role fit. In McLean, A. *Occupational stress*. Springfield, Ill.: Thomas.

French, J. R. P., Jr., and Caplan, R. D. 1973. Organizational stress and individual strain. In Marrow, A. J. (ed.) *The failure of success*. New York: Amacom (American Management Association).

French, J. R. P., Jr., Israel, J. and Aas, D. 1960. An experiment on participation in a Norwegian factory. *Human Relations*, 13, 3–19.

French, J. R. P., Jr. and Kahn, R. L. 1962. A programmatic approach to studying the industrial environment and mental health. *The Journal of Social Issues*, 18, 3, 1–47.

French, J. R. P., Jr., and Raven, B. H. 1960. The bases of social power. In Cartwright, D. and Zander, A. (eds.) *Group dynamics: research and theory*, 2nd. ed. New York: Row, Peterson, 607–623.

French, J. R. P., Jr., Rodgers, W. L. and Cobb, S. 1974. Adjustment as person-environment fit. In Coelho, G., Hamburg, D., and Adams, J. (eds.) *Coping and adaptation*. New York: Basic Books.

French, J. R. P., Jr., Tupper, C. J., and Mueller, E. F. 1965. *Workload of University Professors*. Ann Arbor, Mich.: Institute for Social Research.

French, J. R. P., Jr., and Zander, A. 1949. The group dynamics approach. *Psychological labor-management relations*, Industrial Relations Research Association, 71–80.

French, R. L. 1965. The Motorola case. *The Industrial Psychologist*, 2, 20–50.

Frey, R. L. 1971. The interlocking effects of intergroup behavior and intragroup conflict on the bargaining behavior of representatives. Doctoral dissertation, University of North Carolina.

Frey, R. L., Jr. and Adams, J. S. 1972. The negotiator's dilemma: Simultaneous in-group and out-group conflict. *Journal of Experimental Social Psychology*, 4, 331–341.

Friedlander, F. and Pickle, H. 1968. Components of effectiveness in small organizations. *Administrative Science Quarterly*, 13, 289–304.

Friedlander, F. and Walton, R. E. 1964. Positive and negative motivations toward work. *Administrative Science Quarterly*, 9, 194–207.

Friedman, M. and Rosenman, R. H. 1959. Association of specific covert patterns with blood and cardiovascular findings. *Journal of the American Medical Association,* 169, 1286–1296.

Friedman, M., Rosenman, R. H., and Carroll, V. 1958. Changes in the serum cholesterol and blood clotting time in men subjected to cyclic variation of occupational stress. *Circulation,* 18, 852–861.

Friedrich, C. J. 1940. Public policy and the nature of administrative responsibility. In Friedrich, C. J. and Mason, E. S. (eds.) *Public policy, Yearbook of the Graduate School of Public Administration.* Cambridge, Mass.: Harvard University Press.

Frost, C. F., Wakely, J. H., and Ruh, R. A. 1974. *The Scanlon Plan for organizational development: identity, participation and equity.* Lansing, Mich.: Michigan State University Press.

Gage, N. L. 1953. Accuracy of social perception and effectiveness in interpersonal relationships. *Journal of Personality,* 22, 128–141.

Galbraith, J. 1973. *Designing complex organizations.* Reading, Mass.: Addison-Wesley.

Galbraith, J. and Cummings, L. L. 1967. An empirical investigation of the motivational determinants of task performance: interactive effects between instrumentality-valence and motivation-ability. *Organizational Behavior and Human Performance,* 2, 237–257.

Galbraith, J. K. 1958. *The affluent society,* Boston: Houghton, Mifflin.

Galbraith, J. K. 1967. *The new industrial state.* Boston: Houghton, Mifflin.

Gamson, W. A. 1968. *Power and discontent.* Homewood, Ill.: Dorsey Press.

Ganguli, H. C. 1954. An inquiry into incentives for workers in an engineering factory. *Indian Journal of Social Work,* 15, 30–40.

Gardell, B. 1971. Alienation and mental health in the modern industrial environment. In Levi, L. (ed.) *Society, stress and disease,* Vol. I, *The psychosocial environment and psychosomatic diseases.* London: Oxford University Press, 146–166.

Gardell, B. 1976. Arbetsinnehåll och livskvalitet. Prisma, Stockholm.

Geiger, T. and Hansen, R. D. 1968. The role of information in decision making on foreign aid. In Bauer, R. A. and Gergen, K. S. (eds.) *The study of policy formation.* New York: Free Press, 329–380.

George, A. L. 1967. *The Chinese Communist Army in action.* New York: Columbia University Press.

George, J. R. and Bishop, L. K. 1971. Relationship of organizational structure and teacher personality characteristics to organizational climate. *Administrative Science Quarterly,* 16, 467–475.

Georgopoulos, B. S. 1970. An open-system theory model for organizational research: the case of the contemporary general hospital. In Negandhi, A. R. and Schwitter, J. P. (eds.) *Organizational Behavior Models.* Kent, Ohio: Kent State University, 33–70.

Georgopoulos, B. S. 1975. *Hospital organization research: review and source book.* Philadelphia: W. B. Saunders.

Georgopoulos, B. S., Mahoney, G. M. and Jones, N. W. 1957. A path-goal approach to productivity. *Journal of Applied Psychology,* 41, 345–353.

Georgopoulos, B. S. and Mann, F. C. 1962. *The Community general hospital.* New York: Macmillan.

Georgopoulos, B. S. and Matejko, A. 1967. The American general hospital as a complex social system. *Health Services Research, 2,* 76–112.

Getzels, J. W. 1969. A social psychology of education, in Lindzey, G. and Aronson, E. (eds.) *The handbook of social psychology,* Vol. 5, Reading, Mass.: Addison-Wesley, 459–537.

Getzels, J. W. and Guba, E. G. 1954. Role, role conflict and effectiveness: an empirical study. *American Sociological Review, 19,* 164–175.

Gibb, C. A. 1954. Leadership. In Lindzey, G. (ed.) *Handbook of social psychology,* Vol. 2. Cambridge, Mass.: Addison-Wesley, 877–920.

Gibb, J. R. 1975. A research perspective of the laboratory method. In Benne, K. D., Bradford, L. P., Gibb, J. R., and Lippitt, R. O. (eds.) *The laboratory method of changing and learning.* Palo Alto, Calif.: Science and Behavior Books.

Goffman, E. 1961. *Asylums.* Garden City, N.Y.: Doubleday.

Goldberg, L. R. 1968. Simple models or simple processes? Some research on clinical judgments. *American Psychologist, 23,* 483–496.

Gore, S. 1973. *The influence of social support and related variables in ameliorating the consequences of job loss.* Ph.D. dissertation, Philadelphia: University of Pennsylvania.

Gorman, L. and Malloy, E. 1972. *People, jobs, and organizations.* Dublin: Irish Management Institute.

Gosling, R H. 1958. Peptic ulcer and mental disorder. *Journal of Psychosomatic Research, 2,* 285.

Gough, H. G. 1948. A sociological theory of psychotherapy. *American Journal of Sociology, 53,* 359–366.

Gough, H. G. and Peterson, D. R. 1952. The identification and measurement of predispositional factors in crime and delinquency. *Journal of Consulting Psychology, 16,* 207–212.

Gouldner, A. W. 1954. *Patterns of industrial bureaucracy.* New York: Free Press.

Gouldner, A. W. 1959. Organizational dynamics in Merton, R. K., et al. (eds.) *Sociology Today,* New York: Basic Books.

Gouldner, A. W. 1960. The norm of reciprocity: a preliminary statement. *American Sociological Review, 25,* 161–179.

Graen, G. 1976. Role-making processes in organizations. In Dunnette, M. D. (ed.) *Handbook of industrial and organizational psychology.* Chicago: Rand McNally.

Graen, G., Orris, J. B., and Johnson, T. 1973. Role assimilation processes in a complex organization. *Journal of Vocational Behavior, 3,* 395–420.

Greenspoon, J. 1955. The reinforcing effect of two spoken sounds on the frequency of two responses. *American Journal of Psychology, 68,* 409–416.

Gross, B. M. 1966. The state of the nation: Social systems accounting. In Bauer, R. A. (ed.) *Social Indicators.* Cambridge, Mass.: Massachusetts Institute of Technology Press, 154–271.

Gross, N., Mason, W. and McEachern, A. W. 1958. *Explorations in role analysis: studies of the school superintendency role.* New York: Wiley.

Gruder, D. L. 1968. Effects of perception of opponent's bargaining style and accountability to opponent and partner on interpersonal, mixed motive bargaining. Doctoral dissertation. University of North Carolina at Chapel Hill.

Guetzkow, H. 1965. Communication in organizations. In March, J. G. (ed.) *Handbook of organizations*. Chicago: Rand McNally, 534–573.

Guetzkow, H. and Dill, W. R. 1957. Factors in the organizational development of task-oriented groups. *Sociometry, 20,* 175–204.

Guetzkow, H. and Simon, H. A. 1955. The impact of certain communication nets upon organization and performance in task-oriented groups. *Management Science, 1,* 233–250.

Guion, R. M. 1976. The practice of industrial and organizational psychology. In Dunnette, M. D. (ed.) *Handbook of industrial and organizational psychology.* Chicago: Rand McNally.

Guion, R. M. 1976. Recruiting, selection, and job replacement. In Dunnette, M. D. (ed.) *Handbook of industrial and organizational psychology.* Chicago: Rand McNally.

Gulick, L. and Urwick, L. (eds.) 1937. *Papers on the science of administration.* New York: Institute of Public Administration.

Gumpert, P., Deutsch, M., and Epstein, Y. 1969. Effects of incentive magnitude on cooperation in the Prisoner's Dilemma Game. *Journal of Personality and Social Psychology, 11,* 66–69.

Gupta, N. and Quinn, R. P. 1973. The mirage of trade-offs among job facets. In Quinn, R. P. and Mangione, T. W. (eds.) *The 1969–1970 Survey of working conditions: Chronicles of an unfinished enterprise.* Ann Arbor: Institute for Social Research, University of Michigan, 321–334.

Gurel, L. 1976. The human side of evaluating human services programs: problems and prospects. In Guttentag, M. and Struening, E. L. (eds.) *Handbook of research evaluation.* Beverly Hills: Sage Publications, Vol. 2, 11–28.

Gurin, G., Veroff, J. and Feld, S. 1960. *Americans view their mental health.* New York: Basic Books.

Gurin, P. and Epps, E. 1975. *Black consciousness, identity and achievement: a study of students in historically black colleges.* New York: Wiley.

Gurin, P., Gurin, G., Lao, R. C., and Beattie, M. 1969. Internal-external control in the motivational dynamics of Negro youth. *Journal of Social Issues, 25,* 3, 29–53.

Gutek, B. A. K. 1975. *Social system and psychological contexts of support for the political system.* Doctoral dissertation, University of Michigan.

Guttormsson, U. and Smith, R. Juni 1971. *Attityder till premielon inom Post-Banken Rapport till Statsjanstemannaforbundet,* Stockholm.

Haas, E., Hall, R. H., and Johnson, N. J. 1963. The size of the supportive component in organizations. *Social Forces, 42,* 9–17.

Haas, J. E. and Drabek, T. E. 1970. Community disaster and system stress: a sociological perspective. In McGrath, J. E. (ed.) *Social and psychological factors in stress.* New York: Holt, Rinehart and Winston, 264–286.

Haber, L. D. 1971. Disabling effects of chronic disease and impairment. *Journal of Chronic Diseases, 24,* 482 ff.

Hackman, J. R. and Lawler, E. E. 1971. Employee reactions to job characteristics. *Journal of Applied Psychology, 55,* 259–286.

Hage, J. 1974. *Communication and organizational control: Cybernetics in health and welfare settings.* New York: Wiley.

Hage, J., Aiken, M., and Marrett, C. B. 1971. Organizational structure and communication. *American Sociological Review, 35,* 860–71.

Hahn, D. L. 1977. The importance of pay. In Quinn, R. et al. (eds.) *The 1972–1973 quality of employment survey: continuing chronicles of an unfinished enterprise.* Ann Arbor, Mich.: Survey Research Center, University of Michigan.

Haire, M. 1959. Biological models and empirical histories of the growth of organizations. In Haire, M. (ed.) *Modern organization theory.* New York: Wiley, 272–306.

Haire, M., Ghiselli, E. E. and Porter, L. W. 1966. *Managerial thinking: an international study.* New York: Wiley.

Hall, D. T. and Schneider, B. 1972. Correlates of organizational identification as a function of career pattern and organizational type. *Administrative Science Quarterly, 17,* 340–350.

Hall, D. T., Schneider, B., and Nygren, H. T. 1970. Personal factors in organizational identification. *Administrative Science Quarterly, 15,* 176–190.

Hall, J. November 1971. Decisions, decisions, decisions. *Psychology Today, 5,* 51–54, 85–87.

Hall, R. H. and Tittle, C. 1966. A note on bureaucracy and its correlates. *American Journal of Sociology, 72,* 267–272.

Halperin, S. 1974. Comment on Congress, information and policy making for postsecondary education: "Don't trouble with the facts." (Wolanin, T. R.) *Policy Studies Journal, 4,* 394–399.

Halpin, A. and Winer, B. 1957. A factorial study of the leader behavior descriptions. In Stogdill, R. and Coons, A. (eds.) *Leader behavior: its description and measurement.* Columbus: Bureau of Business Research, Ohio State University.

Halpin, A. U. 1954. The leadership behavior and combat performance of airplane commanders. *Journal of Abnormal and Social Psychology, 49,* 19–32.

Hamburg, D. A. 1962. Plasma and urinary corticoid levels in naturally occurring psychological stresses, in ultrastructure and metabolism of the nervous system. *Association for Research of Nervous Disease Processes, 25,* 406.

Hammond, K. R. and Adelman, L. 1976. Science, values and human judgment. *Science, 194,* 389–396.

Hamr, V. 1956. Hypertense u zeleznicaru (Hypertension in railway personnel). *Pracov. Lek, 8,* 126. (Cited by Brod) In Levi, L. (ed.) *Society, stress and disease,* Vol. 1, *The psycho-social environment and psychosomatic diseases.* London: Oxford University Press.

Hardin, G. 1968. The tragedy of the commons. *Science, 162,* 1243.

Hasenfeld, Y. and English, R. A. 1974. *Human service organizations.* Ann Arbor: University of Michigan Press.

Hausser, D. L., Pecorella, P. A. and Wissler, A. L. 1975. *Survey guided development: a manual for consultants.* Ann Arbor, Mich.: Institute for Social Research.

Havelock, R. G. 1972. *Knowledge utilization and dissemination: a bibliography.* (rev. ed.) Ann Arbor, Mich.: Institute for Social Research.

Havighurst, R. J. 1967. The social and educational implications of interinstitutional cooperation in higher education. In Howard, L. C. (ed.) *Interinstitutional cooperation in higher education*. Milwaukee: Institute of Human Relations, University of Wisconsin, 508–523.

Hayes, C. J. H. 1926. *Essays on nationalism*. New York: Macmillan.

Hebb, D. O. 1958. *A textbook of psychology*. Philadelphia: Saunders.

Hebden, J. E. 1975. Patterns of work identification. *Sociology of Work and Occupations, 2,* 107–132.

Heberle, R. 1968. "Tönnies, Ferdinand." In Sills, D. L. (ed.) *International encyclopedia of the social sciences*. New York: Macmillan and Free Press, Vol. 16, 98–103.

Heise, G. A. and Miller, G. A. 1951. Problem solving by small groups using various communication nets. *Journal of Abnormal and Social Psychology, 46,* 327–335.

Hendershot, G. E. and James, T. F. 1972. Size and growth as determinants of administration-production ratios in organizations. *American Sociological Review, 37,* 149–53.

Herbst, P. G. 1962. *Autonomous group functioning*. London: Tavistock Publications.

Hermanson, R. H. 1964. *Accounting for human assets*. East Lansing: Michigan State University, Bureau of Business and Economic Research.

Hersey, J. 1959. *The war lover*. New York: Knopf.

Hertog, J. F. den and Vries, H. J. J. de. 1977. *Breaking the deadlock*. Eindhoven, Netherlands: Philips' Gloeilampenfabrieken.

Herzberg, F. 1966. *Work and the nature of man*. Cleveland: World Publishing Co.

Herzberg, F. 1968. "One more time: how do you motivate employees?" *Harvard Business Review, 46,* 53–62.

Herzberg, F., Mausner, B., Peterson, R. O. and Capwell, D. F. 1957. *Job attitudes: review of research and opinion*. Pittsburgh: Psychological Services of Pittsburgh.

Hickson, D. J., Pugh, D. S. and Pheysey, D. 1969. Operations technology and organization structure: an empirical reappraisal. *Administrative Science Quarterly, 14,* 378–397.

Hilton, E. T. and Lumsdaine, A. A. 1975. Field trial designs in gauging the impact of family planning programs. In Bennett, C. A. and Lumsdaine, A. A. (eds.) *Evaluation and experiment*. New York: Academic Press, 319–408.

Hinrichs, J. R. 1976. Personnel training. In Dunnette, M. D. (ed.) *Handbook of industrial and organizational psychology*. Chicago: Rand McNally.

Hinton, B. L. and Barrow, J. C. 1976. Personality correlates of the reinforcement propensities of leaders. *Personnel Psychology, 29,* 61–66.

Hoffman, C. 1964. Work incentives in Communist China. *Industrial Relations, 3,* 2, 881.

Hoffman, L. R. and Maier, N. R. F. March 1961. Quality and acceptance of problem solutions by members of homogeneous and heterogeneous groups. *Journal of Abnormal and Social Psychology, 62,* 401–407.

Hoffman, S. 1968. *Gulliver's troubles or the setting of American foreign policy*. New York: McGraw-Hill.

Hollander, E. P. 1964. *Leaders, groups, and influence*. New York: Oxford University Press.

Hollander, E. P. and Julian, J. W. 1969. Contemporary trends in the analysis of the leadership process. *Psychological Bulletin, 71,* 387–397.

Hollingshead, A. B. and Redlich, F. C. 1958. *Social class and mental illness.* New York: Wiley.

Holmes, J. G. 1971. The effects of the structure of intragroup and intergroup conflict on the behavior of representatives. Unpublished doctoral dissertation. University of North Carolina at Chapel Hill.

Holmes, T. H. and Rahe, R. H. 1967. The social readjustment scale. *Journal of Psychosomatic Research, 11,* 213–218.

Holmes, T. H., Joffe, J. R., Ketcham, J. W., et al. 1961. Experimental study of prognosis. *Journal of Psychosomatic Research, 5,* 235–252.

Homans, G. C. 1958. Social behavior as exchange. *American Journal of Sociology, 63,* 597–606.

Hoppe F. 1930. Erfolg und Misserfolg. *Psychologische Forschung, 14,* 1–62.

Hoppock, R. 1935. *Job satisfaction.* New York: Harper.

Horsfall, A. B. and Arensberg, C. M. 1949. Teamwork and productivity in a shoe factory. *Human Organization, 8,* 13–25.

Horwitz, M. 1954. The recall of interrupted group tasks: an experimental study of individual motivation in relation to group goals. *Human Relations, 7,* 3–38.

House, R. J. 1967. T-group education and leadership effectiveness. *Personnel Psychology, 20,* 1–32.

Hughes, E. C. 1958. *Men and their work.* Glencoe, Ill.: Free Press.

Hulin, C. L. 1966. Job satisfaction and turnover in a female clerical population. *Journal of Applied Psychology, 50,* 280–285.

Hulin, C. L. 1968. Effects of changes in job-satisfaction levels on employee turnover. *Journal of Applied Psychology, 52,* 122–126.

Hulin, C. L. and Blood, M. R. 1968. Job enlargement, individual differences and worker responses. *Psychological Bulletin, 69,* 41–55.

Hull, R. L. and Kolstad, A. 1942. Morale on the job. In Watson, G. (ed.) *Civilian morale.* New York: Reynal and Hitchcock.

Hunt, J. McV. 1963. Motivation inherent in information processing and action. In Harvey, O. J. (ed.) *Motivation and social interaction, cognitive determinants.* New York: Ronald Press, 35–94.

Hutchins, E. B. and Nonneman, A. J. 1966. *Construct validity of an environmental assessment technique for medical schools.* Technical Report No. L661. Evanston, Ill.: Association of American Medical Colleges.

Hyman, H. and Katz, D. 1947. Industrial morale and public opinion methods. *International Journal of Opinion and Attitude Research, 1,* 13–30.

Hyman, H. H. and Singer, E. (eds.) 1968. *Readings in reference group theory and research.* New York: Free Press.

Illich. I. 1976. *Medical nemesis: the expropriation of health.* New York: Pantheon Books.

Ima, K. 1962. "Central life interests" of industrial workers: a replication among lumber workers. Unpublished master's thesis, University of Oregon.

Jackson, J. 1960. Structural characteristics of norms. In Henry, N. B. (ed.) *Dynamics of instructional groups.* (The fifty-ninth yearbook of the National Society for the Study of Education). Chicago: University of Chicago Press.

Jacobs, C. D. 1975. Job enrichment of field technical representatives—Xerox Corporation. In Davis, L. E. and Cherns, A. B. (eds.) *The quality of working life*. New York: Free Press, Vol. II, 285–299.

Jacobson, E. 1951. Foremen-steward participation practices and work attitudes in a unionized factory. Unpublished doctoral thesis. Ann Arbor: University of Michigan.

Jahoda, M. 1958. *Current concepts of positive mental health*. New York: Basic Books.

Janis, I. L. 1958. *Psychological stress*. New York: Wiley.

Janis, I. L. 1959. Decisional conflicts: a theoretical analysis. *Journal of Conflict Resolution, 3*, 6–27.

Janis, I. L. 1972. *Victims of groupthink*. Boston: Houghton, Mifflin.

Janowitz, M. 1969. *Institution building in urban education*. New York: Russell Sage Foundation.

Janson, R. 1975. A job enrichment trial in data processing in an insurance organization. In Davis, L. E. and Cherns, A. B. (eds.) *The quality of working life*. New York: Free Press. Vol. II, 300–315.

Jaques, E. 1951. *The changing culture of a factory*. London: Tavistock Publications.

Jaques, E. 1961. *Equitable payment*. New York: Wiley.

Jessner, L., Blom, G. E., and Waldfogel, S. 1952. Emotional implications of tonsillectomy and adenoidectomy on children. *Psycho-analytic Study of the child, 7*, 126–169.

Julian, J. W., Hollander, E. P., and Regula, C. R. 1969. Endorsement of the group spokesman as a function of his source of authority, competence, and success. *Journal of Personality and Social Psychology, 11*, 42–49.

Kahn, R. L. 1952. *Attitudes and opinions of non-supervisory factory employees: About productivity and the time study and incentive system*. Ann Arbor, Mich.: Publications of the Institute for Social Research, Vol. 15, 213–339.

Kahn, R. L. 1958. Human relations on the shop floor. In Hugh-Jones, E. M. (ed.) *Human relations and modern management*. Amsterdam, Holland: North-Holland Publishing Co. 43–74.

Kahn, R. L. 1964. Field studies of power in organizations. In Kahn, R. L. and Boulding, E. (eds.) *Power and conflict in organizations*. New York: Basic Books, 52–66.

Kahn, R. L. 1972. The meaning of work: interpretation and proposals for measurement. In Campbell, A. and Converse, P. E. (eds.) *The human meaning of social change*. New York: Russell Sage Foundation, 159–204.

Kahn, R. L. 1974. Conflict, ambiguity, and overload: three elements in job stress. In McLean, A. (ed.) *Occupational stress*, Springfield, Ill.: Thomas, 47–61.

Kahn, R. L. 1975. In search of the Hawthorne effect. In Cass, E. L. and Zimmer, F. G. (eds.) *Man and work in society*. New York: Van Nostrand Reinhold, 49–62.

Kahn, R. L. and Katz, D. 1960. Leadership in relation to productivity and morale. In Cartwright, D. and Zander, A. (eds.) *Group dynamics: research and theory*, 2nd ed. Evanston, Ill.: Row, Peterson, 554–571 (1953).

Kahn, R. L. and Quinn, R. P. 1970. Role stress: a framework for analysis. In

McLean, A. (ed.) *Mental health and work organizations.* Chicago: Rand McNally.

Kahn, R. L., Wolfe, D. M., Quinn, R. P., Snoek, J. D., and Rosenthal, R. A. 1964. *Organizational stress: studies in role conflict and ambiguity.* New York: Wiley.

Kantrowitz, N. 1971. Hearings Before the House Committee on Rules and Administration.

Karas, T. H. 1974. Secrecy as a reducer of learning capacity in the U.S. foreign policy bureaucracy. *Policy Studies Journal, 3,* 162–166.

Kasarda, J. D. 1974. The structural implications of social system size: a three level analysis. *American Sociological Review, 39,* 19–28.

Katona, G. and Morgan, J. 1950. *Industrial mobility in Michigan.* Ann Arbor, Mich.: Institute for Social Research.

Katz, D. 1973. Patterns of leadership. In Knutson, J. M. (ed.) *Handbook of political psychology.* San Francisco: Jossey-Bass.

Katz, D. 1975. Feedback in social systems: operational and systemic research on production, maintenance, control and adaptive functions. In Bennett, C. A. and Lumsdaine, A. A. (eds.) *Evaluation and experiment.* New York: Academic Press, 465–523.

Katz, D. and Georgopoulos, B. S. 1971. Organizations in a changing world. *Journal of Applied Behavioral Science, 7,* 342–370.

Katz, D. and Golomb, N. 1974. Integration, effectiveness and adaptation in social systems: a comparative analysis of kibbutzim communities. Part I. *Administration and Society, 6,* 283–316. Part II, 1975, *6,* 389–422.

Katz, D., Gutek, B. A., Kahn, R. L., and Barton, E. 1975. *Bureaucratic encounters.* Ann Arbor, Mich.: Institute for Social Research.

Katz, D. and Kahn, R. L. 1952. Some recent findings in human relations research in industry. In Swanson, G. W., Newcomb, T. M., and Hartley, E. L. (eds.) *Readings in social psychology,* 2nd ed. New York: Holt, 650–665.

Katz, D., Maccoby, N., Gurin, G., and Floor, L. 1951. *Productivity, supervision and morale among railroad workers.* Ann Arbor, Mich.: Institute for Social Research.

Katz, D., Maccoby, N., and Morse, N. 1950. *Productivity, supervision and morale in an office situation.* Ann Arbor, Mich.: Institute for Social Research.

Katz, D., Sarnoff, I. and McClintock, C. 1956. Ego-defense and attitude change. *Human Relations, 9,* 27–45.

Katz, D. and Schanck, R. L. 1938. *Social psychology.* New York: Wiley.

Katz, E. and Lazarsfeld, P. 1955. *Personal influence: the part played by people in the flow of mass communication.* New York: Free Press.

Katzell, M. E. 1968. Expectations and dropouts in schools of nursing. *Journal of Applied Psychology, 52,* 154–157.

Katzell, R. A., Yankelovich, D. et al. 1975. *Work, productivity, and job satisfaction.* New York: The Psychological Corporation.

Kaufman, H. 1976. *Are government organizations immortal?* Washington, D.C.: The Brookings Institution.

Kaye, C. 1958. Some effects on organizational change of the personality characteristics of key role occupants. Unpublished doctoral dissertation. Ann Arbor: University of Michigan.

Kelley, H. H. 1952. Two functions of reference groups. In Swanson, G. E.,

Newcomb, T. M. and Hartley, E. L. (eds.) *Readings in social psychology,* 2nd ed. New York: Holt, Rinehart & Winston, 410–414.

Kelley, H. H. and Stahelski, A. J. 1970. Social interaction basis of cooperators' and competitors' beliefs about others. *Journal of Personality and Social Psychology, 16,* 66–91.

Kerr, S. and Schriesheim, C. 1974. Consideration, initiating structure and organizational criteria—an update of Korman's 1966 review. *Personnel Psychology, 27,* 555–568.

Kilometeren. December 1976. Sodertalje, Sweden: Saab-Scania.

Kilpatrick, F., Cummings, M., and Jennings, M. K. 1964. *The image of the Federal Service.* Washington, D.C.: Brookings Institution.

Kissinger, H. 1961. *The necessity for choice.* New York: Harper and Row.

Knejer, A., Gittings, H. and Conway, J. 1976. Serving two masters. Summarized in *Front Line.* Washington, D.C., *2,* 6, 8.

Knowles, M. C. 1964. Personal and job factors affecting labour turnover. *Personnel Practice Bulletin, 20,* 25–37.

Kolko, G. 1969. *The roots of American foreign policy.* Boston: Beacon Press.

Korman, A. K. 1966. Consideration, initiating structure and organizational criteria—a review. *Personnel Psychology, 19,* 349–361.

Kornhauser, A. 1965. *Mental health of the industrial worker.* New York: Wiley.

Krasner, L., Knowles, J. B., and Ullmann, L. P. 1965. Effect of verbal conditioning of attitudes on subsequent motor performance. *Journal of Personality and Social Psychology, 1,* 407–412.

Kraut, A. 1965. A study of role conflicts and their relationships to job satisfaction, tension, and performance. Doctoral dissertation, University of Michigan, Ann Arbor, University Microfilms, 67-8312.

Kraut, A. I. 1970. The prediction of turnover by employee attitudes. *Psychological Bulletin, 80,* 2, 153.

Krech, D. and Crutchfield, R. 1948. *Theory and problems of social psychology.* New York: McGraw-Hill.

Kuriloff, A. H. and Atkins, S. 1966. T-group for a work team. *Journal of Applied Behavioral Science, 2,* 63–94.

Lapp, R. E. 1970. *Arms beyond doubt: the tyranny of weapons technology.* New York: Cowles Book Co., 178.

Latta, L. H. 1968. Occupational attitudes of over-the-road truck drivers. Unpublished manuscript. Michigan State University.

Lawler, E. E. 1965. Managers' perception of their subordinates' pay and of their superiors' pay. *Personnel Psychology, 18,* 413–422.

Lawler, E. E. 1968. Equity theory as a predictor of productivity and work quality. *Psychological Bulletin, 70,* 596–610.

Lawler, E. E. 1971. *Pay and organizational effectiveness: a psychological view.* New York: McGraw-Hill.

Lawler, E. E. and Hackman, J. R. 1969. Impact of employee participation in the development of pay incentive plans: a field experiment. *Journal of Applied Psychology, 53,* 467–471.

Lawler, E. E., Koplin, C. A., Young, T. F., and Fadem, J. A. 1968. Inequity reduction over time in an induced overpayment situation. *Organizational Behavior and Human Performance, 3,* 253–268.

Lawler, E. T. and Porter, L. W. 1963. Perceptions regarding management compensation. *Industrial Relations, 3,* 41–49.

Lawrence, P. R. and Lorsch, J. W. 1967. Differentiation and integration in complex organizations. *Administrative Science Quarterly, 12,* 1–47.

Lawrence, P. R. and Lorsch, J. W. 1967. *Organization and environment.* Boston: Harvard Business School, Division of Research.

Lazarus, R. S. 1966. *Psychological stress and the coping process.* New York: McGraw-Hill.

Leavitt, H. J. 1951. Some effects of certain communication patterns on group performance. *Journal of Abnormal and Social Psychology, 46,* 38–50.

Leavitt, H. J. 1965. Applied organizational change in industry: structural, technological, and humanistic approaches. In March, J. G. (ed.) *Handbook of organizations.* Chicago: Rand McNally.

Leinhart, W. S., Doyle, H. N., Enterline, P. E., Henschel, A., and Kendrick, M. A. 1969. *Pneumoconiosis in Appalachian bituminous coalminers.* Cincinnati: U.S. Department of Health, Education and Welfare.

Lesieur, F. G. and Puckett, E. S. December 1968. The Scanlon Plan: past, present and future. *Proceedings of the Twenty-First Annual Winter Meeting.* Industrial Relations Research Association, Chicago.

Lesieur, F. G. and Puckett, E. S. 1969. The Scanlon Plan has proved itself. *Harvard Business Review, 47,* 109–118.

Levi, L. 1966. Life stress and urinary excretion of adrenaline and noradrenaline. In Raab, W. (ed.) *Prevention of ischemic heart disease.* Springfield, Ill.: Thomas.

Levi, L. 1971. (ed.) *Society, stress and disease,* Vol. 1, The psychosocial environment and psychosomatic diseases. London: Oxford University Press.

Levi, L. 1972(a). *Stress and distress in response to psycho-social stimuli.* Oxford: Pergamon Press.

Levi, L. 1972(b). Conditions of work and sympathoadreno-medullary activity: experimental manipulations in a real life setting. In Levi, L. (ed.) *Stress and distress in response to psycho-social stimuli.* Oxford: Pergamon Press, 106–118.

Levi, L. 1972(c). Psychological and physiological reactions to and psychomotor performance during prolonged and complex stressor exposure. In Levi, L. (ed.) *Stress and distress in response to psycho-social stimuli.* Oxford: Pergamon Press.

Levi, L. 1975. *Society, stress and disease,* Vol. II, Childhood and adolescence. London: Oxford University Press.

Levine, J. and Butler, J. 1952. Lecture vs. group decision in changing behavior. *Journal of Applied Psychology, 36,* 29–33.

Lewicki, R. J. 1969. The effects of cooperative and exploitative relationships on subsequent interpersonal relations. Unpublished doctoral dissertation. New York: Columbia University.

Lewin, K. 1938. *The conceptual representation and measurement of psychological forces.* Durham, N.C.: Duke University Press.

Lewin, K. 1947. Frontiers in group dynamics. *Human Relations, 1,* 5–41.

Lewin, K. 1948. *Resolving social conflicts.* New York: Harper.

Lewin, K. 1951. *Field theory in social science*. Cartwright, D. (ed.) New York: Harper.

Lewin, K. 1952. Group decisions and social change. In Swanson, G. E., Newcomb, T. M., and Hartley, E. L. (eds.) *Readings in social psychology*, 2nd Ed. New York: Holt, 459–473.

Lewis, H. B. and Franklin, M. 1944. An experimental study of the role of ego in work. II. The significance of task orientation in work. *Journal of Experimental Psychology, 34,* 195–215.

Leys, S. 1977. Chinese shadows: bureaucracy, happiness, history. *The New York Review of Books,* Vol. 24, 10.

Lieberman, S. 1956. The effects of changes in roles on the attitudes of role occupants. *Human Relations, 9,* 385–402.

Likert, R. 1961. *New patterns of management*. New York: McGraw-Hill.

Likert, R. 1967. *The human organization*. New York: McGraw-Hill.

Likert, R. and Likert, J. G. 1976. *New ways of managing conflict*. New York: McGraw-Hill.

Lindholm, R. 1972. *The condemned piecework: a study of 73 plants in Swedish industry*. Stockholm: Swedish Employers' Confederation.

Lindholm, R. 1975. *Job Reform in Sweden*. (See Swedish Employers' Confederation).

Lindzey, G. and Aronson, E. 1968. *The handbook of social psychology*. 2nd edition. Reading, Mass.: Addison-Wesley, 5 volumes.

Linton, R. 1936. *The study of man*. New York: Appleton-Century.

Lippitt, R., Watson, J. and Westley, B. 1958. *The dynamics of planned change*. New York: Harcourt Brace Jovanovich.

Lippman, W. 1922. *Public opinion*. New York: Harcourt Brace Jovanovich.

Lipset, S. M., Trow, J. A. and Coleman, J. S. 1956. *Union Democracy*. New York: Free Press.

Litterer, J. A. 1966. Conflict in organizations: A reexamination. *Academy of Management Journal, 9,* 178–186.

Litwin, G. H. and Stringer, R. A. Jr. 1968. Motivation and organizational climate. Cambridge: Harvard University Press.

Locke, E. A. 1976. The nature and causes of job satisfaction. In Dunnette, M. D. (ed.) *Handbook of industrial and organizational psychology*. Chicago: Rand McNally, 1297–1349.

Locke, E. A. and Bryan, J. F. 1967. *Goals and intentions as determinants of performance level, task choice and attitudes*. Washington, D.C.: American Institute for Research.

Locke, E. A., Bryan, J. F., and Kendall, L. M. 1968. Goals and intentions as mediators of the effects of monetary incentives on behavior. *Journal of Applied Psychology, 52,* 104–121.

Luchins, A. S. and Luchins, E. H. 1966. Learning a complex ritualized social role. *Psychological Record, 16,* 177–187.

Luthans, F. and Kreitner, R. 1975. *Organizational behavior modification*. Glenview, Ill.: Scott, Foresman.

Lyons, T. 1971. Role clarity, need for clarity, satisfaction, tension and withdrawal. *Organizational Behavior and Human Performance, 6,* 99–110.

McClelland, D. 1961. *The achieving society.* New York: Van Nostrand Reinhold.

McClintock, C. G. and Moskowitz, J. M. 1976. Children's preferences for individualistic, cooperative and competitive outcomes. *Journal of Personality and Social Psychology, 34,* 543–555.

McFarland, A. S. 1969. Power and leadership in pluralist systems. Stanford, Calif.: Stanford University Press.

McGrath, J. E. (ed.) 1970. *Social and psychological factors in stress.* New York: Holt, Rinehart, Winston.

McGrath, J. E. 1976. Stress and behavior in organizations. In Dunnette, M. D. (ed.) *Handbook of industrial and organizational psychology.* Chicago: Rand McNally.

McGregor, D. 1959. The Scanlon Plan through a psychologist's eyes. In Lesieur, F. G. *The Scanlon Plan.* Cambridge: Massachusetts Institute of Technology Press.

McGregor, D. 1960. *The human side of enterprise.* New York: McGraw-Hill.

McKersie, R. B. 1964. Avoiding written grievances by problem solving: An outside view. *Personnel Psychology, 17,* 367–379.

McLean, A. (ed.) 1970. *Mental health and work organizations.* Chicago: Rand McNally.

McLean, A. 1974. *Occupational stress.* Springfield, Ill.: Thomas.

McNeil, E. B. (ed.) 1965. *The nature of human conflict.* Englewood Cliffs, N. J.: Prentice-Hall.

Macaulay, S. 1963. Non-contractual relations in business: a preliminary study. *American Sociological Review, 28,* 55–67.

Macedonia, R. M. 1969. Expectation-press and survival. Unpublished doctoral dissertation, Graduate School of Public Administration, New York University.

Maher, J. R. (ed.) 1971. *New perspectives in job enrichment.* New York: Van Nostrand Reinhold.

Maier, N. R. F. 1949. *Frustration: the study of behavior without a goal.* New York: McGraw-Hill.

Maier, N. R. F. 1952. *Principles of human relations.* New York: Wiley.

Malinowski, B. 1926. *Crime and custom in savage society.* New York: Harcourt Brace Jovanovich.

Mann, F. C. 1957. Studying and creating change: a means to understanding social organization. *Research in Industrial Human Relations,* Industrial Relations Research Association, *17,* 146–167.

Mann, F. C. 1964. Toward an understanding of the leadership role in formal organizations. In Dubin, R., Homans, G. and Miller, D. (eds.) *Leadership and productivity.* San Francisco: Chandler.

Mann, F. C. and Dent, J. K. 1954. The supervisor: member of two organizational families. *Harvard Business Review, 32,* 103–112.

Mann, F. C. and Hoffman, L. R. 1960. *Automation and the worker: a study of social change in power plants.* New York: Holt.

Mann, M. 1970. The social cohesion of a liberal democracy. *American Sociological Review, 35,* 423–439.

March, J. G. (ed.) 1965. *Handbook of organizations.* Chicago: Rand-McNally.

March, J. G. and Simon, H. A. 1958. *Organizations.* New York: Wiley.

Marlow, D., Gergen, K. J., and Doob, A. N. 1966. Opponents' personality, expectation of social interaction, and interpersonal bargaining. *Journal of Personality and Social Psychology, 3,* 206–213.

Marriott, R. 1957. *Incentive payment systems.* London: Staples Press.

Marrow, A. J., Bowers, D. G., and Seashore, S. E. 1967. *Management by participation.* New York: Harper & Row.

Marschak, T. A. 1965. Economic theories of organization. In March, J. G. (ed.) *Handbook of organizations.* Chicago: Rand McNally, 423–450.

Marx, K. and Engels, F. 1961. The manifesto of the Communist party (1848). In *The Essential Left.* New York: Barnes & Noble, 7–47.

Maslow, A. H. 1943. A theory of human motivation. *Psychological Review, 50,* 370–396.

Maslow, A. H. 1954. *Motivation and personality.* New York: Harper.

Maurer, J. G. 1968. Work as a "central life interest" of industrial supervisors. *Academy of Management Journal, 11,* 329–339.

May, M. A. and Doob, L. W. 1937. Competition and cooperation. *Bulletin 25,* Social Science Research Council.

Mayo, E. 1933. *The human problems of an industrial civilization.* New York: Macmillan.

Mead, G. H. 1934. *Mind, self and society.* Chicago: University of Chicago Press.

Meehl, P. E. 1954. *Clinical versus statistical prediction: a theoretical analysis and review of the literature.* Minneapolis: University of Minnesota Press.

Meehl, P. E. 1965. Clinical versus statistical prediction. *Journal of Experimental Research in Personality, 1,* 27–32.

Meggison, L. C. and Gullett, C. R. 1970. A predictive model of union-management conflict. *Personnel Journal, 49,* 495–503.

Meier, D. L. and Bell, W. 1959. Anomia and differential access to the achievement of life goals. *American Sociological Review, 24,* 189–202.

Meier, R. L. 1961. *Social change in communication-oriented institutions.* Ann Arbor: Mental Health Research Institute, University of Michigan.

Meier, R. L. 1963. Information input overload: features of growth in communications-oriented institutions. *Libri, International Library Review, 13,* 1–44.

Meissner, M. 1976. The language of work. In Dubin, R. (ed.) *Handbook of work, organization, and society.* Chicago: Rand McNally, 205–279.

Melman, S. 1951. The rise of administrative overhead in the manufacturing industries of the United States. *Oxford Economic Papers, 3,* 62–112.

Meltzer, L. 1956. Scientific productivity in organizational settings. *Journal of Social Issues, 12,* 32–40.

Meltzer, L. and Salter, J. 1962. Organizational structure and the performance and job satisfaction of physiologists. *American Sociological Review, 27,* 351–362.

Menzies, I. E. P. 1960. A case study in the functioning of social systems as a defence against anxiety: a report of a study of the nursing services of a general hospital. *Human Relations, 13,* 95–121.

Merton, R. K. 1940. Bureaucratic structure and personality, *Social Forces, 18,* 560–568.

Merton, R. K. 1957. *Social theory and social structure,* Rev. ed. New York: Free Press.

Merton, R. K. and Lazarsfeld, P. F. (eds.) 1950. *Continuities in social research.* New York: Free Press.

Meyer, M. W. 1975. Leadership and organizational structure. *American Journal of Sociology, 81,* 514–542.

Meyers, S. M. and McIntyre, J. 1969. *Welfare policy and its consequences for the recipient population: a study of the AFDC Program.* Washington, D.C.: U.S. Government Printing Office.

Michael, D. N. 1973. *On learning to plan—and planning to learn.* San Francisco: Jossey-Bass.

Michels, R. 1949. *Political parties: a sociological study of the oligarchical tendencies of modern democracy.* New York: Free Press.

Michigan Organizational Assessment Package. 1975. Progress Report II, Ann Arbor, Mich.: Institute for Social Research.

Mikes, P. S. and Hulin, C. L. 1968. Use of importance as a weighting component of job satisfaction. *Journal of Applied Psychology, 52,* 394–398.

Milbrath, L. W. 1965. *Political participation.* Chicago: Rand McNally.

Miles, R. H. 1976. Role requirements as sources of organizational stress. *Journal of Applied Psychology, 61,* 2, 172–179.

Milgram, S. 1965. Some conditions of obedience and disobedience to authority. *Human Relations, 18,* 57–76.

Miller, A. 1974. Political issues and trust in government: 1964–1970. *American Political Science Review, 68,* 951–972.

Miller, D. R. 1963. The study of social relations: situation, identity, and social interaction. In Koch, S. (ed.) *Psychology: a study of a science, 5.* New York: McGraw-Hill.

Miller, F. B. 1958. 'Situational' interactions—a worthwhile concept? *Human Organization, 17,* 4, 39–47.

Miller, J. G. 1955. Toward a general theory for the behavioral sciences. *American Psychologist, 10,* 513–531.

Miller, J. G. 1960. Information input, overload, and psychopathology. *American Journal of Psychiatry, 116,* 695–704.

Miller, J. G. 1965(a). Living systems: basic concepts. *Behavioral Science, 10,* 193–237.

Miller, J. G. 1965(b). Living systems: structure and process. *Behavioral Science, 10,* 337–379.

Miller, L. 1965. The use of knowledge of results in improving the performance of hourly operators. Crotonville, New York: General Electric Company, Behavioral Research Service.

Milsum, J. H. 1972. The hierarchical basis for general living systems. In Klir, G. J. (ed.) *Trends in general systems theory.* New York: Wiley-Interscience, 145–187.

Mindlin, S. E. and Aldrich, H. 1975. Interorganizational dependence: a review of the concept and a reexamination of the findings of the Aston group. *Administrative Science Quarterly, 20,* 3, 382–392.

Miner, Horace M. 1968. Community-society continua. In Sills, D. L. (ed.) *Inter-*

national encyclopedia of the social sciences. New York: Macmillan and Free Press, Vol. 3, 174–180.

Mirvis, P. H. and Berg, D. N. (eds.) 1977. *Failures in organizational development and change.* New York: Wiley Interscience.

Misumi, J. 1960(a). A field study of human relations in Japanese small sized enterprises, I. *Industrial Training, 6,* 3, 2–12.

Misumi, J. 1960(b). A field study of human relations in Japanese small sized enterprises, II. *Industrial Training, 4,* 2–13.

Misumi, J. and Shirakashi, S. 1966. An experimental study of the effects of supervisory behavior on productivity and morale in a hierarchical organization. *Human Relations, 19,* 3, 297–307.

Misumi, J. and Tasaki, T. 1965. A study of the effectiveness of supervisory patterns in a Japanese hierarchical organization. *Japanese Psychological Research, 7,* 4, 151–162.

Mjasnikov, A. L. 1961. Discussion. In *Proceedings of the joint WHO-Czechoslovak cardiological society symposium on the pathogenesis of essential hypertension.* Prague, Czechoslovakia.

Mohr, L. B. 1973. The concept of organizational goal. *American Political Science Review, 67,* 470–481.

Moore, L. M. 1968. Effects of wage inequities on work attitude and performance. Unpublished master's thesis, Wayne State University.

Moreno, J. L. 1934. *Who shall survive?* Beacon, N.Y.: Beacon House.

Morris, J. N., Heady, J. A., and Barley, R. G. 1952. Coronary heart disease in medical practitioners. *British Medical Journal, 1,* 503.

Morse, N. 1953. *Satisfactions in the white collar job.* Ann Arbor, Mich.: Survey Research Center.

Morse, N. and Reimer, E. 1956. The experimental change of a major organizational variable. *Journal of Abnormal and Social Psychology, 52,* 120–129.

Morse, N. C. and Weiss, R. S. 1955. The function and meaning of work and the job. *American Sociological Review, 20,* 191–198.

Morton, R. B. and Wight, A. 1964. A critical incident evaluation of an organizational training laboratory. (Working paper.) Akron, Ohio: Aerojet General Corporation.

Mueller, E. 1965. Psychological and physiological correlates of work overload among university professors. Unpublished Ph.D. dissertation. University of Michigan.

Mueller, E. and Morgan, J. 1962. Location decisions of manufacturers. *American Economic Review,* Proceedings of the American Economic Association, 52, 204–217.

Munro, D. J. 1975. The Chinese view of modeling. *Human Development, 18,* 5, 333–352.

Munsterberg, H. 1913. *Psychology and industrial efficiency.* Boston: Houghton Mifflin.

Nadler, D., Mirvis, P., and Cammann, C. 1976. The ongoing feedback system: experimenting with a new managerial tool. *Organizational Dynamics, 4,* 4, 63–80.

Neal, A. G. and Seeman, M. 1964. Organizations and powerlessness: a test of the mediation hypothesis. *American Sociological Review, 29,* 216–226.

Nieman, L. J. and Hughes, J. W. 1951. The problems of the concept of role—a re-survey of the literature. *Social Forces, 30,* 141–149.

Neustadt, R. E. 1960. *Presidential power: The politics of leadership.* New York: Wiley.

Newcomb, T. M. 1943. *Personality and social change: attitude formation in a student community.* New York: Dryden.

Newcomb, T. M. 1947. Autistic hostility and social reality. *Human Relations, 1,* 69–86.

Newcomb, T. M. 1950. *Social psychology.* New York: Dryden.

Newcomb, T. M., Turner, R. H., and Converse, P. E. 1965. *Social psychology: the study of human interaction.* New York: Holt, Rinehart, Winston.

Norstedt, J. P. and Agurén, S. 1973. *The Saab-Scania report.* Stockholm: Swedish Employers' Confederation.

Nove, A. 1964. *Economic rationality and Soviet politics or was Stalin really necessary?* New York: Praeger.

Nuckolls, K. P., Cassel, J., and Kaplan, B. H. 1972. Psycho-social assets, life crisis and the prognosis of pregnancy. *American Journal of Epidemiology, 95,* 431–441.

Ogburn, W. F. 1922. *Social change with respect to culture and original nature.* New York: Huebsch.

Ohlstrom, B. 1970. *Kockumsrapporten. Om orsaker till missnoje bland varvsarbetare.* Stockholm: Prisma-LO.

Ondrack, D. A. 1975. Socialization in professional schools: a comparative study. *Administrative Science Quarterly, 1,* 97–103.

Opsahl, R. L. and Dunnette, M. D. 1966. The role of financial compensation in industrial motivation. *Psychological Bulletin, 2,* 66, 94–118.

Organ, D. W. 1970. Some factors influencing the behavior of boundary role persons. Unpublished doctoral dissertation. University of North Carolina at Chapel Hill.

Organizational Dynamics, Winter 1973. At Emery Air Freight: Positive reinforcement boosts performance. *1,* 41–50.

Orne, M. T. 1959. The nature of hypnosis: artifact and essence. *Journal of Abnormal and Social Psychology, 58,* 277–299.

Orne, M. T. and Scheibe, K. E. 1964. The contribution of nondeprivation factors in the production of sensory deprivation effects: the psychology of the 'panic button.' *Journal of Abnormal and Social Psychology, 68,* 3–12.

Orzack, L. H. 1959. Work as a 'central life interest' of professionals. *Social Problems, 7,* 125–132.

Osgood, C. E. 1961. An analysis of the cold war mentality. *Journal of Social Issues, 17,* 12–19.

Oshry, B. and Harrison, R. 1966. Transfer from here-and-now to there-and-then. *Journal of Applied Behavioral Science, 2,* 185–198.

Park, R. E. 1926. Behind our masks. *Survey,* New York, *56,* 135–139.

Parker, S. R. 1965. Work and non-work in three occupations. *Sociological Review, 13,* 65–75.

Parkinson, C. N. 1957. *Parkinson's Law.* Boston: Houghton Mifflin.

Parsons, T. 1951. *The social system.* New York: Free Press.

Parsons, T. 1956. Suggestions for a sociological approach to the theory of organizations, I and II. *Administrative Science Quarterly, 1*, 63–85, 225–239.

Parsons, T. 1960. *Structure and process in modern societies.* New York: Free Press.

Participation and Self-Management, 1972–1973. 6 Volumes. Zagreb: Yugoslavia.

Patchen, M. 1960. Absence and employee feelings about fair treatment. *Personnel Psychology, 13,* 349–360.

Patchen, M. 1961. *The choice of wage comparisons.* Englewood Cliffs, N.J.: Prentice-Hall.

Patten, T. H., Jr. 1970. Collective bargaining and consensus: The potential of a laboratory training input. *Management of Personnel Quarterly, 9,* 29–37.

Paul, W. J., Robertson, K. B., and Herzberg, F. 1969. Job enrichment pays off. *Harvard Business Review, 47,* 61–78.

Payne, R. L. and Mansfield, R. M. 1973. Relationships of perceptions of organizational climate to organizational structure, context, and hierarchical position. *Administrative Science Quarterly, 18,* 515–526.

Payne, R. and Pugh, D. S. 1976. Organizational structure and climate. In Dunnette, M. D. (ed.) *Handbook of industrial and organizational psychology.* Chicago: Rand McNally.

Peak, H. 1955. Attitude and motivation. In Jones, M. R. (ed.) *Nebraska symposium on motivation,* Lincoln: University of Nebraska Press, 149–188.

Pelz, D. C. 1951. Leadership within a hierarchical organization. *Journal of Social Issues, 7,* 49–55.

Pelz, D. C. and Andrews, F. M. 1966. *Scientists in organizations: productive climates for research and development.* New York: Wiley.

Pennings, J. M. 1975. The relevance of the structural-contingency model for organizational effectiveness. *Administrative Science Quarterly, 20,* 393–410.

Pennings, J. M. and Goodman, P. S. 1977. *Toward a framework of organizational effectiveness.* In Goodman, P. S., Pennings, J. M., and associates. *New perspectives on organizational effectiveness.* San Francisco: Jossey-Bass.

Perrow, C. 1972. *Complex organizations: a critical essay.* Chicago: Scott Foresman.

Perry, S. E., Silber, E., and Bloch, D. A. 1956. *The child and his family in disaster: a study of the 1953 Vicksburg tornado.* National Research Council, Committee on Disaster Studies, Disaster Study No. 5. Washington: National Academy of Science, National Research Council.

Peter, L. F. and Hull, R. 1969. *The Peter Principle.* New York: W. Morrow.

Peterson, M. W., Blackburn, R. T., Gamson, Z. F., Arce, C., Davenport, R., and Mingle J.R. 1978. *Black students on white campuses: the impacts of black enrollments.* Ann Arbor: Institute for Social Research, University of Michigan.

Pflanz, M., Rosenstein, E., and Von Uexkull, T. 1956. Socio-psychological aspects of peptic ulcer. *Journal of Psychosomatic Research, 1,* 68.

Piel, G. 1961. End of toil: science offers a new world. *The Nation, 192,* 24, 515–519.

Pondy, L. R. 1967. Organizational conflict: concepts and models. *Administrative Science Quarterly, 12,* 296–320.

Porter, L. W., Crampon, W. J., and Smith, F. J. 1976. Organizational commitment and managerial turnover: a longitudinal study. *Organizational Behavior and Human Performance, 15,* 87–98.

Porter, L. W. and Lawler, E. E. III 1965. Properties of organization structure in relation to job attitudes and job behavior. *Psychological Bulletin, 64,* 23–51.

Porter, L. W. and Lawler, E. E. III 1968. *Managerial attitudes and performance.* Homewood, Ill.: Irwin-Dorsey.

Porter, L. W., Lawler, E. E. III, and Hackman, J. R. 1975. *Behavior in organizations.* New York: McGraw-Hill.

Porter, L. W. and Roberts, K. H. 1976. Communication in organizations. In Dunnette, M. D. (ed.) *Handbook of industrial and organizational psychology.* Chicago: Rand McNally, 1553–1589.

Porter, L. W. and Smith, F. J. 1970. The etiology of organizational commitment: a longitudinal study of the initial stages of employee-organization reactions. Unpublished paper. Graduate School of Administration, University of California, Irvine.

Porter, L. W. and Steers, R. M. 1973. Organizational, work and personal factors in employee turnover and absenteeism. *Psychological Bulletin, 80,* 151–176.

Porter, L. W., Steers, R. M., Mowday, R. T., and Boulian, P. V. 1974. Organizational commitment, job satisfaction and turnover among psychiatric technicians. *Journal of Applied Psychology, 59,* 603–609.

Pugh, D. S., et al. 1963. A conceptual scheme for organizational analysis. *Administrative Science Quarterly, 8,* 289–315.

Pugh, D. S., Hickson, D. J., Hinings, C. R., and Turner, C. 1969(a). The context of organization structures. *Administrative Science Quarterly, 14,* 91–114.

Pugh, D. S., Hickson, D. J. and Hinings, C. R. 1969(b). An empirical taxonomy of structures of work organizations. *Administrative Science Quarterly, 14,* 115–126.

Pye, L. W. 1961. Personal identity and political ideology. In Marvick, D. (ed.) *Political decision makers.* Glencoe, Ill.: Free Press, 290–313.

Quinn, R. P. 1973. Personal communication.

Quinn, R. P. and Shepard, L. 1974. *The 1972–1973 quality of employment survey.* Ann Ann Arbor: Survey Research Center, University of Michigan.

Quinn, R. P., Staines, G. L., and McCullough, M. R. 1974. *Job satisfaction: is there a trend?* Manpower Research Monograph, No. 30. U.S. Department of Labor, Washington, D.C.: U.S. Government Printing Office.

Quinn, R. P., Tabor, J. M. and Gordon, L. K. 1968. *The decision to discriminate.* Ann Arbor: Institute for Social Research, University of Michigan.

Raab, W. 1966(a). *Prevention of ischemic heart disease: principles and practice.* Springfield, Ill.: Thomas.

Raab, W. 1966(b). Emotional and sensory stress factors in myocardial pathology. *American Heart Journal, 72,* 538.

Raab, W. and Kimura, H. 1971. The myocardial ionogram—a potential diagnostic tool. *American Journal of Cardiology.*

Radke, M. and Klisurich, D. 1947. Experiments in changing food habits. *Journal of the American Dietetic Association, 23,* 403–409.

Raffle, P. A. B. 1959. Stress as a factor in disease. *Lancet,* II, 839–843.

Rapoport, A. 1960. *Fights, games, and debates.* Ann Arbor: University of Michigan Press.

Rapoport, A. 1970. *N-person game theory.* Ann Arbor: University of Michigan Press.

Rapoport, A. and Chammah, A. M. 1965. *Prisoner's dilemma: A study in conflict and cooperation.* Ann Arbor: University of Michigan Press.

Raven, B. H. and Kruglanski, A. W. 1970. Conflict and power. In Swingle, P. (ed.) *The structure of conflict.* New York: Academic Press, 69–109.

Read, W. 1962. Upward communication in industrial hierarchies. *Human Relations, 15,* 3–16.

Reimer, E. 1970. *School is dead: alternatives in education.* Garden City, N.Y.: Doubleday.

Rein, M. 1972. Determinants of the work-welfare choice in AFDC. *Social Service Review, 46,* 539–566.

Reston, J. September 30, 1976. *International Herald Tribune.* Editorial.

Rice, A. K. 1958. *Productivity and social organization: the Ahmedabad experiment.* London: Tavistock Publications.

Rice, A. K. 1963. *The enterprise and its environment.* London: Tavistock Publications.

Richardson, L. F. 1960. In Rashevsky, N. and Trucco, E. (eds.) *Arms and insecurity: a mathematical study of the causes and origins of war.* Pittsburgh: Boxwood Press.

Richman, B. 1964. Increasing worker productivity: how the Soviets do it. *Personnel, 41,* 1, 8.

Richmond, B. 1969. *Industrial society in Communist China.* New York: Random House.

Riesman, D. 1950. *The lonely crowd.* New Haven: Yale University Press.

Rioch, D. McK. 1971. The development of gastro-intestinal lesions in monkeys. In Levi, L. (ed.) *Society, stress and disease,* Vol. I, *The psycho-social environment and psychosomatic diseases.* London: Oxford University Press.

Ritzer, C. and Trice, H. 1969. An empirical study of Howard Becker's side bet theory. *Social Forces, 47,* 475–479.

Rocheblave-Spenle, A. M. 1962. *La notion de role en psychologie sociale: etude historico-critique. (The concept of role in social psychology: an historical-critical study.)* Paris: Presses Universitaires de France.

Roethlisberger, F. J. 1945. The foreman: master and victim of double-talk. *Harvard Business Review, 23,* 283–298.

Roethlisberger, F. J. and Dickson, W. J. 1939. *Management and the worker.* Cambridge, Mass.: Harvard University Press.

Rogers, E. M. and Shoemaker, F. F. 1971. *Communication of innovations.* New York: Free Press.

Rokeach, M. 1973. *The nature of human values.* New York: Free Press.

Ronan, W. W. 1967. A study of some concepts concerning labour turnover. *Occupational Psychology, 41,* 193–202.

Rosenberg, M. J. 1956. Cognitive structure and attitudinal affect. *Journal of Abnormal and Social Psychology, 53,* 367–372.

Rosenthal, R. A. and Weiss, R. S. 1966. Problems of organizational feedback processes. In Bauer, R. A. (ed.) *Social Indicators.* Cambridge: Massachusetts Institute of Technology Press, 302–340.

Rossi, P. H. 1972. Community social indicators. In Campbell, A. and Converse, P. E. (eds.) *The human meaning of social change.* New York: Russell Sage Foundation, 87–126.

Rowley, V. and Keller, D. 1962. Changes in children's verbal behavior as a function of social approval and manifest anxiety. *Journal of Abnormal and Social Psychology, 65,* 53–57.

Roy, D. 1952. Quota restriction and gold bricking in a machine shop. *American Journal of Sociology, 57,* 427–444.

Rozwadowska-Dowzenko, M., Kotlarska, H. and Zawadskj, M. 1956. Nadcisrienie tetnicze samoistne a wykonywany zawod (Essential hypertension and profession). *Polish Archives of Medicine, 26,* 497.

Rubenstein, A. H. and Haberstroh, C. J. (eds.) 1960. *Some theories of organization.* Homewood, Ill.: Dorsey.

Rundquist, B. S. and Griffith, D. E. 1974. The parochial constraint on foreign policy making. *Policy Studies Journal, 3,* 142–146.

Russek, H. I. 1960. Emotional stress and coronary heart disease in American physicians. *American Journal of Medical Science, 240,* 711.

Russek, H. I. 1962. Emotional stress and coronary heart disease in American physicians, dentists and lawyers. *American Journal of Medical Science, 243,* part 6, 716–725.

Saleh, S. D., Lee, R. J., and Prien, E. P. 1965. Why nurses leave their jobs—an analysis of female turnover.. *Personnel Administration, 28,* 25–28.

Sales, S. M. 1969. Differences among individuals in affective, behavioral, biochemical, and physiological responses to variations in workload. Doctoral dissertation, University of Michigan. *Dissertation Abstracts International, 30,* 2407-B (University Microfilms, 69-18098).

Sapolsky, H. M. 1972. *The polaris system development.* Cambridge, Mass.: Harvard University Press.

Sarason, I. G. and Spielberger, C. D. 1976. *Stress and anxiety,* Vol. III. New York: Wiley.

Sarbin, T. R. and Allen, V. L. 1968. Role theory. In Lindzey, G. and Aronson, E. (eds.) *The handbook of social psychology* (2nd ed.) Reading, Mass.: Addison-Wesley.

Sarbin, T. R. and Jones, D. S. 1956. An experimental analysis of role behavior. *Journal of Abnormal and Social Psychology, 51,* 236–241.

Sarbin, T. R. and Williams, J. D. 1953. Contributions to role-taking theory. V. Role perception on the basis of limited auditory stimuli. Unpublished manuscript.

Schanck, R. L. 1932. A study of a community and its groups and institutions conceived of as behaviors of individuals. *Psychological Monographs, 43,* (2).

Schefler, K. C., Lawler, E. E., and Hackman, J. R. 1971. Long-term impact of employee participation in the development of pay incentive plans: A field experiment. *Journal of Applied Psychology, 55,* 182–186.

Schein, E. H. 1965(a) *Organizational psychology.* Englewood Cliffs, N.J.: Prentice-Hall.

Schein, E. H. 1965(b). Organizational socialization and the profession of management. *Industrial Management Review,* 1–15.

Schelling, T. C. 1960. *The strategy of conflict.* Cambridge: Harvard University Press.

Schiller, B. 1977. Industrial democracy in Scandinavia. *The Annals of the American Academy of Political and Social Science, 431,* 63–73.

Schiller, B. R. 1973. Empirical studies of welfare dependency: a survey. *The Journal of Human Resources,* Supplement Vol. 8, 19–32.

Schlesinger, A. M. 1965. *A thousand days.* Boston: Houghton, Mifflin.

Schmidt, S. M. and Kochan, T. A. 1972. Conflict: toward conceptual clarity. *Administrative Science Quarterly, 17,* 3, 359–370.

Schmidt, W. H. and Tannenbaum, R. 1960. The management of differences. *Harvard Business Review, 38,* 107–115.

Schmookler, J. 1966. *Inventions and economic growth.* Cambridge, Mass.: Harvard University Press.

Schneider, B. 1972. Organizational climate: Individual preferences and organizational realities. *Journal of Applied Psychology, 56,* 211–217.

Schneider, B. and Olson, L. D. 1970. Effort as a correlate of an organization reward system and individual values. *Personnel Psychology, 23,* 313–326.

Schneider, J. and Locke, E. 1971. A critique of Herzberg's incident classification system and a suggested revision. *Organizational Behavior and Human Performance, 6,* 441–457.

Schoettle, E. C. B. 1968. The state of the art in policy studies. In Bauer, R. A. and Gergen, K. S. (eds.) *The study of policy formation.* New York: Free Press, 149–180.

Schriesheim, C. A. and Kerr, S. 1974. Psychometric properties of the Ohio State leadership scales. *Psychological Bulletin, 81,* 756–765.

Schriesheim, C. A. and Murphy, C. J. 1976. Relationships between leader behavior and subordinate satisfaction and performance: A test of some situational moderators. *Journal of Applied Psychology, 61,* 5, 634–641.

Schumacher, E. F. 1973. *Small is beautiful.* New York: Harper.

Schwyhart, W. R. and Smith, P. C. 1972. Factors in the job involvement of middle managers. *Journal of Applied Psychology, 56,* 227–233.

Scott, R. and Howard, A. 1970. Models of stress. In Levine, S. and Scotch, N. A. *Social Stress.* Chicago: Aldine, 259–278.

Scott, W. G. 1965. *The management of conflict: Appeal systems in organizations.* Homewood, Ill.: Irwin-Dorsey.

Scott, W. R. 1977. On the effectiveness of studies of organizational effectiveness. In Goodman, P. S., Pennings, J. M. and associates. *New perspectives on organizational effectiveness.* San Francisco: Jossey-Bass.

Scudder, K. 1954. The open institution. *The Annals.* American Academy of Political and Social Science, *293,* 79–87.

Seashore, S. E. 1954. *Group cohesiveness in the industrial work group.* Ann Arbor, Mich.: Institute for Social Research.

Seashore, S. E. 1964(a). Assessing organizational performance with behavioral measurements. In Seashore, S. E. (ed.) Chapter 7. *Problems of comparative measurement from different business organizations.* Ann Arbor, Mich.: Foundation for Research on Human Behavior.

Seashore, S. E. 1964(b). Field experiments with formal organizations. *Human Organization, 23,* 2. 164–170.

Seashore, S. E. and Bowers, D. G. 1963. *Changing the structure and functioning of an organization.* Ann Arbor, Mich.: Institute for Social Research.

Seashore, S. E. and Bowers, D. G. 1970. The durability of organizational change. *American Psychologist, 25,* 3, 227–233.

Seashore, S. E., Indik, B. P. and Georgopoulos, B. S. 1960. Relationships among criteria of job performance. *Journal of Applied Psychology, 44,* 195–202.

Seashore, S. E. and Yuchtman, E. 1967. Factorial analysis of organizational performance, *Administrative Science Quarterly,* 377–395.

Seeman, M. 1966. Alienation, membership and political knowledge: A comparative study. *Public Opinion Quarterly, 30,* 353–367.

Seeman, M. 1972. Alienation and engagement. In Campbell, A. and Converse, P. E. (eds.) *The human meaning of social change.* New York: Russell Sage Foundation, 467–527.

Seiler, J. A. 1963. Diagnosing interdepartmental conflict. *Harvard Business Review, 41,* 121–132.

Selikoff, I. J. and Hammond, E. C. November 1975. Multiple risk factors in etiology of environmental cancer: implications for prevention and control. Unpublished data. Cited in *Health and Work in America.* Available from the Superintendent of Documents, U.S. Government Printing Office, Washington, D.C.

Selye, H. 1956. *The stress of life.* New York: McGraw-Hill.

Selye, H. 1971. The evolution of the stress concept—stress and cardiovascular disease. In Levi, L. (ed.) *Society, stress and disease,* Vol. I, *The psychosocial environment and psychosomatic diseases.* London: Oxford University Press.

Selznick, P. 1949. *TVA and the grass roots.* Berkeley: University of California Press.

Selznick, P. 1957. *Leadership in administration.* Evanston, Ill.: Row, Peterson.

Sermat, V. 1967. Cited in Deutsch 1973.

Shaw, M. E. 1963. Scaling group tasks: A method for dimensional analysis. Mimeographed. Gainesville: University of Florida.

Shaw, M. E. 1964. Communication networks. In Berkowitz, L. (ed.) *Advances in experimental social psychology.* New York: Academic Press, 111–147.

Shepard, J. M. 1970. Functional specialization, alienation, and job satisfaction. *Industrial and Labor Relations, 23,* 207–219.

Sherif, M. 1936. *The psychology of social norms.* New York: Harper.

Sherif, M. 1958. Superordinate goals in the reduction of intergroup conflict. *The American Journal of Sociology, 63,* 349–356.

Sherif, M. 1966. *In common predicament.* Boston: Houghton Mifflin.

Sherwood, R. 1958. The Bantu clerk: A study of role expectations. *Journal of Social Psychology, 47,* 285–316.

Shipley, T. E. and Veroff, J. 1952. A projective measure of need affiliation. *Journal of Experimental Psychology, 43,* 349–356.

Shirer, W. L. 1960. *The rise and fall of the Third Reich.* New York: Simon and Schuster.

Shure, G. H., Meeker, R. J., and Hansford, E. A. 1965. The effectiveness of pacifist strategies in bargaining games. *Journal of Conflict Resolution, 9,* 106–117.

Sills, D. L. 1957. *The volunteers.* Glencoe, Ill.: The Free Press.

Simon, H. A. 1964. On the concept of organizational goals. *Administrative Science Quarterly, 9,* 1–22.

Singer, D. 1961. The level of analysis problem in international relations. *World Politics, 14,* 77–92.

Skinner, B. F. 1948. *Walden two.* New York: Macmillan.

Skinner, B. F. 1968. The design of experimental communities. In Sills, D. (ed.) *The international encyclopedia of the social sciences.* New York: Macmillan and the Free Press. Vol. 16, pages 271–275.

Skinner, B. F. 1971. *Beyond freedom and dignity.* New York: Knopf.

Skinner, B. F. 1973. Conversation with B. F. Skinner. *Organizational Dynamics, 1,* 31–40.

Sloan, A. P. 1964. *My years with General Motors.* McDonald, J. (ed.) with Stevens, C. Garden City, N.Y.: Doubleday (c. 1963).

Smelser, W. T. 1961. Dominance as a factor in achievement and perception in cooperative problem solving interactions. *Journal of Abnormal and Social Psychology, 62,* 535–542.

Smith, C. G. and King, J. A. 1975. *Mental hospitals: a study in organizational effectiveness.* Lexington, Mass.: D.C. Heath.

Smith, E. E. 1957. The effects of clear and unclear role expectations on group productivity and defensiveness. *Journal of Abnormal and Social Psychology, 55,* 213–217.

Solomon, L. 1960. The influence of some types of power relationships and game strategies upon the development of interpersonal trust. *Journal of Abnormal and Social Psychology, 61,* 223–230.

Solomon, P. et al. (eds.) 1961. *Sensory deprivation.* Cambridge, Mass.: Harvard University Press.

Spitz, R. A. 1945. Hospitalism: an inquiry into the genesis of psychiatric conditions in early childhood. *Psychoanalytic Study of the Child, 1,* 53–74.

Spitzer, M. E. 1964. *Goal-attainment, job satisfaction and behavior.* Doctoral dissertation, New York University. Ann Arbor, Mich.: University Microfilms, No. 64-10, 048.

Srole, L., Langner, T. S., Michael, S. T., Opler, M. K. and Rennie, T. A. C. 1962. *Mental health in the metropolis: The midtown Manhattan study.* Vol. I. New York: McGraw-Hill.

Stagner, R. 1951. Homeostasis as a unifying concept in personality theory. *Psychological Review, 58,* 5–17.

Stagner, R. 1962. Personality variables in union-management relations. *Journal of Applied Psychology, 46,* 350–357.

Stagner, R. and Rosen, H. 1965. *Psychology of union-management relations.* Belmont, Calif.: Brooks/Cole.

Stanton, A. and Schwartz, M. 1954. *The mental hospital.* New York: Basic Books.

Starbuck, W. 1976. Organizations and their environments. In Dunnette, M. D. (ed.) *Handbook of industrial and organizational psychology.* Chicago: Rand McNally.

Statistical abstract. 1963. Washington, D.C.: U.S. Bureau of the Census.

Staw, B. and Szwajkowski, E. 1975. The scarcity-munificence component of organizational environments and the commission of illegal acts. *Administrative Science Quarterly, 20*, 3, 345–354.

Steers, R. M. 1975. Problems in the management of organizational effectiveness. *Administrative Science Quarterly, 20*, 546–558.

Stern, G. G. 1970. *People in context: Measuring person-environment congruence in education and industry.* New York: Wiley.

Stern, I. and Pearse, R. F. 1968. Collective bargaining: A union's program for reducing conflict. *Personnel, 45*, 61–72.

Stieber, H. W. 1956. Interaktionen—ausdruck der sozialen organisation einer arbeitsgruppe. *Kölner Zeitschrift für Soziologie und Sozialpsychologie, 8*, 83–89.

Stogdill, R. M. 1948. Personal factors associated with leadership. *Journal of Psychology, 25*, 35–71.

Stogdill, R. M. 1974. *Handbook of leadership.* New York: Free Press.

Stogdill, R. M. and Coons, A. E. (eds.) 1957. *Leader behavior: Its description and measurement.* Columbus: Ohio State University, Bureau of Business Research, Research Monograph 88.

Stotland, E. and Kobler, A. L. 1965. *Life and death of a mental hospital.* Seattle: University of Washington Press.

Stouffer, S. A. et al. 1949. *The American soldier.* Vols. 1 and 2 of *Studies in Social Psychology during World War II.* Princeton, N.J.: Princeton University Press.

Stouffer, S. A. and Toby, J. 1951. Role conflict and personality. *American Journal of Sociology, 56*, 395–406.

Strauss, G. 1974. Is there a blue-collar revolt against work? In O'Toole, J. (ed.) *Work and the quality of life.* Cambridge: Massachusetts Institute of Technology Press, 40–69.

Strauss, G. 1976. Organization Development. In Dubin, R. (ed.) *Handbook of work, organization, and society.* Chicago: Rand McNally.

Street, D. 1970. The inmate group in custodial and treatment settings. In Grusky, O. and Miller, G. A. (eds.) *The sociology of organizations.* New York: Free Press, 377–391.

Strickland, L. 1958. Surveillance and trust. *Journal of Personality, 26*, 200–215.

Student, K. R. 1966. *Some organizational correlates of supervisory influence.* Doctoral dissertation, University of Michigan.

Student, K. R. 1968. Supervisory influence and work-group performance. *Journal of Applied Psychology, 52*, 188–194.

Sturmthal, A. 1977. Unions and industrial democracy. *The Annals of the American Academy of Political and Social Science, 431*, 12–21.

Super, D. 1939. Occupational level and job satisfaction. *Journal of Applied Psychology, 23*, 547–564.

Swedish Employers' Confederation. (Lindholm, R.) 1975. *Job reform in Sweden.* Stockholm.

Swingle, P. (ed.) 1970. *The structure of conflict.* New York: Academic Press.

Sykes, G. M. 1958. *The society of captives.* Princeton, N.J.: Princeton University Press.

Sykes, G. M. and Messinger, S. L. 1960. The inmate social system. In Cloward,

R. A. et al. (eds.) *Theoretical studies in the social organization of the prison.* New York: Social Science Research Council, 5–18.

Syme, S. L., Borhani, N. O., and Buechley, R. W. 1965. Cultural mobility and coronary heart disease in an urban area. *American Journal of Epidemiology, 82,* 334–346.

Syme, S. L., Hyman, M. M., and Enterline, P. E. 1964. Some social and cultural factors associated with occurrence of coronary heart disease. *Journal of Chronic Diseases, 17,* 277–289.

Takezawa, S. 1976. The quality of working life: trends in Japan. *Laborer and Society, 1,* 29–48.

Talacchi, S. 1960. Organization size, individual attitudes and behavior: An empirical study. *Administrative Science Quarterly, 5,* 398–420.

Tannenbaum, A. S. 1957. Personality change as a result of an experimental change of environmental conditions. *Journal of Abnormal and Social Psychology, 55,* 404–406.

Tannenbaum, A. S. 1962. Control in organizations. *Administrative Science Quarterly, 7,* 236–257.

Tannenbaum, A. S. 1968. *Control in organizations.* New York: McGraw-Hill.

Tannenbaum, A. S. 1974. *Hierarchy in organizations.* San Francisco: Jossey-Bass.

Tannenbaum, A. S. and Cooke, R. A. 1978. Organizational control: a review of research employing the control graph method. In Lammers, C. J. and Hickson, D. J. (eds.) *Organizations alike and unlike.* London: Routledge and Kegan Paul Ltd.

Tannenbaum, A. S. and Donald, M. N. 1957. *A study of the League of Women Voters of the United States. Factors in League functioning.* Ann Arbor, Mich.: Institute for Social Research (mimeograph).

Tannenbaum, R., Weschler, I., and Massarik, F. 1961. *Leadership and organization.* New York: McGraw-Hill.

Tausky, C. and Parke, E. L. 1976. Job enrichment, need theory and reinforcement theory. In Dubin, R. (ed.) *Handbook of work, organization, and society.* Chicago: Rand McNally.

Taylor, F. W. 1923. *The principles of scientific management.* New York: Harper.

Taylor, K. and Weiss, D. 1969. Prediction of individual job termination from measured job satisfaction and biographical data. (Research Report No. 30). Minneapolis: University of Minnesota, Work Adjustment Project.

Telly, C. S., French, W. L., and Scott, W. G. 1971. The relationship of inequity to turnover among hourly workers. *Administrative Science Quarterly, 16,* 164–172.

Tenebaum, A. 1970. Dyadic communications in industry. Unpublished doctoral dissertation, University of California.

Terhune, K. W. 1970. The effects of personality in cooperation and conflict. In Swingle, P. (ed.) *The structure of conflict.* New York: Academic Press.

Terhune, K. W. and Firestone, J. M. Psychological studies in social interaction and motives (STAM), Phase 2: Group motives in an international relations game. CAL Report No. VX-2018-G-2. Cornell Aeronautical Laboratory, March 1967.

Terrien, F. W. and Mills, D. L. 1955. The effect of changing size upon the internal structure of organizations. *American Sociological Review, 20,* 11–13.

Thelen, H. A. 1960(a). Exploration of a growth model for psychic, biological, and social systems. Mimeographed paper.

Thelen, H. A. 1960(b). Personal communication to authors.

Thibaut, J. W. and Kelley, H. H. 1959. *The social psychology of groups.* New York: Wiley.

Thomas, E. J., Polansky, N., and Kounin, J. 1955. The expected behavior of a potentially helpful person. *Human Relations, 8,* 165–174.

Thomas, K. 1976. Conflict and conflict management. In Dunnette, M. D. (ed.) *Handbook of industrial and organizational psychology.* Chicago: Rand McNally.

Thomas, K. W. and Walton, R. E. 1971. Conflict-handling behavior in interdepartmental relations. Research Paper No. 38. Division of Research, Graduate School of Business Administration, University of California, Los Angeles.

Thompson, D. (Sir D'Arcy) 1952. *On growth and form.* Cambridge, England: Cambridge University Press.

Thompson, J. D. 1967. *Organizations in action.* New York: McGraw-Hill.

Thorndike, E. L. 1935. Workers' satisfactions: likes and dislikes of young people for their jobs. *Occupations, 13,* 704–706.

Thorsrud, E. and Emery, F. E. 1969. *Mot en ny bedriftsorganisasjon.* Oslo: Tanum.

Thorsrud, E., Sørensen, B. S., and Gustavsen, B. 1976. Sociotechnical approach to industrial democracy in Norway. In Dubin, R. (ed.) *Handbook of work, organization, and society.* Chicago: Rand McNally.

Tönnies, F. 1887. Gemeinschaft and Gesellschaft. Translated and edited by Loomis, C. P. 1957. East Lansing: Michigan State University Press.

Tolman, E. C. 1932. *Purposive behavior in animals and men.* New York: Appleton-Century.

Torrance, E. 1954. The behavior of small groups under stress conditions of survival. *American Sociological Review, 19,* 751–755.

Tosi, H., Aldag, R., and Storey, R. 1973. On the measurement of the environment: an assessment of the Lawrence and Lorsch environmental uncertainty subscale. *Administrative Science Quarterly, 18,* 1, 27–36.

Touraine, A. 1955. *L'evolution du travail ouvrier aux usines Renault.* Paris: Centre National de la Recherche Scientifique.

Triandis, H. C. 1967. Review of Herzberg, F. Work and the nature of man. *Industrial and Labor Relations Review, 20,* 529–531.

Trist, E. 1976. Toward a postindustrial culture. In Dubin, R. (ed.) *Handbook of work, organization and society.* Chicago: Rand McNally, 1011–1033.

Trist, E. L. and Bamforth, K. W. 1951. Some social and psychological consequences of the long-wall method of coal-getting. *Human Relations, 4,* 3–38.

Trist, E. L., Higgin, G. W., Murray, H., and Pollock, S. B. 1963. *Organizational choice.* London: Tavistock Publications.

Trotsky, L. 1936. *The history of the Russian Revolution.* New York: Simon and Schuster.

Tucker, R. C. 1965. The dictator and totalitarianism, *World Politics, 17*, 555–583.

Turner, A. N. and Lawrence, P. R. 1965. *Industrial jobs and the worker.* Cambridge, Mass.: Harvard University, Graduate School of Business Administration.

Turner, R. H. 1956. Role-taking, role standpoint, and reference-group behavior. *American Journal of Sociology, 61,* 39–46.

Turner, R. H. 1968. Role: sociological aspects. In Sills, D. (ed.) *International encyclopedia of the social sciences.* Crowell, Collier and MacMillan, *13,* 552–557.

Tyroler, H. A. and Cassel, J. 1964. Health consequences of culture change: The effect of urbanization on coronary heart disease mortality in rural residents. *Journal of Chronic Diseases, 17,* 167–177.

Udy, S. H. 1958. Bureaucratic elements in organizations. *American Sociological Review, 23,* 415–418.

Udy, S. H. 1960. Technology, society and production organization. Paper read at American Sociological Association Meetings, New York.

Udy, S. H. 1965. The comparative analysis of organizations. In March, J. G. (ed.) Chapter 16. *Handbook of organizations.* Chicago: Rand McNally, 1965.

Urbrock, R. 1934. Attitudes of 4,430 employees. *Journal of Social Psychology, 5,* 365–377.

Valen, H. and Katz, D. 1964. *Political parties in Norway.* Oslo, Norway: University of Oslo Press.

Van de Ven, A. H. and Delbecq, A. 1976. Determinants of coordination modes within organizations. *American Sociological Review, 41,* 322–338.

Van Doorn, J. A. A. 1966. Conflict in formal organizations. In de Reuck, A. and Knight, J. (eds.) *Conflict in society.* Boston: Little, Brown. 111–133.

Vanek, J. (ed.) 1975. *Self-management.* Harmondsworth, Middlesex, England: Penguin.

Van Maanen, J. 1976. Breaking-in: Socialization to work. In Dubin, R. (ed.) *Handbook of work, organization, and society.* Chicago: Rand McNally, 67–130.

Verplanck, W. 1955. The control of the content of conversation: Reinforcement of statements of opinion. *Journal of Abnormal and Social Psychology, 51,* 668–676.

Vertin, T. G. 1954. Bedrijfsgeneeskundige aspecten van het ulcus pepticum. Thesis, Groningen. Eindhoven: Hermes.

Viteles, M. S. 1953. *Motivation and morale in industry.* New York: Norton.

Vliet, A. van. 1970. *A work structuring experiment in television assembly.* Eindhoven, Netherlands: Philips.

von Bertalanffy, L. 1940. Der organismus als physikalisches system betrachtet. *Naturwissenschaften, 28,* 521 ff.

von Bertalanffy, L. 1950. The theory of open systems in physics and biology. *Science, 111,* 23–28.

von Bertalanffy, L. 1956. General system theory. *General systems.* Yearbook of the Society for General Systems Theory, *1,* 1–10.

Vroom, V. H. 1962. Ego involvement, job satisfaction and job performance. *Personnel Psychology, 15,* 159–177.

Vroom, V. H. 1964. *Work and motivation*. New York: Wiley.

Vroom, V. H. 1976. Leadership. In Dunnette, M. D. (ed.) *Handbook of industrial and organizational psychology*. Chicago: Rand McNally. 1527–1552.

Vroom, V. H. and Deci, E. L. 1971. The stability of past decision dissonance: A follow-up study of job attitudes of business graduates. *Organizational Behavior and Human Performance, 6,* 36–49.

Wager, L. U. 1965. Leadership style, hierarchical influence, and supervisory role obligations. *Administrative Science Quarterly, 9,* 391–420.

Walker, C. R. and Guest, H. 1952. *The man on the assembly line*. Cambridge, Mass.: Harvard University Press.

Walker, C. R., Guest, R. H., and Turner, A. N. 1956. *The foreman on the assembly line*. Cambridge, Mass.: Harvard University Press.

Walker, J. and Marriott, R. 1951. A study of some attitudes to factory work. *Occupational Psychology, 25,* 181–191.

Wall, J. A. 1972. The effects of the constituent's informational environment upon the constituent-boundary role person relationship. Unpublished doctoral dissertation, University of North Carolina at Chapel Hill.

Wall, J. A., Jr., and Adams, J. S. 1974. Some variables affecting a constituent's evaluations of and behavior toward a boundary role occupant. *Organizational Behavior and Human Performance, 11,* 390–408.

Waller, W. 1932. *The sociology of teaching*. New York: Wiley.

Walton, R. E. 1969. *Interpersonal peacemaking: Confrontations and third party consultation*. Reading, Mass.: Addison-Wesley.

Walton, R. E., Dutton, J. M., and Fitch, H. G. 1966. A study of conflict in the process, structure, and attitudes of lateral relationships. In Rubenstein, A. H. and Haberstroh, C. J. (eds.) *Some theories of organization*. Homewood, Ill.: Irwin.

Walton, R. E. and McKersie, R. B. 1966. Behavioral dilemmas in mixed-motive decision making. *Behavioral Science, 11,* 370–384.

Warwick, D. P. 1975. *A theory of public bureaucracy: Politics, personality and organization in the State Department*. Cambridge, Mass.: Harvard University Press.

Waters, L. K. and Roach, D. 1971. Relationship between job attitudes and two forms of withdrawal from the work situation. *Journal of Applied Psychology, 55,* 92–94.

Weber, M. 1947. *The theory of social and economic organization* (translated by Henderson, A. M. and Parsons, T.) Parsons, T. (ed.) New York: Free Press.

Weiner, H. J., Akabas, S. H. and Sommer, J. J. 1973. *Mental health care in the world of work*. New York: Association Press.

Weiss, R. S. and Riesman, D. 1961. Social problems and disorganization in the world of work. In Merton, R. K. and Nisbet, R. L. (eds.) *Contemporary social problems*. New York: Harcourt Brace Jovanovich, 459–514.

Weitz, J. 1956. Job expectancy and survival. *Journal of Applied Psychology, 40,* 245–247.

Weitz, J. and Nuckols, R. C. 1955. Job satisfaction and job survival. *Journal of Applied Psychology, 39,* 294–300.

Westerlund, C. 1952. *Group leadership*. Stockholm: Nordisk Rotogravyr.

White, H. 1961. Management conflict and sociometric structure. *American Journal of Sociology, 67,* 185–199.

White, H. C. 1970. *Chains of opportunity: System models of mobility in organizations.* Cambridge, Mass.: Harvard University Press.

Whyte, M. K. 1973. Bureaucracy and modernization in China: The Maoist Critique, *American Sociological Review, 38,* 149–163.

Whyte, W. F. (ed.) 1955. *Money and motivation.* New York: Harper.

Whyte, W. F. 1972. Skinnerian theory in organizations. *Psychology Today,* Vol. 5, 11, 66.

Wilcox, L. D., Brooks, R. M., Beal, G. M., and Klonglan, G. E. 1972. *Social indicators and societal monitoring.* San Francisco: Jossey-Bass.

Wild, R. 1970. Job needs, job satisfaction, and job behavior of women manual workers. *Journal of Applied Psychology, 54,* 157–162.

Wilensky, H. 1964. The professionalization of everyone? *American Journal of Sociology, 70,* 137–138.

Wildavsky, A. 1964. *The politics of the budgetary process.* Boston: Little, Brown.

Wilson, W. 1887. The study of administration. *Political Science Quarterly,* 197–222.

Wilson, W., Chun, N., and Katanyi, M. 1965. Projection, attraction, and strategy choices in intergroup competition. *Journal of Personality and Social Psychology, 2,* 432–435.

Windmuller, J. P. 1977. Industrial democracy and industrial relations. *The Annals of the American Academy of Political and Social Science, 431,* 22–31.

Woodward, J. 1965. *Industrial organization: theory and practice.* London: Oxford University Press.

Work In America. 1973. Report of a special task force to the Secretary of Health, Education, and Welfare. Cambridge: Massachusetts Institute of Technology Press.

Worthy, J. C. 1950(a). Factors influencing employee morale. *Harvard Business Review, 28,* 61–73.

Worthy, J. C. 1950(b). Organizational structure and employee morale. *American Sociological Review, 15,* 169–179.

Yoder, D. 1947. *Personnel management and industrial relations.* New York: Prentice-Hall.

Youngberg, C. F. 1963. An experimental study of "job satisfaction" and turnover in relation to job expectancies and self expectations. Unpublished doctoral dissertation, New York University.

Yuchtman, E. and Seashore, S. 1967. A system resource approach to organizational effectiveness. *American Sociological Review, 32,* 891–903.

Zald, M. N. 1962. Organizational control structures in five correctional institutions. *American Journal of Sociology, 68,* 335–345.

Zaleznik, A., Christensen, C. R. and Roethlisberger, F. 1958. *The motivation, productivity, and satisfaction of workers: a predictive study.* Boston: Harvard Graduate School of Business Administration.

Zander, A. 1971. *Motives and goals in groups.* New York: Academic Press.

Zander, A. and Medow, H. 1963. Individual and group levels of aspiration. *Human Relations, 16,* 89–105.

Zander, A. and Newcomb, T. 1967. Group levels of aspiration in United Fund campaigns. *Journal of Personality and Social Psychology, 6,* 157–162.

Zeigarnik, B. 1927. Das Behalten erledigter und unerledigter Handlungen, III. The memory of completed and uncompleted actions. *Psychologische Forschung, 9,* 1–85.

Ziller, R. C. 1965. Toward a theory of open and closed groups. *Psychological Bulletin, 64,* 164–182.

NAME INDEX

SUBJECT INDEX